RELIGION, CHARITY AND HUMAN RIGHTS

For the first time in 400 years a number of leading common law nations have, fairly simultaneously, embarked on charity law reform leading to an encoding of key definitional matters in charity legislation. This book provides an analysis of international case law developments on the ever-growing range of issues now being generated by clashes between human rights, religion and charity law. Kerry O'Halloran identifies and assesses the agenda of 'moral imperatives', such as abortion and gay marriage, that delineate the legal interface, and considers their significance for those with and those without religious belief. By assessing jurisdictional differences in the law relating to religion/human rights/charity the author provides a picture of the evolving 'culture wars' that now typify and differentiate societies in Western nations, including the United States, England and Wales, Ireland, Australia, Canada and New Zealand.

KERRY O'HALLORAN is Adjunct Professor at the Australian Centre for Philanthropy and Nonprofit Studies, Queensland University of Technology, Brisbane. He is a professionally qualified lawyer and social worker. His 22 books and many other publications include *The Church of England: Charity Law & Human Rights* (2014), *The Profits of Charity* (2012), *The Politics of Charity* (2011), *Modernising Charity Law* (2010), *Charity Law, 2nd edition* (2009), *Charity Law & Social Policy* (2008) and *Charity Law and Social Inclusion: An International Study* (2006).

RELIGION, CHARITY AND HUMAN RIGHTS

KERRY O'HALLORAN
Queensland University of Technology

CAMBRIDGE
UNIVERSITY PRESS

University Printing House, Cambridge CB2 8BS, United Kingdom

One Liberty Plaza, 20th Floor, New York, NY 10006, USA

477 Williamstown Road, Port Melbourne, VIC 3207, Australia

314-321, 3rd Floor, Plot 3, Splendor Forum, Jasola District Centre, New Delhi - 110025, India

103 Penang Road, #05-06/07, Visioncrest Commercial, Singapore 238467

Cambridge University Press is part of the University of Cambridge.

It furthers the University's mission by disseminating knowledge in the pursuit of education, learning and research at the highest international levels of excellence.

www.cambridge.org
Information on this title: www.cambridge.org/9781107020481

© Cambridge University Press 2014

This publication is in copyright. Subject to statutory exception and to the provisions of relevant collective licensing agreements, no reproduction of any part may take place without the written permission of Cambridge University Press.

First published 2014

A catalogue record for this publication is available from the British Library

Library of Congress Cataloging in Publication data
O'Halloran, Kerry, author.
Religion, charity and human rights / Kerry O'Halloran,
Queensland University of Technology.
pages   cm
ISBN 978-1-107-02048-1 (hardback)
1. Corporations, Religious – Law and legislation – English-speaking
countries.   2. Charitable uses, trusts, and foundations – English-speaking
countries.   3. Religious trusts – English-speaking countries.
4. Freedom of religion – English-speaking countries.   5. Religion and
politics – English-speaking countries.   6. Religion and law – English-speaking
countries.   7. Human rights – English-speaking countries.   I. Title.
K3280.O33   2014
346´.0642–dc23
2013050035

ISBN 978-1-107-02048-1 Hardback

Cambridge University Press has no responsibility for the persistence or accuracy of URLs for external or third-party internet websites referred to in this publication, and does not guarantee that any content on such websites is, or will remain, accurate or appropriate.

This book is dedicated to the memory of Rosemary C Dickson
(24.09.1923 – 15.12.2013).

Her commitment as a Quaker, to religion and charity,
was a support and inspiration to many.

CONTENTS

Acknowledgements   *page* viii

Introduction   1

PART I   **Background**   7

1   Religion, charity and the state: concepts, precepts, relationships and boundaries   9

2   Charity law and religion: the common law context; historical background   42

3   Competing frames of reference: domestic constraints   74

4   The international context: religion, human rights and charity law reform   110

PART II   **Contemporary international perspectives**   155

5   England and Wales   157

6   Ireland   224

7   The United States of America   274

8   Canada   325

9   Australia   374

10   New Zealand   427

PART III   **Future directions**   465

11   A conflicts of laws: canon law, charity law and human rights law   467

Conclusion   509

Index   515

ACKNOWLEDGEMENTS

Sincere thanks are owed to Professor Myles McGregor-Lowndes, Director of the Australian Centre of Philanthropy and Nonprofit Studies, Queensland University of Technology, Brisbane, Australia for his support and friendship, and to the Australian Centre for Philanthropy and Nonprofit Studies for offering me an academic base to conduct the research for this and other books. For his companionship and that of other colleagues, and for all their many acts of friendship to my wife and self during our visits to the Centre, I remain extremely grateful.

Thanks are also due to those who offered comment on draft chapters. In particular, I much appreciated the helpful feedback received from the home team: Myles McGregor-Lowndes, Dr Matthew Turnour, Managing Director, Neumann & Turnour Lawyers, Brisbane, QLD, Australia and Director of the Australian Charity Law Association, and Fr Brian Lucas, General Secretary of the Australian Catholic Bishops Conference; the latter's patient observations were certainly challenging. Among those who made helpful contributions from further afield were: Putnam Barber, a renowned Seattle-based writer and commentator on public policy issues affecting the work of nonprofits (United States); Dr Michael Gousmett, Founding Trustee, The New Zealand Third Sector Educational Trust and co-author of *The Law and Practice of Charities in New Zealand*, and Sue Barker, Director of Sue Barker Charities Law and co-author of *The Law and Practice of Charities in New Zealand* (New Zealand); and Laird Hunter QC, recognised by Lexpert as one of Canada's leading practitioners in charity and nonprofit law and retained by some of Canada's leading charitable foundations (Canada).

I am very thankful to Cambridge University Press for the vote of confidence that resulted in the publication of this book. *Religion, Charity and the Law* was completed during my tenure at the Australian Centre of Philanthropy and Nonprofit Studies, and there may be some overlap of material with other books also written during that period such as *The Church of England: Charity Law & Human Rights* (Springer, 2014), *The*

Profits of Charity (Oxford University Press, 2012), *The Politics of Charity* (Routledge, 2011), *Modernising Charity Law* (Elgar, 2010), *Charity Law & Social Policy* (Springer, 2008) and *Charity Law and Social Inclusion: an International Study* (Routledge, 2006).

Despite editorial diligence, some mistakes, inconsistencies and other faults of omission or commission may have found their way into print, in which case, responsibility for same, as for all views expressed, must rest exclusively with me.

Thank you as always, Elizabeth, but especially for putting up with this in the midst of what for you has been a particularly stressful year.

Introduction

The roles of religion and charity in society have probably always given rise to controversy. In recent years this has centred on doubts regarding their capacity – separately or jointly – to promote equity, equality and pluralism, to deliver public benefit rather than satisfy the needs of a selected few and to further social cohesion instead of fostering social division. Indeed, there is an argument that both are fundamentally discriminatory (each differentiates between their beneficiaries and all others) and, consequently, it is inevitable that in a modern human rights context their functioning will generate serious issues for a democratic society.

It is also apparent that religious organisations, which almost always have charitable status, are now growing in number and are acquiring a more visible social profile. This is something of a paradox, given the well-documented rise in secularism, but the increased variety of 'religions', the volume of faith-based service providers and the more conspicuous presence of some religions – such as Islam – in the developed common law nations would seem irrefutable. Certainly, the secular arm of religion is extending its reach: always a significant contributor to hospital provision, to general health and social care facilities and to education, in recent years the growth in faith-based schooling has been particularly noticeable. It may be that the more general need for all nonprofits to develop new funding streams is resulting in religious organisations also becoming more entrepreneurial and consequently more visible. Whatever the reason, it is clear that as such bodies further develop the secular outworkings of their religious beliefs, so they are inevitably drawn more into the complex web of civil law which, in all developed common law jurisdictions, is giving rise to issues such as those relating to: charitable tax exemption; government funding; discretion not to appoint clergy on grounds of gender or sexual orientation; and to exemption privileges regarding employment laws and the general requirements of equality legislation. For such reasons the debate about the future social role of religion and charity is set to become an acute and pressing concern for governments, academics and others on a national and international basis. The need to prepare the ground for that debate, and contribute some thoughts and data that may help inform it, provides the rationale for this book.

Charity law brings together and governs the relationship between charity and religion. That for the first time in 400 years a number of leading common law nations should, fairly simultaneously, embark on processes of charity law reform – processes which involve defining 'religion' and 'charity' – is both curious, in terms of timing, and clearly important in terms of how process outcomes may affect the future of that relationship. For present purposes, the working hypothesis is that a primary impetus for reform came from the pressing need to square a circle – to bring the principles of charity and religion into alignment with those of human rights. Possibly, however, such an objective is fatally flawed – a basic category error. Matters of faith and equality may be irreconcilable.

Supporting evidence for this view can be found in the jurisdictional logjams caused by what might be termed an agenda of 'moral imperatives' – including abortion, genetic engineering, DNA patenting and gay marriage – which have come to symbolise the modern conflict between faith and equality. These morally driven issues, the number and potency of which would seem to be on the increase, are indicative of an eagerness in all jurisdictions to bring the same type of matters to court, often repeatedly. It is undoubtedly in the public interest that such matters be debated, though there must be some doubt as to the degree to which they are justiciable, but it is clear that the outcome is going to be unacceptable to a large proportion of those who care deeply – altruistically, on behalf of public morality – about the resulting implications for society. The long and embittered confrontation between the pro-life and pro-choice camps in relation to abortion is a case in point and one which demonstrates that while matters of belief may remain impervious to argument they are only too capable of generating a strident and often virulent moralism that itself can have a corrosive effect on public benefit. The nature of the items on this agenda, their common origins and the varied jurisdictional response to them, constitute an important theme throughout this book.

The six jurisdictions chosen to represent the common law jurisdictions are those that have recently completed or continue to undergo processes of charity law reform. In all six, the legal issues relating to matters such as 'religious belief' and 'religious discrimination', to the

INTRODUCTION 3

tax privileges of religious organisations and to government funding of faith-based service providers are not dissimilar: the statutory exemptions provided in all jurisdictions, enabling those of religious belief to behave in ways that would be discriminatory for ordinary citizens, is contentious in public benefit terms. In four, the presence of an Indigenous population with its own separate and distinct set of beliefs has provided a counterpoint to Christianity and an incentive for a policy of religious pluralism; while in the United States, Canada and Australia the subdued social profile of such populations has meant that for generations their beliefs have largely been denied formal State recognition, in New Zealand it was acquired by the Māori because of their relatively strong and coherent culture. In two, the shadow of a Church–State relationship embodied in constitutional arrangements of an earlier age continues to loom over the law governing the social role of religion: in England and Wales the 'established' Church of England enjoys a unique locus standi in relation to the State; in the United States the First Amendment erects a 'wall of separation' between the affairs of Church and State. In one, the role of religion in the social infrastructure of schools and health care is all pervasive: the influence of the Catholic Church in Ireland has no equivalent among the religions of the other jurisdictions being considered. All have had to wrestle, in recent years, with the impact of human rights and equality legislation and the ever-broadening scope of related case law developments upon the traditional religions, particularly upon the Scripturally based doctrines of Christianity.

Religion, as it is now legally understood, neither requires a God nor (at least in the UK jurisdictions) is it necessarily a 'good thing'. These fundamental changes have emerged from the charity law reform processes. The latter, in particular, have set the United Kingdom apart from other common law jurisdictions and apart from its own developmental history. For all religions and religious organisations seeking charitable status in the United Kingdom, the new statutory requirement – to demonstrate how they are adding to the quotient of public benefit and how that contribution outweighs any possible detraction from it – is a challenge. It is one that faces not only all religious entities seeking charitable status in the future, but also all that have already acquired that status and, by virtue of establishing new case law precedents, it has the potential to fundamentally alter the future relationship between charity and religion within the United Kingdom and beyond.

Developments in human rights case law have also effected real changes in that relationship. Perhaps the most significant of these has been the focus on an individual's subjective interpretation as the determining test of what constitutes 'religious belief' in any particular circumstance. This test would seem to be relied upon by judiciary and regulators as a means of coping with the proliferation of New Age religions, of evangelical versions of Christianity and the many and varied forms of faith that are beginning to crowd out the more traditional and institutional religions. Their response to this wave of new and mutating forms of belief systems, all seeking recognition as coming within the definition of 'religion' and therefore within the eligibility criteria for tax exemption, has been to examine the cogency and authenticity of that belief. In terms of 'religion', the existence of a body of doctrines and tenets, the fact or mode of worship and the belief or not in a god or gods have become matters of peripheral importance in determining whether the definition is satisfied.[1] In terms of 'religious belief', it is not the fact of being an adherent of a specific religion that is important, but rather the nature and the subjective understanding of beliefs and the appropriateness of an individual's actions as a manifestation of those beliefs. When taken together with the public benefit test, this exercise in revisionism has added greatly to the current general unease about the role of religion in society: an uncertainty as to when private piety constitutes religious belief and the extent to which a 'religion' necessarily defines the beliefs of its adherents. Needless to say, such uncertainty has not been helped by the revelations of child abuse perpetrated over several generations and continents by some members of religious organisations.

If the competition between the different variants of religion and other forms of belief is accelerating, that is as nothing compared to the increasing mutual antipathy between those with and those without religious faith. Secularists would seem to be growing numerically and in assertiveness in all the jurisdictions considered, and indeed it is this more than anything that now gives added potency to many items on the moral imperatives agenda. A strong secularist lobby is now demanding to know what it is about religious beliefs – as opposed, for example, to Marxism – that confers an entitlement to exemption from human rights principles. While the traditional secular functions of religious organisations have to some extent been impacted by human rights, they have also benefited from specific statutory exemption privileges. In some instances compliance has been enforced by direct legal action: courts have ordered

---

[1] There remains, admittedly, a good deal of jurisdictional variation in the weight given to these factors as determinants of charitable status.

religious hospitals and personnel to offer services that breach their religious beliefs; regulators have forced the closure of religious facilities due to their inability to meet legislative non-discrimination requirements; and legislation has been introduced specifically to override the capacity of medical personnel to exercise a religious veto regarding the availability of abortion. In other areas, the difficulties involved are proving difficult to resolve: the restrictions, for example, within religious organisations on the appointment of clergy to certain posts being dependant upon their satisfying criteria of gender and sexual orientation. Indeed, the exemption privileges in equality legislation, permitting tax-exempt religious organisations to restrict employment opportunities to those that share their religious beliefs, have been condemned by some as statutorily licensing religious discrimination by religious bodies, leading secularists to protest that there is no good reason why taxpayers should be left to subsidise the discriminatory practices (religious, sexual and gender) of religious organisations.

Religion, Charity and Human Rights sets out to examine the relationship between these three subjects. It does so from the perspective of a charity law academic who acknowledges that, while he has a working knowledge of related human rights case law developments, his grasp of Christian theology and 'Natural law' will disappoint some (moreover, that perspective has probably been influenced by the experience of many decades of living in Northern Ireland). Its central axis rests on the relationship between religion and charity law, a relationship originating in the early years of the Protestant Reformation in England and one that transferred with the forces of the Crown to all parts of the British Empire. Since the last half of the twentieth century, both have interfaced with an ever-expanding equality and human rights jurisprudence, thereby setting the scene for the current conflict between canon law, charity law and human rights law. It's a conflict that underpins the spreading 'culture wars'.

This necessarily means that the book is exclusively concerned with Christianity and charity law as practised in the common law jurisdictions. It consists of 11 chapters arranged in three parts under the headings 'Background', 'Contemporary international perspectives' and 'Future directions'. Because of the considerable similarity in the national and international legislative provisions that give effect to this law, the book draws in the main from the cases to compare and contrast jurisdictional differences in relation to certain key issues.

Part I begins with a background section of four chapters. The first two explain core concepts, principles, precepts and legal definitions, provide a historical overview of the developing relationship between religion and charity in a common law context and outline some of the more influential parameters. The second two chapters address the domestic frames of reference that compete with religion and then, in an international context, consider the impact of human rights case law and charity law reform on religion. The objective of this section is to broadly sketch the common law heritage shared by the six jurisdictions that are the subject of detailed study in Part II. Of particular interest is the specific religion-related changes to that heritage recently introduced by developments in charity law and human rights.

Part II, which comprises the bulk of the book, deals with contemporary international perspectives and in six chapters focuses in turn on England and Wales, Ireland, the United States, Canada, Australia and New Zealand. Of these, the first is necessarily the longest as so much of the foundations for the contemporary law governing charity, the advancement of religion as a charitable purpose, the Church–State relationship and the social role of religion, were laid in England. The objective of this section is to examine the inter-relationship between canon law, charity law and human rights law as illustrated in the cases generated within each jurisdiction. In order to facilitate the systematic gathering of information and allow for ease of cross-referencing and comparative analysis, a loosely designed template is utilised but with some elasticity as, particularly in relation to the United States, there is often a need to take account of singular, jurisdiction-specific, material.

Part III, the final section of one chapter, draws from material in the jurisdiction-specific chapters to examine the nature of the present legal impasse confronting 'religion', to consider the implications of the current agenda of 'moral imperatives' and to assess possible future directions.

PART I

Background

1

Religion, charity and the state

Concepts, precepts, relationships and boundaries

Introduction

Beginning with the key building blocks, this chapter considers the definition and social roles of 'religion' and 'charity' and the capacity of religious charities to further both. It reflects on the associated core values of piety and altruism, drawing attention to the significance of de Tocqueville's 'moral tie',[1] the balance between member benefit and public benefit, between individual and collective piety, and the tendency for religion to accentuate social differences. The institutions of Church and State and the evolving relationship between them are then examined with a special focus on theocratic rule, with its fusion of public and private beliefs, suppression of non-State religions and the moral imperatives that emerged from Christian theocracy. Consideration is given to the support of institutional religious bodies for the State, the distinctive role of an Established Church and the significance of religious doctrine and canon law.

This is balanced by an appraisal of secularism and the consequent emerging confrontation between those with religious beliefs and those without, on an agenda of important social issues, in which context religious charities have a tendency to develop a discriminatory role. The modern phenomenon of multiculturalism, resulting from the waves of economic migration that have arrived to challenge Western culture in recent years, is considered together with the implications of ethnic diversity for religion, charity and human rights. This leads into the concluding part of the chapter, which addresses the impact of pluralism on both religion and charity and the role played by government subsidies. The relevance of bonding and bridging forms of social capital are weighed, the capacity of religion to accommodate pluralism is examined and the risks associated with the rising tide of didactic moralism are noted.

---

[1] See, A. de Tocqueville, *Democracy in America*, Saunders and Otley, London, 1835.

Religion and charity: concepts, definitions and social role

It has been said that:

> The importance of religion as a fundamental spring of charity can scarcely be overestimated. It is part of the makeup of Man to want to give. It is part of the ethics of most religions to encourage that.[2]

The problem is that neither 'religion' nor 'charity' has ever been wholly amenable to legal definition. Over time, however, each has acquired its own distinctive set of hallmarks, at least within the common law tradition.

Religion

The law has always approached with considerable caution the question of whether the set of beliefs adhered to by a person or group constitute a 'religion'. While it avoids being drawn into any assessment of the merits or otherwise of any such 'religion', it looks for substantive corroborating evidence of what it is that its adherents collectively believe and the form and manner in which they express their beliefs. Attention may then turn to whether or not a member of a 'religion' does in fact understand and wholly subscribe to its beliefs, is genuinely committed to pursuing them, and is doing so through activities that are designed for and do in fact progress those religious beliefs.

Religions

The gamut of religious groupings is considerable and probably indeterminate. Among the oldest extant religions are those of Christianity, Judaism and Islam, each of which accommodates an ever-growing number of separate and distinct religious groups. Other prominent religions with well-established histories include Buddhism, Hinduism and Sikhism. In addition, there are a large and fluctuating number of organisations with a varying quotient of religious characteristics of which Mormons, Scientologists, Druze and Zoroastrians are perhaps the most notable. Then there are religious-type groupings that derive from and represent a particular ethnic culture, found among the Indigenous people of Australia, Canada and elsewhere, and which include distinctive entities such as the Rastafarians. Outside the range of religious groupings there are various

---

[2] See, Government White Paper, *Charities: A Framework for the Future*, (Cm 694), HMSO, London, 1989 at p.8.

cults which have little in common with religion other than commitment to a central belief, nor with each other except for a common tendency towards abnormal rituals and the 'brainwashing' of members.

Philosophical and other value systems differ from religion by not having a theistic component and by being less reliant upon the supernatural. This renders them more open to empirical testing. They share with religion the fact that the belief of adherents rests on conviction and commitment to a set of principles that informs their world view. Like religious beliefs, a person's philosophy or values is an intrinsically and intensely personal matter, not readily amenable to objective proof, but is equally capable of providing guidance for leading a 'good life' and for managing relationships with others.

Religious doctrine and cannon law

The individuality of religious belief is balanced by the necessarily collective experience of 'religion': while traditionally the former was understood as wholly derived from the latter, there is now an acceptance that 'belonging' to a religion is insufficient to define and corroborate an individual's religious belief; the public and private dimensions both require validation. The traditional means of verification rested on the particular doctrines and such subscribed to by a body of religious adherents. These continue to provide satisfactory evidence of 'religion' – if not of an individual's religious belief.

Just as all beliefs are not necessarily religious, so some associated with a religion are not absolutely integral and essential to it, and of those that are, some are of lesser importance than others. The core mandatory beliefs, upheld as being of central importance to any religion, are established in its doctrines, tenets and creed. Canon law, though restricted to a minority of religions, sets out the powers and duties, the regulations and procedures by which the internal affairs of a religious organisation are to be conducted.

Doctrines, tenets, etc.

A body of core doctrines or creeds comprise the essence of a religion: they serve to affirm the beliefs that commit and bind the members as adherents of a particular religion. Their significance as representing 'terms of membership' – the submission of the individual to the collective – is very evident from the clear statement in the Second

Epistle of Peter that 'no prophecy of the scripture is of any private interpretation'. While some contain beliefs common to a number of religions, the main function of doctrines is to assert those specific beliefs which firmly differentiate one religion from all others. The immortality of the soul, for example, a belief crucial to the doctrine of divine authority of the Scriptures, is central to the Protestant religion, but is also common to other Christian religions and is proclaimed by Buddhists, Jews and Muslims, among others. The doctrines of transubstantiation, immaculate conception and 'purgatory' are, however, specific to Roman Catholicism;[3] the Nicene Creed is a core Christian belief;[4] while a belief in predestination distinguishes Calvinism. The doctrines of a religion exist not just as an inert public document – a record of how and why it was established – but also as a continuing source of inspiration, guidance and direction for its members. As has been said:

> It belongs to the religious convictions of a good many religious people in our society that they ought to base their decisions concerning fundamental issues of justice on their religious convictions. They do not view it as an option whether or not to do it. It is their conviction that they ought to strive for wholeness, integrity, integration in their lives: that they ought to allow the Word of God, the teachings of the Torah, the command and example of Jesus, or whatever, to shape their existence as a whole, including, then, their social and political existence. Their religion is not, for them, about something other than their social and political existence.[5]

The point of religious doctrine is to assure members that the one true way is as ordained in their set of beliefs and require them to demonstrate this and seek to convince others; doctrinal deviation was the road to heresy. The net result, Rivers has argued, is that 'freedom of religion in English law has not simply been about the freedom to believe and to manifest that belief in worship and doctrine, but about the plurality of protected social and material spaces in which believers could live faithfully to their religion'.[6] The implication being, I think, that a religious

---

[3] See, further, P. Ridge, 'The Legal Regulation of Religious Giving' (2006) 157 *Law and Justice* 17.

[4] Formulated in AD 325 at the First Council of Nicaea, the Nicene Creed was based on Christian understanding of the Canonical Gospels, the letters of the New Testament and, to a lesser extent, the Old Testament.

[5] N. Woltersorrf, 'The Role of Religion in Decision and Discussion of Political Issues' in R. Audi and N. Woltersorrf, *Religion in the Public Square: The Place of Religious Convictions in Political Debate*, Rowan and Littlefield, New York, 1997.

[6] J. Rivers, 'Law, Religion and Gender Equality' (2007) 9 *Ecclesiastical Law Journal* 24, 52.

person or organisation must not be corralled in their expression of belief to designated places and times of worship, to prayerful activity and suchlike, but should be permitted to manifest their beliefs through normal daily civic engagements (employment, recreation and the like). This conviction that for 'believers' all conduct must conform to their beliefs is a very potent force which, as has been argued by Jurgen Habermas and others, is capable of divisive social and political consequences.[7]

Canon law

Confined to the Catholic Church, the Greek Orthodox Church and the Anglican Church, canon law consists of a body of 'canons' or rules that have been agreed and adopted by authority of the Church's ecclesiastical body over many centuries. It functions in much the same way as its civil counterpart. It not only gives effect to religious doctrines but extends to set out the rules for managing organisational matters and issues of ordinary daily life.

With its origins in Catholicism and Papal authority, canon law in England pre-dates the Reformation by several centuries.[8] After the Reformation, the enforcement by the Ecclesiastical Courts of the 151 canons that constituted the Canons of 1603[9] formed the foundations of a civic morality that infused the laws, particularly those relating to the family, throughout the common law nations: marriage, for example, remained for centuries within the remit of the Church. A network of some three or four hundred Ecclesiastical Courts then administered ecclesiastical law[10] with jurisdiction over matters dealing with the rights and obligations of church members which, in effect, meant almost all English citizens. The range of offences that fell within the scope of these courts in theory extended to all matters which could be construed as 'sinful' but their chief concern was with matters of moral turpitude (e.g. bastardy, fornication, bigamy, blasphemy, buggery, drunkenness, defamation, perjury, usury and swearing). Until the court reforms in the second half of the nineteenth century, the ecclesiastical jurisdiction extended over a wide

---

[7] J. Habermas, 'Religion in the Public Sphere' (2006) 14:1 *European Journal of Philosophy* 1.

[8] For example, Canon 33 enacted at the Synod of Evira (*c.* AD 305–306) proclaimed the obligation of celibacy for priests.

[9] See, P. Jones, *Lynwood's Provinciale*, edited by J. V. Bullard and C. H. Bell, Faith Press, London, 1929. The *Provinciale* was compiled by William Lynwood in about 1432 and is the principal source of canon law in England.

[10] The ecclesiastical law of England consists of the general principles of the *ius commune ecclesiasticum*: see, further, *Ever* v. *Owen* Godbolt's Report 432, per Whitlock J.

spectrum of personal affairs, including probate, marriage and divorce, tithes, defamation and disciplinary prosecutions involving the laity.

Private immoral conduct was not only a 'sin' and therefore within the remit of the Church, with its concern for the salvation of souls, but it was also a public offence and punishable by the State as a crime. This, perhaps overly Protestant, equation of sin = crime, which governed a wide spread of social behaviour, underpinned the beginnings of accepted civic morality across the common law world.

Nowadays the jurisdiction of canon law has been ousted by civil law, wherever they overlap, leaving it to deal mainly with issues relating to the organisation of the Church and the management of its officials, income and property.

Religious differences

There are attributes of membership that permit, and some that certainly promote, a communal sharing with others, but for each religion the core requirement is generally one of exclusiveness. To belong to one religion, or to belong to none, necessitates rejecting the beliefs of others.

Subliminal permeation

The subliminal quality of religion allows it to discreetly permeate the secular world of politics, institutions and service provision outlets, and influence their content – from adding justification for war to resisting the planting of genetically modified crops. Some of the more contentious disputes arise when the 'hidden' influence of religion is detected: notably in school teaching materials that depict only the Judeo-Christian model of the traditional family unit; possibly, also, in the 'neo-con' politics of the last Bush administration in the United States. As a counterpoint, quite a number of secularly staffed and managed facilities such as hospitals and other health or social care services are owned by religious organisations that prefer not to allow their religious beliefs to impinge upon professional service provision. Further, many nonprofit and charitable agencies (e.g. Amnesty International and Meals-on-Wheels) tend to be similarly staffed.

Public and private interests

Religion generates an interesting mix of public and private interests. Religious beliefs, as experienced by an individual, are clearly an entirely personal and internal matter: the interests served are private, save to the extent that any effect they are seen to have on that individual may serve to influence others. Should such an individual choose to manifest their religious beliefs, by engaging in activities intended to give effect to them, then for better or worse that activity becomes a matter of public interest.

The public sphere

Religious organisations, as physical manifestations of virtuous principles, as deliverers of public benefit services and as institutions representing religious views on current issues to government and the public, are unequivocally players in the public domain.

In this context, the Jurgen Habermas argument carries some weight. For the religious individual, as for the religious organisation, private piety and public conduct must be synonymous: those of faith are doctrinally obliged to strive to shape matters of public interest into conformity with their religious beliefs; their views are necessarily dogmatic because religious dogma leaves them unable to compromise. He notes that this imposes an additional and, arguably, an unreasonable burden on such individuals and organisations as they are not free to take any action or advance any views which may compromise their beliefs. While holding firm to the view that there must be a separating of public from private interests, he suggests that 'the liberal state must not transform the requisite institutional separation of religion and politics into an undue mental and psychological burden for those of its citizens who follow a faith'.[11] The challenge is to find a way of engaging with those of religious belief to ensure that their interests find proportionate representation in the institutions and public policy that constitute contemporary politics; subject to the caveat that the body politic must not in that process allow itself to become hostage to a possible religious veto.

Religion and politics

The Marxian critique of religion as 'the opium of the people'[12] is open to debate, but over the millennia and in many different continents, religion and its adherents have been alternately courted and demonised by secular authorities. Governments in modern Western democracies are

[11] Habermas, 'Religion in the Public Sphere', at p.9.
[12] See, K. Marx, *Critique of Hegel's Philosophy of Right*, edited by J. O'Malley, Cambridge University Press, Cambridge, 1970 [1844].

no longer troubled by having to function within a theocratic context, but the legacy from having once done so is very apparent in the caution with which they now deal with religion, religious organisations and associated adherents. Where Church and State maintain a joint relationship – as with Protestantism in England and to some extent with Catholicism in Ireland – the political nexus thus created provides a distinctive centre of gravity for that society which may well be perceived as alienating by those of other religious belief and those of none. Alternatively, there are some common law countries, most obviously the United States, where Church and State are constitutionally separated and where politics is consequently overshadowed by the need to constantly demonstrate both its immunity from religious influence and disinterest in preferencing any one religion, or the interests of religion per se relative to those of secularism.

Charity

The single most important attribute of 'charity', as this term is known in all countries that share the common law tradition, is that it be unequivocally dedicated to the public benefit. Throughout the centuries the altruism of the individual,[13] generating the voluntary contribution of many for the public good, has always been held to be its vital and distinguishing characteristic.

Altruism

Titmuss, in his seminal and widely quoted work *The Gift Relationship*,[14] explored the nature of altruism. He examined the relationship between donor and recipient in the context of two models of blood donation that prevailed in the 1960s: the philanthropic exchange model in the United Kingdom and the commercial service model in the United States. The former he found to be altruistic as it relied upon an act of 'giving' – blood being donated by the voluntary and selfless act of an individual, constituting ethically based behaviour. The UK National Blood Transfusion Service provided a service to which blood donors made anonymous

---

[13] It was Comte's *Philosophy of the Sciences* (translated by George Lewes, 1890) that first introduced the word 'altruism' (from the French 'alteri huic') into the English language.

[14] See R. A. Titmuss, *The Gift Relationship: From Human Blood to Social Policy*, London, Allen and Unwin, 1970.

contributions, without financial or other reward, and from which recipients took according to need, incurring no cost, and without knowing the identity of the donor. In Titmuss' view, this free gift of blood left the relationship between giver and recipient uncompromised by any 'contract of custom; legal bond; functional determinism; situations of discriminatory power; nor by domination, constraint or compulsion.'[15] This 'gift relationship', it has been argued, is something that can bond us as a society.

Indeed, as Titmuss himself pointed out: 'The social relations set up by gift exchange are among the most powerful forces which bind a social group together.'[16] He argued that altruism lay at the heart of that relationship – and that activities which allowed opportunities for altruism were of value to the individuals concerned and to society generally because ethical conduct was good in itself, generating a sense of shared morality and civic responsibility that served to bond society. Titmuss took the view that altruism was the reason people donated blood without direct reward, at a cost of their own time and effort, to another with whom they would have no direct contact. A regard for the needs of others was the principle that motivated their action. Donors showed a high sense of awareness of belonging to a community and of social responsibility. It followed that it was important for the State to provide the opportunity for individuals to express their commitment to the community in which they lived; indeed, he developed this theme in his final chapter, 'The Right to Give'. The gift was to be valued both for its own sake and because its demonstration of altruism would also encourage others to give. The act of giving modelled ethical conduct, and generated a sense of shared morality and civic responsibility in more caring communities.

In practice this gift is twofold: from the donor and from the State. The first is uncontroversial: in a democracy, any persons of sound mind (subject to the rights of dependants) are free to give their property to whomsoever they choose; this can be by way of charity. The second, when the charity vehicle is used and the State adds considerably to the value of the gift by exempting it from tax, is hedged about with conditions that can give rise to controversy.

Titmuss would still recognise the altruism that underpins modern charity and his defence of the right to give remains valid. However,

---

[15] Ibid. [16] Ibid., at p.73.

18 RELIGION, CHARITY AND THE STATE

although the parties to the gift relationship remain much the same, the nature of the gift itself has changed considerably.

The public good

Blood was the particular gift identified by Titmuss as constituting a 'public good', but the latter has traditionally been interpreted in terms of a gift of funds and/or food and shelter. Increasingly, however, use is now made of assets with potential for achieving more long-term and sustainable improvement. The strategic value of a workshop, farm, or manufacturing plant, for example, can be an effective contribution in situations where those who are to use it, and thereby secure their future independence, have received the necessary preparatory training, and appropriate support systems are in place. The giving of time, as well as or instead of a gift of money or other forms of property, is also a public good.

Member benefit vs. public benefit

Any consideration of religious charities and public benefit must take into account the school of thought which argues that while a particular value of religion and charity lies in their undoubted capacity to generate social capital,[17] religion is essentially a member benefit activity and as such must fail the public benefit test: the 'public' arm being constrained in scope by the number and exclusiveness of its adherents; 'benefit' being restricted to personal and intangible rewards; and more generally that there can be no charity in attempting to save one's soul because charity, that is charity in law, is necessarily altruistic (for the benefit of others).[18] Essentially this view contends that the 'bonding' form of social capital provided by religion is at the price of the 'bridging' form;[19] and, arguably, can serve to emphasise differences, accentuate the marginalisation of minority groups and increase social polarisation. This argument, when extended to take account of the vast range of religious buildings, artefacts, activities and services, etc. (including, but not restricted to churches, chapels, synagogues, temples and mosques; services, rituals,

---

[17] See, further, R. Putnam, *Bowling Alone*, Simon and Schuster, New York, 2000, at p.19.

[18] *In re Delany: Conoley* v. *Quick* [1902] 2 Ch. 642 *per* Farwell J., at p.648.

[19] See Puttnam, *Bowling Alone*. Also see, G. Çelik, 'Breakpoint or Binder: Religious Engagement in Dutch Civil Society' (2013) 9:3 *Journal of Civil Society* 248.

ceremonies and prayers; musical instruments, sheet music, bells, sacred vessels, candles, seating for ministers and choirs; churchyards, cemeteries and burial sites) accompanying such charities, questions how such an array of material that advertises the separateness and exclusiveness of organisations and their respective adherents could be conducive to promoting a collective sense of public good.

Charity and politics

Generating engagement in socially responsible activity has become an attractive proposition for governments striving to cultivate a sufficient mandate to continue in office. Promoting charity has been viewed as politically advantageous: by providing opportunities for concerned individuals to ameliorate the disadvantages of others, government can both reduce costs and accountability for service provision while also promoting civil society. Consequently it is often the policy of governments to support charity and the contribution of volunteers as a means of fostering a sense of civic responsibility and assisting the growth of social capital.[20]

There is, of course, another view which holds that charity has always been the foil of capitalism: it being politically expedient to leave to charity the needs of those who fail and must pay the price for a society driven by the competitive forces that constitute an 'open market' economy. In such a cynical political scenario poverty 'will always be with us' because a capitalist society requires winners and losers; and equally, charity is assured of a permanent role in such a society in order to rescue the victims, salve the conscience of the successful and patch over the cracks sufficiently to allow capitalism to continue.

The relationship between religion and charity

There is a presumption of a natural synergy between religion and charity. As has been stated:

> The importance of religion as a fundamental spring of charity can scarcely be overestimated. It is part of the makeup of Man to want to give. It is part of the ethics of most religions to encourage that. Trusts for the advancement of religion have contributed much to the spiritual welfare of individuals and to the sound development of our society.[21]

---

[20] Ibid.   [21] See Government White Paper, *Charities: A Framework for the Future*, at p.8.

However, this is open to challenge. Despite a requirement in all religions for faith and good works to go hand in hand, history records many acts conducted in the name of religion that were far from charitable. There is also ample proof from contemporary events to demonstrate that religious persons, even excepting Islamic Jihadists, are not necessarily charitable. The evidence is, at best, mixed.

A religious duty to assist others

For many, if not most, being a Christian carries with it the duty to love one's neighbour. This has generally been a requirement for salvation of the soul. Christianity is not unique in this respect: Buddhism teaches the love of mankind as the highest form of righteousness; Islam requires a tithe of income to be given to those in need;[22] and the Jewish religion urges its followers to assist the poor and practice charity. While private piety together with theological doctrines of 'predestination' and 'inherent grace' must be taken into account, religion in all its forms has always also placed a high premium on doing good to others. However, extending the hand of friendship has not always been a prominent feature of religious practice.

Leaving aside the Christian zealatory evident in the Crusades and Inquisition, for many centuries Christianity had no difficulty in accommodating slavery,[23] which was accepted as a social institution by the Church – an approach no different from that adopted by Judaism and Islam. Colonialism, also a crude exercise of power by those with superior means over people considered inferior, was pursued with vigour by Christians, and by the late nineteenth century Christian evangelists were intimately involved in the colonial process at least in southern Africa.[24] The suffragette and anti-apartheid movements, the campaign for gender equality and currently the lobbying for equality opportunities

---

[22] See, further, M. M. Gaudiosi, 'The Influence of the Islamic Law of WAQF on the Development of the Trust in England: The Case of Merton College' (1987–88) 136 *University of Pennsylvania Law Review* 1231.

[23] While the British involvement in the slave trade ended in 1807 (a year before the United States), up until then (from the sixteenth to the nineteenth centuries) the British had played a lead role in the transportation of some 12 million Africans to the Americas. See, further, J. Walvin, *Crossings: Africa, the Americas and the Atlantic Slave Trade*, Reaktion, London, 2013.

[24] See, for example, J. Comaroff and J. L. Comaroff, 'Christianity and Colonialism in South Africa' (1986) 13:1 *American Ethnologist* 1.

for heterosexual and homosexual marriage are among those that have seen Christians manning the barricades to resist change.

Moreover, the religious hand of friendship is perhaps not wholly compatible with 'charity' as it is known to the common law. The latter, unlike the former, requires a charitable act to be at donor discretion, within the parameters of a recognised charitable purpose, and to be made for the public benefit. Religious adherence requires intervention: to stand alongside those seen to be suffering, offering care and compassion; but also to bring the iniquitous circumstances to the attention of the appropriate authorities and seek remedial action. However, 'charity' in the common law tradition forbids advocacy as a primary purpose and this has forced many organisations to choose between pursuing charitable status or advocacy.

Church and State

The traditional role of religious organisations as authoritative social institutions continues to have political resonance in many modern secular States. Religion's span of population permeation and the ability of its organisations to accumulate wealth, together with an inherent capacity to inculcate values, maintain order and thereby contribute to social cohesion had always assured it of special attention from government. The interests of Church and State may at varying times have been wholly united, divided or locked in mutual opposition, but they have also been intimately and lastingly interwoven and form an inescapable backdrop to the history of charity in a common law context.

Theocracy

In England, theocratic rule provided the environment in which the relationships between Church, charity and the State were first formulated. That process, transferred by colonialism, provided a model for all common law jurisdictions: a structure for Church–State relationships; and a format for the social roles of religion and charity. As the following chapters illustrate, the way these relationships have worked out has distanced those jurisdictions from that initial model and, to some extent, from each other.

Theocratic rule

In England, both prior to and following the upheaval of the Reformation, governance was essentially theocratic in nature: before 1534 King Henry

22 RELIGION, CHARITY AND THE STATE

VIII ruled by divine right in support of Catholicism with Papal guidance; afterwards he did so in support of Protestantism without it. Matters deemed to be in breach of religious doctrine, and therefore sinful, continued to receive secular endorsement and attract rigorous punishment by State authorities. The secular enforcement of religious doctrine was through the designation of a range of conduct as 'profane', being both criminal and sinful, including apostasy,[25] heresy[26] and blasphemy.[27] Once a breach was designated a 'sin' it then automatically became a crime and excommunication from the Church could follow (even if the subject was the head of State, as happened to King John in the early thirteenth century).[28]

Theocratic rule and moral imperatives

Christian principles established the moral imperatives that came to inform the law relating to the family and now provide the grounds for those of traditional religious beliefs to challenge the changes being driven by equality and human rights legislation.[29] As Lord Finlay LC commented in *Bowman* v. *Secular Society Ltd.*, when reflecting on previous centuries of case law:

> It has been repeatedly laid down by the Courts that Christianity is part of the law of the land, and it is the fact that our civil polity is to a large extent based upon the Christian religion. This is notably so with regard to the law of marriage and the law affecting the family.[30]

He was quite clear that up until then the courts would have considered themselves bound by such principles when called upon to interpret

---

[25] Apostasy occurs when someone who has been religious explicitly renounces their adherence to that religion and denies its validity.

[26] Heresy occurs when someone pronounces beliefs or principles that are at variance with those of the prevailing religion.

[27] Blasphemy occurs when someone insults or shows contempt or lack of reverence for a religion or for any of its beliefs or practices.

[28] Note that the Ecclesiastical Courts could, by issuing a 'letter of signification', require the secular courts to enforce its sentences.

[29] Laws LJ acknowledged as much in *McFarlane* v. *Relate Avon Ltd.* [2010] IRLR 872; 29 BHRC 249 when he observed that 'the Judaeo-Christian tradition, stretching over many centuries, has no doubt exerted a profound influence upon the judgment of lawmakers as to the objective merits of this or that social policy', at para. 23.

[30] *Bowman* v. *Secular Society Ltd.* (1917) AC 406 (HL), citing: *Briggs* v. *Hartley* (1850) 19 LJ (Ch.) 416; *Cowan* v. *Milbourn* (1867) LR 2 Ex. 230; *De Costa* v. *De Paz* (1754) 2 Swanst, 487; and *In re Bedford Charity* (1819) 2 Swanst, 470, 527.

'religion' in a charity law context.[31] The distinctively Christian dimension to those principles included: monogamous, heterosexual marriage for life; the sanctity of marriage to the exclusion of non-marital sex, any children thereof, and unmarried partnerships; the prohibition of abortion; and the rejection of a Darwinian approach to the meaning of 'life'.

Theocratic rule and charity

The fact that theocratic rule was very much the political context for the birth of charity law, and continued to be so for many years later, is evident from the prosecutions for such profanities as heresy[32] and blasphemy,[33] which were still being conducted after the 1601 Act. Indeed, in England, trial by jury for atheism continued until 1842.[34]

State religions

As distinct from theocratic rule, in which the authority and administrative systems of Church and State are mutually reinforcing if not wholly unified and jointly promulgate the doctrines of a particular religion, State religions are those that are established as the primary religion among others and as such enjoy a varying level of State support rather than State enforcement. The distinction is one not easily drawn and many countries have evolved from the former to the latter.

Contemporary religious States

Barro and McCleary, in their survey of 188 countries, established that, in the year 2000, 40 per cent, or 75 countries, could be classified as having a

---

[31] A long catalogue of cases beginning with *De Costa* v. *De Paz* (1754) 2 Swanst, 487, Chancery, including *Lawrence* v. *Smith, Murray* v. *Benbow* (1822) The Times 2 Feb. 1822, *Briggs* v. *Hartley* (1850) 19 LJ (Ch.) 416, and ending with *Pare* v. *Clegg* (1861) 29 Beav. 589, 54 ER 756, established that 'the Courts will not help in the promotion of objects contrary to the Christian religion'.

[32] The last heretics to be burned at the stake in England were Legate at Smithfield in 1612 upon a writ *de haeretico comburendo*, and Wightman at Lichfield about the same time.

[33] See the trials of Atwood 1618 (Cro. Jac. 421; 2 Roll. Abr. 78) and Taylor 1676 (1 Ventris 293; 3 Kebble 607; 2 Strange 789).

[34] J. Erskine, in sentencing G. J. Holyoake, pronounced: 'we do not assume to be the protectors of our God, but to protect the people from such indecent language'. See, further, The Project Gutenberg e-book of George Jacob Holyoake, *The History of the Last Trial by Jury for Atheism in England* (accessed 20 July 2011) at: www.gutenberg.org/files/36799/36799-h/36799-h.htm

State religion.[35] Of the total, 113 did not have a State-supported religion; 29 did and were Muslim; 22 were Catholic; 10 Protestant; 4 Buddhist; 1 Hindu; and 1 Jewish. Those without included Ireland, Australia, New Zealand, Canada and the United States. Catholicism was typically the State religion in southern Europe (Italy, Spain and Portugal), while in the United Kingdom it was Protestantism. The authors explain that establishing or maintaining a State religion enables a government 'to favor the majority religion by subsidizing its practices and by restricting religious expression of minorities', and that 'these subsidies and restrictions are hallmarks of a State religion'.[36] This view was endorsed in 2011 by Bielefeldt, a Special Rapporteur, who in the process of presenting his latest report on freedom of religion or belief and recognition issues to the UN Human Rights Council in Geneva, cautioned against the use of 'official' religion for purposes of national identity politics and commented that 'it seems difficult, if not impossible, to conceive of an official "State religion" that in practice does not have adverse effects on religious minorities, thus discriminating against their members'.[37] As Rawls once put it: 'How is it possible . . . for those of faith . . . to endorse a constitutional regime even when their comprehensive doctrines may not prosper under it, and indeed may decline?'[38]

Separation of Church and State

As the social context for an evolving charity law in a common law context became less theocratic, with boundaries emerging between the spheres of interest of Church and State, so the shared ground for continued mutual support became gradually based less on matters of religious doctrine. After all, as John Locke once advised, 'neither the right nor the art of ruling does necessarily carry along with it the certain knowledge of other things; and least of all the true religion'.[39]

---

[35] See R. J. Barro and R. M. McCleary, 'Which Countries Have State Religions?' (2005) 120:4 *The Quarterly Journal of Economics* 1331.

[36] Ibid.

[37] See H. Bielefeldt, 'Report of the Special Rapporteur on Freedom of Religion or Belief', presented to the UN General Assembly, Human Rights Council Nineteenth Session, 22 December 2011.

[38] J. Rawls, 'The Idea of Public Reason Revisited' (1997) 64 *The University of Chicago Law Review* 765, at p.781.

[39] See J. Locke, *A Letter on Toleration*, edited by James H. Tully, Hackett Publishing Company, Indianapolis, 1983 [1689], at p.36.

Secularism

The principle of secularism is not without its complications.[40] It broadly suggests that matters of government should be wholly insulated from any religious influence. As Neuhaus once explained, it is an affront to democracy when those who make political points do so on the basis of private truths: 'public decisions must be made by arguments that are public in character'.[41]

This can be interpreted as licensing the State to assume responsibility for all decision-making, facilities, administrative systems and processes associated with matters in the public interest, without any concessions to a religion or religions nor of any input from religious organisations. While the term clearly would not accommodate State religion, or any State preferencing of religion (e.g. favouring Christianity over Islam), there is doubt as to whether it extends to suggesting that religion per se, or religions, or religious values should not be recognised and respected by the State; though not for Jurgen Habermas who urges that the State 'must not discourage religious persons and communities from also expressing themselves politically as such'.[42]

It may also be interpreted as affording religion protection from government interference in all circumstances where there is no evidence of criminality. This might be understood, in the developed Western nations, as starting with constitutional arrangements that clearly separate State and religion. Statute law would declare that government had neither the interest nor the power to impose any form of restriction on religious belief and practice. It would not interfere in the self-governance of religious bodies and would allow such bodies to determine internal arrangements for recruiting staff, teaching and training adherents. It would similarly stand aside from any donation of funds, time or other resources freely made to religious bodies and would permit missionary work or proselytism to be undertaken by such bodies or on their behalf within or outside the jurisdiction.

Essentially, this would seem to lead to a dichotomy: the public arena is either an open market in which all religions are equally free to proclaim and manifest their beliefs, compete for adherents and be assured of equal respect and engagement from State authorities; or, alternatively, the

---

[40] The term 'secularism' was first coined by George Jacob Holyoake (1817–1906).
[41] See R. J. Neuhaus, *The Naked Public Square*, Erdmans, Grand Rapids, 1984, at p.36.
[42] Habermas, 'Religion in the Public Sphere', at p.10.

public arena is one in which all religions are equally prohibited from exercising any presence, that space is reserved entirely for secular entities and their activities, and all religions can be assured that they will be equally ignored by the State authorities. In either case, however the State would function impartially.

Habermas argues that 'every citizen must know and accept that only secular reasons count beyond the institutional threshold that divides the informal public sphere from parliaments, courts, ministries and administrations'.[43] He explains:

> The principle of separation of church and state demands that the institution of the state operate with strict impartiality vis-a-vis religious communities; parliaments, courts, and the administration must not violate the prescription not to privilege one side at the cost of another. But this principle is to be distinguished from the laicist demand that the state should defer from adopting any political stance which would support or constrain religion per se, even if this affects all religious communities equally. That would amount to an overly narrow interpretation of the separation of state and church. At the same time, the rejection of secularism must not succumb to leaving the door wide open for revisions that would undermine the principle itself.[44]

The State, secularism and religious charities

From a secularist perspective, any supportive State role in relation to religion and its works is always going to be fraught and certain choices have to be made.

Quite apart from any socially binding or divisive side effects, the contribution of religion to public benefit rests on the solace, strength and equanimity it may instil in individuals that their beliefs in this life will be rewarded in the next. As there is no direct social utility there can be no State support. Religion and its ancillary organisations must take their place in the open market alongside such other social forces as for-profit concerns, philosophy, philanthropy, etc., compete for their own niche and be subject to the same loose regulatory constraints.

Alternatively, it might be argued that a distinction should be drawn between 'religion' as an institution with its churches, ministers, etc. and any secular public benefit role that a religious organisation may have in

---

[43] Ibid., at p.9. [44] Ibid., at p.6.

the community. The former could be entitled to State support on the grounds that, notwithstanding its purpose to prepare those of faith for a supernatural existence, its beliefs embody mankind's higher aspirations; its values as modelled by adherents contribute to making contemporary society a better place; and, anyway, for some millennia, civilisation has accorded religion a special status. As regards the latter, however, it can be argued that religious organisations will do what they do with or without government input: piety requires good works; such organisations are impelled by their beliefs to engage in public benefit service provision; they need neither charitable status nor tax exemption privileges to continue an established social role that is integral to religious belief. On that basis, all ancillary religious organisations (i.e. those with a community role) would be ineligible for State support and for charitable status in respect of any function that could be performed by a for-profit or other nonprofit organisation: as otherwise it could only be construed that the secular charitable role was to be used as a means to further religious ends. The justification for retaining the advancement of religion as a charitable purpose thus disappears.

More pragmatically, in the pluralist States where economic recession is forcing cutbacks in public benefit provision, there is now a growing likelihood that government will nonetheless look to the wealthy institutional structures of established religions for assistance in making good the public services shortfall.

Government funding of religious charities

A very significant proportion of charity funds come from government, most often in the form of grants for service provision in targeted areas of social need. Some of this goes to religious charities which, operationally, are usually located close to those in need, and have long-established ties with disadvantaged communities. They can therefore more effectively address poverty, hunger, homelessness and drug abuse because they are both more accessible in various ways and because they are more 'mission driven' – impelled by religious beliefs and Church commitment – than their secular counterparts.[45] Whether domestic or overseas, it is often the case that the only possible service providers on hand to address

---

[45] See, for example, R. D. Puttnam and D. E. Campbell, *American Grace: How Religion Divides and Unites Us*, Simon & Schuster, New York, 2010.

concentrations of social need are those operated by churches or other faith-based organisations.

However, the channelling of taxpayers' revenue – from contributions made by adherents of many different religions and by atheists – to specific churches and religious organisations, the majority of which will have hiring or service policies favouring a specific religion and its adherents that significant numbers of taxpayers would not necessarily be sympathetic towards, inevitably generates considerable controversy. Questions arise as to whether this is compatible with a separation of Church and State. Crudely put, the argument is that the government is funding discrimination. Most usually, suggestions of preferencing are countered with claims that government regulators protect public funds from utilisation by religious charities for proselytising purposes and require such charities to separate their religious activities from government-funded programmes. This is a more difficult position to hold when the grants are received by churches for distribution rather than paid directly to religious service providers.

A further argument often advanced is that government funding of religious charities is blurring, if not corrupting, the role of both. Faith-based charities, as they become increasingly dependent on government funds, risk losing their sense of mission, their religious character is subordinated to secular concerns and they come to function largely as another government agency. For government there is a corresponding risk that it will no longer have the sense of responsibility and account-ability that should rest with it as guardian of the public good. Charity is in danger of losing its autonomous character, religion of having its beliefs distorted, and government of slipping into a role of franchising out its responsibilities.

Equality of religions

With the separation of Church and State the principle that the law stands neutral between religions became firmly established by the courts as an indicator of religious tolerance. This stance is very much in keeping with the advice of John Locke that 'the magistrate ought always to be very careful that he do not misuse his authority to the oppression of any Church, under the pretence of public good'.[46]

---

[46] See J. Locke, 'A Letter Concerning Toleration', in *Two Treaties on Government and A Letter Concerning Toleration*, Yale University Press, New Haven, 2005, at pp.236–237.

CHURCH AND STATE

Equality

It was Sir John Romilly MR in *Thornton* v. *Howe*[47] who first author-
atively ruled that the courts would no longer make any distinction
between religions. He then expressed the view that:

> the Court of Chancery makes no distinction between one sort of religion
> and another. They are equally bequests which are included in the general
> term of charitable bequests. Neither does the Court, in this respect, make
> any distinction between one sect and another.[48]

Further, he declared that 'although this court might consider the
opinions sought to be propagated foolish or even devoid of foundation,
it would not, on that account declare it void'.[49] Subsequently, the courts
ruled that they would not inquire into the inherent validity of any
particular religion[50] nor would they examine the relative merits of
different religions.[51]

Atheism and agnostics

Sir John Romilly MR, however, added a significant caveat to his above
ruling, when he warned that the courts would continue to intervene
where 'the tenets of a particular sect inculcate doctrines adverse to the
very foundations of all religion, and . . . are subversive of all morality'.[52]
The line thereby drawn between religious and irreligious beliefs, denying recognition to atheists and agnostics, was still respected a century
later in *Re South Place Ethical Society*[53] when the court determined
that an association whose members advocated a humanistic philosophical concept concerning the excellence of trust, love and beauty,
to the exclusion of anything supernatural, was not a religion for *Pemsel*
purposes.

---

[47] *Thornton* v. *Howe* (1862), 31 Beav. 14.
[48] Ibid., at pp.19–20. Also see, *Re Michael's Trust* (1860) 28 Beav. 39.
[49] *Thornton* v. *Howe* (1862) 31 Beav. 14, at p.20.
[50] See *O'Hanlon* v. *Logue* [1906] 1 IR 247 where Lord Walker advised that 'the Court does
not enter into an inquiry as to the truth or soundness of any religious doctrine, provided
it is not contrary to morals, or contain anything contrary to law', at p.259.
[51] See *Nelan* v. *Downes* (1917) 23 CLR 546.
[52] *Thornton* v. *Howe* (1862) 31 Beav. 14, at pp.19–20; 54 ER 1042.
[53] *Re South Place Ethical Society* [1980] 1 WLR 1565 (sub. nom. *Barralet* v. *A.G.*) [1980] 3
All ER 918 (English Chancery Division).

The impact of multiculturalism

The relative population homogeneity that formerly characterised so many nations, perhaps particularly those of Western Europe, became diluted with ever increasing rapidity in the latter half of the twentieth century. Regions and countries once firmly stamped with a religious and cultural identity in which citizens learned a sense of belonging, of inter-dependency and collective strength that united families and societies, gradually lost a good deal of their distinctiveness and cohesion. The onset of globalisation did much to undo but offered little to replace the social coherence that came with the ties of 'family', locality, Church, etc.

The ties that bind

Pluralism was probably the last thing on the minds of testators. This was mostly evident in a family context where resistance to the possibility of a relative betraying the family's established religious allegiance, principally by 'marrying out', indicated the defensive nature of many religious adherents. In Northern Ireland, for example, recent research found that Protestant testators' charitable bequests have for generations been directed almost exclusively to Protestant beneficiaries.[54]

The practice, whereby the courts upheld the right of donors and institutions to attach quite stringent discriminatory religious conditions of access, persisted for many generations to become an accepted aspect of charity law jurisprudence. In the process an anti-pluralism ethos was legitimated which prepared the ground for contemporary tensions between the principles of charity law and human rights law.

Testators' religious conditions

A considerable body of case law illustrates the importance many testators gave to ensuring the perpetuation of their religious beliefs by the succeeding generation: the inducement of a bequest to a relative beneficiary was offered with entitlement made conditional upon their adhering to an explicit religious requirement; and the right to attach such discriminatory conditions was repeatedly upheld by the judiciary. The

---

[54] See N. Dawson, *Dying to Give: Trends in Charitable Giving by Will*, The Stationery Office, Belfast, 2003.

THE IMPACT OF MULTICULTURALISM 31

precedents established in England were duly transferred to other common law jurisdictions and applied by courts and regulators.

Discriminatory religious prejudices were also evident in the public arena. In some instances this was a consequence of public institutions, like private individuals, being the beneficiaries of testators' biased gifts, and at other times it was due to an institution imposing exclusionary religious access criteria. Unlike gifts made in a private context, however, such practices involving public institutions were likely to be challenged on the grounds of breaching public policy: a challenge that met with an equivocating judicial response in England; but a more robust rejection of any suggested compliance elsewhere.

Discriminatory practice in an institutional setting often differed from testator family bequests in that the effect of religious conditions were prejudicial rather than merely defensive: the public benefit was restricted and distorted in the former; in the latter it was largely avoided in favour of private interests. Both reflected the capacity of religion and charity to function in a partisan and protectionist manner.

Promoting multiculturalism

Catering for difference has become a significant challenge for all institutions of Western society. The recognition given to ethnic, racial, religious and other differences has multiplied exponentially in recent years and equality legislation requires that any such persons or groups must be respected, accommodated and treated equitably within modern social service infrastructures. Initially, neither religion nor charity law had a credible record in that regard.

Religion: from intolerance to acceptance

From approximately the sixteenth century to the early nineteenth, the intolerance shown by theocratic English rulers toward any form of religion or associated organisation and activity, other than that of the Established Church, spread with their armed forces throughout an expanding empire. Not until the late nineteenth and early twentieth centuries did intolerance begin to abate and a more liberal approach to religious diversity take hold. It was then that the reputation of Britain (and subsequently that of other common law countries such as the United States and Canada) as a safe haven for waves of refugee groups fleeing persecution became established. In that context it was perhaps only natural that a sense of cultural affinity would be reflected in the evolving trends relating to donor gifts. As has been pointed out:

> Historically, many minority populations have attempted to avoid, in various ways, assimilation becoming erasure. For those with property and wealth, keeping that wealth 'within the family' in this case meaning the wider family of the minority community, has often been one way of attempting to ensure the continuation of the community itself.[55]

Such concerns directed a flow of funds primarily through private trusts, but also via charitable trusts and bequests, to those conjoined in a cultural nexus with the donor. Huguenots, Jews and many other distinct religious and ethnic groups, finding themselves socially isolated in a foreign land, looked inward to the family circle for support. It was a strategy not restricted to immigrant groups. Indigenous minorities, including Roman Catholics in England and Protestants in Ireland, have traditionally suffered much the same experience and adopted similar methods of coping.

From religious tolerance to ethnic diversity

By the end of the nineteenth century the law in general, including charity law, had extended its recognition of religion beyond the confines of the Established Church to include all forms of Christianity and Judaism. By the twentieth century, the major religions of the East – Islam, Buddhism, Hinduism and Taoism – had been added to a list that then grew to accommodate more philosophical beliefs such as Freemasonry.

In keeping with their acceptance of religiously discriminatory donor conditions attached to charitable bequests, the courts developed an approach that viewed gifts subject to a discriminatory condition favouring persons on the basis of their race or gender as similarly not necessarily constituting a derogation from a donor's property rights, as being public policy compliant and thus eligible for charitable status. Donor targeting of disadvantaged groups, the essence of charity, grew by logical extension to accommodate minority groups – identified, for example, by a shared ethnicity, locality or religion – the members of which need not be poor. In England, the courts had little difficulty in finding that a trust restricted to persons of a specified race or gender could be a valid

---

[55] See D. Herman, *An Unfortunate Coincidence: Jews, Jewishness and English Law*, Oxford University Press, Oxford, 2011, at p.51.

charity.[56] The Charity Commission extended charitable status to trusts for: the promotion of equality of women with men;[57] promoting good race relations, endeavouring to eliminate discrimination on the grounds of race and encouraging equality of opportunity between persons of different racial groups;[58] and for promoting equality and diversity for the benefit of the public.[59]

The challenge of pluralism

Arguably, one of the most challenging issues facing democracy in the twenty-first century is how to resolve the distorted legacy of Church–State relationships, within and between States, inherited from our undemocratic past. Many current dynamics have an unsettling resonance with those of several centuries ago, and earlier, echoing the despairing comment of Lucretius *'tantum religio potuit suadere malorum'* (so potent was religion in persuading to evil deeds).[60] They serve as a reminder of enduring failure, political and religious, to grapple effectively with what can be a destabilising social force. Layered onto this inherited risk is the increasingly acrimonious standoff between those with and those without religious belief in respect of an agenda of morally driven issues that impact significantly on matters constituting public benefit in contemporary Western societies.

Pluralism

The concept of pluralism rests on the assumption that it is for the greater good of all if as broad a mix of social groups as possible are enabled to interact equally. When operationalised by government policy, pluralism implies a positive duty on the State to facilitate and promote opportunities

---

[56] See, for example, *Re Lysaght* [1966] Ch. 191.
[57] *Women's Service Trust* [1977] Ch. Com Rep 14–15 (paras 34–36).
[58] [1983] Ch. Com Rep 9–11 (paras 15–20). As cited by D. Morris, 'Charities and the Modern Equality Framework: Heading for a Collision?' (2012) 65 *Current Legal Problems* 295 at p.299.
[59] See Charity Commission, *Promotion of Equality and Diversity for the Benefit of the Public*, 2003. See, further, at: www.charitycommission.gov.uk/detailed-guidance/charitable-purposes-and-public-benefit/guidance-on-charitable-purposes/promotion-of-equality-and-diversity-for-the-benefit-of-the-public (accessed 20 December 2013).
[60] A quotation from the Roman poet, Lucretius (96 BC–55 BC). See, further, 1911 Encyclopaedia Britannica at: www.studylight.org/enc/bri/view.cgi?n=20770&search=span (accessed 20 December 2013).

for all minorities, special interest groups, etc. to participate alongside established bodies and interests in the public arena. This has proven difficult to realise in practice.

Entrenched interests

Preparations for a pluralistic society entails making room available for the interests of emerging groups both structurally and psychologically: providing a more level playing field and evidence of welcome. There are many areas where old vested interests have become accustomed to a sphere of influence that needs to shrink in order to accommodate new minority groups. These include: the government, armed forces and the for-profit sectors; professional and trade union organisations; and the ever-growing panoply of civil society entities.

However, where, for example, a society is heavily freighted with the trappings of Christianity, within which an Established Church has for some time exercised considerable influence on matters of State, then the realities of pluralism would seem to demand particularly determined and conspicuous efforts to engineer a reduction of that presence proportionate to other religious entities. In Ireland and England, perhaps exceptionally among the common law countries, such efforts require greater conviction if pluralism is to prevail.

Subsidies and multiculturalism

For many Western governments, giving effect to pluralism has been by way of subsidising the running costs of organisations established to represent and further the interests of minority groups. Such funding is intended to empower recipient groups to counterbalance the institutionalised status quo provided by government and other agencies. It has also brought its own set of problems.

The funding is necessarily discriminatory: the more marginal the group, the greater the level of funding needed if parity with the social standing of similar groups is to be achieved. Some emerging groups, however, are less civil society compliant than others, a few of which may deliberately subvert pluralism, while others may attract or avoid subsidies, depending on size of membership, lobbying skills and current relevance of their social objectives. Subsidy may also, of course, be achieved by granting charitable status. As this is constrained by the common law definition of charitable purpose it has served as an incentive for charity law reform in order to broaden that definition and with it the type of organisations that may qualify for charitable tax exemption.

A side effect of subsidies is to reinforce differences: targeted grants induce prospective recipient groups to emphasise their distinctive cultural or ethnic identity to gain government recognition; thereby triggering a cycle which becomes self-fulfilling. In the long run the cumulative effect may well be to fuel competition among minority groups, exacerbate greater awareness of cultural separateness and incentivise the spin-off of splinter entities, each claiming subsidised autonomy.

Pluralism and religion

In so far as pluralism rests on a premise that different groups should retain the integrity and autonomy of their respective cultural identities, then religion can act as a reinforcing agent. Perhaps particularly when religion conflates with ethnic identity, affirmed by a government subsidy, the separate and distinct nature of the recipient group is readily established. Clearly, however, this gives rise to issues for pluralism.

Bonding

Where a facility is representative of prevailing community religious beliefs, for example a closed monastic order in Ireland, then it often functions as a public good – serving as a rallying point for common values, and a source of inspiration and motivation for those who identify with all that it represents. Similarly, immigrant ethnic groups may rely on their religion as a 'badge of difference', a means of asserting their cultural values, language and traditions which provides a sense of commonality in an unfamiliar environment. Given a sufficient body mass, religion acts as a binding force, enabling individuals, families and communities to cohere around and share in values that encourage public benefit activity and the growth of a caring society. In particular, where a society perceives itself as under threat – from military action, poverty, disease, perhaps economic recession, or other danger – then religious belief or a mix of beliefs may well be a positive public good in fostering solidarity and generating mutual care.

Not bridging

Unfortunately, the magnetic pull towards an inner core of shared religious beliefs can be at the price of repelling those not shared: essentially this 'member benefit' activity negates both 'charity' and pluralism. Also, as religion is primarily manifested through private prayer and religious activity, the cumulative effect tends to be one of inducing isolationism rather than integration – promoting group bonding and thereby accentuating rather than bridging social differences. This is a tendency often manifested in the felt need to ensure that religious values are passed on to and represented by the next generation. This is borne out by the many and varied litigious disputes regarding parental attempts to control the religious upbringing of their children.[61]

Indeed, there are circumstances in which the capacity of religion to accommodate, let alone promote, pluralism is questionable; any sense in which private piety can be interpreted as a public good tends to disappear when that piety manifests itself in a facility perceived as excluding those who do not subscribe to the relevant belief system. Where a facility is wholly secular, but operates a service which offends the beliefs of religious people, then the effect can be divisive for that community – for example, the presence of an abortion clinic, a registry office offering marriage services for gay or lesbian couples or an adoption agency that will place children with such couples. Similarly divisive is the presence of a facility which represents beliefs not shared by the community within which it is located – for example, a 'closed' convent, a mosque, a halal butcher's shop, a faith-based school with compulsory religious/cultural attire requirements or any one of a number of such religion-specific facilities. In fact, some facilities may be overtly discriminatory, providing services and facilities to which access and employment opportunities are restricted by religion. Where this is pursued in order to positively discriminate in favour of socially disadvantaged groups which, by receiving services not made available to others are then uplifted towards parity with those others, this makes a significant contribution to pluralism in that society. It also, however, gives rise to issues of discrimination – particularly in a human rights context – a theme to be tracked through the subsequent jurisdiction-specific chapters.

---

[61] See, for example: *Re T (Minors) (Custody: Religious Upbringing)* (1975) 2 FLR 239; and *Re R (A Minor) (Religious Sect)* [1993] 2 FCR 525. Also see *Re J (Child's Religious Upbringing and Circumcision)* [2000] 1 Fam (CA) 307, which concerned J who lived with his non-practising Christian mother and whose Muslim father sought an order that he be circumcised. Refusing the order but acknowledging the emblematic significance of circumcision, the judge commented that J was 'not going to grow up in an environment in which circumcision is a part of family life; or in which circumcision will be in conformity with the religion practised by his parimary carer; or in which his peers have all been circumcised and for him not to be so would render him either unusual or an outsider'.

THE CHALLENGE OF PLURALISM

Pluralism and religious charities

Targeting resources towards specific needs is what many charities do best. Religious charities tend to do so with an additional filter. Being more partisan than pluralist, they function particularly well in societies where either entrenched irreligious interests dominate or a healthy diversity already flourishes, when their discriminatory role can ensure that the needs of marginalised groups are not overlooked. They are then in a position to compensate for uneven State provision by directing sufficient resources to enable fuller social participation for such a group. The corollary is equally true: in a social context dominated by an Established Church and/or a particular religious culture, religious charities can only be drawn into either a complementary or competing role, neither of which serves to promote pluralism.

Charity and faith-based provision

The importance of service provision by a religious organisation in an area of acute social deprivation cannot be overstated. Quite apart from its utility function, such an organisation often provides the only social facility available to represent civic values in a marginalised and alienated community; whether domestic or overseas. By offering a source of comfort, acceptance and generous goodwill across an undifferentiated range of need, it attracts and mediates between different social groups. Where religious charities provide broad-based access to services for those otherwise unable to obtain them due to economic, geographic, cultural or other constraints, then undoubtedly they contribute to making society more pluralistic.

However, service provision by religious charities is not always directed towards poverty relief. The spread of faith-based schools, particularly in the wealthier and more pluralist Western societies, is a relatively recent and growing phenomenon. Together with the escalating involvement of religious organisations in health care, nursing homes and residential homes for the elderly, etc., this phenomenon draws attention to: the subliminal nature of religion that enables it to penetrate and become an integral part of commonplace social facilities; the view that there is no good reason why secularists should have a monopoly on public benefit service provision; the fact that religious charities are increasingly becoming providers of services that could equally be furnished by for-profit or other nonprofit entities and are often in competition with them; and, in the latter case, that charitable status with possible added government grants is preferencing faith-based providers and distorting the 'level playing field' principle. While this development may be interpreted as contributing to pluralism, it is also open to the challenge that it provides a subsidised platform for proselytism, and one which can disproportionately further the interests of an Established Church or dominant culture.

Religion, secularism and democracy: towards/away from a pluralistic society

There is evidence of a creeping polarisation, within and between some contemporary societies, on faith-based differences. Internationally, the political significance of religion, apparent before 9/11, has become steadily consolidated ever since, drawing in more countries and ratcheting up the tension between some elements of Islam and some nations of the Judeo-Christian tradition. Domestically, there are now few countries in the Western world with societies that are not riven with disputes between those who share conservative religious beliefs and those who do not on much the same agenda of moral issues. On both fronts, as confrontations become more violent, so pluralism becomes more elusive. Nationally and internationally the frontline between religious and secular authorities is becoming longer, studded with minefields, and evermore confrontational.

The moral imperatives

The irreconcilability of traditional religious beliefs with contemporary values and the lifestyle choices available in modern civil society would seem to be driving a wave of didactic moralism: polarising views and politicising the role of religion within many developed nations and between them and other, largely Islamic, nations, while reducing the likelihood of negotiable change. This has been particularly evident in regard to Christian dogma and its core moral imperatives associated with the 'Nazarene family'[62] model, which under theocratic rule had for so long seen Church and State staunchly maintain that any form of sexual relationship outside the marital family unit was prohibited and punishable by God and the courts. For many centuries, Christian religious doctrine had been underpinned by statute and common law to prohibit any infringement of Church-approved marital family relationships (e.g. bigamy, incest, abortion, sodomy, etc.). In recent decades the

---

[62] A reference to the original Christian family unit in Nazareth consisting of married parents and the child 'of their marriage'.

THE CHALLENGE OF PLURALISM 39

range of prohibition has extended well beyond matters relating to the nuclear marital family unit (see, further, Chapter 11).

The latter part of the twentieth century, in a rehearsal of issues that would later emerge in a human rights context, saw State and Church in Western nations begin to disengage in relation to family matters. In several Muslim countries, however, as in Israel and to some extent still in Ireland, a traditional conservative ideology ensured that family law continued to be at least heavily influenced by religion and could serve as an alternative to secular civil law. Elsewhere among Western developed nations, the agenda of moral imperatives is being further extended in keeping with the ebb and flow of advances in science, collapse of confidence in social institutions and retreat into conservative values.

The need for rules of engagement between those of religious belief and secularists to facilitate negotiation on their common agenda of issues, largely associated with the moral imperatives inherited from a theocratic regime, would seem quite pressing. Jurgen Habermas, in an observation that applies domestically and internationally, sees the problem as one requiring a change of perspective on the part of secularists:

> As long as secular citizens are convinced that religious traditions and religious communities are to a certain extent archaic relics of pre-modern societies that continue to exist in the present, they will understand freedom of religion as the cultural version of the conservation of a species in danger of becoming extinct. ... The insight by secular citizens that they live in a post-secular society that is epistemically adjusted to the continued existence of religious communities first requires a change in mentality that is no less cognitively exacting than the adaptation of religious awareness to the challenges of an ever more secularized environment.[63]

There is some way to go before State and citizens can reach agreement on the agenda of moral imperatives that now divide the religious and irreligious within and between nations.

The moral imperatives and the 'culture wars'

The sociological phenomenon referred to as the 'culture wars' was probably first recognised as such in the United States in the early 1990s[64] and was then, and in subsequent debates,[65] addressed in terms of a perceived

---

[63] Habermas, 'Religion in the Public Sphere', at p.15.
[64] See J. D. Hunter, *Culture Wars: The Struggle to Define America*, Basic Books, New York, 1991.
[65] See, for example: A. I. Abramowitz, *The Polarized Public*, Pearson Education, Upper Saddle River, 2012; M. Fiorina, *Culture War? The Myth of a Polarized America* (3rd edn),

growing social and political polarisation that separated religious, conservative Americans from their more liberal or progressive fellow citizens. The dividing line in this clash between opposing sets of values was seen to be one of morality and picked out by such 'hot-button issues' as gun control, the death penalty, abortion and homosexuality, and later extended to matters such as genetic engineering, gay marriage and the use of drones (see also Chapter 7). While this was not necessarily a confrontation between Christians and secularists, and neither were the moral imperatives necessarily religious, this was nevertheless largely the case.

For the purposes of this book, it may be fairly said that although the moral imperatives theme, together with the argument that such imperatives derive from canon law doctrinal underpinnings, would remain coherent and viable without any reference to cultural wars, the reverse is not the case.

The moral imperatives and 'fundamentalism'

The contemporary tendency towards 'fundamentalism' – equally apparent in Islam, Judaism and Christianity – increasingly practised by minorities in the developed nations of the West, if not as lethally as in parts of Africa and the Middle East, is serving as intended to accentuate religious differences. The consequent hardening of interfaces, reinforced by the theocratic rule persisting in some politically unstable parts of the world, has given rise to al-Qaeda, Hezbollah and others. Echoing, to some extent, the much earlier role of the Knights Templar,[66] these zealots are similarly determined to use military violence to further perceived religious ends. The 9/11 and subsequent attacks seemed to pause the drift towards secularisation. Together with the wars in Iraq and Afghanistan, the recurring use of sophisticated Western military weaponry in impoverished Muslim nations and the implacable stance of Israel, they primarily caused an international heightening of religious tension. Contemporary conflicts in parts of Africa, Southeast Asia, and in the Indian subcontinent, which often conflate with local ethnic disputes and increasingly involve militant Islamic factions, also provide further evidence of a steady ramping up of religious confrontation. At the same time, sectarianism, once thought to have been consigned to history, is

---

Pearson Education, New York, 2010; and R. A. Dahl, *How Democratic is the American Constitution?* (2nd edn), Yale University Press, New Haven, 2001.

[66] Knights Templar was an elite, powerful and international Christian military force that existed for nearly two centuries during the Middle Ages, 1129–1312, and played an important role in the Crusades. It was organised as a monastic order and treated as a charity.

CONCLUSION 41

showing every sign of undergoing a revival: anti-Semitism, that most invidious benchmark of religious intolerance, is becoming more common.[67]

Conclusion

As traditionally understood, both 'religion' and 'charity' were uncomplicated concepts with straightforward social roles within which the virtuous conduct of the individual, together with an allied public benefit premium, were of central importance. The social revolution that constituted the Reformation in England saw both become core components of State authority – reinforced by statue law and Protestant precepts – and remain so for some centuries, during which they and related case law precedents were disseminated throughout the British Empire. As society became less homogenous, shedding its theocratic underpinnings and allowing the interests of Church and State to become separate and distinct, so the space created allowed other entities to flourish, mutate and, in so doing, to alter the established pattern of public subservience to both. The dominance of public over private interests that had been such a prominent characteristic of religion and charity in the early post-Reformation period, loosened up as both slowly shrank as social institutions, though never losing their mutual affinity.

As the common law countries made their transition into developed Western societies they brought with them their shared legacy of religion and charity as evolved in and transmitted from the laws of post-Reformation England. While the principles of both (stated in canon law and case law, respectively) have remained essentially intact, the social context they must now relate to has changed enormously. Among the challenges they now face are those that accompany the modern phenomenon of multiculturalism. Pluralism, the social policy of choice for the governments concerned, necessitates holding a balance between the interests of an increasing range of religions and also between those of religious faith and secularists. Simultaneously, governments must manage the increasing tension between those of religious belief and those of none on an agenda of morally driven issues that impact significantly on matters constituting public benefit in contemporary Western societies. The resulting implications for charity and religion in some of the leading common law nations in the twenty-first century is largely what this book is about.

---

[67] See, for example, the European Monitoring Centre on Racism and Xenophobia, *Manifestations of Anti-Semitism in the EU: 2002–03*, Vienna, 2004; J. Horowitz, The Second OSCE Conference on Anti-Semitism (Berlin, 28–29 April 2004), Papers in the Theory and Practice of Human Rights, Human Rights Centre, University of Essex, 2004.

2

Charity law and religion

The common law context; historical background

Introduction

The mixing of the sacred and the secular in public benefit activity preceded the Statute of Charitable Uses 1601 by several centuries.[1] Nonetheless, for all common law nations, the law governing the interaction of charity and religion is customarily dated from this statute, or rather from the provisions listed in its Preamble, as subsequently classified by Lord Macnaghten in *Pemsel* and thereafter developed by the courts and Charity Commission in England and Wales.[2] Consequently, the advancement of religion has become recognised as a charitable purpose, legally presumed to be for the public benefit and, as such, automatically entitled to tax exemptions and other privileges. Religion and charity, fused together under the broad umbrella of charity law, have been responsible for the foundations of our current social infrastructure – particularly in health and education – and for the accompanying sense of civic responsibility and a collective, if at times partisan, grasp of social identity across the common law world.

Religious charities have also tended to conform to much the same model. All common law nations have required certain essential components to be present if a religious organisation, or a donation or gift to such an organisation, was to be accorded charitable status: a belief in a 'Supreme Being' and a shared commitment to faith and worship – although for some there are signs that this is now set to change. The following historical background provides a narrative that introduces the main concerns of the book: identifying the key components within both charity law and religion, and the matters crucial to their relationship; enabling these to be tracked through the subsequent chapters; and allowing the main themes to emerge that will form the basis for the comparative jurisdictional analysis of the law governing the contemporary relationship

---

[1] 43 Eliz. I, c.4.
[2] *Commissioners for Special Purposes of Income Tax* v. *Pemsel* [1891] AC 531.

between charity and religion. Beginning with an account of religious organisations as charities, this chapter explains the meaning of 'charity' and 'religion' in a common law context and the significance of their core conceptual characteristics, while outlining the importance of the 'public benefit' test. Attention is given to the main charity law precedents which fixed the boundaries for construing what does and does not constitute a religion, a religious organisation, or a charitable gift to such, across the common law jurisdictions. It then considers the role of religious charities, the related development of charity law and the gradual evolution of the charitable purpose known as 'the advancement of religion'. The common law constraints on the judicial shaping of this charitable purpose are examined: the limits imposed on donor discretion; the relevance of the restraint on political activity; and the importance of ensuring compliance with public policy. The chapter closes with a brief exploration of early case law relating to religious discrimination.

RELIGIOUS ORGANISATIONS, CHARITY AND THE COMMON LAW: THE HISTORICAL BACKGROUND

Charities have existed for at least the last millennium.[3] While the essential elements of the present law governing charity in a common law context date from the Statute of Charitable Uses 1601, its roots lie in pre-Reformation England.[4] There they were entwined with religious concerns to ensure salvation of the soul and given effect through the law governing pious uses[5] and equitable trusts,[6] as administered first by the Ecclesiastical Courts then by the Courts of Chancery.[7]

Medieval origins of charity law

As Church and king emerged as the twin national institutions, charity took its place as the default position for hierarchical authorities that

---

[3] See H. Picarda, *The Law and Practice Relating to Charities* (3rd edn), Butterworths, London, 1999.

[4] The oldest, and still existing, charity being (perhaps) King's School Canterbury, founded in 597.

[5] See G. Jones, *History of the Law of Charity, 1532–1827*, Cambridge University Press, Cambridge, 1969, at pp.16–18.

[6] See, for example, J. Duddington, *Essentials of Equity and Trusts Law*, Pearson Education, Harlow, 2006.

[7] See D. R. Klinck, *Conscience, Equity and the Court of Chancery in Early Modern England*, Ashgate, Farnham, 2010.

44 CHARITY LAW AND RELIGION

prescribed the rights and duties of all loyal subjects within the realm.
Those too poor, infirm or otherwise incapacitated to play a useful role in
a heavily structured society would be cared for and maintained, and kept
in their place, by services paid for by parish tithes imposed and administered by worthy men of both institutions. This system provided for the
inbuilt reciprocity of two sets of needs – those who wished to be fed in
this life and those who by feeding them hoped to save their souls in the
next – the dutiful role conformity of both contributing to maintaining
the established authority of lord and bishop. At that time many schools
and hospitals[8] were founded by religious organisations and they in turn
received powerful support from the State which, through laws proclaim-
ing that 'God's churches are entitled to their rights',[9] required taxes to be
paid to the Church and imposed severe penalties for non-payment.[10]

Instilling and supporting Christian beliefs, accompanied by charitable
provision for the disadvantaged, was thus recognised at an early stage as
of common interest to both Church and State.

Basic structures uniting the holy and the secular

Following the Norman Conquest in 1066, feudalism became established
in England. This centralised hierarchical system, based on land ownership, determined the loyalty, services and tithes due to the king and
proportionately thereafter to local representatives of the ruling elite.

Alongside the feudal system, ecclesiastical bodies had jurisdiction over
charitable testamentary causes, known as *ad pias causas* (or causes
dedicated to the honour of God and his Church). It was customary for
a penitent donor to make a gift to the Church for a pious use coupled
with a request that prayers or masses be offered for the salvation of the
donor's soul, charity being a means of expiating sin. Indeed, the soul, not
just of the giver but of those already deceased, could be saved by acts of
generosity to the poor: masses offered for the dead being accompanied

---

[8] See, for example, St John's Hospital in Malmesbury, which dates from the early tenth
century.
[9] See King Edward's code, promulgated at Andover (*c.*963). Also see the laws of the West
Saxon King Ine (688–694) which directed that 'Church-scot is to be given by
Martinmass; if anyone does not discharge it, he is liable to 60 shillings and to render
the church-scott twelve-fold', as cited in J. C. Brady, *Religion and the Law of Charities in
Ireland*, Northern Ireland Legal Quarterly, Belfast, 1975, at p.6.
[10] See D. Whitelock (ed.), *English Historical Documents 500–1042*, Oxford University
Press, New York, 1955, at p.365; as cited in Brady, *Religion and the Law of Charities in
Ireland*.

by alms for the poor of the parish; chantries by endowments for the Church and monasteries;[11] and guilds by bequests of property for the use of the Church. Such was the extent of this practice that it was feared that the Church would 'garner in all the land of the kingdom'[12] as clerics would 'terrorise them ("the dying" *sic*) into making death-bed devises *ad pias causas* to the ruin of their heirs'.[13]

Doing good in this life as a down payment for saving one's soul in the next has a long history. In *The Parish Gilds of Mediaeval England*,[14] for example, it was mentioned that 'the gild of the Blessed Virgin Mary in the parish church of St Botolph at Boston founded in 1260, gave a yearly distribution of bread and herrings to the poor in alms for the souls of its benefactors'. It was similarly customary for the Church to administer probate more generally and to channel testamentary gifts of money and property towards secular public benefit purposes. So, as has been pointed out, there are 'early-fifteenth century examples of the Church regulating bequests for the repair of roads and other such infrastructural investments, justified as pious contributions to the public weal'.[15]

Gradually, responsibility for the pious use was assumed by the Court of Chancery, which provided the means for their enforcement,[16] until it was replaced by the trust (see Chapter 3) as the means whereby a donor could impose a legal requirement upon a trustee or trustees to receive, retain and utilise a gift for purposes specified by the donor. In its initial religious context, charity was thus 'more a means to the salvation of the soul of the benefactor than an endeavour to diagnose and alleviate the needs of the beneficiary'.[17]

---

[11] A 'chantry' (from the Chanting of the Mass) was a religious service founded and endowed by a benefactor for the repose of the soul of one or more persons. See K. Wood-Leigh, *Church Life under Edward III*, Cambridge University Press, Cambridge, 1934, at p.91; cited in Brady, *Religion and the Law of Charities in Ireland*, at p.12.

[12] See G. Jones, *History of the Law of Charity 1532 –1827*, Cambridge University Press, Cambridge, 1969, at p.109.

[13] Ibid.

[14] See H. Westlake, *The Parish Gilds of Mediaeval England*, Society for Promoting Christian Knowledge, London, 1919; cited in Brady, *Religion and the Law of Charities in Ireland*, at p.14.

[15] See J. Getzler, '*Morice* v. *The Bishop of Durham 1805*', in C. Mitchell and P. Mitchell (eds), *Landmark Cases in Equity*, Hart Publishing, Oxford, 2012, at p.162.

[16] See Jones, *History of the Law of Charity 1532 –1827*, at pp.3–4.

[17] See, *Report of the Committee on the Law and Practice Relating to Charitable Trusts* (Cmnd. 8710), HMSO, London, 1952, at para. 36

The law of mortmain

This Norman French term *morte meyn* or 'dead hand' referred to the practice whereby a donor would tie-up lands in perpetuity by gifting them to the Roman Catholic Church. Once property passed into the 'dead hand of the Church' it remained there as the latter prohibited any alienation of its property. Much land came to be owned by the Church on this basis. Feudal rulers regarded a grant of land to the Church by a subject as incompatible with the latter's feudal duties and sought to curtail this practice through successive statutes.[18] However, the continued systematic avoidance of statutory constraints allowed the Church, and particularly the religious orders, to acquire power, land and political influence. In the process, the feudal powers of the king and his retinue were being simultaneously drained.

From the time of Magna Carta in 1215,[19] rulers in England sought, through the mortmain legislation,[20] to prevent land from being removed in this way from the feudal economy. The rule against perpetuities, which dates from the statute of Quia Emptores 1290,[21] established the principle that property must not be made non-transferable, and ever since the law relating to property has sought to facilitate freedom of disposition. Once vested, a charitable trust – being exempt from this rule – could in theory exist in perpetuity, as since confirmed by many cases.[22]

Religion and the State

The lessons of this period, when the Church amassed land and wealth which it sought to retain in perpetuity, causing a corresponding diminution of State powers and depletion of its tax revenues, have reverberated

---

[18] Including the Statute of Mortmain 1279 (7 Edw. I, St 2) and the Statute of Westminster III 1290 (18 Edw. I) and in particular the Statute of Mortmain 1391 (15 Ric. 2, c. 5).

[19] See Clause 43, which provided:

> It shall not be lawful from henceforth to any to give his lands to any religious house and to take the same land again to hold of the same house: nor shall it be lawful to any house of religion to take the lands of any and to have the same of him of whom he received it. If any from henceforth give his lands to any religious house, and thereupon be convict, the gift shall be utterly void, and the land shall accrue to the lord of the fee.

[20] Including the Statute of Mortmain 1279 (7 Edw. I, St 2) and the Statute of Westminster III 1290 (18 Edw. I), and in particular the Statute of Mortmain 1391 (15 Ric. 2, c. 5).

[21] 18 Edw. 1 cc. 1–3.

[22] See, for example, *A-G* v. *National Provincial Bank* [1924] AC 262.

down the centuries. The funding of charities, religious and otherwise, continues to be contentious.

The Reformation

The 'Reformation' saw Henry VIII taking vigorous action to suppress the Church, dissolve the monasteries and confiscate their property. By the mid-sixteenth century a large number of abbeys and monasteries had been forcibly closed and their lands appropriated by the Crown.

Dissolution of the monasteries had several important consequences for charities. First, it had the immediate effect of removing the single most important source of housing, care and education for the poor; the homeless and destitute were left to roam town and countryside in search of alms and shelter. Second, it ended the possibility of making grants of property to the Church in exchange for spiritual benefits. Third, and crucially for the unfolding relationship between religion, charity and the State, it was followed in Tudor England by confirmation that Protestantism would be the Established Church, thereby ensuring that all religions other than the Church of England were denied the privileges that were to be reserved solely for it.

This was a time when the hold of the Church on charity had been broken, the saintly were displaced by the secular and charity became more aligned with the agenda of government, though the latter never quite lost its deference to religious institutions. Whether supplementing or substituting for government provision, charity continued to deal mainly with the effects of poverty as the majority of Englishmen 'reflected less on their souls and became more concerned with the worldly needs of their fellow men'.[23]

The emergence of charitable trusts from ecclesiastic origins

In a common law context, the deeply rooted interdependent relationship of charity and religion stems from the law governing pious uses, as first administered by the Ecclesiastical courts in England, transferred to charitable trusts and came to form a singular and rather esoteric branch of the law, but one with but considerable influence. As has been said: 'The enormous status and prestige of the early and mediaeval

---

[23] G. Jones, *History of the Law of Charity 1532–1827*, Wm. W. Gaunt & Sons, Inc., Holmes Beach, Florida, 1986, at p.10.

Church enabled her to assume jurisdiction over whole areas of social life which today would rightly be considered the concern of secular government.'[24]

Private and public interests in charity were thus harmoniously balanced in their Christian origins. One aspect of the ecclesiastic origins of charity with important consequences for the future was the discretionary power exercised by the Church in respect of gifts it received for pious uses. Any such gift was not permitted to fail due merely to a lack of certainty in framing the charitable objects. Instead, wherever possible, Church administrators interpreted the donor's intention to ensure that the gift could be saved for charity and then directed it towards an appropriate area of need.[25]

Chancery

During and following the protracted struggle between Church and State, the jurisdiction of the king as *parens patriae*[26] was exercised by the Court of Chancery in relation to the wardship of minors and lunatics, and also in relation to charitable trusts. The use of judicial discretion, a hallmark of this jurisdiction, allowed the judiciary to formulate a body of principles to guide the determination of matters affecting trusts and charitable trusts. A general power to enforce trusts was recognised and additional common law powers were also used in relation to charities.[27]

Elizabethan legislative developments in charity law

The Elizabethan era began with the attempt to establish a new and comprehensive national Protestant religion regulated by statute: other

---

[24] See Brady, *Religion and the Law of Charities in Ireland*, at p.6.

[25] See, for example, *Porter's Case* (1592) 1 Co. 22b, *Partridge* v. *Walker* (1595) 4 Co. 116b and *Martidale* v. *Martin* (1593) Cro. Eliz. 288. But also see *Eyre* v. *Shaftesbury* (1722) 2 P. Wms 119.

[26] From perhaps the fourteenth century, the monarch was responsible for those declared *sui juris* and who because they lacked the necessary capacity could neither protect their own interests nor fulfil their feudal duties and therefore 'belonged to the King as *Pater patriae*, and fell under the direction of this court, as charities, infants, idiots, lunatics, etc' (*per* Lord Somers LC in *Falkland* v. *Bertie* (1696) 2 Vern 333, at p.342; 23 ER 814, at p.818).

[27] See, for example, *Porter's Case* (1592) 1 Co. 22b, *Partridge* v. *Walker* (1595) 4 Co. 116b and *Martidale* v. *Martin* (1593) Cro. Eliz. 288. But also see *Eyre* v. *Shaftesbury* (1722) 2 P. Wms 119.

religions were not to be tolerated; the only permissible object of a religious charity was an endowment for the national Church; all other gifts or purposes intended for religious ends were not only not charitable, they were illegal.

Elizabethan Poor Laws

The Statute of Uses 1535[28] sought to prevent the evasion of feudal dues by the creation of uses.[29] It simply legislated that all equitable owners were also the legal owners. This restored to the Crown all feudal incidents, with Parliament being persuaded by a provision which protected all current titles. Subsequently, the Statute of Wills 1540[30] gave landowners the ability to devise by will their land (which had previously been denied) but not to a corporation. Thereafter, the corporation was never the preferred vehicle for charitable gifts and instead trusts became the dominant legal form for charities in England. Then, in 1547, the Statute of Chantries[31] essentially allowed all pre-Reformation endowments to the Catholic Church, in respect of masses to be said for the souls of the deceased, to be vested in the Crown.

In 1597 the earliest form of State public service provision for the socially disadvantaged in Europe was introduced[32] and subsequently amended by the Act for the Relief of the Poor 1601.[33]

The Statute of Charitable Uses 1601

The Statute of Charitable Uses 1601,[34] of fundamental importance to charity law, has for four centuries provided a basic framework for the role and responsibilities of charity in many different common law societies. Entitled 'an Acte to redresse the Misemployment of Landes, Goodes, and Stockes of Money heretofore given to Charitable Uses', its intent was quite explicit. It sought to regulate private charitable

---

[28] 27 Hen 8 c 10. This statute enabled Henry VIII to abolish the power of devising land which had been acquired by means of uses. It subsequently gave rise to the modern system of trusts, i.e. the enforcement of a use upon a use as a trust.

[29] An alternative view credits the Franciscan friars with introducing uses into England in the thirteenth century. See, further, M. M. Gaudiosi, 'The Influence of the Islamic Law of WAQF on the Development of the Trust in England: The Case of Merton College' (1987–1988) 136 *University of Pennsylvania Law Review* 1231, at p.1240.

[30] 32 Hen. 8, c.1.   [31] 1 Edw. 6 c.14.   [32] Statute of Uses 1597, 39 Eliz. 1. c.6.

[33] 43 Eliz. I c.2.   [34] A modified version of the Statute of Uses 1597 (39 Eliz. I, c.6).

50   CHARITY LAW AND RELIGION

donations, reduce abuse and identify the public benefit purposes to be addressed by charity. It also established the functions which would thereafter be served by charity law, implicitly giving recognition to altruism, as represented by religious organisations and by the gifts and activities of religious people. Most importantly, the charitable purposes as listed in the Preamble to the 1601 Act in effect laid down an agenda for what was thereafter to become a public benefit contract between the State and charity. The State then considered that charity could bear responsibility for the following matters:

> The relief of aged, impotent and poor people; the maintenance of sick and maimed soldiers and mariners, schools of learning, free schools and scholars of universities; the repair of bridges, havens, causeways, churches, sea banks and highways; the education and preferment of orphans; the relief, stock or maintenance of houses of correction; marriages of poor maids; supportation, aid and help of young tradesmen, handicraftsmen and persons decayed; the relief or redemption of prisoners or captives and the aid or ease of any poor inhabitants concerning payments of fifteens, setting out of soldiers, and other taxes.[35]

These charitable purposes were treated from the outset as being illustrative rather than definitive. The courts would not regard a purpose as charitable unless it could be defined as coming within 'the spirit and intendment' of the Preamble. An element of 'public benefit' was also crucial.

State secularisation of charity is generally considered to have been formalised by the Charitable Uses Act 1601: the charitable purposes enumerated in the Preamble are indeed of general social utility and almost exclusively secular in nature. The law, however, continued to accommodate religious trusts and donations, even if this was restricted for many years to those made in favour of the Protestant religion, until formally acknowledged as the 'advancement of religion' constituting the third *Pemsel* head of charity.[36] To a large extent, charity, then as now, reflects the political realities of the day: the 1601 Act denoted not only State recognition of a need to share social utility costs with charity, but also its capacity to use charity law to forge expedient political allegiances; and religion has, in the meantime, been

---

[35] As noted in O. Tudor, *Charities* (9th edn), Sweet & Maxwell, London, 2003, at p.3, the wording of the Preamble closely resembles a passage in *The Vision of Piers Plowman*.

[36] See ruling of Macnaghten LJ in *Commissioners for Special Purposes of Income Tax* v. *Pemsel* [1891] AC 531, at p.583.

at least subliminally present as a driving force in 'the creation and sustaining of significant charitable activities across all the heads and the ages'.[37]

Early judicial developments in charity law

The *parens patriae*[38] jurisdiction of the king passed to the Court of Chancery and was in time assumed by the High Court as an aspect of its inherent jurisdiction. This was long considered to offer appropriate and sufficient authority for resolving issues affecting charitable trusts, all of which shared the unique privilege of being both enforceable by the Attorney-General and of being amenable to adjustment by the court, using its *cy-près* powers, to remedy technical deficiencies in what would otherwise be a good charitable gift.

A paternalistic use of judicial discretion coupled with access to prerogative powers gave this court the flexibility to build a case law structure of principles on the foundations laid by the Elizabethan statutes. During the ensuing two centuries neither statute nor judiciary intervened to classify the charitable purposes listed in the Elizabethan statutes.[39] When such classification came it ordered the judicial approach to charities and to charitable activity thereafter.

The ruling in Morice v. The Bishop of Durham

In the ruling in *Morice* v. *The Bishop of Durham*[40] Sir William Grant MR (and Lord Eldon on appeal) stated that a fixed principle existed in the law of England that purposes deemed to be charitable are those 'which that Statute enumerates' and those 'which by analogies are deemed within its spirit and intendment'.[41] He suggested four heads: the relief of the indigent; advancement of learning; advancement of religion; and the

---

[37] See M. McGregor-Lowndes, 'Introduction', in M. McGregor-Lowndes, and K. O'Halloran (eds), *Modernising Charity Law: Recent Developments and Future Directions*, Elgar Publications, Cheltenham, 2010, at p.7.

[38] See J. Seymour, '*Parens Patriae* and Wardship Powers: Their Nature and Origins' (1994) 14:2 *Oxford Journal of Legal Studies* 159.

[39] Note that the Mortmain Act of 1736, which rendered void testamentary gifts of land given to a charitable purpose, served as a reminder that the charitability of religious purposes was not always advantageous.

[40] *Morice* v. *The Bishop of Durham* (1804) 9 Ves 405.

[41] See also *Kendall* v. *Grainger* (1842) 5 Beav. 302, *per* Lord Langdale MR and *Dolan* v. *MacDermott* (1868) LR 3 Ch. App 678.

advancement of 'objects of general public utility'. The effect of this landmark ruling, in what was essentially a mortmain case, has been interpreted as imposing 'a curb on the ancient role of the Church in administering charitable uses and forming social and political projects alongside and in tension with secular society'[42] as it effectively served notice that its customary discretionary default remit in probate matters would no longer be passively accepted by the judiciary.[43]

The ruling in Commissioners for Special Purposes of Income Tax v. Pemsel

Lord Macnaghten accepted Sir Samuel Romilly's classification, but added some significant refinements. In *Commissioners for Special Purposes of Income Tax* v. *Pemsel*,[44] he classified all recognised charitable purposes under four heads and added that to be charitable a gift must be 'beneficial to the community'. He ruled as follows:

> 'Charity' in its legal sense comprises four principal divisions: trusts for the relief of poverty; trusts for the advancement of education; trusts for the advancement of religion; and trusts beneficial to the community not falling under any of the preceding heads. The trusts last referred to are not any the less charitable in the eye of the law, because incidentally they benefit the rich as well as the poor, as indeed, every charity that deserves the name must do directly or indirectly.[45]

To be considered charitable in law, a trust had to fall into one of these four separate but not necessarily mutually exclusive categories. Thereafter the Macnaghten ruling has been universally accepted and followed as the single most important charity law precedent.

The ruling in Williams Trustees v. IRC

The judgment in *Williams Trustees* v. *IRC*,[46] delivered by Lord Simonds, indicated that in determining whether a trust is charitable,

---

[42] See Getzler, '*Morice* v. *The Bishop of Durham 1805*', at p.161.

[43] See, further, R. Helmholz, *The Canon Law and Ecclesiastical Jurisdiction from 597 to the 1640s, Volume 1 of The Oxford History of the Laws of England*, Oxford University Press, Oxford, 2004, pp.387–432, as cited in C. Mitchell and P. Mitchell (eds), *Landmark Cases in Equity*, Hart Publishing, Oxford, 2012.

[44] *Commissioners for Special Purposes of Income Tax* v. *Pemsel* [1891] AC 531, at p.583.

[45] Ibid., at p.583.

[46] *Williams Trustees* v. *IRC* [1947] AC 447, *per* Lord Simonds, at p.519.

the trust must first be properly regarded as being within the 'spirit and intendment of the Preamble'[47] and, second, that its purpose must be beneficial to the community in a way that was charitable.

Equity

Over time, judicial discretion in interpreting gifts as coming within the spirit and intendment of the 1601 statute served to broaden the range of charitable purposes in an empirical rather than logical fashion; by a process of precedent and analogy the judiciary greatly extended the original list. The Preamble to the 1601 Act, as ordered by the ruling in *Pemsel* and further developed through judicial interpretation, laid the statutory foundation for charity law as we now know it throughout the common law world.

Tax

The steady migration of charity from private to public law has mostly been due to charitable organisations becoming enveloped by the tax regime: fundamentally, private/public interests are reflected in the balance struck between charitable purposes and tax liability, as evidenced by the traditional role of the Revenue as the agency responsible for determining charitable status. The further charity encroaches on mainstream taxable activity, through involvement in government service provision and commerce, the more it moves into the domain of public law and risks being made subject to the same sanctions as other public bodies. This is becoming steadily more evident in some leading common law jurisdictions.

Tax law

Charities have been tax exempt since the first taxation statute, the Income Tax Act 1799,[48] which declared 'That no corporation, fraternity, or society of persons established for charitable purposes only, shall be

---

[47] The development of charity within the common law was dependent upon the courts interpreting a novel purpose as charitable because it could be defined as coming within 'the spirit and intendment' of the Preamble to the 1601 Act. Thus enabling charity to be adapted to meet emerging areas of social need.

[48] 39 Geo III c. 13, s. 5. See, further, M. Gousmett, 'The Charitable Purposes Exemption from Income Tax: Pitt to Pemsel 1798–1891', unpublished PhD thesis, Canterbury

chargeable under this Act, in respect of the income of such corporation, fraternity, or society.' Ever since, eligibility for a range of tax concessions has been a primary reason for acquiring charitable status. This entitlement is broadly justified on the basis that as charities do what government would otherwise have to do, so the public interest is served by facilitating their altruistic activities.

RELIGION AND CHARITABLE PURPOSE

In a charity law context, a trust for the advancement of religion must also be of public benefit. There is case law evidence illustrating an early judicial willingness to accept that such trusts may be presumed to be so in the absence of evidence to the contrary.[49] Nonetheless, the presumption is rebuttable. It is a subject the courts have tended to approach with caution. As was explained in *Gilmour* v. *Coats and others*:[50]

> Before the Reformation only one religion was recognized by the law and in fact the overwhelming majority of the people accepted it. . . . But since diversity of religious beliefs arose and became lawful the law has shown no preference in this matter to any church and other religious body. . . . It does not now in this matter prefer one religion to another. It assumes that it is good for man to have and practice a religion, but, where a particular belief is accepted by one religion and rejected by another, the law can neither accept nor reject it. The law must accept the position that it is right that different religions should each be supported, irrespective of whether or not all its beliefs are true.

The presumption that religion per se is conducive to the public benefit nonetheless leaves the judiciary and other regulators with the responsibility to consider whether the beliefs of an organisation or its adherents actually constitute a religion for the purposes of charity law, and to filter out cults.[51]

University, New Zealand, at: www.google.co.uk/#q=Gousmett%2C+M.%2C+'The+Charitable+Purposes+Exemption+from+Income+Tax%3A+Pitt+to+Pemsel+1798-1891'%2C++unpublished+Ph.D.+thesis%2C+Canterbury+University%2C+New+Zealand+ (accessed 21 December 2013).

[49] See, for example: *Gass* v. *Wilhite*, 32 Ky 170 (Ct App, 1834); *Holland* v. *Peck*, 37 NC 255, 258 (1842); and *People ex rel Seminary of Our Lady of Angels* v. *Barber*, 3 NY St Rep 367 (1886), affd 13 NE 936 (1887).

[50] *Gilmour* v. *Coats and others* [1949] AC 426, *per* Lord Reid at p.457. Sentiments echoed in the more recent judgement of Laws LJ in *McFarlane* v. *Relate Avon Ltd.* [2010] IRLR 872; 29 BHRC 249.

[51] Not always successfully – see, for example, *Thornton* v. *Howe*, 1862, 31 Beav. 14, where a trust for 'printing, publishing, and propagating the sacred writings of the late Joanna Southcote' was held good by Romilly MR.

RELIGION AND CHARITABLE PURPOSE

Religious charities and the definitional common law conceptual components of 'charity'

Charitable status confers eligibility for tax exemption, permits existence in perpetuity and grants entitlement to the protection of the Attorney General. However, in relation to religion, it also requires compliance with civilised moral standards: as was pointed out in *Cocks* v. *Manners*,[52] entities that are 'adverse to the very foundation of all religion'[53] or are 'subversive of all morality'[54] are not charities. While the common law conceptual basis is the same for religious charities as for those registered under any other *Pemsel* heading, this requires the core components to be in place, and additional obligations in respect of the definition of 'religion' and the 'public benefit test' to be satisfied.

Core conceptual requirements

The core legal requirements for a charity to be recognised as such are that an entity must be confined exclusively to charitable purposes, be for the public benefit, be independent, non-profit-distributing and non-political. There are some jurisdictional variations in the interpretation of these definitional criteria, and donor intention can also be relevant, but throughout the common law world these have long been held to be the basic legal components for any charity, including a religious charity. Indeed, some have a particular significance for such charities.

- Donor intent

Where the donor's intention is malicious, illegal[55] or against public policy then the gift is not charitable. Where the intention is charitable but the gift has no intrinsic merit,[56] is given for non-charitable purposes or could possibly be so used, then again the gift is not charitable.[57]

- Exclusiveness

For a trust to be charitable its purposes must be confined exclusively to charitable purposes. The courts look for an exclusive charitable intent

---

[52] *Cocks* v. *Manners* (1871) 12 LR Eq 574.
[53] See *Re Watson; Hobbs* v. *Smith* [1973] 1 WLR 1472, 1473.
[54] See *Thornton* v. *Howe* (1862) 31 Beav. 14; 54 ER 1042.
[55] See *National Anti-Vivisection Society* v. *IRC* [1948] AC 31.
[56] *Re Pinion* [1965] Ch. 85.
[57] *Anglo-Swedish Society* v. *Commissioners of Inland Revenue* (1931) 16 TC 34.

and have resolutely declined to save gifts as charitable where the donor had failed to unequivocally and unambiguously state such intent or had expressed mixed intentions, some charitable and some not. If a donor's gift included both charitable and non-charitable purposes, and allowed for the possibility of trustees using at their discretion some or all of the gift for non-charitable purposes, then the courts would refuse to recognise it as charitable.[58]

- Non-profit distributing

A charity does not compromise its standing by making a profit, but any profit gained must not accrue to the benefit of individuals but be directed towards the fulfilment of the charity's objects. There must be benefit for the community or a section of the community.[59] The tension between concepts of 'profit' and 'charitable purpose' is considerably exacerbated when both are being pursued in tandem by a religious charity.

- Non-political

An organisation intending to pursue political activity as its primary purpose, or in fact doing so, will be denied charitable status. The extent to which any political activity, lobbying or campaigning may be safely undertaken by a charity has long been fraught with uncertainty and varies to a degree among the common law jurisdictions.[60] The restrictions on advocacy/political activity by charities appear increasingly controversial and incongruous in an era where openness, transparency and accountability are now accepted as the appropriate benchmarks for conduct in public life.

- Independent

A charity is required under common law to be a free-standing, independent entity founded by and bound to fulfil the terms of the donor's gift. The duty resting on trustees to honour the terms of their trust and ensure that the objects of the charity prevail has always been seen as the primary means whereby the integrity of the donor's gift could be protected. Fulfilling this duty has required trustees to be resolutely

---

[58] *Boyle* v. *Boyle* (1877) IR 11 Eq 433.
[59] *Commissioners of Inland Revenue* v. *Oldham Training and Enterprise Council* (1996) 69 TC 231.
[60] *McGovern* v. *Attorney General* [1982] 1 Ch. 321.

committed to the charity's objects and free from any influence which may deflect from that focus.[61] Increasingly, courts and regulators are closely examining the nature and extent of government/charity relations, where the latter appears to be acting as a proxy government service delivery agent, to establish whether in doing so a charity has fatally compromised its independence.[62]

Charity law and the definition of religion

Religion, for the purposes of charity law, has been defined as 'the promotion of spiritual teaching in a wide sense, and the maintenance of the doctrines on which it rests, and the observances that serve to promote and manifest it.'[63] The legal inseparableness of charity and religion was confirmed by the decision in *Pemsel*[64] when Macnaghten LJ ruled that 'the advancement of religion' was a charitable purpose. Subsequently, the judiciary have added that for it to do so two conditions must be met:[65] the organisation or gift must contribute to the advancement of 'religion', as interpreted by the courts;[66] and it must promote the religious instruction or education of the public.[67] A non-theistic organisation was initially held not to satisfy such conditions.[68]

- **Belief in a Supreme Being**

For the purposes of charity law, 'religion' has been tied to a belief in a Supreme Being which, until relatively recently, was most usually

---

[61] See, for example, *Hallows* v. *Lloyd* (1888) 39 Ch.D. 686.

[62] See, for example, *Cali & Figli SrL* v. *SEPG* [1997] ECR I-1547; [1997] 5 CMLR 484, when a charity was found to be functioning as a mere emanation of the State.

[63] *Keren Kayemeth Le Jisroel* v. *Inland Revenue Commissioners* (1931) 48 TLR 459, at p.477.

[64] *The Commissioners for Special Purposes of the Income Tax* v. *Pemsel* [1879] AC 531.

[65] As explained in, *Tudor on Charities*, edited by J. Warburton, D. Morris and N. Riddle (9th edn), London, Sweet & Maxwell, 2003, at p.73.

[66] See *Dunne* v. *Byrne* [1912] AC 407.

[67] *Cocks* v. *Manners* (1871) LR 12 Eq 574, at p.585; *Yeap* v. *Cheah Neo* v. *One Cheng Neo* (1875) LR 6 PC 381; *Re Joy* (1888) 60 LT 175; *Re Macduff* [1896] 2 Ch. 451; *Re Delaney* [1902] 2 Ch. 642, at 648; *Chesterman* v. *Federal Commissioners of Income Tax* [1926] AC 128; *Gilmour* v. *Coats* [1949] AC 426.

[68] See, for example, *Re Hummeltenberg* [1923] 1 Ch. 237, when spiritualism was held not to meet the definition of 'religion' and *Bowman* v. *Secular Society Ltd.* [1917] AC 406, where doubts were cast by Parker LJ on 'humanism'.

58 CHARITY LAW AND RELIGION

interpreted in all common law countries to mean a Christian deity[69] until case law extended recognition beyond the monotheistic Christian religions.

- Worship of a Supreme Being

In addition to belief in a god or gods, members of a religion must practice a common form of worship and have a shared faith. As Dillon J stated in *Re South Place Ethical Society*,[70] which concerned a society with objects that included 'the study and dissemination of ethical principles and the cultivation of a rational religious sentiment', the 'two essential attributes of religion are faith and worship: faith in a god and worship of that god'.[71] He explicitly rejected the view that the legal definition of religion could be satisfied by a system of belief which did not involve faith in a god, nor would it seem possible to worship with reverence a mere ethical or philosophical ideal. As he explained:

> religion, as I see it, is concerned with man's relations with God and ethics are concerned with man's relations with man. The two are not the same and are not made the same by sincere inquiry into the question – what is God? If reason leads people not to accept Christianity or any known religion but they do believe in the excellence of qualities such as truth, beauty, and love, or believe in the platonic concept of the ideal, their belief may be to them the equivalent of a religion but viewed objectively they are not a religion.

Worship must have at least some of the following characteristics: submission to the object worshipped, veneration of that object, praise, thanksgiving, prayer or intercession. This requirement can vary in interpretation across the common law world – as illustrated by the varying fortunes of the Church of Scientology, which was refused charitable status in England because its core practices of training and auditing (counselling) did not constitute worship of a Supreme Being,[72] even though it had been deemed charitable in the United States[73] and Australia.[74]

---

[69] Although, in the United States, the Inland Revenue Service (IRS) took an early and clear view that charitable trusts could not be restricted to those that declared their belief in one 'Supreme Being'.

[70] *Re South Place Ethical Society, Barralet v. Attorney General* [1980] 1 WLR 1565; (1980) 124 SJ 774; [1980] 3 All ER 918.

[71] Ibid., at p.924.

[72] *Application for Registration as a Charity by the Church of Scientology (England and Wales)*, Charity Commissioners Decision, 17th November 1999 at p.24.

[73] In 1993, the United States' IRS recognised Scientology as a 'non-profit charitable organisation'.

[74] *Church of the New Faith v. Commissioner for Pay Roll Tax* (1983) 49 ALR 65.

RELIGION AND CHARITABLE PURPOSE

- Religious doctrines

As Lord Halsbury once put it:

> Speaking generally, one would say that the identity of a religious community described as a Church must consist in the unity of its doctrines. Its creeds, confessions, formularies, tests, and so forth are apparently intended to ensure the unity of the faith which its adherents profess, and certainly among all Christian Churches the essential idea of a creed or confession of faith appears to be the public acknowledgment of such and such religious views as the bond of union which binds them together as one Christian community.[75]

The presence of a body of beliefs or teachings, to which an organisation or individual is fully committed, has always provided good supportive evidence of the existence of a religion, although 'a religion can be regarded as beneficial without it being necessary to assume that all its beliefs are true'.[76] This point finds support in the corollary: a gift to a religious body will fail if in the meantime the congregation has so changed its tenets that it is no longer identifiable as the religion previously known to the donor.[77] However, that the significance of doctrines can be overstated was evident in *Re Allen*,[78] when Birkett LJ stated:

> when a testator uses the words 'a member of the Church of England', he must not be assumed to be speaking as a learned theologian or an ecclesiastical historian, with special meanings in his mind, or with refinements and reservations. He must be assumed to be an ordinary man using ordinary language.

Charity law and religions

The law, as judicially articulated in the courts of the United Kingdom and broadly followed thereafter throughout the common law world, now holds that all religions are to be treated equally. While any religion is deemed better than none,[79] no one is deemed better than any

---

[75] See *Free Church of Scotland* v. *Overtoun* [1904] AC 515, HL (Sc), *per* Lord Halsbury LC at pp.612–613.

[76] *Gilmour* v. *Coats and others* [1949] AC 426.   [77] *A-G* v. *Bunce* (1868) LR 6 Eq 563.

[78] *Re Allen* [1953] Ch. 116, at p.834.

[79] *Gilmour* v. *Coats* [1949] AC 426, *per* Lord Reid at pp.457–458. Also see *Neville Etates Ltd.* v. *Madden* [1962] Ch. 832, at p.853, where it was stated that:

> the court is entitled to assume that some benefit accrues to the public from the attendance at places of worship of persons who live in this world and mix with their fellow citizens. As between different religions the law stands neutral, but it assumes that any religion is at least likely to be better than none.

other.[80] Paradoxically, however, even if a gift deliberately discriminates against particular religions it may still be charitable.[81]

Charity law, religion and the public benefit

Both the 'public' and the 'benefit' arms of the test must be satisfied. The challenge of marrying the concept of public benefit to the charitable purpose of advancing religion has, however, been considerably eased by the traditional legal presumption that gifts or trusts for this purpose are *ipso facto* for the public benefit.[82] This was a perspective confidently asserted by Newark in 1946, who was certain that charities for the advancement of religion were by definition for the public benefit.[83]

• Public

Charitable status requires benefit to be provided to the public or, as the test is sometimes described, 'an appreciably important class of the community'.[84] The number constituting a sufficient proportion of 'the public' has never been determined. The class of persons who might benefit may be either a section of the public,[85] a class of the community[86] or a section of the community.[87] Conversely, it will not be met and the trust will not be charitable if those who might benefit are merely 'a fluctuating body of private individuals'.[88] The rule does not impose an

---

[80] *Nelan v. Downes* (1917) 23 CLR 546 at p.568. See also, *Thornton v. Howe* (1862) 31 Beav. 14 and *Re Pinion (deceased)* [1965] Ch. 85.

[81] See *Re Lysaght; Hill v. Royal College of Surgeons of England* [1966] Ch. 191; [1965] 2 All ER 888, which concerned a trust to establish a medical scholarship unavailable to both Roman Catholics and Jews.

[82] See *National Anti-Vivisection Society v. IRC* [1948] AC 31.

[83] See F. H. Newark, *'Public Benefit and Religious Trusts'* (1946) 62 LQR 234.

[84] *Verge v. Somerville* [1924] AC 496, *per* Lord Wrenbury, at p.499.

[85] See *Re Tree* [1945] 1 Ch. 325, 327, *per* Evershed J.

[86] See *Verge v. Somerville* [1924] AC 496, *per* Lord Wrenbury, at p. 499; and *IRC v. Baddeley* [1955] AC 572, *per* Lord Simmonds LC, at p.593.

[87] See *Trustees of Sir HJ William's Trust v. IRC* (1944) 27 TC 409, *per* Lawrence LJ, at p.418.

[88] See *Re Drummond* [1914] 2 Ch. 91 *per* Eve J, at p.97; *Verge v. Somerville* [1924] AC 496, *per* Lord Wrenbury, at p.499; *Trustees of Sir HJ William's Trust v. IRC* (1944) 27 TC 409, *per* Lawrence LJ, at p.418; *Re Tree* [1945] 1 Ch. 325, 327, *per* Evershed J, at p.327; *IRC v. Baddeley* [1955] AC 572, *per* Lord Simmonds LC, at p.593; and *Davies v. Perpetual Trustee Co. Ltd.* [1959] AC 439, *per* Lord Morton, at p.456.

absolute bar on any private benefit accruing from a charitable gift, only that any private benefit conferred is incidental. Where the access of potential beneficiaries to the benefits made available are in some way restricted, this may compromise charitable status.

Where the class of potential beneficiaries is defined by its faith then the courts construe this as a non-personal relationship nexus and therefore intrinsically public in nature.[89] Typically, a religious charity is entitled to restrict access to its place of worship to the followers or adherents of that religion. However, the well-known hypothetical instance cited by Simonds LJ, when he pointed out that a bridge restricted to impecunious Methodists would breach the 'public' requirement, nicely illustrates an underlying dilemma.[90] As he then noted, such a trust would fail the public requirement because the formally restricted class of beneficiaries means that the trust 'does not serve the public purpose which its nature qualifies it to serve.'[91] Such a restriction dooms the trust because 'it is not for the benefit of the adherents of the religion themselves that the law confers charitable status, it is in the interest of the public'.[92]

Access is also often restricted by fees, which can again give rise to controversy. Fee-charging schools and hospitals may well be driven as much if not more by profit than public benefit considerations, but the fact that they nonetheless relieve pressure on the State, by diverting paying customers away from equivalent public services and so leaving greater service availability for others, can suffice to qualify for charitable status.[93]

- Benefit

The requirement that organisations, or gifts to them, should also satisfy the benefit arm of the public benefit test has proven controversial. This is partly because in the words of Wright LJ, what is construed as 'benefit' in the charity law sense will 'vary from generation to generation'.[94] Mainly, however, in a religious context the difficulty lies in the extent to which private piety can be construed to be of public benefit. This has been particularly contentious in relation to gifts made to, or for the use of, a

---

[89] See *IRC* v. *Baddeley* [1955] AC 572, and a class of 'Methodists'. [90] Ibid., at p.592.
[91] Ibid., at p.592. [92] *Holmes and others* v. *HM Attorney General* [1981], transcript.
[93] *Re Resch's Will Trusts, Le Cras* v. *Perpetual Trustee Co. Ltd.* [1968] 1 AC 514 (PC). Also see *Joseph Rowntree Memorial Trust Housing Association Limited* v. *AG* [1983] Ch. 159.
[94] See *National Anti-Vivisection Society* v. *IRC* [1948] AC 31, at p.42.

closed contemplative religious order,[95] for the saying of a private mass[96] or for services in a private chapel,[97] which, in some jurisdictions, have been found not to be charitable both because of their long association with superstitious uses and because intercessory prayers and the example set by leading pious lives were viewed as being too vague in terms of their benefit to the public.[98] Masses to be said for the repose of the souls of the dead have always been accorded charitable status in Ireland, Canada and Australia, but not in the UK jurisdictions, regardless of whether such masses were held in public or private. The approach taken in the United Kingdom was summarised by Harman J in *Re Warre's Will Trusts*, a case concerning a retreat house, when he said: 'Pious contemplation and prayer are, no doubt, good for the soul, and may be of benefit by some intercessory process, of which the law takes no notice, but they are not charitable activities.'[99] In *Cocks* v. *Manners*[100] it was asserted that such cases contravene both aspects of the public benefit requirement because 'any benefit by prayer or example is incapable of proof in the legal sense, and any element of edification is limited to a private, not public, class of those present'.[101] Similarly, religious practices that are restricted to a familial group cannot be charitable for, it is claimed, they 'can lead to no public advantage, and can benefit or solace only the family itself'.[102]

Moreover, far from making a beneficial contribution, some religious practices can be detrimental to the public. This potential for religion to be more malign than benign was a matter of concern to Lord Scott of Foscote, who spoke for the House of Lords in *Gallagher* v. *Church of Jesus Christ of Latter-Day Saints*:[103]

---

[95] See, for example, *Cocks* v. *Manners* [1871] 12 Eq 574, where a contemplative order of nuns was found to be not charitable in contrast to the Irish case *Maguire* v. *Attorney General* [1943] IR 238, when a similar convent was held to be a 'spiritual powerhouse', and a bequest to it was charitable.

[96] See, for example, *Kehoe* v. *Wilson* (1880) 7 LR Ir 10. Also see *Re Hetherington's Will Trusts* [1990] Ch. 1.

[97] *Hoare* v. *Hoare* (1886) 56 LT 147.

[98] *Gilmour* v. *Coates* [1949] AC 426. Also see *Trustees of the Congregation of Poor Clares of the Immaculate Conception* v. *The Commissioner of Valuation* [1971] NI 114, at 169, *per* Lowry LJ.

[99] *Re Warre's Will Trusts* [1953] 1 WLR 725.   [100] *Cocks* v. *Manners* [1871] 12 Eq 574.

[101] *In re Hetherington decd* [1990] Ch. 1, 12 (Sir Nicholas Browne-Wilkinson VC). See also *Gilmour* v. *Coates* [1949] AC 426.

[102] See, for example, *Yeap Cheah Neo* v. *Ong Cheng Neo* (1875) LR 6 PC 381, at p.396.

[103] *Gallagher* v. *Church of Jesus Christ of Latter-Day Saints* [2008] 1 WLR 1852, 1867 [51].

RELIGION AND CHARITABLE PURPOSE 63

[S]tates may.... recognise that, although religion may be beneficial both to individuals and to the community, it is capable also of being divisive and, sometimes, of becoming dangerously so. No one who lives in a country such as ours, with a community of diverse ethnic and racial origins and of diverse cultures and religions, can be unaware of this. Religion can bind communities together; but it can also emphasise their differences. In these circumstances secrecy in religious practices provides the soil in which suspicions and unfounded prejudices can take root and grow; openness in religious practices, on the other hand, can dispel suspicions and contradict prejudices.

- Presumption of public benefit

By 1893, as was acknowledged in *In re White*, gifts for religious purposes were considered charitable unless shown otherwise:

the authorities shew that a bequest to a religious institution, or for a religious purpose, is *prima facie* a bequest for a 'charitable' purpose, and that the law applicable to 'charitable' bequests, as distinguished from the law applicable to ordinary bequests, ought to be applied to a bequest to a religious institution, or for a religious purpose.[104]

Once the court recognised a religious body as such then, unless the purpose of a gift was clearly in some way illegal or immoral, it was generally presumed charitable. As Lord Langdale MR stated in *Baker* v. *Sutton*, 'all the cases, with one exception, go to support the proposition, that a religious purpose is a charitable purpose'.[105]

From an early stage, however, some judges were arguing that even religious purposes must demonstrate a public benefit.[106] In 1871, in *Cocks* v. *Manners*, the presumption was challenged when the court explicitly held that purposes for the advancement of religion must provide a public benefit. In finding that the purposes of an enclosed order of Roman Catholic nuns could not be charitable, as no benefit to those outside the order could be proved, the court ended the presumption in England.

Further, in certain circumstances the presumption will be rebutted and the gift will not be considered to be of public benefit. This will be the

---

[104] *In re White* [1893] 2 Ch. 41; followed in *In re Bain, Public Trustee* v. *Ross* [1930] 1 Ch. 224.
[105] *Baker* v. *Sutton* (1836) 1 Keen 224.
[106] See, for example, *Heath* v. *Chapman* (1854) 2 Drewry 417, 426; 61 ER 781, *per* Sir Kindersley VC, at p.784.

64 CHARITY LAW AND RELIGION

case, for example, if the organisation in question operates solely for profit, or if it employs oppressive psychological manipulation of its followers or potential followers.[107]

Activities test

Generally, courts and regulators throughout the common law nations have come more firmly to the view that applying an activities test is necessary in circumstances where there is doubt regarding the alignment between a charity's purpose and its practice.[108] An entity's activities should further its charitable purpose: the reality and substance of its declared purpose must be substantiated (i.e. confirmed, corroborated or demonstrated) by its actual activities.[109]

THE ADVANCEMENT OF RELIGION

To be charitable, an organisation or gift must 'advance' religion. Charity law in a common law context requires a religious charity to be not only so constituted as to satisfy the legal definition of religion, by having objects or purposes of a religious nature, but its activities and gifts to it must also advance religion, meaning that they must 'promote or maintain or practice it and increase belief in the Supreme Being or entity that is the object or focus of the religion'.[110]

Advancement

To advance religion is to do something positive in the name of that religion and directly relevant to its beliefs. As Denning LJ once

---

[107] It was Wickens VC in *Cocks* v. *Manners* (1871) LR 12 Eq 574, at p.585 who initially suggested that the 'benefit' quotient of a religious organisation for the 'public' lay in its moral and spiritual values which could be found in its beliefs, doctrines and practices.

[108] See, for example, Charity Commission, RR2 *Promotion of Urban and Rural Regeneration* (Version – March 1999), 'Tests for charitable status'. To be charitable, an organisation will need to demonstrate that 'the public benefit from its activities outweighs any private benefit', at para. 4.

[109] See new guidelines on public benefit issued by the Charity Commission, which make clear that charitable status will in the future be an organisation's purpose, rather than its activities (16 September 2013). See more at: www.charitycommission.gov.uk/news/new-public-benefit-guidance (accessed 21 December 2013).

[110] See Charity Commission, 'The Advancement of Religion for the Public Benefit', December 2008, at para. C3.

remarked: 'The word "advancement" connotes to my mind the concept of public benefit. ... When a man says his prayers in the privacy of his own bedroom, he may truly be concerned with religion but not with "the advancement of religion".'[111]

In the UK jurisdictions, public benefit must now be proven, but in all other jurisdictions the traditional presumption continues and any such organisational activity will be presumed to be for public benefit unless the contrary can be shown.

Whether or not the presumption prevails, the activities of a religious entity must in fact be linked to and actually further the essence of the religion: they must not be merely supplementary, tangential or in furtherance of an ancillary, non-charitable purpose. Similarly, the members or staff of such an organisation will not be furthering the religion if they are engaged solely in activities that are of peripheral significance; a functional relationship of some significance for the accountability of those engaged, for example, as janitors in a school run by a religious order. Indeed, as will become evident in later chapters, there are significant differences, with accompanying legal consequences, between: a religious adherent furthering their religion and giving effect to their religious beliefs through the terms and conditions of their chosen employment; such a person undertaking work in furtherance of a secular purpose; and a non-religious person undertaking work on behalf of a religious body.

It is also the case that the beneficiaries must be appropriate. These are normally the followers or adherents, the wider church and the public generally, or, in the case of a charitable religious order, the beneficiaries are the members of that order and the wider public.

Traditional types of 'advancement'

Perhaps the most characteristic activity associated with religious bodies, and one always assumed to be furthering its intrinsic message, is the virtuous lifestyle modelled by its adherents. Where the actions of its members reflect and give effect to a religion's particular set of religious beliefs or doctrines, and so encourage members of the wider community to conduct themselves in a socially responsible way, then the latter are customarily viewed as the beneficiaries of the former's actions undertaken to advance their religion. In the UK jurisdictions, however, it is

---

[111] *National Deposit Friendly Society Trustees* v. *Skegness UDC* [1958] 2 All ER 601. Also see *Keren Kayrmeth Le Jisroel, Ltd.* v. *Inland Revenue Commissioners* [1931] 2 KB 465.

probable that more tangible public benefit outcomes would be required by, for example, the followers or adherents putting the values of their religion into practice by taking positive actions to help others in society, such as visiting people who are distressed, sick or dying, or providing food and shelter to the homeless.

There is a long tradition of certain types of gift being recognised as advancing religion, including the following.

- Churches and their fixtures

A range of gifts, made for the benefit of churches and their fixtures, have historically been upheld as charitable, including: gifts for the provision of ornaments in a church,[112] for the erection of a pulpit,[113] for an organ,[114] for the maintenance of a choir,[115] for the construction of an organ gallery,[116] for the repair of a parish churchyard,[117] for the repair of a rectory,[118] a gift to a church *eo nomine*[119] and a gift to a parish *eo nomine*.[120]

- Gifts for the upkeep of graves

Gifts for the upkeep of graves and burial vaults, etc., where the facility is an integral part of the fabric of a church, have similarly been upheld as charitable. This has been so whether the gift was restricted to a particular grave[121] or provided for the maintenance of a whole cemetery.[122]

- Gifts for the support of clergy

Such gifts, for example for the relief of infirm, sick and aged Roman Catholic priests, have usually been upheld as charitable.[123]

- Masses

Bequests for masses to be said for the repose of the souls of the dead was one of the earliest and most traditional forms of religious charitable gift. These were refused charitable status in England after the Reformation, where for centuries it was thought that gifts for the celebration of masses

---

[112] *Hart* v. *Brewer* (1595) Cro. Eliz. 449. [113] *Sir Baptist Hender's Case*, Poph 139.
[114] *Attorney-General* v. *Oakover* (1736) cited: 1 Ves Sen 536.
[115] *Re Palatine Estate Charity* (1888) 39 Ch D 54.
[116] *Adam* v. *Cole* (1843) 6 Beav. 353. [117] *Re Vaughan* (1886) 33 Ch D 187.
[118] *Attorney-General* v. *The Bishop of Chester* (1785) 1 Bro CC 444.
[119] *Cresswell* v. *Cresswell* (1868) LR 6 Eq 69. [120] *West* v. *Knight* (1670) 1 Ch Ca 134.
[121] *Re Eighmie* [1935] Ch. 524. [122] *Re Vaughan* (1886) 33 Ch D 187.
[123] *Re Foster* [1939] 1 Ch. 22.

THE ADVANCEMENT OF RELIGION 67

were unlawful as 'superstitious uses' and in breach of the Statute of Chantries 1547.[124] Not until the House of Lords decision in *Bourne* v. *Keane* did such gifts again become lawful,[125] and not until *Re Caus* did they regain charitable status.[126]

- Missionaries

The courts have had little difficulty in finding that missionary work serves to advance religion. All bona fide missionary work is regarded as equally charitable: whether seeking to advance Christianity in general or the interests of a particular religion. As Donovan J has advised:

> To advance religion means to promote it, to spread the message ever wider among mankind; to take some positive steps to sustain and increase religious belief; and these things are done in a variety of ways which may be comprehensively described as pastoral and missionary.[127]

Proselytising or 'spreading the word', while naturally intrinsic to religious bodies, is associated also with the activities of religious charities and indeed provided the grounds for charity law's most famous case. *Commissioners for Special Purposes of the Income Tax Act* v. *Pemsel*[128] concerned the Moravian Church and its charitable purpose of 'maintaining, supporting and advancing the missionary establishments among heathen nations'. It was the decision of the Commissioners to discontinue granting income tax exemption for this missionary work that brought John Pemsel before the court in his ultimately successful action.[129]

- Support services

As with other charitable purposes, gifts and organisations dedicated to indirectly advancing religion by providing necessary support services have also qualified for charitable status. For example, in England, a

---

[124] See, for example, *West* v. *Shuttleworth* (1835) 2 My & K 684 and *Heath* v. *Chapman* (1854) 2 Drew 416.
[125] *Bourne* v. *Keane* [1919] AC 815. Also see *Re Hetherington* [1989] 2 WLR 1094.
[126] *Re Caus* [1934] Ch. 162.
[127] See *United Grand Lodge of Free and Accepted Masons of England and Wales* v. *Holborn Borough Council* [1957] 1 WLR 1080; 121 JP 595; 101 SJ 851; [1957] 3 All ER 281.
[128] *Commissioners for Special Purposes of the Income Tax Act* v. *Pemsel* [1891] AC 531 (HL).
[129] See, further, K. Bromley, '*The Definition of Religion in Charity Law in the Age of Fundamental Human Rights*', paper presented at ISTR conference, Dublin, 2000.

68 CHARITY LAW AND RELIGION

bequest for the relief of infirm, sick and aged Roman Catholic priests was found to be charitable,[130] as was the provision of rest homes for members of a religious community[131] and so also, in New South Wales, was a gift of cottages for retired missionaries.[132]

Contemporary types of 'advancement'

Any of the following are now generally accepted as activities that may advance religion:[133]

(1) the provision of sacred spaces, churches and worship services;
(2) the provision of public rituals and ceremonies;
(3) contributing to the spiritual and moral education of children;
(4) contributing towards a better society – for example by promoting social cohesion and social capital;
(5) carrying out, as a practical expression of religious beliefs, other activities (such as advancing education or conflict resolution, or relieving poverty), which may also be charitable;
(6) contributing to followers' or adherents' good mental and physical health; aiding the prevention of ill health, speeding recovery and fostering composure in the face of ill health;
(7) providing comfort to the bereaved; and
(8) health care and social care.

In some jurisdictions, other than the United Kingdom, this list would extend to include gifts for private prayer,[134] private masses[135] and to closed religious orders.[136] It must of course be borne in mind that a religious body may decide to channel its charitable activity not directly into the advancement of religion but through an alternative charitable purpose such as the advancement of education or the relief of poverty. Also, as has been explained:[137]

---

[130] *Re Foster* [1939] 1 Ch. 22. [131] *Re James* [1932] 2 Ch. 25.
[132] *Re Macgregor* (1932) 32 SRNSW 483.
[133] See Charity Commission, 'The Advancement of Religion for the Public Benefit', December 2008, at para. D2.
[134] See *Re White* [1893] 2 Ch. 41.
[135] See, for example, *Kehoe* v. *Wilson* (1880) 7 LR Ir 10. Also see *Re Hetherington's Will Trusts* [1990] Ch. 1.
[136] See *In re Macduff; Macduff* v. *Macduff* [1896] 2 Ch. 451.
[137] See *Catholic Care* v. *Charity Commission and Human Rights Commission* [2010] EWHC 520 (Ch), *per* Briggs J., at para. 87.

THE PRE-HUMAN RIGHTS ERA 69

Charities do not, strictly, exist to serve a beneficial class, they serve publicly beneficial purposes. Nonetheless, even if certain familiar types of charity may loosely be described as serving a beneficial class, it is by no means uncommon for them to achieve that purpose by conferring benefits on persons outside that class. For example, a charity for the relief of sickness may serve that purpose by providing benefits to nurses or to the hospital employing those nurses.[138]

RELIGIOUS DISCRIMINATION: CHARITIES AND THE LAW IN THE PRE-HUMAN RIGHTS ERA

Donor discretion, within the boundaries long established by the Preamble and *Pemsel*, as subsequently judicially enlarged, lies at the heart of charity law. Any such exercise of discretion is necessarily accompanied by exclusionary criteria: the targeted beneficiaries are identified by a specification broad enough to be 'public' but sufficiently precise to exclude those outside donor intent.

Discriminatory religious conditions

It has always been the case that donor discretion may be exercised in a manner that is discriminatory but wholly legal, or discriminatory and not. The distinction cannot always be readily drawn: matters construed as unlawful or contrary to public policy are liable to fluctuate over time. Motivation may also play a part in determining into which camp a charitable trust or donor's gift will fall.

Religious conditions and unlawfulness

In England before the introduction of religious toleration legislation, many donor gifts intended for charitable purposes were struck down on the grounds of unlawfulness. In *De Costa* v. *De Paz*,[139] for example, Lord Hardwicke held that a gift for the advancement of the Jewish religion was illegal as this was contrary to the Christian religion. Similarly, in *Cowan* v. *Milbourn*[140] the refusal to allow a room which had been hired to be used for the delivery of lectures impeaching the character and teachings of Christ was held to be justified on the ground that the intended use was for an unlawful purpose as Christianity was part and

---

[138] Citing *Re White's Will Trusts* [1951] 1 All ER 528.
[139] *De Costa* v. *De Paz* (1754) 2 Swanst 487.   [140] *Cowan* v. *Milbourn* (1867) LR 2 Ex 230.

70 CHARITY LAW AND RELIGION

parcel of the law of the land. Again, societies founded to pursue secularism were viewed as subversive of both religion and the law of the land, illegal and incapable of receiving bequests.[141]

Religious conditions and public policy

There is a tradition of judicial respect for charitable trusts and gifts made subject to conditions that unequivocally favour a particular religion. This practice, termed 'conditions in restraint of religion' by Lord Greene in *Re Samuel*,[142] refers to a broad category of gifts and trusts, most usually created by testators but occasionally by donors, that require a prospective beneficiary to commit to or renounce a specified religion, often set in the context of marriage and/or the upbringing of children.[143] By the late nineteenth century the courts had become well accustomed to and accepting of such conditions. For example, the view of Hall VC in *Hodgson v. Halford*,[144] that property holders were 'perfectly justified' in imposing such conditions, was endorsed by the comment of Naish J in *Re Knox*[145] that since such conditions have been 'repeatedly held valid ... it is now too late to question their validity' and they were held to be 'beyond question' by Lord Romer in *Clayton v. Ramsden*.[146]

Even when the courts were prepared to strike a condition of religious discrimination attached to a donor's gift, for breach of public policy, the rulings fell short of unequivocally stating that an exercise of property rights must defer to anti-discrimination principles. This tended to occur in relation to matters of legal status such as, as noted above, when an exercise of property rights impinged upon marriage[147] and parenthood – for example, when a settlor sought to use the enticement

---

[141] See, for example: *Thompson v. Thompson* (1844) 1 Coll 381, 397; *Thornton v. Howe* (1862) 31 Beav. 14, 20; *In re Bedford Charity* (1819) 2 Swanst. 470, 527; and *Bowman v. Secular Society Ltd.* [1917] AC 406.

[142] *Re Samuel* (1941) [1942] 1 Ch. 1, at 30 (CA).

[143] See, further, S. Grattan and H. Conway, 'Testamentary Conditions in Restraint of Religion in the Twenty-first Century: An Anglo-Canadian Perspective' (2005) 50 *McGill Law Journal* 511.

[144] *Hodgson v. Halford* (1879) 11 Ch D 959, at p.967.

[145] *Re Knox* (1889) 23 LR Ir 542 (Ch.), at p.544.

[146] *Clayton v. Ramsden* [1943] 1 AC 320, at p.332.

[147] See *Trustee of Church Property of the Diocese of Newcastle v. Ebbeck* (1960) 104 CLR 394, at para. 5, *per* Windeyer J.

THE PRE-HUMAN RIGHTS ERA 71

of property to induce the termination of an existing marriage.[148] Parachin makes this point very well:[149]

> So, if a beneficiary is already married to (or about to marry) a person of a particular faith, it is against public policy for a settlor to either delay vesting until this is no longer the case or to divest the beneficiary if this still remains the case by a future date.[150] But even here it seems that the condition is invalid only if it is capable of interfering with an existing relationship, which turns on factors that have nothing to do with anti-discrimination norms. If a beneficiary is single, there is no existing marriage being interfered with. In this context, a condition restraining marriage on religious grounds will be enforceable as either a condition precedent or a condition of forfeiture.[151] If the cases were truly about enforcing anti-discrimination norms in property law, it would not matter whether an existing or a future marriage was being targeted. A similar point applies in relation to conditions requiring beneficiaries to provide (or not to provide) certain religious instructions to minor children. The basis for striking such conditions is not that they are discriminatory, but rather that it is against public policy to interfere in a parental–child relationship.[152] Again, if the cases were really about equality, the controlling issue would be the religious distinction not the context in which it was being drawn.[153]

He goes on to assert that it was, and remains, very rare for religious conditions to be struck on the express ground of being in breach of public policy against discrimination. The overwhelming tendency has instead been

---

[148] See *Trustee of Church Property of the Diocese of Newcastle* v. *Ebbeck* (1960) 104 CLR 394 and *Re Hurshman, Mindlin* v. *Hurshman* (1957) 6 DLR (2d) 615. More recently, see *In re Estate of Max Feinberg* (2009) 235 Ill. 2d 256, at 266.

[149] See, further, A. Parachin, 'The Definition of Charity and Public Law Equality Norms', paper presented at the conference Private and Public Law – Intersections in Law and Method, the T.C. Beirne Law School at the University of Queensland, Brisbane, July 2011.

[150] It was key in both *Ebbeck* and *Hurshman* that the testator was aware at the time of drafting the restraint on marriage that the beneficiaries would be in breach due to existing marriage.

[151] Such a condition is valid because it 'involves the decision to marry, not an incentive to divorce'. See *In re Estate of Max Feinberg* (2009) 235 Ill. 2d 256, at 274.

[152] See, for example, *In re Tegg* [1936] 2 All ER 878.

[153] Contrast cases such as *In re Tegg* (where the beneficiary is the parent and the condition requires the parent to provide a certain kind of religious instruction to a child) with cases where the beneficiary is the minor and the condition requires the minor to meet a religious adherence requirement. Courts have struck the former but upheld the latter, though the minor must be given until a reasonable time after attaining majority to meet the religious condition (see *Blathwayt* v. *Lord Cawley* [1976] 1 AC 397 (HL) and *In re May* [1917] 2 Ch. 126). If equality were the controlling factor no distinction would be recognised between the two contexts.

72 CHARITY LAW AND RELIGION

to protect the property law right of disposal and allow conditions that restrain religion (either requiring or prohibiting the practice of a particular religion) or marriage (either requiring or prohibiting marriage to a person of a particular religious persuasion, ethnicity or class).[154]

Conditions and the common law

There was always a greater probability of an attached condition threatening the charitable status of a trust on grounds of it being in breach of the common law than of public policy. The difficulties likely to result in such an outcome arose not specifically from the religious nature of a restrictive condition, but either because the discriminatory clause was indefinite,[155] uncertain[156] or otherwise rendered the charitable trust impracticable or impossible to administer; or by so identifying the class of potential beneficiaries the trust failed the public benefit test. This remains the case.

In the former category, despite application of the 'benignant construction' rule,[157] many trusts have failed for uncertainty.[158] Where uncertain language is used by a donor, as where a purpose or object has been described as 'philanthropic', 'benevolent' or 'for a worthy cause', etc., it would be denied charitable status. Ultimately the objects must be sufficiently certain to be able to provide for the proper administration of a charity and to enable its property to be applied pursuant to its charitable objects.[159] The general principle is that a trust for purposes which are not limited to, but are broad enough to include charity, fails altogether.[160] Where the uncertainty is attributable to a religious condition

---

[154] Parachin,'The Definition of Charity and Public Law Equality Norms', citing in support an impressive list of cases with rulings to the same effect covering several jurisdictions.
[155] *Morice* v. *Bishop of Durham* [1804] 9 VES 399; 32 ER 656.
[156] See, for example, *Re Hurshman, Mindlin* v. *Hurshman* (1957) 6 DLR (2d) 615, *per* McInnes J, at p.619.
[157] See, for example, *Mills* v. *Farmer* (1815) 1 Mer 55, *per* Eldon LJ.
[158] For a trust to be created, the three certainties must be satisfied: the subject matter must be certain; the objects of the trust must be certain; and the words relied on as creating the trust must have been used in an imperative sense so as to show that the testator intends to create an obligation. See *Wright* v. *Atkyns* (1823) Turn & R. 143, *per* Lord Eldon, at p.157; and *Knight* v. *Knight* (1840) 3 Beav. 148, *per* Lord Langdale MR, at p.173.
[159] *Re Koeppler's Will Trusts, Barclays Bank Trust Plc* v. *Slack and others* [1984] Ch. 243, at pp.257–258 and [1985] 2 All ER 869 CA, at p.874 approved.
[160] *Morice* v. *Bishop of Durham* (1804) 9 VES 399. Also see *Biscoe* v. *Jackson* (1887) 35 Ch D 460, where the court was able to infer such a general charitable intention in a bequest to the poor of a parish.

CONCLUSION

then only where there is evidence of paramount charitable intent[161] can the trust be retrieved for its charitable purpose by using a *cy-près* scheme to remove that condition.

In the latter category, the terms used in delineating the religious condition may irreparably damage the charitable status of the trust by preventing either the 'public' or the 'benefit' components of the public benefit test from being satisfied by, respectively: the specification being such as to narrow the class of intended beneficiaries to the point where it is insufficiently 'public';[162] or by the discriminatory effect being more harmful than beneficial.

Conclusion

The common law foundations for charity law lie in the Statute of Charitable Uses 1601, particularly in the wording of its Preamble and in the judicial principles and precedents, most notably the decision in *Pemsel*, established over the following centuries. In the post-Reformation years 'religion' and 'charity' were defined and practised in accordance with clear terms of reference, mutually agreed and jointly applied by Church and State, within a resolutely Protestant culture. For some centuries there was no uncertainty as to the duality of their social roles: a monotheistic deity was to be worshipped in the manner required by Church of England doctrines; with related public and private morality issues policed by the Ecclesiastical Courts; and charity law administered accordingly. During this period, and in that particular Protestant theocratic context, the interpretation of activities now held to constitute 'the advancement of religion' throughout the common law world was first formulated.

---

[161] In a line of cases, from *In re Harwood; Coleman* v. *Innes* [1936] 1 Ch. 285 to *In re Spence dec'd; Ogden* v. *Shackleton* [1979] Ch. 483, the UK courts have held that no charitable intent could be inferred from a testator's will.

[162] In *Gilmour* v. *Coats* [1949] AC 426 (HL) the House of Lords considered the restriction to a group of Carmelite nuns practising intercessory prayer and spiritual edification failed to satisfy either arm of the test.

3

Competing frames of reference

Domestic constraints

Introduction

As the twentieth century progressed, the social infrastructure of many developed nations succumbed to a process of creeping secularisation which reduced the necessity to rely on the voluntary, morally driven and, ultimately, discretionary acts – characteristic of charity and religion in previous centuries – to address social need. This allowed, and perhaps stimulated, mounting scepticism as to the public benefit inherent in the role of religion. By the close of that century, a raft of national legislation and international conventions – underpinning entitlements to legal rights per se, and addressing an ever-broadening social justice agenda – was in place to cast corresponding doubt on the equivalent role of charity. This chapter considers the impact of such changes, the resulting interface tensions and areas of boundary permeability in the social structures that constitute a modern framework for public benefit provision.

Beginning with the more traditional frameworks and their constraints, the chapter considers the fading importance of the 'family' and 'community' as transmitters/enforcers of religion and its values and then identifies the common law constraints that have inhibited the charitable acts of donors. It briefly surveys the range of alternative organisational forms historically deployed to achieve public benefit outcomes: from formative beginnings in the rights of 'association', through to the 'collectivism' movement of the late nineteenth century, noting the significant steps taken by the modern trade union movement and including an appraisal of the role of cooperatives and other mutual-benefit entities. A discussion follows on the implications of the current and growing entanglement of charities with commerce and government, the proliferating range of competing philanthropic vehicles such as social enterprises, and the likely consequences of such developments for the future of charity. This leads into an exploration of the inter-relationships between justice, morality, charity and religion which, to some extent, found expression in the Hart–Devlin debate which some may see as the first transatlantic shots in the culture wars. There is a focus on the impact of legal rights and social justice, which carry an assertion of individual and group entitlement, and then on to an assessment of the restrictions imposed by politics, as demonstrated by the contemporary crises-ridden global context, on the remit of both religion and charity. An extension of that focus brings the discussion to a review of the public policy constraint on charity and concludes the chapter.

Charity, religion and the boundaries between individual/family/society

As the traditional sources for our sense of belonging, of sharing in a collective identity with all the security that offered, have slowly melted away, there has been a corresponding adjustment to the social roles of charity and religion. The former was once confined to the margins of family and Church, operating to salvage society's victims – the poor, the frail and the failed – restoring them as far as possible to their place in society, but is now a much more diffuse entity and no longer defined mainly by its relationship to the helpless. The latter, displaced by creeping secularisation and tarnished by revelations of systemic child abuse, has been similarly diminished in its capacity to maintain the values and institutions of contemporary society and contribute to furthering social coherence and homogeneity.

Changes in the 'family'

The Victorian ideal family model – characterised by the monogamous, lifelong union of a heterosexual couple, parenting the children of their marriage – has not, for some time, been the ubiquitous norm it once was.[1] Developments in medicine and law have greatly impacted upon parenting: increasing the extent to which maternity is now a chosen option as pregnancy may be achieved by artificial insemination and surrogacy, avoided through the use of improved contraceptives or terminated by abortion; while decreasing the relevance of paternity and rendering obsolete any residual traces of patriarchy. The traditional

---

[1] See, for example, A. S. Wohl (ed.), *The Victorian family: Structure and Stresses*, Croom Helm Ltd, London, 1978.

kith and kin support networks and good neighbour relationships of settled communities have faded in significance, leaving families to become more nuclear, impermanent and mobile, often featuring transient and serial parenting arrangements. Such developments, together with a decline in the rates of both fertility and marriage in modern Western nations, with childbirth being a great deal less dependent upon marriage, has led to a general loosening of the previously tightly structured relationship between family and State.

The Christian marital family unit

The Victorian family was also very much a Christian – and in England an overtly Protestant – model, based on the original Nazarene unit of married parents and the child 'of their marriage' and providing a cornerstone for the communities of the common law nations. 'Family', in effect, was defined by marriage, which in turn had been defined by Christianity: none of the legal characteristics of a marital family applied to its non-marital or 'extra-marital' counterparts; these were seen as deviant and all parties involved were legally and socially stigmatised.

The sacrament of marriage bound the spouses in an exclusive mutually supportive union for procreative purposes, granted legal rights to maintenance and property and provided the only context in which sexual relations and the children born thereof could be legitimate. It also bound the families and relatives of the spouses in a kinship network and the marital family to the State as a unit that conformed to the latter's laws. For centuries, culminating in the moral code of the Victorian era, the legal status of marriage was upheld by Church and State as an inviolable building block for constructing a sound Christian society: a contract between family, Church and State, perpetuating a code of morality that set recognisable standards for acceptable conduct in public and private life and for family relationships.

Charity, professional services and family support

It would seem that as the traditional sources of family support weaken or disappear, their functions are often displaced onto charity or absorbed into the commercial sector. In either case it results in family problems being passed to professionals as the private becomes more public. Exposure to family sanctions, and to the prevailing norms of Christian morality, which may have previously exercised a restraining influence on individual action, are now readily avoided in our more mobile society where relocation to a safely anonymous environment offering opportunities for replicating a similar package of employment, housing and lifestyle can be swiftly organised.

Changes in 'religion'

Like the 'family', religion is no longer the social force it once was. Lamenting the loss, Scrutton comments that: 'Western societies are organised by secular institutions, secular customs and secular laws, and there is little or no mention of the transcendental either as the ground of worldly authority or the ultimate court of appeal in all our conflicts.'[2]

The impact of modern science and scientific rationality

Some might contend that religion, with its accompanying belief systems and spiritual and moral values for leading a 'good life' has merely been displaced by, or swapped for, the verities of scientifically established knowledge, the derived values from which have come to inform the way we now live. Indeed, for all religions, the inroads made by modern scientific discoveries into areas hitherto clothed in religious belief have been and will continue to pose a significant and challenging alternative frame of reference.

As noted above, developments in medicine and law have greatly impacted upon parenting, increasing the extent to which maternity is now a chosen option as pregnancy may be achieved by artificial insemination, avoided through the use of improved contraceptives or terminated by abortion. Surrogacy, while decreasing the relevance of paternity and rendering obsolete any residual traces of patriarchy, has also rendered the choice to parent a gender-free option: its availability to single prospective parents[3] as well as to same-sex couples has done much to broaden the diversity of contemporary family forms. At the other end of the scale, medical advances are now such that people are living longer and assisted euthanasia can offer relief for the terminally ill, even if this is not yet lawful.

---

[2] See R. Scruton, *Arguments for Conservatism: A Political Philosophy*, Continuum, London, 2006, at p.142.
[3] See, for example, I. Mucklejohn, *And Then There Were Three: The Exceptional Story of a Remarkable Surrogacy Family*, Gibson Square Books Ltd, London, 2005.

78   COMPETING FRAMES OF REFERENCE

But medical intervention in life more broadly – in the form of bio-genetic engineering, synthetic biology, cloning and discoveries in sequencing the human genome which are believed likely to advance the diagnosis and treatment of diseases – offer new insights and lead to an understanding of human evolution itself. The ongoing process of having to make room for alternative, evidenced-based explanations for matters handed down through the previous generations as inviolable religious truths is inevitably weakening the authority of all religions.

The impact of pluralism

In the United Kingdom and in Europe more generally, the dilution in population homogeneity has been accompanied by a general decline in the role of established religions and the traditional powerful position of the Church: fewer people now have religious convictions, belong to a Church or, most tellingly, attend religious services; and respect for religious organisations has been greatly damaged by evidence of their role in promoting mass sectarian violence, involvement in genocide and revelations of child abuse.[4] In the United States, and to a lesser extent Australia and Canada, however, there has been something of a resurgence in the social role of religion, while all modern Western societies in recent years have placed an increased reliance upon faith-based social facilities (mainly schools).

Fundamentalism, however, although more readily associated with Islam, is also very apparent in the many and varied strains of evangelism recently metastasised from Christianity. Wherever its origins, fundamentalism then functions, as intended, to emphasise differences, which can lead more in the direction of social polarisation than pluralism.

Secularism and religion

From at least the mid nineteenth century, secularism[5] has had a marginal if expanding social profile, but the interface between religious belief and what to some has since evolved into 'a militant secularism'[6] is one that,

---

[4] See, for example, the *Report of the Commission to Inquire Into Child Abuse* (the Ryan Report), Dublin, May 2009.

[5] The term 'secularism' was first coined by George Jacob Holyoake (1817–1906).

[6] A term used by Baronness Warsi, Britain's first Muslim cabinet minister and chair of the Conservative Party.

although already tense in the closing decades of the twentieth century, is set to become more so in the twenty-first.

The State and religion

The question of whether all matters of government should be entirely separate and insulated from religion is one that has exercised policy makers in many countries. In England there is no equivalent to the constitutional separation of Church and State in the United States. Indeed, following the Reformation, all State institutions were permeated by and aligned with Protestantism, and although this symbiotic Church–State relationship has faded somewhat over the past century it remains formally in place and still retains a good deal of potency.

It may be argued that in circumstances where the cultural identity of a nation has become indivisible from its association with a particular religion (e.g. the Catholic Church in Italy, Ireland and Spain), then there is justification for the State to permit its public institutions to reflect that mutuality and for it to preference the interests of related religious organisations against all others. On the other hand, the equality principle as upheld by the ECtHR does seem to require the State to be neutral in its relationship with religion. In this case the public arena needs to be treated as either an open market in which all religions are equally free to proclaim and manifest their beliefs, compete for adherents and be assured of equal respect and engagement with State authorities; or, alternatively, as one in which all religions are equally prohibited from exercising any presence, that space is reserved entirely for secular entities and their activities, and all religions can be equally assured that they will be ignored by the State authorities.

Those with and those without religious beliefs

The rift between these two groups has become steadily more contentious as secularists grow in number and both adopt opposing and intransigent positions on an increasing range of matters. The area of contention is partially to do with the propriety of any form of government support for, or engagement with, religion, particularly in relation to a specific religion, and of its links to bodies associated with a religion. Secularists would be very alert, for example, to the vulnerability of public institutions, such as schools, to penetration by covert proselytism either in the classroom (through use of teachers, teaching materials or fixtures that suggest particular, or any, religious belief) or in pastoral care (through the role of chaplain, etc).[7] In recent decades contention has grown more acrimonious in respect of an ever-extending agenda of social issues with a high moral content. While the interface between the religious and the secular is fraught, so also are those that lie between and within religions and, to a lesser extent, those which lie between religion and philosophy or other belief systems.

Charity, the nonprofit sector and the citizen

Whereas family and religion required loyalty of its members, gave them a sense of affiliation and built for them a collective value base and enduring identity, the nonprofit sector offers individuals a shopping mall and recycling depot for identity accessories. Local community support networks that used to be localised, organised around a sense of belonging to a congregation and focused on the parish church are now likely to take the form of very individualised attachments to an eclectic array of nonprofit bodies, some accessed solely via the internet.

Secular 'sense of mission'

While the sector provides diverse 'belonging' opportunities, it also opens the door for individuals to lend their weight to mission-driven collaborative enterprises that demand commitment, obey definite principles and strive to achieve beneficial outcomes for its members or for others who are more disadvantaged. This 'missionary zeal' is evident in the very many projects currently being led by philanthropic funds and the idealism that focuses on challenges such as eliminating malaria. In the space left by government and market, philanthropy is a growing presence affording opportunities for values-led, collective contributions to furthering the public benefit which, in the process, generate social capital of both the 'bonding' and 'bridging' varieties.[8]

---

[7] This wariness is not confined to instances where the Christian religion intrudes on public institutions. The founding of the Islamic Sharia Council in 1982, with its remit to address issues such as marriage breakdown, has also caused controversy. The 85 Sharia 'courts' in Britain have since processed many thousands of cases and there is concern that they may exercise an intimidating influence on Islamic communities: see, BBC's *Panorama* programme at: www.familylawweek.co.uk/site.aspx?i=ed112864 (accessed 21 December 2013).

[8] See R. D. Putnam, *Bowling Alone: The Collapse and Revival of American Community*, Simon & Schuster, New York, 2000.

THE COMMON LAW CONSTRAINTS

81

Charity law, religion and the common law constraints

The discretionary right of a donor, to give to whomsoever he or she pleases, remains the basic starting point for charity – just as the freedom of association is for charitable organisations. Subject to the rights of dependents, creditors, etc., and provided the gift meets the public benefit test, complies with other customary common law rules, is public policy compliant and falls within the parameters of the *Pemsel* charitable purposes (as subsequently judicially and legislatively extended), such a discretionary gift has also always satisfied the definition of 'charity' for the purposes of charity law. However, in recent years the traditional scope for discretionary action by donor or charity within the parameters of that law has become more exposed to challenge.

Donor discretion

For many centuries property rights have been consistently viewed by the judiciary as sacrosanct: the law has always sought to facilitate freedom of disposal; the right of an owner to transfer ownership – to dispose of their goods, whether in the form of money, real estate or other valuables – by contract, bequest or gift has been of fundamental importance. It is a right that, when exercised by a donor within the parameters of charity law, may be subject to certain restrictions.

Donor constraints

As Panachin has shown,[9] the courts have been most reluctant to allow the right of an owner to dispose of their property to be obstructed in any way,[10] firmly asserting that convincing justification is required for the removal of any restrictive condition a donor may have attached to an otherwise charitable gift – for example: that property holders are 'perfectly justified' in imposing such conditions[11] and invalidity should follow only where the condition is 'unquestionably against public morality';[12] the case against the condition must be 'concrete';[13] and that a condition must be 'self-evidently

---

[9] See A. Parachin, 'Human Rights and the Definition of Charity', paper presented at ARNOVA conference, 2010.

[10] See, for example, *Blathwayt* v. *Lord Cawley* [1976] 1 AC 397 (HL).

[11] *Hodgson* v. *Halford* (1879) 11 Ch D 959, *per* Hall VC, at p.967.

[12] Ibid., *per* Hall VC, at p.966.

[13] *Blathwayt* v. *Lord Cawley* [1976] 1 AC 397 (HL), *per* Lord Wilberforce at p.427.

82 COMPETING FRAMES OF REFERENCE

against public policy'.[14] The mere fact that a condition is 'inconsistent with standards now widely accepted' has been held insufficient to justify a finding of invalidity.[15] Donor-imposed religious constraints would normally be judicially respected.[16]

In time, however, while the burgeoning multicultural environment of modern common law nations correspondingly increased the probability of donor gifts being made on a culture-specific basis, it also led to the ubiquity of human rights legislative provisions designed to prevent any inequality of treatment of persons on the basis of their belonging to a group defined by characteristics such as race, gender or religion.[17] Case law precedents forged in a pre-human rights legislative era, when social homogeneity was more prevalent, would not necessarily be sustainable in a more fractious climate of competing human rights, clashing religious sensitivities and cultural politics (see Chapter 4).[18]

Common law conceptual constraints

Charitable status requires that an entity is confined exclusively to charitable purposes, is for the public benefit, independent, non-profit-distributing and non-political (see Chapter 2). In particular, the concepts of 'charitable purpose' and 'public benefit', as defined and elucidated through many generations of case law, have imposed very real constraints on the ambit of charity.

Charitable purpose constraints

An entity is 'charitable' within the meaning ascribed to this term by charity law, only if it fits within one of the charitable purposes identified by that body of law: the four *Pemsel* heads, although broadened under the 'spirit and intendment' rule,[19] have long imposed legal parameters

---

[14] Ibid., *per* Lord Edmond-Davies at p.441.

[15] *Blathwayt* v. *Lord Cawley* [1976] 1 AC 397 (HL), at p.426 *per* Lord Wilberforce.

[16] See, for example, *Re Lysaght* [1966] Ch. 191 and *Re Dominion Students Trust* [1947] 1 Ch. 183.

[17] In particular, the European Convention for the Protection of Human Rights and Fundamental Freedoms 1950 and the International Covenant on Civil and Political Rights (ICCPR) 1966.

[18] See, for example, *R(E)* v. *Governing Body of JFS* [2010] IRLR 136.

[19] Although not strictly falling within one of the four *Pemsel* heads of charity, a gift could nonetheless be defined as charitable if it could be construed as coming within the 'spirit or intendment' of the statute (i.e. Statute of Charitable Uses 1601).

upon the scope of charity throughout the common law world. Ultimately, this became one of the more significant driving forces for charity law reform: it was widely recognised that the *Pemsel* classification had ceased to provide an appropriate or sufficient framework for charity to address contemporary social needs.

Public benefit constraints

The crucial and distinctive requirement for charitable status has always been that an entity must satisfy the public benefit test:[20] there must be a real, verifiable benefit, and this must accrue to the public or to a significant section of it. In all common law jurisdictions, with the exception of England and Wales, this test was applied by the revenue agency which, given its statutory duty to protect the nation's tax revenue base, was prone to doing so with a defensiveness that restricted the number and categories of entities entitled to such status. Nonetheless, over time it became accepted by the judiciary and regulators in most jurisdictions that a presumption of public benefit compatibility existed in relation to gifts made or to organisations that functioned under the first three *Pemsel* heads, remaining to be proven only in relation to the fourth. Significantly, in all jurisdictions, religious organisations and gifts or bequests made to them were presumed charitable, excepting 'closed' religious orders in the United Kingdom.[21]

Charity as a legal entity: the constraints of new boundaries

The nonprofit sector has always provided a home for many different forms of associational activity, but none have occupied a more clearly defined role, nor for longer, than charities in general and religious charities in particular. These have been readily recognised by their conservative and institutional functions, conforming to a settled public benefit role and operating within a fairly clearly defined social space with well-established constituencies. The security of their traditional social

---

[20] 'It is a general rule that a trust or gift in order to be charitable in the legal sense must be for the benefit of the public or some section of the public', *per* Jenkins LJ in *Re Scarisbrick* [1951] Ch. 622, at pp.648–649.

[21] See *Gilmour* v. *Coats* [1949] AC 426; *Cocks* v. *Manners* 12 EQ 574; and *Dunne* v. *Byrne* [1912] AC 407.

position has been under threat for some time, but in recent years the pressures for change have increased as new factors have come into play.

Beginnings: the basic legal structures for charitable and nonprofit activity

Organised charitable activity requires a legal structure.[22] In the common law jurisdictions this was provided by the trust; indeed, charity in England, having emerged from its origins as a pious use, first assumed the legal form of a trust as early as the fifteenth century. In time, although the gift relationship continued to revolve around a gift that was most usually legally packaged as a trust, a charity could also be established as an unincorporated association or company;[23] all three now provide alternative legal structures for a 'charitable organisation' for the purposes of charity law. The trust continues to be the means for giving effect to the charitable intentions of a donor: the charitable trust and the charitable foundation are much the same thing in some but not all common law jurisdictions. The legal significance of the 'trust' to the development of charity is matched by that of the 'association' in relation to the nonprofit sector.

The trust

A trust provides a means whereby a donor can impose a legal requirement upon a trustee or trustees to receive, retain and utilise a gift for purposes specified by the donor. Such a trust will arise either during the lifetime of a donor by agreement or deed drawn up for that purpose, or after death from the terms of a donor's will. A charitable trust is a species of trust, but what distinguishes it from all other forms, as Mummery LJ pointed out, is that 'it is a public trust for the promotion of purposes beneficial to the community, not a trust for private individuals'.[24] Those

---

[22] See, for example, the ruling of the European Court in App. No. 8317/78, *McFeeley* v. *United Kingdom*, 20 DR 44 (1980).

[23] Although the charitable trust was initially the preferred legal structure for charity, and continued to be so for some centuries in the United Kingdom and Irish jurisdictions, elsewhere incorporation offered an alternative that from an early stage proved more attractive.

[24] See *Gaudiya Mission* v. *Brahmachary* [1997] 4 All ER 957, at p.963.

CHARITY AS A LEGAL ENTITY

purposes are defined by *Pemsel* unless subsequently statutorily extended (see Chapter 2). This common law institution, with its roots in the law of equity, has survived due to its singular strengths.

Its unique strength lies in its independence. A trust/foundation is always self-governing, nonprofit, dedicated to public purposes (whether charitable or not) with, to a varying degree, its own resources. It need not necessarily be established by endowment, but in that event it then has guaranteed long-term financial independence, free from any obligation to appease a particular constituency. The freedom of not having to fundraise and/or seek government grants or contracts means that it is not hostage to the goodwill of government or the general public. As long as it stays within the parameters of its donor's stated purposes, a trust/foundation is free to be innovative, to take risks and to lend its support to other causes. Perhaps most importantly, its independence in theory allows it to operate without fear or favour and without having to negotiate vested interests. Their size, capacity and prominent social profile makes them both difficult to ignore when they adopt an advocacy role and attractive partners for government bodies engaged in the provision of health, social care and education services.

The trust/foundation does have some weaknesses. Of these, donor discretion is most notable: the charitable purpose and related recipients are chosen entirely at donor discretion, which may have no bearing on social priorities. As has often been pointed out, it is the fact that control over the gift is retained by the donor, and subsequently by trustees, that distinguishes it from other forms of charitable giving and this is so regardless of whether the donor is an individual or a corporation.[25] The fact that a trust/foundation can exist in perpetuity means that eventually, although the initial gift may well have grown into a considerable sum, the donor-determined purpose will either no longer be necessary or perhaps be incapable of fulfilment. The law, however, has always attached great importance to protecting the expressed wishes of a donor and confining the use of the gift to the terms on which it was given, which can give rise to situations where the donor rules from the grave and resources are wasted.

---

[25] See H. Anheier and D. Leat, *From Charity to Creativity: Philanthropic Foundations in the 21st Century*, Comedia, Stroud, 2002, at p.64.

Associations

The right of citizens to form, join or not to join associations constitutes a hallmark of democracy;[26] indeed, the very existence of non-government organisations, and therefore that of the nonprofit sector, is conditional upon this right. Its significance has been recognised by the legislatures of democratic states for centuries and the constitutions of most countries in the world contain articles protecting freedoms of association and assembly.[27] The judiciary has also stressed its importance: in *Sidiropoulos and Others* v. *Greece*,[28] for example, the ECtHR held that the ability of citizens to form a legal entity in order to act collectively in a field of mutual interest is 'one of the most important aspects of the right to freedom of association, without which that right would be deprived of any meaning'.[29]

Religion is a type of voluntary association. As such it requires a legal structure and this, in the common law jurisdictions, was initially provided by the 'corporation' established by special charter created by Parliament in England at the time of its colonial expansion.[30] In due course, religious organisations came to be legally constituted as either a charitable trust, an unincorporated association,[31] a corporation sole, a religious corporation or as a nonprofit corporation.

Collectivism and organisational structures

Long before the emergence of the current 'rights conscious' age, with its emphasis on the entitlements of individuals, a more collective approach

---

[26] The International Covenant on Civil and Political Rights (ICCPR) and the Universal Declaration of Human Rights both guarantee freedom of association internationally, as do the Helsinki Accords of the Organisation (former Conference) on Security and Cooperation in Europe (OSCE). Also see the Freedom of Association and Protection of the Right to Organise Convention, 1948 (No. 87) and the Right to Organise and Collective Bargaining Convention 1949 (No. 98).

[27] See, for example: Canada, and the Canadian Charter of Rights and Freedoms, where the freedom of association has become an entrenched right; and the First Amendment to the US Constitution.

[28] *Sidiropoulos and Others* v. *Greece* (26695/95) 27 EHRR (1998).

[29] Ibid., at para. 40.

[30] See P. Gerstenblith, 'Associational Structures of Religious Organisations' (1995) 2 *Bringham Young University Law Review* 439, at: www.law2.byu.edu/lawreview/archives/1995/2/ger.pdf (accessed 21 December 2013).

[31] See, J. Warburton, D. Morris and N. Riddle, *Tudor on Charities*, Sweet & Maxwell, London, 1995, at p.163.

CHARITY AS A LEGAL ENTITY

was evident. In part this was political in nature, as ideology shaped the expectations of different societies, permeated the culture and mobilised some social sectors and professional groups (see Chapter 4). However, at a deeper and more pervasive level the concepts of 'collectivism', of group representation, of bargaining and contract had also taken hold and over time these have undoubtedly done much to erode certain attitudes – submissiveness, acceptance and compliance with authority – which contributed to sustaining the social functions of charity and religion.

Collectivism

In England, towards the end of the nineteenth century, as the State poor law regime faded, collectivism as a basis for organised mutual support became evident in initiatives such as those that launched the Friendly Societies.[32] There was also greater awareness of the extent and effects of poverty as a result of a series of late-Victorian and early Edwardian social surveys, notably those conducted by the wealthy liberal businessmen Charles Booth[33] and Seebohm Rowntree.[34] A new pattern of social activism emerged which was most fully embodied in the creation of Associational Charities.[35] Prominent liberal activists, including Mary Wollstonecraft,[36] Mary Carpenter[37] and Octavia Hill[38] generated public awareness of contemporary issues of social inequity. Leadership for a new approach was provided by 'chocolate philanthropists' from the

---

[32] The 1874 report of the Royal Commission on Friendly Societies offered support for the new forms of intervention into the circumstances of the poor.

[33] Charles Booth (1840–1916), a social researcher noted for his studies into pauperism in London; see, *Life and Labour of the People of London*, Macmillan, London, 1891–1903.

[34] Seebohm Rowntree (1871–1954), noted for his studies which measured poverty and analysed its effects in York at the turn of the century; see further his reports, for example *Poverty: A Study of Town Life* (1901), *Poverty and Progress* (1936) and *Poverty and the Welfare State* (1951).

[35] See T. Hitchcock, 'Paupers and Preachers: The SPCK and the Parochial Workhouse Movement', in L. Davison, T. Hitchcock, T. Keirn and R. Shoemaker (eds), *Stilling the Grumbling Hive: The Response to Social and Economic Problems in England, 1689–1750*, Palgrave Macmillan, Stroud, 1992, pp.145–166.

[36] See, for example, L. Gordon, *Mary Wollstonecraft: A New Genus*, Little Brown, London, 2004.

[37] See M. Carpenter, *Reformatory Schools for the Perishing and Dangerous Classes and for the Prevention of Juvenile Delinquency*, published in 1851.

[38] Founder member of the Charity Organisation Society; see, O. Hill, *Homes of the London Poor*, Macmillan, London, 1875.

Quaker families of Fry, Cadbury and Rowntree.[39] Their construction of model villages enabling whole communities to be self-sufficient and mutually supportive were motivated by their religious principles and offered a new challenging interpretation of philanthropy.

Mutual benefit and other organisational structures

The new ethos saw the birth of organisations formed to provide sustained economic security for its members, such as mutual benefit associations and the Methodist-led Credit Union movement,[40] which were organised around principles that required ownership, labour and profits to be shared among their members. The Industrial and Provident Societies, a member benefit type of non-government organisation, usually a commercial organisation, were established under the Industrial and Provident Societies Acts 1893–1978. It was formed 'for carrying on any industries, businesses or trades', which included agricultural producers, group water schemes and housing cooperatives. The Friendly Societies, another member benefit type of non-government organisation, was a mutual assurance association, established under the Friendly Societies Act 1896. They included mutual insurance and assurance bodies, benevolent societies and other societies formed for purposes such as the promotion of science, literature and education. Although an Industrial and Provident Society and a Friendly Society were quite different, both were established under the Friendly Societies Acts 1875 and 1896 (as amended). Again, cooperatives and community benefit societies have been in existence since the late eighteenth century, but the Rochdale Society of Equitable Pioneers, founded in 1844, is usually considered the first successful cooperative enterprise and was used as a model for others. All such entities, whose business is conducted for the benefit of their members or community, required profits and assets to remain dedicated to that purpose.

To an extent the emergence of umbrella or 'apex' bodies within the nonprofit sector can be seen as a further step down that road. While they vary greatly and can operate at local, national or international levels, all tend to provide services such as membership support, coordination,

---

[39] See, further, D. Cadbury, *Chocolate Wars*, Harper Press, London, 2010.

[40] Organisations set up for the mutual benefit of members have, of course, consistently been refused charitable status: see, for example, *Nuffield (Lord)* v. *Inland Revenue Commissioners* (1946) 175 LT 465.

advocacy and representation together with research, policy development and capacity building for their nonprofit member organisations. Some emphasise their role in developing, not merely implementing, government policy.

The emergence of all such bodies indicated an awareness of unacceptable restraints and a recognition that the time was right for them to operate alongside and in competition with the traditional role of charities.

Trade unions, contracts and negotiated rights

Trade unions not only improved conditions for workers, but also provided debating forums and social facilities that offered a supportive environment within which members could build a sense of collective solidarity and learn self-help strategies. Collective bargaining broke the reliance on employers' discretion that had contained previous generations of 'the working class'. Arguably, it similarly proved to be an equally formidable antidote to acquired dependency on charity and religion. Deference and dependency were no longer automatically in-built components of any such relationship between 'man' and his maker, employer or benefactor. Negotiated rights, as embodied in contracts, empowered swathes of sector-based employees, gave permission for hierarchical social arrangements to be challenged and, in time, came to provide the terms of reference for all transactional relationships.

Charities as 'public bodies': relationships with government and commerce

A new emphasis on competing in the market is imposing its own constraints on the freedom of action traditionally characteristic of charities. This is apparent, for example, in: a general 'muting of dissent' as charities are either subject to explicit 'gagging' clauses in their contracts with government or have become more circumspect in their criticism of policies pursued by bodies with which they have or hope to have a contractual relationship; a consequent absence of effective advocacy on behalf of the socially disadvantaged as charities attend more to the requirements of immediate service provision rather than to needs, their causes and long-term strategies for improvement; and charities being diverted into developing the next marketing opportunity in order to secure their funding base.

'Public bodies'

Among the legal hallmarks that distinguish charities from all other trusts and nonprofit entities is the requirement that they serve the public benefit. This, not unnaturally, often results in their assuming functions normally viewed as the responsibility of government, such as the provision of health and social care, education and housing, etc. However, the legal safeguard preventing their absorption into the machinery of government service provision is the obligation on trustees to maintain the independence of their charitable trust. Not unless it can be demonstrated that a charity has surrendered such key legal features as 'its constitution, its activities, its history and its control'[41] will its charitable status be open to challenge.

The principle–agency relationship

The common law principle of 'agency' found early expression in the Latin maxim *qui facit per alium, facit per se* (the one who acts through another, acts in his or her own interests). It has been defined as 'the relationship between a principal and an agent whereby the principal, expressly or impliedly, authorizes the agent to work under his control and on his behalf'.[42] Whether an agency relationship exists turns on the facts in each case: not all delegated authority necessarily constitutes agency and the span of control exercised is crucial.

An agent who acts within the scope of authority conferred by the principal binds the principal in the obligations created against third parties; the authority may be expressly conferred by the principal or may arise by implication. The acts of an agent, acting within the scope of delegated authority, are imputed to the principal; failings in service delivery are the responsibility of the principal, and in matters governed by public law, the principal can be held accountable. This is of importance in the present context because of an increasing trend in many jurisdictions for government to franchise out its public service responsibilities to charities, including religious organisations (thereby getting a cheaper service as, although government pays the charities' costs, the true service price is subsidised by public donations to those charities).

---

[41] As per Lockhart J in *Cronulla Sutherland Leagues Club Ltd.* v. *Federal Commissioner of Taxation* 89 ATC 4936 (1989); 20 ATR 1404.

[42] See, e.g. B. S. Markesinis and R. J. C. Munday, *An Outline of the Law of Agency* (4th edn), LexisNexis, London, 1998.

Where, as in a growing number of cases,[43] there is evidence that a charity has allowed itself to become subsumed into an agency–principal relationship with a government body, then there is every likelihood that it will be found to be functioning as a public body. As the ECJ stated in *Calì & Figli* v. *Servizi Ecologici Porto de Genova*, an entity acts as a public body when it is performing 'a task in the public interest which forms part of the essential functions of the state and where the activity is connected by its nature, its aims and rules to which it is subject with the exercise of powers . . . which are typically those of a public authority'.[44] In that event such a charity, even if a religious organisation, will then share the same level of accountability and on the same terms as a public body.

Government

As state tax revenues shrink – due to the invidious demographic equation of a declining working population relative to growing numbers of pensioners, outsourcing of production, the cost of wars, etc. – governments in all major developed nations are withdrawing from much direct public service provision and ensuring that responsibility is devolved where feasible to nonprofits. In health, social care and education, these organisations are most usually charities and very often they are religious charities. In addition, the roles of government and charity had in many countries already been adjusted as the former replaced direct grants to organisations for core funding with short-term contracts for service delivery. This strategy has allowed government to avoid paying full service costs while also shifting the associated risks and accountability.

Competition from old and new legal forms of nonprofit activity

The 'social economy'[45] – the middle ground between the public and private sectors, or between the economic interests of government and

---

[43] See, for example: *National Union of Teachers* v. *Governing Body of St Mary's Church of England (Aided) Junior School* [1997] 3 CMLR 630; *R (Weaver)* v. *London & Quadrant Housing Trust* [2009] EWCA Civ 587; [2008] EWHC 1377 (Admin); [2008] WLR (D) 207; and *Poplar Housing and Regeneration Community Association Ltd.* v. *Donoghue* [2001] EWCA Civ 595; [2002] QB 48.

[44] *Calì & Figli* v. *Servizi Ecologici Porto de Genova* [1997] ECR I-1547, at para. 23.

[45] See, for example, S. Bridge, B. Murtagh and K. O'Neil, *Understanding the Social Economy and the Third Sector*, Palgrave Macmillan, Basingstoke, 2008.

market – is the territory occupied by organisations with an economic role to provide public benefit services in collaboration with those in need and to do so through methods that allow for minimal private profit. Such organisations typically share a mission to provide new and innovative solutions to issues (whether they be socially, economically or environmentally based) and to meet the needs of those members and users ignored or inadequately addressed by the private or public sectors.

Cooperatives

This form of nonprofit is generally in decline, except in the United Kingdom, where government intervention has triggered a revival in its fortunes.[46] There are very many different types, including those based in agriculture and manufacturing, but it has been the cooperatives with a brief for public utilities and housing in particular that have made considerable inroads into the role usually associated with charity. More recently, at least in the United Kingdom, the ongoing financial crisis with the accompanying revelations of corruption and exploitation has prompted a flight of investment from the high street banks into such ethics-led entities as credit unions and cooperative banking.

Social enterprises

These are businesses with primarily social objectives, the surpluses of which are principally reinvested for that purpose in the business or in the community, rather than being driven by the need to maximise profit for shareholders and owners.[47] They are mission-driven but profit-making businesses that trade in goods or services to achieve a social goal. Aiming to accomplish targets that are social and environmental as well as financial, social enterprises can include housing associations, credit unions and the trading arms of registered charities. Originating in the United States, they are now widespread in Europe and elsewhere, are increasing rapidly and are often viewed as preferable to charity,

---

[46] See, further, J. Curl, 'The Cooperative Movement in Century 21', at: http://affinities journal.org/index.php/affinities/article/view/50/169 (accessed 21 December 2013).
[47] See R. Ridley-Duff and M. Bull, *Understanding Social Enterprise: Theory and Practice*, SAGE Publications, London, 2011.

particularly to religious charities, because they provide a more acceptably neutral vehicle for intervention in areas of social disadvantage.

Other contemporary public benefit vehicles

The pace of government withdrawal from public service provision in recent years has prompted a rapid growth in intersectoral activity, as a range of commercial and nonprofit organisations compete or cooperate to fill the gap, and governments experiment with variations of public–private finance initiatives. Venture philanthropy, limited liability companies, social bonds and corporate philanthropy in many different shapes and sizes are among the contenders that have now entered the market to challenge the role formerly reserved for charity.

Justice and morality, charity and religion

The secularisation of social infrastructure together with the spread of national and international human rights legislation have brought a broadening entitlement to legal rights, equity, equality and non-discrimination in contemporary developed nations. This has done much to dislodge the social roles traditionally performed by charity and religion. Such developments have provided a context for the reworking of the above relationships: not just between religion and charity or between justice and morality, but also with challenging cross-tensions emerging between all four.[48]

Law and principles

Law is generally understood either in terms of a body of inter-related rules,[49] enforced with penalties by designated agencies for the common good, or as a body of principles, drawn from religious belief, that are held to inform and govern the law which is in turn enforced and adjusted by agencies and rules to ensure compliance with those principles. Known respectively as the schools of 'legal positivism' and 'natural law', they

---

[48] See L. L. Fuller, *The Morality of Law* (revised edn), Yale University Press, New Haven, 1969.

[49] See N. E. Simmonds, *Central Issues in Jurisprudence: Justice, Law and Rights* (2nd edn.), Sweet & Maxwell, London, 2002.

form the background against which the relationship between religion, charity and human rights presently falls to be explored.

The school of 'legal positivism' is based to some degree on the political philosophy of Thomas Hobbes,[50] of which Jeremy Bentham[51] and John Austin[52] have been leading advocates. Legal positivists hold that the validity and authority of law derives wholly from, is a technical response to and is explicable only in terms of, actual social circumstances. They argue that law in itself does not necessarily equate with morality or, as Simmonds comments, 'the concept of law, for positivists, is a concept with no intrinsic moral import'.[53] The 'natural law' school is more ideological and based upon early Christian teachings with such eminent exponents as St. Thomas Aquinas,[54] Aristotle,[55] John Locke[56] and Emile Durkheim.[57] Natural law scholars maintain that validity and authority originate in moral principles that transcend the confines of any set of social circumstances and cannot be subject to or explained by wholly temporal terms of reference.

Principles have an important role to play in guiding the application of law and in providing the underpinning necessary to extend that application beyond prescribed circumstances and so allow for continuity in legal practice. This is particularly the case with 'grundnorms', or overarching norms which command wide acceptance and are powerful enough to govern other principles, as posited by Kelsen (e.g. the 'public benefit' principle in charity law).[58] Principles inject an added dimension to the law, lifting it beyond being merely a technical response to a particular set of circumstances and setting standards for future conduct. However, principles are not dogma: their validity is rooted in a general acceptance and so they are amenable to adjustment or

---

[50] See T. Hobbes, *Leviathan*, 1668 (reissued by Oxford Paperbacks, 2008).

[51] See, for example, J. Bentham, *Introduction to Principles of Morals and Legislation* (printed for publication 1780, published 1789, reissued by Dover Publications, 2007).

[52] See, for example, J. Austin, *The Province of Jurisprudence Determined*, 1832 (reissued by General Books LLC, 2012).

[53] Simmonds, *Central Issues in Jurisprudence*, at p.5.

[54] See, for example, St. Thomas Aquinas, the *Summa Theologiae* (written 1265–1274, reissued by Ave Maria Press, 2000).

[55] See, for example, Aristotle, the *Corpus Aristotelicum*, 2nd century AD.

[56] See, for example, J. Locke, *Two Treatises of Government and a Letter Concerning Toleration* (1689, reissued by Classic Books International, 2010).

[57] See, for example, E. Durkheim, *Rules of Sociological Method*, The Free Press, New York, 1982 [1895].

[58] See, for example, Hans Kelsen, *Pure Theory of Law* (1934, reissued by the Lawbook Exchange Ltd, 1967).

abandonment in keeping with what has usually been a gradual pace of change in the broad consensus – as, for example, in the principle that marriage is a monogamous, heterosexual, lifelong commitment. In the complex, multicultural, contemporary societies typified by the jurisdictions currently being considered, an untidy mix of principles – some conflicting, but each mandated by acceptance within their cultural constituency – must learn to co-exist. The resulting tensions can be seen in the 'culture wars' that are now a feature of life in all those jurisdictions.

Justice and morality

The contention between the two above schools as to whether or not there is, necessarily, a connection between law and morality is at its most heated in relation to the concept of 'justice'. For natural law theorists this concept is inexplicable without an acknowledgement that a set of moral principles lie at its core with the corollary, as encapsulated in that often-quoted dictum of Saint Augustine, '*lex iniusta non est lex*' (unjust law is not law). For legal positivists justice is a more pragmatic affair, often amounting to little more than adherence to the rule that like cases should be treated alike. This requires a common understanding of and agreement with the basis for making any such differentiation and a consensus that circumstantial factors should either play no part in mitigating the outcome or the part played will be strictly in accordance with accepted rules. Arguably, both approaches depend on a common acceptance of the values employed to identify 'justice occasions' and measure the significance of a breach. To that extent, justice functions as an attribute of its social context and is prone to variations from society to society and from time to time within the same society, in keeping with fluctuations in the social moral compass (e.g. acceptance of homosexuality).[59]

The Hart–Devlin debate

The view that the coherence and identity of a society at any point in time is dependant upon it having a core of moral principles embodied in and protected by its laws is probably of theocratic origin and was certainly very evident in post-Reformation England. That it continued to

---

[59] See, further: H. L. A. Hart, *Law, Liberty and Morality*, Oxford University Press, Oxford, 1963; P. Devlin, *The Enforcement of Morals*, Oxford University Press, Oxford, 1965.

command widespread respect was evidenced by the Hart–Devlin debate in the 1960s. The position of Devlin LJ, as he then expressed it, was that:

> Societies disintegrate from within more frequently than they are broken up by external pressures. There is disintegration when no common morality is observed and history shows that the loosening of moral bonds is often the first stage of disintegration.[60]

Therefore, he maintained, State intervention to control the conduct of persons, organisations or other entities judged to be acting contrary to the established morality norms of society was not only wholly justified, but was actually essential to ensure its survival: 'it is wrong to talk of private morality or of the law not being concerned with immorality as such';[61] 'society must be the judge of what is necessary to its own integrity'.[62] Hart, on the other hand, being an exponent of the John Stewart Mill[63] philosophy of liberalism, was certain that 'there is no evidence that the preservation of a society requires the enforcement of its morality "as such"'.[64] He warned that:

> It seems fatally easy to believe that loyalty to democratic principles entails acceptance of what may be termed moral populism: the view that the majority should have a moral right to dictate how all should live. This is a misunderstanding of democracy which still menaces individual liberty.[65]

Hart pointed out that societies survive changes in basic moral views.

This debate is itself indicative of morality at work in a democratic society. The issues raised form a backdrop to the theme of 'moral imperatives' that threads its way through this book and can fairly be viewed as indicating an awareness that the culture wars would migrate from the United States to other common law jurisdictions – and elsewhere. Advance warning of the spread of this conflict had been signalled by G. K. Chesterton a century ago:

> The next great heresy is going to be simply an attack on morality; and especially on sexual morality. ... The madness of tomorrow is not in Moscow but Manhattan – but most of what was in Broadway is already in Piccadilly.[66]

---

[60] See Devlin, *The Enforcement of Morals*, at p.13. [61] Ibid., at p.14.

[62] Ibid., at p.118.

[63] See J. S. Mill, *On Liberty*, London, 1859. See, further, at: www.gutenberg.org/ebooks/34901 (accessed 2 January 2014).

[64] See Hart, *Law, Liberty and Morality*, at p.82. [65] Ibid., at p.79.

[66] See 'Selections from GK Chesterton' at: www.personal.reading.ac.uk/~spsolley/GKC/Chesterton_selections.html (accessed 21 December 2013).

Legal rights, charity and religion

For most developed common law nations, the displacing of charity by rights was a phenomenon that gathered pace through the last half of the twentieth century. International conventions and national legislation began to assert basic entitlements and displace reliance upon charitable acts of gratuitous compassion. Litigation, or the threat of it, pushed aside the controls of price or grace and favour that had hitherto determined access to some of the more basic necessities of life.

Legal rights

A legal rights approach specifies entitlements, and the grounds under which they may be claimed, within a range of legislation that includes human rights, equity and non-discrimination provisions. Many every-day aspects of life, now taken for granted as governed by universally applied rights (to maternity leave, holiday pay, health and safety stand-ards in the workplace, etc.), and by processes for enforcing them (legal aid, ombudsmen, regulators, etc.), have only become so relatively recently. Legal rights and corresponding legal duties, usually under-pinned by principles and enforced by legal powers, form the basis for: a formal recognition of individual entitlement; objective adjudication on alleged breach and appropriate recompense; and a process for enforce-ment.[67] As nation states became steadily less cohesive, unicultural, homogenous, and more independent entities, so legal rights acquired a transnational remit. Where need can be met by established legal rights, charity has no role: need is then entitled to a legal remedy.

Charity

Dealing with the needs of those suffering from the many, often complex, interwoven or systemic forms of contemporary social disadvantage, charity can provide opportunities for donors and beneficiaries within public benefit parameters as defined by charity law. It serves to amelio-rate hardship, demonstrate altruism, enrich the fabric of society and generate social cohesion. While charity continues to carry vestiges of the traditional model, which rested on private acts of benevolence favouring impoverished or otherwise dependent beneficiaries, it has long since

---

[67] See H. L. A. Hart, *The Concept of Law* (2nd edn), Oxford University Press, Oxford, 1994.

98   COMPETING FRAMES OF REFERENCE

spread to accommodate the ever growing range of organisations, activities and gifts that, in a contemporary sophisticated Western society, conform to a charitable purpose and satisfy the public benefit test. However, charity rests on donor discretion while recipient eligibility is dependent upon their needs fitting within the designated charitable purpose.

Religion

Arguably, the adversarial assertion of legal rights by individuals, according to public laws facilitated by State institutions and processes, runs counter to the religious ethos of private individuals striving to achieve eternal redemption by subjecting oneself to a belief system as ordained by the relevant 'Church': in the former case it must be demonstrated that behaviour conforms to a universally accepted code; in the latter that it transcends accepted norms. While the two may be compatible, this is not always so: legal rights can be at variance with religious beliefs (e.g. abortion and homosexual marriage). Where both systems are congruent, then public and private interests are satisfied, but otherwise a serious disconnect may arise with divisive social consequences.

Social justice, charity and religion

In contrast to an approach based on the rights of the individual, social justice requires universal standards of equity, equality and non-discrimination to be entrenched in legislation, applied uniformly across society, largely through the procedures and practice of government agencies, with a right of access to the courts.

Charity

Some of the expansion secured by social justice is at the price of reducing the areas left to charity. All modern Western societies have now put into place, for example, much the same legislation to ensure equal opportunities for citizens regardless of factors such as gender, age or disability, and establish entitlements to equal pay and fair employment, etc. Such provisions also provide for an independent overview by regulatory bodies, commissions or tribunals coupled with power of referral to the court. This approach can, of course, restrict as well as facilitate opportunities; illustrated by the collective recourse of many nations to anti-terrorist measures as required by the United Nations Security Council Resolution 1373.[68]

Moreover, it is an approach which by categorising areas of social need – disability, gay relationships, age, etc. – requires the law and charities to address instances of need en bloc and, arguably, thereby reduces the capacity to respond flexibly to individual or newly emerging variants of need: forcing the individuals concerned to think of themselves in terms of categories, while prompting a rigid response that objectifies and stereotypes personal and particular circumstances.

Social justice

In contrast to an approach based on the rights of the individual, but complementary to it, social justice provides a blanket safety net of provisions. It requires universal standards of equity, equality and non-discrimination to be entrenched in legislation and applied uniformly across society. In particular, the prohibiting of discrimination is now to be found in many laws applying that principle in relation specifically and separately to disability, race, religion or belief, sexual orientation, equal pay and fair employment, etc., requiring more general social legislation to be proofed against those principles and providing for an independent overview by regulatory bodies, commissions or tribunals coupled with power of referral to the court.

The international dimension and religion

Charity law must now operate within the constraints imposed by the growing number of international conventions, protocols and treaties, etc. introduced since 1945 when the United Nations declared its commitment to international cooperation 'in promoting and encouraging respect for human rights and for fundamental freedoms for all without distinction as to race, sex, language, or religion'.[69] The Universal

---

[68] On 28 September 2001, the UN Security Council unanimously adopted a wide-ranging, comprehensive resolution with steps and strategies to combat international terrorism. Resolution 1373 gave rise to a wave of anti-terrorism legislation across the Western world.

[69] On 24 October 1945 the United Nations was established by 51 countries in order to: maintain international peace and security; develop friendly relations among nations; cooperate in solving international problems and in promoting respect for human rights; and to be a centre for harmonising the actions of nations.

Declaration of Human Rights,[70] finalised in 1948, declared the basic principles of international human rights and directed that the freedoms declared therein were to be exercised subject only to those set out in Article 29(2):

> In the exercise of his rights and freedoms, everyone shall be subject only to such limitations as are determined by law solely for the purpose of securing due recognition and respect for the rights and freedoms of others and of meeting the just requirements of morality, public order and the general welfare in a democratic society.

In 1976 the two covenants containing binding legal norms for international rights came into force: the International Covenant on Civil and Political Rights and the International Covenant on Economic, Social, and Cultural Rights (see Chapter 4).

Charity law, religion and politics: contemporary constraints

The use of law to regulate charity is a political matter.[71] Whether it is used at all and, if used, the type of government agency empowered with regulatory responsibility – and whether this is applied with a differentiating application, with or without donor incentives, or falls evenly on all charities – provides insight to the political considerations in play.

Charity and the political frame of reference

In law the public benefit remit of charity is mandatory; using its resources to address an area of social need, as defined by its declared charitable purpose, is its entire *raison d'être*. The remit of government, while uncertain and varying between nations, is assuredly broader than that of charity, must be responsive to ever changing priorities and has never proven to have had any particular capacity to resolve poverty and its associated disadvantages. Even if politics held the answer to social need, effective intervention may necessitate non-government involvement. Democratic governments lack the necessary authority, resources and tenure of office to tackle all major areas of social need and may not be best positioned to reach those most socially alienated. The exigencies of government will always require a flexibility of response and the capacity

---

[70] GA Res 217A (III), UN GAOR, 3rd sess, 183rd plen mtg, UN Doc A/810 (10 December 1948).

[71] See, further, K. O'Halloran, *The Politics of Charity*, Routledge, London, 2011.

to divert resources to address changing priorities. In contrast, charities and other nonprofits, often with decades and sometimes centuries of close alignment with social need, have acquired the knowledge, trust and resources and are able to hold focus on the issues long enough to gain traction on causal factors.

Politics

Politics as we now know it – collective movements, organised around an agreed agenda of policy and principles, intending to acquire the authority necessary to effect nationwide change and then organising to do so – is a relatively recent phenomenon and for many is one which has undoubtedly impacted upon their relationship with religion and charity. While it is usually perfectly compatible with religion, politics or, more accurately, political ideology, can itself become the higher authority – transcending circumstantial everyday concerns – to which individuals can turn for a sense of belonging, fulfilment and a feeling of contributing to a greater good. Incompatibility is also clearly possible, particularly on the agenda of contemporary social issues involving medical intervention on matters relating to life and death (including but certainly not limited to abortion, birth control and euthanasia) where religious belief and social policy can often be in conflict. Then again, strands of politics and religion can merge, as in the conjoining of neoconservatism and evangelical Christianity in the United States at the end of the twentieth century.

For those accustomed to investing their trust in evidence-based outcomes, where accountability can be readily established, the political route has proved attractive; though not necessarily to the exclusion of religious belief.

The constraints on politics

A particular problem for government in all modern democracies is the fading importance of politics in the lives of citizens: not just party politics, but politics itself;[72] a trend reinforced by the perceived inability of governments to foresee or have any positive effect on a succession of global threats to public benefit (war, terrorism, climate change, financial

---

[72] See Advisory Group, *Report on Campaigning and the Voluntary Sector* (chaired by Baroness Helena Kennedy QC), London, 2007.

crisis, flu pandemics, etc.). Government concern regarding this seeping away of political penetration has, in some developed nations, prompted an engineering of new structures to bridge the gap between government and citizen: formal partnerships forged with sectoral bodies; colonisation of the nonprofit sector; positioning of mediatory agencies between government and the sector; the development of participative as well as representative forums; and, not least, a rewriting of the law governing government–charity relations as first stated in the Preamble. An aspect of this strategy would seem to involve developing a more pluralist approach: one which makes more room for religion, for the role of religious charities and other faith-based entities in public benefit service provision.

Religion and the constraints imposed by politics

Most obviously, when used to designate a particular religion (in a theo-cratic state) or to outlaw all religions (in a communist state) politics then wields a determining power over religion; indeed, one of the biggest challenges for religion in recent years (Christianity and Islam) arrived with the opportunity to proselytise in the former communist countries of Eastern Europe. Also, however, it ultimately rests with politics to deter-mine which purposes are to be construed in law as charitable and whether appropriate organisational structures are to be available for giving effect to those purposes; politics thereby determines the legal parameters for char-itable activity, including that of religious organisations. Among the polit-ical choices to be made, in that context, are: how to define a religious charity; the distinction, if any, to be made between its religious and secular activities; and the recognition that should be given to secular charities established by religious organisations. There is also the political pressure to ensure that the global movement of resources between charities does not by default also permit a flow of information and funds for use by terrorists. Then there is the added pressure placed on international char-ities not to compromise aid/trade policies pursued by powerful bodies such as the World Bank and the World Health Organisation.

Equality legislation and religious schism

For Christianity and other traditional religions, nationally and interna-tionally, there has been no greater political imposition upon doctrinal beliefs and the social role of religion than the recent introduction of statutory provisions giving effect to human rights principles requiring sexual and gender equality and non-discrimination. In relation, for example, to the Church of England this has resulted in disputes regarding: equality of opportunity for the ordination of female clergy to posts of deacons and bishops; the similar equality of opportunity for Church appointments and promotion of active gay and lesbian applicants; the blessing, provision of celebrant and service, and the use of Church premises, in relation to same-sex marriages. Throughout the Anglican Communion of some 60 countries these and ancillary issues (e.g. same-sex adopters) are causing varying degrees of difficulty, but in some – such as Canada, the United States and increasingly so in England – they are deeply divisive, inducing schisms in Churches and in religious communities and triggering litigation regarding ownership of Church property. This new human rights environment presents a challenge for all Christian religions (also for Muslims and others) which now feel gravely compromised as their Scriptural beliefs would seemingly place them in direct opposition to emerging legal principles.

Charities and political activity

Charity law has considerably restricted the freedom of charities to engage in political activity as a means of effecting change. While this obstructs the work of all, it has a singular impact upon those committed to the advancement of religion. An organisation dedicated to a charitable purpose that entails proselytising, missionary work and the provision of aid to those in need on a domestic and international basis, must inevitably also relate to its political context.

Constraints on the involvement of charities in political activity are of fairly recent origin. There is no historical record of their hands being tied in this way. In England during the Victorian era, many important initiatives resulting in policy changes by government were led by charities, often religious charities.[73] They were to the fore in the rallies against the slave trade, they lobbied to halt the practice of 'baby-farming' and they campaigned in support of the suffragette movement. Charities, in

---

[73] For example: the protests against the conditions suffered by children employed in factories or as chimney sweeps were led by charities such as Dr Barnardo's and the NSPCC; the Infant Life Protection Society, founded in 1870, campaigned for the introduction of the Infant Life Protection Act 1872; and the Charity Organisation Society, established in 1869, mixed provision for the poor with research into the causes of poverty.

short, have a proud tradition of involvement in advocacy even if, in recent years, that has given way to the general muting of dissent in the nonprofit sectors of the common law nations, with its resulting chilling effect on political activity by charities.[74]

Charity law constraints

A legal distinction is drawn between bodies with a primary political purpose and bodies that engage in political activities: the former are not charitable; the latter will be charitable if the activities are ancillary but subordinate to and in furtherance of its non-political purposes and are within its powers. This rule varies to some degree between the common law jurisdictions. Essentially, courts take the view that matters of law and policy are for government to determine: any organisation with a purpose of changing or supporting existing law or policy cannot be a charity as there is no way of establishing whether such activity would in fact be compatible with the public benefit test.[75] The judicial dilemma, when faced with policy issues arising from action or inaction by government, remains as stated by Simons LJ, 'it is not for the court to judge and the court has no means of judging'.[76]

Unfortunately, no definitive statement has yet been given by court or regulator as to what constitutes 'political purposes'. The nearest to a definition is the list of purposes identified by Slade J in *McGovern* v. *Attorney General*,[77] also known as the Amnesty International case. Basically, it is clear that an organisation cannot be a charity, nor can it remain one, if its principal or sole purpose is to campaign to support or oppose a particular political party or its doctrines[78] or to further policies such as the promotion of peace,[79] international understanding[80] or the

---

[74] See Advisory Group on Campaigning and the Voluntary Sector (chaired by Baroness Helena Kennedy QC), *Campaigning and the Voluntary Sector*, Advisory Group on Campaigning and the Voluntary Sector, London, 2007.

[75] See *National Anti-Vivisection Society* v. *Inland Revenue Comrs* [1948] AC 31; *McGovern* v. *Attorney General* [1982] Ch. 321; *Southwood* v. *Attorney General* [2000] WTLR 1199.

[76] See Advisory Group, *Campaigning and the Voluntary Sector*, at p.62. Also, see, *Bowman* v. *Secular Society Ltd.* [1917] AC 406 and *McGovern* v. *A-G* [1982] Ch. 321.

[77] *McGovern* v. *Attorney General* [1982] 1 Ch. 321.

[78] See *Re Jones* [1929] 45 TLR 259; in Australia see, for example, *Bacon* v. *Pianta* [1966] ALR 1044.

[79] *Re Southwood* v. *AG* [2000] EWCA (Civ) 204.

[80] *Anglo-Swedish Society* v. *IRC* (1931) 47 TLR 295. In the United States such a trust would be charitable.

CHARITY LAW, RELIGION AND POLITICS

removal of injustice;[81] though, where such purpose or purposes are not political, then it may engage in political activity, provided that it does so in ways that are ancillary and incidental. Nor can a charity engage in political activity in order to organise public opinion in support of or to seek to change matters of law or government policy,[82] or to resist any proposed change,[83] or where such activity may more generally tend to usurp the role of government.[84]

Religion, charities and political activity

The case law history of involvement by religious charities in political activity began, and continues today, with issues of morals. In a succession of temperance cases the judiciary first rehearsed the arguments for separately ring-fencing charity and political activity. In the *Temperance Council of Christian Churches* case[85] in 1926 an English court denied charitable status to a trust established to promote temperance through the introduction of legislation, an approach followed by the courts in New Zealand[86] and Tasmania.[87] The grounds for the decisions were stated as being the 'political' nature of the organisation's purposes. Where the purpose of promoting temperance was to be given effect by means of circulating educational propaganda rather than by seeking to introduce legislation, as in *Re Hood*,[88] this could be charitable.

It is likely that the temperance cases in the early twentieth century were influenced by the 1907 judgment of Lord Parker in *Bowman* v. *Secular Society Ltd*,[89] in which he grounded his finding that a society, with objects that included the abolition of religious texts and the disestablishment of the Church, could not be charitable because 'a trust for the attainment of political objects has always been held invalid ... because the law has no way of judging whether a proposed change in the law will or will not be for the public benefit. ... Equity has always refused to recognize such objects as charitable.' The moral issues

---

[81] *McGovern* v. *AG* [1982] Ch. 321, *per* Slade J, at p.354.

[82] See *Hanchett-Stamford* v. *Attorney-General* [2009] Ch. 173, where Lewison J held that the 2006 Act did not change 'the fundamental principle that if one of the objects or purposes of an organisation is to change the law, it cannot be charitable', at pp.181–182.

[83] *Re Hopkinson* [1949] 1 All ER 346.

[84] See, for example, *Southwood* v. *Attorney General* [2000] WTLR 1199.

[85] *Inland Revenue Commissioners* v. *Temperance Council of Christian Churches of England and Wales* (1926) 136 LT 27.

[86] *Knowles* v. *Stamp Duties Comr* [1945] NZLR 522.   [87] *Re Cripps* [1941] Tas SR 19.

[88] *Re Hood* [1931] 1 Ch. 240 (CA).   [89] *Bowman* v. *Secular Society Ltd.* [1907] SALR 190.

associated with temperance and which generated case law involving churches and religious charities at the beginning of the twentieth century have, a century later, been replaced by issues that now bring the same parties to court to contest politically approved changes to traditional human relationships, such as the introduction of gay marriage, adoption and other rights of LGBT persons, genetic engineering and medical interventions to induce fertility or terminate pregnancies. The contemporary political context, both domestic and international, is also producing an abundance of moral issues grounded in more secular concerns – not least the extortionate abuse of good governance principles that triggered the ongoing financial crisis, the pursuit of high-tech warfare in undeveloped countries and the consequent rise in the poverty levels of Western nations – that are similarly engaging the interest of such bodies and leading to political activity on their part (see Chapter 4).

Advancement of religion and advocacy

Charities, including religious charities, can undertake advocacy, campaigning or other forms of political activity where this is directly linked to and in furtherance of their charitable purpose: but only when the issues are relevant to that purpose are they free to engage in advocacy to change or retain any related law or policy. It cannot become the continuing or sole activity of the charity.

Advocacy

Advocacy is a hallmark of charity. The capacity, willingness and indeed the obligation to represent the interests of the socially disadvantaged: to speak on their behalf, articulate their grievances, protect their interests and mediate between them and relevant authorities have been among the key attributes traditionally associated with the role of charities. This is no less the case with religious charities: indeed, such expectations are perhaps strongest in respect of those bodies whose *raison d'être* uniquely combines religious principles and charitable purpose.

Advocacy in the advancement of religion

Advocacy can contribute to the advancement of religion through the proactive dissemination of material that educates the public as to its particular doctrines or liturgy. When used on behalf of a particular religious or philosophical charity, such education would naturally be selective and persuasive rather than impartial, and often amounts to frank proselytism.

Proselytising is an accepted and much used means whereby charities can advance religion. Persuasion, inducement by example, or the sharing of and induction in religious beliefs, are among the established bona fide methods of attracting new followers or adherents. In some religions proselytising is seen as an essential part of the outworking of the religion. Christians, for example, regard evangelising as a central part of their religion and this has become a significant aspect of religious practice in some jurisdictions.

Charities and the public policy constraint

The rule that an organisation, or a gift to it, cannot be designated as charitable if this would be *contra bonos mores* (or contrary to public policy) is well established and most usually associated with the fourth *Pemsel* head.[90] This rule, which probably dates back to the nineteenth century, has a broad application to all charitable trusts, whether religious or otherwise.

Public policy and the donor

The simple statement that a 'settlor's freedom to dispose of property through the creation of a charitable trust ... must give way to current principles of public policy'[91] has proven difficult to apply. In practice a donor's right to give is seldom found to be in breach of public policy. Lord Cross, contemporaneously with the introduction in the United Kingdom of the Race Relations Act 1976, explained in *Blathwayt* v. *Lord Cawley* that

> it is widely thought nowadays that it is wrong for a government to treat some of its citizens less favourably than others because of differences in their religious beliefs; but it does not follow from that that it is against

---

[90] As asserted by M. R. Evershed in *Camille and Henry Dreyfus Foundation Inc* v. *Inland Revenue Commissioners* [1932] AC 650 (HL). See *Habershon* v. *Varnon* (1851) 4 De G & Sm 467 (trust to establish Jewish settlement in Jerusalem at a time when it was under Turkish rule).

[91] *Canada Trust Co.* v. *Ontario Human Rights Commission* (1990) 69 DLR (4th) 321, *per* Robins JA, at para. 38.

108 COMPETING FRAMES OF REFERENCE

> public policy for an adherent of one religion to distinguish in disposing of
> his property between adherents of his faith and those of another.[92]

In the same case, Lord Wilberforce confidently asserted that 'neither by express provision nor by implication has private selection yet become a matter of public policy'.[93]

Of course, where it is clear that the donor's intention is to further a political rather than a charitable purpose, then the court will intervene. Otherwise, public policy has been permitted to encroach only when it represents principles considered to be of equal or greater weight. This will certainly occur when the donor's gift not only breaches public policy, but is also illegal,[94] in which case the gift is irretrievable for charity.

Testamentary bequests, religion and public policy

There is a long-standing judicial rule that every effort must be made to give effect to a testator's wishes – *voluntas testatoris servanda est* – as expressed in their last will and testament.[95] Testamentary dispositions of private property, executed in the twentieth century and earlier,[96] are clearly not central to the flux of contemporary issues involving charity, religion and the law, although in some jurisdictions they continue to be significant both in volume and in social divisiveness. There is an unmistakeable carryover of principles forged in relation to early testamentary case law that has undoubtedly coloured the evolving judicial and regulatory approach to the current social role of religion and religious charities, and shaped the related public policy context.

Initially the courts, employing the 'benignant construction rule',[97] leaned conspicuously towards respecting the donor's charitable intent, thereby allowing gifts to be defined as charitable rather than as illegal or contrary to public policy, which in turn permitted gifts to be saved, by employing *cy-près* to excise any obstructive discriminatory conditions,

---

[92] *Blathwayt* v. *Lord Cawley* [1976] 397 (HL), at p.429.   [93] Ibid., at p.426.

[94] See, for example: *Thrupp* v. *Collett (No. 1)* (1858) 26 Beav. 125 (a bequest to procure the discharge of imprisoned poachers); *A-G* v. *Vint* (1850) 3 De G & Sm 704 (a gift to provide those inmates of a workhouse, aged 60 or more, with a porter).

[95] *Robertson* v. *Robertson's Executors* 1914 AD 503, 507.

[96] See Parachin, 'Human Rights and the Definition of Charity', which cites many such cases.

[97] Broadly meaning that if the wording of a charitable gift permits a construction that will save it, that construction will be adopted. See, for example, *Weir* v. *Crum-Brown* [1908] AC 162 and *Re Worth Library* [1994] 1 ILRM 161.

CONCLUSION 109

for their intended charitable purpose. This approach was, for example, evident in *Re Dominion Students Trust*[98] which concerned the gift, from a testator domiciled in England of land in South Africa, for the purpose of establishing a student hostel for male students 'of European origin'. Concluding that the ethnic restriction rendered impossible or impracticable the attainment of its purpose to promote a community of citizenship, the court employed its *cy-près* powers to delete the restriction and save the gift for charity. In such cases, greater judicial weight was placed upon upholding the traditional claim of a donor's discretionary right than on any counter claim that such right be exercised in a manner that did not adversely discriminate against the interests of a socially disadvantaged minority and thereby breach public policy.

Conclusion

For the common law countries, the moral code represented by and articulated through the symbiotic religion–charity relationship was largely a product of the politics of post-Reformation England. State authority for the Scriptural beliefs of Protestantism was crucial to the imprinting of a related morality on the public and private lives of its citizens and its subsequent transfer to subjects overseas. As the passage of time saw a loosening of the bonds between State, religion and charity, the moral code reverted to its Scriptural origins to become, in the main, the business of the Church. Boundaries gradually firmed up between State, Church and charity as political realities shaped and confined their respective roles.

However, the central importance of family-oriented morality proved to be an enduring strand in the social function of all three parties. Once enforced with something approaching fanatical zeal, it has now become the final frontier in the present relationship of the Church to State and charity. As the following chapter reveals, the recent impact of reform on charity and human rights has radically readjusted that set of relationships, leaving the Church (or religion and religious organisations more generally) conspicuously isolated, particularly as regards issues relating to 'the family' as Scripturally defined.

---

[98] *Re Dominion Students Trust* [1947] 1 Ch. 183.

4

The international context

Religion, human rights and charity law reform

Introduction

Until relatively recently, the law governing charity, religion and the relationship between them was broadly shared by the 60 or so common law nations. That platform, largely comprising centuries of case law precedents, although somewhat reduced by the more recent incremental incursions of legal rights, has been shaken by two waves of law reform: the international assertion and extension of fundamental human rights; and the outcomes of a prolonged series of national charity law reform processes. The latter had a direct bearing on the former. The import in some jurisdictions, by statute or case law, of new definitions of 'religion', 'religious beliefs' and of activities that could be construed as constituting the charitable purpose of 'advancing religion', has compromised the capacity for future sharing and added considerably to the complexities of life for religious charities in the twenty-first century. Consequently, religious bodies in all developed common law nations are now struggling to achieve congruity in a tripartite conflict of laws: canon law, and the doctrines of their particular religion; human rights law, with particular reference to discrimination; and meeting the requirements of reformed charity law, with its definitions of 'religion' and regard for public benefit. It is a struggle that lies at the heart of this book.

This chapter examines the broad nature of the changes introduced by international law reform on the relationship between religion and charity. Beginning with a brief reflection on the significance of ideological context, the link between the fall of totalitarian regimes and the rise of religion and the growth of the nonprofit sector are explored. This context is one in which the roles of aid/trade and international anti-terrorism legislation also arise for consideration. The chapter then identifies those fundamental rights, established by the European Convention on Human

110

Rights (ECHR)[1] but also present in the constitutions and legislation of many developed nations, that have become benchmarks against which issues resulting from the interplay of religion and charity law must now be measured. It considers the nature of these issues, analyses the related ECtHR[2] case law and sets out the core principles and standards that have emerged to govern the development of Convention law in this area. The chapter then moves on to outline and assess the sequence of national charity law reform processes and the implications of their varied outcomes for religious charities. It notes that while reform outcomes have largely focused on the regulatory framework, with some extensions to charitable purposes, all jurisdictions have broadly settled for statutorily encoding the established common law approach to definitional matters (i.e. *Pemsel* purposes,[3] public benefit,[4] exclusive,[5] independent,[6] non-profit distributing[7] and non-political[8]). However, it is the difference in approach to the public benefit test as it relates to the advancement of religion that now divides the jurisdictions and is likely to raise the most significant challenge for the future.

Charity, religion and the international context

As Taylor rightly notes, 'religious intolerance continues to fuel a high proportion of the situations of armed conflict around the world'.[9] But even within many developed Western nations there are signs of growing

---

[1] The European Convention on Fundamental Human Rights (ECHR), formally known as the Convention for the Protection of Human Rights and Fundamental Freedoms, was drafted in 1950 and took effect on 3 September 1953.

[2] The European Court of Human Rights (ECtHR) was established by the Convention and adjudicates on alleged breaches of Convention rights.

[3] See *Commissioners for Special Purposes of Income Tax* v. *Pemsel* [1891] AC 531, at 583, *per* Macnaghten LJ, who then stated:

> 'Charity' in its legal sense comprises four principal divisions: trusts for the relief of poverty; trusts for the advancement of education; trusts for the advancement of religion; and trusts beneficial to the community not falling under any of the preceding heads.

[4] See *National Anti-Vivisection Society* v. *IRC* [1948] AC 31.

[5] See *Boyle* v. *Boyle* (1877) IR 11 Eq 433.   [6] See *Hallows* v. *Lloyd* (1888) 39 Ch D 686.

[7] See *Commissioners of Inland Revenue* v. *Oldham Training and Enterprise Council* (1996) 69 TC 231.

[8] See *McGovern* v. *Attorney General* [1982] 1 Ch. 321.

[9] P. M. Taylor, *Freedom of Religion: UN and European Rights, Law and Practice*, Cambridge University Press, Cambridge, 2005, p.ix.

tensions between different religious and ethnic groups which threaten government policy to accommodate the current population influx from underdeveloped countries by building multicultural and pluralistic civil societies. Religious charities now have a crucial but difficult role to play.

A background of ideological change

The transition from the twentieth to the twenty-first century has been marked by momentous political change.[10] The fall of communism, the rise of militant Islam, followed by the 'Arab Spring',[11] with its challenge to theocracy – all testified to the relative superiority of Western democracy. That the latter should then trigger a global economic recession revealed a structural flaw that called its own political credentials into question, as it seemingly originated in and destructively expressed an imbalance between democracy and capitalism. It is against that broad political background, much of which is still unfolding and awaiting analysis, that the dynamics currently being played out in the relationships between charity, human rights and religious belief must be considered.

Re-calibrating the political framework

The fall of the Berlin Wall on 9 November 1989 signalled the collapse of communism, the end of the Cold War[12] and virtually the end of ideology as an international polarising and dividing force: Western democracy no longer had a credible ideological opponent. Among the consequences that followed, some had implications for religion and religious entities.

The barriers that for many decades had shielded the regimes of Eastern Europe from outside influence were abruptly removed. This paved the way for the countries concerned to put in place democratic institutions, build more egalitarian social infrastructures and allow for the revival of religion.

---

[10] See, for example, T. Judt, *Ill Fares the Land: A Treatise on Our Present Discontents*, Allen Lane, London, 2010.

[11] A term used to describe the phenomenon of civil unrest and uprisings that affected a sequence of Middle East Arab countries (Libya, Tunisia, Yemen, Syria) starting in the spring of 2010. At the time it seemed that they signified a revolt against traditional feudal rule and a step towards democratic rule, but this assessment is currently being revised.

[12] The Cold War, signifying the political standoff and brinkmanship between the communist bloc nations led by Russia and the Western democratic nations led by the United States, is generally accepted as lasting from 1981 to 1992.

This, in turn, led those countries into the EU,[13] into the legal framework established by the ECHR and to eventual participation in a range of international conventions, protocols, treaties, etc. The removal of defensive frontiers and the embracing of human rights have ensured that contemporary Western legal and social developments relating to religion and charity will now be shared with the countries of Eastern Europe. This constitutes a very real change in the quality of life for the many millions of former subjects of totalitarian rule; the human rights platform has been instrumental in securing their citizenship rights.

The end of the Cold War instilled greater confidence in the governments of Western democracies, as evidenced by: the rise of neoconservatism in the United States and to some degree in the United Kingdom and Australia; the move to a spreading engagement in war; the latter often being coupled with a 'regime change' agenda to at least encourage a transition to democratic rule. On the domestic front, there has been a corresponding weakening in the political potency of socialism and the 'welfare state' approach to public benefit service provision: government cutbacks on unemployment and disability benefits became the norm; campaigns to drive down taxes became increasingly common; trade unions decreased in number and negotiating power; and for-profit companies competed for a greater share of public benefit service provision, especially in the fields of health, education and social care.

The collapse of communism also seemed to give free rein to entrepreneurial capitalism and to the market excesses that led to the global financial crisis of 2008. Indeed, it would be hard not to construe a causal link between the demise of the enemy of capitalism and the latter's ensuing exploitative practices which were, after all, politically endorsed until they culminated in global economic recession. The resulting sharp decline in living standards and the spread of poverty in many 'developed' nations has damaged the credibility of government and questioned the morality and voracity of free-market capitalism, while raising the profile and stretching the resources of charities and the nonprofit sector.

As communism followed fascism, Maoism and others into the ideology graveyard, a counter movement gathered strength – which itself is in

---

[13] The European Union (EU), which developed from the European Coal and Steel Community and the European Economic Community established in 1951 and 1958, respectively, is now an economic and political entity comprising 28 Member States, almost all of which are located in Europe.

danger of acquiring some of the characteristics of ideology. Across many Western or Westernised nations there has been a growing demand for governments to put in place (and encourage others to do so) the institutions and infrastructures necessary to establish or consolidate 'civil society'.[14] While there is some uncertainty as to precisely how such a society should be defined,[15] for present purposes it is perhaps sufficient just to note that it is hoped that civil society would: provide for a more structured relationship between government and the nonprofit sector; accommodate a diversity of religions, beliefs and cultures; and operate within a comprehensive legal framework, such as a more inclusive charity and nonprofit law, embracing all public benefit entities. It might also be borne in mind that scholars such as Schnabel[16] are strongly of the view that 'believers' have traditionally formed the cornerstone of civil society, while Çelik argues that 'whereas the traditional Christian civil society is becoming smaller, there is a significant role for new religious groups in which religion often has a stronger role in members' everyday life'.[17]

Charity and the nonprofit sector

For Eastern Europe the transition to democracy had the incidental effect of opening the door to organised 'charity' or philanthropy in the many countries concerned. This opportunity has been accompanied by the challenge to ensure that charitable intervention meets the needs of the citizenry as well as those of the governments of these new or incipient democratic states. It will take time before it becomes clear how non-indigenous charities will, for example: accommodate the restrictions of working within very corporatist systems; transcend an immediate role of dealing with the effects of poverty and assisting government to adopt the legal and social infrastructure of democracy; maintain established levels of functioning in the face of reduced resources and increased domestic demand; and respond to government as it wrestles with the unfamiliar

---

[14] 'Civil society' refers to the range of entities, their resources and social roles, which fill the space between the public and private sectors.

[15] See J. Bothwell, 'Indicators of a Healthy Civil Society', in J. Burbridge (ed.), *Beyond Prince and Merchant*, Institute of Cultural Affairs International, Brussels, 1997.

[16] See P. Schnabel and P. Giesen (eds), *What Everyone Should Know About the Humanities*, publisher unknown, Amsterdam, 2011, pp.198–202.

[17] G. Çelik, 'Breakpoint or Binder: Religious Engagement in Dutch Civil Society' (2013) 9:3 *Journal of Civil Society* 248 at p.261.

problems associated with addressing the cohering collective strength of charities and other nonprofits.

The collapse of communism was also not without domestic consequences for charities in the Western democracies: not least of which has recently been the need to spread their resources that much further in a time of economic recession. In addition, that phenomenon, alongside the more recent but deep-seated public disenchantment with government (for its perceived failure to provide protection from international terrorists, from Church-based child abuse and from corrupt banking practices) and with the for-profit sector (for avariciousness that triggered global recession), would seem to have created a more neutral political space on the boundary between citizen and State. The signs are that public trust, now being diverted towards the nonprofit sector as this is perceived as a relatively safer custodian of public benefit services, will be instrumental in nudging the sector into filling that space.

Religion

In the aftermath of the collapse of communism the social role of religion has experienced something of a resurgence. This does not always translate into an increase in religious belief or in numbers of religious adherents (judging from decreased attendance for religious worship and increased deconsecration of churches in the United Kingdom and mainland Europe), but it is evident in the spread of faith-based schools and, to a lesser extent, in faith-based health care facilities. It is also apparent in the emergence and spread of a distinctive evangelical strain within the Christian religions: a tendency towards 'fundamentalism' and sectarianism, resulting in a fusion of religious beliefs and social values and consequent polarised views regarding the public benefit inherent in gay marriages, abortion, etc. This has been particularly noticeable in the United States and to some degree in the United Kingdom and Australia.

There has clearly also been a revival of religion in the former communist states, where it had been suppressed for many decades, and in the Middle East and Africa as despotic rule has given way to democracy. While it may well have been anticipated that Islam, like Christianity, would flower in the space vacated by totalitarianism, the spread and ferocity of a militant variant of Islam was perhaps less predictable.

116 THE INTERNATIONAL CONTEXT

International aid/trade and anti-terrorism measures

Charities have long had a reputation for swift action in coordinating the transfer of personnel, resources and funds for disaster relief or remedial intervention in countries not readily accessed. For religious charities this role has traditionally been blended with missionary activity, but in recent years it is a role that has become somewhat compromised.

Aid/trade

Only governments, acting alone or jointly with others, have the resources to tackle structural problems such as poverty in developing countries. The bilateral government-to-government aid budgets of Western nations dwarf any possible input by charities; the latter cannot command equivalent resources. Aid and/or preferential trading agreements have the potential to assist such countries to achieve sustainable economic growth and this has been the established approach of governments in Western nations, though the present capacity-building role of China in Africa presents, perhaps, a challenging re-interpretation of that approach.[18] The 'rescue' role initiated centuries ago by charities, most usually religious charities, continues into the twenty-first century. However, charities can find themselves under considerable pressure to channel resources in directions that are compliant with government policies as determined by trade agreements and by strategic defence considerations. Some contemporary charities, for example the Bill and Melinda Gates Foundation[19] and Make Poverty History,[20] have the critical mass of resources and skill to achieve a greater impact on health and wellbeing in sub-Saharan Africa than was ever achieved through the many preceding decades of government aid/trade.

Anti-terrorism

By the early years of the twenty-first century, it had become clear that tighter regulatory supervision of nonprofits was necessary to achieve

---

[18] See D. Li, *Does the 21st Century Belong to China: The Munk Debate on China*, Anansi Press, Toronto, 2011.
[19] See, further, at: www.gatesfoundation.org (accessed 22 December 2013).
[20] Launched in 2005, this was the biggest and most media-promoted anti-poverty campaign in history. See, further, at: www.makepovertyhistory.org/takeaction (accessed 22 December 2013).

CHARITY, RELIGION AND HUMAN RIGHTS

greater compliance with government policy, safeguard against fiscal abuse, promote better governance arrangements and track the flow of funds so as to prevent their use by terrorists. As the internet allowed charitable causes to become global in scope and facilitated the flow of an ever-increasing volume of funds across continents, issues of probity became more pressing and then, following the terrorist attacks of 9/11 and in the wake of subsequent incidents, this became an urgent priority for governments. The introduction of anti-terrorism legislation[21] imposed new powers requiring the registration of non-government organisations and permitting covert surveillance of their funds, activities and staff. The 'chilling' effect of such measures on charities in general, including religious charities, has inhibited and slowed the overseas movement of funds and other resources.[22]

Charity, religion and human rights

The more fundamental human rights, having gained recognition as being of greater importance than others, are now entrenched in international conventions[23] or in national constitutions.[24] The work and reports generated by the United Nations,[25] the judgments of the European Court of Human Rights (ECtHR) and the evidence provided by such other organisations as Amnesty International,[26] speaks to both the increasing importance of these rights and to their continued abuse. While their assertion is a responsibility that generally falls more to government than charity, some rights, such as those of assembly, expression and association, lie at the heart of the modus operandi of charities

---

[21] Required by the United Nations Security Council Resolution 1373.

[22] See Advisory Group, *Campaigning and the Voluntary Sector*, London, 2007, in which Baroness Helena Kennedy QC warns of this 'chilling effect'.

[23] See, in particular, the European Convention for the Protection of Human Rights and Fundamental Freedoms 1950, which is now binding upon all Member States of the EU.

[24] See, for Canada, the Charter of Rights and Freedoms.

[25] Founded in 1945 after the Second World War, the United Nations is a multi-national organisation of almost 200 Member States that aims to promote and facilitate cooperation in matters of international law, security and economic development while also progressing human rights, civil liberties, democracy and world peace. See more at: www.un.org/en/aboutun (accessed 22 December 2013).

[26] This international non- government organisation monitors breaches of human rights and advocates on behalf of victims. See, further, at: www.amnesty.org/en/who-we-are (accessed 22 December 2013).

118   THE INTERNATIONAL CONTEXT

and indeed could be construed as representing the *raison d'être* of the nonprofit sector. As the ECtHR noted in *Sidiropoulos and Others* v. *Greece*,[27] the ability of citizens to form a legal entity in order to act collectively in a field of mutual interest is 'one of the most important aspects of the right to freedom of association, without which that right would be deprived of any meaning'.[28]

From its inception, the EU attached great importance to maintaining a balanced approach to religion. The sensitivity of this subject was reflected in the final text of the Preamble to the draft Constitution of the European Union, which conspicuously omits any theistic reference and instead adopts a neutral formulation that refers to drawing 'inspiration from the religious inheritance of Europe'.

Human rights and religion

All developed common law nations now provide formal legal recognition of and protection for much the same set of internationally recognised basic human rights. These include the freedom of association and assembly, of expression, of religion, of access to justice and the right to family life. The body of principles and case law assembled under the umbrella of the European Convention of Human Rights (ECHR),[29] and extended by a series of protocols, have a direct bearing on some common law jurisdictions and are not unrepresentative of similar developments in others. The European Court of Human Rights, which was established by the European Convention and in 1998 replaced the European Commission of Human Rights, hears complaints that a contracting Member State has violated rights enshrined in the Convention and its protocols.[30] In making its determinations, the ECtHR is guided by principles such as: 'proportionality', which requires a fair balance to be

---

[27] *Sidiropoulos and Others* v. *Greece* (26695/95) 27 EHRR, (1998).

[28] Ibid., at para. 40.

[29] The ECHR is a treaty of international law, authorised by the Council of Europe in 1950, which came into effect in 1953. It has since been ratified by all 47 Member States and now provides a legal rights framework for some 800 million citizens.

[30] Applications are first registered with the Court before being assigned to a judge rapporteur who determines admissibility. If admissible, the case is then referred to a Chamber of the Court which may determine and rule on the issues presented. Cases which raise serious questions of interpretation and application of the European Convention on Human Rights, a serious issue of general importance, or which may depart from previous case law can be heard in the Grand Chamber if all parties agree.

struck between the demands of the general interests of the community and the requirements of the protection of the individual's fundamental rights;[31] and 'compatibility with democracy',[32] which imports a liberal measure of balance and tolerance. Its decisions are reached with regard to 'a margin of appreciation' which permits States a degree of latitude in their interpretation of human rights obligations.[33]

Freedom of religion

Article 9 of the European Convention provides for the right to freedom of religion. This right, available to and enforceable by individuals and collective entities,[34] provides as follows:

(1) Everyone has the right to freedom of thought, conscience and religion; this right includes freedom to change his religion or belief and freedom, either alone or in community with others and in public or private, to manifest his religion or belief, in worship, teaching, practice and observance.

(2) Freedom to manifest one's religion or beliefs shall be subject only to such limitations as are prescribed by law and are necessary in a democratic society in the interests of public safety, for the protection of public order, health or morals, or for the protection of the rights and freedoms of others.

The exercise of this freedom is, as it has been said:

> one of the most vital elements that go to make up the identity of believers and their conception of life, but it is also a precious asset for atheists, agnostics, sceptics and the unconcerned. The pluralism indissociable

---

[31] See: *Olson* v. *Sweden (No 1)* (1988) 11 EHRR 299; *Sporrong* v. *Sweden* [1982] 5 EHRR 35, at para. 69; *Tsirlis and Kouloumpas* v. *Greece* (1997) 25 EHRR 198, at para. 116; *Razgar* v. *Secretary of State for Home Department* [2004] UKHL 27, at para. 20; and *Kozac* v. *Poland* [2010] ECHR 280; (2010) 51 EHRR 16.

[32] See *Refah Partisi* v. *Turkey* (2003) 37 EHRR 1; [2003] ECHR 87, when the ECtHR ruled that shariah law is not consistent with democracy and therefore the Turkish government was justified in banning a political party seeking to introduce such law.

[33] See, for example, *Lithgow* v. *United Kingdom* (1986) 8 EHRR 329; *Fredin* v. *Sweden* (1991) 13 EHRR 784; *Abdulaziz, Cabales and Balkandali* v. *United Kingdom* (1985) 7 EHRR 471. See, further, A. Legg, *The Margin of Appreciation in International Human Rights Law*, Oxford University Press, Oxford, 2012.

[34] That a church body is capable of possessing and exercising Article 9 rights was confirmed in cases such as *X & Church of Scientology* v. *Sweden* (1979) DR 16.

120   THE INTERNATIONAL CONTEXT

from a democratic society, which has been dearly won over the centuries, depends on it.[35]

Article 9 rights may be supported by the right to freedom of expression under Article 10, a freestanding right, which can also impact on the right to manifest religious belief.[36] Article 2 of the First Protocol[37] also has a bearing on the exercise of Article 9 rights. This provides for the right to education as follows:

> No person shall be denied the right to education. In the exercise of any functions which it assumes in relation to education and to teaching, the State shall respect the right of parents to ensure such education and teaching in conformity with their own religious and philosophical convictions.

Other international instruments, relevant for present purposes, include the International Covenant on Civil and Political Rights (ICCPR),[38] Article 2 of which binds every signatory nation to 'respect and ensure all individuals within its territory and subject to its jurisdiction the rights recognised in the present Covenant without distinction of any kind'. Article 18 of the ICCPR extends specific protection to religion:

(1) Everyone shall have the right to freedom of thought, conscience and religion. This right shall include freedom to have or to adopt a religion or belief of his choice, and freedom, either individually or in community with others and in public or private, to manifest his religion or belief in worship, observance, practice and teaching.

(2) No one shall be subject to coercion which would impair his freedom to have or to adopt a religion or belief of his choice.

(3) Freedom to manifest one's religion or beliefs may be subject only to such limitations as are prescribed by law and are necessary to protect public safety, order, health, or morals or the fundamental rights and freedoms of others.[39]

---

[35] *Moscow Branch of the Salvation Army* v. *Russia* [2006] ECHR 7288/01 [57].

[36] See, for example, *Otto-Preminger Institute* v. *Austria*, Judgment A 295 (1994).

[37] This Protocol was established on 20 March 1952. The leading case on Protocol 1 Article 2 is *Belgian Linguistic* (1968) 1 EHRR 252.

[38] Opened for signature by General Assembly resolution 2200A (XXI) of 16 December 1966 and entered into force 23 March 1976. As of March 2012 the Covenant had 74 signatories and 167 parties.

[39] The preferred interpretation is that 'public' is a descriptor of 'order, health, or morals' as well as 'safety': see, M. D. Evans, *Religious Liberty and International Law in Europe*, Cambridge University Press, Cambridge, 1997, at p.223.

CHARITY, RELIGION AND HUMAN RIGHTS

(4) The States Parties to the present Covenant undertake to have respect for the liberty of parents and, when applicable, legal guardians to ensure the religious and moral education of their children in conformity with their own convictions.

Unlike the right to freedom of belief, the right to manifest religion recognised by Article 18(1) is subject to restrictions in circumstances as specified by Article 18(3). In fact, all relevant major international declarations and conventions recognise the social reality that religious belief and its manifestation through practice are integrated, and extend protection to both.[40] Article 18 is reinforced by Articles 2(1) and 26 in relation to discrimination on the basis of religion.[41]

Elaborating upon Article 18 obligations, the United Nations Human Rights Committee issued 'General Comment 22', which defined the right to freedom of religion or belief as:

> protect[ing] theistic, non-theistic and atheistic beliefs, as well as the right not to profess any religion or belief. The terms 'belief' and 'religion' are to be broadly construed. Article 18 is not limited in its application to traditional religions or to religions and beliefs with institutional characteristics or practices analogous to those of traditional religions.[42]

Importantly, the Committee then went on to explain other matters. First, that the concluding words of Article 18 'worship, observance, practice, and teaching' should be interpreted to 'include not only ceremonial acts but also such customs as the observance of dietary regulations, the wearing of distinctive clothing or headcoverings, participation in rituals

---

[40] See, for example: Article 18 of the Universal Declaration of Human Rights; Article 18(1) of the International Covenant on Civil and Political Rights; Article 9(1) of the European Convention for the Protection of Human Rights and Fundamental Freedoms; Article 12(1) of the American Convention on Human Rights; and Article 1 of the Declaration on the Elimination of all Forms of Intolerance and of Discrimination Based on Religion or Belief.

[41] Article 2(1): 'Each state Party to the present Covenant undertakes to respect and to ensure to all individuals within its territory, and subject to its jurisdiction the rights recognised in the present Covenant, without distinction of any kind, such as race, colour, sex, language, religion, political or other opinion, national or social origin, property, birth or other status.' Article 26: 'All persons are equal before the law and are entitled without any discrimination to the equal protection of the law. In this respect, the law shall prohibit any discrimination and guarantee to all persons equal and effective protection against discrimination on any ground such as race, colour, sex, language, religion, political or other opinion, national or social origin, property, birth or other status.'

[42] General Comment No. 22, UN Doc CCPR/C/21/Rev.1/Add.4 [8].

122   THE INTERNATIONAL CONTEXT

associated with certain stages of life, and the use of a particular language customarily spoken by a group'. Second, the State may interfere in the right to manifest a religion or belief but only if it can show that this was both 'prescribed by law', 'necessary to protect public safety, order, health, or morals or the fundamental rights and freedoms of others' and that any restrictions 'must be directly related and proportionate to the specific need on which they are predicated'.

Article 20(2) provides that 'any advocacy of national, racial or religious hatred that constitutes incitement to discrimination, hostility or violence shall be prohibited by law'.

The Convention on the Rights of the Child (UNCROC) is also important, but more relevant for present purposes is the International Labour Organisation Discrimination (Employment and Occupation) Convention 1958 (ILOC).[43] The ILOC provides in Article 1.2 an exemption relating to the employment of people by 'religious institutions', where discrimination is 'required by the tenets and doctrines of the religion, is not arbitrary, is consistently applied' or 'is an inherent requirement of a particular job'. One of the most important UN documents protecting religious freedom is the UN Declaration on the Elimination of All Forms of Intolerance and of Discrimination based on Religion or Belief which, in addition to elaborating upon the right to 'manifest' one's religion in Article 18,[44] sets out in considerable detail what the international community regards as basic standards for protection of religious freedom and in Article 3 cautions that 'discrimination between human beings on grounds of religion or belief constitutes an affront to human dignity'. However, an inability to agree on issues such as the freedom to change religion prevented the Declaration from attaining Convention status. This was attributable in part to the fact that Islamic nations are unable to consider the possibility of a freedom to change religion as part of religious freedom. Indeed, 'apostasy,' or conversion from Islam, can attract the death penalty.

It is also important to note the work of the UN Committee on the Elimination of Discrimination Against Women, in particular its 'general

---

[43] Adopted by the General Conference of the International Labour Organisation on 25 June 1958 and came into effect on 15 June 1960. As of May 2011 the Convention had been ratified by 169 out of 183 ILO members.

[44] GA Res 36/55, UN GAOR, 36th sess, UN Doc A/36/684 (1981). It includes the freedom: '(a) to worship or assemble in connection with a religion or belief, and to establish and maintain places for these purposes; (b) To establish and maintain appropriate charitable or humanitarian institutions', and '(f) to solicit and receive voluntary financial and other contributions from individuals and institutions'.

recommendations'.[45] More recently there has been Resolution 16/18 which was initially introduced in March 2011 at the UN Human Rights Council by the Organisation of Islamic Co-operation. This calls upon UN Member States to combat 'intolerance, negative stereotyping and stigmatization of, and discrimination, incitement to violence and violence against, persons based on religion or belief'. Following that introduction, the Istanbul Process was created in July 2011 and continues in being; it last met in Geneva in June 2013.

By 1998 the Committee had adopted and issued 23 such recommendations, of which 'general recommendation 23', dealing with equality in marriage and the family, is relevant in the present context. Also significant is the European Directive 2000/78 of 27 November 2000, the purpose of which, as stated in Article 1, is to 'lay down a general framework for combating discrimination on the further grounds of religion or belief, disability, age or sexual orientation, as regards employment and occupation'. This Directive limits discrimination on the grounds of religion to 'occupational activities within churches and other public or private organisations the ethos of which is based on religious belief'. In that context, it is further limited to circumstances where 'by reason of the nature of these activities or of the context in which they are carried out, a person's religion or belief constitute a genuine, legitimate and justified occupational requirement, having regard to the organisation's ethos'.

This should be read alongside the European Directive on Race, also issued in 2000 (both known as 'the Article 13 Directives'), which refers to beliefs as 'more than just mere opinions or deeply held feelings' but which involve 'a holding of spiritual or philosophical convictions which have an identifiable formal content' and which have 'a certain level of cogency, seriousness, cohesion and importance'.

Rights and religion

Religious beliefs and human rights would seem mutually exclusive in certain areas. Religious charities are fundamentally unable, for example, to reconcile traditional theological precepts of marriage as a lifelong monogamous and heterosexual union with the contemporary statutory human rights recognition of it as a union that may encompass homosexual relationships. The orthodox view of marriage, central to Christian religious belief,

---

[45] The Committee was launched in 1982. See more at UN Doc HRI/Gen/Rev3, at pp.117–157.

124 THE INTERNATIONAL CONTEXT

stands in blunt opposition to the modern statutory requirement that it and LGBT partnerships be treated as equal before the law.

Religious belief

The Convention requires any interpretation of 'religion' to be applied objectively, have reasonable justification[46] and be non-discriminatory; any differential treatment must comply with strict standards. This approach has broadened the range of beliefs that now qualify in charity law as 'religious' to beyond those that could be called 'new', 'minority' or 'nontraditional',[47] allowing the ECtHR to extend its protection to include Scientology,[48] Druidism,[49] Divine Light Zentrum,[50] and Krishna Consciousness.[51] It is a development of particular significance in view of the established judicial principle that it is not for the court to inquire into any asserted belief and judge its validity by some objective standard: the right to freedom of religion protects the subjective belief of an individual;[52] there is no power to assess the legitimacy of religious beliefs;[53] and States are required to ensure that conflicting groups tolerate each other, even where they have their origins in the same group.[54]

---

[46] See, for example, *Tsirlis and Kouloumpas* v. *Greece* (1997) 25 EHRR 198. Also see the *Belgian Linguistic Case* (1968)(No. 2) 1 EHRR 252, where the ECHR held that there must be an objective and reasonable justification for differential treatment and this will only exist where there is a 'legitimate aim' for the action and where the action taken is 'proportionate' to that aim.

[47] See T. J. Gunn, 'Adjudicating Rights of Conscience Under the European Convention on Human Rights', in J. D. Van der Vyver and J. D. Witte (eds), *Religious Human Rights in Global Perspective: Legal Perspectives*, Martinus Nijhoff, The Hague, 1996, at p.311.

[48] See *X and the Church of Scientology* v. *Sweden* (1976) 16 D&R 68.

[49] See *Chappel* v. *UK* (1988) 10 EHRR 510 (Eur. Comm. HR); *Pendragon* v. *UK* (1998) EHRR CD 179.

[50] See *Swami Omkaramamda and the Divine light Zentrum* v. *Switzerland* (1981) 25 D&R 105 (Eur. Comm. HR).

[51] See *ISKCON* v. *UK* (1994) 76A D&R 90.

[52] See Laws LJ in *McFarlane* v. *Relate Avon Ltd.* [2010] EWCA Civ B1 (29 April 2010), where he said that 'in the eye of everyone save the believer religious faith is necessarily subjective'.

[53] However, see *Kosteski* v. *'The Former Yugoslav Republic of Macedonia'* [2006] ECHR 403, where the ECtHR accepted that investigations as to whether an employee in fact held a particular belief were not inappropriate in the context of an employment dispute.

[54] *Metropolitan Church of Bessarabia* v. *Moldova*, App. No. 45701/99, 13 December 2001.

Such 'beliefs', as defined in European Convention case law, must amount to 'more than just mere opinions or deeply held feelings', they must involve 'a holding of spiritual or philosophical convictions which have an identifiable formal content'. In *Campbell and Cosans* v. *United Kingdom*,[55] for example, the complainants successfully alleged that the system of corporal punishment in Scottish State schools offended their philosophical convictions under Article 2 of the First Protocol of the ECHR, while in *H* v. *UK*,[56] veganism similarly won recognition.

Manifesting religious belief

While Article 9 of the Convention affords a more or less absolute right to hold a religious belief, it provides only a heavily qualified right to manifest that belief by conduct: the more public and secular the sphere in which the conduct takes place, the less protection it provides. In *C* v. *the United Kingdom*,[57] for example, the refusal of a Quaker to pay a proportion of tax judged to correspond to the proportion of government revenue directed towards military purposes was found not to fall within the protection of Article 9. As expressed by the Commission:

> Article 9 primarily protects the sphere of personal beliefs and religious creeds, i.e. the area which is sometimes called the forum internum. In addition, it protects acts which are intimately linked to these attitudes, such as acts of worship or devotion which are aspects of the practice of a religion or belief in a generally recognised form.

In the similar case of *Arrowsmith* v. *the United Kingdom*,[58] the Commission then stated the principle that 'the term "practice" as employed in Article 9(1) does not cover each act which is motivated or influenced by a religion or a belief'. Again, in *X* v. *UK*,[59] it was held that the practice of wearing a turban did not absolve Sikh motorcyclists from the obligation to wear crash helmets.

The personal choices of those seeking to manifest their religious beliefs may also be a contributory factor by placing them in a position that consequently gives rise to the alleged infringement of their Article 9

---

[55] *Campbell and Cosans* v. *United Kingdom* [1982] 4 EHRR 293.
[56] *H* v. *UK* (1993) 16 EHRR CD 44.
[57] App. No. 10358/83, 37 ECHR D&R 142, at 147.
[58] App. No. 7050/75, Comm. Report para. 71 DR 19, at p.5.
[59] App. No. 7992/77, 14 DR 234 (1978).

126 THE INTERNATIONAL CONTEXT

rights. In *Kalac* v. *Turkey*[60] the applicant was subject to compulsory retirement from the military as his alleged involvement with a fundamental Muslim sect was contrary to the secular nature of the Turkish State. However, as the ECtHR pointed out, 'Article 9 does not protect every act motivated or inspired by a religion or belief. Moreover, in exercising his freedom to manifest his religion, an applicant may need to take his specific situation into account.'[61] In choosing a military career the applicant was accepting a military system that placed limitations on individuals that would not be imposed on civilians.

That the right to freedom of expression, afforded protection by Article 10, can be the focus of issues relating to manifesting religious belief was illustrated by *Otto-Preminger*,[62] which concerned the Austrian government's 'seizure and forfeiture' of a satirical religious film due to be shown to the public deemed to be deriding the Eucharist and negatively portraying 'God the Father, Christ and Mary Mother of God'. The Austrian government justified its actions on the grounds that it had a 'legitimate aim' in protecting 'the rights of others', 'particularly the right to respect for one's religious feelings', and 'the prevention of disorder'. Referring to the *Kokkinakis* decision,[63] the ECtHR found that the Austrian government's measure fell within the parameters of a 'legitimate aim', and took the view that 'the respect for the religious feelings of believers as guaranteed in Article 9 can legitimately be thought to have been violated by provocative portrayals of objects of religious veneration; and such portrayals can be regarded as malicious violation of the spirit of tolerance which must also be a feature of democratic society'. The court reasoned that:

> Those who choose to exercise the freedom to manifest their religion, irrespective of whether they do so as members of a religious majority or a minority, cannot reasonably expect to be exempt from all criticism. They must tolerate and accept the denial by others of their religious beliefs and even the propagation by others of doctrines hostile to their faith. However, the manner in which religious beliefs and doctrines are opposed or denied is a matter which may engage the responsibility of the State, notably its responsibility to ensure the peaceful enjoyment of the rights guaranteed under Article 9 to the holders of those beliefs and doctrines. Indeed, in extreme cases the effect of particular methods of opposing or

---

[60] *Kalac* v. *Turkey* [1997] EHRR 552.   [61] Ibid., at para. 27.
[62] *Otto-Preminger-Institut* v. *Austria* (1994) 19 EHRR 34.
[63] *Kokkinakis* v. *Greece* (A/260-A) (1994) 17 EHRR 397.

CHARITY, RELIGION AND HUMAN RIGHTS 127

denying religious beliefs can be such as to inhibit those who hold such beliefs from exercising their freedom to hold and express them.[64]

The right to manifest religious belief by worship, teaching, practice and observance may also be considered in the light of both Article 10 and Article 11 (which provides for the freedom of assembly and association). Attention was drawn to this overlap by the ECtHR in *Ollinger* v. *Austria*,[65] which concerned the applicant's proposal to hold a meeting at the Saltzburg Municipal Cemetery in front of the War Memorial to commemorate the Saltzburg Jews killed by the SS during the Second World War. The meeting was to coincide with a gathering of Comradeship IV in memory of SS soldiers killed in the Second World War. The applicant's meeting was banned and the ECtHR held the prohibition to be disproportionate. In its consideration of the bearing, the ECtHR found that Article 11 had to be considered in the light of Article 10 as the protection of opinions and the freedom to express them was one of the objectives of freedom of assembly and association enshrined in Article 11.

Traditional religious belief and the modern 'family'

As the frontiers of medicine push forward they are increasingly bumping up against areas where social institutions, customs, etc. have traditionally transmitted religious principles. In the context of Christianity, clashes now tend to occur when religious principles rooted in the traditional model of the Nazarene family unit are found to be incompatible with modern civic requirements emanating from human rights provisions.[66] The range of related issues, already considerable and guaranteed to grow further, includes: birth control and infertility treatment in various forms; genetic engineering and stem cell research; transgender medical intervention; and adoption by same-sex couples. In relation to the latter, the ECtHR has taken a cautious approach. In *Gas and Dubois* v. *France*,[67] for example, it ruled that a French court did not breach Articles 8 and 14 when it refused to allow one partner in a homosexual relationship to adopt the child of the other. This accords with its earlier ruling in *Schalk*

---

[64] Ibid., at para. 47.   [65] *Ollinger* v. *Austria* [2006] (No. 76900/01) (29 June 2006).

[66] The Nazarene family unit is a reference to the 'original Christian family of Nazareth', i.e. Joseph, his wife Mary and Jesus Christ, the child of their marriage.

[67] *Gas and Dubois* v. *France* (2012), App. No. 25951/07.

128 THE INTERNATIONAL CONTEXT

and Kopf v. *Austria*[68] to the effect that it would not force States to make marriage available for same-sex couples. The court then noted that the right to marry is granted to 'men and women', and includes the right to found a family, which could be interpreted as granting the right to two men or two women, because, as the court observed, all other Convention rights are granted to 'everyone'. The court stated that it would no longer consider that the right to marry enshrined in Article 12 must in all circumstances be limited to marriage between two persons of the opposite sex and, consequently, it could not be said that Article 12 was therefore inapplicable.[69] It took the view that same-sex couples were just as capable as different-sex couples of entering into stable, committed relationships and, consequently, were in a relevantly similar situation to a different-sex couple as regards their need for legal recognition and protection of their relationship.[70] The court took the opportunity to pointedly reject the reasoning of earlier decisions and to state its acceptance of the view that a same-sex couple can enjoy 'family life' within the meaning of Article 8 of the European Convention (the right to private and family life). Previously, in the eyes of the court same-sex couples had been restricted to being able to enjoy 'private' but not 'family life'.

Religious charities

'Religion' in the charity law of common law nations, traditionally defined or in practice largely restricted to theistic beliefs within the Judeo-Christian tradition, has since the latter part of the twentieth century come to be interpreted more broadly. Courts and regulators in many common law nations have now become accustomed to adjudicating on issues where a person or organisation claims that an alleged breach of human rights was a natural consequence of giving effect to a particular set of beliefs or doctrines of central importance to their non-Christian religion. This has occurred, for example, in respect of Muslims in England,[71] Jews in Canada[72] and Sikhs in the United States.[73]

In all modern states, governments are intent on ensuring that private rights are exercised in a manner that respects public law principles of equity,

---

[68] *Schalk and Kopf* v. *Austria*, App. No. 30141/04, Council of Europe: European Court of Human Rights, 24 June 2010.

[69] Ibid., at para. 61. [70] Ibid., at para. 99.

[71] See *JH Walker Ltd.* v. *Hussain* [1996] IRLR 11 EAT.

[72] See *Syndicat Northcrest* v. *Amselem* 2004 SCC 47; [2004] 2 SCR 551.

[73] See *Cooper* v. *Eugene Sch. Dist. No. 4J* 723 P.2d 298 (Oregon 1986).

CHARITY, RELIGION AND HUMAN RIGHTS 129

equality and non-discrimination as established by human rights legislation. The resulting tension is evident, for example, in staff selection, training and treatment (with regard to beliefs, values and lifestyle); in religious practice or religious symbols in the workplace; in the choice of goods or services provided or not by religious charities; and in the criteria used by those charities for excluding or restricting access to such goods and services.

The State, its institutions and religious belief

The centuries-old Christian beliefs that have characterised the identity of most common law nations, informing their institutional infrastructures and enduring as cornerstones of their cultural heritage, are now facing serious challenges. The judicial struggle to find the principles needed to balance the rights of newly emerging minority groups with those of an established majority – so as to do justice to the cultural identity of both and facilitate the continuing growth of a pluralistic, multicultural society – is very apparent in the unfolding human rights case law; the failure to achieve adequate protection for the established cultural identity of European nation states is a repeated political refrain in countries such as Britain.

Secularism and the State

The ECtHR in some of its earlier rulings[74] seemed to draw a line requiring the institutions of Member States to remain neutral and impartial in their treatment of religious matters.[75] In *Kokkinakis* v. *Greece*[76] and *Manoussakis* v. *Greece*,[77] for example, it ruled respectively that the Greek anti-proselytism law impermissibly interfered with freedom of religion and 'the right to freedom of religion . . . excludes any discretion on the part of the State to determine whether religious beliefs or the means used to express such beliefs are legitimate'. As it emphasised in *Refah Partisi (The Welfare Party) and Others* v. *Turkey*,[78] 'the State's duty of neutrality

---

[74] See, for example, *Dahlab* v. *Switzerland*, App. No. 42393/98, 2001-V Eur. Ct. H.R 449 and *Leyla Sahin* v. *Turkey*, App. No. 44774/98, 2005-XI Eur. Ct. H.R. 819.

[75] For an analysis of the relationship between religion, the right to religious freedom and democracy, see K. Boyle, 'Human Rights, Religion and Democracy: The Refah Party Case' (2004) 1:1 *Essex Human Rights Review* 1.

[76] *Kokkinakis* v. *Greece* (A/260-A) (1994) 17 EHRR 397.

[77] *Manoussakis* v. *Greece* (18748/91) (1996) 21 EHRR CD3.

[78] *Refah Partisi (The Welfare Party) and Others* v. *Turkey*, 13 February 2003 [ECtHR]. Case nos 41340/98, 41342/98, 41343/98, at para. 91.

130   THE INTERNATIONAL CONTEXT

and impartiality [among beliefs] is incompatible with any power on the State's part to assess the legitimacy of religious beliefs and requires the State to ensure mutual tolerance between opposing groups'. The ECtHR has returned to this theme in some of its more recent decisions. In *Bayatyan v. Armenia*,[79] for example, the Grand Chamber stressed that:

> The Court reiterates that, as enshrined in article 9, freedom of thought, conscience and religion is one of the foundations of a 'democratic society' within the meaning of the Convention. This freedom is, in its religious dimension, one of the most vital elements that go to make up the identity of believers and their conception of life, but it is also a precious asset for atheists, agnostics, sceptics and the unconcerned. The pluralism indissociable from a democratic society, which has been dearly won over the centuries, depends on it. That freedom entails, inter alia, freedom to hold or not to hold religious beliefs and to practise or not to practise a religion.

This emphasis on the importance of State impartiality firmed up into a more positive secularist approach, as was clearly evident in an education context. So, for example, in *Kjeldsen, Busk Madsen and Pedersen* v. *Denmark*,[80] parents with strong Christian beliefs objected to compulsory sex education lessons in Danish State schools and sought to assert their right to choose the religious and moral education of their children under Article 2 of the First Protocol. While their application was rejected, the court declared that 'the State is forbidden to pursue an aim of indoctrination that might be considered as not respecting parents' religious and philosophical convictions'. Respect for such parental religious convictions, however, did not divert the court from adopting a strictly secular approach towards the introduction of symbols that manifested religious beliefs in the public sphere.[81] This gradually became tempered by a concern to ensure that the established cultural identity of a Member State did not become neutralised by the secularism of its institutions. *Folgerø & Others* v. *Norway*,[82] for example, concerned an objection to the compulsory teaching in State schools of religious knowledge that

---

[79] *Bayatyan v. Armenia* (2012) 54 EHRR 15, 494.
[80] *Kjeldsen, Busk Madsen and Pedersen v. Denmark* (1979–1980) 1 EHRR 711.
[81] See, for example, *Dogru v. France*, App. No. 27058/05, and *Kervanci v. France*, App. No. 31645/04, handed down on 4 December 2008, when the Court upheld the expulsion of two girls from their schools for refusing to remove their Islamic headscarves, ruling that such State action was not a violation of the private right to manifest one's religion under Article 9. Also see J. Habermas, 'Religion in the Public Sphere' (2006) 14:1 *European Journal of Philosophy* 1.
[82] *Folgerø & Others v. Norway*, App. No. 15472/02 (Eur. Ct. H.R. [GC] 29 June 2007).

CHARITY, RELIGION AND HUMAN RIGHTS 131

concentrated on Christianity to the detriment of other religions. Finding that such an institutional representation of a nation's majority religion did not in itself contravene Article 2 of the First Protocol, the Grand Chamber ruled as follows:

> [T]he fact that knowledge about Christianity represented a greater part of the Curriculum for primary and lower secondary schools than knowledge about other religions and philosophies cannot, in the Court's opinion, of its own be viewed as a departure from the principles of pluralism and objectivity amounting to indoctrination. . . . In view of the place occupied by Christianity in the national history and tradition of the respondent State, this must be regarded as falling within the respondent State's margin of appreciation in planning and setting the curriculum.[83]

At much the same time there was evidence of judicial notice being taken that adherents of traditional religious beliefs are as entitled to court protection from discrimination as those minority groups wishing to assert their newly established human rights:

> The belief in question is the orthodox Christian belief that the practice of homosexuality is sinful. The manifestation in question is by teaching, practice and observance to maintain the choice not to accept, endorse or encourage homosexuality. Whether the belief is to be accepted or rejected is not the issue. The belief is a long established part of the belief system of the world's major religions. This is not a belief that is unworthy of recognition. I am satisfied that Article 9 [of the European Convention, *sic*] is engaged in the present case. The extent to which the manifestation of the belief may be limited is a different issue.[84]

The evolving nature of the case law was evident in the recent decision in *Lautsi* v. *Italy*,[85] which revealed how far the ECtHR had retreated from the secular high ground of earlier rulings. This long-running, landmark case began in 2001 when Ms Lautsi objected that her two children, then aged 11 and 13 and attending a State secondary school in Italy, were exposed to crucifixes displayed in every classroom. Arguing that such a

---

[83] Ibid., at para. 89.
[84] See *Christian Institute and Others* v. *Office of First Minister and Deputy First Minister*, Neutral Citation no. [2007] NIQB 66, *per* Weatherup J, at para. 50. In this case the Northern Ireland Human Rights Commission contended that the applicants' religious beliefs concerning homosexuality did not satisfy the threshold requirements for protection under Article 9 because the belief was not consistent with the basic standards of human dignity and integrity. A position described by counsel for the applicants as 'fundamental secularism', as it involved the rejection of what was regarded as orthodox religious belief.
[85] *Lautsi* v. *Italy*, App. No. 30814/06 (Eur. Ct. H.R. 18 March 2011).

practice was contrary to the principle of secularism by which she wished to bring up her children, she requested that the crucifixes be removed. Following a succession of failed national court hearings, the plaintiff appealled to the European Court claiming that this practice violated her right to educate her children in accordance with her philosophical convictions, as protected by Article 2 of the First Protocol, as well as her and her children's right to freedom of conscience guaranteed by Article 9 of the Convention. In 2009 a Chamber of the Court unanimously upheld the applicant's claim,[86] ruling that the presence of crucifixes in State schools could not be reconciled with 'the educational pluralism which is essential for the preservation of "democratic society"', and that the compulsory display of this symbol, especially in classrooms, was 'incompatible with the State's duty to respect neutrality in the exercise of public authority'[87] and violated Article 2 of the First Protocol taken together with Article 9.[88] In January 2010 the case was referred to the Grand Chamber, which affirmed the approach adopted in previous cases and emphasised that Article 2 of the First Protocol did not prohibit a State from including any matters touching on religion in schools' curriculum; rather, the aim of the provision was to safeguard pluralism in education and to prevent indoctrination by the State.[89] It emphasised that the State's duty to respect parents' religious and philosophical convictions was also relevant to the organisation of the school environment. Finding that the crucifix was primarily a religious symbol, the Grand Chamber held that it was nevertheless impossible to conclude that its presence in classrooms was capable of influencing school children. The applicant's subjective perception in that regard – although recognised by the Grand Chamber as being understandable – was not in itself sufficient to establish a breach of Article 2 of the First Protocol. Crucially, the Grand Chamber ruled that the presence of crucifixes in classrooms was a matter falling within the margin of appreciation of the respondent State which was justified by the need to 'take into account the fact that Europe is marked by a great diversity between the States of which it is composed, particularly in the sphere of cultural and historical development';[90] and that the contracting States' decisions in such matters, including the place they accord to religion, should in principle be respected. It held that 'a crucifix on a wall is an essentially passive

---

[86] *Lautsi* v. *Italy*, App. No. 30814/06 (Eur. Ct. H.R. 3 November 2009).
[87] *Lautsi* v. *Italy*, App. No. 30814/06 (Eur. Ct. H.R. 18 March 2011), at para. 56.
[88] Ibid., at para. 59.   [89] Ibid., at para. 66.   [90] Ibid., at para. 68.

CHARITY, RELIGION AND HUMAN RIGHTS 133

symbol' that cannot be regarded as having an effect on pupils comparable to that of didactic speech or the requirement to participate in religious activities and therefore could not constitute indoctrination.[91] The Grand Chamber concluded that Italy had acted within its margin of appreciation in deciding how to 'respect' the rights of parents under Article 2 of the First Protocol; it had not violated that provision; and further that no separate issue arose under Article 9 of the Convention.[92]

The secular, the sacred and discrimination

Over time a body of jurisprudence had managed to accommodate religion, charity and discrimination.[93] In the face of increasing secularisation and a rising tide of human rights litigation, that position is now becoming more difficult to hold. Aligning the purpose and activities of religious charities with the modern, clinically secular, and an ever more reductionist approach to human rights is presenting significant challenges for courts and regulators. This is particularly the case in those common law jurisdictions – such as the United States, Canada and Australia – currently experiencing a resurgence in religious belief.

Discrimination

Article 14 of the European Convention provides a right to non-discrimination as follows:

> The enjoyment of the rights and freedoms set forth in this Convention shall be secured without discrimination on any ground such as sex, race, colour, language, religion, political or other opinion, national or social origin, association with a national minority, property, birth or other status.

This was subsequently amplified by the United Nations Human Rights Committee, which defined 'discrimination' as:

> any distinction, exclusion, restriction or preference which is based on any ground such as race, colour, sex, language, religion, political or other opinion, national or social origin, property, birth, or other status, and which has the purpose or effect of nullifying or impairing the recognition,

---

[91] Ibid., at para. 72. [92] Ibid., at paras 76–77.
[93] See, for example, *Re Dominion Students Hall Trust* [1947] Ch. 183 and *Re Lysaght* [1966] Ch. 191.

134 THE INTERNATIONAL CONTEXT

> enjoyment or exercise by all persons, on an equal footing, of all rights and freedoms.[94]

This right, as the EHtCR has stated, is violated when a State fails to treat differently persons whose situations are significantly different, without objective and reasonable justification.[95] As explained in *EB v. France*:[96] 'the Court reiterates that, for the purposes of Article 14, a difference in treatment is discriminatory if it has no objective and reasonable justification',[97] which means that it does not pursue a 'legitimate aim' or that there is no 'reasonable proportionality between the means employed and the aim sought to be realised'. The salient elements being: a difference in treatment in comparable situations; without justification, a legitimate aim, nor with regard for proportionality; and where the State cannot claim a 'margin of appreciation'. The corrolary is also true: discrimination can be justified if 'the criteria for [differentiation of treatment] are reasonable and objective and if the aim is to achieve a purpose which is legitimate under the ICCPR';[98] Daniel Moeckli describes this as a two-pronged test requiring a legitimate aim on the part of the State and proportionality in its execution.[99] *Francesco Sessa* v. *Italy*[100] perhaps illustrates the test in action. This case concerned the complaint of a Jewish lawyer that the refusal to adjourn his case to a date which did not coincide with the Jewish holidays of Yom Kippur and Sukkot was an interference with his right to manifest his religion. His complaint was dismissed by a majority but a powerful minority pointed out that, for a measure to be proportionate, the State must choose the means which is least restrictive of rights and freedoms. Thus, seeking a reasonable accommodation may, in some circumstances, constitute a less restrictive means of achieving the aim pursued. Mr Sessa had given

---

[94] See United Nations Human Rights Committee, 'General Comment relating to discrimination under the International Covenant on Civil and Political Rights', (No.18, para. 7), 1989.

[95] See *Thlimmenos* v. *Greece*, App. No. 34369/97 (2001).

[96] See *E.B.* v. *France* (App. No. 43546/02), 22 January 2008, at para. 90.

[97] See *Tsirlis & Kouloumpas* v. *Greece* (1997) 25 EHRR 198; *Belgian Linguistic Case* (1968) (No 2) 1 EHRR 252, paras 9–10.

[98] Human Rights Committee, General Comment 18, HRI/GEN/1/Rev 9 (Vol. 1) 195, para. 13. See D. Moeckli, 'Equality and Non-Discrimination', in D. Moeckli, S. Shah and S. Sivakumaran (eds), *International Human Rights Law*, Oxford University Press, Oxford, 2010, pp.201–202.

[99] Moeckli, 'Equality and Non-Discrimination'. See also in relation to Article 14 of the European Convention, *Jehovah's Witnesses* v. *Austria* (2009) 48 EHRR 17 [87], [96].

[100] App. No. 28790/08, Judgment of 3 April 2012.

the Italian court ample notice of the problem and reorganising the lists to accommodate him would cause minimal disruption to the administration of justice – 'a small price to be paid in order to ensure respect for freedom of religion in a multi-cultural society'.[101] The State should ensure a 'reasonable relationship of proportionality between the means employed and the aim sought to be achieved'.[102] The majority decision, which does not sit very well alongside earlier rulings,[103] and from which it can perhaps be distinguished, would seem to reflect a view that the restrictions imposed on the applicant were a consequence of his contractual obligations and therefore had little or nothing to do with the freedom of religion.[104]

Discrimination: direct and indirect

Discrimination may be direct or indirect: 'direct' involves treating people differently who are the same or treating people the same who are different; 'indirect' occurs when an apparently neutral practice or condition has a disproportionate and negative effect on one of the groups against whom it is unlawful to discriminate, and the practice or condition cannot be justified objectively. Article 14 operates not by way of conferring a freestanding right not to be discriminated against, but rather by way of complementing the other substantive provisions of the Convention and the Protocols. It has no independent existence, since it has effect solely in relation to the enjoyment of the rights and freedoms safeguarded by those other provisions.[105]

Discrimination: affirmative action

Unequal treatment in itself does not necessarily constitute discrimination. As the UN Human Rights Committee has noted:

> the principle of equality sometimes requires states to take affirmative action in order to diminish or eliminate conditions which cause or help to perpetuate discrimination prohibited by the Covenant. For example, in a state where the general conditions of a certain part of the population

---

[101] Ibid., at para. 13. [102] Ibid., at para. 38.
[103] See, for example, *Jakobski* v. *Poland* (2010) 30 BHRC 417 and *Gatis Kovalkovs* v. *Latvia*, App. No. 35021/05 (2012).
[104] In keeping with, for example, *Stedman* v. *the United Kingdom* (1997) 23 EHRR CD 168 and *Konttinnen* v. *Finland* (App. No. 249/49/94, 3 December 1996).
[105] See *Schmidt* v. *Germany* [1994] EHRR 513, 526, at para. 22.

prevent or impair their enjoyment of human rights, the state should take
specific action to correct those conditions.[106]

This gives credence to action which might otherwise be interpreted as
'positive discrimination' which, by definition, would be in breach of
Article 14.

Discrimination: conflated

Even when unequal treatment does constitute discrimination, only in some
instances is it solely religious in nature. The causes of discrimination can be
conflated. Religious discrimination, for example, is at times imputed to
circumstances of unequal treatment which in fact derive from differences
in ethnicity.[107] The same conflation would seem to occur more consistently where that inequality is generated by differences in sexual practices or in religious beliefs: most particularly, perhaps, in the eyes of those
who adhere to a more traditional strand of Christianity, but also often
from Islamic, Jewish and other religious perspectives. Even where religious discrimination can be confirmed, it may not necessarily impact
upon charity and when it does that impact can be incidental.[108] Negotiating
the boundaries and areas of overlap between charity law, religious belief
and human rights is complicated and requires a broad understanding of
how 'discrimination' may operate.

Discrimination against a class

A leading case in this area is *D.H. v. Czech Republic*,[109] which concerned the
routine practice whereby Roma children were diverted into 'special' schools
designated for those with learning difficulties. The ECtHR confirmed that a
difference in treatment may take the form of disproportionately prejudicial

---

[106] See United Nations Human Rights Committee, 'General Comment relating to discrimination under the ICCPR', 1989 (No.18, para. 10).

[107] See, for example, *Crown Supplies (PSA) v. Dawkins* [1991] ICR 583 (EAT); *Dawkins* v.
Department of Environment [1993] IRLR 284 (CA), where the issue was whether
Rastafarians could be recognised as a distinct racial/cultural entity. Similarly, in
Mandla v. Dowell-Lee [1983] 2 AC 548, where the distinct ethnicity of Sikhs was at
issue. In both, religion was a secondary matter.

[108] See, for example, *McFarlane v. Relate Avon Ltd.* [2010] EWCA Civ B1 (29 April 2010),
where the issue arose in an employment context that coincidentally was one where a
charity was the employer.

[109] *D.H. v. Czech Republic*, App. No. 57325/00 (2007).

CHARITY, RELIGION AND HUMAN RIGHTS 137

effects of a general policy or measure which, though couched in neutral terms, discriminates against a racial or ethnic group. Intent was not required. The court also talked about shifting the burden of proof: where the applicant established a rebuttable presumption that the effect of a measure or practice was discriminatory, the burden shifted to the State to show the difference in treatment is not discriminatory. There may in effect be an 'obligation to make reasonable adjustments'.

Religious organisations and discrimination

The identification of a class of beneficiaries, selected as the recipients of a charitable gift or bequest or the focus of intervention by a charitable organisation, is intended to confer preferential benefit to the exclusion of all others. To the extent that the others excluded by such a differentiation are in all respects identical to the beneficiaries except for a difference of race, religion, gender, etc., that exclusion is discriminatory. So, for example, in *Pla* v. *Andorra* a majority of the ECtHR found that the Andorran High Court of Justice had acted in breach of the ECHR by upholding a testamentary settlement that discriminated against adoptive children.[110] Where any such discriminatory practice involves a religious charity then the question arises as to whether it can be excused compliance on grounds of established judicial precedent or by statutory exemption; indeed, charities are often expressly excused, by statute, from being subject to human rights provisions.

Religious beliefs and proselytism

While neither evangelism (advocacy to advance religious doctrines) nor proselytism (persuasion to convert) *per se* breach human rights, improper proselytism (inducing conversion through the use of undue influence, intimidation or reward) will do so. Article 18(1) of the ICCPR has direct relevance in this context. It provides that no one shall be subject to coercion which would impair his ability to choose his religion and that freedom to manifest one's religion may be subject to domestic legal restrictions such as are 'necessary to protect public safety, order, health, or morals or the fundamental rights and freedoms of others'.[111]

---

[110] See *Pla and Puncernau* v. *Andorra*, App. No. 69498/01 (2006) 42 EHRR 25.
[111] See, for example: *Larissis and others* v. *Greece* (Ser. A). No. 65 [1998-V] ECtHR 363; *Murphy* v. *Ireland*, App. No. 44179/98) [2004] 38 EHRR 212;

138 THE INTERNATIONAL CONTEXT

In the above mentioned *Kokkinakis* case,[112] for example, the ECtHR drew a distinction between 'evangelism' and 'improper proselytism' when it found that the Greek courts were wrong to convict a Jehovah's witness for 'improper proselytism' following his attempt to bring his neighbour 'good news' by entering her house and offering to sell to her some booklets advertising that religion. As the court then noted:

> Article 9 refers only to 'freedom to manifest one's religion or belief'. In so doing, it recognises that in democratic societies, in which several religions coexist within one and the same population, it may be necessary to place restrictions on this freedom in order to reconcile the interests of the various groups and ensure that everyone's beliefs are respected.[113]

The court did, however, maintain that:

> a distinction has to be made between bearing Christian witness and improper proselytism. The former corresponds to true evangelism, which a report drawn up in 1956 under the auspices of the World Council of Churches describes as an essential mission and a responsibility of every Christian and every Church. The latter represents a corruption or deformation of it. It may, according to the same report, take the form of activities offering material or social advantages with a view to gaining new members for a Church or exerting improper pressure on people in distress or in need; it may even entail the use of violence or brainwashing; more generally, it is not compatible with respect for the freedom of thought, conscience and religion of others.

Moreover, as Pettiti J then stated, 'religion is one of the foundations of a democratic society within the meaning of the Convention and the pluralism that cannot be disassociated from a democratic society depends on religious freedom'.

However, there are circumstances in which the proactive dissemination of doctrines and observances might include activities that others may find objectionable and some could experience as discriminatory. The use of symbols, for example, has been found to have such an effect as in *D.H.* v. *Czech Republic*,[114] when the ECtHR considered that the Islamic veil was a 'powerful external symbol' capable of having a proselytising effect, at least on very young children. Although, as in *Lautsi* v. *Italy*,[115] it would seem that where the symbols manifesting religious

---

Otto-Preminger-Institut v. Austria (Ser. A) 19 EHRR 34; and *Wingrove* v. *United Kingdom* [1997] 24 EHRR 1.

[112] *Kokkinakis* v. *Greece* (A/260-A) (1994) 17 EHRR 397. [113] Ibid., at p.14.

[114] App. No. 42393/98 (2001-V) Eur. Ct. H.R 449.

[115] App. No. 30814/06 (Eur. Ct. H.R. 18 March 2011).

beliefs are of a passive nature, not such as to constitute indoctrination or misplaced proselytism, then they should be accommodated. However, when evangelism is directed towards those already in a dependant relationship with the religious organisation (for example, being children in a youth camp, prisoners in a jail or mentally ill persons receiving counselling), then such activities may well constitute discrimination. On the other hand it is arguable that parents wishing to disseminate their religious beliefs by establishing faith-based schools could claim a right to do so under Article 2 of the First Protocol.[116]

Organisational issues and discrimination

It is often not so much doctrinal issues, matters of medical or social intervention or even the basic aspects of the charity transaction (donor to organisation or organisation to beneficiary) that give rise to contention, but the downstream activities of a religious charity: aspects of organisational staffing, administration and management that have been adapted to reflect a particular religious ethos. As Evans and Hood rightly point out:

> For . . . employees, the increased regulation of the workplace gives rise to questions over the extent to which ordinary employment laws are or should be applicable in religious workplaces. The debate is made particularly complex because of the competing legitimate claims on both sides based on human rights. Employees rely on their rights to equality, non-discrimination, fair processes and other employment rights to protect them from unfair treatment in the workplace. Religious employers, however, argue that undue regulation of religious workplaces leads to undermining of religious freedom and religious autonomy.[117]

In *Thlimmenos* v. *Greece*,[118] for example, the complainant was refused an appointment as a chartered accountant because of a conviction resulting from his refusal to wear a military uniform, which was against his religious beliefs as a Jehovah's Witness. He argued successfully that a distinction should have been made between offences committed exclusively because of a religious belief and other offences. Equality of rights

---

[116] See *Ingrid Jordebo Foundation of Christian Schools Ingrid Jordebo* v. *Sweden* (1987) 51 DR 125.

[117] C. Evans and A. Hood, 'Religious Autonomy and Labour Law: A Comparison of the Jurisprudence of the United States and the European Court of Human Rights' (2012) *Oxford Journal of Religion and the Law*, DOI: 10.1093/ojlr/rwr030.

[118] *Thlimmenos* v. *Greece*, App. No. 34369/97 (2001).

140   THE INTERNATIONAL CONTEXT

on a gender-free basis can lead to issues relating to employment opportunities in general and access to posts in the Church ministry in particular.

In this context the protection for religious interests provided for in Article 4(2) of EC Directive 2000/78/EC is important.[119] This general framework, established to provide for equal treatment in employment and occupation, attracted the following comment from a leading Irish human rights academic:

> First, one now has to show that, by virtue of the occupational activities of the employer or the context in which they are carried out, the employee's religion or belief constitutes a genuine, legitimate and justified occupational requirement, having regard to the employer's ethos. Thus Bolger argues that 'it will be necessary to show that a person's religion is a determining factor in her actual ability to discharge the duties of her job, rather than simply showing the employer's perception that such religion or belief is fitting in light of the organisation's ethos'. Second, the religious discrimination will only be upheld provided that it does not also constitute discrimination on any one of the other prohibited grounds in addition to gender. Thus, the dismissal of an openly homosexual teacher could not be justified under this provision as the dismissal would constitute sexual orientation discrimination.[120]

Charitable status

In *Religionsgemeinschaft der Zeugen Jehovas* v. *Austria* (*Jehovah's Witnesses* v. *Austria*),[121] the ECtHR was concerned with Article 9 (the right to manifest religion) read in conjunction with Article 14 (the right to non-discrimination) and appeared to give considerable weight to the importance of legal privileges to religious groups.[122] The case involved a refusal by Austria to register the Jehovah's Witnesses as a 'religious society' (making the group eligible for the fullest range of legal privileges possible for a religious group), rather than as a 'recognised religious community'. The alleged violations by Austria also included lengthy delays in the

---

[119] [2000] O.J. L303/16. Effective from 2 December 2003.

[120] See G. Whyte, 'Religion and Education: The Irish Constitution' paper presented at the TCD/IHRC conference on *Religion and Education: A Human Rights Perspective, Dublin*, 27 November 2010, at p.7.

[121] *Jehovah's Witnesses* v. *Austria* (2009) 48 EHRR 17.

[122] See, further, C. Evans, 'Individual and Group Religious Freedom in the European Court of Human Rights: Cracks in the Intellectual Architecture' (2010–2011) 26 *Journal of Law and Religion*, 321.

CHARITY, RELIGION AND HUMAN RIGHTS

registration processes. The Court emphasised the importance in Austria of the privileges associated with status as a religious society (privileges analogous to charitable status), including: 'exemption from military service and civilian service, reduced tax liability or exemption from specific taxes, facilitation of the founding of schools, and membership of various boards' which suggested that 'this special treatment undoubtedly facilitates a religious society's pursuance of its religious aims'.[123] It could be implied from this that the Court considered the withholding of such substantial legal privileges to have restricted the group's right to manifest their religion pursuant to Article 9, but the Court went on to decide that Austria had discriminated against the Jehovah's Witnesses, thus violating Article 14, rather than finding unequivocally that Article 9 had been breached. On the other hand, Judge Steiner in his partly dissenting opinion argued that Article 9's protection extended only to the ability of religious groups to acquire legal personality (which the group could have done by seeking status as an association) and ability to organise their internal affairs free from State interference. The withholding of the privileges associated with status as a 'religious society' did not interfere with the group's ability to manifest religion.[124]

Sexual orientation of staff

The sexual orientation of staff can give rise to discriminatory practices in religious organisations.[125] As the court emphasised in *EB* v. *France*,[126] '[w]here sexual orientation is in issue, there is a need for particularly convincing and weighty reasons to justify a difference in treatment regarding rights falling within article 8.' More recently, in *Kozak* v. *Poland*,[127] the ECtHR has stated that in relation to the justification of differential treatment on grounds of sexual orientation, the State's margin of appreciation is narrow, and that the principle of proportionality requires that the measure chosen to realise the legitimate aim must be both suitable in general, and necessary in the circumstances.[128]

---

[123] *Jehovah's Witnesses* v. *Austria* (2009) 48 EHRR 17, 445.   [124] Ibid.

[125] See, for example, *Salguerio da Silva Mouta* v. *Portugal* (2001) 31 EHRR 47; and *EB* v. *France* (2008) 47 EHRR 21.

[126] *EB* v. *France* (2008) 47 EHRR 21, at para. 90.

[127] *Kozak* v. *Poland* [2010] ECHR 280, at para. 92.

[128] See, further, C. Stychin, 'Faith in the Future: Sexuality, Religion and the Public Sphere' (2009) 29 *Oxford Journal of Legal Studies* 729.

Charity law reform

Beginning in England and Wales – then spreading to the neighbouring jurisdictions of Scotland, Northern Ireland and Ireland, and spilling over to include New Zealand, Australia, Canada, Singapore, to some extent the United States, and most recently reaching Hong Kong – the phenomenon of charity law reform has, since the closing years of the twentieth century, gradually embraced most developed common law nations.[129] One aspect of these processes, attracting a varying degree of attention, concerned the future role of religion in relation to charity and included issues such as: the legal definition of 'religion' and 'religious organisation'; the part to be played by religious bodies in public benefit service delivery; the weighting to be given to the charitable purpose of 'advancing religion'; and the interpretation of activities which could be construed as constituting such 'advancement'.

Reform drivers

Appropriately, the first steps towards reform were taken by England,[130] the progenitor of charity law throughout the common law world. Although the push was undoubtedly multifactorial, much the same set of pressures and inducements were evident in all the jurisdictions involved, notwithstanding differences in the timing and priority of various elements. It was no coincidence that so many governments embarked fairly simultaneously on the task of modernising charity law.[131]

Failures in the common law approach

For 400 years the legislature had scrupulously avoided any attempt to modernise charity law: in particular, there had been no interference with matters of definition; defining and interpreting the core concepts of charity were viewed as strictly the responsibility of the judiciary. The latter were left to deploy the *Pemsel* classification of charitable purposes together with the public benefit test and the 'spirit and intendment'

---

[129] See, further, M. McGregor-Lowndes and K. O'Halloran (eds), *Modernising Charity Law: Recent Developments and Future Directions*, Elgar Publications, Cheltenham, 2010.

[130] See Cabinet Office Strategy Unit, *Private Action, Public Benefit: A Review of Charities and the Wider Not-For-Profit Sector*, London, 2002.

[131] Barbados made an early start by introducing a detailed statutory definition of charitable purposes in the Charities Act 1979, Cap. 243.

rule,[132] and continue their arcane interpretation of 'charity'. By the early years of the twenty-first century, however, the governments of Canada,[133] Australia,[134] New Zealand,[135] the United States,[136] the United Kingdom[137] and Singapore[138] had come to the realisation that the traditional common law approach, designed to address the social needs of Elizabethan England, no longer provided an appropriate or sufficient legal framework for charity in their respective jurisdictions. Charity law and social need had fallen seriously out of synch. The crux of the problem was not that the judiciary were no longer up to the task of developing the law: it was more that their opportunities to do so were decreasing relative to the pace of social change. The functioning of the common law was predicated on a steady flow of judicial judgments without which it tended to ossify. This stream, needed to refresh and progress charity law development, was drying up as litigation became constrained by mounting costs, the protracted delays of court processes and charity concerns regarding unwelcome public exposure: in some jurisdictions, decades passed without any significant charity law cases being heard in the higher courts.[139]

Need for an improved regulatory system

Up until the closing decades of the twentieth century there had been no real pressure to introduce legislation to extend or adjust what was a

---

[132] Broadly speaking, this rule holds that even if a purpose cannot be defined as coming under one of the established heads of charity, it will nonetheless be construed as charitable if it can be interpreted as falling broadly within the scope of the Preamble to the 1601 Act.

[133] See Ontario Law Reform Commission, *Report on the Law of Charities*, Ontario, 1996.

[134] See the Charity Law Reform Committee Report, *Inquiry into the Definition of Charities and Related Organisations*, Canberra, June 2001.

[135] See the Working Party on Charities and Sporting Bodies, *Report on the Accountability of Charities & Sporting Bodies*, 1997.

[136] See Panel on the Nonprofit Sector, *Strengthening Transparency, Governance, Accountability of Charitable Organisations*, final report to Congress and the Nonprofit Sector, Washington, DC, 2005.

[137] See, for England and Wales: the National Council for Voluntary Organisations, *For the Public Benefit? A Consultation Document on Charity Law Reform*, London, 2001 and *Private Action, Public Benefit, a Review of Charities and the Wider Not-For-Profit Sector*, London, September 2002.

[138] See, for Singapore, the final report of the Inter-Ministry Committee on *The Regulation of Charities and Institutions of Public Character*, 2006.

[139] In Australia, for example, no charity law cases were heard by the High Court between *Commissioner of Land Tax (NSW) v. Joyce* (1974) 132 CLR 22 and *Bathurst City Council v. PWC Properties* (1998) 195 CLR 566.

benign regulatory framework that had seemed adequate to facilitate and monitor the workings of what had been a not particularly significant part of the nonprofit sector.[140] In all jurisdictions, except England and Wales, the Revenue had assumed responsibility as the lead regulatory body for charity and determined both charitable status and entitlement to tax relief. Other bodies traditionally associated with charities, but with less importance than formerly, included the High Court, the offices of the Attorney General and Customs and Excise, all of which had some statutory powers but very little regulatory control. Different areas of responsibility were distributed across different sets of statutes while government responsibility was diffuse and spread between different departments. The disparate nature of these traditional regulatory mechanisms was obstructive and accentuated the overall lack of coherence. It was the growing threat from international terrorism, accompanied by the suspicion that charities could unwittingly or otherwise become conduits for the illegal transfer of funds, that eventually provided the impetus for regulatory reform. The tracking of charity finances, the capacity to impose a regime for auditing income and inspecting charity affairs and the ability to compare and coordinate information with other agencies within and between jurisdictions all depended at least on the existence of a mandatory registration system specifically for charities.

Good governance concerns

The widespread media coverage given to corporate scandals in the United States (e.g. Enron[141]) had a ripple effect in the nonprofit sector, where levels of inefficiency, duplication and poor administration had long been considered an acceptable price to pay for greater flexibility and user involvement. Corporate corruption and mismanagement in the business world alerted governments to the potential for similar scandals in the charitable sector and stimulated awareness of the need to facilitate transparency, greater accountability, proper

---

[140] Excepting the Recreational Charities Act 1958 in England and Wales, as subsequently replicated in many common law jurisdictions, which extended definitional boundaries to accommodate recreational sports.

[141] The Enron scandal, revealed in October 2001, eventually led to the bankruptcy of the Enron Corporation, an American energy company based in Houston, Texas. This, the largest bankruptcy reorganisation in American history at that time, was attributed to audit failure.

models of governance and ensure that adequate standards of propriety prevailed in all corporate boardrooms, including those of charities. The lack of a regulatory charity-specific system was readily acknowledged to be a serious weakness which provided opportunities for fiduciary abuse.

Fundraising concerns

Fundraising for charitable and other purposes had traditionally been treated separately from charity regulation by statutes and by agencies that were concerned more with outlining authorised procedures than identifying and proscribing abuses. While fundraising law continued to focus on raffles, church collections, door-to-door and street collections, contemporary practice featured professional and entertainment-based techniques with the capacity to attract and possibly transfer overseas, within a very short period, a large volume of funds. There was a general recognition that reform of the law relating to fundraising by charities had become necessary in order to ensure accountability and to protect against abuse of charitable status and fraud.

Need to broaden the charity share of public benefit service provision

In part the rationale for charity law review was technical. The *Pemsel* classification no longer provided an appropriate and sufficient agenda of charitable purposes; new manifestations of social need were constantly emerging; there was every good reason to update the classification to accommodate a modern and broader vision of matters that charitable organisations might address. Moreover, the presumption that the benefit test was satisfied in relation to organisations and gifts that could fit within the first three *Pemsel* heads was controversial; particularly in respect of religion, the requirement to prove public benefit for all organisations and gifts under the fourth head was arguably discriminatory, and there was uncertainty as to the thresholds of proof for both the 'public' and the 'benefit' components of the test. In the main, however, the rationale was cost driven: the burden of responsibility for present services had to be shifted to some extent towards the nonprofit sector as governments, embroiled in foreign wars and struggling with the revenue implications of unfavourable demographic

146   THE INTERNATIONAL CONTEXT

trends,[142] lacked the spare capacity to meet the health, education and social care needs of its citizens.

Basis for building government/nonprofit sector partnership

Throughout the common law world the principal means of orchestrating not just the balance to be struck between government and charity in relation to responsibility for public benefit service provision, but also the broader strategic relationship between government and the nonprofit sector, has rested largely on charity law. This has been by default as no other legal framework has yet been devised to govern a relationship only recently formally acknowledged in a few jurisdictions and yet to be fully developed in any.[143] In all developed common law jurisdictions, however, by the late twentieth century the retraction of the State and the corresponding rolling forward of the nonprofit sector brought the nature of this relationship to the fore as governments sought to shift more responsibility for public benefit service provision towards the sector and came to view the relationship as the central axis on which to build or consolidate civil society.

In the UK jurisdictions, as in Ireland and New Zealand, where government had already cultivated a model of social partnership with representative organisations in the nonprofit sector as a platform for social policy planning, it became evident that charity law needed to be revised if it was to reflect the reality of contemporary rules of engagement between government and the sector and facilitate the further development of that partnership.

Basis for promoting civic/political engagement

The growing gap between government and the electorate was a matter of concern to the former in many jurisdictions. As had been observed:

---

[142] See V. Tanzi, *Government versus Markets: The Changing Economic Role of the State,* Cambridge University Press, Cambridge, 2011.

[143] Some academics have called for a sector-wide legal framework: see, for example, J. Garton, 'The Future of Civil Society Organizations: Towards a Theory of Regulations for Organized Civil Society' and M. Turnour, 'Modernising Charity Law: Steps to an Alternative Architecture for Common Law Charity Jurisprudence', in M. McGregor-Lowndes and K. O'Halloran (eds), *Modernising Charity Law: Recent Developments and Future Directions,* Elgar Publications, Cheltenham, 2010.

CHARITY LAW REFORM

> There is a growing crisis at the heart of democratic accountability. The public's disengagement from organised politics has gathered pace as they have lost faith in the more traditional forms of political engagement.[144]

Modernising charity law, by broadening the range of charitable activities, was seen by government as also providing an opportunity to enhance the capacity of democratic politics: encouraging the use of volunteers in public service provision being viewed as a means of promoting civic engagement and building social capital. Drafting the architecture for civil society may not have been on the political horizon at that time, but governments' need to generate a greater sense of civic responsibility had become pressing in order to increase volunteer input and thereby ease the service delivery onus resting on government bodies; generate the social capital necessary to build more cohesive and caring communities; and to bridge the gap with the electorate by demonstrating how government and citizens could work together and deliver tangible benefits to local communities. The review process was viewed as providing an opportunity to broaden and formalise the relationship between government and citizens, allowing the latter more participation in the democratic process with the hope of thereby facilitating greater social cohesion.

Reform outcomes

Following the lead given by England and Wales in the Charities Act 2006, certain key outcomes were achieved by the law reform process in some jurisdictions, as evidenced in their respective new charity statutes, while for others the obstacles on the road to reform proved insurmountable, at least in the short term. The key components, with variable distribution among the jurisdictions, were: statutory statements of core common law concepts; a new extended list of charitable purposes; changes to the regulatory framework; and the testing and, in some cases, the consolidation of the relationship between government and the sector.

Changes to the regulatory system

An outcome of considerable importance has been the decision in Scotland, Northern Ireland, Ireland, Singapore and to a lesser extent

---

[144] See Advisory Group, *Report on Campaigning and the Voluntary Sector* (chaired by Baroness Helena Kennedy QC), London, 2007, at p.1.

148 THE INTERNATIONAL CONTEXT

New Zealand and prospectively Australia and Hong Kong, to follow the lead given earlier by England and Wales and decouple the regulatory mechanisms for charities and for determining charitable status from those traditionally used to regulate tax liability. These jurisdictions have now established relatively independent, charity-specific, lead regulatory bodies statutorily responsible for: sector support; maintaining a register of charities; determining charitable status; providing advice and improving governance; monitoring through annual reports and financial statements; and conducting audits and investigations.[145] Their reforms have also variously introduced provisions for: an appeals tribunal or procedure; adjusting the traditional roles of court and Attorney General; and an updating of the law relating to other matters such as trustees, fundraising, *cy-près* and legal structures for charitable activity.

Changes to the common law

In England and Wales,[146] Scotland,[147] Northern Ireland[148] and Ireland,[149] the review processes concluded with – and in New Zealand,[150] Australia,[151] Canada[152] and Singapore,[153] concluded without – changes to some core definitional matters. In all, the statutory definition of 'charity' simply restates the legal meaning given to it under the common law. In the UK and Irish jurisdictions, change has taken the form of a significant redefinition of 'public benefit', adjustments to the 'poor relations' rule and a statutory restatement of all other common law

---

[145] The new bodies vested with responsibility for determining charitable status and registering and supervising charities are: in Scotland, the Office of the Scottish Charity Regulator; in Northern Ireland, the Charity Commission for Northern Ireland; in Singapore, the Commissioner of Charities; and in New Zealand, the Charities Commission.

[146] Concluded with the introduction of the Charities Act 2006, now the Charities Act 2011.

[147] Concluded with the introduction of the Charities and Trustee Investment (Scotland) Act 2005.

[148] Concluded with the introduction of the Charities Act (Northern Ireland) 2008.

[149] Concluded with the introduction of the Charities Act 2009.

[150] Concluded with the introduction of the Charities Act 2005.

[151] Concluded, temporarily, with the withdrawal of the draft Charities Bill in May 2004 and the introduction of the Extension of Charitable Purpose Act 2004.

[152] Concluded, for the time being, with the submission of the Joint Table Report.

[153] Currently at the stage of implementing the recommendations of the Inter-Ministry Committee on the regulation of Charities and Institutions of Public Character established in October 2005.

concepts.[154] In Australia, Canada, New Zealand and Singapore, all common law concepts remained unchanged and no legislative steps were taken to alter the public benefit presumption. However, and unlike Canada, both New Zealand and Singapore have now placed the key common law concepts onto the statute books, thereby, in keeping with the UK and Irish jurisdictions, giving their governments the future capacity to: add, subtract from, or otherwise qualify, the list of charitable purposes; and amend or adjust the rules relating to matters such as public benefit, exclusiveness and independence. Additionally, although the UK and Irish jurisdictions reversed the public benefit presumption traditionally granted to the first three *Pemsel* heads (excepting religion in Ireland) this initiative has not been adopted elsewhere. Moreover, the precise criteria of such a test and the calibration and weighting to be given to it, in application to traditional institutional religions as opposed to emergent minority religious groups and to philosophical, moral or ethical belief systems, has yet to be determined. In this context, the warning given by the ECtHR in *Jehovah's Witnesses* v. *Austria* must be borne in mind:

> if a State sets up a framework for conferring legal personality on religious groups to which a specific status is linked, all religious groups which so wish must have a fair opportunity to apply for this status and the criteria established must be applied in a non-discriminatory manner.[155]

Consequently, the traditionally shared common law conceptual basis of charity has been left in considerable disarray.

A broadened range of charitable purposes

The fact that all reforming jurisdictions choose to retain as charitable the set of purposes first identified and listed in the 1601 Statute[156] and classified in *Pemsel* means that: the currency of all related case law will maintain its value; all jurisdictions, whether or not engaged in law reform, will continue to share the basic common law platform; and they will keep the same associated public benefit service provision opportunities. However, of the handful of nations to embark on reform, a minority took an important

---

[154] Note that both s.8(2)(a) of the Charities and Trustee Investment (Scotland) Act 2005 and s.3(3)(a)(ii) of the Charities Act (Northern Ireland) 2008 insert a statutory requirement that when applying the public benefit test regard must also be had to any possible negative side effects.

[155] *Jehovah's Witnesses* v. *Austria* (2009) 48 EHRR 17, 445.

[156] Statute of Charitable Uses 1601 (43 Eliz. 1. Cap. 4).

150 THE INTERNATIONAL CONTEXT

further step. The UK jurisdictions and Ireland introduced legislation to give effect to government's plans for broadening charity's contribution by adding to the Preamble list of charitable purposes. This set of '*Pemsel*-plus' charitable purposes, as has been recently explained,[157] identifies with remarkable consistency clusters of new purposes, cohering around clear social policy themes that reveal matters central to government's intended partnership arrangement with charity. These are: the advancement of human rights, conflict resolution or reconciliation, and promotion of multiculturalism, etc.; the advancement of civil society; the advancement of health and related services; and promoting the welfare of specific socially disadvantaged groups. In addition, the reform processes in these jurisdictions concluded with statutory provisions allowing charitable purposes concerned with matters of poverty and health to accommodate a preventative dimension. Also, a statutory definition of 'religion' now forms part of charity law in the UK jurisdictions and, to a lesser extent, in Ireland.

Four centuries after the initial declaration of matters it considered should be addressed by charity, government has again resorted to statute law for that purpose. In updating the public benefit agenda and distributing the responsibility for related service provision, the governments concerned have reset the basis for its partnership relationship with charity and the broader nonprofit sector and provided a model for other common law jurisdictions.

The government/nonprofit sector relationship

It was in England and Wales, where the strategic function of the Charity Commission in that relationship had been augmented by an institutional infrastructure constructed by the successive Labour and Coalition governments at the turn of the century, and where nonprofit sector umbrella bodies had developed considerable negotiating power, that the most far-reaching reforms were achieved. In some jurisdictions, the political leverage of the sector was virtually nullified by government either choosing not to facilitate sector engagement (Singapore) or to give only token regard to it (Australia under the liberal administration). In others, that leverage was, perhaps, compromised by dependency on government funds whether through direct grants or through contracts (United

---

[157] See M. McGregor-Lowndes and K. O'Halloran (eds), *Modernising Charity Law*, Elgar Publishing, London, 2010; and also K. O'Halloran, *The Politics of Charity*, Routledge, London, 2011.

Kingdom and Ireland). In the United States, the prospect of government/ sector negotiations never arose, while in Canada various attempts at province and federal levels largely ended in stalemate. The process in New Zealand started promisingly, with extensive government/sector consultations, but produced anodyne outcomes, although reform was further progressed through tax law adjustments.

However, with hindsight it has to be noted that the unfortunate juxtaposition of charity law reform followed by global economic recession has resulted in some erosion of the painfully crafted government–sector partnerships that produced the widely acclaimed legislative outcomes, and in doing so it reveals the political realities governing that relationship. As governments resort to austerity measures to reduce levels of public debt, the costs associated with maintaining the sector's administrative regime are among the first to be cut. As governments retrench and public services shrink, the nonprofit sector as a whole and charities in particular are under increasing pressure to make good the shortfall, which in turn is undermining the basis of trust sustained through the reform process and with it the future for any government–sector partnership.

Charity law reform outcomes and religion

For many generations the charity law framework allowed those nations comprising the common law world to share much the same legal definition of religion and the accompanying case law in determining when a religion, a religious organisation and gifts to them could be construed as charitable. Such jurisdictional differences as existed[158] were relatively insignificant compared to the changes statutorily introduced by some nations as a consequence of charity law reform. While the detail of such reforms fall to be examined in the jurisdiction-specific chapters, it is necessary to take account of their broad effect in the present context.

Religious charitable purposes: from common law to statutory definition

Allowing for the fact that only a small minority of common law nations engaged in charity law reform, of which only a few actually introduced

---

[158] Largely centred on matters such as: the charitable status of 'closed' religious orders; gifts for the saying of private masses; and whether non-theistic entities could be construed as 'religious'.

152 THE INTERNATIONAL CONTEXT

changes to core concepts, and of those even fewer made changes relating to religion, nonetheless the nature of those changes, together with the lead status of the main jurisdiction involved, will generate repercussions elsewhere. In particular, the encoding of provisions relating to religion enables the governments concerned to thereafter adjust the law governing the definition of religious bodies and the obligations and entitlements of religious charities.

The changes

Before the reforms, the essential requirements for a religious organisation, or for a donation to such an organisation, to be legally recognised as charitable, were broadly the same in all common law nations: a belief in a 'Supreme Being' and a shared commitment to faith and worship;[159] though these requirements were assisted by the legal presumption that such organisations and gifts to them were for the public benefit[160] (see Chapter 2). In addition, importance has traditionally been attached to 'the laws, canons, ordinances and tenets of the religion concerned'.[161] The reform process, however, introduced a statutory definition of 'religion' to form part of charity law in the UK jurisdictions and, to a lesser extent, in Ireland. In the UK jurisdictions, but not in Ireland nor in any of the other reforming jurisdictions, the definition now includes an express reference to faiths that do not profess belief in a god, as well as to polytheistic religions. This new legislative definition has: excised any need for a belief in a god, and allows the belief in multiple gods;[162] removed the need for worship or liturgy; and reversed the public benefit presumption so that any such organisation or gift must now demonstrably satisfy the public benefit test.[163] It is not impossible that other common

---

[159] See Charity Commission, 'Analysis of the Law Underpinning *Public Benefit and the Advancement of Religion*', February 2008 at para. 2.14. Also see Charity Commission in *Church of Scientology of California* v. *Customs and Excise Comms.* [1980] CMLR 114; [1979] STC 297; [1979] T.R. 59; *affd* [1981] 1 All ER 1035; [1981] STC 65, Ca.

[160] The advancement of religion has been presumed to be for the public benefit in all common law jurisdictions; in some, such as Ireland, this presumption has statutory endorsement.

[161] It was Wickens VC in *Cocks* v. *Manners* (1871) LR 12 Eq 574, who initially suggested that the 'benefit' quotient of a religious organisation for the 'public' lay in its moral and spiritual values which could be found in its beliefs, doctrines and practices (at p.585).

[162] See: the Charities Act 2006, s.2(3)(a); Charities and Trustee Investment (Scotland) Act 2005, s.7(2A)(e); and the Charities Act (Northern Ireland) 2008, s.2(3)(a)(i).

[163] See the Charities Act 2006, s.3.

law countries will in due course, either explicitly by statute or by following case precedents, accept the changes made by the UK jurisdictions. This, in all probability, will encourage further faith-based initiatives in service provision.

Conclusion

It would be difficult to overstate the importance of the effect of developments in human rights upon traditional religious beliefs and associated organisations, including religious charities. Charity law reform, which took into account such developments, has added to the impact and together both are now presenting a formidable challenge to some of the core doctrines that have sustained religion and its adherents for many generations.

PART II

Contemporary international perspectives

5

England and Wales

Introduction

From 1983 to 2011, according to the British Social Attitudes Survey, religious affiliation dropped from 68 per cent to 53 per cent of the population and as a consequence it advises that 'we can expect to see a continued increase in liberal attitudes towards a range of issues such as abortion, homosexuality, same-sex marriage, and euthanasia, as the influence of considerations grounded in religion declines'.[1] The corollary, of course, being an expectation of matching antipathy from the resolutely religious towards the same agenda of issues, leading to increased recourse to the courts. The growing confrontation between religious beliefs and human rights in this jurisdiction would seem set to become more strident.

This chapter begins with an explanatory overview of the evolving relationship between Church, State and religious charities in England and Wales, one of the three jurisdictions that constitute the United Kingdom, but the only one with a charity-specific regulator in place for the past 150 years. It then examines the role of that regulator, the Charity Commission[2] and other key agencies and the charity law framework in setting and adjusting the parameters of that relationship. It considers the legal definition and interpretation of 'religion', 'religious beliefs' and the activities held to constitute the charitable purpose of 'advancing religion'. The chapter then explains and traces the public policy approach to religious charities before focusing on the contemporary law and judicial rulings relating to the tension between human rights and religious beliefs in this jurisdiction. As the latter forms the

---

[1] See the National Centre for Social Research, annual publications of BSAS results since 1983, at www.secularism.org.uk/british-social-attitudes-survey.html (accessed 3 January 2014).

[2] See the Charity Commission for England and Wales at: www.gov.uk/government/organisations/the-charity-commission-for-england-and-wales (accessed 3 January 2014).

core of the chapter, a good deal of attention is given to identifying the circumstances in which issues arise, assessing the difficulties encountered by religious charities and analysing what in law and practice constitutes discrimination. The chapter concludes by considering the type of religious charitable activity statutorily exempt from the law governing discrimination.

Church, State and religious charities

It would be difficult to overstate the importance of the relationship between Church and State in this jurisdiction for setting the parameters of charity law, determining the definition of 'religion' and shaping the role of religious charities throughout the common law world.

Historical background: the Church–State relationship

The strong links initially forged between Church and State and the preferential standing of Anglicanism as the established Church are among the more important continuing and distinguishing constitutional characteristics of England.

The State, Protestantism, charity and religious discrimination

From an early stage in the Elizabethan era, discrimination in favour of charitable trusts for the benefit of Protestant causes was very apparent.[3] In 1606, for example, a trust to support students studying for the Roman Catholic priesthood was disallowed[4] while, in 1639, one for the purpose of maintaining a preaching minister was upheld.[5] State suppression of the Roman Catholic Church led to the systematic judicial voiding of many trusts that would have previously been found charitable, including trusts to maintain popish priests,[6] and gifts dedicated to the advancement of any religion other than that of the Established Church.[7] Suppression was not restricted to Catholicism, as was evident in the similar judicial approach to trusts for the purposes of assisting Judaism

---

[3] See, further, H. Picarda, *The Law and Practice Relating to Charities* (4th edn), Bloomsbury Professional, London, 2010, at pp.89–90.
[4] See, for example, *Croft* v. *Evetts* (1606) Moore KB 784.
[5] *Pember* v. *Inhabitants of Knighton* (1639) 1 Eq Cas 95.
[6] See, for example, *A-G* v. *Baxter* (1684) 1 Vern 248.
[7] *De Costa* v. *De Paz* (1754) 2 Swan 487n; *Cary* v. *Abbot* (1802) 7 Ves 490.

CHURCH, STATE AND RELIGIOUS CHARITIES 159

or its adherents and in relation to support for non-conformist minis-ters.[8] Only gradually, following the Toleration Act 1689 (which extended freedom of worship rights to some religions but not to Catholicism),[9] did this situation begin to improve.

As Rivers has pointed out,[10] up until at least the early eighteenth century religious minorities were barely tolerated by the State, as was illustrated in *AG* v. *Eades*,[11] when doubts were still being expressed as to whether a gift to poor Anabaptists was a good charity. The Papists Act 1778 was the first statute to address legal discrimination against Roman Catholics, but it was the Roman Catholic Relief Act 1829 that finally emancipated Catholics and not until the early part of the nineteenth century did legislation[12] gradually allow the courts to endorse as charitable those trusts made for the promotion of the religious purposes of Unitarians,[13] Roman Catholics[14] and those of the Jewish faith.[15]

With the introduction of the Places of Religious Worship Registration Act 1855,[16] equal opportunities were finally provided for all religious bodies or denominations to establish their own places of meeting for religious worship and have these certified as such by the Registrar General. Even then the courts were reluctant to embrace the ethos of equality. In 1943, for example, the House of Lords felt able to rule that 'Jewish faith' was so uncertain a term as to render a will void.[17]

State enforcement of Christianity

For several centuries the Christian nature of the State was not to be questioned; no other religions would be granted equal legal status. As Lord Eldon C asserted:

---

[8] See, for example, *Gates* v. *Jones* (1690), cited in 2 Vern 266.   [9] 1 Will. & Mar. c.18.

[10] J. Rivers, *The Law of Organized Religions: Between Establishment and Secularism*, Oxford University Press, Oxford, 2010, p.16.

[11] *AG* v. *Eades* (1713), unreported; see *AG* v. *Cock* (1751) 2 Ves Sen 273; 28 ER 177, at 274.

[12] Unitarian Relief Act 1813; Roman Catholic Charities Act 1832; and the Religious Disabilities Act 1846, which provided that in respect of schools, places of religious worship, educational and charitable purposes and property held by them, Jews shall be subject to the same laws as Protestants who dissent from the Church of England.

[13] *Shore* v. *Wilson* (1842) 9 CI & Fin 355; *Shrewsbury* v. *Hornby* (1846) 5 Hare 406.

[14] *Bradshaw* v. *Tasker* (1834) 2 My & K 221.

[15] *Straus* v. *Goldsmid* (1837) 8 Sim 614; *Re Braham* (1892) 36 Sol Jo 712.

[16] 1855 c. 81 (Regnal. 18 and 19 Vict). Not until the House of Lords ruling in *Bourne* v. *Keane* [1919] AC 815 did gifts for the saying of masses again become legal.

[17] *Clayton* v. *Ramsden* [1943] AC 320 (HL). See also *Re Moss's Will Trusts* [1945] 1 All ER 207.

160   ENGLAND AND WALES

> I apprehend that it is the duty of every judge presiding in an English Court of Justice, when he is told that there is no difference between worshipping the Supreme Being in chapel, church, or synagogue, to recollect that Christianity is part of the law of England ... he is not at liberty to forget that Christianity is the law of the land.[18]

Such views were commonly expressed by the judiciary and rigorously enforced,[19] as illustrated by the long history of blasphemy in which that offence was often treated as seditious. Christianity was also to be exported for the benefit of the State's overseas subjects. A. Picarda notes:[20]

> A trust for spreading Christianity among infidels was upheld in 1790.[21] In the heyday of the British Empire there was very considerable missionary activity, and numerous societies carrying on such work were recognized as charitable, for example the society for Promoting Christian Knowledge,[22] the Society for the Propagation of the Gospel in Foreign Parts,[23] the Church Missionary Society[24] and the Sunday School Association.[25]

Blackstone, in dealing with offences against religion, refers to the heinous offence 'of blasphemy against the Almighty, by denying his being or providence; or by contumelious reproaches of our Saviour Christ ... these are offences punishable at common law by fine and imprisonment, or other infamous corporal punishment: for Christianity is part of the laws of England.'[26] The gravity of the offence was demonstrated in the prosecutions of both Atwood (1618)[27] and Taylor (1676).[28] While blasphemy was referred to in 1842 by the House of Lords in disarming terms as 'scoffingly or irreverently to ridicule or impugn the doctrines of the

---

[18] See *In re Masters & C. of the Bedford Charity* (1818) 2 Swans 470, at p.527.

[19] See, for example: Best CJ, 'There is no act which Christianity forbids, that the law will not reach: if it were otherwise, Christianity would not be, as it has always been held to be, part of the law of England', in *Bird* v. *Holbrook* (1828) 4 Bing. 628, at p.641; and Sumner LJ 'Ours is, and always has been, a Christian State. The English family is built on Christian ideas', in *Bowman* v. *Secular Society Limited* [1917] AC 406.

[20] See Picarda, *The Law and Practice Relating to Charities*, at p.109.

[21] Citing *A-G* v. *City of London* (1790) 1 Ves 243.

[22] Citing *Re Clergy Society* (1856) 2 K&J 615.

[23] Citing *Re Maguire* (1870) LR 9 Eq 632.   [24] Ibid.

[25] Citing *R* v. *Special Comrs of Income Tax, ex p Essex Hall* [1931] 2 KB 434.

[26] See W. Blackstone, *Commentaries on the Laws of England*, (Book 4, c. 4, s. iv), Yale Law School, at: http://avalon.law.yale.edu/18th_century/blackstone_bk4ch14.asp (accessed 3 January 2014).

[27] Cro. Jac. 421; 2 Roll. Abr. 78.

[28] 1 Ventris 293; 3 Kebble 607; 2 Strange 789. See also *Regina* v. *Woolston*, 1729 (Fitz-G. 64; 1 Barn. Ch. 162, 266; 2 Stra. 832).

CHURCH, STATE AND RELIGIOUS CHARITIES

Christian faith',[29] it did once attract severe punishment, including banishment, being placed in the pillory or, in Scotland until 1813, in certain circumstances it could merit the death penalty. More recently a fine and imprisonment could be imposed at the discretion of the court, as was the case with John William Gott who, on 9 December 1921, became the last person in Britain to be sent to prison for blasphemy.

Atheism was also viewed as essentially subversive. The solemn swearing of an oath (usually a declaration of loyalty and fealty to the Crown, ending typically with the words 'So help me God') was a precondition for taking any form of office in public life, including being a Member of Parliament, until at least 1888 when the Oaths Act allowed the substitution of an affirmation. As an oath required the swearer to believe in a god or gods,[30] an atheist could not do so,[31] which in turn precluded such non-believers from being considered for almost all positions in public life.

The special position of the Church of England

The institutional presence of the Church of England has been a source of religious and secular authority in English society since the reign of Henry VIII. As the 'established' Church of England it has prevailed over all other religions under constitutional arrangements which provide for the reigning monarch to be both its Supreme Governor and Head of State:[32] the monarch on coronation being blessed by the Archbishop who in turn may be appointed by exercise of the royal prerogative; in effect, this particular religion has a special status as it is dually licensed by Crown and State. Indeed, Anglican bishops once ruled by divine right, even exercising a penal jurisdiction, not in the name of the King, but as a parallel source of authority in the land. Anglican canon law has become assimilated into national law and therefore it and Protestantism more broadly, to that extent, continue to have a favoured legal status relative to all other religions, the conversion from which to Anglicanism has been deemed charitable.[33]

---

[29] See *Shore* v. *Wilson* (1842) 9 Cl. & Fin. 355, *per* Erskine LJ, at p.524. Also see W. S. Holdsworth, 'State and Religious Nonconformity: An Historical Retrospect' (1920) 36 *Law Quarterly Review* 339.

[30] See *Omichund* v. *Barker* (1744) 1 Willes 538; 125 ER 1310, which held that although such an oath was necesaarily religious, it did not have to be Christian.

[31] See *A-G* v. *Bradlaugh* (1885) 14 QBD 667.

[32] Under the Act of Union 1707, Article 2, the monarch is required to belong to the Church of England; the position is restricted exclusively to that religion.

[33] *A-G* v. *Becher* [1910] 2 IR 251.

The appointment of its chaplains to prisons is a statutory requirement;[34] and even its church bells are relatively privileged as they (and only the bells of churches of that denomination) are statutorily required to be rung morning and evening. It also enjoys a stronger relationship with government:[35] the hierarchy of Church officials hold their posts by government appointment rather than election, an arrangement dating from the civil war and designed to guard against religious fundamentalism; and all 26 Anglican bishops (the Lords Spiritual) sit as a right in the House of Lords on the government benches.[36] With that right comes the entitlement not just to contribute an ethical dimension to the shaping of government policy on matters such as family planning and child care, but to have a say in determining more secular matters such as foreign policy. No other religion has such legal or political standing and no initiative by government or Church has ever been taken to change it.

Moreover, a privilege accorded to the Established Church has traditionally allowed many of its constituent religious entities to be treated as 'excepted charities' by the Charity Commission and so enjoy the benefits of charitable status without the requirement to register and demonstrate public benefit.[37] Not until the introduction of special provisions in the Charities Act 2006, now the Charities Act 2011, was this privilege withdrawn.[38]

Building a modern Church–State relationship

From being essentially a theocratic State – with monarchy, parliament and the Protestant Church united in a consensus to uphold and defend the same body of religious beliefs – this jurisdiction has evolved to function as a more measured secular entity.

---

[34] The Prison Act 1952, s.74.

[35] Illustrated by the fact that the Church of England is often the only named religious organisation in legislation dealing with such entities. Note, however, 'The Governance of Britain (Cm. 7170)', which presents the government's proposals for constitutional renewal including an intention to abolish the prerogative power to appoint bishops (July 2007); see, further, at: www.parliament.uk/documents/commons/lib/research/rp2007/RP07-072.pdf (accessed 3 January 2014).

[36] The Bishopric of Manchester Act of 1847 limited the number of places for Lords Spiritual to 26. From at least the time of King Edward's parliament in 1300, the Lords Spiritual have sat alongside the Lords Temporal in the House of Lords to consider matters of state.

[37] Maintaining the Church of England is expensive, costing just over £1,000 million each year to finance its 13,000 parishes and 43 cathedrals, with each component part having charitable status.

[38] See the Charities Act 2011, s.30(2)(b)–(c).

Religion(s)

Religious adherents would now seem to be a minority: according to the British Social Attitudes Survey for 2009 a total of 50.7 per cent of the UK population declared they had no religion; although, paradoxically, 33.2 million people in England and Wales described themselves as Christians in the 2011 census. Of those subscribing to a religious belief, most are Christians with Anglicanism being the most widely practised and declared religion. Islam and Hinduism are numerically the next most popular. In the past ten years there has been a decrease in people in England and Wales identifying as Christian, from 71.7 per cent to 59.3 per cent of the population while, in the same period, the number of Muslims in England and Wales has risen from 3 per cent of the population to 4.8 per cent.[39] The Jewish culture and the Jewish population are also significant.

Secularisation

Church attendance, according to the British Social Attitudes survey,[40] remains at an all-time low, with only some 14 per cent of the population regularly attending services; the prediction from Christian Research is for a continued decline.[41] In general, compared with its European neighbours, Britain has been quite relaxed about the public display of private religious affiliation: for example, there is no legal prohibition on adults wearing turbans or other headwear denoting religious affiliation in their places of employment. However, some limits to British tolerance became evident in 2013: Murphy J at London's Blackfriars Crown Court, commenting that 'the niqab has become the elephant in the courtroom', ruled that a Muslim woman defendant must remove her niqab when giving evidence;[42] and public controversy was generated by news reports

---

[39] See further, for example, at: www.dailymail.co.uk/news/article-2332998/One-country-religions-telling-pictures-The-pews-churches-just-yards-overcrowded-mosque.html#i xzz2ZO2VLRjH (accessed 3 January 2014).

[40] According to the 28th report (2011) of the British Social Attitudes Survey, 56 per cent of people who were brought up in a religion never attend services and only 14 per cent do so on a weekly basis. In the 26th survey it was found that 62 per cent of the population never attend any form of service. See further at: www.brin.ac.uk/news/tag/british-social-attitudes-survey (accessed 3 January 2014).

[41] See at: www.christian.org.uk (accessed 3 January 2014).

[42] While the hijab is an obligatory code of dress for Muslim women, the majority of Muslim scholars would seem to be in agreement that a woman is not obliged to wear the niqab or

164   ENGLAND AND WALES

that wearing the burqa is mandatory for attendance at some Islamic schools.[43] Nonetheless, two-thirds of schools in England remain secular and many long-established British charities with strong evangelical Christian traditions, such as Barnardo's and the YMCA,[44] have in recent years distanced themselves from their religious origins and embraced instead an equality and diversity ethos; some others, such as Catholic adoption agencies, when faced with the statutory requirement to accept and treat equally adoption applications from homosexual and hetero-sexual couples, have chosen to do so even though this has necessitated formally severing their ties with the Church.[45]

Paradoxically, however, the evidence of secularisation is mixed. On the one hand these and other indicators point to religion becoming more marginal to British civic life. On the other, there has been a recent and rapid spread of faith schools. Then there is the fact that the United Kingdom is one of only four EU Member States to have an Established Church.

An 'established' religion

The courts now tread a rigorously neutral path when dealing with issues that touch upon the relationship between Church and State. The require-ment that the courts maintain such an impartial role has attracted academic[46] and judicial[47] support and was recently and directly raised in *McFarlane* v. *Relate Avon Ltd*,[48] a religious discrimination case con-cerning the charity Relate. Lord Carey, the former Archbishop of Canterbury, sought to intervene by making suggestions as to the desired composition of the court (deemed by Laws LJ to be 'deeply inimical to

---

the burqa. See further at: www.theguardian.com/world/2013/sep/16/veil-biggest-issue-uk-niqab-debate (accessed 3 January 2014).

[43] See, further, at: www.dailymail.co.uk/news/article-2424241/Islamic-schools-Britain-forcing-girls-young-11-wear-face-veils.html (accessed 3 January 2014).

[44] In January 2011 the Young Women's Christian Association dropped its historic title after 156 years because 'it no longer stands for who we are' and adopted the name 'Platform 51'.

[45] Since this statutory requirement was introduced in 2007, 10 of the 11 Catholic adoption agencies in the United Kingdom have severed their ties to the Church or ceased operations.

[46] See, for example, J. Habermas, 'Religion in the Public Sphere' (2006) 14:1 *European Journal of Philosophy*, 1, at p.10, where he warns that 'every citizen must know and accept that only secular reasons count beyond the institutional threshold that divides the informal public sphere from parliament, courts, ministries and administrations'.

[47] See, for example, Munby J in *X* v. *X* [2002] 1 FLR 508, where he states that 'although historically this country is part of the Christian west, and although it has an established church which is Christian, I sit as a secular judge serving a multi-cultural community', at para. 112.

[48] *McFarlane* v. *Relate Avon Ltd*. [2010] IRLR 872; 29 BHRC 249.

the public interest'[49]) and the need to address what he perceived to be an alleged 'lack of sensitivity to religious belief'[50] by the judiciary when dealing with such cases. In response, Laws LJ drew attention to two principles generally considered to be central to liberal democracy: that the State should remain neutral in relation to religion; and that public policy should be rigorously secular. He pointed out that:

> In a free constitution such as ours there is an important distinction to be drawn between the law's protection of the right to hold and express a belief and the law's protection of that belief's substance or content. The common law and ECHR Article 9 offer vigorous protection of the Christian's right (and every other person's right) to hold and express his or her beliefs. And so they should. By contrast they do not, and should not, offer any protection whatever of the substance or content of those beliefs on the ground only that they are based on religious precepts. These are twin conditions of a free society.[51]

While acknowledging that 'the liturgy and practice of the established Church are to some extent prescribed by law', Laws LJ added 'but the conferment of any legal protection or preference upon a particular substantive moral position on the ground only that it is espoused by the adherents of a particular faith, however long its tradition, however rich its culture, is deeply unprincipled'.[52]

More recently, another sacred–secular boundary dispute generated much controversy when, in February 2012, the High Court in *NSS* v. *Bideford Town Council*[53] ruled against Bideford Town Council, holding that it was unconstitutional for councils to continue with the long-standing practice of holding prayers at the beginning of their meetings. Prayer, Ouseley J ruled, is a private matter that has no place in the formal proceedings of a legal assembly. This judgment attracted the comment from Britain's first Muslim cabinet minister 'that a militant secularisation is taking hold of our societies'.[54] She went on to claim that religion is being 'sidelined, marginalised and downgraded in the public sphere'. In response to the ruling, the government promptly introduced amending legislation with the effect that councils which want to continue holding formal prayers may now do so. This brief skirmish illustrates both the neutrality of the courts and the political reality of government support for the 'Established' Church.

---

[49] Ibid., at para. 26.   [50] Ibid., at para. 20.   [51] Ibid., at para. 22.
[52] Ibid., at para. 23.   [53] *NSS* v. *Bideford Town Council* [2012] EWHC 175 (Admin).
[54] See Baroness Warsi, minister without portfolio and chair of the Conservative Party, who used the term in response to the ruling of Ouseley J.

Equality of religions

The principle that the law must treat all religions equally has been firmly established since at least *Re Pinion (deceased)*,[55] when it was held that 'the court cannot discriminate between religions'. It was reiterated more recently by Laws J, in *McFarlane* above; when continuing his peroration against religious preferencing he advised that:

> The promulgation of law for the protection of a position held purely on religious grounds cannot therefore be justified. It is irrational, as preferring the subjective over the objective. But it is also divisive, capricious and arbitrary. We do not live in a society where all the people share uniform religious beliefs. The precepts of any one religion – any belief system – cannot, by force of their religious origins, sound any louder in the general law than the precepts of any other. If they did, those out in the cold would be less than citizens; and our constitution would be on the way to a theocracy.[56]

Religious organisations and the nonprofit sector

In addition to organisations that clearly proclaim their particular religious identity, others are permeated by and give effect to religious influences. Many of the United Kingdom's earliest charities were off-shoots of religious movements: some of the country's first schools were set up by faith groups, while religious charities provided health and social care before the welfare state existed. Indeed, religious communities have long protested that the metrics employed by government bodies fail to capture the full story with regard to faith-based charitable activity. It would probably not be an exaggeration to say that in this jurisdiction religious entities are the longest established, most numerous and wealthiest category of charity, and the one which continues to attract the proportionately largest share of total charitable donations.

Religious charities

The Charity Commission estimates that of the approximately 164,000 charities on its register, some 29,000 have declared aims that include advancing religion; a number that is growing as those previously

---

[55] *Re Pinion (deceased)* [1965] Ch. 85. Also see *Nelan* v. *Downes* (1917) 23 CLR 546.
[56] *McFarlane* v. *Relate Avon Ltd.* [2010] EWCA Civ 880; [2010] IRLR 872, *per* Laws LJ, at para. 24.

CHURCH, STATE AND RELIGIOUS CHARITIES

'excepted' are now required to register.[57] 'Excepted' charities are those with an annual income of less than £100,000, most of which are either: connected with certain churches and chapels belonging to various Christian denominations; charitable service funds of the armed forces; or are scout and guide groups. Their right to be 'excepted' from the requirement to register ceased in February 2009 and by 2012 most had been registered.

Many of the larger religious charities pursue their charitable purposes of advancing religion and relieving poverty overseas in the underdeveloped countries of Africa and Asia. Christian Aid, for example, has been engaged in both treating the effects and lobbying for action to change the causes of poverty for several decades. Religion has been ranked as the sixth most popular cause for individual donations, with 13 per cent of donors giving to religions amounting to 16 per cent of the total amount.[58]

Religious umbrella bodies

Religious umbrella bodies include: Caritas Social Action Network (CSAN), an umbrella organisation for charities with a Catholic ethos; Churches Together in Britain and Ireland (CTBI), the umbrella body for the Christian churches dealing with issues relevant to England, Scotland, Ireland and Wales; the Britain Yearly Meeting, which is the umbrella body for the Religious Society of Friends (Quakers); the League of British Muslims (LBM), an umbrella body providing support for Muslim voluntary and community groups nationwide; and the National Council of Hindu Temples UK (NCHT), a Hindu umbrella body linking over 200 Hindu temples and faith organisations across the United Kingdom.

Government funding: the sector and religious charities

The funding relationship between the nonprofit sector and the State has changed considerably in recent years. The 2012 edition of the *Voluntary Sector Almanac* notes that: 'income from statutory grants has declined

---

[57] See the Charity Commission, 'The Advancement of Religion for the Public Benefit' (Version: December 2008, as amended December 2011), at: www.charitycommission. gov.uk/detailed-guidance/charitable-purposes-and-public-benefit/charities-and-pub lic-benefit/the-advancement-of-religion-for-the-public-benefit/#sthash.k5fXlAvD.dpuf (accessed 3 January 2014).

[58] See Charities Aid Foundation, UK Giving 2011 (2011), at: www.cafonline.org/publica tions/2011-publications/uk-giving-2011.aspx (accessed 3 January 2014).

168 ENGLAND AND WALES

steadily from a peak of £5.3 billion in real terms in 2003/4 to £3 billion in 2009/10. At the same time, the decade saw a significant increase in contract income as voluntary organisations' role in public service delivery expanded, from £4.3 billion in 2000/1 to £10.9 billion in 2009/10.'[59] Whereas in 2001 less than 50 per cent of government funding to the sector came in the form of contracts rather than grants, by 2009/2010 this had risen to almost 80 per cent, indicating that government funding is becoming increasingly sharply focused.[60]

Government funding of religious charities: the policy

Religious charities and other faith-based organisations have always played a leading role in the provision of public benefit services, in developing countries[61] and on a domestic basis,[62] assisted by government grants or under government contracts. The latter has been the subject of considerable public policy debate in recent years. The government White Paper *Communities in Control: Real People, Real Power*, launched in July 2008 and one of a number of policy documents issued by various bodies, announced that:

> There are over 23,000 religious charities in the UK and many more faith-based organisations, involving tens of thousands of people motivated by their faith, working at a local and national level to provide support and services to communities. At times there has been reluctance on the part of local authorities and agencies to commission services from faith-based groups, in part because of some confusion about the propriety of doing so. Building on the Faithworks Charter,[63] we intend to work with faith communities to clarify the issues and to remove the barriers to commissioning services from faith-based groups.

---

[59] See, further, at www.ncvo-vol.org.uk (accessed 3 January 2014).

[60] Ibid. See also D. Brindle, 'The Worst is Yet to Come', *Guardian*, 18 February 2009.

[61] The Department for International Development (DfID), for example, gave £20.9 million to religious NGOs in 2008, compared with £17.4 million in 2003. Christian Aid, Islamic Relief, the international development charity Progressio and World Vision are among the religious charities currently receiving DfID funds.

[62] Figures produced to Parliament show that grants to faith-based groups from two government funding pots alone in 2010 amounted to £13 million.

[63] The Faithworks Charter comprises a set of 15 principles that commits signatory churches and Christian agencies to meet the needs of their local communities in a professional and trustworthy manner, consistent with the Christian ethos, when providing local public benefit services, including 'never imposing our Christian faith or belief on others'. See further at www.faithworks.info/about-us/faithworks-charter (accessed 3 January 2014).

Government funding of religious charities with discriminatory practices

In July 2008 the Secretary for the Communities and Local Government Department explained: 'I am concerned to ensure that if faith groups become involved, they do so on a proper footing – not by evangelising or proselytising, but by providing services in a non-discriminatory way to the whole community.'[64] The resulting increase in government service provision contracts going to local faith-based groups was demonstrated most graphically, with its attendant problems, in education.

At a cost of disrupting holistic local authority planning for community-based education, and probably exacerbating local social divisions, schooling is becoming more diversified, with most independent schools now being granted charitable status (82 per cent in 2010), of which the growth in the number of faith-based academies is particularly significant. According to the Department of Education, the 6,814 faith-based schools now constitute 34 per cent of the maintained sector, of which about 67 per cent are Church of England and 29 per cent are Catholic.[65] Whether structured as 'foundation or trust schools',[66] 'academies'[67] or 'free schools',[68] they most often: have charitable status; receive government grants of up to 90 per cent of the total cost towards capital costs of the buildings and 100 per cent of running costs (including teachers' salaries); and are allowed to impose faith restrictions on staff employment, admissions, curriculum content and on school worship.

---

[64] Explanation given in response to a question in the House of Commons following the introduction of the government White Paper *Communities in Control: Real People, Real Power*.

[65] See, further, at www.education.gov.uk/aboutdfe/foi/disclosuresaboutschools/a0065446/maintained-faith-schools (accessed 3 January 2014).

[66] Foundation schools are run by their own governing body, which employs the staff and sets the admissions criteria. Land and buildings are usually owned by the governing body or a charitable foundation. A trust school is a type of foundation school that forms a charitable trust with an outside partner – for example, a business or educational charity – aiming to raise standards and explore new ways of working. Established by the School Standards and Framework Act 1998 to replace grant maintained schools, as the name suggests these schools have charitable status but often also allow for private investment.

[67] Academies are schools judged to be 'outstanding', which, with official encouragement, have been allowed to break away from local authority control to seek independence with charitable status, sponsored by commerce or charity. These schools have more freedom over the curriculum but continue to be funded by the State.

[68] These are new-build, all-ability, independent but State-funded schools, set up in response to parental demand, which like academies have charitable status.

The considerable curriculum freedom coupled with independent governance arrangements and generous state funding has presented a significant growth opportunity for faith-based charities. The Academies Act 2010 has given all grant-maintained schools the right to unilaterally opt out of local authority control and become academies, and the Church of England[69] alone estimates that 70 per cent (3,360) of its 4,800 State schools will have done so within the next five years.[70]

Some faith schools see their mission as the transference of religious belief and culture from one generation to another, and have closed admission procedures with the majority of places allocated to those from their own faith community. In autumn 2006, religious bodies overturned government plans to oblige faith schools to reserve up to 25 per cent of school places for pupils with other or no faith, where there is local demand. Moreover, late amendments to the Education and Inspections Act 2006 allowed voluntary-controlled faith schools, although fully funded by the local authority, to stipulate the religious belief of employees, including support staff, and to do the same for headship applicants. In short, government-funded, faith-based schools permit an extensive range of discriminatory practices: preferential treatment in terms of funding to become established; permission to discriminate in pupil admissions and staffing; a teaching curriculum skewed in favour of religious belief; and a corresponding alignment of social values in regard to issues such as gay marriage, abortion, etc.

Charity law and the regulatory framework

The Charity Commission, rather than the Revenue, has long been the lead regulatory body for charity in England and Wales. This fact, together with complex institutional links between government and the

---

[69] See the *Chadwick Report* published by the Church of England (March 2012). It outlines as a 'key premise that applies equally to children of the faith, of other faiths and of no faith' that (somewhat presumptively) the schools would 'work towards every child and young person having a life-enhancing encounter with the Christian faith and the person of Jesus Christ'.

[70] See, e.g. T. Judt, *The Memory Chalet*, Penguin Press, London, 2010, at p.144, where he comments:

> Successive education ministers have authorised and encouraged 'academies' – furtively introducing (with the help of private money) the very process of selection of whose abolition on egalitarian grounds they once so proudly boasted.

CHARITY LAW AND THE REGULATORY FRAMEWORK   171

nonprofit sector, already provided a quite distinctive environment for the operation of charity law. Against that background the Charities Act 2006, now the Charities Act 2011, introduced significant changes to established common law definitions and rules, which further distanced this jurisdiction from all others presently being considered. In particular, the reversal of the public benefit presumption and its replacement with a mandatory statutory public benefit requirement, even in respect of the advancement of religion, constituted a step change in charity law and a challenge to all other common law jurisdictions. The extension to the *Pemsel* heads of charitable purposes,[71] combined with their transfer from a common law to a statutory context thereby making them amenable to government amendment, was itself a fundamental change.

Legislation

The separation of tax and charity regulatory systems, each governed by its own specific legislation, is an established and distinctive characteristic of the law relating to charity in this jurisdiction. That law functions in tandem with the rights guaranteed by the European Convention on Human Rights,[72] as applied within the jurisdiction by the Human Rights Act 1998.[73] Also relevant is the International Covenant on Civil and Political Rights (ICCPR), which the government ratified in 1976, with certain reservations and declarations.

For present purposes, the influence of Article 9 of the European Convention and the protections against religious discrimination introduced by the Employment Equality (Religion or Belief) Regulations 2003, and now provided by the Equality Act 2010, bring an added significance. Under s.3 of the Human Rights Act 1998, as has been rightly pointed out, 'it is incumbent on domestic courts to construe domestic laws compatibly with Convention rights, and therefore the same (or at least no less favourable) approach must be adopted to the concept of religion and belief'.[74]

---

[71] See *Income Tax Special Purposes Commissioners* v. *Pemsel* [1891] AC 531.

[72] Specifically: Article 9(1); Article 14; and Article 2 of Protocol No. 1 (see, further, Chapter 4).

[73] For a review of the compatibility of the Human Rights Act 1998 and the Charities Act 2006, see B. Bromley, 'Submission to the Charity Commission: Consultation on Draft Public Benefit Guidance', June 2007, at: http://beneficgroup.com/paperpres.php (accessed 3 January 2014).

[74] See *Eweida* v. *British Airways plc* [2009] ICR 303, *per* Elias P, at para. 27.

The charity regulator

For more than 150 years the Charity Commission has functioned as lead regulator, its Commissioners being statutorily entrusted, as restated in the 1993 Act and more recently in the 2011 Act, with the duty of 'promoting the effective use of charitable resources'.[75] The Commission is vested with the statutory authority to determine charitable status and it maintains a register of all charities which provides the basis for supervising and holding to account all organisations so registered.

Charity law

The Charities Act 2011, which came into effect on 14 March 2012 (replacing most of the Charities Acts 1992, 1993 and 2006, and all of the Recreational Charities Act 1958), provides the current relevant statutory framework. Section 2, under the heading 'Meaning of charity', states that 'for the purposes of the law of England and Wales, "charity" means an institution which: (a) is established for charitable purposes only, and (b) falls to be subject to the control of the High Court in the exercise of its jurisdiction in respect of charities.' The Companies Acts of 1985, 1989 and 2006 are also relevant.

The common law

The core, traditional, common law requirements that an entity must be confined exclusively to charitable purposes, be for the public benefit, be independent, non-profit-distributing and non-political (see Chapter 2), continue in force but are now vested with statutory authority.

Charity law reform

The process of charity law reform in England and Wales[76] concluded with some important adjustments to the regulatory framework but, for present purposes, the more significant changes were those made to certain core definitional matters. In the main, these have taken the form of a reworking of the public benefit test, an expanded list of charitable purposes and their encoding in legislation.

---

[75] Section 14(4) of the Charities Act 2011.
[76] Concluded with the introduction of the Charities Act 2006 as consolidated in the Charities Act 2011.

CHARITY LAW AND THE REGULATORY FRAMEWORK   173

The reforms: public benefit

The Charities Act 2006 reversed the public benefit presumption traditionally granted to the first three *Pemsel* heads[77] to give the public benefit
test an unequivocal mandatory application in respect of all charitable
purposes in England and Wales; a reversal with potentially important
implications for the Commission's role. As declared in what is now s.4 of
the 2011 Act:

> (3) In determining whether that requirement is satisfied in relation to any
> such purpose, it is not to be presumed that a purpose of a particular
> description is for the public benefit.

This provision explicitly states what is perhaps the most important
change to be made in charity law in many decades: all purposes identified
in the 2011 Act or otherwise hitherto recognised in the common law as
charitable, will only be so if in addition they can also be shown to satisfy
the public benefit test. It is possible that organisations with purposes
which for generations have been commonly regarded as charitable, such
as those for the advancement of religion,[78] may in future be found not to
be for the public benefit and therefore not charitable.

The reforms: charitable purposes

The Charities Act 2006 introduced a new set of '*Pemsel*-plus' purposes,
which together with the existing four *Pemsel* heads now constitute the
full complement of purposes defined as charitable under the 2011 Act.
While these largely give statutory recognition to those already judicially
established as charitable, many are central to government's new partnership agenda with charity, thereby giving a clear message that government
will encourage organisations to become established in these areas and

---

[77] It should be noted that on introducing the 2006 Bill in the House of Commons the then
Minister for the Cabinet Office assured the House that 'The Bill preserves the existing
law on the definition and test of public benefit' (Hansard, 26 June 2006; Vol. 448, c.
24–25). However, the new statutory test in fact proved to be radically different from the
established common law interpretation. All three UK jurisdictions and Ireland have
modified this common law test by introducing statutory rules to guide interpretation
and provide powers for further guidance to be supplied by the regulator.

[78] The presumption in English law that gifts for the advancement of religion satisfy the
public benefit test probably dates from the decision in *Morice* v. *The Bishop of Durham*
(1804) 9 Ves 405, when Lord Eldon made a finding which in effect over-ruled the
decision of Thurlow LJ in *Brown* v. *Yeall* 7 Ves 59 which rejected as charitable trusts
providing for the distribution of religious books.

they will be rewarded with charitable status and tax exemption. Of even greater significance is the fact that all charitable purposes are now placed on the statute book, thereby enabling any future government to swiftly and directly delete, adjust or add charitable purposes by simply amending the legislation.

Post reform: the public benefit test and religious organisations

The reversal of the public benefit presumption as a determinant of the charitable status of religious organisations has been and continues to be contentious:[79] many questioned what seemed to be a reductionist approach whereby religion was viewed purely in secular terms, its social worth left to be treated the same as any other 'charitable purpose' and measured against the common benchmark of public benefit, thereby elevating the significance of public benefit to the corresponding diminution of religious values. Others considered it to be verging on the heretical that judiciary or regulators should be empowered or required to question the bona fides of traditional religious organisations that have survived and flourished for centuries, venerated by adherents who unquestionably accepted their public benefit. Under the Charities Act 2011, all who seek charitable status for their purpose must now satisfy the test by argument and proof, even if that purpose is listed in the Act as prima facie charitable.[80]

The test

In its published guidance, the Charity Commission explains the two key principles of the public benefit test: (1) there must be an identifiable benefit or benefits; and (2) that benefit must be to the public, or a section of the public.[81] The first has the following requirements: it must be clear what the benefits are; the benefits must be related to the aims; and the

---

[79] Harding, for example, has argued that incorporating a positive public benefit test for charitable status could violate the right to manifest religion pursuant to Article 9 of the Convention. See also B. Bromley and K. Chan, 'Submission to the House of Lords Joint Committee on the Draft Charities Bill', June 2004, at: http://beneficgroup.com/paper-pres.php

[80] Charities Act 2011, ss.4(1) and 4(2). Note that the Charity Commission undertook 20 public benefit assessments between 2009 and 2011.

[81] See the Charity Commission for England and Wales, *The Advancement of Religion for the Public Benefit*.

benefits must be balanced against any detriment or harm. The second requires that: the beneficiaries are appropriate to the aims; and where benefit is to a section of the public, the opportunity to benefit must not be unreasonably limited by geographical or other restrictions; people in poverty must not be excluded from the opportunity to benefit; and any private benefits must be incidental.[82]

Public

The 'public' dimension of the test must be satisfied: it is not sufficient that an organisation is established solely for the benefit of the followers or adherents of a religion; there must also be benefit to the wider public or a section of the public.

In this jurisdiction the established view of the judiciary and regulators has been that religious practices cannot be private or limited to a private class of individuals or not extend to the public more generally.[83] In particular, closed religious orders have been denied charitable status. The traditional interpretation of this test,[84] illustrated by the Court of Appeal decision in *R* v. *Registrar General, ex p Segerdal*[85] when the 'chapel' used by the Scientology movement was held not to be a place of worship, has been continued by the 2011 Act. However, the Charity Commission acknowledges that reasonable restrictions may be permissible:

> where the class of people who can benefit is sufficiently wide or open in nature (given the charitable objects to be carried out and the resources available to the charity) to constitute a sufficient section of the public; or because the class of people whom the aims are intended to benefit have a particular charitable need which justifies restricting the benefits to them; or where there are restrictions on the class of people who may be followers or adherents of the religion but the wider public benefits from

---

[82] Ibid., at para. E3. Note that in response to the tribunal's ruling, the Charity Commission issued revised guidance in September 2013. See, further, at: www.charitycommission.gov.uk/ detailed-guidance/charitable-purposes-and-public-benefit (accessed 3 January 2014).

[83] As Wrenbury LJ explained in *Verge* v. *Somerville* [1924] AC 496, at p.499:

> a first enquiry must be made whether it is public ... whether it is for the benefit of the community or an appreciably important class of the community.

[84] See the Charity Commission for England and Wales, *Analysis of the Law Underpinning the Advancement of Religion for the Public Benefit* (2008). See, further, at: www.charitycommission.gov.uk/media/94857/lawrel1208.pdf (accessed 3 January 2014).

[85] *R* v. *Registrar General, ex p Segerdal* [1970] 2 QB 697.

176 ENGLAND AND WALES

the positive behaviours of the followers or adherents promoted by the doctrines of that religion.[86]

The latter caveat would seem to allude to the decision in *Neville Estates Ltd.* v. *Madden*,[87] when Cross J was prepared to confirm the charitable status of a Jewish synagogue that was not open to members of the general public, on the basis that 'some benefit accrues to the public from the attendance at places of worship of persons who live in this world and mix with their fellow citizens'.[88] This approach allows a religious organisation to simultaneously restrict its activities to its own adherents and to satisfy the test by claiming that the wider public will thereby benefit from both the fact that religious beliefs are being practised and by the edification which may flow from that practice into the wider community (unlike the practice of such beliefs by a closed order) and teach people to behave better. Arguably it is an interpretation that would seem to elide the need for the test to include any extraneous objective measures.

Recently, in the leading case of *Gallagher* v. *Church of Jesus Christ of Latter-Day Saints*,[89] the House of Lords considered whether the Temple of the Mormon Church in the Borough of Chorley in Lancashire was a hereditament that could be defined as a 'place of public religious worship' such as to qualify for charitable exemption from rates under the Local Government Finance Act 1988. The premises were not open to the public, and not even open to all Mormons, as a right of entry was reserved to those members who had acquired a 'recommend' from their bishop. The court considered itself bound by an earlier decision of the House[90] when it held that the Mormon Temple at Godstone was not exempt from rates as a 'place of public religious worship' because the term could not apply to such places from which the public was excluded. It also considered and dismissed a claim that to deny exemption would

---

[86] See the Charity Commission for England and Wales, *The Advancement of Religion for the Public Benefit*, at para. E3.

[87] *Neville Estates Ltd.* v. *Madden* [1962] 1 Ch. 832.

[88] Ibid., 853 (Cross J). See further, A. Iwobi, 'Out With the Old, in With the New: Religion, Charitable Status and the Charities Act 2006' (2009) 29 *Legal Studies* 619, at p.635–636, citing T. Haddock, 'Charitable Trusts for the Advancement of Religion: Judicial Rejection of Metaphysical Benefits and the Emergence of Public Interaction' (2001) 7 *Charity Law and Practice Review* 151, at p.152.

[89] *Gallagher* v. *Church of Jesus Christ of Latter-Day Saints* [2008] 1 WLR 1852, 1867 [51].

[90] *Church of Jesus Christ of Latter-Day Saints* v. *Henning (Valuation Officer)* [1964] AC 420. See also, *Broxtowe Borough Council* v. *Birch* [1983] 1 WLR 314, where buildings used for religious worship by the Exclusive Brethren were similarly not entitled to the exemption.

be to discriminate against the Church on the grounds of religion (see below). Nor could a claim be sustained that the Temple was entitled to exemption on the ground that its use was ancillary to the use of other buildings which were so entitled because, as Lord Denning MR had said 40 years earlier:

> The short answer is that this temple is not a church hall, chapel hall nor a similar building. It is not in the least on the same footing as a church hall or chapel hall. It is a very sacred sanctuary, quite different from a building of that category.[91]

In a more recent and not dissimilar case, the Charity Commission refused to accept an application by the Preston Down Trust to be registered as a charity as it was unconvinced that the Trust was established for the advancement of religion for public benefit.[92] The Plymouth Brethren, to which the Trust belonged, is a religious group, established in 1828, which had been a registered charity for 50 years, with about 16,000 adherents. Far from being a closed sect, this organisation welcomed the public to participate in its activities and undertook a wide programme of community-based public benefit activities. Unlike its approach in *ex p Segerdal*, the Commission considered that it was not bound by an earlier court ruling.[93] Its key concern appeared to be openness; that is, that non-Brethren members of the public might not be able to participate in their services. It questioned whether a notice board identifying the Preston Down Trust's meeting hall as a public place of worship, with contact details, 'is sufficient to demonstrate meaningful access to participate in public worship'. The Commission expressed 'concerns about the lack of public access to participation in ... Holy Communion'. It also commented on the beneficial impact of the Preston Down Trust, saying that it is 'perhaps more limited than other Christian organisations as their adherence limits their engagement with the wider public' and that 'the evidence in relation to any beneficial impact on the wider public is perhaps marginal and insufficient to satisfy us as to the benefit of the

---

[91] *Henning (Valuation Officer)* v. *Church of Jesus Christ of Latter-Day Saints* [1962] 1 WLR 1091, at p.1099.

[92] *Preston Down Trust (Exclusive Plymouth Brethren)* v. *Charity Commission for England & Wales*, June 2012.

[93] See *Holmes* v. *Attorney-General* [1981], when the High Court ruled that the Plymouth Brethren's Kingston Meeting Rooms Trust was a valid charitable trust, despite the Brethren's well-known 'separatist distinctives'.

community'. This is the first time that charitable status has been refused to a religious group since the introduction of the Charities Act 2006, which reversed the public benefit test. The outcome of the appeal, listed for hearing by the First-tier Tribunal, may well have implications for many religious organisations registered as charities before the Charities Act 2006 took effect.

In the meantime, the Supreme Court entered the fray with its ruling in *R (on the application of Hodkin and another)* v. *Registrar General of Births, Deaths and Marriages*.[94] It then unanimously decided that a Scientologist chapel is 'a place of meeting for religious worship' for the purposes of s.2 of the Places of Worship Registration Act 1855 (the same legislative provision, appellants and grounds of appeal that had featured in *Segerdal*) and may therefore be licensed for the solemnisation of marriages. The differentiating factor for the Supreme Court was the absence in contemporary law of the requirement in *Segerdal* for 'religious worship' to include an object of veneration if the appellants were to qualify as a religious organization. It also accepted evidence from the organization that 'all congregational services are open to the public'.[95] The form of words 'place of meeting for religious worship' was no longer to be interpreted as 'a place for the worship of God . . . I am sure that would be the meaning attached by those who framed this legislation of 1855' as Denning LJ had then asserted.[96] Instead, in a finding that will have significant future consequences for the law relating to religion and to religious charities, the court held that the phrase 'has to be interpreted in accordance with contemporary understanding of religion and not by reference to the culture of 1855'.[97] To recognise Scientology as a religion (see, further, below) but to then deny its chapel registration as a place of worship would be 'illogical, discriminatory and unjust'.[98] It is hard to see how the decision in *Preston Down Trust* can survive this Supreme Court ruling.

---

[94] *R (on the application of Hodkin and another)* v. *Registrar General of Births, Deaths and Marriages* [2013] UKSC 77.

[95] Ibid., at para. 18.

[96] *R* v. *Registrar General, ex p Segerdal* [1970] 2 QB 697, *per* Denning LJ, at p.707.

[97] *R (on the application of Hodkin and another)* v. *Registrar General of Births, Deaths and Marriages* [2013] UKSC 77, *per* Toulson LJ, at para. 34. Citing in support the judgment of Adams CJ in *Malnak* v. *Yogi* 592 F.2d 197 (1979) and *Church of the New Faith* v. *Comr of Pay-Roll Tax (Victoria)* (1983) 154 CLR.

[98] *R (on the application of Hodkin and another)* v. *Registrar General of Births, Deaths and Marriages* [2013] UKSC 77, *per* Toulson LJ, at para. 64.

Benefit

Proving the public benefit of a religious organisation is an exercise to be undertaken in accordance with the statutory guidance issued by the Charity Commission, which requires that 'the benefits to the public should be capable of being recognised, identified, defined or described', though not necessarily capable of being quantified, and the Commission is willing in principle to consider intangible benefits.[99] It is now clear, however, from the decision in *R (Independent Schools Council)* v. *Charity Commission for England and Wales*,[100] that a trust excluding the poor from benefit cannot be a charity. The tribunal then held that while the Charity Commission was correct to so rule, it had been mistaken to find that this required 'reasonable' provision to be made for the poor. This was a matter best left to the trustees' discretion, subject only to the proviso that any provision made must be 'beyond the merely de minimis or token'.[101] It also warned that trustees 'need to consider the question of access ... and how to treat all their potential beneficiaries fairly'.[102]

Detriment

Although the 2011 Act does not expressly mention the concept of 'detriment' (introduced in equivalent Scottish legislation), the Charity Commission, when assessing the public benefit of a charity, including one for the advancement of religion, will consider any evidence of significant detrimental or harmful effects that arise, or may do so, from the charity carrying out its aims.[103] In so doing, the Commission advises that it will take into account 'public opinion where there are objective and informed public concerns about, or evidence that, the beliefs or practices of an organisation advancing religion causes detriment or harm'.[104]

---

[99] See the Charity Commission for England and Wales, *The Advancement of Religion for the Public Benefit*, at para. D2. Also see revised guidance issued in September 2013 at: www.charitycommission.gov.uk/detailed-guidance/charitable-purposes-and-public-benefit (accessed 3 January 2014).

[100] *R (Independent Schools Council)* v. *Charity Commission for England and Wales* [2012] Ch. 214, 269–275 [162]–[186].

[101] Ibid., 288 [233]. See also at 287 [230].

[102] *Independent Schools Council* [2012] Ch. 214, 283 [218].

[103] See, further, at: www.charitycommission.gov.uk/search/?q=detriment+principle (accessed 3 January 2014).

[104] See the Charity Commission for England and Wales, *The Advancement of Religion for the Public Benefit*.

As Briggs J has explained, 'an organisation which proposes to fulfil a purpose for the public benefit will only qualify as a charity if, taking into account any dis-benefit arising from its modus operandi, its activities nonetheless yield a net public benefit'.[105] The Charity Commission points out that the conduct of religious groups might meet the definition of detriment – for example 'the current charitable status of Christian Scientists and Jehovah's Witnesses might be ... compromised by their absolute refusal to allow blood transfusions even for a child in a life-threatening situation'.

Religion, religious beliefs and the advancement of religion

The Charities Act 2011 sought, among other objectives, to align charity law with the requirements of the Human Rights Act 1998. This included ensuring that human rights principles and standards were sufficiently incorporated into charity law to address the inequities and discrimination that had sometimes seemed to characterise the treatment of non-Judeo Christian religious organisations. The 2011 Act, however, goes a step further and, arguably, a step away from the definition of religion which, hitherto, this jurisdiction had shared with other common law nations, by extending that definition to accommodate non-theistic and philosophical beliefs. Moreover, whereas in the past a person could be construed as having a religious belief by the mere fact of their belonging to an organisation with an established commitment to such beliefs, in future the authenticity of an individual's beliefs, judged in accordance with basic threshold requirements, would be crucial.

Religion

The Charities Act 2011, s.3(2), now states that 'religion' includes: 'a religion which involves a belief in more than one god, and; a religion which does not involve a belief in a god'. When considering whether or not a system of belief constitutes a religion for the purposes of charity law, the Charity Commission has identified certain key characteristics such as:

> belief in a god (or gods) or goddess (or goddesses), or supreme being, or divine or transcendental being or entity or spiritual principle ('supreme being or entity') which is the object or focus of the religion;

[105] See *Catholic Care (Diocese of Leeds)* v. *the Charity Commission for England and Wales and the Equality and Human Rights Commission* [2010] EWHC 520 (Ch), 17 March 2010, *per* Briggs J, at para. 97.

THE ADVANCEMENT OF RELIGION

a relationship between the believer and the supreme being or entity by showing worship of, reverence for or veneration of the supreme being or entity;

a degree of cogency, cohesion, seriousness and importance; and an identifiable positive, beneficial, moral or ethical framework.[106]

However, as Toulson LJ recently noted 'ideas about the nature of God are the stuff of theological debate' and therefore are not readily justiciable.[107] He did, however, go on to offer the following guidance:

> I would describe religion in summary as a spiritual or non-secular belief system, held by a group of adherents, which claims to explain mankind's place in the universe and relationship with the infinite, and to teach its adherents how they are to live their lives in conformity with the spiritual understanding associated with the belief system. By spiritual or non-secular I mean a belief system which goes beyond that which can be perceived by the senses or ascertained by the application of science. I prefer not to use the word 'supernatural' to express this element because it is a loaded word which can carry a variety of connotations. Such a belief system may or may not involve belief in a supreme being, but it does involve a belief that there is more to be understood about mankind's nature and relationship to the universe than can be gained from the senses or from science.[108]

Belief in a Supreme Being

The basic indices, traditionally employed by the judiciary to differentiate a religious body from other bodies, have been a belief in a 'Supreme Being' together with a shared commitment to faith and worship[109] (see Chapter 2). The necessity for the first was emphasised in the judgment of the House of Lords in *Bowman* v. *Secular Society*.[110] This approach was adopted by the Charity Commission as illustrated in its rejection of charitable status for the Church of Scientology[111] but acceptance for the Druid

---

[106] See the Charity Commission, *The Advancement of Religion for the Public Benefit*.

[107] See *R (on the application of Hodkin and another)* v. *Registrar General of Births, Deaths and Marriages* [2013] UKSC 77, *per* Toulson LJ, at para. 52.

[108] Ibid., at para. 57.

[109] See the Charity Commission, *Analysis of the Law Underpinning Public Benefit and the Advancement of Religion*, February 2008, at para. 2.14.

[110] *Bowman* v. *Secular Society* [1917] AC 406.

[111] See *Church of Scientology of California* v. *Customs and Excise Comms.* [1980] CMLR 114; [1979] STC 297; [1979] TR 59; affd [1981] 1 All ER 1035; [1981] STC 65, C.a. See also the decision of the Charity Commission on the application for registration as a charity by the Church of Scientology, 17 November 1999. See, further, at: www. charitycommission.gov.uk/media/100909/cosfulldoc.pdf (accessed 3 January 2014).

Network.[112] The decision in the first case was accompanied by an explanation that belief in a Supreme Being remains a necessary characteristic of religion and that Scientology could not be defined as a religion for the purpose of charity law as it provides 'no legally recognised benefit to the public in terms of the advancement of a religion or spiritual welfare'. In the second, the Commission decided that the combination of Druid belief in a Supreme Being, its rationale for connecting with 'sacred nature', its emphasis on the importance of ancestors, cultural heritage and the natural environment and its common elements of worship and their integration into an ethical and moral system were a sufficient demonstration of an 'identifiable positive, beneficial, moral or ethical framework' to qualify for charitable status.

Worship, religious tenets, doctrines, etc.

Traditionally, courts and regulators, in their interpretation of what constitutes a 'religion', have required evidence of worship. This component, as noted by Dillon J in *South Place Ethical Society*,[113] has been held to comprise submission to the object worshipped, veneration of that object, praise, thanksgiving, prayer or intercession. In that case, an association whose members advocated a humanistic philosophical concept concerning the excellence of trust, love and beauty, to the exclusion of anything supernatural, was deemed not to be a religion for *Pemsel* purposes. The members were agnostics, cultivating a 'rational religious sentiment'.

In recent years a more relaxed approach has been taken towards this requirement, although where a doctrinal dispute arises then the court will take note of the differences, not for the purpose of adjudicating on the respective religious merits[114] of the parties concerned but simply to determine whether the differences constitute a re-defining of the former religious organisation.[115] Otherwise, it is clear that courts and regulators

---

[112] See *The Druid Network* [2010] Ch. Comm Decision (21 September 2010).

[113] *South Place Ethical Society* [1980] 1 WLR 1565; (1980) 124 SJ 774; [1980] 3 All ER 918, at p.1573A. The association was ultimately held to be a charity under the education and 'other public benefit' heads.

[114] *HH Sant Baba Jeet Singh Ji Maharaj* v. *Eastern Media Group Limited and Hardeep Singh* [2010] EWHC (QB) 1294 (17 May 2010): an action for defamation was stayed by the High Court because of 'the well-known principle of English law to the effect that the courts will not attempt to rule upon doctrinal issues or intervene in the regulation or governance of religious groups'.

[115] See, for example, *Dean* v. *Burne* [2009] EWHC 1250 (Ch).

THE ADVANCEMENT OF RELIGION   183

have moved away from examining institutional structures or referencing doctrines and tenets, which were the customary indicators for defining an 'organised religion', while also shifting their focus from religion as an institution to the authenticity of an individual's subjective interpretation and experience of it.[116]

Philosophy and other value systems

The 2011 Act accommodates non-theistic beliefs in the definition of 'religion', thereby ending the requirement for a Supreme Being, over-ruling the decision in *Bowman*[117] and also negating Lord Denning's reservations regarding Scientology that it 'seems to be more a philosophy of the existence of man or of life, rather than a religion'.[118]

The ground for this development had, however, been well prepared by earlier judicial[119] and Charity Commission decisions.[120] Indeed, the judgment of the ECtHR in *Campbell and Cosans* v. *United Kingdom*[121] some decades earlier had served notice that non-theistic beliefs would be human rights compliant when it ruled in favour of complainants who alleged that the system of corporal punishment in Scottish State schools offended their philosophical convictions under Article 2 of the First Protocol of the ECHR. This interpretation was endorsed by the Employment Equality (Religion or Belief) Regulations 2003, which made provision for a philosophical belief to have a similar weight and significance as a religious belief in the context of human rights jurisprudence. Adopting such an approach, and in recognition of an evolving interpretation of religion, the Charity Commission had examined faith healing and spiritualism and deemed them to be charitable when open to members of the public.[122] For example, it examined the standing of spiritualism in a charity law context when it gave consideration to an application from the Sacred Hands Spiritual Centre for registration as a

---

[116] See P. W. Edge, 'Determining Religion in English Courts' (2012) *Oxford Journal of Law and Religion*, doi: 10.1093/ojlr/rwr005.

[117] *Bowman* v. *Secular Society* [1917] AC 406.

[118] *R* v. *Registrar General; Ex parte Segerdal* [1970] 1 QB 430, *per* Denning LJ, at p.707.

[119] Note the judgment in *Arrowsmith* v. *United Kingdom* [1978] 3 EHRR 218.

[120] Ibid., at para. 69, where the Commission was of the opinion that pacifism is a philosophy.

[121] *Campbell and Cosans* v. *United Kingdom* [1982] 4 EHRR 293.

[122] *Funnell* v. *Stewart* (1996) 1 WLR 288. Contrary to the more traditional approach in *Re Hummeltenberg* [1923] 1 Ch. 237 and *Bowman* v. *Secular Society Ltd.* [1917] AC 406.

charity.[123] The Commission concluded that Sacred Hands would satisfy the criteria applicable to the charitable purpose of advancement of religion with its proposed objects. Shortly afterwards, Walker LJ in *Willamson*[124] felt able to confidently assert that 'pacifism, vegetarianism and total abstinence from alcohol are uncontroversial examples of beliefs which would fall within Article 9 (of course pacifism or any comparable belief may be based on religious convictions, equally it may be based on ethical convictions which are not religious but humanist)'.[125] Following the introduction of definitional change in the 2006 Act, a number of cases further explored the range of beliefs that could now qualify for charitable status alongside the traditional religious bodies. In *Grainger* v. *Nicholson*,[126] for example, the Employment Appeal Tribunal considered whether the appellant Mr Nicholson's allegedly strongly held philosophical belief about climate change and the alleged morality thereof (that carbon emissions must be urgently cut to avoid catastrophic climate change) were capable of constituting a philosophical belief within the meaning of paragraph 2(1) of the 2003 Regulations, which states that '"belief" means any religious or philosophical belief'. The tribunal found that 'the claimant has settled views about climate change, and acts upon those views in the way in which he leads his life ... his belief goes beyond mere opinion'.[127] Within a year other tribunals had applied this test to extend recognition to a range of belief systems, such as anti-fox hunting[128] and a belief in the higher purpose of public service broadcasting.[129] However, a limit of sorts was reached when an employment tribunal rejected a claim that wearing a poppy in commemoration of the sacrifices made by the British armed forces military personnel constituted a philosophical belief deserving protection under the Equality Act 2010.[130] The tribunal took the view that 'the belief that one should wear a poppy to show respect to servicemen, however admirable ... seems to lack the characteristics of cogency, cohesion and importance'.

---

[123] See Charity Commission, 'Decision to Register Sacred Hands Spiritual Centre as a Charity', 9 May 2003. This was a review of the decision on 24 July 2001 which rejected an application for registration.

[124] *R (Williamson)* v. *Secretary of State for Education and Employment* [2005] 2 AC 246.

[125] Ibid., at para. 55.   [126] *Grainger* v. *Nicholson* [2009] UKEAT 0219 09 0311 (EAT).

[127] Ibid., at para. 13.

[128] See *Hashman* v. *Milton Park (Dorset) Ltd. (t/a Orchard Park)* ET/3105555/09.

[129] See *Maistry* v. *BBC* ET/1313142/10.

[130] See *Lisk* v. *Shield Guardian Co. Ltd.* ET/3300873/11.

THE ADVANCEMENT OF RELIGION   185

In October 2011, the Commission registered the British Humanist Association as a charity, thereby recognising as charitable the Association's aim to pursue the 'advancement of humanism, namely a non-religious ethical life stance, the essential elements of which are a commitment to human wellbeing and a reliance on reason, experience and a naturalistic view of the world'.[131] Then, in December 2013 the Supreme Court in a landmark ruling[132] revisited the decision in *Segerdal*[133] and reversed its effect to determine that Scientology was indeed a religion. In coming to this conclusion the court accepted uncontested evidence from Scientology representatives that 'Scientology involves belief in and worship of a supernatural power, also known as God, the Supreme Being or the Creator'; and held that 'it bears some similarity to Buddhism'.[134] The court made the finding that:[135]

> religion should not be confined to religions which recognise a supreme deity. First and foremost, to do so would be a form of religious discrimination unacceptable in today's society. It would exclude Buddhism, along with other faiths such as Jainism, Taoism, Theosophy and part of Hinduism.

Religious and philosophical beliefs

For charity law the evidential challenges involved in establishing the existence of religious or philosophical beliefs are considerable. In at least two areas there are obvious difficulties: in ascertaining whether the views or convictions constitute religious or philosophical beliefs; and in determining whether or not professed beliefs are actually genuinely held.

Religious beliefs

As Nicholls LJ observed in *Ex parte Williamson*,[136] a case determined by the House of Lords, immediately preceding the introduction of the 2006 Act:

---

[131] See, further, at: https://humanism.org.uk/humanism (accessed 3 January 2014).

[132] *R (on the application of Hodkin and another)* v. *Registrar General of Births, Deaths and Marriages* [2013] UKSC 77.

[133] See *R* v. *Registrar General, ex parte Segerdal* [1970] 2 QB 697.

[134] Ibid., at para. 16.

[135] *R (on the application of Hodkin and another)* v. *Registrar General of Births, Deaths and Marriages* [2013] UKSC 77, *per* Toulson LJ, at para. 51.

[136] *Ex parte Williamson* [2005] UKHL 15; [2005] 2 AC 246 (HL), at para. 75. An approach very much in keeping with the views expressed by Lord Greene MR in *Re Samuel* [1942] 1 Ch. 1, CA, at p.17.

186 ENGLAND AND WALES

> Typically, religion involves belief in the supernatural. It is not always susceptible to lucid exposition or, still less, rational justification. The language used is often the language of allegory, symbol and metaphor.[137]

This was a case which concerned a number of schools collectively seeking to be exempted from the statutory ban on the use of corporal punishment on the grounds that the claimants represented a large body of the Christian community whose fundamental beliefs included the use of such punishment on behalf of parents.[138] Notwithstanding the challenge posed by the above observation, where adherents profess a shared belief or beliefs of central importance to their sense of collective identity, this calls for some examination. It is permissible and necessary for the court or regulator to enquire into the basis for it and whether it is held in good faith without going as far as to assess its validity.[139] As Baroness Hale warned:

> The court is not required to consider the nature of religion, still less is it required to consider whether a particular belief is soundly based in religious texts. The court's concern is with what the belief is, whether it is sincerely held, and whether it qualifies for protection under the Convention.

Walker LJ, while noting the difficulty involved in defining religion, expressed the view that this was not of central importance as 'it is not in dispute that Christianity is a religion and that the appellants are sincere, practicing, Christians'.[140] What was of central importance, in the opinion of Nicholls LJ, in any case where the genuineness of a claimant's professed belief was at issue, was whether:

> an assertion of religious belief is made in good faith: 'neither fictitious, nor capricious, and that it is not an artifice'.[141] . . . But, emphatically, it is not for the court to embark on an enquiry into the asserted belief and judge its 'validity' by some objective standard such as the source material

---

[137] Ibid., at para. 23.
[138] See also *Campbell and Cosans* v. *United Kingdom* [1982] 4 EHRR 293, where the complainants were successful in their claim that the system of corporal punishment in Scottish State schools offended their philosophical convictions under Article 2 of Protocol No. 1 of the ECHR.
[139] *R (Williamson)* v. *Secretary of State for Education and Employment* [2005] 2 AC 246, where the shared belief was that of teachers and parents in independent private schools who supported corporal punishment.
[140] Ibid., at para. 56.
[141] Citing Iacobucci J in *Syndicat Northcrest* v. *Amselem* (2004) 241 DLR (4th) 1, 27, at para. 52.

upon which the claimant founds his belief or the orthodox teaching of the religion in question or the extent to which the claimant's belief conforms to or differs from the views of others professing the same religion. Freedom of religion protects the subjective belief of an individual.[142]

These and other judicial views expressed in this landmark case have set standards for regulators and courts. Indeed, in the following year the House of Lords in *Begum*[143] considered the wish of a schoolgirl to wear the jilbab in keeping with the professed religious beliefs of herself and her family, despite the prohibition on doing so in the school dress code. The court heard evidence that the wearing of the jilbab was not considered necessary by a large proportion of those who shared the plaintiff's religious beliefs, but nonetheless upheld her right to consider it to be so. Lord Bingham of Cornhill added that 'it was not the less a religious belief because her belief may have changed, as it probably did, or because it was a belief shared by a small minority of people'.[144] The court found that wearing the jilbab is associated with a particular variant of Muslim religious beliefs and that the claimant genuinely adhered to that belief (before going on to rule that, nonetheless, in the interests of proportionality, her right in this instance could be interfered with). So also in *Azmi*,[145] the court upheld the earlier employment tribunal finding that the claimant's beliefs concerning the veil were 'genuine and held by a sizeable minority of Muslim women'.[146] In the same year, Weatherup J determined *Christian Institute*,[147] which concerned an application from a coalition of Christian organisations protesting against a perceived inequality of treatment in the Equality Act (Sexual Orientation) Regulations (Northern Ireland) 2006 between anti-discrimination measures on the grounds of sexual orientation and orthodox religious beliefs. In an analysis of the legal requirements for a properly constituted 'religious belief', which owed much to the earlier pronouncement by Nicholls LJ, he advised that:

> issues as to the manifestation of a belief must satisfy certain modest objective minimum requirements. The 'threshold requirements' are

---

[142] *Ex parte Williamson* [2005] UKHL 15; [2005] 2 AC 246 (HL), at para. 22; though expressed obiter.

[143] *R (On the application of Begum (by her litigation friend, Rahman)* v. *Headteacher and Governors of Denbigh High School* [2006] UKHL 15 (HL).

[144] Ibid., at para. 18.

[145] *Azmi* v. *Kirkless Metropolitan Borough Council* [2007] UKEAT/009/07.

[146] Ibid., at para. 101.

[147] *Christian Institute and Others* v. *Office of First Minister and Deputy First Minister*, Neutral Citation no. [2007] NIQB 66.

188 ENGLAND AND WALES

> that the belief must be consistent with basic standards of human dignity
> or integrity, it must possess an adequate degree of seriousness and impor-
> tance and it must be intelligible and capable of being understood ... the
> conduct that constitutes the manifestation of a belief must be intimately
> connected to the belief. In deciding whether the conduct constitutes
> manifesting a belief in practice it is first necessary to identify the nature
> and scope of the belief. If the belief takes the form of a perceived
> obligation to act in a specific way then the act will be intimately linked to
> the belief and will be a manifestation of that belief. However, a perceived
> obligation is not a prerequisite to manifestation of a belief in practice.[148]

More recently, in *Ghai*,[149] the Court of Appeal considered a request from Ghai, a Hindu, that the council make available some land outside the city precincts to allow the practice of open-air cremation as his religion required that cremation take place by traditional fire, in direct sunlight and away from man-made structures. This had been rejected by the council as in breach of the Cremation Act 1902, but it also argued that to fall within the protective ambit of Article 9 a belief must be of central importance to the religion concerned, and open-air cremation was only peripheral to Hindu religious beliefs. The judicial view, however, was quite different and the court held that Mr Ghai's wishes as to how, after his death, his remains were to be cremated could be accommodated under the Act. Of particular significance is the fact that the Master of the Rolls, following the approach taken earlier by Baroness Hale in *Williamson*,[150] emphasised the importance of the individual's belief: 'What we are concerned with in this case is, of course, what Mr Ghai's belief involves when it comes to cremation, and it matters not for present purposes whether it is a universal, orthodox or unusual belief for a Hindu.'[151] This accords with the views expressed earlier by Elias P in *Eweida*:

> it is not necessary for a belief to be shared by others in order for it to be a
> religious belief, nor need a specific belief be a mandatory requirement of
> an established religion for it to qualify as a religious belief. A person
> could, for example, be part of the mainstream Christian religion but hold
> additional beliefs which are not widely shared by other Christians, or
> indeed shared at all by anyone.[152]

[148] Ibid., at para. 48.
[149] *Ghai, R (on the application of)* v. *Newcastle City Council & Ors* [2010] EWCA Civ 59.
[150] *R (Williamson)* v. *Secretary of State for Education and Employment* [2005] 2 AC 246.
[151] *Ghai, R (on the application of)* v. *Newcastle City Council & Ors* [2010] EWCA Civ 59, at para. 19.
[152] *Eweida* v. *British Airways PLC* [2008] UKEAT 0123 08_2011 (20 November 2008), at para. 29. Also see *Kelly and Others* v. *Unison* (2010) Case No 2203854/08, ET.

Non-religious beliefs

Views relating to religious matters, even if genuinely and fervently held, will not necessarily constitute a religious belief. In *Playfoot (a minor), R (on the application of)* v. *Millais School,*[153] the court found that an item of jewellery (a 'purity ring') was used as an ornamental accoutrement reflecting the wearer's personal preferences rather than her religious beliefs or, as it was put, 'representative of a moral stance and not a necessary symbol of Christian faith'.[154]

Non-philosophical beliefs

In *McClintock* v. *Department of Constitutional Affairs,*[155] a case concerning a member of a statutory panel who declined to officiate in cases where he might have to decide whether same-sex partners should adopt children, Elias P examined the basis for a philosophical belief. In his view 'the test for determining whether views can properly be considered to fall into the category of a philosophical belief is whether they have sufficient cogency, seriousness, cohesion and importance and are worthy of respect in a democratic society'.[156] Applying the test to the facts of that case he upheld the earlier decision of the employment tribunal that Mr McClintock's objection was not based on a philosophical belief:

> As the tribunal in our view correctly observed, to constitute a belief there must be a religious or philosophical viewpoint in which one actually believes. It is not enough to have an opinion based on some real or perceived logic or based on information or lack of information available.[157]

This is clearly a complex matter.

Religious and philosophical beliefs: differences in approach

According to Burton J in *Grainger* v. *Nicholson,*[158] 'to establish a religious belief the claimant may only need to show that he is an

---

[153] *Playfoot (a minor), R (on the application of)* v. *Millais School* [2007] EWHC 1698 Admin.
[154] Ibid., at para. 8. A finding that resonates with positions taken in the US culture wars.
[155] *McClintock* v. *Department of Constitutional Affairs* [2008] IRLR 29.
[156] Ibid., at para. 41.   [157] Ibid., at para. 45.
[158] *Grainger* v. *Nicholson* [2010] IRLR 4 (EAT).

adherent to a particular religion'.[159] In relation to 'philosophical belief', however, both he and Nicholls LJ were clear that the same exercise would necessitate imposing limitations to the scope of possible interpretation. Nicholls LJ considered that this could be achieved by applying a threshold test, comprising certain requirements implicit in Article 9 of the European Convention, and comparable guarantees in other human rights instruments. Burton J, drawing from the expositions of Nicholls LJ in *Williamson* and Weatherup J in *Christian Institute*, suggested the following criteria:

(i) The belief must be genuinely held.
(ii) It must be a belief and not, as in *McClintock*, an opinion or viewpoint based on the present state of information available.
(iii) It must be a belief as to a weighty and substantial aspect of human life and behaviour.
(iv) It must attain a certain level of cogency, seriousness, cohesion and importance.
(v) It must be worthy of respect in a democratic society, be not incompatible with human dignity and not conflict with the fundamental rights of others (paragraph 36 of *Campbell* and paragraph 23 of *Williamson*).[160]

However, while having some ground rules to establish what does or does not constitute a philosophical belief may be helpful, if this amounts to applying a different approach in assessing religious and philosophical beliefs this could be discriminatory. The above mentioned approach of Burton J seems both inappropriate as, in the context of the same statutory provision, the burden of proof should surely not be any the less on the religious believer than on his or her philosophical counterpart, and insufficient because merely belonging to a religious body clearly provides no guarantee of having an informed and sincerely held religious belief. The following observation of Nicholls LJ in *Williamson* seems nearer the mark:

> Article 9 embraces freedom of thought, conscience and religion. The atheist, the agnostic, and the sceptic are as much entitled to freedom to hold and manifest their beliefs as the theist. These beliefs are placed on an equal footing for the purpose of this guaranteed freedom.[161]

---

[159] Ibid., at para. 6.   [160] Ibid., at para. 24.
[161] *Ex parte Williamson* [2005] UKHL 15; [2005] 2 AC 246 (HL), at para. 24.

THE ADVANCEMENT OF RELIGION

Beliefs, the believer and manifestations of belief

As Nicholls LJ pointed out in *Williamson*, 'everyone is entitled to hold whatever beliefs he wishes'.[162] Problems only arise when action is taken to manifest that belief.

The personal nature of beliefs

The assertion by Nicholls LJ in *Williamson*[163] that 'the freedom of religion protects the subjective belief of an individual', was echoed by the employment appeal tribunal (EAT) view in *Eweida*[164] that 'it is not necessary for a belief to be shared by others in order for it to be a religious belief',[165] and by the comment of Baroness Hale for the Court of Appeal in *Ghai*[166] that 'it matters not for present purposes whether it is a universal, orthodox or unusual belief'. Such judicial and regulatory pronouncements would seem to firmly establish the subjective interpretation of a religion or philosophy as all-important. This is clearly problematic. The subjective belief of an individual is arguably insufficient: any such belief must first be capable of being construed as religious or philosophical; and there must be a dividing line between an individual's particular beliefs, whatever importance and sincerity the subject attaches to them, and the significance of those beliefs – as objectively determined – for the religion or belief system concerned.

Moreover, as always when the law revolves around a central, subjectively understood concept (e.g. 'welfare' in child care or 'reasonableness' in matrimonial proceedings), this brings its own problems. Importing the perception of an individual, as a significant factor in determining the veracity of their purported beliefs leaves court or regulator hostage to fortune when the individual then changes that belief, as in *Begum*, or has a seemingly shallow understanding of what constitutes a belief, as in *Playfoot*. Laws LJ in *McFarlane* v. *Relate Avon Ltd*[167] drew attention to the inherent contradictions and dangers for legal objectivity in attaching undue weight to subjectively perceived 'truths':

---

[162] Ibid., at para. 23.

[163] Ibid., at para. 22. An approach very much in keeping with the views expressed by Lord Greene MR in *Re Samuel* [1942] 1 Ch. 1, CA, at p.17.

[164] *Eweida* v. *British Airways PLC* [2010] EWCA Civ, 80 (12 February 2010).

[165] *Eweida* v. *British Airways* [2008] UKEAT 0123, 08, 2011 (EAT), at para. 29.

[166] *Ghai, R (on the application of)* v. *Newcastle City Council & Ors* [2010] EWCA Civ 59.

[167] *McFarlane* v. *Relate Avon Ltd.* [2010] EWCA Civ B1 (29 April 2010).

the conferment of any legal protection or preference upon a particular substantive moral position on the ground only that it is espoused by the adherents of a particular faith, however long its tradition, however rich its culture, is deeply unprincipled. It imposes compulsory law, not to advance the general good on objective grounds, but to give effect to the force of subjective opinion. This must be so, since in the eye of everyone save the believer religious faith is necessarily subjective, being incommunicable by any kind of proof or evidence. It may of course be true; but the ascertainment of such a truth lies beyond the means by which laws are made in a reasonable society. Therefore it lies only in the heart of the believer, who is alone bound by it. No one else is or can be so bound, unless by his own free choice he accepts its claims.[168]

The manifestation of beliefs

Clearly there are circumstances when it can be difficult to judge from the nature of an action whether this in fact constitutes a manifestation of religious or philosophical beliefs: whether it is necessarily causally and substantively related to, and adequately reflective of, something that falls within a definition of such beliefs as understood for the purposes of the 2011 Act. It may instead, for example, be a facile posture, a hollow pretence, an induced response or be simply criminal. It could also: be related but unintended or peripheral; emanate from something else entirely, such as the idiosyncratic convictions of an individual or minority group; or be fervently held but random, opportunistic or fleetingly transient in nature.

The advancement of religion

For a religious body to be charitable it must demonstrate that it is advancing religion, meaning that it is promoting, maintaining or practising it, increasing belief and thereby furthering the public benefit.[169] The Charity Commission sees religion being effectively advanced through practices which further develop the belief of adherents and which may thereby, if incidentally, generate a stronger sense of civic responsibility among the wider public. However, the Commission has also sounded a warning that 'the promotion of a

---

[168] Ibid., at paras 23–24.
[169] See Charity Commission for England and Wales, *The Advancement of Religion for the Public Benefit*, at paras D2 and E2.

particular religious doctrine is not necessarily advancement of religion in the charitable sense'.[170] This is now well illustrated by the legal status of Scientology: recognised by the highest court in the land as a religion;[171] but yet to be recognised by the Charity Commission as sufficiently engaged in the advancement of religion to warrant registration as a charity.

In *Berry* v. *St Marylebone*,[172] the Theosophy Society sought exemption from rates as a charity but the court held that theosophy did not come within the third head of charity because it provided no answer to the question 'what religion does the society advance and how does it advance it?'. In that same year Donovan J, in *United Grand Lodge of Free and Accepted Masons of England and Wales* v. *Holborn Borough Council*,[173] considered whether the activities of freemasons could be said to advance religion. In concluding that they did not, he reasoned that 'to advance religion means to promote it, to spread the message ever wider among mankind; to take some positive steps to sustain and increase religious belief; and these things are done in a variety of ways which may be comprehensively described as pastoral and missionary'.

The means for advancing religion

The means traditionally recognised by the judiciary in England and Wales for advancing religion are very similar to those given equivalent recognition elsewhere in the common law world (see Chapter 2); indeed, they were spread there by judicial precedents emanating from this jurisdiction. The broader interpretation of 'religion' now provided for under the 2011 Act and encompassing philosophical belief systems will continue to allow a commensurate broadening of 'advancement' as illustrated by *Grainger* v. *Nicholson*[174] and the registration of the British Humanist Association as a charity.

---

[170] See, for example, Charity Commission, *Application for Registration of Good News for Israel* (5 February 2004), at para. 2.1: www.charitycommission.gov.uk/media/100949/gnfidecision.pdf (accessed 3 January 2014).

[171] See *R (on the application of Hodkin and another)* v. *Registrar General of Births, Deaths and Marriages* [2013] UKSC 77.

[172] *Berry* v. *St Marylebone* [1957] 3 All ER 677.

[173] *United Grand Lodge of Free and Accepted Masons of England and Wales* v. *Holborn Borough Council* [1957] 1 WLR 1080; 121 JP 595; 101 SJ 851; [1957] 3 All ER 281.

[174] *Grainger* v. *Nicholson* [2009] UKEAT 0219 09 0311 (EAT).

Public policy, religious charities and common law constraints

In this jurisdiction a considerable body of case law testifies to the traditional presumption of charitable status for gifts and for activities intended to further religious purposes. As human rights litigation gathers momentum, however, the tensions between the traditional approach towards discretionary rights and a public policy objective to reduce opportunities for discrimination are becoming steadily more acute.

Testamentary conditions and the common law

Government concern to uphold the right of owners to freely dispose of their property dates from the Reformation and has been defended by the courts ever since (see Chapter 2). Gifts to charity, including those made to religious organisations, are generally viewed as an incident of that right and similarly worthy of support. The legacy of respect for a testator's expressed wishes regarding the use to be made of their gift continues to have an influential role. Attaching conditions, whether of a religious nature or otherwise, to donors' bequests is still more likely to breach the traditional common law requirements for charitable status than offend public policy.

Failure due to breach of common law rules

Traditionally, the freedom of testamentary disposition rule has meant that the court will do its utmost to give effect to a testator's intent. It was an approach that survived through the twentieth century and into the twenty-first. The parameters of a testator's intentions are crucial: where a gift is restricted to family members or friends or framed so widely as to possibly permit non-charitable purposes, it will fail; in neither instance will the public benefit test be satisfied. This may occur where a donor couples his gift with a direction that an appointee exercise his or her discretion.[175] As Sir William Grant pointed out, 'the question is not whether the trustee may not apply it upon purposes strictly charitable, but whether he is bound so to apply it'.[176] For example, the House of Lords held that a gift to a vicar and churchwardens of a parish 'for parish work' failed because it was too wide to be construed as exclusively

---

[175] *Doe d. Toone* v. *Copestake* (1805) 6 east 328. Also see *Re Davidson, Minty* v. *Bourne* [1909] 1 Ch. 567.

[176] *Morice* v. *The Bishop of Durham* (1804) 9 Ves 399.

PUBLIC POLICY AND COMMON LAW CONSTRAINTS   195

charitable.[177] Where the gift is clearly identified and intended to go to a religious institution, the fact that the institution has not been named will not invalidate its charitable nature; nor will it fail to gain charitable status simply because it has been restricted to one specified religion.

The charitable purposes may be ambiguously expressed. A reference made to both 'charitable' and 'religious' purposes would not prevent a trust from being upheld as charitable.[178] However, where the terms allowed for the possibility that a non-charitable purpose could have been intended, as where a gift was expressed to be for 'charitable, religious or other societies, institutions, persons or objects'[179] or for 'such Roman Catholic purposes in the parish of Coleraine and elsewhere' as the trustees may determine,[180] then it failed. As explained by Chatterton VC in *Copinger*: 'where there is discretion to apply it to charitable purposes, or to other purposes not charitable, and the trust is indefinite, the gift fails'.[181] Also, where there is uncertainty, as where a gift of £10,000 was made 'to his holiness ... the Pope ... to use and apply at his sole discretion in the carrying out of the sacred office',[182] it will fail.

Bequests subject to a religious condition

As Grattan and Conway point out, the term 'conditions in restraint of religion' was first coined by Lord Greene in *Re Samuel*[183] and 'is most typically associated with clauses in wills that require a beneficiary to continue with, convert to, or become involved with a particular religion on threat of forfeiture of the gift'.[184] There is a long history, in this jurisdiction, of sympathetic judicial treatment being given to donor bequests made subject to religious constraints. As Parachin has noted,[185] such explicitly discriminatory intentions are very evident in an endless list of cases confirming donor religious conditions such as: *Hodgson* v. *Halford*,[186] a condition against forsaking Jewish religion or marrying a non-Jew; *In*

---

[177] *Fairley* v. *Westminster Bank* [1939] AC 430.   [178] *Re Salter* [1911] 1 IR 289.
[179] *Re Davidson* [1909] 1 Ch. 567.   [180] *MacLaughlin* v. *Campbell* [1906] 1 IR 588.
[181] *Copinger* v. *Crehane* (1877) IR 11 Eq 429, at p.431.   [182] *Re Moore* [1919] 1 IR 316.
[183] *Re Samuel* (1941) [1942] 1 Ch. 1 at 30 (CA).
[184] S. Grattan and H. Conway, 'Testamentary Conditions in Restraint of Religion in the Twenty-first Century: An Anglo-Canadian Perspective', at p.4.
[185] See, A. Parachin, 'The Definition of Charity and Public Law Equality Norms', paper presented at the conference Private and Public Law – Intersections in Law and Method, the T.C. Beirne Law School at the University of Queensland, Brisbane, July 2011.
[186] *Hodgson* v. *Halford* [1977] EWCA Civ 11; [1978] 1 All ER 1047.

re Joseph, Pain v. *Joseph,*[187] a condition requiring adherence to Judaism; *Blathwayt* v. *Lord Cawley,*[188] a condition prohibiting becoming a Roman Catholic; *In re May, Eggar* v. *May,*[189] a condition prohibiting practice of Roman Catholicism; *In re Morrison's Will Trusts, Walsingham* v. *Blathwayt,*[190] a condition against becoming or marrying a Roman Catholic; *Clavering* v. *Ellison,*[191] a condition requiring education in the Protestant religion; *Hay* v. *Brown,*[192] a condition requiring practice of the Roman Catholic religion; *In re Allen,*[193] a condition of membership in and adherence to doctrines of the Church of England; *Re Tuck's Settlement Trusts, Public Trustee* v. *Tuck,*[194] a condition of belonging to the Jewish faith; and *Wainwright* v. *Miller,*[195] a condition requiring membership in the Roman Catholic Church or any sisterhood. In these and many similar cases,[196] the right of English testators to exercise direct religious discrimination when disposing of their estates was upheld in the courts, the established judicial view being that such conditions were not void for being in breach of public policy. As Naish J observed in *Re Knox,*[197] since such conditions had been 'repeatedly held valid ... it is now too late to question their validity'. This was a view endorsed by Lord Romer, who declared, in *Clayton* v. *Ramsden,* that the enforceability of unambiguous religious conditions was 'beyond question'.[198]

Religious preferences and public policy

Simonds LJ, in the course of delivering his judgment in *National Anti-Vivisection Society* v. *IRC,*[199] reflected on the case law history illustrating the benign liberal approach of the judiciary towards the development of the doctrine of general charitable intention. He noted that quite often,

---

[187] *In re Joseph, Pain* v. *Joseph* [1908] 1 Ch. 599.
[188] *Blathwayt* v. *Lord Cawley* [1976] 1 AC 397 (HL).
[189] *In re May, Eggar* v. *May* [1932] 1 Ch. 99.
[190] *In re Morrison's Will Trusts, Walsingham* v. *Blathwayt* [1940] Ch. 102.
[191] *Clavering* v. *Ellison* (1859) 7 HLC 282.
[192] *Hay* v. *Brown* (1883) 10 R (Ct. of Sess.) 460.   [193] *In re Allen* [1953] 1 Ch. 810.
[194] *Re Tuck's Settlement Trusts, Public Trustee* v. *Tuck* [1977] EWCA Civ 11; [1978] 1 All ER 1047.
[195] *Wainwright* v. *Miller* [1897] 2 Ch. 255.
[196] For example, *Lysaght* v. *Edwards* (1876) 2 Ch D 499.
[197] *Re Knox* (1889) 23 LR Ir 542 (Ch.), at p.544.
[198] *Clayton* v. *Ramsden* [1943] 1 AC 320, at p.332.
[199] *National Anti-Vivisection Society* v. *IRC* [1948] AC 31.

even in cases where the testator's intent was manifestly against public policy, the courts would find there was a general charitable intention and then proceed to save the gift for charity by applying the bequest to some other charitable purpose. As examples he cited *De Costa* v. *De Pas*,[200] where Lord Hardwicke had applied a bequest for instructing the people in the Jewish religion (then regarded as an illegal purpose) for the benefit of the Foundling Hospital, and *Cary* v. *Abbot*,[201] where Grant MR directed that the residue of an estate, which had been bequeathed for the instruction of children in the Roman Catholic faith, should be applied as the King by Sign Manual should direct.

More recently, in *Re Lysaght*,[202] a testamentary gift to fund the enrolment of medical students at the Royal College of Surgeons was subject to the donor's stipulation that eligibility for such scholarships was restricted to male medical students 'not of Jewish or Roman Catholic faith'. When the Royal College of Surgeons objected to the religious restriction (but not that relating to gender) and refused to administer the fund, the issue came before the court, where it was found that the motivation of the testatrix was to establish a fund for studentships: the restrictive condition was only an incidental aspect of the fund's administration. Although the bequest as such might not have been regarded as being against public policy,[203] the court struck out the words 'and not of the Jewish or Roman Catholic faith' from the testatrix's will, thereby enabling the college to administer the bursaries by the application of a *cy-près* scheme.

In 1976 the tension between freedom of testamentary disposition and public policy was again explored, this time by the House of Lords in *Blathwayt* v. *Lord Cawley*,[204] when the court was asked to pronounce on the validity of a clause requiring the forfeiture of a child's inheritance if he should 'be or become a Roman Catholic'. Rejecting the claim that the condition should be declared void on the grounds of constituting a breach in public policy, as such a direction would be likely to influence the parental upbringing of that child, Lord Wilberforce expressed the view that to do so would be to licence an unwarranted intrusion into the exercise of parental rights. His Lordship commented that 'discrimination is not the same thing as choice, it operates over a larger

---

[200] *De Costa* v. *De Pas* (1753) Amb. 228.   [201] *Cary* v. *Abbot* (1802) 7 Ves 490, 496.
[202] *Re Lysaght* [1966] Ch. 191.   [203] Ibid., 206.
[204] *Blathwayt* v. *Lord Cawley* [1976] AC 397; [1975] 3 All ER 625 (HL) *per* Lord Wilberforce, at p.637.

Public policy constraints

That not all dispositions with a declared religious preference would be regarded as charitable was demonstrated at an early stage when, in *De Themmines* v. *De Bonneville*,[206] the court found a trust to promote the doctrine of papal supremacy to be void, and did so on grounds of public policy. Again, in *Keren Kayemeth Le Jisroel Ltd.* v. *Commissioners of Inland Revenue*,[207] when considering the entitlement of a company to charitable status, the House of Lords took the view that facilitating the settlement of Jews in Palestine and elsewhere did not advance religion. It was not charitable because it involved considerations of public policy. Again, the Commission's intervention in the affairs of the North London Central Mosque Trust, which operated the Finsbury Park Mosque, was partially necessitated by public policy concerns. The Commission became concerned that the Trust had been taken over by Islamic extremists who were not adhering to the Trust's charitable purposes. Acting on evidence that the radical cleric, Sheikh Abu Hamza Al-Masri, was abusing his position within the Trust by broadcasting inflammatory Islamic rhetoric and posting such material on the Trust's website, the Commission closed down the mosque for a period.[208]

Advocacy

This well-established method of advancing a charitable purpose is one which can give rise to public policy issues: as occurred in *De Themmines* v. *De Bonneville*,[209] when the court found a trust to promote the doctrine of papal supremacy to be void. However, many uncontroversial methods of advocating in a religious context have been identified by the Charity

---

[205] *Blathwayt* v. *Lord Cawley* [1976] AC 397, at p.426. See also *Re Harding; Gibbs* v. *Harding* [2007] EWHC 3 (Ch).
[206] *De Themmines* v. *De Bonneville* [1828] 5 Russel 288.
[207] *Keren Kayemeth Le Jisroel Ltd.* v. *Commissioners of Inland Revenue* [1932] AC 650.
[208] See Charity Commission of England and Wales, *North London Central Mosque Trust* (1 July 2003). See, further, at: www.m2.com/m2/web/story.php/200315EB4F17EEE 4E1F585256D56003DBD46 (accessed 3 January 2014).
[209] *De Themmines* v. *De Bonneville* [1828] 5 Russel 288.

Commission,[210] but when advocacy becomes propaganda then it ceases to be charitable.

Proselytism

'Evangelising' or 'proselytising' have as their objective the conversion of someone to a specific faith or religion. Such activity is, as the Charity Commission point out, 'used by many charities advancing religion as an established and accepted means of attracting new followers or adherents'.[211] For some religions this is seen as an essential part of the outworking of their beliefs.

Public policy and the Pemsel-plus charitable purposes

The 2011 Act, s.3(1)(h), by formally recognising 'the advancement of human rights, conflict resolution or reconciliation or the promotion of religious or racial harmony or equality and diversity' as a charitable purpose, brought into sharper focus the tension between the advancement of religion and the constraints of public policy. In earlier cases the judiciary had already begun to wrestle with charity law issues arising on the difficult political interface between promoting cultural diversity and protecting cultural identity. In *Re Strakosch*,[212] for example, the court ruled to the effect that 'appeasing racial feeling within the community' was a political purpose and therefore non-charitable, and thereby established a precedent followed by courts and regulators in many common law countries.

Human rights, discrimination and religious charities: contemporary issues

The complexity for regulators and judiciary is considerable as they strive to resolve issues of discrimination by cross-referencing the provisions of charity law, equality law and the growing body of European Convention jurisprudence. This has not been helped by the absence of a definition for

---

[210] See Charity Commission, 'The Advancement of Religion for the Public Benefit', at Annex B.

[211] See, further, at: www.charitycommission.gov.uk/detailed-guidance/charitable-purpo ses-and-public-benefit/charities-and-public-benefit/the-advancement-of-religion-for-the-public-benefit/#sthash.vF7Bt6Oe.dpuf (accessed 3 January 2014).

[212] *Re Strakosch* [1949] 1 Ch. 529 (CA).

the key component in these overlapping areas of law – the meaning of 'religion'. Nevertheless, as Toulson LJ summarily noted:

> Religion and English law meet today at various points. Charity law protects trusts as charitable if they are for the advancement of religion. Individuals have a right to freedom of thought, conscience and religion under article 9 of the European Convention. They enjoy the right not to be discriminated against on grounds of religion or belief under EU Council Directive 2000/78/EC and under domestic equality legislation. ... More recently Parliament provided partial definitions of religion in section 2 the Charities Act 2006 (now section 3 of the Charities Act 2011) and section 10 of the Equality Act 2010 for the purposes of those Acts.[213]

Human rights

As Baroness Hale stated in *Ghaidan* v. *Godin-Mendoza*: 'It is the purpose of all human rights instruments to secure the protection of the essential rights of members of minority groups even when they are unpopular with the majority.'[214] However, the House of Lords has cautioned against abandoning established domestic case law precedents and slavishly following each new ECtHR judgment. For example, in *Kay* v. *London Borough of Lambeth*,[215] the House clearly stated that in order to ensure certainty in the law, courts should adhere, even in the Convention context, to the rules of precedent. Bingham LJ went on to say:

> The Strasbourg Court authoritatively expounds the interpretation of the rights embodied in the Convention and its protocols, as it must if the Convention is to be uniformly understood by all member states. But in its decisions on particular cases the Strasbourg Court records a margin of appreciation, often generous, to the decisions of national authorities and attaches much importance to the peculiar facts of the case. Thus it is for national authorities, including national courts particularly, to decide in the first instance how the principles expounded in Strasbourg should be applied in the special context of national legislation, law, practice and social and other conditions. It is by the decisions of national courts that the domestic standard must be initially set and to those decisions the ordinary rules of precedence should apply.[216]

---

[213] See *R (on the application of Hodkin and another)* v. *Registrar General of Births, Deaths and Marriages* [2013] UKSC 77, *per* Toulson LJ, at paras 32–33.

[214] *Ghaidan* v. *Godin-Mendoza* [2004] 3 WLR 113 HL, at para. 131.

[215] *Kay* v. *London Borough of Lambeth* [2006] UKHL 10. [216] Ibid., at para. 44.

While the Act specifically requires public authorities to act in accordance with Convention rights, it has remained controversial as to whether or to what extent organisations such as religious charities, when undertaking functions as agents of public authorities, are also subject to the same requirement.

The European Convention

For the purposes of religious charities and discrimination, the important Convention provisions are Articles 9 and 14. The first, fully incorporated into UK domestic law by Article 9 of the Human Rights Act 1998,[217] provides for the right to freedom of thought, conscience and religion. The second broadly prohibits discrimination 'on any ground' including, specifically, discrimination on religious grounds. It can only be used in conjunction with another Convention provision, and has similarly been incorporated into UK domestic law by the corresponding Article 14 of the 1998 Act. Although not specifically referred to, sexual orientation discrimination is plainly within the ambit of Article 14.[218] As with other Convention provisions, the State enjoys a margin of appreciation in assessing what constitutes 'discrimination' and the extent to which differences in otherwise similar situations may justify a difference in treatment. However, as the ECtHR has stressed, 'if a restriction on fundamental rights applies to a particularly vulnerable group in society that has suffered considerable discrimination in the past, then the State's margin of appreciation is substantially narrower and it must have very weighty reasons for the restrictions in question'[219] (see Chapter 3). The Court had previously drawn attention to the narrowness of that margin in relation to the justification of differential treatment on grounds of sexual orientation, in which circumstances the principle of proportionality requires that the measure chosen to realise

---

[217] Together with the associated ECtHR case law, including: *Buscarini and Others* v. *San Marino* (App. No. 24645/94), 1998; *Kokkinakis* v. *Greece* (App. No. 14307/88), 1993; *Leyla Sahin* v. *Turkey* (App. No. 44774/98), 2004; *Pichon and Sajous* v. *France* (App. No. 49853/99); *Leela Forderkeis E.V. and Others* v. *Germany* (App. No. 58911/00), 2008; *Universelles Leben E.V.* v. *Germany* (App. No. 29745/96), 1996; and *Lautsi* v. *Italy* (App. No. 30814/06), 2011.

[218] As noted in *Catholic Care (Diocese of Leeds)* v. *the Charity Commission for England and Wales and the Equality and Human Rights Commission* [2010] EWHC 520 (Ch), *per* Briggs J, at para. 57, citing *Salgueiro Da Silva Mouta* v. *Portugal* (2001) 31 EHRR 47.

[219] *Kiyutin* v. *Russia*, (App. No. 2700/10), March 2011.

the legitimate aim must be both suitable in general, and necessary in the circumstances.[220]

The Equality Act 2010, public bodies and exemption for charities

The 2010 Act,[221] which mostly came into effect in October of that year, now provides, along with, *inter alia*, the Human Rights Act 1998, a consolidated statutory anti-discrimination framework for the United Kingdom which prohibits unfair treatment on any of nine 'protected grounds', whether occurring in the workplace, when providing goods, facilities and services, when exercising public functions, in the disposal and management of premises, or in education and by associations (such as private clubs); and whether the discrimination takes the form of direct, indirect, harassment or victimisation. The nine grounds are the established six (sex, race, disability, sexual orientation, religion or belief and age) together with an additional three (marriage and civil partnership, gender reassignment and pregnancy and maternity) transferred from the Sex Discrimination Act. Despite the new legislation, the law is substantially unchanged: the definitions of direct and indirect discrimination now appear in sections 13(1) and 19; the statement regarding the immaterial differences between marriage and civil partnership is to be found in s.23(3); the prohibition of discrimination in providing services is located in s.29; while other carried over provisions are in the Schedules. Essentially, the same set of principles is now applied uniformly, including to all charities, religious or otherwise, unless relieved by a statutory exemption.

Additional protection continues to be available in the provisions of the Racial and Religious Hatred Act 2006 (amending the Public Order Act 1986), of which s.29B(i) provides that 'a person who uses threatening words or behaviour, or displays any written material which is threatening, is guilty of an offence if he intends thereby to stir up religious hatred'. Significantly, this legislation stops well short of prohibiting activity that might be merely persuasive, provocative or even insulting. The following caveat, embedded in the statute, reveals the legislative intent to achieve proportionality when licensing intervention in the right of an individual to manifest his or her religious beliefs:

---

[220] See *Kozak v. Poland* [2010] ECHR 280, at para. 92.   [221] Equality Act 2010, c. 15.

s.29J. Nothing in this Part shall be read or given effect in a way which prohibits or restricts discussion, criticism or expressions of antipathy, dislike, ridicule, insult or abuse of particular religions or the beliefs or practices of their adherents, or of any other belief system or the beliefs or practices of its adherents, or proselytising or urging adherents of a different religion or belief system to cease practising their religion or belief system.

This serves as a reminder that freedom of speech is an important right that must not be lightly interfered with. Possibly Briggs J had this in mind when, in *Smith* v. *Trafford Housing Trust*,[222] he considered whether the charity concerned was entitled to discipline an employee, a Christian manager, for posting on Facebook his view that holding civil partnership ceremonies in churches was 'an equality too far'. Expressing his opinion that the posting was not 'viewed objectively, judgmental, disrespectful or liable to cause upset or offence', Briggs J accepted that the complainant could have considered this as homophobic and have been offended but 'her interpretation was not in my view objectively reasonable'.[223] The judge advised that:

> The frank but lawful expression of religious or political views may frequently cause a degree of upset, and even offence, to those with deeply held contrary views, even where none is intended by the speaker. This is a necessary price to be paid for freedom of speech.[224]

Religious charities, discrimination and exemptions

The prohibition against religious discrimination in this jurisdiction is of fairly recent origin. It dates from the issue of EC Framework Directive 2000/78 when, as a direct consequence, the Employment Equality (Religion or Belief) Regulations 2003 were implemented in the UK by amendments to the Disability Discrimination Act and by regulations dealing with discrimination on grounds of religion or belief, age and sexual orientation in those fields (see the Employment Equality (Religion or Belief) Regulations 2003, the Employment Equality (Sexual Orientation) Regulations 2003 and the Employment Equality (Age) Regulations 2006). These were subsequently extended under the Equality Act 2006 to include philosophical beliefs and non-belief before being revoked but substantially reinstated in the Equality Act 2010, Sched 2.

---

[222] *Smith* v. *Trafford Housing Trust* [2012] EWHC 3221. [223] Ibid., at para. 85.
[224] Ibid., at para. 82.

Specific exemptions for charities from the laws governing discrimination – previously to be found in Regulation 18[225] – are now more restricted than formerly and consigned to s.193 of the Equality Act 2010.[226] These allow a charity to limit its benefits to people who share a 'protected' characteristic where either: the restriction is justified as a means of furthering the charity's aim to tackle a particular disadvantage borne by people with such a characteristic; or the charity is seeking to achieve some other legitimate aim in a fair, balanced and reasonable ('proportionate') way. Section 193 also exempts any charity which, prior to 18 May 2005, made acceptance of a particular religion or belief a condition of membership with an entitlement to the benefit, service or facility provided by that charity, and has since continued to impose that condition, from being in contravention of the Act. Certain schools and associations also benefit from exemptions. In addition to this exemption, the 'positive action' provisions enable charities to target their resources on what would ordinarily be considered a discriminatory basis where this is either a proportionate means to achieve a legitimate aim or for the purpose of preventing or compensating for disadvantage.

Religious charities as public bodies

Public bodies, for the purposes of human rights law, include non-government organisations such as a religious charity, functioning in an agency capacity on behalf of a government body. Any religious charity when so acting is bound by the laws governing discrimination.

Determining whether or not an agency relationship exists between government and charity is an imperfect science which turns on the facts in each case: not all delegated authority necessarily constitutes agency; the span of control exercised is crucial.[227] Where the evidence points to the charity performing a function that is wholly government controlled then, when so doing, the charity will be held to be acting as a public body. In that event, the charity, even if it is a religious organisation, will be fully bound by human rights requirements. Religious and belief

---

[225] The Sexual Orientation Regulations 2007, Regulation 18, was issued under powers provided by the Equality Act 2006.

[226] Possibly tightened as a result of the important ruling given by Richards J in *R (Amicus – MSF section)* v. *Secretary of State for Trade and Industry* [2004] IRLR 430.

[227] See, for example, B. S. Markesinis and R. J. C. Munday, *An Outline of the Law of Agency* (4th edn), LexisNexis, London, 1998.

organisations, for example, are prohibited from discriminatory practice in respect of sexual orientation in circumstances where they are providing a service under contract on behalf of a public authority. A case in point is that of *National Union of Teachers* v. *Governing Body of St Mary's Church of England (Aided) Junior School*,[228] where the Court of Appeal found that the Church of England school was in the State system, the governors were a body charged by the State with the running of the school and were exercising their functions with a view to securing provision by the school of the national curriculum. In these circumstances the governors were to be regarded as an emanation of the State for the purposes of the doctrine of direct effect. As the ECJ stated in *Calì & Figli*, an entity acts as a public body when it is performing 'a task in the public interest which forms part of the essential functions of the State and where the activity is connected by its nature, its aims and rules to which it is subject with the exercise of powers ... which are typically those of a public authority'.[229]

Freedom of religion

This right, guaranteed by Article 9 of the 1998 Act, includes the freedom: to change religion or belief; to exercise religion or belief publicly or privately, alone or with others; and to exercise religion or belief in worship, teaching, practice and observance. It also provides for the right to have no religion and to have non-religious beliefs protected.

Interference with the manifestation of religious belief

Article 9 is a qualified right and as such the freedom to manifest a religion or belief can be limited, or subject to 'interference', so long as that limitation: is prescribed by law; is necessary and proportionate; and pursues a legitimate aim (namely, the interests of public safety, the protection of public order, health or morals or the protection of the rights and freedoms of others). This allows the provision of services or 'benefits' to a certain section of society if such actions are a proportionate means of achieving a legitimate aim, such as improving health or the

---

[228] *National Union of Teachers* v. *Governing Body of St Mary's Church of England (Aided) Junior School* [1997] 3 CMLR 630.

[229] *Calì & Figli SrL* v. *SEPG* [1997] ECR I-1547; [1997] 5 CMLR 484, at para. 23.

206 ENGLAND AND WALES

protection of children. Weatherup J, in *Christian Institute*,[230] provided the following useful appraisal of what constitutes 'interference' in this context:[231]

> It is not every impact on the manifestation of religious belief that constitutes 'interference' for the purposes of Article 9. To constitute sufficient interference for the purposes of Article 9 it must be shown that [it] interfere[s] 'materially, that is, to an extent which was significant in practice, with the claimant's freedom to manifest their beliefs in this way'.[232] ... The position in which persons seeking to manifest religious belief have placed themselves may bear on whether the matter to which they object constitutes interference.[233] ... There will be instances where the impact on the individual does not amount to an interference with the right to manifest religious belief.

Subsequently, additional authority for this approach was provided by the ruling of the House of Lords in *Gallagher* v. *Church of Jesus Christ of Latter-Day Saints*,[234] when it considered the argument that s.3 of the Human Rights Act 1998 required the ratings legislation (the 1988 Act) to be 'read and given effect' in a manner compatible with Convention rights: whether restricting a rating exemption to places of 'public religious worship' contravened the Article 9 rights of a group (the Mormon Church) which excluded the public from some of its worship spaces. This argument rested on the assertion that the exclusion of the public from the Temple (their place of worship) was a manifestation by the Mormons of their religion and, therefore, to deny them rates exemption would be to discriminate against them on the grounds of religion, contrary to Articles 9 and 14 of the Convention. Lords Hoffmann and Hope held that the rating legislation did not prevent the group manifesting its religion. As Hoffmann LJ pointed out:

> the present case is not one in which the Mormons are taxed on account of their religion. It is only that their religion prevents them from providing

---

[230] *Christian Institute and Others* v. *Office of First Minister and Deputy First Minister*, Neutral Citation no. [2007] NIQB 66.

[231] Ibid., at paras 66 and 68.

[232] Ibid., citing *R (Williamson)* v. *Secretary of State for Education and Employment* [2005] 2 AC 246, *per* Lord Nicholls.

[233] Ibid., at para. 68, citing *Kalac* v. *Turkey* [1997] EHRR 552.

[234] *Gallagher* v. *Church of Jesus Christ of Latter-Day Saints* [2008] 1 WLR 1852, 1867. Note this matter has since been referred to the ECtHR: *The Church of Jesus Christ of Latter-day Saints* v. *United Kingdom* (App. No. 7552/09).

the public benefit necessary to secure a tax advantage. That seems to me an altogether different matter.[235]

Possibly the ultimate decision to deny rates exemption was coloured by the precedent set in the earlier decision of *Henning (Valuation Officer)* v. *Church of Jesus Christ of Latter-Day Saints*.[236]

Discrimination

The ECtHR has defined discrimination as 'treating differently, without an objective and reasonable justification, persons in analogous, or relevantly similar, situations'.[237] For the purposes of Article 14, no 'objective and reasonable justification' is understood as meaning 'that it does not pursue a "legitimate aim" or that there is no "reasonable proportionality between the means employed and the aim sought to be realised" '.[238] The Equality Act 2010 prohibits discrimination against an individual on the basis of a protected characteristic, in relation to several areas including employment and the provision of goods and services, while also providing exemptions for religious charities in certain circumstances. The principles established in the case law leading up to the Equality Act 2010 retain their currency and continue to serve as benchmarks for the rulings of judiciary and regulators in the post-2010 era.

Legitimate aim

According to the Charity Commission, a legitimate aim is one that: has a reasonable social policy objective (e.g. health improvement or the protection of children); is consistent with the lawful carrying out of the charity's stated purpose for the public benefit, though not necessarily identical with that purpose (e.g. a purpose of relieving poverty and sickness could be a legitimate aim and a subsidiary aim of helping children out of poverty could also be a legitimate aim); and is not itself discriminatory.[239]

---

[235] Ibid., at para. 13, citing *M* v. *Secretary of State for Work and Pensions* [2006] UKHL 11; [2006] 2 AC 91.

[236] *Henning (Valuation Officer)* v. *Church of Jesus Christ of Latter-Day Saints* [1962] 1 WLR 1091.

[237] See *Kiyutin* v. *Russia* (App. No. 2700/10), March 2011.

[238] See *EB* v. *France* (2008) 47 EHRR 21, at para. 91.

[239] See Charity Commission, 'Equality Act Guidance for Charities: Restricting Who Can Benefit from Charities', 2012, at para. C4.

Proportionality

In assessing what constitutes 'proportionality', Mummery LJ in *Elias*[240] adopted a three-stage approach:

> First, is the objective sufficiently important to justify limiting a fundamental right? Secondly, is the measure rationally connected to the objective? Thirdly, are the means chosen no more than is necessary to accomplish the objective?

Shortly afterwards the House of Lords, in *Huang* v. *Secretary of State for the Home Department*,[241] explained the principle of proportionality as 'the need to balance the interests of society with those of individuals and groups'.

Discrimination and same-sex marriage

The recently passed Marriage (Same Sex Couples) Bill 2012–13 is inevitably going to raise human rights issues: particularly for the Church of England as its canons clearly restrict marriage to heterosexual relationships.[242] The fact that under the proposed new legislation, accompanied by amendments to the Equalities Act 2010, the Church is to be relieved of any duty to conduct gay marriages, is going to be problematic.[243] It is thereby statutorily handicapped relative to other religions, its functional capacity diminished by the State. Moreover, it will also compromise the equality principle and give rise to a charge that the law operates in a discriminatory fashion to the clear detriment of Anglican same-gender couples. There can be no right without a reciprocal duty. Once the law recognises a right to same-sex marriage it cannot be Convention-compliant to then relieve one specific religious organisation of an

---

[240] *R (Elias)* v. *Secretary of State for Defence* [2006] EWCA Civ 1293.

[241] *Huang* v. *Secretary of State for the Home Department* [2007] UKHL 11. See also: *De Freitas* v. *Permanent Secretary of the Ministry of Agriculture Fisheries, Lands and Housing* [1999] 1 AC 69, *per* the Privy Council; *R* v. *Oakes* [1986] 1 SCR 103, *per* Dickson CJ; and *Christian Institute and Others* v. *Office of First Minister and Deputy First Minister*, Neutral Citation no. [2007] NIQB 66, *per* Weatherup J.

[242] In July 2002, the General Synod resolved: that this Synod affirm in accordance with the doctrine of the Church of England as set out in Canon B 30, that marriage should always be undertaken as a 'solemn, public and life-long covenant between a man and a woman'.

[243] The Church of England, as the established Church, will be able of its own accord, under the Church of England Assembly (Powers) Act 1919, to bring legislation before Parliament to enable it to 'opt in'.

obligation imposed on other similar religious organisations to respond to an exercise of that right by permitting a church wedding. There is, of course, also the fact that the permission not to officiate at same-sex marriages is restricted exclusively to the Church: all other religious institutions, wishing for similar exemption, may well protest that this provision discriminates against them.

Religious discrimination in practice

The Equality Act 2010 identifies four types of religious discrimination: direct, indirect, harassment or victimisation. The first takes the form of unequal treatment whereby some are directly treated less favourably than others because of their religious beliefs. The second incidentally disadvantages a certain religious group, such as when a service provider's provision, criterion or practice imposes restrictions that affect their ability to access services available to others.[244] The third results from 'whistleblower' circumstances involving a complaint about religious discrimination; the fourth is behaviour that may range from physical attack or verbal abuse to causing discomfort because of a religious or racial difference.

Unequal but not discriminatory

For a charity to provide services and benefits only to persons of a certain religion or belief does not constitute discrimination. The Equality Act 2010, s.193, provides exemptions for charities: unequal treatment is permissible in respect of persons who share one or more of the protected characteristics; but any charity that wishes to limit benefits to such people, even if this conforms wholly to the aims set out in its governing documents, must now also justify that restriction. The justification can be provided by satisfying one of two tests outlined by the Charity Commission:[245] where the governing document restricts benefits to people with a shared protected characteristic and are provided in order

---

[244] In *Board of Governors of St Matthias Church of England School* v. *Crizzle* [1995] ICR 401, the complaint of an unsuccessful Asian applicant for the post of headteacher that the criterion of being 'a committed communicant Christian' constituted discrimination was treated as indirect discrimination on the grounds of race and therefore justifiable as it sought to protect the religious ethos of the school.

[245] See Charity Commission, 'Equality Act Guidance for Charities: Restricting Who Can Benefit from Charities', at para. C.

to tackle a particular disadvantage or need linked to that protected characteristic; and, otherwise, where the governing document restricts benefits to people with a shared protected characteristic and the restriction can be justified as being a fair, balanced and reasonably necessary way of carrying out a legitimate aim, taking into account the discrimination involved. The Commission adds that: in deference to a person's religion or belief or their sexual orientation, religious or belief-based charities can impose restrictions on membership, participation in their activities, the services they provide or the use of their premises, and in doing so are exempted from the justification tests.[246] A restriction can only be made: on the grounds of religion or belief, where necessary because of the organisation's purpose, or to avoid causing offence to followers of the religion or belief on which the organisation is founded; and in relation to sexual orientation, if this is necessary to comply with the organisation's doctrine or to avoid conflict with the religious or belief-based convictions of many followers of the religion or belief on which the organisation is founded. Further, if an organisation contracts with a public body to carry out an activity, such as the provision of services, then it cannot discriminate because of sexual orientation in relation to that activity.

In recent years, however, the courts have tended to adopt a more rigorous approach to policing unequal treatment that disadvantages those with personal characteristics (including sex, race and sexual orientation) which they cannot change and in regard to which discrimination could be particularly demeaning.[247] As Briggs J has warned, 'a charity which proposed to apply differential treatment on grounds of sexual orientation otherwise than as a proportionate means of achieving a legitimate aim might thereby fail to achieve charitable status (or lose it, if it sought to pursue such activities by amendment of its objects)'.[248] In deciding whether unequal treatment is justified, it will be relevant to take into account whether the aim could have been achieved through other means or, effectively, whether 'reasonable adjustments' could have been made.[249] This principle was evident in the approach developed by the House of Lords when considering *R (Begum)* v. *Head Teacher and*

---

[246] Ibid., at para. F5.
[247] See, for example, *R (Carson)* v. *Work and Pensions Secretary* [2006] 1 AC 173, *per* Walker LJ, at p.192E.
[248] *Catholic Care (Diocese of Leeds)* v. *the Charity Commission for England and Wales and the Equality and Human Rights Commission* [2010] EWHC 520 (Ch).
[249] See, for example, *Glor* v. *Switzerland* (App. No. 13444/04), April 2009.

Governors of Denbigh High School,[250] which concerned the compatibility of a school uniform requirement and the wearing of the jilbab. Ms Begum had attended the school for two years and adhered to the normal dress code, but then changed her position on the basis of a change in her religious belief. The school Head, herself a Muslim, sought advice from two London mosques as to whether the school uniform offended Islamic propriety and, on being informed that it did not, banned the jilbab with the effect of denying Ms Begum access to her classes. When, eventually, the case came before the House of Lords, a majority found that there had been no interference with her right to manifest her belief in practice or observance. In choosing to attend Denbigh High School Ms Begum found limitations imposed on the manifestation of her religious belief, but was otherwise uninhibited in that regard. For the many religious charities engaged in the advancement of education this decision is of considerable significance.

Unequal but not discriminatory: contractual obligations

Prior to the 2010 Act, a charity benefited from a series of wide exemptions which provided that so long as its constitution set out the class of people which it could benefit, and that class was not defined by reference to skin colour, then any consequent discrimination would not be unlawful. Those exemptions included: an occupational requirement having regard to the nature or context of the work; where employment was for the purposes of an 'organised religion';[251] and for employers with a faith-based ethos. The rationale developed in *Begum*[252] resonates with three earlier decisions. In the first, *Esson* v. *London Transport Executive*,[253] the appeal of a Seventh Day Adventist, dismissed after trying to take Saturdays off for religious reasons, was rejected with the court ruling that it was his duty to reconcile the 'insurmountable conflict' between his religious beliefs and his contractual obligations. In the second, *Ahmad* v.

---

[250] *R (Begum)* v. *Head Teacher and Governors of Denbigh High School* [2006] 2 All ER 487.
[251] A term used in the Employment Equality (Religion or Belief) Regulations 2003/1660, regulation 20(3); Employment Equality (Sexual Orientation) Regulations 2003, SI 2003/1661, regulation 20(3); and the Discrimination Act 1975, s.19(2).
[252] *R (Begum)* v. *Head Teacher and Governors of Denbigh High School* [2006] 2 All ER 487. See also *Copsey* v. *WWB Minerals Ltd.* [2005] IRLR 811, when a Christian worker objected to the introduction of a new shift system at his place of work which would involve Sunday working. His eventual dismissal was held, on the facts, to be not unfair.
[253] *Esson* v. *London Transport Executive* [1975] IRLR 48.

Inner London Education Authority,[254] the Court of Appeal held that the right to freedom of thought, conscience and religion established by Article 9 of the European Convention on Human Rights does not entitle an employee to be absent from work for the purpose of religious worship in breach of contract. This decision was subsequently upheld by the ECtHR,[255] which reiterated that Article 9(1) rights must necessarily be subject to Article 9(2) limitations: the Court held that freedom of religion 'may, as regards the modality of a particular religious manifestation, be influenced by the situation of the person claiming that freedom'.[256] Finally, in *Stedman* v. *UK*,[257] a dismissal for refusal to work on a Sunday was held not to constitute a breach of the right to freedom of religion: the employee's freedom to resign effectively guaranteed her Convention rights; she remained free to leave her job in order to exercise her religious freedom (which, it has to be said, is a curious interpretation of 'freedom'). So, also, in *MBA* v. *London Borough of Merton*,[258] when the Court of appeal dismissed a discrimination appeal by a Christian care worker who had been told to work on Sundays contrary to her beliefs.

This approach was duly followed in a number of cases where courts and regulators were required to weigh the alleged unequal treatment against the contractual duties that provided the context for such treatment and to which the claimant had willingly subscribed. One such case was *McClintock* v. *Department of Constitutional Affairs*,[259] which concerned the request of a member of a statutory panel (a Justice of the Peace) that he be excused from officiating in cases where he might have to decide whether same-sex partners should adopt children. When his request was refused he resigned from the Family Panel and commenced proceedings alleging that he had been subject to direct and indirect discrimination and harassment on the grounds of religion and belief.

---

[254] *Ahmad* v. *Inner London Education Authority* [1978] QB 36, CA. A decision seemingly followed in *Safouane & Bouterfas* v. *Joseph Ltd. and Hannah* [1996] Case No. 12506/95/LS & 12569/95, when the appeal of two Muslims dismissed for praying during breaks was rejected. However, both seem at variance with *JH Walker Ltd.* v. *Hussain* [1996] IRLR 11 EAT, when it was decided that actions taken by an employer causing detriment to Muslims as a class, such as refusal to allow time off for religious holidays, might be held to constitute indirect racial discrimination against those from an ethnic or national origin that is predominantly Muslim.

[255] *Ahmad* v. *Inner London Education Authority* (1982) 4 EHRR 126.

[256] Ibid., at p.11.

[257] *Stedman* v. *UK* (1997) 23 EHRR CD168, following *Ahmad* v. *UK* (1981) 4 EHRR 126.

[258] *MBA* v. *London Borough of Merton* [2013] EWCA Civ 1562.

[259] *McClintock* v. *Department of Constitutional Affairs* [2008] IRLR 29.

The employment appeal tribunal found that McClintock had not been disadvantaged because of any religious belief he held and, even if he had been, such discrimination would have been justified.

A year later, in *Ladele v. London Borough of Islington*,[260] the Court of Appeal considered the dismissal of Ms Ladele, a Christian marriage registrar, who refused to be involved in registering same-sex 'civil partnerships' in accordance with newly introduced statutory procedures. She had been working at the office for some years before same-sex partnerships were allowed to be registered and it was clear that her unavailability would not have impeded the registrations as other registrars were available and willing to do the work. The Court of Appeal took the view that the registration process was a public service, that it had significant human rights implications for the community and that administering the process formed part of Ms Ladele's contractual duties. It noted that 'the effect on Ms Ladele of implementing the policy did not impinge on her religious beliefs: she remained free to hold those beliefs, and free to worship as she wished'.[261] It concluded that:

> Ms Ladele was employed in a public job and was working for a public authority; she was being required to perform a purely secular task, which was being treated as part of her job; Ms Ladele's refusal to perform that task involved discriminating against gay people in the course of that job; ... Ms Ladele's objection was based on her view of marriage, which was not a core part of her religion; and Islington's requirement in no way prevented her from worshipping as she wished.[262]

Eweida v. British Airways plc[263] concerned Ms Eweida, a committed Christian working for British Airways (BA) in a customer service area, who wanted to display a small cross around her neck contrary to BA policy that no jewellery was to be visible. She claimed that BA's refusal to allow this was indirect discrimination, as a general policy was applied to all visible jewellery (though exceptions were allowed for apparel that could not be worn discreetly such as a hijab, a turban and a skullcap worn by other staff). It was rejected by the employment tribunal and then again on appeal to EAT, which upheld the original tribunal finding of no

---

[260] *Ladele v. London Borough of Islington* [2009] EWCA (Civ) 1357 (15 December 2009).
[261] Ibid., *per* Lord Neuberger, at para. 51.
[262] Ibid., the Master of the Rolls (with whom Dyson and Smith LJJ agreed), at para. 52.
[263] *Eweida v. British Airways plc* [2010] EWCA Civ 80 (12 February 2010).

indirect discrimination, because the claimant had been unable to demonstrate that there were any other Christians who wanted to wear a visible cross but had been prevented from doing so. The Court of Appeal confirmed the previous decisions, rejecting the appellant's argument that the test of indirect discrimination was met, even if she was alone in being disadvantaged by the policy.

McFarlane v. *Relate Avon Ltd*[264] concerned a charity that provided relationship support, including counselling for couples, families, young people and individuals, sex therapy, mediation and training courses. Mr M, a relationship counsellor, had been dismissed when he indicated to his employer that he did not approve of same-sex relationships on biblical grounds and did not wish to be involved in counselling such couples. The court, following the approach it had earlier adopted in *Ladele*,[265] ruled that Mr M had not suffered religious discrimination.

These cases were appealed to the ECtHR, which eventually issued its ruling in January 2013. Only the *Eweida* case succeeded, with the court determining that BA had breached Ms Eweida's human rights, in particular her right to freedom of thought, conscience and religion, when it banned her from wearing a crucifix while at work. The court took the view that her desire to wear a cross openly was a sincere manifestation of her religious beliefs and there was no evidence that in so doing she was encroaching on the rights of others. In the *Ladele* and *McFarlane* cases, however, where the appellants argued that their Christian beliefs concerning homosexuality were in conflict with the duties of their jobs, which required them to perform services for gay couples, the court was not convinced and both appeals failed. The most important factor in these cases was that the employers had taken the actions they had because they were committed to providing services without discrimination and the employees had willingly accepted their jobs knowing that the conditions of employment would affect their ability to demonstrate their religious beliefs. The ECtHR endorsed the approach of the English judiciary and regulators that an individual's right to manifest religious beliefs in the workplace is subject to the employer's right not to accommodate them in circumstances where to do so may conflict with their obligation to protect the rights of others.

[264] *McFarlane* v. *Relate Avon Ltd.* [2010] EWCA Civ B1 (29 April 2010). Also see *R (Johns* v. *Derby City Council* [2011] EWHC 375 (Admin); [2011] 1 FLR 2094.
[265] *Ladele* v. *London Borough of Islington* [2009] EWCA Civ 1357; [2010] IRLR 211.

The same rationale, with the proportionality principle prominently in play, can be seen in other decisions such as *Cherfi*,[266] *Chaplin*[267] and even in *Playfoot*,[268] where in each case the claimant had knowingly placed themselves in positions which could potentially compromise their beliefs. The observation of Weatherup J in 2007 seems equally applicable to the circumstances of the claimants in the above cases:

> 'in exercising his freedom to manifest his religion, an applicant may need to take his specific situation into account'.[269] . . . By electing to participate in certain activities individuals may find that those activities engage others of different sexual orientation. There will be instances where the impact on the individual does not amount to an interference with the right to manifest religious belief.[270]

Unequal and discriminatory: restricting employment opportunities

A religious charity is permitted to give preference to employing staff that share its religious ethos where to do so enables the charity to give effect to its purpose.[271] The 'organised religion' exemption, which permits such a

---

[266] *Cherfi v. G4S Security Services Ltd.* [2011] UKEAT 0379 10 2405 (24 May 2011), where Mr Cherfi's right to attend the mosque on Fridays did not override his contractual obligations to his employer; in part because the employer had offered to let him work on Saturdays and he declined the offer.

[267] *Chaplin v. Royal Devon & Exeter Hospital NHS Foundation Trust* [2010] ET 1702886/ 2009 concerned a nurse who refused on religious grounds to stop wearing a crucifix with her uniform contrary to the Trust's health and safety policy. The ECtHR upheld the earlier ruling that the nurse had not been subjected to direct or indirect discrimination. It differentiated the ruling from the *Eweida* case on the basis that the health and safety dimension placed Ms Chaplin in a position where her wish to manifest her religious belief might well impact upon the interests of others. Similarly in *X v. UK*, No. 7992/77, 14 DR 234 (1978), where it was held that the practice of wearing a turban did not absolve Sikh motorcyclists from the obligation, on health and safety grounds, to wear crash helmets.

[268] *Playfoot (a minor), R (on the application of) v. Millais School* [2007] EWHC 1698, where a schoolgirl challenged the decision of her school to prohibit her wearing a 'purity ring' as a symbol of her Christian commitment to celibacy before marriage.

[269] Citing *Kalac v. Turkey* [1997] EHRR 552, at para. 27.

[270] See *Christian Institute and Others v. Office of First Minister and Deputy First Minister*, Neutral Citation no. [2007] NIQB 66, *per* Weatherup J, at para. 68.

[271] See, for example, the 'organised religion' exception (at f/n 277) and the Equality Act 2010, Sched 9. Also, see the School Standards Framework Act 1998, s.60, which provides that foundation or voluntary schools with a religious character can give preference in employment, remuneration and promotion to teachers whose beliefs are in accordance with the tenets of that religion.

body to restrict employment opportunities on religious or sexual grounds where such criteria constitute a genuine occupational requirement of the post to be filled, was unsuccessfully challenged in *R (Amicus)* v. *Secretary of State for Trade and Industry*.[272] While the claim that it was framed so broadly as to license unwarranted discrimination, particularly in relation to sexual orientation, was rejected, the court warned that the exemption must not be narrowly construed. Subsequently, this exemption was recast in the Equality Act 2010, where it now permits such a body to impose explicitly discriminatory restrictions on employment opportunities in relation to gender, marital status and sexual orientation. However, the problems associated with its former statutory iteration have not gone away. It remains uncertain as to where the line may be drawn between an 'organised religion' and a religious organisation, and between the different types of post that may be entitled to protection under the 2010 Act.

It is at least certain that this exemption privilege must be exercised reasonably. For example, in *Reaney* v. *Hereford Diocesan Board of Finance*,[273] the employment tribunal held that where a homosexual was committed to working for the Church of England, an organised religion, he could expect to discuss the perceptions of homosexuality within the Church during a job interview and, as the questions put to the job applicant (about his sexuality and future intentions about relationships) had been reasonable and had been expected by him, he had not been subjected to harassment. The tribunal found the requirement (that the applicant declare either that he had made a positive choice of celibacy for the future or that he would abstain from sexual behaviour) was both for compliance with the doctrines of the Church of England and to avoid conflict with the strongly held religious convictions of a significant number of the religion's followers. However, as he had been the preferred candidate after competitive interview, the failure to offer him the job was an act of direct sexual orientation discrimination. The defence of a genuine occupational requirement was not available to the Church.

Exemption from the discrimination prohibition is directly linked to the religious functions of the charity and is not to be interpreted as carte blanche for operating a 'closed shop' employment policy exclusively

---

[272] *R (Amicus)* v. *Secretary of State for Trade and Industry* [2004] EWHC 860 (Admin) 26 April 2004.

[273] *Reaney* v. *Hereford Diocesan Board of Finance*, 1602844/2006, (April 2007).

favouring persons of a designated religion or belief. This was clearly illustrated in *Hinder & Sheridan* v. *Prospects for People with Learning Disabilities*,[274] which concerned Prospects, a Christian charity and therefore a religious organisation, that provided housing and day-care for people with learning disabilities. Prospects introduced a policy based on its Christian ethos whereby it would recruit only practising Christians for the vast majority of roles (except cooking, cleaning, gardening and maintenance), as those in post might have to lead prayers or give spiritual guidance,[275] and told existing non-Christian employees that they were no longer eligible for promotion. The tribunal found that it was insufficient to assume that, as a matter of principle, every job in a Christian organisation should be done by Christians. In order to comply with the provisions of the 2003 Regulations it was necessary to carry out a job evaluation for every post. In a decision that sent a clear message to faith-based organisations regarding blanket policies which discriminate on this protected characteristic, the tribunal held that the charity had unlawfully discriminated against one of its managers by requiring him to only employ Christians and not to promote its existing non-Christian employees. Again, in *Glasgow City Council* v. *McNab*,[276] the EAT upheld a tribunal's decision that an atheist teacher employed by a Catholic school maintained by the council had suffered direct discrimination under the Employment Equality (Religion or Belief) Regulations 2003 when he was refused an interview for the post of Principal Teacher of Pastoral Care. The tribunal had been entitled to conclude that the post was not on the list of those for which the Roman Catholic Church required a teacher to be a Catholic.

The provisions in the 2010 Act that frame employment-related exemptions to the prohibition against discrimination have further narrowed the scope of permissible restrictions and present a challenge to the established policies and practices of some religious charities. For example, some of the current practices in the Church of England, an organised religion, would normally be clearly discriminatory: restricting opportunities for ordination to the office of bishop to those of one gender is clearly prejudicial to all possible candidates of the other and to

---

[274] *Hender & Sheridan* v. *Prospects for People with Learning Disabilities* [2008] employment tribunal (nos. 2902090/2006 and 2901366) (2008).
[275] Thereby ostensibly complying with the 'genuine occupational requirement' of the Employment Equality (Religion or Belief) Regulations 2003.
[276] *Glasgow City Council* v. *McNab*, UKEATS/0037/06/MT; [2007] IRLR 476.

218   ENGLAND AND WALES

trans-sexuals;[277] and restricting the ordination of gay priests to those who undertake to remain celibate and the consecration of gay bishops to those who are not sexually active. The Church can avail of the 'islands of exclusivity' policy,[278] given effect by schedule 9 of the 2010 Act, thereby avoiding human rights constraints, but in doing so it risks further compounding its moral stance.

Unequal and discriminatory: restricting access to services

Article 2 of the First Protocol to the European Convention on Human Rights recognises a right to educate children in the religious beliefs of their parents. The leading English case on such matters has long been *Mandla (Sewa Singh) and another* v. *Dowell Lee and others*,[279] which concerned a Sikh boy, Gurinder Singh, who was denied admittance to Park Grove School, a private foundation school, because he refused to comply with a school uniform requirement to cut his hair and remove his turban. The House of Lords held that it was unlawful indirect discrimination for a headmaster of an independent school to insist on a uniform requirement of short hair and caps for boys, thus excluding Sikhs who wear turbans with long hair. More recently, a contrary judicial view was taken in relation to the significance of an individual's right to present themselves in a manner emblematic of their religious affiliation. In August 2013, echoing a similar incident in New Zealand in 2004,[280] a Crown Court judge in London refused to hear the submission of a Muslim woman wearing a full-length burqa on the grounds that the need to confirm her identity was greater than her right to so manifest her religious beliefs.[281] Proportionality, and standards compatible with

---

[277] Note that the ordination of women bishops is expressly prohibited by Canon C2 *Of the consecration of bishops*:

> 5. Nothing in this Canon shall make it lawful for a woman to be con-secrated to the office of bishop.

[278] See A. Esau, '"Islands of Exclusivity": Religious Organisations and Employment Discrimination' (1993) 33 UB Col LR 719). Cited by J. Rivers, *The Law of Organized Religions*, who declares: 'It is right for the State to recognise "islands of exclusivity" at any rate in the core dimension of collective religious activity', at p.135.

[279] *Mandla (Sewa Singh) and another* v. *Dowell Lee and others* [1983] 2 AC 548.

[280] See, further, at: www.hrc.co.nz (accessed 3 January 2014).

[281] See, further, at: www.dailymail.co.uk/news/article-2400844/Judge-orders-Muslim-woman-remove-burkha-court-appearance-bans-entering-plea-refuses.html (accessed 3 January 2014).

HUMAN RIGHTS, DISCRIMINATION & RELIGIOUS CHARITIES 219

democracy, would again seem to be crucial: for an adversarial system of justice, the need to establish the identity of the parties is of fundamental importance; in contrast, the need of an educational system to require all pupils in a particular school to conform to uniform requirements is of a lower order of importance.

Article 2 of the First Protocol, which provides the rationale for exempting faith schools[282] from the prohibition on religious discrimination and is now part of domestic statute law, was tested in *R (on the application of E)* v. *Governing Body of JFS and the Admissions Appeal Panel of JFS*,[283] which concerned the rules of admission to a Jewish school that had, for 52 years, required a child to have a mother who was born Jewish. The issue for the court was whether the school could claim an exemption against a charge of racial discrimination on the grounds of their religious commitments. The High Court ruled that a school that accepts State funding must not discriminate in its admission policy on the basis of ethnicity. Subsequently, the UK Supreme Court, in a majority ruling, held that such a matrilineal religious condition was direct racial discrimination. It found that what in the High Court had been characterised as religious grounds were in fact racial grounds, notwithstanding their theological motivation, and no faith school could be excused from the prohibition on race discrimination.

Allegations of a discriminatory restriction on access to services also formed the basis for recent rulings by judicial and regulatory authorities in relation to the policy of a Catholic adoption agency to confine adoption services to heterosexual couples.[284] Catholic Care, a charity based in Leeds and one of 11 UK Catholic adoption agencies, with strong connections to the Roman Catholic Church, which provided much of its

---

[282] Where a faith school is a voluntary aided school, as JFS is, and so maintained by public funding, its religious character has to be designated by the Secretary of State (School Standards and Framework Act 1998, s.69).

[283] *R(E)* v. *Governing Body of JFS* [2010] IRLR 136; [2009] UKSC 15, on appeal from [2009] EWCA Civ 626.

[284] A decision in keeping with the policy statement made by Tony Blair, the then Prime Minister, on announcing the preparation of the Sexual Orientation Regulations 2007:

> there is no place in our society for discrimination. That is why I support the right of gay couples to apply to adopt like any other couple. And that is why there can be no exemptions for faith-based adoption agencies offering publicly-funded services from regulations which prevent discrimination.

As posted on the Downing Street office website (www.no10.gov.uk).

funding, sought exemption from the 2007 Sexual Orientation Regulations.[285] These required it to consider gay and lesbian couples as prospective parents. The agency took the position that it was outside the tenets of the Roman Catholic Church to provide adoption services to same-sex cohabiting couples or civil partners and, in fact, provided adoption services only to married couples. The Commission noted that other such agencies, for example those under the auspices of the Anglican Church, had found a way of accommodating the prohibition on sexual orientation discrimination within their continued activities, without breaking their ties with that Church. Some, including a number formerly operating under the auspices of the Roman Catholic Church, had severed their ties with that Church so as to be able to provide adoption services for same-sex couples. Some faith-based charities had hived-off their adoption agency work while retaining their Church ties. However, Catholic Care, in common with a number of Roman Catholic adoption agencies, had found it impossible or at least impracticable to pursue any of those alternatives and instead sought to bring itself within the exemption provided for charities by Regulation 18 from the statutory prohibition on discrimination on grounds of sexual orientation in the provision of services to the public.

Following rejection by the Charity Commission, the charity appealed to the High Court, where Briggs J remitted the case back to the Commission to reconsider the issues in the light of certain principles he set out in his judgment.[286] The Commission followed his reasoning that, although applicable human rights law allowed charities to restrict services on the basis of sexual orientation, this was only possible if the restriction amounted to a proportionate means of achieving a legitimate aim. Noting that the intended beneficiaries of Catholic Care's adoption service were children in need of adoption rather than prospective adoptive parents, the Commission concluded that this test was not made out, reasoning that religious conviction was insufficient to justify the discrimination by the charity because of the public nature of the charity's activities. This decision was then appealed to the First-tier Tribunal

---

[285] See the Equality Act 2006, s.81, together with the Equality Act (Sexual Orientation) Regulations 2007. A main effect of the regulations was, subject to important exceptions, to make it unlawful for a person to discriminate on grounds of sexual orientation in the provision of goods, facilities or services to the public or a section of the public.

[286] *Catholic Care (Diocese of Leeds)* v. *the Charity Commission for England and Wales and the Equality and Human Rights Commission* [2010] EWHC 520 (Ch).

(Charity),[287] where it was dismissed following the tribunal's finding that the charity had failed to meet the statutory test imposed by s.193 of the Equality Act 2010, which required it to demonstrate that the less favourable treatment it proposed to offer same-sex couples would constitute a proportionate means of achieving its legitimate aim of providing suitable adoptive parents for a significant number of 'hard to place' children. Because adoption is a public service, funded in part by local authorities, Catholic Care could not avail itself of the protection afforded by the exemptions under the 2010 Act. This decision is significant as it indicates that charities which restrict their services on certain protected grounds (including sex and religion) may find it increasingly difficult to maintain such restrictions in the future; and those that provide services on behalf of the State, such as adoption or nursing home places, may have to choose between complying with the requirements of the State or otherwise re-aligning the manner in which the services can be provided.

Most recently, the Supreme Court in *Bull* v. *Hall and Preddy*[288] confirmed that it was unlawful discrimination for Christian hotel owners to refuse a double-bedded room to a same-sex couple, and dismissed their argument that they should not be compelled to run their business in a way which conflicts with their deeply held religious beliefs. The relevant legal framework was provided by the Sexual Orientation Regulations 2007: Regulation 4(1), which makes it unlawful for a 'person ("A") concerned with the provision to the public or a section of the public of goods, facilities or services to discriminate against a person ("B") who seeks to obtain or to use those goods, facilities or services by . . . refusing to provide B with goods, facilities or services'; Regulation 4(2) states that this 'applies, in particular, to . . . accommodation in a hotel, boarding house or similar establishment'; while Regulation 14 specifically exempts religious organisations from the Regulation 4 prohibition. Lady Hale emphasised that the decision did not amount to replacing legal oppression of one community (homosexual couples) with legal oppression of another (Christians and others who shared the appellants' beliefs about marriage), as the law equally prohibits a hotel keeper from refusing a particular room to a couple because they are heterosexual or because they have certain religious beliefs.

---

[287] *Catholic Care (Diocese of Leeds)* v. *The Charity Commission for England and Wales* [2011] Eq LR 597.
[288] *Bull* v. *Hall and Preddy* [2013] UKSC 73. Also, see the similar case *Black* v. *Wilkinson* [2013] EWCA Civ 820; [2013] 1 WLR 2490.

Unequal but 'positive action'

The positive action provisions, which became law as part of the Equality Act 2010 and have been in effect since April 2011, provide specific opportunities for charities to take action in circumstances that would otherwise constitute unlawful discrimination. These provisions, which are additional to the charities' exemption privileges available under s.193, permit positive action if it is a proportionate means of addressing the disadvantages of a group with shared protected characteristics,[289] and if it serves to encourage a more proportionate take-up in activities or services by members of such a protected group. Contrary to the government minister's interpretation of service provision policy as that of 'providing services in a non-discriminary way to the whole community',[290] discriminatory targeting in favour of disadvantaged groups is wholly permissible and, indeed, necessary in many situations. Any doubt was removed by the ruling in *R (Kaur and Shah)* v. *Ealing LBC*,[291] when Southall Black Sisters (SBS)[292] appealed the decision of Ealing council to withdraw its funding because the SBS focus on black and Asian minority communities was considered contrary to the council's perceived obligation to sponsor a non-discriminatory service. As Moses J explained:

> There is no dichotomy between the promotion of equality and cohesion and the provision of specialist services to an ethnic minority. ... [I]n certain circumstances the purposes of [the public sector equality duty] may only be met by specialist services from a specialist source.[293]

Whether a charity and/or faith based, a service provider is permitted by law and government policy to deliver services in certain circumstances on a discriminatory basis. The general positive action provisions allow employers to target measures such as training towards groups such as ethnic minorities, which are under-represented or disadvantaged in the workplace, or to in other ways address their particular needs.

---

[289] The 'protected characteristics' being age, disability, gender reassignment, marriage and civil partnership, pregnancy and maternity, race, religion or belief, sex and sexual orientation.

[290] [2008] EWHC 2062 (Admin).

[291] *R (Kaur and Shah)* v. *Ealing LBC* [2008] EWHC 2062 (Admin).

[292] This nonprofit was established in 1979 to address the needs of black (Asian and African-Caribbean) women experiencing domestic violence.

[293] *R (Kaur and Shah)* v. *Ealing LBC* [2008] EWHC 2062 (Admin), at paras 55–56.

Conclusion

As progenitor of both Anglicanism and charity law, it is somewhat ironic that England should now find itself in a position where its primary religion and religious organisations are facing serious challenges. The status of the Church of England as the 'established' religion of the nation is under threat due to its inability to compromise its canons to meet the principles established in equality legislation: its discriminatory policies regarding gender and sexuality as preconditions for appointment to certain posts, coupled with its Scripture-led rejection of same-sex relationships is leading towards a sundering of the nearly 500-year-old Church–State relationship. Human rights law has brought developments with regard to the definition of 'discrimination': restrictions on the exemptions available to religious organisations are matched by increased recognition given to the rights of secularists; employers have to be more vigilant to ensure service access and a non-discriminatory workplace; government must exercise caution in relation to contracting with religious organisations; proselytism is not always permissible; and discrimination on the basis of gender or sexuality is becoming more rigorously policed. At the same time, charity law reform has placed on the statute books a broader definition of 'religion', one which: no longer requires a God; reverses the public benefit presumption, thereby raising the question as to whether or not the role and functions of a religious entity are necessarily conducive to the public benefit; and looks to the subjective understanding of the individual, rather than to doctrines and tenets, for evidence of what constitutes religious belief. The combined effect of charity and human rights law reform has been to isolate, as comparatively anachronistic and dogmatic, some doctrines of canon law. The resulting compromised position of the national religion and its institutional framework may well also compromise government policy to further promote the development of a pluralist society.

6

Ireland

Introduction

Ireland in the twenty-first century is no longer the homogenous Catholic society it once was. Being an island off an island off continental Europe, it remained relatively culturally intact until the effects of an abrupt change from emigration to immigration, during the closing decades of the twentieth century, transformed it from a mono-cultural white Catholic society coalesced around the Church and with the highest level of regular church attendance in Europe, to a much more multicultural and multi-faith society. Exposure to 30 years of religious-based violence in the adjoining jurisdiction, at times spilling over into Irish towns and into the heart of the capital city, has undoubtedly also done much to disrupt inherited values and community loyalties. Added to which, the current deep and ongoing economic crisis is making its own contribution to what has been experienced, in the space of a generation or so, as a general erosion of social cohesion. Religion no longer holds its traditional, very special, position in this increasingly secular society; it has diminished considerably since the introduction of the Charities Act 1961 and even more so since the Constitution, with its Roman Catholic ethos, was adopted in 1937. In particular, the Catholic religion has been severely impacted by a loss of trust and respect following the revelations of systemic child abuse perpetrated over many years by previously revered religious organisations.

Indeed, in the aftermath of a conflict that destroyed the fabric of many towns and caused the violent deaths of some 3,500 people, religion on this island has become a demonstrably divisive influence, polarising communities and hindering the consolidation of a pluralist civil society. However, the legacy of religious values – specifically those derived from Catholic teachings – continues to pervade much of the law and institutions of the Irish State. This is evident in the governing principles of the Constitution, and also in the Charities Acts 1961 and 1973, which still provide the framework within which religious charities must operate, while the reforming provisions of the Charities Act 2009 remain in abeyance.

Although charity law therefore reflects the more traditional religious values of previous generations, Ireland has not avoided the surge of equality and human rights legislation that has grafted a new agenda of personal legal rights onto the domestic civil law of all developed nations. The result has been a growing disconnect in this jurisdiction between traditional religious values and the requirements of modern human rights. The principles constantly being generated by ECtHR case law present a real challenge to the established practice of government and charities in relation to a growing agenda of social issues (including contraception, abortion and IVF treatment) that now map out the interface between religion and secularism.

This chapter begins by tracing the historical background of what was a symbiotic Church–State relationship in Ireland and analyses the crucial role played by the courts in progressing institutional separation. It considers the prominence of the Catholic Church relative to other religions, and the resulting significance for religious charities, particularly those engaged in education and health care. The recent and growing socio-economic importance of the nonprofit sector, the partnership arrangements with government, together with the central importance of religious charities, and the differentiated nature and effect of government funding are assessed. The current law and regulatory framework for charities is then outlined, and the related law reform process evaluated, with a focus on the potential offered by the, as yet, unimplemented provisions of the Charities Act 2009. This leads into a consideration of the changed and unchanged statutory definitions of such core common law concepts as 'religion', 'religious beliefs', the 'public benefit' and the 'advancement of religion', with an assessment of the implications arising for religious charities. The constraints imposed by public policy and traditional common law rules on the remit of charity and religious bodies are identified. The chapter then explores the impact of a modern human rights approach to matters customarily left to charity. In particular, it examines the difficulties emerging for the established practice of domestic religious charities as a consequence of ECtHR case law. It draws from contemporary judicial rulings on issues of discrimination to gauge the nature and extent of the gap between the requirements of the Convention and domestic charity law in relation to matters affecting the role of religious charities.

Church, State and religious charities

Church and State in Ireland have long had a close relationship. Religion, specifically Roman Catholicism, has provided a basis for social cohesion: before independence it united by far the majority of the population, differentiating them from the ruling Protestant ascendancy, and offering a platform for stoical resistance to colonialism; afterwards it imbued and united rulers and ruled in a common allegiance to build a national civic polity. This adherence to Catholicism has probably been the factor most responsible for setting the development of charity law in Ireland down a somewhat different road than that taken in England as signposted by different founding statutes: the Statute of Charitable Uses 1601 in England[1] and the Statute of Pious Uses 1634 in Ireland.[2] Indeed, although the source for charity law in all common law nations lies in the Preamble to the 1601 Act, only Ireland had its own formative statute.

Background: government and the nonprofit sector

Entitled 'An Act for the Maintenance and Execution of Pious Uses', the 1634 Act[3] identifies the following charitable purposes in its Preamble:

> for the erection, maintenance, or support of any college, school, lecture in divinity or in any of the liberal arts or sciences;
>
> or for the relief or maintenance of any manner of poor, succourless, distressed, or impotent persons;
>
> or for the building, re-edifying, or maintaining in repair any church, college, school or hospital;
>
> or for the maintenance of any minister and preacher of the Holy Word of God;
>
> or for the erection, building, maintenance, or repair of any bridges, causeyes, cashes, paces, and highways within this realm;
>
> or for any other like lawful and charitable uses and uses, warranted by the laws of this realm now established and in force.

Although very closely resembling the 1601 Act, the purposes listed in the Irish statute differ from those in its English counterpart in their pointed inclusion of religious matters; a difference emphasised by the reference to 'pious uses' in the title.[4] This difference is indicative of a

---

[1] 43 Eliz. 1 cap. 4, also known as the Statute of Elizabeth.
[2] 10 Car. 1 sess. 3 cap. 1, also known as the Statute of Charles.
[3] Repealed by the Statute Law Revision Act (Ireland) 1878.
[4] In marked contrast to the more emphatically secular nature of the corresponding title to the 1601 Act: 'An Acte to redresse the Misemployment of Landes, Goodes, and Stockes of Money heretofore given to Charitable Uses'.

CHURCH, STATE AND RELIGIOUS CHARITIES 227

deep and enduring change of direction taken by charity law in the two jurisdictions in relation to religion.

Pious uses

'Pious uses' may have been one of the more potent triggers for the Reformation. Feudalism, as established in England and extended to Ireland in the years following the Norman Conquest, was a centralised system based on land ownership which determined the loyalty, services and tithes due to rulers. It was a system that, over time, was brought to its knees by the growing practice of mortmain, whereby a donor would seek to atone for his sins in this life and save his soul in the next by assigning his lands, in whole or in part, in perpetuity to the Church as a gift for a pious use coupled with a request that prayers or masses be offered for the salvation of his soul. In both England and Ireland, gifts for pious uses were recognised as charitable gifts in the years prior to the Reformation (see, further, Chapter 2).

The State, Catholicism and charity

The Statute of Chantries 1547,[5] giving effect to a 1545 statute, provided for the dissolution of chantries and gifted the Crown with ownership of all Catholic colleges, chapels, chantries and related lands and endowments. It also led to gifts for the saying of masses being deemed 'superstitious' and illegal in England and Wales but, as the Statute of Chantries never applied to Ireland, the validity of such gifts continued to be recognised as both legal and charitable in this jurisdiction.[6] As Keane J has explained:

> Before the Reformation such gifts were clearly lawful and in Ireland their legality remained unaffected by the Statute of Chantries which did not extend to this country. In England it was thought for centuries that the statute had the effect of rendering unlawful as 'superstitious uses' gifts for the celebration of masses: the cases which so decided were, however, over-ruled by the House of Lords led by Lord Birkenhead in the famous decision of *Bourne* v. *Keane*.[7] Accordingly when the penal laws came to

---

[5] 1 Edw. VI cap. 14.

[6] See *Commissioners of Charitable Donations and Bequests* v. *Walsh* (1828) 7 IR Eq R 34 and *Read* v. *Hodgins* (1844) 7 IR Eq R 17.

[7] *Bourne* v. *Keane* [1919] AC 815.

228　　　　　　　　　　　　　IRELAND

an end, there was no question of a gift for the celebration of masses being unlawful, as it was believed to be in England.[8]

The validity of gifts for the saying of masses for the souls of the deceased was recognised by Lord Manners LC in *Commissioners of Charitable Donations and Bequests* v. *Walsh*[9] and confirmed by Blackburne MR in *Read* v. *Hodgins*,[10] and has since always been a valid charitable gift.[11] Nonetheless, charity law as it related to Roman Catholicism during the years prior to independence endured a long period of adverse treatment[12] typified by the ruling of the Court of Appeal in *MacLaughlin* v. *Campbell*,[13] which held that a gift 'for such Roman Catholic purposes' as the trustees saw fit was not charitable partly because those 'purposes' would not necessarily be conducive to the advancement of religion. This changed abruptly when Ireland acquired independence.

Building a modern Church–State relationship

The Constitution marked a new start for Ireland. This was true in many respects, but perhaps particularly in the early decades of independence it was evident in the affirmation given to Roman Catholicism as a hallmark of the nation's cultural identity in constitutional and legislative provisions. While Article 44 prohibited any State establishment or endowment of religion,[14] or any State discrimination on the basis of religious belief, it nonetheless gave clear precedence to monotheism, to Christianity and to Catholicism, in that order. In a charity law context, while the judiciary and Commissioners were at pains to ensure the general continuity of established common law case precedents and

---

[8] See R. Keane, *Equity and the Law of Trusts in the Republic of Ireland* (2nd edn), Bloomsbury Professional, Dublin, at p.142.

[9] *Donations and Bequests* v. *Walsh* (1828) 7 IR Eq R 34n.

[10] *Read* v. *Hodgins* (1844) 7 IR Eq R 17.

[11] The ruling in *Bourne* v. *Keane* [1919] AC 815, ending the prohibition on such gifts as 'superstitious uses' had no relevance for Ireland, where such gifts had always been recognised as being for the advancement of religion.

[12] See the effect of the Roman Catholic Relief Act 1829 and s.15 of the Charitable Donations and Bequests (Irl) Act 1844. See also, J. Brady, *Religion and the Law of Charities in Ireland*, Northern Ireland Legal Quarterly, Belfast, 1975.

[13] *MacLaughlin* v. *Campbell* [1906] 1 IR 588. The precedent value of this decision did not survive s.49 of the 1961 Act.

[14] The Irish Church Act 1869 dis-established the Church of Ireland.

that further development proceeded in tandem with like developments elsewhere, they were also alert to opportunities for registering the distinctive religious characteristics distinguishing Irish law from its UK counterpart.

Religion(s)

In 1937 the government introduced Bunreacht na hÉireann, the Irish Constitution. Article 44.1.2 declared: 'The State recognises the special position of the Holy Catholic Apostolic and Roman Church as the guardian of the Faith professed by the great majority of the citizens.' This provision, reflecting Irish social mores until the 1960s, gave a degree of primacy to Catholicism as was broadly acknowledged by O'Higgins CJ in *Norris* v. *AG*,[15] although there was also some judicial opinion to the effect that this provision did not confer any special privileges on the Roman Catholic religion or on Roman Catholics.[16] Article 44.1.3 also extended State recognition to:

> the Church of Ireland, the Presbyterian Church in Ireland, the Methodist Church in Ireland, the religious Society of Friends in Ireland, as well as the Jewish Congregations and the other religious denominations existing in Ireland at the date of the coming into operation of this Constitution.

There can be little doubt that the Constitution, by specifying certain religions and not others, intended and achieved a conferring of preferential status on those mentioned. While the Fifth Amendment of the Constitution Act 1972 deleted both provisions, as they had come to be viewed as dated and potentially discriminatory, Article 44 continues to make special reference to the Christian nature of the State.[17] It pledges the State to uphold its duty to pay 'the homage ... due to Almighty God' and religious values are commended as being of central importance to Irish society. It remains the case that there is no express reference to faiths that do not profess belief in a god nor to polytheistic religions nor to beliefs of a wider philosophical nature such as humanism. Moreover, the continued leaning towards a theistic rather

---

[15] *Norris* v. *AG* [1984] IR 36.
[16] See *In re Tilson, Infants* [1951] IR 1, *per* Black J, at p.36.
[17] But, see also the remarks of Barrington J in *Corway* v. *Independent Newspapers (Ireland) Ltd.* [1999] 4 IR 484, at p.502.

230   IRELAND

than a secular State can be seen in the enduring constitutional and statutory ban on blasphemy.[18]

Private piety

The 'contract' at the heart of the pious use was the understanding that a personal material sacrifice offered up for use by the Church would earn a degree of redemption for the donor's soul in the next life: a reduction in time spent in purgatory before admission to eternal life in God's presence. In charity law terms such an act of private piety, contentious due to the absence of any tangible evidence of public benefit, became an issue in relation to situations where the 'offering' was conducted by way of a private mass or through the devotions of a cloistered religious order.[19]

In relation to the former, the validity of such gifts was steadfastly denied in England[20] and initially also refuted in Ireland,[21] but was conclusively established in this jurisdiction by the ruling of the Court of Appeal in *O'Hanlon* v. *Logue*[22] and subsequently legislatively endorsed by s.45(2) of the Charities Act 1961.[23] In relation to the latter, the line was drawn in England by the ruling in *Cocks* v. *Manners*,[24] when Sir Wickens VC held that the Dominican Convent, a contemplative order of nuns, was not charitable and explained:

> A voluntary association of women for the purpose of working out their own salvation by religious exercises and self-denial seems to me to have

---

[18] See Article 40.6.1 of Bunreacht na hÉireann and the Defamation Act.

[19] See, further, M. Blakeney, 'Sequestered Piety and Charity: A Comparative Analysis' (1981) 2 *Journal of Legal History* 207.

[20] See, for example, *Re Hetherington's Will Trusts* [1990] Ch. 1.

[21] See *Attorney General* v. *Delaney* (1875) IR 10 CL 104.

[22] *O'Hanlon* v. *Logue* [1906] 1 IR 247.

[23] Under the Charities Act 1961, s.45:

> (2) For the avoidance of the difficulties which arise in giving effect to the intentions of donors of certain gifts for the purpose of the advancement of religion and in order not to frustrate those intentions and notwithstanding that certain gifts for the purpose aforesaid, including gifts for the celebration of Masses, whether in public or in private, are valid charitable gifts, it is hereby enacted that a valid charitable gift for the purpose of the advancement of religion shall have effect and, as respects its having effect, shall be construed in accordance with the laws, canons, ordinances and tenets of the religion concerned.

[24] *Cocks* v. *Manners* (1871) LR 12 Eq 574. Also see *Re White* [1893] 2 ch. 41 and *In Re Delany: Conoley* v. *Quick* [1902] 2 ch. 642.

CHURCH, STATE AND RELIGIOUS CHARITIES   231

none of the requisites of a charitable institution, whether the word
'charitable' is used in its popular sense or in its legal sense.

Initially, as for example in *Re Byrne; Shaw* v. *The Attorney-General and
Others*,[25] this approach was also adopted in Ireland. Then, in *Re
Howley*,[26] Gavan Duffy J declared: 'The assumption that the Irish public
finds no edification in cloistered lives, devoted purely to spiritual ends,
postulates a close assimilation of the Irish outlook to the English, not
obviously warranted by the traditions and mores of the Irish people.' He
followed this, in *Maguire* v. *Attorney General*,[27] with the pronouncement
that: 'It is a shock to one's sense of propriety and a grave discredit to the
law that there should, in this Catholic country, be any doubt about
the validity of a trust to expend money in founding a convent for the
perpetual adoration of the Blessed Sacrament.' As Gannon J eventually
noted in *O'huadhaigh* v. *Attorney General*,[28] 'in significant respects the
law on charities in England and Ireland has diverged and *Cocks* v. *Manners*
is no longer an acceptable authority in Ireland'.[29] Private piety would be,
and remains, sufficient to warrant charitable status in Ireland.

Secularisation

Ireland is ostensibly a secular State. The national census results, published in December 2012, showed a four-fold increase in the number of
people who said they had no religion, or were either atheist or agnostic,
between 1991 and 2011. The 2011 census revealed that: 84.2 per cent of
Irish citizens self-identified as Roman Catholic; 2.8 per cent Church of
Ireland; 1 per cent Muslim; 1.8 per cent of no religion; with the remainder unstated or of various religions. In terms of ethnicity: 85 per cent
described themselves as white Irish; 0.6 per cent as Irish Travellers;
while 58,697 people described themselves as Black or Black Irish. It
is also one in which many of its institutions such as hospitals and

[25] *Re Byrne; Shaw* v. *The Attorney-General and Others* [1935] IR 782. Also see O'Connor
MR in *Commissioners of Charitable Donations and Bequests* v. *McCartan* [1943] IR 238.
[26] *Re Howley* [1940] IR 109.   [27] *Maguire* v. *Attorney General* [1943] IR 238.
[28] Unreported, High Court, 5 February 1979; also see *Re Keogh's Estate* [1945] IR 13. See,
further, J. C. Wylie, *A Casebook on Equity & Trusts in Ireland*, Butterworths, Dublin,
1998, at pp.917–926.
[29] See *Re Cranston: Webb* v. *Oldfield* [1898] 1 IR 431; *O'Hanlon* v. *Logue* [1906] 1 IR 260;
Attorney General v. *Becher* [1910] IR 260; *Maguire deceased: Maguire* v. *Attorney
General* [1943] IR 238; *Sheridan deceased: Bank of Ireland* v. *Attorney General* [1957]
IR 257.

residential care facilities, but most notably its schools, have retained their capacity for religious permeability.

In recent decades, Catholicism and religion in general have faded as distinctive characteristics of Irish society and the nation has become visibly more multicultural, but there is reason to doubt whether this has been accompanied by any slackening of the traditional hold that Catholicism has had on the organs of State. Concern has been expressed regarding the authenticity of a State commitment to secularity by a former president who refers to 'the dubious relationship between the State and the Catholic Church, the constitutional prohibition on divorce, the ban on the use of contraception, the criminalisation of homosexuality',[30] as well as on the availability of information and advice to women about abortion, and equal rights and equal status for women in the workplace and in the family.

An 'established' religion

For many decades after Ireland achieved independence, it could be argued that government policy demonstrated such a strong preference for supporting Catholicism that this was in all but name the 'established' religion.

The courts follow case precedents by not inquiring into the inherent validity of a particular religion nor do they examine the relative merits of different religions. The broad governing principle remains as initially expressed by Walker LC in the Irish case of *O'Hanlon* v. *Logue*:

> a gift for the advancement of 'religion' is a charitable gift; and that in applying this principle, the Court does not enter into an inquiry as to the truth or soundness of any religious doctrine, provided it be not contrary to morals or contain nothing contrary to law. . . . Whether the subject of the gift be religious or for an educational purpose, the Court does not set up its own opinion. It is enough that it is not illegal, or contrary to public policy, or opposed to the settled principles of morality.[31]

With a weakening of the Catholic influence and a diversification of values and lifestyle choices in Irish society, the courts are increasingly called upon to broaden their interpretation of 'religion' to accommodate contemporary philosophical perspectives. This has yet to occur. The effect of judicial consideration of constitutional guarantees is to retain a traditional emphasis on theism, if balanced with respect for other beliefs. As Barrington J put it:

---

[30] See M. Robinson, *Everybody Matters: A Memoir*, Hodder and Stoughton, London, 2012.
[31] *O'Hanlon* v. *Logue* [1906] IR 247.

CHURCH, STATE AND RELIGIOUS CHARITIES   233

> The effect of these various guarantees is that the State acknowledges that
> the homage of public worship is due to Almighty God. It promises to hold
> his name in reverence and to respect and honour religion. At the same
> time it guarantees freedom of conscience, the free profession and practice
> of religion and equality before the law to all citizens be they Roman
> Catholics, Protestants, Jews, Muslims, agnostics or atheists.[32]

As Whyte has pointed out,[33] the constitutional constraints in Article 44 –
prohibiting State endowment of religion and State discrimination on
grounds of religious profession, belief or status – have been considered in
a series of cases. The earlier cases were concerned with religious practices[34]
and decisions of ecclesiastical authorities,[35] but more recently they have
embraced the promotion of social conditions which are conducive to,
though not strictly necessary for, the fostering of religious beliefs.[36] The
record also provides evidence of judicial diligence in policing the
Church–State interface and ensuring that the former is free from interference from the latter.[37]

Equality of religions

Any suggestion that the Constitution inferred preferential treatment
for Christian religions was refuted by Walsh J in *Quinn's Supermarket
v. Attorney General*,[38] who expressed the view that there was no constitutional provision restricting charitable trusts for religious purposes
to those which advance Christian religions. Subsequently, Barrington J,
in the Supreme Court case of *Corway v. Independent Newspapers
(Ireland) Ltd*,[39] when considering the standing of the Muslim, Hindu
and Jewish religions under Article 44 of the Constitution, commented
that it:

---

[32] See *Corway v. Independent Newspapers (Ireland) Ltd.* [1999] 4 IR 484.

[33] See G. Whyte, 'Religion and Education: the Irish Constitution', paper presented at the
TCD/IHRC conference on *Religion and Education: A Human Rights Perspective*, Dublin,
27 November 2010.

[34] *Quinn's Supermarket Ltd. v. Attorney General* [1972] IR 1.

[35] *McGrath and Ó Ruairc v. Trustees of Maynooth College* [1979] ILRM 166.

[36] See: *Re Article 26 and the Employment Equality Bill 1996* [1997] 2 IR 321; *Greally v.
Minister for Education (No 2)* [1999] 1 IR 1; [1999] 2 ILRM 296; and *Campaign to
Separate Church and State Ltd. v. Minister for Education* [1998] 2 ILRM 81.

[37] See, for example, *Re Article 26 and the Employment Equality Bill 1996* [1997] 2 IR 321 at
p.359.

[38] *Quinn's Supermarket v. Attorney General* [1972] IR 1, 23.

[39] *Corway v. Independent Newspapers (Ireland) Ltd.* [1999] 4 IR 484, at p.502.

234 IRELAND

is an express recognition of the separate co-existence of the religious denominations, named and unnamed. It does not prefer one to the other and it does not confer any privilege or impose any disability or diminution of status upon any religious denomination, and it does not permit the State to do so.

Religious organisations and the nonprofit sector

J.C. Brady once commented that 'Religion is still inextricably interwoven with the whole fabric of life in Ireland and the Irishman's commitment to institutionalised Christianity is nowhere more clearly reflected than in his charitable benefactions.'[40] However, the nature of the relationship between religion and charity has since changed considerably. While the contribution of religious organisations to total charitable activity, to the work of the wider nonprofit sector and to the development and delivery of statutory services is inestimable, the State does now provide an infrastructure of public service provision. Those religious organisations, once most obviously prominent in activities serving to advance religion but also active across all other heads of charity, perhaps particularly in relation to the broad front of education and social care, have in recent years been in decline. This has been due in part to an ageing cohort of adherents, but revelations of domestic and international instances of abuse, perpetrated by some members of religious orders in relation to children entrusted to their care, has also had an adverse impact.[41]

Religious charities

Within the Irish nonprofit sector there are probably upwards of 7,200 charities.[42] However, in the absence of a national registration system, obtaining accurate statistical information in relation to those that are religious and continue to be active is impossible.

Religious umbrella bodies

Some bodies are denomination specific and/or are established to pursue particular secular activities. Others are more broad based coordinating

---

[40] See Brady, *Religion and the Law of Charities in Ireland*, at p.xiii.

[41] See, for example, the *Ferns Report* and the report of the Investigation Committee and Confidential Committee of the *Commission to Inquire into Child Abuse*, Dublin, May 2009.

[42] See G. Harrahill, Collector General, '*Charities and Taxation: Service and Compliance*', paper presented at the ICTRG conference *Charities Towards 2012*, 8 November 2007, at p.20.

organisations, such as the Irish Council of Churches, an ecumenical umbrella body for Christian denominations in Ireland, and Churches Together in Britain and Ireland, an umbrella body for the Christian churches dealing with issues relevant to England, Wales, Scotland and Ireland.

Government funding: the sector and religious charities

As has recently been noted, 'most Irish nonprofits receive part of their funding from the government, and for many, government provides most of their funding'.[43] Government sources account for not less than 60 per cent of the funding required by nonprofits,[44] mostly in respect of service delivery in the areas of health and social services, education and social housing.[45] A large part of the educational infrastructure in this juris-diction has been and continues to be provided by religious bodies. As many of the buildings and teachers comprising the educational system are provided by religious bodies or to a lesser extent by other independent organisations, religious charities continue to have a real significance.

Government funding of religious charities: the policy

The government commitment to supporting the work of religious char-ities in Ireland, by means that include direct funding, has never been in question. In practice this policy has been one directed almost exclusively towards assisting Roman Catholic organisations, most usually in their role as service providers in health care and education. Many hospitals have been built, and continue to be managed by, Catholic bodies and the permeation of religious belief has on occasions resulted in medical treat-ment being made available subject to religious doctrine: abortion and

---

[43] See M. T. Mullen, F. Nolan (lead developer and database administrator), M. Regan, C. Yena Kim and P. Quinn, *Irish Nonprofits: What Do We Know?*, Irish Nonprofits Knowledge Exchange, 2012, at p.9.

[44] See F. Donoghue, G. Prizeman, A. O'Regan and V. Nöel, *The Hidden Landscape: First Forays into Mapping Nonprofit Organisations in Ireland*, Centre for Nonprofit Management, School of Business, Trinity College, Dublin, 2006. Also see F. Donohue, A. O'Regan, S. McGee and A. M. Donovan, *Exploring the Irish Fundraising Landscape: A Report on the Practice and Scale of Charitable Fundraising from the Public in Ireland*, Centre for Non-Profit Management, School of Business, Trinity College, Dublin, 2007.

[45] See, for example, Office of the Comptroller and Auditor General, *Report on Value for Money Examination: Health Service Executive – Provision of Disability Services by Nonprofit Organisations*, Dublin, 2005.

236   IRELAND

contraception being two areas where religious sanctions have generated most social controversy.

Government funding of religious charities with discriminatory practices

The long established government practice of subsidising the Catholic-controlled provision of services in hospitals and schools is set to continue for the foreseeable future.

In recent years, religiously discriminatory practices in a health care context have been the subject of considerable national and international controversy. In *A, B and C* v. *Ireland*,[46] the ECtHR held that the Article 8 rights of a Lithuanian national resident in Ireland, suffering from a rare form of cancer, had been violated because

> the criminal provisions of the [Offences Against the Person Act 1861] . . . would constitute a significant chilling factor for both women and doctors in the medical consultation process, regardless of whether or not prosecutions have in fact been pursued under that Act. Both the third applicant and any doctor ran a risk of a serious criminal conviction and imprisonment in the event that a decision taken in medical consultation, that the woman was entitled to an abortion in Ireland given the risk to her life, was later found not to accord with Article 40.3.3 of the Constitution.

This case proved to be a sad precursor to the 2012 tragedy of an Indian woman who died in an Irish hospital after being told by a midwife at the hospital that was treating her that she could not have an abortion because Ireland was 'a Catholic country'. As a direct consequence, the Irish government introduced legislation in May 2013 to make abortion available on a limited basis.

In the context of education, the Equal Status Act 2000, s.7(3)(c) allows schools, including schools in receipt of public funding, to discriminate on grounds of religion in relation to admission policy where the objective of the school is to provide education in an environment which promotes certain religious values. The leading case on this matter is *Crowley* v. *Ireland*,[47] which clearly established that the State could support denominationally controlled education in discharging its obligation to provide for free primary education (see below). For many years the vast majority

---

[46] *A, B and C* v. *Ireland* [2010] ECtHR (GC) (No. 25579/05) (16 December 2010).
[47] *Crowley* v. *Ireland* [1980] IR 102.

of parents were content to rely on the system of denominationally controlled education for the schooling of their children. However, in more recent times some parents have asserted their right to educate their children outside of this system, either in non-denominational or multi-denominational schools.

Charity law and the regulatory framework

Charity law and the related regulatory framework have been in a state of limbo for the past four years – one among the many casualties of the economic recession that has so severely impacted the development of social infrastructure in this jurisdiction. Consequently, while the charity law reform process concluded with the comprehensive provisions of the Charities Act 2009, which makes it possible to foresee the future scheme of things, the fact that it remains largely unimplemented means that the pre-reform regime, with all its deficiencies, continues to provide the current operational framework.

Legislation

The Charities Act 2009 was signed into law in February 2009 thereby, seemingly, signalling the end of the traditional Revenue-governed and tax-driven approach to charities. However, much of the 2009 Act is held in abeyance with only seven sections commenced and 92 sections awaiting Ministerial commencement.[48] The few activated provisions of that Act, together with the Charities Acts 1961 and 1973 and the Street and House-to-House Collections Act 1962, provide the current regulatory framework for charities. In addition, the activities of many charities come within the scope of statutes such as the Companies Acts of 1963 and 1990, the Tax Consolidation Act 1997 and the Freedom of Information Act 1997, while all are required to be compliant with the provisions of the European Convention on Human Rights Act 2003.

The charity regulator

In particular, as provisions of the 2009 Act relating to the new Charities Regulatory Authority (CRA) have yet to be implemented,

---

[48] Charities Act 2009, sections 1, 2, 4, 5, 10 (other than subsections 3 and 4), 90 and 99, as commenced by SI 284 of 2009 and SI 315 of 2010.

the Charities Section of the Revenue Commissioners maintains its traditional role as the lead regulatory body for charities in Ireland. Similarly, provisions providing for the winding up of the Commissioners of Charitable Donations and Bequests, in existence since 1845 with a brief to provide support mainly to religious bodies (which were always heavily involved in the work of Irish charities), remain unactivated and this organisation continues its customary administrative functions. Both the Attorney General and the High Court retain their traditional common law functions, as do bodies such as the Probate Office, the Companies Registry Office and the Garda Síochána. The long-standing deficiencies of this regulatory regime – the absence of both a mandatory register of charities[49] and a lead regulatory body with charity-specific supervisory duties – persist, with reliance being instead placed on a voluntary code of practice[50] intended to encourage charities to publish annual accounts and information in the public domain.

Charity law

Charity law in Ireland remains rooted in the common law and anchored on both the Statute of Pious Uses 1634[51] and its English predecessor, the Statute of Charitable Uses 1601.[52] It has developed to become more facilitative than interventionist and remains dependent upon an outdated statutory framework consisting of the Charities Acts of 1961 and 1973, since modified by the Social Welfare Consolidation Act 2005 (as amended), which are closely modelled on the provisions of the English Charities Act 1960. Aspects of fundraising by charities are addressed by the Street and House-to-House Collections Act 1962 and the Casual Trading Act 1995. The law has long been given effect through a range of government bodies and legal structures which have quite traditional legal functions. The decision to defer implementation of the 2009 Act leaves charity law in Ireland very largely governed by this regulatory framework.

---

[49] Note that a list of bodies accepted as charitable organisations for the purposes of s.11 of Table 2 of Schedule 3 of the Social Welfare Consolidation Act 2005 (as amended), is kept by the Dept of Social Protection. See, further, at: www.welfare.ie/EN/Operational Guidelines/pages/meanslist.aspx (accessed 3 January 2014).

[50] Developed by the Irish Charities and Tax Research association, the industry's coordinating body.

[51] 10 Car. 1, Sess. 3, Cap. 1.   [52] 43 Eliz. 1, Cap. 4.

The common law

The traditional common law definitions, concepts and rules remain in place (See Chapter 2). Charitable purposes in Ireland are as classified by *Pemsel*: for the relief of poverty, the advancement of education and religion and for other purposes beneficial to the community, as broadened in keeping with 'the spirit and intendment rule'; accompanied by the public benefit presumption in relation to the first three *Pemsel* heads. The public benefit test, however, has important and distinctive features (see below) while the rule requiring exclusiveness in relation to charitable purposes has been applied with some equivocation by the Irish judiciary. So, for example, in *Jackson* v. *Attorney General*,[53] 'missionary purposes' were held not to be exclusively charitable, therefore there was no charitable trust. Similarly, in *Re Moore*[54] a gift for the Pope was found not to be exclusively charitable but, particularly where religious orders or institutions were involved,[55] the rule was not strictly applied. Eventually it was displaced by the Charities Act 1961, s.49(1), which provided that 'where any of the purposes of a gift includes or could be deemed to include both charitable and non-charitable objects, its terms shall be so construed and given effect as to exclude the non-charitable objects and the purpose shall, accordingly, be treated as charitable'.[56]

Charity law reform

The drivers for reform were much the same in Ireland as in other common law jurisdictions where charity matters were customarily addressed by the Revenue as an aspect of its remit for tax administration. Essentially, the main difficulties with this approach were: the lack of a charity register with no reliable information as to how many charities existed, where they were located, their size, wealth or type; the absence of a charity-specific regulator responsible for policing charitable status and supervising standards of probity; uncoordinated government agency involvement with charities; no requirement that all charities should adhere

---

[53] *Jackson* v. *Attorney General* (1917) 1 IR 332.   [54] *Re Moore* (1919) 1 IR 316.

[55] See, for example: *Phelan* v. *Slattery* (1887) 19 LR Ir 177; *Bradshaw* v. *Jackman* (1887) 21 LR Ir 12; *Reichenbach* v. *Quin* (1888) 21 LR Ir 138; *Armstrong* v. *Reeves* (1890) 25 LR Ir 325; *Re Gibbons* [1917] 1 IR 448; *Re Ryan's Will Trusts* (1926) 60 ILTR 57; *Re Byrne* [1935] IR 782; *Re Keogh's Estate* [1945] IR 13.

[56] This relaxed approach to the rule was ended by the 2009 Act, s.2.

240   IRELAND

to uniform standards of accountability and transparency, including annual reports on their activities, income and assets. In this jurisdiction the High Court remained the only body vested with sufficient powers to broaden the interpretation of public benefit and thereby able to adjust the definition of charitable purposes to meet the contemporary pattern of social need. However, as in other common law nations, its capacity to do so had become severely constrained as opportunities to develop case precedents faded due to the expense, time and negative media exposure that stemmed the flow of litigation.

Reform process

The need for reform had been noted repeatedly in the closing years of the twentieth century. In the 1990s, both the Costello report[57] and the Advisory Group[58] had called for the reform of the law relating to the administration and regulation of charities, and this had been reinforced by some well-publicised scandals.[59] The government responded with a 'green paper',[60] a 'white paper'[61] and then silence. Subsequently, a report from the Law Society[62] followed by the Arthur Cox-led Review[63] triggered a new government resolve and it declared in the 2002 *Agreed Programme for Government* its commitment to reform the law relating to charity: 'A comprehensive reform of the law relating to charities will be enacted to ensure accountability and to protect against abuse of charitable status and fraud.'[64]

---

[57] See the *Report of the Committee on Fundraising Activities for Charitable and Other Purposes*, Stationery Office, Dublin, 1990 (also known as the Costello Report).

[58] See *Report of the Advisory Group on Charities/Fundraising Legislation*, Department of Equality and Law Reform, November 1996.

[59] Notably, the long-running media exposure of improper practice in the Irish Society for the Prevention of Cruelty to Children.

[60] See Department of Social Welfare, *Supporting Voluntary Activity: A Green Paper on the Community Voluntary Sector and its Relationship with the State*, Stationery Office, Dublin, 1997.

[61] See Department of Social Welfare, *Supporting Voluntary Activity: A White Paper for Supporting Voluntary Activity and for Developing the Relationship between the State and the Community and Voluntary Sector*, Stationery Office, Dublin, 2001.

[62] See Law Society of Ireland Law Reform Committee, *Charity Law: The Case for Reform* (July 2002), pp.73–76, at: www.lawsociety.ie/Gazette/Search-Gazette-Archive (accessed 3 January 2014).

[63] See Arthur Cox and the Centre for Voluntary Action Studies, *Charity Law Review*, Dublin, March 2002.

[64] *Agreed Programme for Government*, Dublin, June 2002.

The reform process, which included a consultation process and the issue of two bills,[65] concluded in February 2009 with the introduction of the 2009 Act[66] but then, after a change of government, plans for implementation were suspended. In 2011 departmental responsibility for charity regulation was transferred to Justice and Equality and in the following year a public consultation was announced to progress plans for implementation.

Reform outcomes

The Charities Act 2009 provided for certain regulatory changes: the decoupling of tax administration from charitable status determination;[67] establishing the CRA with defined powers, duties and functions (although ultimate responsibility for designating tax-exempt status between the CRA and Revenue remains unclear);[68] the dissolution of the Board of the Commissioners of Charitable Donations and Bequests for Ireland; the consolidation and updating of powers to assist the administration of charities previously vested in said Board and now in the CRA; the establishment of a register of charities, with a mandatory registration requirement for all entities wishing to acquire or retain charitable status; and the setting up of the Charity Appeals Board. It also addressed the traditional common law conceptual basis of charity, providing for: a broader range of charitable purposes; a new definition of 'charity'; and the assertion of a defined 'public benefit' test to be applied to all charitable purposes excepting the advancement of religion. In relation to religion and religious charities, the most significant changes effected by the 2009 Act are likely to be found in the broader range of charitable purposes and in the public benefit test.

Charitable purposes

Until the relevant provisions of the 2009 Act are implemented the law will continue to be framed by the four *Pemsel* heads. Once implemented, the 2009 Act will define a purpose as charitable if it is of public benefit

---

[65] The Irish Charities General Scheme Bill 2006 and Irish Charities Bill 2007.

[66] The 2009 Act was signed into law by President Mary McAleese on 28 February 2009.

[67] See the Charities Act 2009, s.7.

[68] Ibid. This section provides that in performing its functions under tax legislation, Revenue shall not be bound by the CRA determination as to whether a purpose is of public benefit.

242   IRELAND

and if its aim is: the prevention or relief of poverty or economic hardship; the advancement of education; the advancement of religion; or any
other purpose that is of benefit to the community. In addition to
enlarging the first head to allow for the prevention as well as the
relief of poverty, s.(3)(1)(d) restates the fourth head but adds, under
s.3(11), that this is to include 12 specific new charitable purposes.

For present purposes, the most distinctive aspects of the *Pemsel*-
plus list embodied in the Charities Act 2009, differentiating it from
its UK counterparts, are: an absence of any reference to human
rights[69] or of equality and diversity; and the mention of the advancement of conflict resolution or reconciliation as supplemented by the
promotion of religious or racial harmony and harmonious community relations.

The public benefit test and religious organisations

The concept of public benefit lies at the heart of charity law. It was
central to the legal concept of charity in the common law and continues
to be so in statute law: s.3 of the 2009 Act clearly states that '(2) a purpose
shall not be a charitable purpose unless it is of public benefit'. There is no
equivalent to the requirement in Scotland that account be taken of any
possible 'dis-benefit' that might be likely to arise as a consequence of the
intended method of pursuing such a purpose.

The test

The 'public' arm of the test has been interpreted in a remarkably
generous fashion in this jurisdiction. While the number constituting a
sufficient proportion of 'the public' has never been determined, Keane
J in *Re the Worth Library*[70] by implication found three named individuals
adequate to warrant charitable status. Also, unlike the UK jurisdictions,
with their broad interpretations of 'religion', in this jurisdiction the test
is applied to a narrower, more traditional definition.

In Ireland, the public benefit test has long had the following distinctive
characteristics: an entity, gift or bequest dedicated to the purpose of

---

[69] See O. Breen, 'Too Political to be Charitable? The Charities Act 2009 and the Future of
Human Rights Organisations in Ireland' (2012) *Public Law* 268.
[70] *Re the Worth Library* [1994] 1 ILRM 161.

CHARITY LAW AND THE REGULATORY FRAMEWORK 243

advancing religion is presumed to satisfy the test;[71] that presumption has for many years been given statutory recognition;[72] the presumption extends to private piety whether in the form of masses[73] or closed religious orders;[74] and it has been customary to apply a subjective test to determine whether or not a gift satisfies the public benefit test[75] (i.e. the courts will pose the question: did the donor believe that the purpose to which he or she was directing a gift was of a charitable nature?[76]). As Fitzgibbon LJ explained in *In re Cranston, Webb* v. *Oldfield*,[77] 'the benefit must be one which the founder believes to be of public advantage, and his belief must be at least rational and not contrary either to the general law of the land or to the principles of morality'. Moreover, s.45 of the Charities Act 1961 gives statutory effect to the ruling in *O'Hanlon* v. *Logue*,[78] where Palles CB established that a gift for the saying of masses, whether in public or private, satisfied the public benefit test and, being affirmed by the subjective judicial approach,[79] was determinative of a donor's charitable intent.

Under the 2009 Act, s.3, '(4) It shall be presumed, unless the contrary is proved, that a gift for the advancement of religion is of public benefit.' This provision changes the law only to the extent that it substitutes a rebuttable presumption for the previous prescriptive approach,

---

[71] See: *Powerscourt* v. *Powerscourt* 1 Moll 616; *Arnott* v. *Arnott* [1906] [1911] 1 IR 289; and *Rickerby* v. *Nicholson* [1912] 1 IR 343, in which Ross J declared that 'according to our law a bequest for a religious purpose is *prima facie* charitable'.

[72] See the Charities Act 1961, s.45(1).

[73] The Statute of Chantries 1547 led to gifts for the saying of masses being deemed illegal in England and Wales but it never applied to Ireland, where the validity of such gifts was recognised: see *Commissioners of Charitable Donations and Bequests* v. *Walsh* (1828) 7 IR Eq R 34n and *Read* v. *Hodgins* (1844) 7 IR Eq R 1.

[74] See *Re Howley* [1940] IR 109, which stands in direct contrast to the corresponding decision taken in *Cocks* v. *Manners* (1871) LR 12 Eq 574, where the view of the English courts was that a gift for a closed Dominican convent could not be charitable.

[75] Initially established by Palles CB in *O'Hanlon* v. *Logue* [1906] IR 247, the leading Irish case in this context is *In re Cranston, Webb* v. *Oldfield* [1898] 1 IR 431.

[76] See *In re the Worth Library* [1994] 1 ILRM 161, *per* Keane J, where he stated:

> In every case, the intention of the testator is of paramount importance. If he intended to advance a charitable object recognised as such by the law, his gift will be a charitable gift.

[77] *In re Cranston, Webb* v. *Oldfield* [1898] 1 IR 431, at p.447.

[78] *O'Hanlon* v. *Logue* [1906] IR 247. See also: *Arnott* v. *Arnott (No 2)* [1906] 1 IR 127; and *Rickerby* v. *Nicholson* [1912] 1 IR 343.

[79] In *Gilmour* v. *Coats* [1949] AC 426, the House of Lords took the view that the subjective approach had no relevance to trusts for religious purposes.

which declared that such gifts were conclusively presumed to be for the public benefit.[80] Basically, it remains the case that once the court or regulatory authority recognises a religious body as such then, unless the purpose of a gift to it is clearly in some way illegal or immoral, it will be presumed charitable; this may be rebutted. Even where there is evidence suggesting that grounds exist for such a rebuttal, the regulatory authority must first obtain the consent of the Attorney General before denying charitable status to a religious organisation,[81] but thereafter its decision is final.[82] Keane J, in *Campaign to Separate Church and State* v. *Minister for Education*,[83] reasoned that the presumption of public benefit in relation to religious charitable status is due to the centrality of religious belief and activity to Irish culture and society.

The Act also clarifies that the charitable purpose includes any financial provision made by a religious organisation or community for the accommodation and care of its members. It is also worthy of note that the distinctive approach to religious institutions in Ireland is reinforced by an additional privilege granted to them in the definition of 'charitable organisation' provided in s.2 of the 2009 Act. Within that definition an exception is made to the general rule that to satisfy the definition such an organisation 'under its constitution, is required to apply all of its property (both real and personal) in furtherance of that purpose'. The provision goes on to provide an exemption from the restrictions solely in favour of 'a religious organisation or community, on accommodation and care of members of the organisation or community'. In addition, one of the four main exemptions from the requirement to register, under s.48(6) of the 2009 Act, is in relation to an 'education body'.[84] As many of

---

[80] Under the Charities Act 1961, s.45(1):

> In determining whether or not a gift for the purpose of the advancement of religion is a valid charitable gift it shall be conclusively presumed that the purpose includes and will occasion public benefit.

Note the view of the Law Society's Law Reform Committee in *Charity Law: The Case for Reform*, Dublin, July 2002: 'We recommend that no change be made to section 45 of the Charities Act 1961.'

[81] Charities Act 2009, s.3(5).

[82] Charities Act 2009, s.3(9), specifically preventing any further appeal process.

[83] *Campaign to Separate Church and State* v. *Minister for Education* [1998] 3 IR 321, *per* Keane J, at pp.330–331.

[84] See the Education Act 1998, s.18, and Universities Act 1997, s.39, both of which impose upon such bodies the same requirement to 'keep all proper and usual accounts and records of all monies received by it or expenditure of such monies incurred by it' for inspection by relevant government authorities.

these are owned and/or managed by religious organisations this will have the effect of enabling them to avoid the levels of fiscal monitoring, regulatory accountability and public transparency now expected of all other charities. To some extent this is counterbalanced by the removal of an anomolous privilege hitherto available that exempted incorporated religious charities from filing annual returns under company law:[85] s.52(5) will require full financial accounts from religious charities, whether incorporated or unincorporated.

Religion, religious beliefs and the advancement of religion

The impact of charity law reform in this jurisdiction has left religious charities largely untouched. Despite the very considerable cultural changes it has experienced over recent decades, particularly as regards the traditional congruity between citizenship and Catholicism, there is nothing in the 2009 Act to reflect the religious pluralism that Ireland has attained in the early years of the twenty-first century.

Religion

A statutory definition of 'religion', introduced by the 2009 Act, restates the common law interpretation but allows the determination of what constitutes the advancement of any religion to be defined on the religion's own terms, i.e. in accordance with 'the laws, canons, ordinances and tenets of the religion concerned'. The broad principle remains as expressed by Walker LC in *O'Hanlon* v. *Logue*:

> a gift for the advancement of 'religion' is a charitable gift; and that in applying this principle, the Court does not enter into an inquiry as to the truth or soundness of any religious doctrine, provided it be not contrary to morals or contain nothing contrary to law. . . . Whether the subject of the gift be religious or for an educational purpose, the Court does not set up its own opinion. It is enough that it is not illegal, or contrary to public policy, or opposed to the settled principles of morality.[86]

The basic indicators, judicially employed to differentiate a religious body from others, continue to be a belief in a Supreme Being, together with a shared commitment to faith and worship. Nor is any statutory recognition given to philosophical beliefs, though s.3(10) of the 2009 Act

---

[85] See the Companies (Amendment) Act 1986, s.2.
[86] *O'Hanlon* v. *Logue* [1906] 1 IR 247, at pp.259–260.

denies charitable status to any organisation or cult, and of gifts to any such entity.

Belief in a Supreme Being

A religion will not gain judicial recognition as such unless its adherents at least profess belief in a 'Supreme Being'. The view that a legal definition of religion could be satisfied by a system of belief not involving faith in a god has been consistently rejected and the legislators have clearly chosen not to avail of the opportunity to break with tradition by extending recognition to non-theistic faiths nor to philosophical beliefs in the 2009 Act.[87] However, while Irish statutory law retains the traditional requirement of a belief in god, the case law explicitly extends the constitutional guarantee of freedom of religion beyond monotheistic Christian religions.[88]

Worship, religious tenets, doctrines, etc.

In addition to a belief in god or gods, members of a religion must practise a common form of worship and have a shared faith that draws from the same body of beliefs. The importance of the latter is evident from s.3(6) of the 2009 Act, reiterating the wording of the equivalent provision in s.45 of the 1961 Act, stating that 'a charitable gift for the purpose of the advancement of religion shall have effect, and the terms upon which it is given shall be construed, in accordance with the laws, canons, ordinances and tenets of the religion concerned'. The court or regulatory authority have traditionally examined such matters in order to ascertain the moral and spiritual values of the religion concerned and to be assured that they are beneficial. Worship must have at least some of the following characteristics: submission to the object worshipped; veneration of that object; praise, thanksgiving, prayer or intercession.

The necessity for doctrinal evidence to substantiate an ostensible religious practice was demonstrated recently in *McNally & Anor* v.

---

[87] See comments of Minister Curran, Report Stage Debates of the Charities Bill, 2007 Vol. 192 No. 16 *Seanad Debates* 1059.

[88] See O. Breen, 'Neighbouring Perspectives: Legal and Practical Implications of Charity Regulatory Reform in Ireland and Northern Ireland' (2008) 59:2 *Northern Ireland Legal Quarterly* 223, at p.230, citing *Corway* v. *Independent Newspapers (Ireland) Ltd.* [1999] 4 IR 484, *per* Barrington J, at p.502.

Ireland & Ors,[89] which concerned the distribution and sale of mass cards contrary to s.99 of the Charities Act 2009.[90] As MacMenamin J noted, 'the purchase of mass cards is a Roman Catholic practice, governed by canon law and the regulation of that faith'.[91] It is significant that in determining the issue, MacMenamin J felt the need to call expert witnesses to give evidence on canon law doctrine.

Philosophy and other value systems

There is no specific provision in the Irish statutory definition of charitable purposes for recognition of philosophical beliefs. Attempts to introduce recognition for humanism as charitable under the advancement of religion heading failed and instead it is registered under education.[92] The interpretation of 'religion' remains close to the definition given to it in *Bowman* v. *Secular Society,*[93] when it was held to mean a faith in a higher power, to the exclusion of ethical principles or rationalism.

After implementation of the 2009 Act, any recognition for a philosophical or other value system, as charitable under any other heading than as a religious purpose, will first require it to satisfy the public benefit test.

The advancement of religion

A religious entity, or any gift to such an entity, must promote, maintain or practise that religion, and thereby spread awareness of its particular beliefs and increase the number of its adherents, if it is to acquire or retain charitable status. In Ireland this has often been achieved by conferring gifts in aid of private piety; a distinctive characteristic of religious charitable trusts in this jurisdiction.[94] Such gifts include those

---

[89] *McNally & Anor* v. *Ireland & Ors* [2009] IEHC 573.

[90] Ibid. Judicial notice was taken of the scale of this business: the plaintiff's sales amounted to €250,000 for 2008; the Irish market was estimated at approximately €4 million. A practice traditionally known as 'simony' and defined in the *Oxford Dictionary* (2nd edn) as the buying and selling benefices, ecclesiastical preferments or other spiritual things.

[91] Ibid., at para. 8.   [92] See Breen, 'Neighbouring Perspectives', at p.231.

[93] *Bowman* v. *Secular Society* [1917] AC 406.

[94] See: *Attorney General* v. *Hall* [1897] 2 IR 426; *O'Hanlon* v. *Logue* [1906] 1 IR 247 (holding bequests for masses to be valid charitable gifts); *Maguire* v. *Attorney General* [1943] 1 IR 238 (holding a bequest to establish a convent for an enclosed order of Catholic nuns to be a valid charitable gift under *Irish Bank of Ireland Trustee Co. Ltd.* v. *Attorney General* [1957] 1 IR 257, at pp.274–277. As cited in Breen, 'Neighbouring Perspectives', at p.234.

248   IRELAND

for the celebration of masses, in public or private. Gifts of this nature have long been a distinctive characteristic of Irish charitable activity, traditionally distinguishing it in particular from the non-charitable status of such activity in the United Kingdom.[95] When, however, a gift for masses to be said is attached as a condition to the vesting of a primary gift then the former will lapse due to unenforceability.[96] Again, a gift for masses may fail if it is too remote[97] or if it consists simply of an annual sum for masses to be said it will then be void for being in breach of the rule against perpetuities.[98]

This approach has been evident also in gifts to closed contemplative religious orders, as opposed to those actively engaged in good works in the community.[99] The decision taken by the Irish courts in *Re Howley*[100] stands in direct contrast to that taken in *Gilmour* v. *Coats*.[101] Gavan Duffy J, in *Maguire* v. *Attorney General*,[102] gave a reasoned rejection of the relevance of English case law and set the law in Ireland on a different course. The court received testimony that:

> Perpetual adoration is an expression well known to members of the Catholic Church. It is a form of devotion to the Blessed Sacrament whereby in some suitable church or chapel arrangements are made, necessarily by a community for an unbroken succession of persons to be present in private prayer and in contemplation before the Blessed Sacrament exposed to the full view of the worshippers. ... The adoration of the Blessed Sacrament might be considered an extension of the ceremony and sacrifice of the Mass. ... The existence of a convent devoted to Perpetual Adoration was unquestionably a source of edification and of spiritual and moral benefit to all Catholics.

---

[95] See *Re Hetherington* [1989] 2 All ER 129, where it was finally confirmed that such gifts are *prima facie* charitable.

[96] See *Brannigan* v. *Murphy* [1896] 1 IR 418.

[97] See *In re Stratheden* [1894] 3 Ch. 265.

[98] See *Thompson* v. *Shakespeare* [1860] 1 De G F & J 399 and *Chamberlayne* v. *Brockett* (1872) LR 8 Ch. App. 206.

[99] See, for example, *Cocks* v. *Manners* (1871) LR 12 Eq 574.

[100] *Re Howley* [1940] IR 109.   [101] *Gilmour* v. *Coats* [1949] AC 426.

[102] *Maguire* v. *Attorney General* [1943] IR 238. See also *Re Howley* [1940] IR 109, where Gavan Duffy J stated:

> The assumption that the Irish public find no edification in cloistered lives, devoted purely to spiritual ends, postulates a close assimilation of the Irish outlook to the English, not obviously warranted by the traditions and mores of the Irish people.

THE ADVANCEMENT OF RELIGION 249

Referring to such a convent as a 'spiritual powerhouse', Gavan Duffy J commented that:

> it is a shock to one's sense of propriety and a grave discredit to the law that there should, in this Catholic country, be any doubt about the validity of a trust to expend money in founding a convent for the perpetual adoration of the Blessed Sacrament.

Reaching behind the Elizabethan statutes to the common law, Gavan Duffy J found ample authority for the proposition that gifts for religious purposes, which served to neither instruct nor edify the public, could nevertheless be charitable. As had been previously noted by Black J, 'example is sometimes better than precept, and the pattern of a self-sacrificing life may impress some more than an indifferent sermon'.[103] Gavan Duffy J accordingly ruled that religious activity of devoted dedication was sufficient to qualify the bequest as charitable.

Other gifts traditionally guaranteed charitable status include: to build, maintain or repair churches and their fixtures; the upkeep of graves; the support of clergy; and for missionary purposes. In Ireland, as a consequence of s.45 of the 1961 Act, the public benefit test had no application to trusts for the advancement of religion; a prescriptive approach moderated somewhat by s.3(4) of the 2009 Act.

The means for advancing religion

A gift expressed to be for 'religious purposes' or for the advancement of religion in general will usually be considered charitable.[104] Romilly MR upheld as charitable a testamentary annuity for three persons forever to study the Bible and to say a prayer on his anniversary in praise of God.[105] Equally, where the gift is intended for a specific religion it will be similarly upheld, as in *Copinger* v. *Crehane*[106] concerning a gift 'for the advancement and benefit of the Roman Catholic religion', and in *re Bonnet dec'd.; Johnston* v. *Langheld*,[107] where the court dealt with the question of general charitable intention of a gift to the Lutheran Church, giving rise to a query as to whether the gift was to the Lutheran Church or to the Protestant Church in general – as the testator had been a member of the Lutheran Church the court held that it had been her

---

[103] See *Munster and Leinster Bank Ltd.* v. *Attorney General* [1940] IR 19, at p.30.
[104] *Arnott* v. *Arnott* [1906] 1 IR 127.   [105] *In Re Michel* (1860) 28 Beav. 39.
[106] *Copinger* v. *Crehane* (1877) IR 11 Eq 429.
[107] *Re Bonnet dec'd.; Johnston* v. *Langheld* [1983] ILRM 359.

intention to confer a benefit on that body. The reverse proposition is also true: if a gift is clearly stated and intended to go to a religious institution, the fact that the institution has not been named will not invalidate its charitable nature.

A gift may be made not to a particular religious body but in support of a specified service or enterprise. The purpose must then be clearly identified. So, a gift to enable invalids to travel to Lourdes was upheld by Budd J as charitable on the grounds that this would fall within the definition of an 'organised religious pilgrimage' as approved by the relevant religious body and incorporating a public benefit element.[108] In relation to missionary work, gifts to 'the Christian Brethren',[109] to 'foreign missions'[110] to enable Church of Ireland missionaries to convert Roman Catholic Irishmen[111] and to 'Presbyterian missions and orphans'[112] have been upheld as charitable, while gifts for 'missionary purposes'[113] have failed due to vagueness.

Public policy, charity and common law constraints

Charitable activity in Ireland has been dominated by and focused upon religious purposes as defined by Catholicism. This largely continues to be the case. The constitutional endorsement of Catholicism, together with the protection provided by a statutory declaration that religious purposes are presumed to be for the public benefit, within a nation that has traditionally been characterised by its collective adherence to the same religious belief, have contributed to an innate Irish blend of religion, charity and public policy.

Testamentary conditions and the common law

The traditional judicial approach of respect for bequests made subject to religious conditions has been continued in Ireland as in other common law jurisdictions.[114] Following English precedents, unless a gift by donor

---

[108] *Re McCarthy's Wills' Trusts* [1958] IR 311.   [109] *Re Browne* [1898] 1 IR 423.

[110] *Dunne* v. *Duignan* [1908] 1 IR 228.

[111] *Attorney-General* v. *Becher* [1910] 2 IR 251.

[112] *Jackson* v. *Attorney General* [1917] 1 IR 332.

[113] *Scott* v. *Brownrigg* (1881) 9 LR IR 246.

[114] See, further, S. Grattan and H. Conway, 'Testamentary Conditions in Restraint of Religion in the Twenty-first Century: An Anglo-Canadian Perspective' (2005) 50 *McGill Law Journal* 511.

PUBLIC POLICY AND COMMON LAW CONSTRAINTS   251

or testator failed for technical reasons, was in breach of the criminal law or public policy, was morally subversive,[115] devoid of all merit,[116] made with an improper motive[117] or was compromised by a relationship nexus with the intended beneficiaries, then it would normally be valid. The law in this context must in future be read subject to the Charities Act 2009, s.3(7), which provides that 'in determining whether a gift is of public benefit or not, account shall be taken of – (a) any limitation imposed by the donor of the gift on the class of persons who may benefit from the gift and whether or not such limitation is justified and reasonable, having regard to the nature of the purpose of the gift'.

Failure due to breach of common law rules

Of the common law rules, a breach of the 'exclusivity' requirement has often in the past proven fatal for an intended charitable bequest (see Chapter 2). This has been the case where there is an uncertainty factor in relation to the testator's intention, such as where a gift of £10,000 was made 'to his holiness ... the Pope ... to use and apply at his sole discretion in the carrying out of the sacred office';[118] or where the terms allow for the possibility that a non-charitable purpose could have been intended, as where a gift was expressed to be for 'charitable, religious or other societies, institutions, persons or objects' or for 'such Roman Catholic purposes in the parish of Coleraine and elsewhere' as the trustees may determine.[119] As explained by Chatterton VC in *Copinger*, 'where there is discretion to apply it to charitable purposes, or to other purposes not charitable, and the trust is indefinite, the gift fails'.[120]

The law on the effect of mixing charitable and non-charitable purposes was thoroughly reviewed by Black J in *Munster and Leinster Bank v. Attorney- General*,[121] in which he placed great reliance on the earlier judgment of the Supreme Court in *Re Byrne*.[122] Black J had to determine

---

[115] *Thornton* v. *Howe* (1862) 31 Beav. 14.
[116] See *Re Watson* [1973] 1 WLR 1472, where it was stated that 'a religious charity can only be shown not to be for the public benefit if its doctrines are adverse to the foundations of all religion and subversive of all morality'.
[117] *Tempest* v. *Lord Camoys* (1882) 21 Ch D 571 (CA).   [118] *Re Moore* [1919] 1 IR 316.
[119] *MacLaughlin* v. *Campbell* [1906] 1 IR 588.
[120] *Copinger* v. *Crehane* (1877) IR 11 Eq 429, at p.431.
[121] *Munster and Leinster Bank* v. *Attorney- General* [1940] IR 19.
[122] *Re Byrne* [1935] IR 782.

whether a gift to a branch of the Catholic Young Men's Society of Ireland was a charitable gift. He examined the constitution and rules of the Society and noted that 'the promotion of the religious welfare of the members is intended to be, and is beyond doubt, an object of the Society'. However, closer inspection revealed that the Society also had a number of other non-charitable objects, so inextricably entangled with its charitable object, as to render the whole gift non-charitable. The introduction of the 1961 Act brought this well-litigated area of law to an end and with it the possibility of a whole trust failing to acquire charitable status because a part of it addressed, or allowed for the possibility that it might address, a non-charitable purpose.

Bequests subject to a religious condition

Parachin notes that in Ireland the courts followed the precedents established in English courts.[123] For example in *Duggan* v. *Kelly*,[124] a condition against marrying a Papist was upheld and so, in *Re McKenna*,[125] was a condition against marrying a Roman Catholic, while in *Re Knox*[126] the court upheld a condition restricting marriage to a Protestant wife with Protestant parents. However, in *Re Doyle*[127] the condition required the donee to be a Roman Catholic at the testator's death and to give an undertaking to her parish priest that she would remain one. Justice Kenny held the condition void as being impossible to perform, but added that it was also void as being unconstitutional.

Religious preferences and public policy

Although charity law in Ireland has in most respects followed the precedents established in England, it has evolved a more benign approach when issues arise relating to the compatibility of matters of religion and public policy. Where the neighbouring jurisdiction has turned away from extending charitable status to pious uses, closed religious orders, etc., Ireland has embraced these as appropriately charitable.

---

[123] See A. Parachin, 'The Definition of Charity and Public Law Equality Norms', paper presented at the conference *Private and Public Law: Intersections in Law and Method*, the T.C. Beirne Law School at the University of Queensland, Brisbane, July 2011.
[124] *Duggan* v. *Kelly* (1847) 10 IR Eq R 295.   [125] *Re McKenna* [1947] IR 277.
[126] *Re Knox* (1889) 23 LR Ir 542 (Ch.).   [127] Unreported, High Court, Kenny J (1972).

Public policy constraints

The 2009 Act specifically excludes the following bodies from having charitable status:[128] a body that promotes purposes that are (1) unlawful, (2) contrary to public morality, (3) contrary to public policy, (4) in support of terrorism or terrorist activities, whether in the State or outside the State, (5) for the benefit of an organisation of which membership is unlawful.

The leading Irish case in this context is still *In re Cranston, Webb* v. *Oldfield,*[129] where, in relation to the particular issue of whether or not a gift to certain vegetarian societies could be construed as charitable, Ashborne LJ took a broad view that had a more general applicability:

> It may be that this idea of vegetarianism has not yet made its way in the world. It may be showing no growth. The vast majority may be opposed to it. It may be disapproved of by medical men. Possibly no member of the Bench may believe in it. But these considerations cannot be regarded as decisive to exclude it from the wide class of gifts regarded by the law as charitable. . . . I do not feel at liberty to sit in judgment upon objects or purposes, or to measure the success they now have, or hereafter may attain to.

This approach, a surprisingly accurate precursor to that currently deployed in other jurisdictions to confer judicial recognition on emerging variants of religious or philosophical belief, was wholly endorsed by Keane J in *In re the Worth Library.*[130] Also, in *Re Ni Brudair,*[131] Gannon J held that a bequest for the benefit of republicans was too vague to be charitable but that had it been properly defined it would still have amounted to a broad statement of political objectives and would not have constituted a valid charitable trust. In *Colgan* v. *Independent Radio and Television Commission,*[132] the Irish High Court defined a 'political end' within the context of the Radio and Television Act 1988, as being an activity that is:

> directed towards furthering the interests of a particular political party or towards procuring changes in the laws of this country or . . . countering suggested changes in those laws, or towards procuring changes in the laws of a foreign country or countering suggested changes in those laws

---

[128] 2009 Act, s.2(1). [129] *In re Cranston, Webb* v. *Oldfield* [1898] 1 IR 431.
[130] *In re the Worth Library* [1994] 1 ILRM 161, at p.193.
[131] Unreported, High Court, Gannon J, 5 February 1979.
[132] *Colgan* v. *Independent Radio and Television Commission* [2000] 2 IR 490 (HC). Also see *Gurhy* v. *Goff* [1980] ILRM 103 (SC).

254   IRELAND

> or procuring a reversal of government policy or of particular decisions of
> governmental authorities in this country or ... countering suggested
> reversals thereof or procuring a reversal of governmental policy or of
> particular decisions of governmental authorities in a foreign country or
> countering suggested reversals thereof.[133]

The crucial issue is whether an organisation intends to pursue political activity as its principal objective or whether it is merely pursued ancillary to and in support of a main objective which is not itself political: the former being definitely incompatible with charitable status.

Advocacy

In relation to the common law rule that an organisation seeking to acquire or retain charitable status and qualify for attendant tax privileges must avoid having political purposes and engaging in most forms of advocacy, Ireland has followed English precedents.[134] Under s.2(b) of the 2009 Act, organisations that advocate in favour of a political cause, which is directly related to the advancement of their charitable purpose, will be able to register as charities. This leaves the law in as an unsatisfactory state after as before the 2009 Act: an organisation intending to campaign for a change in the law, as its sole or main objective, will still have to forego charitable status.

Proselytism

The experience of proselytism in Ireland is largely an aspect of its colonial history, when England pursued a forceful policy of inducing the conversion of its Catholic neighbours to Protestantism, a policy which in Ireland is irredeemably associated with the mid nineteenth-century famine. More recently the Irish contribution to Catholic missionary work in Africa and elsewhere has been very considerable and in that context, proselytism was undoubtedly vigorously pursued.

In *Murphy* v. *Ireland*[135] the ECtHR upheld the State's restriction of a radio advertisement on a local independent commercial radio station

---

[133] *Colgan* v. *Independent Radio and Television Commission* [2000] 2 IR 490 (HC), *per* O'Sullivan J, at p.504.
[134] See, for example, *Bowman* v. *Secular Society* [1917] AC 406, *National Anti-vivisection Society* v. *Inland Revenue Commissioners* [1948] AC 31 (HL) and *McGovern* v. *Attorney General* [1982] Ch. 321.
[135] App. No. 44179/98 [2004] 38 EHRR 212.

that promoted the screening of a film in praise of the Christian faith. The prohibited religious advertisement in fact neither opposed, nor denied the religious claims of other groups, apart from to the degree to which, as the Irish government put it 'the simple proclamation of the truth of one religion necessarily proclaims the untruth of another' and 'as such, even innocuous religious expression can lead to volatile and explosive reactions'.[136]

In the future, proselytism in Ireland will be governed to some extent by s.3(10) of the 2009 Act. This provision denies charitable status to any entity that has used 'oppressive psychological manipulation' as a means of acquiring adherents.

Public policy and the Pemsel-plus charitable purposes

Ireland has statutorily introduced much the same set of *Pemsel*-plus charitable purposes as in the UK jurisdictions, including the advancement of human rights, conflict resolution or reconciliation and the promotion of multiculturalism, etc.[137] A notable difference from the corresponding provisions in all the UK jurisdictions is the Irish exemption of religious purposes from the public benefit test. The *Pemsel*-plus list creates a new and more inclusive statutory platform that will facilitate the future contribution of charity to specific public benefit activity and clarify the terms of reference of government's intended partnership with the sector.

Human rights, discrimination and religious charities: contemporary issues

The constitutional fusion of State institutions, citizenship and Catholicism, in which the independent Republic of Ireland was launched, to a considerable extent continues to provide the contemporary context for dealing with issues involving the role of religious charities and discrimination. This legacy is largely responsible for the conflation of issues of sexuality and religion which now seem to characterise many of the cases that result in Ireland appearing before the ECtHR.

---

[136] Ibid., at para. 38.
[137] See the Charities Act 2009, s.3(11)(e): 'the advancement of conflict resolution or reconciliation', as supplemented by (f) 'the promotion of religious or racial harmony and harmonious community relations'. The Act is singular in that no mention is made of human rights nor of equality and diversity.

Human rights

The Human Rights Act 2003 came into force on 31 December 2003. The statute does not directly incorporate the European Convention into domestic law but partially incorporates it and several of its protocols, which the State has ratified since 1953. Domestic courts are now subject to the instruction in s.2 that 'in interpreting and applying any statutory provision or rule of law, a court shall, in so far as is possible, subject to the rules of law relating to such interpretation and application, do so in a manner compatible with the State's obligations under the Convention provisions'.[138] Surprisingly, the Charities Act 2009 failed to give any recognition to the new standing of human rights in Irish law.

The European Convention

The Convention guarantees religious freedom and prohibits discrimination on religious grounds. It requires that any interpretation of 'religion' be applied objectively, have reasonable justification[139] and be non-discriminatory; any differential treatment must comply with strict standards. Article 14 of the Convention, as supported by Article 9 (the right to freedom of thought, conscience and religion) and by Article 1 of the First Protocol (the right to peaceful enjoyment of property), now have a direct bearing upon Irish domestic law. These provisions require the government and other public bodies to give parity of recognition to Christian and non-Christian religions. Moreover, express provision is made for EU law to prevail over Irish domestic law, by Article 29.4.6 of the Constitution, where the two are in conflict but only to the extent that such EU law is 'necessitated' by Ireland's membership. In making its determinations, the ECtHR allows States a wide margin of appreciation when it comes to placing limitations on the manifestation of one's religion and belief. In deciding whether there has been a limitation or interference on the exercise of the applicant's religion, the infringement must be: (a) prescribed by law and (b) necessary in a democratic society

---

[138] See *Foy* v. *An t-Ard Chlaraitheoir & Others* [2007] IEHC 470, where a declaration of incompatibility was made concerning the lack of legal recognition for transgender people under Irish law.

[139] See, for example, *Tsirlis and Kouloumpas* v. *Greece* (1997) 25 EHRR 198. Also see the *Belgian Linguistic Case* (1968) (no. 2) 1 EHRR 252, where the ECtHR held that there must be an objective and reasonable justification for differential treatment and this will only exist where there is a 'legitimate aim' for the action and where the action taken is 'proportionate' to that aim.

for a permissible purpose, i.e. directed to a legitimate purpose and proportionate in scope and effect.

The Constitution

In *Norris* v. *Attorney General*,[140] O'Higgins CJ declared that, as he understood it, the Irish people had proclaimed in the Preamble to the Constitution a 'deeply religious conviction and faith and an intention to adopt a Constitution consistent with that conviction and faith and with Christian beliefs'. There is a considerable body of case law, accruing before and since that pronouncement, testifying to its accuracy.

Articles 40–44 of the Constitution specifically provide protection for fundamental rights. Article 40.1. states:

> All citizens shall, as human persons, be held equal before the law. This shall not be held to mean that the State shall not in its enactments have due regard to differences of capacity, physical and moral, and of social function.

As Henchy J commented in *Dillane* v. *Ireland*:

> When the State ... makes a discrimination in favour of, or against, a person or category of persons, on the express or implied grounds of a difference of social function the courts will not condemn such discrimination as being in breach of Article 40.1 if it is not arbitrary, capricious, or otherwise not reasonably capable, when objectively viewed in the light of the social function involved, of supporting the selection or classification complained of.[141]

This provision has been held to debar a body corporate as such an entity would be incapable of coming within the ambit of a provision which related solely to 'human persons'.[142] In addition, the constitutional guarantee of equal treatment is subject to the important caveat of 'public order and morality'. One example of what this might mean was brought before the Court of Criminal Appeal in *The People (DPP)* v. *Draper*,[143] which dismissed the appeal against conviction in the case of a person convicted of malicious damage to religious statues. In relation to the belief of the defendant that he had been sent by God, McCarthy J stated that the guarantee of free practice and profession of religion was in this case limited by the requirement of public order.

---

[140] *Norris* v. *Attorney General* [1984] IR 36, at p.64.
[141] *Dillane* v. *Ireland* [1980] ILRM 167.
[142] See *Quinn's Supermarket* v. *Attorney General* [1972] IR 1.
[143] Unreported, Court of Criminal Appeal, *Irish Times*, 24 March 1988.

Articles 41 and 42, which address family rights, are important for present purposes, but it is important to note the continuing differences between the concept of 'family' as defined in the Constitution (Articles 41 and 42) and as defined in the Convention (Article 8), a difference emphasised by the court rulings made in respect of each. In keeping with the religious ethos (specifically, that of Roman Catholicism) pervading the Constitution, there is a strong implication that in law the term 'family' refers to a marital family unit. Article 41.1.1 'recognises the Family as the natural primary and fundamental unit group of Society, and as a moral institution possessing inalienable and imprescriptible rights, antecedent and superior to all positive law', and guarantees its protection by the State; Article 41.3 avows that 'the State pledges itself to guard with special care the institution of marriage, on which the Family is founded, and to protect it against attack'. The inescapable corollary is that non-marital families, one-parent families and those families where the parents are of the same gender are all disadvantaged in the eyes of the Constitution relative to the family based on marriage. A whole nexus of issues about the relative rights of parent and child, as compounded by the marital status of those concerned, revolve around the constitutional presumption favouring the marital family. For that reason, in Ireland the non-marital family has always attracted less protection in law than the family based on marriage.[144] This in turn gives rise to the probability that the protection afforded human rights in Ireland may be structurally flawed: being inherently discriminatory in its prejudicial treatment of non-marital parents and children (and, also its treatment of family units led by single parents or by same gender couples) relative to members of a marital family; and by implicitly favouring Christianity, with an overlay of Roman Catholicism, it is also open to challenge on the ground of possibly adversely discriminating against all others.

Equality and diversity legislation, public bodies and exemption for charities

The primary body of legislative provisions governing matters of equality and diversity is composed of the Employment Equality Act 1998–2008,

---

[144] See, for example, *The State (Nicolaou)* v. *An Bord Uchtála* [1966] IR 567. The then Mr Justice Walsh of the Supreme Court stated that 'the family referred to in [Art.41 was] the family which is founded on the institution of marriage'. See also *G* v. *An Bord Uchtála* [1980] IR 32; and *WO'R* v. *EH (Guardianship)* [1996] 2 IR 248.

and the Equal Status Act 2000–2008. This legislation prohibits discrimination in employment, vocational training, advertising, collective agreements, the provision of goods and services and other opportunities to which the public generally have access on nine distinct grounds: gender; civil status; family status; age; disability; race; sexual orientation; religious belief; and membership of the Traveller Community. The Equality Authority, established in October 1999, is the independent body responsible for regulating equality matters arising under the above legislation.[145]

Other statutes may also be relevant: the Pensions Act 1990–2008; the Unfair Dismissals Act 1977–2007; the Social Welfare (Miscellaneous Provisions) Act 2004 prohibits discrimination in the provision of occupational pensions; the Prohibition on the Incitement to Hatred Act 1989, which criminalises hate speech; and the Intoxicating Liquor Act 2003, which provides for enforcement of discrimination law in the context of premises licensed for the sale of alcohol.

The government has announced controversial plans to merge the existing Equality Authority and Irish Human Rights Commission into a new single body.

Religious charities, discrimination and exemptions

There is clearly a tension between the assurance of Article 40.1, that 'all citizens shall, as human persons, be held equal before the law', and the exemption permitted by statutory and Convention provisions from the normal operation of secular law which is available only to those of religious belief.

Article 44.2.1 of the Constitution affords citizens the right to freely express their conscience as well as the profession and practise of their religion subject to public order and morality. However, any restriction on this right would have to be proportionate under the Constitution, meaning that the restriction would have to be rational, intrude as little as possible and be proportionate to the aim that it seeks to achieve.[146] While, in *Quinn's Supermarket Ltd.* v. *Attorney General*[147] and *Re*

---

[145] The Tribunal website discloses 98 case reports on religious issues. See, further, at: www.equalitytribunal.ie/search.aspx?zoom_query=religion&zoom_page=3&zoom_per_page=10&zoom_and=0&zoom_sort=0&zoom_xml=0 (accessed 20 May 2013).

[146] See *Heaney* v. *Ireland* [1994] 3 IR 531.

[147] *Quinn's Supermarket Ltd.* v. *Attorney General* [1972] IR 1.

260   IRELAND

Article 26 and the Employment Equality Bill 1996,[148] the Supreme Court
confirmed that a religious action may be exempt from general laws if a
failure to provide an exemption would restrict or prevent the free profession and practice of religion, it is clear that not every 'distinction
necessary to achieve this overriding objective will be valid'.[149]

Religious charities as public bodies

Determining whether a religious charity is functioning as a public body
is a matter that turns on a particular set of circumstances. While it is
probable that government funding is in itself insufficient to transform an
otherwise independent entity into an agency of government, where that
funding relationship is substantive, occurs within a more enveloping
context of government policy setting, administrative control and a
specific body of statutory provisions, then in effect the entity may well
have become a public body. An awareness of such a principal–agency
relationship may be implicit in the observation offered by Barrington J in
Campaign to Separate Church and State v. *Min for Education*,[150] that 'the
Constitution contemplated that if a school was in receipt of public funds
any child, no matter what his religion, would be entitled to attend it'.[151]
This, in fact, has for many years been an area of contention.

   In Ireland, State education is faith based: some 91 per cent of primary
schools and perhaps 50 per cent of secondary schools are managed by the
Catholic Church. As a recent report notes, 'primary schools in Ireland
have remained predominantly denominational, chiefly Catholic, in both
ownership and management'.[152] In *Crowley* v. *Ireland*,[153] Kenny J, with
whom Henchy and Griffin JJ agreed, emphasised that the duty laid upon
the State by Article 42.4 was not to 'provide', but to 'provide for' free
primary education. The significance of this distinction being that the
Constitution could be construed as endorsing the existing system of
denominationally controlled primary school management. While
Crowley was concerned with primary education, the courts have also

---

[148] *Re Article 26 and the Employment Equality Bill 1996* [1997] 2 IR 321, at p.358.
[149] See J. Casey, *Constitutional Law in Ireland* (3rd edn), Thomson & Maxwell, Dublin,
2000, at p.698.
[150] *Campaign to Separate Church and State* v. *Min for Education* [1998] 3 IR 321.
[151] Ibid., at p.356.
[152] See the Economic and Social Research Institute, *School Sector Variation among Primary
Schools in Ireland*, Dublin, October 2012.
[153] *Crowley* v. *Ireland* [1980] IR 102.

accepted the constitutionality of denominationally controlled secondary education.[154]

The issue of the very considerable Catholic influence upon the State education system came before the courts in *Campaign to Separate Church and State Ltd.* v. *Minister for Education*,[155] when both Barrington and Keane JJ invoked Article 44.2.4 in support of the proposition that the public funding of denominational schools did not constitute an endowment of religion. According to Keane J:

> [Article 44.2.4] makes it clear beyond argument, not merely that the State is entitled to provide aid to schools under the management of different religious denominations, but that such schools may also include religious instruction as a subject in their curricula. It is subject to two qualifications; first, the legislation must not discriminate between schools under the management of different religious denominations and, secondly, it must respect the right of a child not to attend religious instruction in a school in receipt of public funds.[156]

Elaborating on this latter point, Barrington J said that the Constitution distinguished between religious 'education' and religious 'instruction' and that the right of a child not to attend religious instruction at a publicly funded school did not protect that child from being influenced, to some degree, by the religious ethos of the school. However, while government funding does not constitute 'endowment' it may suggest a level of involvement that, taken in conjunction with other factors, could indicate a controlling relationship.

The government retains responsibility for school funding and for curriculum development (excepting religious instruction) and staffing. Given the extent of government control, in a relationship where the ownership of most schools rests with the Catholic Church, as does the management and delivery of educational services, it is at least arguable that the role of the Church in the national education system for children in Ireland can be construed as that of a public body. This is important because, if that were the case then, while functioning as such, that organisation cannot avail of the statutory exemption provided for religious bodies (that also have charitable status).

---

[154] See *Campaign to Separate Church and State Ltd.* v. *Minister for Education* [1998] 3 IR 321; [1998] 2 ILRM 81; and comments of Geoghegan J in *Greally* v. *Minister for Education (No 2)* [1999] 1 IR 1; [1999] 2 ILRM 296.

[155] *Campaign to Separate Church and State Ltd.* v. *Minister for Education* [1998] 3 IR 321; [1998] 2 ILRM 81.

[156] Ibid., at pp.84.

On the face of it, it would seem that all children should have equal access to all government-funded schools, with a range of different religious beliefs being matched by a corresponding range of accessible denominational-specific schools, as and if required. The Education Act 1998 obliges every person concerned with the implementation of the Act: 'to give practical effect to the constitutional rights of children';[157] 'to promote equality of access to and participation in education'; and 'promotes the means whereby pupils may benefit from education'.[158] This is endorsed by the provisions of the Equal Status Acts 2000–2008, which provide that an educational establishment shall not discriminate in relation to: the admission of a student, including the terms or conditions of admission of a student; the access of a student to a course, facility or benefit provided by the school; any other term or condition of participation in the school; and the expulsion of a student and any other sanction.[159] However, the State is clearly free, under the Constitution, to finance denominationally controlled education and this may entail allowing such schools the freedom to have regard to religion in their admissions policy.[160] This, indeed, is expressly permitted by s.7(3)(c) of the Equal Status Acts 2000–2008, which enables schools to offer preferential treatment in admittance of pupils of certain religious backgrounds where 'the objective of the school is to provide education in an environment which promotes certain religious values'; and by s.7(2), which enables a school to refuse admittance to a pupil who is not of its denomination where it can prove that 'the refusal is essential to maintain the ethos of the school'. This discretionary power to restrict admission does not sit comfortably alongside constitutional and statutory directives to the opposite effect. When this results, as it did in early 2007, in a number of children of Nigerian origin failing to access any local schools in an area of north Co Dublin because they did not hold Catholic baptismal certificates,[161] in the absence of an appropriate range of alternative and accessible denominational schools, a question arises as to the relative authority of the constitutional guarantee vis-à-vis the religious exemption.

---

[157] Education Act 1998, s.6(a).   [158] Education Act 1998, s.6(c).
[159] The Equal Status Acts 2000–2008, s.7(2).
[160] See *Crowley* v. *Ireland* [1980] IR 102.
[161] See: 'Is Your Child Catholic Enough to Get a Place at School?', *The Irish Times*, 1 May 2007; 'New Catholic School Policy Could Produce Unintended "Apartheid"', *The Irish Times*, 8 September 2007; 'Faith before Fairness', *The Irish Times*, 8 September 2007; and 'Ireland Forced to Open Immigrant School', *Guardian*, 25 September 2007.

While this is not the place to debate the intricacies of the Irish Constitution, three matters would seem relevant to such a discussion: the legislative intent underpinning discrimination provisions; the exemption entitlement of a religious service delivery body within a government-controlled system of national education; and, in the context of such an entitlement, the choice of exemption or non-discrimination by the religious body. The first surely intends to protect minority interests from the danger of being ignored or abused by those of the majority – not vice versa; to employ statutory exemption privileges to protect the vested and well-entrenched interests of a national institutional body seems in danger of inverting constitutional intent. The second requires the service delivery agency to subordinate its religious ethos to the needs of the educational system – this is not to imply a total substitution of the secular for the sacred – but the balance struck would need to be respectful of rights to access the service. The third recognises the right and responsibility of the religious body to choose exemption or non-discriminatory practice – indices of incompatibility between religious belief and the education of children would surely be so tightly construed as to rarely suggest exemption as the preferred choice.

Freedom of religion

Article 44.1 of the Constitution declares:

> the State acknowledges that the homage of public worship is due to Almighty God. It shall hold His Name in reverence, and shall respect and honour religion.

This provision is reinforced by: Article 44.2.1, which guarantees a citizen's freedom of religious conscience, practice and worship, 'subject to public order and morality'; Article 44.2.2, which declares that the State may not 'endow' any religion; and Article 44.2.3, which provides that 'the State shall not ... make any discrimination on the ground of religious belief, profession or status'. Barrington J, in *Corway* v. *Independent Newspapers (Ireland) Ltd*,[162] commenting on the locus standi of the Muslim, Hindu and Jewish religions, opined that Article 44 'is an express recognition of the separate co-existence of the religious denominations, named and unnamed. It does not prefer one to the other and it does not confer any privilege or impose any disability or diminution of status

---

[162] *Corway* v. *Independent Newspapers (Ireland) Ltd.* [1999] 4 IR 484, at p.502 (SC).

upon any religious denomination, and it does not permit the State to do so.' An interpretation endorsed most recently by Hogan J who considered that:

> Article 44.2.1 protects not only the traditional and popular religions and religious denominations – such as, for example, Roman Catholicism, the Church of Ireland and the Presbyterian Church – but perhaps just as importantly, it provides a vital safeguard for minority religions and religious denominations whose tenets are regarded by many as unconventional.[163]

Article 14 of the Convention, as supported by Article 9, by Article 1 of the First Protocol and by various Directives, together with domestic statutory provisions, particularly of the Charities and Employment Equality legislation, may also come into play. Consequently, it might be reasonable to assume, in the words of McKechnie J in *Foy* v. *An t-Ard Chlaraitheoir & Others*, that:

> Everyone as a member of society has the right to human dignity, and with individual personalities, has the right to develop his being as he sees fit; subject only to the most minimal of State interference being essential for the convergence of the common good. Together with human freedom, a person, subject to the acquired rights of others, should be free to shape his personality in the way best suited to his person and to his life.[164]

However, it is clear from the relatively limited jurisprudence on the constitutional guarantee of freedom of religion, that in practice the rights of individuals and of organisations will often have to give way to the protection of religious interests: the exemption privileges available to those of religious belief will trump the constitutional guarantees given to others.

Interference with manifestations of religious belief

Article 44 of the Constitution declares 'the free practice and profession of religion ... subject to public order and morality' to be 'guaranteed to every citizen'. This 'free practice' clause, similar in form and effect as its US Constitutional counterpart – the 'free exercise' clause – has been subjected to some examination in the Irish courts.

One such case, *Quinn's Supermarket* v. *Attorney General*,[165] concerned a challenge to ministerial regulations that exempted Jewish

---

[163] See *Temple Street* v. *D. & Anor* [2011] IEHC 1, *per* Hogan J, at para. 27.
[164] *Foy* v. *An t-Ard Chlaraitheoir & Others* [2007] IEHC 470.
[165] *Quinn's Supermarket* v. *Attorney General* [1972] IR 1.

kosher shops from restrictions on hours of trading applicable to other shops selling meat. The plaintiff, a supermarket representative, argued that the differential treatment was contrary to Article 44.2.3 of the Constitution, as it imposed discrimination on grounds of religion. Walsh J considered evidence provided by the Chief Rabbi of Ireland that a majority of Jews in Ireland believed they were prohibited from eating meat other than that prepared according to the kosher method. It was also held that since kosher meat shops do not open 'between sunset on Friday afternoons and sunset on Saturday afternoons', the regulations in question had legitimately sought to compensate for this by exempting these shops completely from ordinary opening hours. The Supreme Court accepted that Article 44.2.3 precludes all distinctions based upon religious belief, profession or status. Thus, the aforementioned regulations were 'unconstitutional on [their] face'. However, the Supreme Court noted that Article 44.2.1 guarantees the free practise and profession of religion. In order to resolve the potential clash between the two sections, the Court looked to ascertain the 'overall purpose' of Article 44 and deemed this to be 'the freedom of practise of religion'. Consequently, any legislative provision which created a distinction on the basis of religious affiliation was not repugnant to the Constitution if its purpose could be similarly construed as permitting the free practice of religion. As Walsh J explained:

> Any law which by virtue of the generality of its application would by its effect restrict or prevent the free profession and practice of religion . . . would be invalid having regard to the provisions of the Constitution, unless it contained provisions which saved from such restriction or prevention the practice of religion of the person or persons who would otherwise be so restricted or prevented.[166]

It was therefore held that such legislative distinctions were not only valid, but necessitated by the 'freedom of practice of religion' of religious groups. This ruling creates difficulties, as Daly points out, because:

> It suggests that the State is not only entitled, but obliged, to exempt religious groupings from laws of general applicability, not merely where such laws actually conflict with the practice of religion, but also where the law does not make allowances for the fact that the observance of religious rituals may in some sense disadvantage certain persons.[167]

[166] Ibid., at p.24.

[167] See E. Daly, 'Religious Discrimination Under the Irish Constitution: A Critique of the Supreme Court Jurisprudence' (2008) 2008 *Cork Online Law Review* 28, at p.32. See,

The ruling implies that the Constitution, specifically the 'free practise' clause of Article 44.2.1, mandates positive discrimination for those of religious belief which, Daly claims, is surely a step too far.[168] Indeed, it would seem to overstep by a considerable margin Walsh J's otherwise sound point that 'Article 40 does not require identical treatment of all persons without recognition of differences in relevant circumstances'.[169]

More recently, in *Temple Street* v. *D. & Anor*,[170] the issue of State intervention arose in a case where a blood transfusion, urgently required by a three-month-old baby, was refused by his parents who, as committed Jehovah's Witnesses, opposed the procedure on grounds of religious belief. Acknowledging that the right of a properly informed adult with full capacity to refuse medical treatment – whether for religious or other reasons – is constitutionally protected,[171] Hogan J was firmly of the view that this did not extend to an adult taking such a decision on behalf of a very ill child whose twin sister had just died. He was certain that 'this Court is given a jurisdiction (and, indeed, a duty) to override the religious objections of the parents where adherence to these beliefs would threaten the life and general welfare of their child'.[172] While the decision cannot be faulted, the rationale would seem to indicate that the freedom to manifest religion is subject to a 'reasonableness' (or proportionality principle) test.

The manifestation of religion can occur indirectly, as through the display of religious icons or ornaments in what would otherwise be neutral public places. A prime example, which gives rise to controversy in many countries, is the presence of Catholic icons or artwork in classrooms. This issue arose in *Campaign to Separate Church and State* v. *Min. for Education*,[173] where Barrington J ruled that publicly funded schools are not obliged 'to change the general atmosphere of its school

---

further, at: http://corkonlinelawreview.com/index.php/2008/03/11/2008 (accessed 3 January 2014).

[168] Contrast with *Braunfeld* v. *Brown* 366 (1961) US 599; Warren CJ held that although a Sunday closing law placed a substantial economic burden on Jewish retailers, this burden was an indirect consequence of a law which had a legitimate secular purpose. It did not forbid or prohibit the religious practice in question, but merely meant that such practices involved a commercial disadvantage (as cited by Daly, 'Religious Discrimination Under the Irish Constitution').

[169] See *Quinn's Supermarket* v. *Attorney General* [1972] IR 1, *per* Walsh J, citing *O'Brien* v. *Keogh* [1972] IR 144.

[170] *Temple Street* v. *D. & Anor* [2011] IEHC 1.

[171] Citing *Fitzpatrick* v. *FK (No.2)* [2008] IEHC 104; [2009] 2 IR 7.

[172] *Temple Street* v. *D. & Anor* [2011] IEHC 1, at para. 38.

[173] *Campaign to Separate Church and State* v. *Min. for Education* [1998] 3 IR 321.

merely to accommodate a child of a different religious persuasion'. This, of course, is more difficult to refute when that 'atmosphere' simply reflects the prevailing national cultural norms than when the school is part of a pluralist society, but arguably such a cultural imbalance makes it all the more necessary that arrangements are in place to offset the predictable alienation of minority groups. Given the above rationale of Walsh J in *Quinn's Supermarket,* and bearing in mind the open question as to whether national schools are functioning as public bodies or to some extent as religious bodies in their delivery of education services then, contrary to the approach advocated by Barrington J, a case could be made for assertive measures to recognise and promote the religious identity of minority groups in such schools.

Discrimination

The legal framework governing discrimination in Ireland is provided by: the European Convention, EU Directives, decisions of the ECtHR and of the European Court of Justice as it interprets the Directives and rights under the EU Treaty; the Constitution, particularly Article 44.2.3, which prohibits the State from imposing any disabilities or making any discrimination on the ground of religious profession, belief or status; and the Employment Equality Act 1998 together with the Equal Status Act 2000 as amended by the Equality Act 2004, which prohibits discrimination in employment, vocational training, advertising, collective agreements and the provision of goods and services, etc.

Discrimination, same-sex marriage and religious organisations

In an interesting anti-discriminatory initiative, the first Irish female bishop was appointed in September 2013 which, in the light of the tiny minority of female clergy in this country, is quite a significant step.[174] However, Ireland as yet has made no legislative provision for same-sex marriage. The Civil Partnership Act 2010 provides the only means available for same-sex couples to acquire formal legal recognition of their status.[175]

---

[174] The Church of Ireland appointed the Revd Pat Storey as the new Bishop of Meath and Kildare. See, further, at www.irishcentral.com/news/Church-of-Ireland-appoints-first-female-bishop-in-historic-move-224609821.html (accessed 3 January 2014).

[175] Properly entitled the Civil Partnership and Certain Rights and Obligations of Cohabitants Act 2010, it came into effect on 1 January 2011.

The legislative road towards equal access to marital status has been bumpy, which as Buckley has pointed out, is unsurprising in a country where Catholicism had such a powerful constraining effect for so long on sex and gender issues.[176] In 2004 the Civil Registration Act was introduced, which prohibited same-sex marriage, explicitly stating that there was an 'impediment to a marriage' if 'both parties are of the same sex'. In December 2006 the High Court held that marriage as defined in the Irish Constitution was between a man and a woman and that there was no breach of rights in the refusal of the Revenue Commissioners to recognise foreign same-sex marriages.[177] Dunne J found that although a 'living document', the Irish Constitution had always meant for marriage to be between a man and a woman, but added: 'It is to be hoped that the legislative changes to ameliorate these difficulties will not be long in coming. Ultimately, it is for the legislature to determine the extent to which such changes should be made.' In July 2012 the Dáil referred the issue of whether to make provision for same-sex marriage to a Convention on the Constitution, which in April 2013 voted overwhelmingly in favour of provisions allowing for same-sex marriage. This has cleared the way for the probable introduction of legislation by 2015, which will undoubtedly include exemption provisions for religious organisations.

Religious discrimination in practice

The 1998 Act defines and proscribes two forms of discrimination – direct and indirect. Discrimination itself is defined as less favourable treatment. The Act provides authority for the Equality Tribunal, which is established to hear and determine claims of discrimination arising on any of nine grounds, including religion. The fact that indirect discrimination can be difficult to detect, and the importance of so doing, was demonstrated in the recent query raised by the Advisory Group to the Forum on

---

[176] Only in 1973 was the ban on married women working in the civil service lifted. Women were not allowed to sit on juries before this date either. Nor were single mothers entitled to social assistance. Contraceptives became available to everyone only in 1984. Divorce – limited – arrived in 1986. In 1991 it became illegal for a man to rape his wife. Two years later homosexuality was decriminalised. See the work of S. A. Buckley (a social historian at National University of Ireland in Galway), at: http://nuigalway. academia.edu/SarahAnneBuckley.

[177] Senator Katherine Zappone and Ann Louise Gilligan, who had married in Canada in 2003 and had sought to have that marriage recognised in Ireland, instigated legal proceedings when the State and the Revenue Commissioners failed to recognise their marital status.

Patronage and Pluralism,[178] questioning Rule 68 of the Rules for National Schools which states that 'a religious ethos should inform and vivify the whole work of the school' with its implied discrimination against secularists.

Unequal but not discriminatory

The Employment Equality Directive,[179] introduced in 2000, requires all Member States to protect against discrimination on grounds of religion and belief in employment, occupation and vocational training. However, the right of schools to discriminate on grounds of religion in employment policies is provided for by s.37(1) of the Employment Equality Act 1998 and has been endorsed in the Irish courts. For example, in *Re Article 26 and the Employment Equality Bill 1996*[180] the Supreme Court was asked to rule on the constitutionality of, inter alia, sections 12 and 37(1) of the Employment Equality Bill 1996, which purported to allow certain vocational training bodies and certain employers to discriminate on grounds of religion in order to protect their religious ethos. It upheld both provisions on the basis that it is constitutionally permissible to discriminate on grounds of religious profession, belief or status if this is necessary to 'give life and reality' to the constitutional guarantee of freedom of religion.[181] In *Campaign to Separate Church and State Ltd.* v. *Minister for Education*[182] a challenge to the constitutionality of the State funding of school chaplains was taken by an organisation opposed to State involvement with religion, arguing that this use of funding discriminated against those of non-Christian beliefs and secularists and would be better directed towards improving non-religious education services. The court found that parents had the right to have religious education provided in the schools which their children attend and were not obliged to settle merely for religious 'instruction'. The role of the chaplain helped to provide this extra dimension to the religious education of children and therefore:

---

[178] See *Report of the Advisory Group to the Forum on Patronage and Pluralism in the Primary Sector*, April 2012; Also see further at: www.education.ie

[179] 2000/78/EC, establishing a general framework for equal treatment in employment and occupation.

[180] *Re Article 26 and the Employment Equality Bill 1996* [1997] 2 IR 32.

[181] The 1996 bill was declared unconstitutional on other grounds, but s.37(1) of the 1998 Act, its replacement, virtually replicates its predecessor.

[182] *Campaign to Separate Church and State Ltd.* v. *Minister for Education* [1998] 3 IR 321; [1998] 2 ILRM 81.

270 IRELAND

the present system whereby the salaries of chaplains in community schools are paid by the State is merely a manifestation, under modern conditions, of principles which are recognised and approved by Articles 44 and 42 of the Constitution.[183]

Barrington J concluded his judgment by adding two caveats to his decision. First, the system of salaried chaplains had to be available to all community schools of whatever denomination on an equal basis in accordance with their needs and, second, it was constitutionally impermissible for a chaplain to instruct a child in a religion other than its own without the knowledge and consent of its parents.

In *Greally v. Minister for Education (No 2)*,[184] Geoghegan J upheld the constitutionality of a recruitment system for secondary school teachers that gave priority to the employment of clerical over non-clerical teachers. This was held to be justified in light of the constitutional right of parents to have their children educated in denominational schools. Again, in *O'Shiel v. Minister for Education*,[185] Laffoy J held the requirements that publicly funded schools only employ teachers with qualifications generally recognised by the State, and that such schools employ teachers with qualifications that enable them to teach Irish to a reasonable standard, were valid conditions having regard to the Constitution.

Unequal but not discriminatory: contractual obligations

In this context *Re Article 26 and the Employment Equality Bill 1996*[186] is worthy of note as the Supreme Court then upheld the constitutionality of s.37(1) of the Employment Equality Bill 1996. That provision exempted from the statutory ban on religious discrimination in employment any 'religious, educational or medical institution which is under the direction or control of a body established for religious purposes or whose objectives include the provision of services in an environment which promotes certain religious values'. Such institutions were permitted to give 'favourable treatment' on grounds of religion to employees, and to prospective employees in terms of recruitment – if necessary 'to uphold the religious ethos of the institution'.[187] Indeed,

---

[183] Ibid., at p.358.
[184] *Greally v. Minister for Education (No 2)* [1999] 1 IR 1; [1999] 2 ILRM 296.
[185] *O'Shiel v. Minister for Education* [1999] 2 IR 321; [1999] 2 ILRM 241.
[186] *Re Article 26 and the Employment Equality Bill 1996* [1997] 2 IR 321.
[187] Ibid., at p.351.

s.12 provided that the prohibition on religious discrimination would not apply to the selection of nurses or primary teachers for these institutions, which was termed 'positive discrimination' by counsel for the Attorney General.

However, if a plaintiff has knowingly placed themselves in a position where contractual obligations will impair their freedom to manifest personal religious beliefs then he or she may not have any rightful cause for complaint if their position in fact becomes so compromised. An inverted version of this problem was brought before the court in *Flynn* v. *Power*,[188] which concerned an unmarried teacher working in a convent school who was dismissed after becoming pregnant by her married partner. Costello J held that as she had been openly having a relationship with a married person, the dismissal was reasonable in order to prevent the undermining of the religious ethos of the school: her lifestyle was openly in conflict with the values the school sought to promote.

Unequal and discriminatory: restricting employment opportunities

Recently, in *Tavoraite* v. *Dunnes Stores*,[189] the Employment Appeals Tribunal in Cork heard an unfair dismissal case concerning a conflict between an employee's religious belief and the dress standards of the employing agency. The Muslim employee had her employment terminated after two years of warnings that, while at work, she was required to conform to the company's dress code and desist from wearing a hijab, despite her protests that this was necessitated by her religious beliefs. The Tribunal hearing ended when the plaintiff reached a settlement with the company. While it is not possible to guess the probable outcome of this case, relevant factors to be taken into account would have included: the fact that the plaintiff converted to Islam after some years of employment in the same post; her firm belief that her religion required her to now wear the hijab; the effect of the hijab on her capacity to perform her duties (including health and safety considerations); and the extent to which other staff were permitted to wear similar religion/culture-specific apparel in addition to or instead of the company uniform (for example, Sikh turbans).

---

[188] *Flynn* v. *Power* [1985] ILRM 336.
[189] Unreported, Employment Appeals Tribunal, Dublin, 13 November 2012.

272 IRELAND

Unequal and discriminatory: restricting access to services

As mentioned above, in *Campaign to Separate Church and State Ltd.* v. *Minister for Education*,[190] the court considered the right of a child not to receive religious instruction: that such a child was suffering discrimination by being burdened with instruction that was detrimental to their needs as a non-believer or believer in another religion. Both Barrington and Keane JJ were of the view that Article 44.2.4 imposed a duty upon any school receiving government funding to provide alternative arrangements for such a child.

Unequal but 'positive action'

The rationale for Walsh J's decision in *Quinn's Supermarket* was unequivocally based upon a perceived need to extend 'positive discrimination' to the interests of a religious minority. Not only was the plaintiff's argument rejected – that special exemption for Jewish kosher butchers from the Sunday trading laws was discriminatory against non-Jewish shop keepers – but the exception was upheld on the basis that it was necessary in order to adequately protect the freedom of religion of the Jewish community. Again, in *Re Article 26*, s.12 of the Bill provided that the prohibition on religious discrimination would not apply to the selection of nurses or primary teachers for these institutions. This was termed 'positive discrimination' by counsel for the Attorney General.

Conclusion

Along with the UK jurisdictions, Ireland has entered a new *Pemsel*-plus list of charitable purposes onto its statute books, but unlike them has chosen to retain both the presumption that those for the advancement of religion are for the public benefit and the traditional reliance upon a Supreme Being, worship and tenets, etc. as definitional components of 'religion'. In common with all UK jurisdictions, other than England, there is no 'established' religion, but Ireland does continue a traditional cultural adherence to Catholicism which is reflected in its Constitution and permeates some core elements of its public services infrastructure. Notwithstanding Ireland's embracing of pluralism in recent decades, the

---

[190] *Campaign to Separate Church and State Ltd.* v. *Minister for Education* [1998] 3 IR 321.

legacy of its particular religious culture is one which is likely to trigger further difficulties as it struggles to synchronise domestic law and practice (particularly in the context of education and health care) with international legal requirements as benchmarked by evolving ECtHR case law.

7

The United States of America

Introduction

Of all the former British colonies, the United States has the greatest concentration of billionaires, the strongest reputation for forming associations for religious purposes and it holds the record for promoting philanthropic activity at home and abroad. Its aversion to 'established' religion is reflected in a history crammed with legislative and judicial evidence of a determination to keep separate matters of Church and State. Primarily, the right to practise religion is ensured by restraining the power of government to intervene in matters of religious belief which, like the right to bear arms, is viewed as an incident of the constitutionally protected freedom of the individual.

This chapter begins with a brief sector profile. It analyses contemporary statistics and trends, identifies the different funding arrangements for the sector, considers the changes affecting the role of charities, particularly religious charities, within the broader nonprofit world, and assesses the difficulties in achieving sector cohesion within a federated jurisdiction. This leads into an outline of the steps so far taken to build a relationship between government and the sector, including government funding of charities and religious charities, the importance of the Charitable Choice initiative and the relative insignificance of the charity law reform process. It examines the regulatory framework for monitoring charities and the role played by the Inland Revenue Service (IRS) within a tax-driven approach to the sector. It then considers the definition of 'religion' and 'belief' and explains the activities held to constitute the 'advancement of religion'. The constraints of public policy and of traditional common law rules on charitable activity associated with religion and religious organisations are reviewed. The final and largest part of the chapter deals in some detail with the interplay of human rights, discrimination and religious charities. Essentially, this exploration of contemporary issues is conducted through an examination of the unfolding case law.

Church, State and religious charities

The United States is distinctive among the common law jurisdictions presently studied, not just because of the sheer volume of litigation on religious matters, but because the cases are as much concerned with contested issues on the Church–State interface as with religious discrimination. In general, much litigation is concerned with whether or not any government resources received by a religious organisation are used for religious purposes.

Background: government and the nonprofit sector

In the United States, the term 'nonprofit sector' is arguably a misnomer: the commonality for many of its constituent entities is no longer the absence of profit but the basis for its distribution; although the term 'sector' implies a coherence, a shared sense of direction and an agreed voice on an agenda of issues, this has yet to be achieved. Moreover, the overall incoherence is exacerbated by the sheer unwieldiness of a system that formally allows nonprofits to be organised under the different state laws, while their operations are largely shaped by the requirements of the federal Internal Revenue Code (IRC). This is exacerbated by the Tenth Amendment to the US Constitution by which: 'The powers not delegated to the United States by the Constitution, nor prohibited by it to the States, are reserved to the States respectively, or to the people.' This allocation of authority to the state governments creates difficulties in terms of overlapping federal and state powers, where state tax-exemption statutes are often not synchronised with federal standards and their numerous operating requirements, which can be further muddled by state financing. There is, arguably, a significant disconnect between embedded federal presumptions of law and policy, which are particularly influential in the case of nonprofits, and the decision-making processes of local elected state officials, which can often be idiosyncratic.

Government policy

Historically, it has not been found necessary to have government bodies or formal structures to bridge the gap between government and the sector. The many hundreds of thousands of organisations that constitute the sector, ranging from churches and hospitals to trade associations and political organisations, and including sports clubs and neighbourhood associations, are linked neither to each other nor to government by any body of legal principles (perhaps soon to be remedied by the 'Principles of the Law of Charitable Nonprofit Organizations' currently being finalised by the American Law Institute).

Frameworks for facilitating government–sector relationships

Alexis de Tocqueville, that great observer of American society in the early nineteenth century, once commented that:

> Religion in America takes no direct part in the government of society, but it must be regarded as the first of their political institutions; for if it does not impart a taste for freedom, it facilitates the use of it. Indeed, it is in this same point of view that the inhabitants of the United States themselves look upon religious belief. I do not know whether all Americans have a sincere faith in their religion for who can search the human heart? – but I am certain that they hold it to be indispensable to the maintenance of republican institutions. This opinion is not peculiar to a class of citizens or to a party, but it belongs to the whole nation and to every rank of society.[1]

On the other hand, it is also worth noting that 'as late as 1890, thirty-seven of the existing forty-two states recognised the authority of God in the preambles or in the text of their constitutions'[2] and two years later in *Church of the Holy Trinity* v. *United States*[3] the Supreme Court was sufficiently confident as to the nation's religious identity to declare that 'American life as expressed by its laws, its business, its customs and its society, we find everywhere a clear recognition of the same truth . . . that this is a Christian nation.'[4] Whether this is added testimony to de Tocqueville's point about the absence of any formal input to State affairs, or detracts from it, is difficult to judge.

While the absence of any formal linkage between State and Church can be attributed to deliberate constitutional prohibition, the similar absence of any framework for facilitating government–sector relationships is as much

---

[1] See A. de Tocqueville, *Democracy in America*, edited by H. C. Mansfield and D. Winthrop, University of Chicago Press, Chicago, IL, 2000 [1835].

[2] See C. Taylor, 'Why We Need a Radical Redefinition of Secularism', in E. Mendieta and J. Vanantwerpen (eds), *The Power of Religion in the Public Sphere*, Columbia University Press, New York, 2011, at p.38.

[3] *Church of the Holy Trinity* v. *United States*, 143 US 457 (1892).   [4] Ibid., at p.471.

CHURCH, STATE AND RELIGIOUS CHARITIES 277

due to a traditional *laissez faire* approach that valued the freedom of associational forms of social activity.

Building a modern Church–State relationship

The independence of associations, in particular the right to establish such entities and to manage them free from government interference, has been an enduring hallmark of society in this jurisdiction,[5] and one quite probably related to the Clarendon Code prohibition on associations for religious purposes enacted in the country from which many US citizens had fled in order to avoid such constraints.[6] The framing of the US Constitution and its Bill of Rights sought to ensure, among other things, that federal powers would not interfere with the independence of law-abiding individuals, communities and their associational activity. This has not proved conducive to building a formal relationship between government and the sector.

In recent years, however, the context for such a relationship has changed. The ongoing global war against terrorism, coupled with prolonged economic recession, has triggered an increase in demand for public benefit services that government cannot hope to fully fund. Moreover, the collapse of major financial institutions, and with them much of the credibility of the business sector, has raised the profile of altruistic entities and encouraged government to look towards the sector – in particular towards the community-oriented, faith-based entities – as possible partners in its struggle to provide more cost-effective public benefit services. Faith-based initiatives now fit well with the more conservative approach of recent administrations in which fiscal rectitude and civic responsibility have been policy keynotes. In the wake of a litany of national setbacks and their attendant hardships for citizens, the strategy of building a closer affiliation with the most demonstrably values-led part of the nonprofit sector has had an understandably strong appeal for a hard-pressed government.

---

[5] See de Tocqueville, *Democracy in America*, at p.513 ('In every case, at the head of a great new undertaking, where in France you would find the government or in England some territorial magnate, in the U.S. you are sure to find an association'). Also see *NAACP* v. *Button*, 371 US 415, 430 (1958), which affirmed the right to 'engage in association for the advancement of beliefs and ideas' and *Boy Scouts of America* v. *Dale*, 120 S.Ct. 2446 (2000).

[6] See, the Conventicles Act 1670 (22 Car II c 1), s.1, which made it an offence for five or more persons to be present at 'any assembly, coventicle or meeting, under colour or pretence of any exercise of religion, in any other manner than according to the liturgy and practice of the Church of England'.

278   THE UNITED STATES OF AMERICA

Religion(s)

The Pew Forum's US Religious Landscape Survey provides an interesting picture of religion in contemporary American society.[7] Broadly, it found that some 78 per cent of the sample were Christian: 51 per cent Protestant; 24 per cent Catholic; and 2 per cent Mormon. Of the remainder: 2 per cent were Jews; 0.7 per cent were Buddhists and slightly fewer were Muslims and Hindus. Among the main findings were that: 44 per cent of adults have either switched religious affiliation, moved from being unaffiliated with any religion to being affiliated with a particular faith, or dropped any connection to a specific religious tradition altogether; the number of people who say they are unaffiliated with any particular faith today (16.1 per cent) is more than double the number who say they were not affiliated with any particular religion as children. The largest religious grouping continues to be Protestantism, but the number who report that they are members of Protestant denominations now stands at barely 51 per cent and is characterised by significant internal diversity and fragmentation, encompassing hundreds of different denominations. Evangelical Protestant churches are the largest (26.3 per cent of the overall adult population).

Secularisation

In 2012 some 73 per cent of polled Americans identified themselves as Christian,[8] which represented a considerable fall from 86 per cent in 1990, and continued the decline from the 78.6 per cent recorded in 2001.[9] This trajectory is viewed as evidence of a growing rate of secularisation and one which will play an important role in the unfolding 'culture wars' of the United States, a phenomenon depicted by Williams:

> The major political cleavage in contemporary American politics is no longer class, race, region, or any of the many social-structural differences that divide the population. Rather, a major realignment of sensibilities and controversial issues means that the body politic is now rent by a

---

[7] See the Pew Forum on Religion & Public Life, *U.S. Religious Landscape Survey*, 2007 at: http://religions.pewforum.org/reports (accessed 7 January 2014).

[8] Ibid.

[9] See CUNY Graduate Center, *American Religious Identification Survey*, 2001, at: www.gc. cuny.edu/CUNY_GC/media/CUNY-Graduate-Center/PDF/ARIS/ARIS-PDF-version.pdf (accessed 7 January 2014).

cultural conflict in which values, moral codes, and lifestyles are the primary objects of contention.[10]

It is a phenomenon which in this book is seen in terms of an agenda of 'moral imperatives'. Both perspectives can be traced back to their shared canon law roots.

As firmer trends indicate a continuing loosening of the religious grip on society – such as the number of Americans now choosing not to attend church,[11] or to get married or to be buried without any form of religious ceremony, together with the climbing rates of divorce and the annual proportion of non-marital births – it can be safely predicted that the current tensions between abortion and pro-life groups, between LGBT libertarians and advocates for traditional family units, will increase. However, Charles Taylor, in *A Secular Age*,[12] draws attention to what he interprets as an inherently contradictory aspect of secularisation in the United States: it simultaneously describes both the withdrawal of religion from public life, a playing out of the constitutionally required Church–State separation; and the withdrawal from, or reduction in attendance at, places of public worship; while disguising the resilient private commitment to religious or other forms of belief which continues to be a durable characteristic of citizenship in this jurisdiction.

An 'established' religion

Government is constitutionally prevented from having an 'established' Church; it cannot 'set up a church', or 'adopt ... teach or practice religion'.[13] The explicit separation of Church and State is one of the most distinctive and heavily litigated constitutional characteristics of the United States. The authority for such a separation derives from the

---

[10] See R. H. Williams (ed.), *Cultural Wars in American Politics: Critical Reviews of a Popular Myth*, Aldine de Gruyter, New York, 1997, at p.1. Also, see, R. D. Putnam and D. E. Campbell, *American Grace: How Religion Divides and Unites Us*, Simon Schuster, New York, 2010.

[11] However, current statistics indicate that church attendance in the United States is considerably stronger than in other countries: 41.6 per cent of American citizens report they regularly attend, compared with 10 per cent in the United Kingdom and 7.5 per cent in Australia. See Gallup International polls for further information.

[12] C. Taylor, *A Secular Age*, Belknap Press of Harvard University, Cambridge, MA, 2007. Also see L. B. Berger, 'Reflections on the Sociology of Religion Today' (2001) 62 *Sociology of Religion* 443, at pp.446–447.

[13] See *Everson* v. *Board of Education* 330 US, at pp.15–16 (1947).

Establishment Clause[14] of the First Amendment to the US Constitution, and was confirmed by the majority decision of the US Supreme Court in cases such as *Everson* v. *Board of Education.*[15] Under the Establishment Clause, the US Supreme Court has held that federal, state and local government may not, directly or indirectly, demonstrate a preference for any religious belief.[16] Among the many tests that have at various times found favour with the Supreme Court for establishing whether or not the wall has been breached is the 'excessive entanglement' test. This was relied upon by the Supreme Court in *Walz* v. *Tax Commission*[17] when it declined to base the rationale for upholding the exemption on the 'good works' of churches but rather looked to whether or not the exemption created excessive entanglement with religion (see, further, below).[18]

Arguably, however, the courts in recent years have moved away from interpreting the Establishment Clause as requiring government to maintain its 'separation' from religion towards favouring instead an interpretation that requires government to maintain a position of 'neutrality'.

Equality of religions

Although, since the early settlements, Protestant Christians have con-stituted the largest religious group, the United States does not give precedence to any particular religion. In this most open market of jurisdictions, government tends to regulate with a view to maintaining a level playing field between religions, and between those with and those

---

[14] The now iconic significance of the separation of Church and State derives from a personal letter written by Thomas Jefferson to the Danbury Baptist Association on 1 January 1802, in which he said:

> Believing with you that religion is a matter which lies solely between man and his God, that he owes account to none other for his faith or his worship, that the legislative powers of government reach actions only, and not opinions, I contemplate with sovereign reverence that act of the whole American people which declared that their legislature should 'make no law respecting an establishment of religion, or prohibiting the free exercise thereof', thus building a wall of separation between church and State.

[15] *Everson* v. *Board of Education*, 330 US 1 (1947).

[16] See, for example, *Sch. Dist. of Abington Twp., Pa.* v. *Schempp*, 374 US 203, 305 (1963), where it was stated that the religion clauses 'require that government neither engage in nor compel religious practices, that it effect no favoritism among sects or between religion and nonreligion, and that it work deterrence of no religious belief'.

[17] *Walz* v. *Tax Commission*, 397 US 664 (1970).   [18] Ibid., at pp.675–676.

CHURCH, STATE AND RELIGIOUS CHARITIES 281

without religious belief, while ensuring that it does not lend its resources to favouring any particular religion.

Religious organisations and the nonprofit sector

The contribution of nonprofits, particlarly faith-based entities, to the collective public benefit of the community has a well-established history in the United States. Indeed, Alex de Tocqueville in the 1830s 'noted with special interest the prominent place of voluntary associations in American society. . . . Churches, community groups, fraternal associations and civil organizations ... did for themselves through these voluntary efforts what people in other societies expected governments and elites to do to them.'[19]

Religious charities

Religious corporations have a long history and their exemption from taxes has been held not to violate the Constitution.[20] There were an estimated 317,751 congregations in 2013.[21] In all 50 states, religious organisations have an established track record of providing social services. Many larger religious organisations have been a part of the traditional provision of social services through separate nonprofit agencies such as the Catholic Charities and Lutheran Social Services. These agencies are religiously influenced, but maintain separate nonprofit organisations registered with the IRS under §501(c)(3) and thereby separate their social service functions from their purely religious functions: a bright line that represents the separation of Church and State.[22] Religious corporations constitute a strong and growing segment of the US nonprofit sector with, as has been said, 'the largest piece of America's charitable pie going to the sustenance of religious groups – for their

---

[19] As cited in R. Wuthnow, 'The Voluntary Sector: Legacy of the Past, Hope for the Future', in R. Wuthnow (ed.), *Between States and Markets: The Voluntary Sector in Comparative Perspective*, Princeton University Press, Princeton, NJ, 1991, at p.3.

[20] See, for example, *Walz* v. *Tax Commission of the City of New York*, 397 US 664 (1970).

[21] See American Church Lists at: http://nccs.urban.org/statistics/quickfacts.cfm (accessed 7 January 2014).

[22] Proselytisation with federal funds would violate the First Amendment to the Constitution. See *Hein* v. *Freedom From Religion Foundation*, 551 US 587 (2007). See also: *Flast* v. *Cohen*, 392 US 83 (1968); *Bowen* v. *Kendrick*, 487 US 589 (1988); and *Valley Forge Christian College* v. *Americans United for Separation of Church & State*, 454 US 464 (1982).

facilities, their operating costs, and their clergy salaries'.[23] There is no definitive legal requirement placed upon religious organisations to demonstrate how their activities satisfy the public benefit test, and their relative autonomy has been considerably strengthened by a recent Supreme Court decision vindicating their right to hire and fire ministry personnel in accordance with the organisation's religious beliefs, even where such action may conflict with the human rights of the personnel concerned.[24]

Many religious congregations and thousands of churches are not required by law to register with the IRS and choose not to do so. Because of the broad range of entities not linked explicitly to pursuing a *Pemsel* charitable purpose,[25] the IRS consistently refers to 'exempt purposes' (i.e. those specified in the statute) rather than using the undefined term 'charitable', and indeed has named its bureau that has been assigned supervisory responsibility as the Tax-Exempt and Government Entities (TEGE) division.

Religious organisations receive by far and away the biggest segment of donations provided to the sector.[26]

Religious umbrella bodies

The Christian religion has several umbrella bodies. For example: the National Council of Churches (NCC) is the largest ecumenical organisation of Christians in the United States; the National Association of Evangelicals (NAE) is the largest conservative Protestant group in the United States; the National Conference of Catholic Bishops (NCCB), the North American Presbyterian and Reformed Council (NAPARC), the Association of Gospel Rescue Missions and the National Association

---

[23] See M. Brown, *Giving USA 2005, the Annual Report on Philanthropy for the Year 2004*, (50th edn), Giving USA Foundation, AAFRC Trust for Philanthropy, New York, 2005.

[24] See *Hosanna-Tabor Evangelical Lutheran Church & School* v. *EEOC*, 132 S Ct 694 (2012).

[25] It was the Tariff Act of 1913 that initially excluded public benefit nonprofits such as churches from paying federal income tax. See, further, B. R. Hopkins, *The Law of Tax-Exempt Organizations*, Wiley, New York, 1998, at p.32.

[26] See *Giving USA*, the American Association of Fund-Raising Counsel and the Center on Philanthropy at Indiana University. The 2012 edition gives a figure of 32 per cent for the share of contributions received by religious organisations and reports a downward trend over the past several years. E. Brody, estimates that churches attract slightly over 50 per cent of total annual philanthropic donations (personal communication, 18 September 2011).

of Evangelicals are also significant. Christian Churches Together is a new cooperative effort involving faith groups from five families within Christianity: Evangelical/Pentecostal, historic Protestant, orthodox, racial/ethnic and Roman Catholic.

The Office of Faith-Based and Community Initiatives

Beginning in 1996, during the Clinton administration, a body of legislation accompanied by a network of government offices, funding bodies and a good deal of controversy has since come into existence in relation to faith-based public benefit service provision initiatives. In January 2001, President George W. Bush created the White House Office of Faith-Based and Community Initiatives within the Executive Office of the President by an executive order.[27] Later executive orders created centres for the Office within the Departments of Justice, Labor, Health and Human Services, Housing and Urban Development, Education, and Agriculture, as well as at the Agency for International Development. Since then, some 22 states have created state Offices of Faith-Based and Community Initiatives, 39 have appointed persons into Faith-Based Liaison positions and 41 have passed legislation or enacted administrative policy changes to give effect to faith-based initiatives. Critics have argued that this represents a violation of the Establishment Clause.

Government funding: the sector and religious charities

As the Aspen Institute has noted, 'religiously affiliated colleges and universities, social service agencies, hospitals, and other institutions have been central actors in government-financed human service activities almost from the founding of the republic'.[28] In recent years a distinct trend has emerged: a growing proportion of sector funding, including funds flowing into religious charities, now comes from earned income: both from commercial enterprises and from government service contracts. Fees for services have become a major, if not *the* major, source of revenue, and

---

[27] The White House Office of Faith-Based and Community Initiatives was rechristened by the Obama administration as the White House Office of Faith-based and Neighborhood Partnerships. See Office of Faith-based and Neighborhood Partnerships, Office of the White House, www.whitehouse.gov/administration/eop/ofbnp/about (accessed 7 January 2014).

[28] Aspen Institute, *Religious Organizations and Government*, 2001, at p.5: www.aspeninstitute.org/topics/religion (accessed 7 January 2014).

faith-based service providers are to the fore in attracting government funding, though initially legal constraints appeared to bar government funding to 'pervasively sectarian' organisations. This growth has been facilitated by the 'Charitable Choice' initiative, which requires that social service providers be permitted to participate in government grant programmes without regard to their religious character. The principle of equal treatment or non-discrimination, which is applied generally to government-funded public benefit service provision, is an acknowledgement of the Establishment Clause restraints and is usually viewed as an aspect of the 'neutrality theory.'[29]

Government funding of religious charities: the policy

The second Bush administration allowed federal money, for the first time, to go directly to churches rather than to nonprofit charitable organisations, making the contracts and grants far less transparent and fuelling the suspicion that the federal government was illegally subsidising religion. The policies of that administration also included exempting faith-based groups from compliance with federal anti-discrimination statutes, thereby permitting religious groups with federal contracts to refuse, for example, to employ LGBT persons if this would be in conflict with the group's religious beliefs.

President Obama largely left in place the federal faith-based infrastructure created by his republican predecessor. He also increased the amount of federal dollars flowing to religious groups and, acknowledging the need for a firewall between evangelising and serving clients, he has warned religious charities that 'If you get a federal grant, you can't use that grant money to proselytise to the people you help, and you can't discriminate against them – or against the people you hire – on the basis of their religion' and that 'Federal dollars that go directly to churches, temples, and mosques can only be used on secular programs.'[30] Under

---

[29] See, for example, *Spencer v. World Vision, Inc.*, 619 F.3d 1109 (9th Cir. 2010), where O'Scannlain J stated that the Establishment Clause commands 'neutrality among religious groups'. He explained that if the exemption was limited to churches, it would exclude religious groups simply because they are not traditional houses of worship and such an interpretation would not be neutral. Also see *Epperson v. Arkansas*, 393 US 97, 103–104 (1968).

[30] Quotes from the Obama 2008 election campaign speech given in Zanesville, Ohio. See further at: www.motherjones.com/politics/2012/02/what-war-religion-obama-catholic-charitiea (accessed 7 January 2014).

CHURCH, STATE AND RELIGIOUS CHARITIES   285

his administration, Catholic religious charities alone have received more than $650 million, according to a spokeswoman from the US Department of Health and Human Services, which provides much of the funding. Indeed, government grants currently provide two-thirds of the funding for Catholic Charities USA, and the Jewish Board of Family and Children Services receives 75 per cent of its funding from the government.[31]

Government funding of religious charities: the practice

A recurring issue for the courts is whether government funding of religious charities violates the Establishment Clause of the First Amendment. This issue is one that arises most frequently in the context of state aid to religious schools: under what circumstances, if any, may government provide assistance to religious schools without breaching the wall demarcating the business of Church and State?

So, for example, the courts have: struck down government loans to religious schools of maps, photos, films, projectors, recorders and laboratory equipment, as well as disallowed services for counselling, remedial and accelerated teaching, psychological, speech and hearing therapy[32] and the use of public school personnel to provide guidance, remedial and therapeutic speech and hearing services away from the religious school campus;[33] disallowed the use of public buildings for optional religious instruction;[34] disallowed the loan of instructional materials to religious schools, as well as disallowed transportation for field trips by religious school students;[35] upheld the use of federal funds for construction work at a religious hospital;[36] and required that equal funding be granted to evangelical Christian groups.[37] The ruling in *Mitchell* v. *Helms*[38]

---

[31] See, L. Goodstein, 'Churches May Not Be Able to Patch Welfare Cuts', *Washington Post*, 22 February 1995. Also see R. Levy, 'The Federalist Case Against Faith-Based Initiatives', American Spectator Online. See, further, at: www.cato.org/publications/commentary/federalist-case-against-faithbased-initiatives (accessed 7 January 2014).

[32] *Meek* v. *Pittenger*, 421 US 349 (1975).   [33] *Wolman* v. *Walter*, 433 US 229 (1977).

[34] *Illinois ex rel. McCollum* v. *Board of Education of School District* 333 US 203 (1948).

[35] *Bowen* v. *Kendrick*, 487 US 589 (1989).   [36] *Bradfield* v. *Roberts*, 15 US 291 (1899).

[37] *Rosenberger* v. *Rector and Visitors of Univ. of Va.*, 515 US 819 (1995).

[38] *Mitchell* v. *Helms* 530 US 793, 120 S Ct 2530 (2000). Having indicated that programme neutrality is an important but not sufficient factor in determining the constitutionality of direct aid, Justice O'Connor went on to say that: (a) *Meek* v. *Pittenger* and *Wolman* v. *Walter* should be overruled; (b) the Court should do away with presumptions of unconstitutionality, hence, the 'pervasively sectarian' test would seem to be no longer relevant to the Court's analysis; and (c) proof of actual diversion of government aid to religious indoctrination would be violative of the Establishment Clause.

286   THE UNITED STATES OF AMERICA

introduced further uncertainty to this area of law. This case concerned the scope of the Establishment Clause when evaluating a programme of governmental assistance entailing direct aid to organisations, including religious organisations. The federal programme at issue entailed federal aid to k-12 schools, public and private, secular and religious, allocated on a per-student basis. Guided by the analysis used in *Agostini* v. *Felton*,[39] O'Connor J employed 'the Lemon test' (see below) in the following process of analysis. First, does the programme of aid have a secular purpose? Second, does the programme of aid have the primary effect of advancing religion: is the aid actually diverted to religious indoctrination; does the programme define the eligibility of participating organisations without regard to religion; and does the programme create excessive administrative entanglement? She noted, in that case, that the educational aid in question was to supplement rather than supplant monies from private sources, that the nature of the aid was such that it could not reach the coffers of a religious school and that the use of the aid was statutorily restricted to 'secular, neutral, and nonideological' purposes. She noted also that the aid consisted of materials and equipment rather than cash, and that the materials were loaned to the religious schools with government retaining title. O'Connor J went on to reject a rule of unconstitutionality where the character of aid is capable of diversion to religious indoctrination. The effect of this decision was to overrule the two 1970s cases and to hold that the government may provide instructional equipment to parochial schools.[40] This approach is consistent with that adopted in *Bowen* v. *Kendrick*,[41] when the court approved cash grants to religious organisations, even in the particularly 'sensitive' area of teenage sexual behaviour, as long as there is no 'use of public funds to promote religious doctrines'.

Recently the courts have addressed more subtle attempts to cross that line in the particularly sensitive context of children's education – for example: ordering the removal of stickers placed on science books stating that 'evolution is a theory, not a fact'[42] and ruling that an 'Intelligent

---

[39] *Agostini* v. *Felton*, 521 US 203 (1997). This landmark decision of the Supreme Court, reversing *Aguilar* v. *Felton* (1985), found that it was not a violation of the Establishment Clause for a state-sponsored education initiative to allow public school teachers to instruct at religious schools, so long as the material was secular and neutral in nature and no 'excessive entanglement' between government and religion was apparent.

[40] See, further, C. H. Esbeck, 'The Establishment Clause as a Structural Restraint on Governmental Power'(1998) 84 *Iowa Law Review* 1.

[41] *Bowen* v. *Kendrick*, 487 US 589, 623 (1988).

[42] *Selman* v. *Cobb County School District*, 449 F.3d 1320 (11th Cir. 2006).

Design Policy' requiring teachers to inform students of the 'gaps/problems in Darwin's Theory' and to introduce 'other theories of evolution including, but not limited to, intelligent design' violated the First Amendment.[43]

The issue is by no means confined to an educational context. It has also arisen in a number of cases involving vulnerable groups such as prisoners and children. In 2007 the civil rights group Freedom From Religion Foundation filed a lawsuit challenging the legality of the White House Office of Faith-Based and Community Initiatives, alleging that any such preferencing of religious organisations breached the Establishment Clause and violated the constitutional imperative that Church and State remain separate.[44] The resulting decision of the Supreme Court in *Hein* v. *Freedom From Religion Foundation*[45] ruled that taxpayers do not have the right to challenge the constitutionality of expenditures by the executive branch of the government, a decision that in effect gave the green light to further government faith-based initiatives. *Americans United For Separation of Church and State* v. *Prison Fellowship Ministries*[46] concerned the Iowa Inner Change Freedom Initiative (IFI), a faith-based pre-release programme for prisoners, which had a record of successfully rehabilitating criminals. This was part of the Prison Fellowship Ministries, launched in 1976, which operated the IFI in states such as Texas, Minnesota, Kansas, Arkansas and Missouri with federal funding of $56 million per year. The IFI, an intensely religious rehabilitation programme, required an enrolled prisoner to constantly satisfy the evangelical Christian programme organisers that he or she was making acceptable spiritual progress. It aimed to reduce recidivism by inspiring prisoners to follow a more Christian way of life. In return for enrolling in the programme, prisoners were rewarded with access to better facilities within the prison. The programme had been a matter of concern to Roman Catholic inmates, who found their faith being criticised by staff members and volunteers from local evangelical churches, while Jews and Muslim participants were required to participate in Christian worship services even if that deeply offended their own religious beliefs. In June 2006 the district court held that the programme violated the

---

[43] *Kitzmiller* v. *Dover Area School District*, 400 F. Supp. 2d 707 (2005).

[44] The plaintiffs relied on the authority of precedents established by the Supreme Court in *Flast* v. *Cohen*, 392 US 83 (1968), *Bowen* v. *Kendrick*, 487 US 589 (1988) and *Valley Forge Christian College* v. *Americans United for Separation of Church & State*, 454 US 464 (1982).

[45] *Hein* v. *Freedom From Religion Foundation*, 551 US 587 (2007).

[46] *Americans United For Separation of Church and State* v. *Prison Fellowship Ministries*, 432 F. Supp. 2d 862 (S.D. Iowa 2006).

288 THE UNITED STATES OF AMERICA

Establishment Clause, expelled the programme from the prison and directed IFI to repay the Department of Corrections the $1.5 million that it had been paid by the state. The defendants appealed to the US Court of Appeals for the Eighth Circuit, which, in December 2007, largely upheld the district court's decision. It held that Iowa's involvement with IFI violated the Establishment Clause by supporting the indoctrination of inmates, that IFI's discriminated against non-Christian inmates and that IFI was 'pervasively sectarian'. In March 2008 Iowa terminated the IFI programme.

Charitable Choice

Charitable Choice refers to a policy, developed during the George W. Bush administration, of providing direct government funding to religious organisations for the provision of social services.[47] Charitable Choice was launched as part of a government welfare reform strategy intended to replace public welfare benefit entitlement with nonprofit and privatised service provision by s.104 of the Personal Responsibility and Work Opportunity Reconciliation Act 1996. It states that those jurisdictions that contract with nonprofit organisations for delivery of social services must include religious organisations as eligible contractees; it also allows government officials to purchase those services from religious providers using Temporary Assistance for Needy Families (TANF), Welfare-to-Work and Community Services Block Grant (CSBG) funds. Implemented primarily through a variety of executive orders issued by President Clinton, it was incorporated into the Community Services Block Grant Act of 1998, included in the Substance Abuse and Mental Health Services Administration's (SAMHSA) block grant in October 2000 and made part of the Children's Health Act of 2003 by President George W. Bush. Most recently, the Obama administration has announced an expansion of government funding for 'faith-based initiatives'.[48]

In programmes subject to Charitable Choice, when funding goes directly to the social service providers the ultimate beneficiaries are empowered with a choice. Beneficiaries who want to receive services from a faith-based organisation may do so. On the other hand, if a beneficiary objects on religious grounds to receiving services at a faith-based organisation, then the state is the alternative provider. If a beneficiary selects

---

[47] See Executive Order No. 13,279, 67 Fed. Reg. 77141 (12 December 2002).
[48] President Obama's White House Office of Faith-based and Neighborhood Partnerships has developed a comprehensive partnership guide, *Partnerships for the Common Good.*

CHURCH, STATE AND RELIGIOUS CHARITIES 289

a faith-based organisation that receives funding, the provider cannot discriminate against beneficiaries on account of their religion or their refusal to participate actively in a religious practice. Faith-based organisations retain their exemption from federal employment discrimination laws, which enables them to select staff on a religious basis.[49]

However, in several cases the judiciary have criticised the operation of a Charitable Choice programme both because they have been offered to participants who lack true freedom of choice (children and prisoners, in particular[50]) and because they can in practice allow government funds to flow along channels that discriminate between recipients and non-recipients on religious grounds, contrary to the constitutional imperative that Church and State remain separate (see below).

Government funding and religious charities as public bodies

There is a clear danger that programmes such as Charitable Choice introduce, in effect, government service provision by proxy: religious charities end up performing as wholly signed-up agents of government. The decisions in both *Bowen* v. *Kendrick*[51] and *Mitchell* v. *Helms*[52] reveal a strong judicial awareness of circumstances in which a consequence of government funding could entail an imputing of functional responsibility from nonprofit service deliverer to government funder in accordance with the agent–principal rule (see Chapter 3).

---

[49] See Department of Health and Human Services, *Charitable Choice Provisions and Regulations; Final Rules*, 2003. See further at: www.twc.state.tx.us/svcs/charchoice/chchoice.html (accessed 7 January 2014).

[50] In recent years, several judges have concluded that children and teenagers, like prisoners, have too few options and too little power to make the voluntary choices the Supreme Court requires when public money flows to programmes involving religious instruction or indoctrination. That was the conclusion of a federal judge in Michigan in *Teen Ranch* v. *UDOW*, 389 F. Supp. 2d 827 (W.D. Mich. 2005), a case filed by Teen Ranch, a nonprofit Christian facility that provides residential care for troubled or abused children aged 11–17. In 2003 state officials imposed a moratorium on placements of children there, primarily because of the facility's intensively religious programming. In another case, *Freedom From Religion Foundation* v. *Towey*, No. 04-C-381-S, 2005 U.S. Dist. LEXIS 39444 (W.D. Wis. 11 January 2005), a federal judge struck down a federal grant in 2003 to MentorKids USA, a ministry based in Phoenix, to provide mentors for the children of prisoners. In this case, filed by the Freedom From Religion Foundation in Madison, Wisconsin, the judge noted that the exclusively Christian mentors had to regularly assess whether the young people in their care seemed 'to be progressing in relationship with God'.

[51] *Bowen* v. *Kendrick*, 487 US 589, 623 (1988).

[52] *Mitchell* v. *Helms*, 530 US 793, 120 S Ct 2530 (2000).

Arguably, the volume of government funding to a charity may indicate that the latter is in effect acting as a public body, its public benefit service provision being virtually government provision by proxy. For example, in *Dodge* v. *Salvation Army*[53] the court ruled that a Salvation Army domestic violence shelter was wrong to terminate the employment of a counsellor because of her religious beliefs. As the employing religious corporation was in receipt of substantial government funding it was not entitled to rely on the exemption normally available to such bodies from laws prohibiting religious discrimination. Because the charity was heavily reliant upon government funding, it was appropriate for the court to apply the Lemon test and, in doing so, it was found that the termination constituted a violation of the second prong – government activity and funding had essentially advanced religion. It was a ruling that raised a crucial issue, particularly in the context of the so-called 'faith-based funding': should religious groups be required to choose between an entitlement to discriminate and eligibility for government funding? However, in *Rendell-Baker* v. *Kohn*,[54] it was found that although a private school was being heavily funded by the State, this did not make the school a state actor. Again, in *Flagg Bros., Inc.* v. *Brooks*,[55] it was stated that mere acquiescence with the requirements of law did not convert the private actions of a warehouse into those of the state. Finally, in *Young* v. *Shawnee Mission Med. Ctr.*,[56] the court determined that a religious hospital did not lose its Title VII exemption simply because it received thousands of dollars in federal Medicare payments because such payments did not 'transform [the hospital] into a federally funded institution'. In these cases the judicial view was clear in holding that funding in itself did not transform a relationship to the extent that the resulting actions of the recipient could be imputed to the funder on the principal–agent rule. However, it remains uncertain whether this would still be the position where the funding strand of that relationship is accompanied by a constraining policy and procedure strand with the effect that the aims and objectives of the funder, together with the wherewithal for achieving them, are wholly controlled by the funder.

The comments made by O'Connor J in *Mitchell* v. *Helms*[57] stand as a warning to all religious charities in receipt of government funding:

---

[53] *Dodge* v. *Salvation Army*, 1989, WL 53857 (S.D. Miss).
[54] *Rendell-Baker* v. *Kohn*, 457 US 830 (1982).
[55] *Flagg Bros., Inc.* v. *Brooks*, 436 US 149, 164 (1978).
[56] *Young* v. *Shawnee Mission Med. Ctr.*, No. 88-2321-S, 1988 U.S. Dist. LEXIS 12248 (D. Kan. 21 October 1988).
[57] *Mitchell* v. *Helms*, 530 US793, 120 S Ct 2530 (2000).

religious organisations should monitor and 'compartmentalise' government funding received in the form of aid for education programmes. Where the aid is used for secular educational functions, then there would be no problem. If, however, the aid flowed into the entirety of an educational activity, and some 'religious indoctrination [is] taking place therein', then that indoctrination 'would be directly attributable to the government'.[58] In effect, a principal–agent relationship will then have arisen which, among other consequences, will transform the religious charity into a public body (in so far as it has assumed government functionality) and which in turn will result in the charity losing the exemption privileges it would otherwise have as a religious body (see also, *Spencer* v. *World Vision, Inc.* below[59]).

Charity law and the regulatory framework

The framework of charity law, providing in other common law jurisdictions a web of principles and charitable purposes for government and sector to recognise their separate sets of interests, and forming a policy agenda for negotiating a relationship, has not had a similar role in the United States. The only operational framework linking sector entities and sector to government has been the regulatory regime for determining income tax exemption through the Department of Treasury and its IRS. The traditional roles and responsibilities of the Revenue department and the Office of State Attorneys General, reinforced by the customary range of regulatory bodies have, by and large, been seen as sufficient to mediate between the interests of government and sector.

Legislation

As Fishman points out:[60]

> There is no single law of charities in the United States.[61] Instead there are several statutes that apply, depending on the form of organization – trust

---

[58] See also *School District* v. *Ball*, 473 US 373, 398–400 (1985).
[59] *Spencer* v. *World Vision, Inc.*, No. 08-35532, 2011 WL 208356 (9th Cir. 25 January 2011).
[60] J. Fishman, 'Nonprofit Organizations in the United States', in K.J. Hopt and T. Von Hippel (eds), *Comparative Corporate Governance of Non-Profit Organizations*, Cambridge University Press, Cambridge, 2010, at p.130.
[61] One effort towards creating unified fiduciary standards for charities is the American Law Institute's project on the Principles of the Law of Nonprofit Organizations.

or corporation; the focus of the regulator – state or federal, and even local; and the purpose of the regulation.[62]

However, some legislation with federal application has emerged: for example, the Model Protection of Charitable Assets Act 2011 was adopted by the Uniform Laws Commission in summer 2011. The unifying influence of the IRS, as it applies the IRC to all the nation's nonprofits, brings some administrative coherence to the sector.

The charity regulator

There is no charity-specific regulator. The regulatory regime for determining income tax exemption through the Department of Treasury and its IRS also accommodates responsibility for governing charities. Constitutional arrangements, specifically the powers reserved to the federal government under the Tenth Amendment, allow the IRS to administer a uniform tax regime across all states, including assessing eligibility for tax exemption on charitable grounds. The IRS maintains a register of tax-exempt nonprofit organisations, of which 'public charities' (the term sometimes used to describe 'charities' or 'charitable organizations' in the United States) receive the highest level of tax benefits (including tax-preferred donations). It provides a level of supervision and accountability through a system of annual returns, audits, penalties and fines.

Charity law

The tax-driven regulatory framework that has long typified all common law jurisdictions other than England and Wales also governs charities in the United States. The courts, the customs and excise and the state attorneys general have their customary roles in respect of charities, albeit this is somewhat complicated by operating within a federated jurisdiction.

The common law

The distinct legal status of 'charity' is recognised in accordance with the usual common law principles[63] governing exclusivity,[64] public

---

[62] For example, protecting charitable assets is covered under certain statutes, protecting the public is covered under others.

[63] See *Vidal* v. *Girards Executors*, 2 How 127 (US) (1844).

[64] A charity's activities must be restricted to furthering its purpose or purposes as identified at registration.

CHARITY LAW AND THE REGULATORY FRAMEWORK 293

benefit,[65] private benefit,[66] political activity[67] and public policy[68] (see Chapter 1). As has been said:

> A charity, in the legal sense, may be more fully defined as a gift, to be applied consistently with existing laws, for the benefit of an indefinite number of persons, either by bringing their minds or hearts under the influence of education or religion, by relieving their bodies from disease, suffering or constraint, by assisting them to establish themselves in life, or by erecting or maintaining public buildings or works or otherwise lessening the burdens of government.[69]

However, some caveats must be added; for example, charitable intent has never been a necessary legal constituent of charitable status in the United States; the utility of a gift may compensate for an absence of altruism;[70] the exclusivity requirement has been interpreted more flexibly; the operational test applied by the IRS interprets 'exclusively' to mean 'primarily' or 'substantially';[71] and charity has developed a considerable and distinctive 'private' dimension alongside the common law public benefit benchmark.

In general, the charity law distinction between charities and all other nonprofits is not so clear-cut as in other common law jurisdictions: for example, charitable 'purpose' for the IRS has long been as listed below rather than as classified by *Pemsel*. The distinct legal status of 'charity' is recognised in accordance with common law principles, but other classes of organisations are also held to have charitable characteristics, and the nonprofit sector as a whole is classified in a graduated scheme, encompassing in separate blocks 'public benefit' and 'mutual benefit' nonprofit

---

[65] Both the 'public' and the 'benefit' requirements must be satisfied: §1.501(c)(3)–1(d)(1)(ii). In a state case construing a bequest, see the influential decision in *Jackson* v. *Phillips*, 14 Allen (Mass.) 539, 556 (1867), which made it clear that 'a charity in the legal sense, may be more fully defined as a gift, to be applied consistently with existing laws, for the benefit of an indefinite number of persons'.

[66] A charity must ensure that no private benefit inures to any individual. See *United Cancer Council* v. *Commissioner*, 165 F.3d 1173 (7th Cir. 1999) and *Ginsberg* v. *Commissioner*, 46 TC 47 (1966).

[67] IRC Section 4911 imposes an 'excise tax' on excess lobbying expenses. See *Christian Echoes National Ministry, Inc.* v. *United States*, 470 F.2d 849 (10th Cir. 1972).

[68] A charity must not violate fundamental public policy: Rev. Rul. 75–384, 1975–2 C.B. 204. See, for example, *Bob Jones University* v. *United States*, 461 US 574 (1983).

[69] *Jackson* v. *Phillips*, 96 Mass. 539, 556 (1867), quoted in M. Fremont-Smith, *Governing Nonprofit Organisations: Federal and State Law and Regulations*, Belknap Press, Cambridge, MA, 2004.

[70] See, for example, *Fire Insurance Patrol* v. *Boyd*, 120 Pa. 624, 643 (1888).

[71] Treas. Reg. §1.501(c)(3)–1(c)(1).

294   THE UNITED STATES OF AMERICA

corporations. Many states, however, make no formal statutory distinction between 'mutual benefit' corporations and 'public benefit' organisations.

Congress has determined what constitutes charitable 'exempt purposes' in the IRC, moving somewhat beyond the charitable purposes approach set by the Preamble/*Pemsel* parameters to define the equivalent of a 'charitable organisation' as an entity whose public benefit activities are organised for:

(1) relief of the poor, the distressed, or the underprivileged;
(2) advancement of religion;
(3) advancement of education or science;
(4) erection or maintenance of public buildings, monuments or works;
(5) lessening the burdens of government;
(6) lessening of neighbourhood tensions;
(7) elimination of prejudice and discrimination;
(8) defence of human and civil rights secured by law; and
(9) combating community deterioration and juvenile delinquency.[72]

Charitable exempt organisations are of two types: public charities[73] and private foundations.[74] Public charities constitute the largest part of the nonprofit sector and, as Fishman has succinctly observed, 'Churches, schools and hospitals fall into the charmed public charities circle as they are the most venerable and influential members of the charitable sector.'[75] Being presumed to be for the public good, religious organisations are also presumptively exempt from taxation and have been since 1894.[76]

Charity law reform

Law reform has been mooted for many years.[77] The eventual commencement of the US review, undertaken at federal level in the middle of the first decade of this century, was not really a process of 'charity law reform'. It was not particularly concerned with charity law as that regime is understood elsewhere in the common law world: 'charity' is treated in law and for tax purposes very largely as just another word for nonprofit.

---

[72] IRC §501(c)(3).   [73] A public charity is defined in §170(b)(1)(A)(i)–(vi).

[74] See IRC §§509, 501(c)(3). A private foundation is neither a public charity nor a supporting organisation.

[75] See Fishman, 'Nonprofit Organizations in the United States', at p.145.

[76] Revenue Act 1894, ch. 349, §27, 28 Stat 556.

[77] See, for example, J. Fishman, 'The Development of Nonprofit Corporation Law and an Agenda for Reform' (1985) 34 *Emory Law Journal* 1.

Nor was law itself necessarily the focus of attention; it was rules and regulations, and the roles of the bodies involved in determining tax liability that preoccupied most of the process. This was a review of the legal framework for nonprofits, driven primarily by the customary government urge to prevent abuse and financial irregularities, intended to result in greater transparency and accountability, with more rigorous measures for increasing the efficiency and effectiveness of regulatory agencies. Launched in 2004, with the US Senate Finance Committee hearings on *Charity Oversight and Reform: Keeping Bad Things from Happening to Good Charities*,[78] it was and continues to be in the main a review of tax administration, and as such is the most comprehensive review of the governance, regulations and operations of the charitable community undertaken for at least three decades.[79]

Reforms

The review of the tax system by Congress did not dwell unduly on the definitional matters crucial to charity law in a common law context. Whether the public benefit test should or should not be statutorily defined, the continuation of existing presumptions in respect of it – and its potential application to religious organisations – did not seem to warrant much attention. Neither did the need for, or the feasibility of extending, the *Pemsel* heads of charity to better address contemporary areas of social disadvantage attract prolonged debate. Nor was much consideration given to the question as to whether determining charitable status should be decoupled from determining tax liability, and whether the IRS should be displaced by a new charity-specific body as the lead regulatory agency with responsibility for matters relating to charitable status.

At the federal level, the IRS sought reform to increase broad compliance with tax-exemption requirements, with greater transparency, accountability and better surveillance of nonprofit funds. At the state level, the authorities were concerned about nonprofit governance, fundraising and clarification of the responsibilities of the Attorney General. The sector, meanwhile, was focused mostly on the need to reduce the

---

[78] This contained proposals to tighten the definition of public charity, or simply to force all public benefit organisations to abide by the same strict self-dealing rules that currently apply only to private foundations. See, further, 108th Cong. (2004), available at www.finance.senate.gov/hearings/hearing/?id=48ca4cce-afe1-db95-0fcb-8ff9255e780a (accessed 7 January 2014).

[79] See P. Barber, 'Tending the Commons: Charities Reform in Britain and the United States at the Start of the 21st Century' (2007) 55:2 *Exempt Organization Tax Review* 203.

onerous burdens of reporting requirements, adjust taxes to favour non-profits and improve fundraising capacity.

There is no comparison between the US law reform process and that of other common law nations. It was not seen by either government or sector as an opportunity to revisit the core principles and mechanics of charity law, to ensure that it became a framework that better represented their interests, and to reset the terms of their relationship for the twenty-first century. Charity law was not the focus of reform because it was not as relevant to the management of the tax administration system in the United States as it was elsewhere. However, running alongside the latter stages of the tax administration reform process a study group launched by the American Law Institute[80] has been taking slow steps to formulate and agree 'Nonprofit Principles' (see Tentative Drafts adopted in 2007–2008, 2009 and 2011 to assist practising lawyers, regulators and judges dealing with charitable legal issues).[81]

The public benefit test and religious organisations

To be recognised as charitable an entity must satisfy the IRS that it is established for, and its activities do in fact serve, purposes beneficial to the public interest.[82] The long-established common law rule that trusts and gifts for the advancement of religion are *prima facie* charitable and presumed to be for the public benefit continues to apply in the United States.

The test

Both arms of the public benefit test must be satisfied. The judiciary and the IRS apply the public benefit requirement to disallow charitable status to closed and purely contemplative religious orders. Actual benefit must result from the activities of a religious organisation if it is to attain or retain charitable exemption status. So, for example, in *Southern Church of Universal Brotherhood Assembled* v. *Commissioner of Internal*

---

[80]   The American Law Institute (ALI) is described on its website as 'the leading independent organization in the United States producing scholarly work to clarify, modernize, and otherwise improve the law'. See further at: www.ali.org (accessed 7 January 2014).

[81]   See www.ali.org/index.cfm?fuseaction=meetings.detail&meetingid=126 (accessed 7 January 2014).

[82]   See IRS document P557.

Revenue,[83] where the financial arrangements were such as to indicate that the primary purpose being served were those of the founder of the Church, then both the IRS and the judiciary held that the organisation was not a religion. More recently, in the *Provena* case,[84] the appellant claimed that its nonprofit hospital, owned by three Roman Catholic religious orders, should be charitably exempt from property tax on the grounds that its property was used exclusively for the pursuit of its charitable purpose. The court found that, on the contrary:

> the primary purpose for which the [Provena] property was used was providing medical care to patients for a fee. Although the provision of such medical services may have provided an opportunity for various individuals affiliated with the hospital to express and to share their Catholic principles and beliefs, medical care, while potentially miraculous, is not intrinsically, necessarily, or even normally religious in nature.

Its declared charitable purpose proved, under judicial examination, to be of only nominal significance as the organisation's activities were in fact focused on securing healthy profit margins. Admittedly this state-level judicial ruling carries limited precedent weight, but it is indicative of a more stringently forensic approach by courts and regulators towards religious charities than would formerly have been regarded as appropriate.

Religion, religious beliefs and the advancement of religion

The number and diversity of religions in the United States, and the fervour with which those with and those without religious beliefs dispute the same agenda of morally based social issues, has no equivalent among the common law jurisdictions currently being examined. The politics of religion in this jurisdiction is a complex area of study in its own right and, unsurprisingly, the difficulties are reflected in the law as it relates to charity.

Religion

In *Fellowship of Humanity* v. *County of Alameda*[85] the court identified four characteristics of religion: 'A belief not necessarily referring to

---

[83] *Southern Church of Universal Brotherhood Assembled* v. *Commissioner of Internal Revenue*, 74 US TCR 1223.

[84] *Provena Covenant Medical Centre* v. *Department of Revenue*, Docket No. 107328 (Ill. 18 March 2010).

[85] *Fellowship of Humanity* v. *County of Alameda*, 153 Cal. App. 2d 673 (1957).

298 THE UNITED STATES OF AMERICA

supernatural power, a cult involving a gregarious association openly expressing the belief, a system of moral practice resulting from adherence to the belief, and an organization within the cult designed to observe the tenets of the belief.' For Clark J, in *United States* v. *Seeger*,[86] religion involved 'a sincere and meaningful belief, which occupies in the life of its possessor a place parallel to that filled by the God of those admittedly qualifying for the exemption on the grounds of religion comes within the statutory definition'. In general the cases requiring the judiciary to define 'religion' have arisen in the context of the Free Exercise Clause of the First Amendment.

Belief in a Supreme Being

It has been said that: 'the theistic theme has always been well to the fore in definitions of religion in American cases'.[87] So, for example, in *United States* v. *Mackintosh*,[88] Hughes CJ saw 'the essence of religion' as 'belief in a relation to God involving duties superior to those arising from any human relation',[89] and consequently the lack of such a belief resulted in the Freethinkers in America being found not to be a religion.[90] Although the courts in the United States were indeed once reliant upon a theistic component for religion,[91] they moved away from this earlier than their UK counterparts, and the IRS took an early and clear view that charitable trusts could not be restricted to those that declared their belief in one 'Supreme Being'.

Worship, religious tenets and doctrines

That worship, understood as conduct indicating reverence or veneration of a Supreme Being, does not extend to include any lawful means for formally observing the tenets of a cult, was noted in *Fellowship of Humanity* v. *County of Almeda*.[92] In *Founding Church of Scientology* v.

---

[86] *United States* v. *Seeger*, 350 US 163 (1965), at p.176.
[87] H. Picarda, *The Law and Practice Relating to Charities* (3rd edn), Butterworths, London, 1999, at p.73.
[88] *United States* v. *Mackintosh*, 283 US 605 (1931).   [89] Ibid., at pp.633–634.
[90] See *Old Colony Trust Co* v. *Welch* 25 F. Supp. 45, at 49 (1938), cited in Picarda, *The Law and Practice Relating to Charities*, at p.83.
[91] See, for example, *Davis* v. *Beason* [1890] USCC 39; (1890) 133 US 333 (33 Law Ed 637).
[92] *Fellowship of Humanity* v. *County of Almeda* 153 Cal. App. 2d 673 (1957). Formally rejected in the *Church of Scientology* case. Note that in 1993 the IRS granted Scientology charitable status (Rev. Rul. 93–73, 1993–2 C.B. 75).

THE ADVANCEMENT OF RELIGION 299

United States,[93] while the IRS did not find it necessary to rule on the claim of the Scientology Church and its various branches that they were 'organized and operated exclusively for religious ... or educational purposes', it did dismiss the case because of aspects of the way in which the organisations were operated. There is little indication in the cases that matters of worship, religious tenets and doctrines have played much part in assisting judiciary or regulators in their decision-making as to an organisation's entitlement to charitable exempt status.

Philosophy and other value systems

The assertion of the right of individuals and associations to prevail against any prescriptive State ordering of matters relating to belief was judicially enunciated at an early stage. As Jackson J declaimed in *West Virginia Board of Education* v. *Barnette*:

> If there is any fixed star in our constitutional constellation, it is that no official, high or petty, can prescribe what shall be orthodox in politics, nationalism, religion or other matters of opinion or force citizens to confess by word or act their faith therein.[94]

The exclusively theistic approach was rejected in 1961 by Black J in *Torcaso* v. *Watkins*,[95] when the Supreme Court struck down a Maryland law requiring officials to declare a belief in God in order to hold office in that state and referred to a list of what could be termed 'religions' – including 'Buddhism, Taoism, Ethical Culture, Secular Humanism and others' – even though they were not defined solely in terms of a Supreme Being. This was followed four years later when, in *United States* v. *Seeger*,[96] the statutory provisions for conscientious objection to military service on religious grounds were extended to anyone holding 'a sincere and meaningful belief which occupies in the life of its possessor a place parallel to that filled by the God of those admittedly qualifying for the exemption'. Mere personal belief, however, which 'in no way related to a Supreme Being', was not a religion. The court found that 'religious training and belief' included non-theistic faiths, provided that they were 'based upon a power or being, or upon

---

[93] *Founding Church of Scientology* v. *United States*, 412 F. 2d 1197 (Ct. Cl. 1969).
[94] *West Virginia Board of Education* v. *Barnette*, 319 US 624 (1943).
[95] *Torcaso* v. *Watkins*, 367 US 488 (1961).
[96] *United States* v. *Seeger*, 380 US 163, 186 (1965).

a faith, to which all else is subordinate or upon which all else is ultimately dependent'.

The interpretation to be given to 'belief' was examined by the courts in *Wooley* v. *Maynard*[97] when it was held to include mere written or verbal affirmations or other manifestations of what one does (or does not) believe. Later, in *Malnak* v. *Yogi*,[98] the US judiciary went further than their counterparts in Australia and New Zealand were prepared to go in recognition of what constitutes a religion. Adams J then described the criteria developed by American courts as: first, a set of ideas that deal with the ultimate concerns of man; second, ideas that *in toto* constitute an integrated belief system; and, third, forms and ceremonies that are found in accepted religions. This was subsequently endorsed by Wilson and Deane JJ, who said their view of 'religion' 'accords broadly with the newer, more expansive, reading of that term' as set out by Adams J.

The advancement of religion

In this jurisdiction there is a legal presumption, though not in legislative form, that religious organisations per se satisfy the public benefit test. Under the First Amendment of the Constitution, Congress is forbidden to enact a law 'respecting an establishment of religion or prohibiting the free exercise thereof'. Interference in any way with religious practice is frowned upon and religion receives special deference in American law. Religious charitable trusts enjoy the same privileges as religious corporations.

The means for advancing religion

The IRS has acknowledged that the 'statutory term "religion" cannot be defined with precision' and that 'serious Constitutional difficulties would be presented if this section were interpreted to exclude those beliefs that do not encompass a Supreme Being'.[99] From time to time various tests have applied to preclude certain religious organisations from receiving tax-exempt status, including: too many political activities, as in *Christian Echoes National Ministry, Inc.* v. *United States*;[100] and

---

[97] *Wooley* v. *Maynard*, 430 US 705, 713 (1977).
[98] *Malnak* v. *Yogi*, 592 F.2d 197 (1979). [99] Treas. Reg. 1.501(c)(3)–1(d).
[100] *Christian Echoes Nat. Ministry, Inc.* v. *United States*, 470 F.2d 849 (10th Cir. 1972).

engaging in impermissible activities in support of or opposed to a candidate for public office, as in *Branch Ministries v. Rossotti*;[101] commercial activity being disproportionate to charitable purpose activity, as in *Scripture Press Foundation v. US*,[102] *People ex rel. Groman v. Sinai Temple*[103] and *Living Faith, Inc. v. Comm'r*;[104] providing too many private benefits to the founders and other insiders, as in *Church of Scientology of California v. Commissioner*[105] and *Founding Church of Scientology v. United States*.[106]

As the IRS has explained, because activities often serve more than one purpose, an organisation that is 'advancing religion' within the meaning of Reg. 1.501(c)(3)–1(d)(2) may also qualify under IRC §501(c)(3) as a charitable or educational organisation.[107]

Public policy, charity and common law constraints

The US has a long-standing reputation as the destination of choice for emigrants. Consequently, American society is in a constant state of flux as different incoming racial groups add to its rich diversity of cultures. It also endured a prolonged period of strife with its Native American population during the colonial period and a bitter civil war, in both of which racial issues played a prominent part. For such reasons it is a society well attuned to the damaging effects of discrimination and this has given rise to a legal presumption that discrimination is contrary to public policy, with some notable exceptions.

Testamentary conditions and the common law

In keeping with the approach adopted in other common law jurisdictions, testators' gifts, made subject to conditions favouring beneficiaries of a particular religious persuasion, are virtually immune from public

---

[101] *Branch Ministries v. Rossotti*, 211 F.3d 137 (D.C. Cir. 2000).
[102] *Scripture Press Foundation v. US*, 285 F.2d 800 (Ct. Cl. 1961).
[103] *People ex rel. Groman v. Sinai Temple*, 20 Cal. App. 3d 614 (Cal. Ct. App. 1971).
[104] *Living Faith, Inc. v. Comm'r*, 60 TCM 710 (1990).
[105] *Church of Scientology of California v. Commissioner*, 823 F.2d 1310 (9th Cir. 1987).
[106] *Founding Church of Scientology v. United States*, 412 F.2d 1197 (Ct. Cl. 1969). See also *Hernandez v. Commissioner*, 490 US 680, 109 S Ct 2136 (1989).
[107] See IRS, 'Part 7: Rulings and Agreements', at: www.irs.gov/irm/part7/irm_07-025-003.html (accessed 7 January 2014).

policy considerations. Although contentious in this jurisdiction, they will normally be valid.[108]

Failure due to breach of common law rules

Broadly speaking, the usual common law rules relating to charity (see, further, Chapter 1) are also applied in the United States. For example, the 'exclusivity' rule came into play in *Slee* v. *Commissioner*[109] when Judge Learned Hand advised that the American Birth Control League was not entitled to tax exemption as it was not operated exclusively for charitable purposes. This was because it disseminated 'propaganda' to legislators and the public in lobbying for the repeal of birth control laws. Again, the common law rule that the viability of a testator's charitable bequest is dependent upon the existence of a valid charitable intent (or at least an absence of malice) has played a part in cases such as *Evans* v. *Abney*,[110] concerning a conveyance of a trust of land to the city for the creation of a park for the exclusive use of white people, where no such intent existed. Where, such as in *Trustees of University of Delaware* v. *Gebelin*[111] and *Wooten* v. *Fitzgerald*,[112] gifts to educational institutions have been restricted by racial conditions, the courts can save the gift by using *cy-près* to eliminate the offending restrictions. The outcome in such cases is, however, dependent upon the testator having had a general charitable intent. Frequent use of *cy-près* is found where there are unconstitutional or illegal conditions in a trust, such as provisions that would violate law and public policy against racial discrimination. Generally, contention arises in relation to whether an organisation to which charitable assets were to be diverted had purposes that were close enough to those of the dissolving corporation.[113]

---

[108] See, further, S. Grattan and H. Conway, 'Testamentary Conditions in Restraint of Religion in the Twenty-first Century: An Anglo-Canadian Perspective' (2005) 50 *McGill Law Journal* 511.

[109] *Slee* v. *Commissioner*, 42 F.2d 184 (2nd Cir. 1930).

[110] *Evans* v. *Abney*, 224 Ga. 826, 165 SE 2d 160, (1968), aff'd 396 US 435, 90 S Ct 628 (1970).

[111] *Trustees of University of Del.* v. *Gebelin*, 420 A.2d 1191 (Del. Ch. 1980) (racial restriction removed but not gender restriction).

[112] *Wooten* v. *Fitzgerald*, 440 SW 2d 719 (Tex. Civ. App. 1969). See, generally, D. Luria, 'Prying Loose the Dead Hand of the Past: How Courts Apply the *Cy-près* to Race, Gender, and Religiously Restricted Trusts' (1986) 21 *University of San Francisco Law Review* 41.

[113] See, for example, the *Matter of Multiple Sclerosis Service Organisation of New York, Inc.*, 68 NY 2d 32 (1986).

The IRS has demonstrated a willingness to stretch the boundaries of accepted common law definitions, particularly in light of the *Bob Jones University* decision (see, further, below).[114] For example, in Private Letter Ruling 8910001,[115] the IRS held that a privately administered trust will not be considered charitable if the beneficiaries are restricted to 'worthy and deserving white persons'. The IRS stated that in its view the decision in *Bob Jones* 'was not limited to racial discrimination in education'.

Bequests subject to a religious condition

The freedom of a testator to divest himself or herself of their property, even if this gift is made subject to an explicitly discriminatory religious condition, can constitute a valid charitable disposition. In *Shapira* v. *Union National Bank*,[116] for example, a father left his money to Israel, his wife and their three sons. The bequests to his sons were contingent on each son being married to a Jewish girl or marrying a Jewish girl within seven years of his father's demise. The court found that the father's unmistakable testamentary plan was that his possessions be used to encourage the preservation of the Jewish faith and blood. The court considered it was duty bound to honour the testator's intention and accordingly rejected the sons' claims that the conditions were invalid. Similarly, in *re the Estate of Max Feinberg*,[117] the Illinois Supreme Court upheld a condition in the will of a deceased Chicago dentist which prohibited marriage outside the Jewish faith with the effect of disinheriting his four grandchildren. In reaching its decision the court explained its rationale, which balanced conflicting considerations:

> [b]ecause a testator or the settlor of a trust is not a state actor, there are no constitutional dimensions to his choice of beneficiaries. Equal protection does not require that all children be treated equally; due process does not require notice of conditions precedent to potential beneficiaries; and the free exercise clause does not require a grandparent to treat grandchildren who reject his religious beliefs and customs in the same manner as he treats those who conform to his traditions.

---

[114] *Bob Jones University*, 461 US 574 (1983).
[115] PLR 8910001 (30 November 1988). The ruling cites Rev. Rul. 67–325, 1967–2 C.B. 113, which held that a racially restrictive community centre was not charitable.
[116] 39 Ohio Misc. 28, 315 NE 2d 825 (1974).
[117] *re the Estate of Max Feinberg* 235 Ill. 2d 256 (2009).

304 THE UNITED STATES OF AMERICA

Religious preferences and public policy

It was in *United States* v. *Carolene Producte Co.*[118] that Stone J, in his famous footnote 4, declared that one of the grounds on which legislation could be subjected to 'more exacting judicial scrutiny' was if it was directed at particular religious, national or racial minorities or expressed prejudice against 'discrete and insular minorities'.[119] This approach has since been followed by the IRS in a number of rulings which have upheld the charitable status of organisations that: are set up to eliminate the discrimination that limit employment opportunities for qualified minority workers;[120] to educate the public on the merits of racially integrated neighbourhoods;[121] to investigate the causes of deterioration in a particular community and inform residents and city officials of possible corrective measures;[122] and to conduct investigations and research on discrimination against minority groups in housing and public accommodation.[123] It was not followed, however, in *State ex rel. Grant* v. *Brown*,[124] when the Supreme Court of Ohio upheld the decision of the Secretary of State to not incorporate an organisation with similar objectives on the ground that it would violate public policy.

Public policy constraints

The constraints imposed by the criminal law on the latitude otherwise available in the Free Exercise Clause were firmly underlined in *Reynolds* v. *United States*,[125] when the Supreme Court upheld the conviction of a Mormon for polygamy (see, further, below). A century later, in *Bob Jones University* v. *United States*,[126] the Supreme Court found that a university with a racially discriminatory admissions policy, and other policies relating to religious beliefs against interracial dating and marriage, was not charitable and therefore did not qualify for the tax exemption and

---

[118] *United States* v. *Carolene Producte Co.*, 304 US 144 (1938). There are three aspects to this test – there must be a compelling state interest, the law or policy must be narrowly tailored to meet it and the law or policy must be the least restrictive means for achieving it.

[119] Ibid., at p.152.   [120] See Rev. Rul. 68–70, 1968–1 C.B. 248.

[121] See Rev. Rul. 68–655, 1968–1 C.B. 248.   [122] See Rev. Rul. 68–15, 1968–1 C.B. 244.

[123] See Rev. Rul. 68–438, 1968–2 C.B. 209.

[124] *State ex rel. Grant* v. *Brown*, 39 Ohio St. 2d 112, 313 NE 2d 847, 68 O.O. 2d 65 (Ohio 1974).

[125] *Reynolds* v. *United States*, 98 US 145 (1878).

[126] *Bob Jones University* v. *United States*, 461 US 574 (1983).

PUBLIC POLICY AND COMMON LAW CONSTRAINTS 305

other benefits available to charities. Burger J reasoned that, given the income tax privileges of charitable status, charities 'must serve a public purpose and not be contrary to established public policy'.[127] This approach was followed more recently in *Home for Incurables of Baltimore City* v. *University of Maryland Medical System Corporation*,[128] which concerned a medical rehabilitation centre that received a gift under charitable bequest for 'white patients' only. The Maryland Court of Appeals struck the racial restriction from the testator's will through application of the *cy-près* doctrine, thus enabling the centre to retain the charitable gift free from the racial restriction. Eason claims that, in so doing, the court rejected the substitute beneficiary's individual-donor 'freedom of testation' argument, which if true would certainly be an important break with tradition.[129]

Advocacy

This traditional limitation on the advocacy capacity of charities is embodied in two parts of §501(c)(3) – the restriction on lobbying ('no substantial part' of the activities of an organisation may constitute 'carrying on propaganda, or otherwise attempting to influence legislation') and the absolute prohibition on engaging in election-related activities 'on behalf of (or in opposition to) any candidate for public office'. Although exempt charities may elect to use a quantitative test, set out in §§501(h) and 4911, for the purpose of staying within the limits of permissible lobbying activities, applying the rules is extremely complicated and thus provides little comfort unless an organisation is going to engage in a highly visible campaign.

In *Roberts* v. *United States Jaycees*[130] the Supreme Court ruled that 'implicit in the right to engage in activities protected by the First Amendment' is a 'corresponding right to associate with others in pursuit of a wide variety of ... religious ... ends'. However, where the group association takes the form of a religious organisation, and that body is in

---

[127] Ibid.

[128] *Home for Incurables of Baltimore City* v. *University of Maryland Medical System Corporation*, 797 A.2d 746 (Md 2002). Also see, *Big Mama Rag, Inc.* v. *United States*, 631 F.2d 1030 (D.C. Cir. 1980).

[129] See, further, J. K. Eason, 'Motive, Duty, and the Management of Restricted Charitable Gifts' (2010) 45 *Wake Forest Law Review* 123.

[130] See *Roberts* v. *United States Jaycees*, 468 US 609, 104 S Ct 3244, 82 L Ed 2d 462, 1984. Also see, *NAACP* v. *Alabama ex rel. Patterson* 357 US 449 (1958), *Regan* v. *Taxation With Representation of Washington, Inc.*, 461 US 540, 103 S Ct 197 (1983) and *Branch Ministries* v. *Rossoti*, 211 F.3d 137 (D.C. Cir. 2000).

receipt of government assistance then, as always, there is a risk that the advocacy role may be constrained by funding considerations. Indeed, as the Aspen Institute has warned, 'special care needs to be taken to avoid having the receipt of government support compromise the ability of religious organizations to perform other roles in the pursuit of social justice, including their role of speaking "truth to power" and attempting to promote more humane public policies'.[131]

The line between assertive but permissible advocacy and impermissible propaganda can be difficult to draw, but once the advocates become abusive and threatening then their actions will cease to be legal.[132]

Proselytism

The advancement of religion by means of proselytism finds stronger recognition in the United States than elsewhere due to the protection offered by the First Amendment. That any impairment of the right to distribute pamphlets anonymously is contrary to the First Amendment's Free Exercise Clause was recognised in *McIntyre* v. *Ohio Elections Comm'n*.[133] Where, however, as in *Heffron* v. *International Society for Krishna Consciousness*,[134] such distribution would interfere with the State's legitimate interest in ensuring the orderly movement and control of crowds at a fair, then a state ordinance preventing this will be upheld: even if the plaintiff's peripatetic solicitation is part of a church ritual it does not entitle church members to solicitation rights in a public forum superior to those of members of other religious groups that raise money but do not purport to ritualise the process.

More recently, *Watchtower Bible and Tract Society of New York* v. *Village of Stratton*[135] concerned town ordinances that made it a misdemeanour to engage in door-to-door advocacy without first registering with town officials and receiving a permit. Jehovah's Witnesses argued that these ordinances violated their First Amendment right to canvass

---

[131] Aspen Institute, *Religious Organizations and Government*, 2001, at p.9, at: www.aspeninstitute.org/topics/religion (accessed 7 January 2014).

[132] See, for example, *Bray* v. *Alexandria Women's Health Clinic*, 506 US 263 (1993) and protests outside abortion clinics.

[133] *McIntyre* v. *Ohio Elections Comm'n*, 514 US 334 (1995).

[134] *Heffron* v. *International Society for Krishna Consciousness*, 452 US 640 (1981). Also, see, *Int'l Society for Krishna Consciousness Inc* v. *Lee*, 505 US 672 (1992).

[135] *Watchtower Bible and Tract Society of New York* v. *Village of Stratton*, 122 S Ct 2080 (2002).

door-to-door as part of their religious belief that they should share the Gospel with others. The Supreme Court agreed and stated that the ordinances were 'offensive, not only to the values protected by the First Amendment, but to the very notion of a free society'.[136]

Moreover, the US Supreme Court has ruled that proselytisation with federal funds would violate the First Amendment.[137]

Human rights, discrimination and religious charities: contemporary issues

'On June 1, 1660, magistrates from the Massachusetts Bay Colony hanged Mary Dyer on Boston Commons for her persistence in believing and proselytizing the Quaker faith.'[138] In 1791 the first 16 words of the First Amendment of the Bill of Rights declared 'Congress shall make no law respecting an establishment of religion, or prohibiting the free exercise thereof', thereby guaranteeing the free exercise of religion at the national level. 'What had happened in the intervening 131 years was not the secularization of American society or politics, or the triumph of Enlightenment rationalism, but the mutual development of religious doctrine and political culture.'[139]

Human rights

The US Constitution, its Bill of Rights (the first ten amendments), together with the Thirteenth, Fourteenth and Fifteenth Amendments, may be considered to provide a body of provisions equivalent to the European Convention on Human Rights, with nationwide application. In addition, the United States has signed and ratified the International Covenant on Civil and Political Rights (albeit with significant 'reservations, understandings and declarations'), but declined to sign the Optional Protocol and the American Convention of Human Rights. Currently, the United States has a complex and at times contradictory relationship with human rights which nonetheless enables it to claim that it is a

---

[136] Ibid., at p.2087.
[137] See *Hein* v. *Freedom From Religion Foundation*, 551 US 587 (2007).
[138] K. S. Hasson, *The Right to Be Wrong: Ending the Culture War Over Religion in America*, Encounter Books, San Francisco, 2005, at pp.40–42.
[139] See, T. F. Farr, 'Bringing Religious Freedom Back into American Religious Freedom Policy' (2011), winter *Cardus Policy in Public.*

308 THE UNITED STATES OF AMERICA

country that protects human rights and is entitled to annually criticise other countries for their human rights record.[140]

The Constitution

The American Constitution is credited with erecting a wall to separate matters of Church and State. In particular, the First Amendment, as stated above, formulated the two key rules for constraining State interference in religious affairs: the Establishment Clause and the Free Exercise Clause. The first operates to prevent any attempt by Congress to identify an official or national Church or collect taxes or provide public money to support any specific religion. The second prohibits Congress from interfering with the manner in which any person chooses to worship. Black J, in *Everson* v. *Board of Education*,[141] drew attention to the wall analogy when, after tracing the historical purpose of the First Amendment, he described the Establishment Clause as preventing federal and state governments from passing laws 'which aid one religion, aid all religions, or prefer one religion over another' and as 'intended to erect "a wall of separation between Church and State"'. We must determine, he explained, 'whether there has been a violation of the constitutionally required separation of church and state ... [i.e.] whether the funded activity has a secular purpose and, even if it does, whether the funded activity has a primary effect of advancing or inhibiting religion'.

The Constitution contains other clauses that also have a bearing on religious freedom. The Speech Clause of the First Amendment, for example, which prohibits government action abridging the freedoms of expression and association,[142] has been held to extend to religious speech and association[143] and has been so judicially deployed, particularly in respect of religious speech by Jehovah's Witnesses.[144] The Fourteenth

---

[140] The US Department of State issues annual 'Human Rights Country Reports', which are available at www.state.gov/g/drl/rls/hrrpt (accessed 7 January 2014).

[141] *Everson* v. *Board of Education*, 330 US 1 (1947).

[142] See *Gitlow* v. *New York*, 268 US 652, 666 (1925).

[143] See, for example, *Good News Club* v. *Milford Cent. Sch.*, 533 US 98 (2001); *Rosenberger* v. *Rector*, 515 US 819 (1995); *Capital Square Review and Advisory Bd.* v. *Pinette*, 515 US 753 (1995); *Lamb's Chapel* v. *Center Moriches Union Free Sch. Dist.*, 508 US 384 (1993); *Bd. of Educ.* v. *Mergens*, 496 US 226 (1990); and *Widmar* v. *Vincent*, 454 US 263 (1981).

[144] See, for example, *Marsh* v. *Alabama*, 326 US 501 (1946); *W. Va. State Bd. Educ.* v. *Barnette*, 319 US 624 (1943); *Martin* v. *City of Struthers*, 319 US 141 (1943); *Cox* v. *New Hampshire*, 312 US 569 (1941); and *Cantwell* v. *Connecticut*, 310 US 296, 309–310 (1940).

HUMAN RIGHTS, DISCRIMINATION & RELIGIOUS CHARITIES 309

Amendment – which declares that the states may not 'deprive any person of life, liberty, or property, without due process of law' – is also important as the courts have held that its protections are fundamental and therefore extend to the states' due processes of law and provides constitutional protection against religious discrimination.[145] When read in conjunction with the First Amendment, the effect is that neither the states nor the federal government may pass laws 'respecting an establishment of religion, or prohibiting the free exercise thereof'.

Equality and diversity legislation

For most practical purposes, the legislative provisions governing equality and diversity on a nationwide basis are to be found in the Civil Rights Act 1964. Title VII of this Act forbids employers with 15 or more employees to discriminate on the basis of race, colour, sex, religion or national origin.[146] The law applies to federal, state and local employers. There are also a number of federal statutes (and much state-specific legislation), some quite dated, that address matters of equality and diversity, including the Age Discrimination in Employment Act 1967, the Equal Pay Act 1963 and the Americans with Disabilities Act 1990.

Religious charities, discrimination and exemptions

The general rule in federal non-discrimination law, that private employers ignore religion in making employment decisions, is subject to the proviso that an accommodation may be allowed for 'a religious corporation, association, educational institution, or society'. This allows religious organisations to give employment preference to members of their own religion. In addition, the courts have held that clergy members generally cannot bring claims under the federal employment discrimination laws, including Title VII and the above-mentioned equality and diversity legislation. This 'ministerial exception' comes not from the text of the statutes, but from the First Amendment principle that governmental regulation of Church administration, including the appointment of clergy, impedes the free exercise of religion and

---

[145] See, for example, *Bolling* v. *Sharpe*, 347 US 497 (1954).

[146] Congress in 1972 added an exemption, codified in s.702 of the Act, for 'religious corporation[s], association[s], educational institution[s], or societ[ies]' to the prohibition against religion-based discrimination.

constitutes impermissible government entanglement with church authority. The exception applies only to employees who perform essentially religious functions, namely those whose primary duties consist of engaging in church governance, supervising a religious order or conducting religious ritual, worship or instruction.

However, in practice it is the Title VII exemption for religious organisations that is important. This applies only to those institutions whose 'purpose and character are primarily religious' and has been interpreted narrowly in recent years: religious entities will not as a matter of course be able to claim immunity from state laws intended to have universal application.[147]

Freedom of religion

The first steps in recognition of the right of religious freedom were taken in Virginia in 1776 with the proclamation of a Bill of Rights, inspired by the French Revolution. James Madison took responsibility for crafting the section on freedom of religion, which repudiated the Established Church model of religious practice in England, and set the United States on its own singular path. Article 16 of the Bill of Rights provided a guarantee of freedom of religion as the basic right of citizens in a democratic republic but most often its recognition is subsumed within other statutory entitlements and prohibitions rather than asserted as a standalone right.

Subsequently, the judiciary made several important contributions to consolidating and elucidating the freedom of religion. The formulation of the Lemon test by Chief Justice Warren Burger in *Lemon v. Kurtzman*,[148] to aid interpretation of the Establishment Clause and determine when a law has the effect of establishing religion, is one such contribution. This case concerned the practice of state authorities in Rhode Island and Pennsylvania of supplementing the salaries of teachers in religiously based, private schools for teaching secular subjects – a practice which was found to violate the Establishment Clause. The test, as then articulated by Burger CJ, has three parts: first, the statute must have a secular legislative purpose; second, its principal or primary effect must be one that neither advances nor inhibits religion;

---

[147] For example, in *Alamo Foundation* v. *Secretary of Labor*, 471 US 290 (1985). Also see *United States* v. *Lee*, 455 US 252 (1982).
[148] *Lemon* v. *Kurtzman*, 403 US 602 (1971).

finally, the statute must not foster 'an excessive government entanglement with religion'.

More recently, the United States has introduced federal legislation to reinforce the principles first declared in 1776. This includes the Religious Freedom Restoration Act 1993;[149] the International Religious Freedom Act 1998, which requires the State Department to focus its international intervention on the humanitarian objectives of denouncing persecution and saving victims; and the Religious Land Use and Institutionalized Persons Act 2000. Individual states often have similar provisions in their own constitutions and statutes.

Interference with the manifestation of religious belief

As declared in *Cantwell* v. *Connecticut*,[150] the Free Exercise Clause 'embraces two concepts – freedom to believe and freedom to act. The first is absolute, but in the nature of things, the second cannot be. Conduct remains subject to regulation for the protection of society.'[151] This principle probably dates from the US Supreme Court ruling in *Reynolds* v. *United States*,[152] which concerned George Reynolds, a Mormon residing in Utah, who challenged his 1878 polygamy conviction under federal law by arguing that this marital practice was sanctioned by his religion. In rejecting his argument, the Supreme Court applied a distinction between religious belief and religious conduct: while the right to religious belief was absolute, the government had a responsibility to curb religious conduct that conflicted with the broader interests of the community.[153] As the Court put it, to excuse polygamy on religious grounds would 'make the professed doctrines of religious belief superior to the law of the land, and in effect . . . permit every citizen to become a law unto himself'.[154]

Gedicks has written that:

> freedom of religion in the United States is less a liberty right than an equality right. Since the Supreme Court's 1990 decision in *Employment Division* v. *Smith*,[155] the U.S. Constitution has been understood to

---

[149] See *City of Boerne* v. *Flores*, 521 US 507, 509 (1997).
[150] *Cantwell* v. *Connecticut*, 310 US 296 (1940).   [151] Ibid., at pp.303–304.
[152] *Reynolds* v. *United States*, 98 US (8 Otto.) 145 (1878).
[153] See, further, S. Pepper, 'Reynolds, Yoder, and Beyond: Alternatives for the Free Exercise Clause' (1981) 1981 *Utah Law Review* 309.
[154] *Reynolds* v. *United States* 98 US 145, at p.167 (1879); 25 Law Ed 244, at p.250.
[155] *Employment Division* v. *Smith*, 494 US 872 (1990).

protect against government action that *intentionally* burdens religious liberty, but not against action that *incidentally* burdens religious liberty.[156] In other words, government action that purposely targets religious activity for a regulatory burden is constitutionally invalid, whereas government action that burdens religious activity along with similarly situated secular activity as the consequence of the government's pursuit of a legitimate regulatory goal is presumptively valid.[157]

Over time, the Supreme Court has formulated several different tests which courts and regulators have relied upon to determine whether or not there has been an unwarranted encroachment on the freedom to manifest religious beliefs.[158] The tests serve to benchmark different stages in the judicial interpretation of the degree of protection that manifestations of religious belief warranted relative to other considerations.

- The 'exemption doctrine'

The exemption doctrine emerged in the 1960s and provided special protection for religion in the form of religious exemptions under the Free Exercise Clause as this seemed a permissible way to balance the special disabilities imposed on religious activity under the Establishment Clause. It empowered courts to excuse individuals from complying with a law if they could show that the law unduly burdened their sincere religious practices, unless the government could show that mandating uniform obedience to the law was required by a compelling interest that could not be protected in any less intrusive manner. In practice the Court rejected most exemption claims.[159] As the majority in *Employment Division* v. *Smith*[160] characterised the matter, the exemption doctrine permitted any person to obtain disposition to disobey the law, to become a 'law unto himself', merely by asserting that a particular government action burdened that person's religious beliefs or practices, even though the burden was incidental rather than intentional.[161] The Court finally abandoned the doctrine in *Smith* in 1990 when it held that 'where

---

[156] Ibid., citing P. M. McFadden, 'Provincialism in United States Courts' (1995) 81 *Cornell Law Review* 4, at p.4.

[157] See F. M. Gedicks, 'The Permissible Scope of Legal Limitations on the Freedom of Religion or Belief in the United States' (2005) 19 *Emory International Law Review*, at p.1187. Also see P. Kurland, *Religion and the Law: Of Church and State and the Supreme Court*, University of Chicago Press, Chicago, IL, 1961.

[158] See, for example, K. M. Sands (ed.), *God Forbid: Religion and Sex in American Public Life*, Oxford University Press, New York, 2000.

[159] See, for example, *Thomas* v. *Colins*, 323 US 65 S Ct 315. 89 L Ed 430.

[160] *Employment Division* v. *Smith*, 494 US 872 (1990).   [161] Ibid., at p.885.

the State has in place a system of individualized exemptions, it may not refuse to extend that system to cases of "religious hardship" without compelling reason'.[162]

- The 'compelling interest' test

Under the Religious Freedom Restoration Act 1993, the government is required to demonstrate a 'compelling interest' of the 'highest order' before interfering with a manifestation of religious belief. This test has a long history.[163] In applying it the Supreme Court has held that the test was not satisfied where criminal penalties were imposed upon Amish parents for refusing to send their children to high school, the Amish claims being said to be based on 'deep religious conviction, shared by an organised group, and intimately related to daily living',[164] nor did the denial of unemployment benefits to a Seventh Day Adventist who was dismissed after she refused to work on Saturday.[165] In *Muhammad v. City of N.Y. Dept. of Corrections*[166] it was held that provision of 'generic' worship services by the state prison for Protestant, Catholic, Jewish and Muslim inmates, but not to Nation of Islam inmates, satisfied the compelling interest test, where the prison lacked sufficient officers, space and time to provide additional services while still maintaining internal order, and where the plaintiffs had access to a Nation of Islam clergyman. The scope of the test was extended under the Religious Land Use and Institutionalized Persons Act 2000.

- The 'pervasively sectarian' test

As Thomas J, speaking for the Supreme Court, explained in *Columbia Union College* v. *Edward O. Clark, Jr., et al*:[167]

---

[162] Ibid., at p.884.

[163] See, for example: *United States* v. *Lee*, 455 US 252, 257 (1982) ('The State may justify a limitation on religious liberty by showing that it is essential to accomplish an overriding government interest'); *Church of Lukumi Babalu Aye* v. *Hialeah*, 508 US 520, 578 (1993) ('When the State enacts legislation that intentionally or unintentionally places a burden upon religiously motivated practice, it must justify that burden by showing that it is the least restrictive means of achieving some compelling State interest'); and *City of Boerne* v. *Flores*, US Lexis 4035, 46 (1997) ('Requiring a State to demonstrate a compelling interest and show that it has adopted the least restrictive means of achieving that interest is the most demanding test known to constitutional law').

[164] *Wisconsin* v. *Yoder*, 406 US 205, 32 L Ed 15, 92 S Ct 1526.

[165] *Sherbert* v. *Verner*, 374 US 398 (1963).

[166] *Muhammad* v. *City of N.Y. Dept. of Corrections*, 904 F. Supp. 161, 193–195 (S.D. N.Y. 1995).

[167] *Columbia Union College* v. *Edward O. Clark, Jr., et al*, 119 S Ct 2357 (1999).

314   THE UNITED STATES OF AMERICA

> We invented the 'pervasively sectarian' test as a way to distinguish
> between schools that carefully segregate religious and secular activities
> and schools that consider their religious and educational missions indi-
> visible and therefore require religion to permeate all activities. In my
> view, the 'pervasively sectarian' test rests upon two assumptions that
> cannot be squared with our more recent jurisprudence. The first of these
> assumptions is that the Establishment Clause prohibits government
> funds from ever benefiting, either directly or indirectly, 'religious' activ-
> ities.[168] The other is that any institution that takes religion seriously
> cannot be trusted to observe this prohibition.[169]

Nonetheless, in *Americans United For Separation of Church and State* v. *Prison Fellowship Ministries*,[170] the IFI, an intensely religious rehabilitation programme delivered under the auspices of the Prison Fellowship Ministries, which required an enrolled prisoner to constantly satisfy an evangelical Christian programme, was found to be 'pervasively sectarian'.

- The 'neutrality test'

This test reflects the view that law must function in a manner that is neutral towards religion: religion is being treated exactly the same as other subjects of the legislative intent; and that a law will lack neutrality if its purpose is to restrict religious practices because they are religious. The test was deployed in *Church of Lukumi Babalu Aye, Inc.* v. *City of Hialeah*,[171] which concerned city ordinances forbidding animal slaughter, except kosher slaughter, within city limits. The court found that the ordinances were intended to prevent adherents of Santeria from conducting animal sacrifices in accordance with the rites of their religion. As the court explained: 'although a law targeting religious beliefs is never permissible, if the object of the law is to infringe upon or restrict practices because of their religious motivation, the law is not neutral'.[172] Such a religiously discriminatory purpose may be evident from the text of the law, as well as from its effect. The neutrality test has most often

---

[168] Citing *Roemer* v. *Board of Public Works of Md.*, 426 US 736 (1976), at p.755.
[169] Citing the plurality's statement in *Tilton* v. *Richardson*, 403 US 672, 681 (1971), that '[t]here is no evidence that religion seeps into the use of any of these facilities ... the schools were characterized by an atmosphere of academic freedom rather than religious indoctrination.'
[170] *Americans United For Separation of Church and State* v. *Prison Fellowship Ministries*, 432 F. Supp. 2d 862 (S.D. Iowa 2006).
[171] *Church of Lukumi Babalu Aye, Inc.* v. *City of Hialeah*, 508 US 520 (1993).
[172] Ibid., at p.533.

HUMAN RIGHTS, DISCRIMINATION & RELIGIOUS CHARITIES 315

been used to invalidate state laws in an educational context.[173] For example, the *School Prayer* cases established that any memorial service sponsored or organised by a school and involving a prayer would be invalid.[174] Most recently it has been affirmed and applied by the Supreme Court in *Mitchell v. Helms*,[175] which concerned the scope of the Establishment Clause when evaluating a programme of governmental assistance entailing direct aid to organisations, including religious organisations. The test has also been applied in relation to employment law.[176]

- The 'permissive accommodations' test

This asks what religious accommodations are allowed – but not required – by the Constitution. Because the neutrality test operates to prevent government from extending any special advantages to religion, and because religious exemptions are no longer required under the Free Exercise Clause, 'permissive accommodations' provides a degree of latitude in a small number of cases to counter-balance a special disability suffered by religion under the Establishment Clause or otherwise. For example, the Court has upheld a statutory exemption of nonprofit religious groups from the anti-discrimination provisions of Title VII[177] 'to equalize religious entities with nonreligious entities that face no comparable statutory impediment to hiring those with ideological loyalty'. In general the interpretation of the duty to accommodate has been somewhat restrictive, with accommodation only required where it is reasonable, and where it does not cause undue hardship.[178] Undue hardship has been interpreted to mean that there must be no more than

---

[173] See, for example: *Edwards v. Aguillard*, 482 US 578 (1987) (invalidating mandatory teaching of creationism); *Stone v. Graham*, 449 US 39 (1980) (invalidating mandatory display of the Ten Commandments); *Epperson v. Arkansas*, 393 U.S. 97 (1968) (invalidating prohibition on teaching evolution); *McCollum v. Bd. of Educ.*, 333 US 203 (1948) (prohibition of in-class sectarian religious instruction); and *Bd. of Educ. of Kiryas Joel Vill. Sch. Dist. v. Grumet*, 512 US 687, 705 (1994), where it was noted that 'the Religion Clauses do not require the government to be oblivious to impositions that legitimate exercises of state power may place on religious belief and practice'.

[174] See: *Santa Fe Indep. Sch. Dist. v. Doe*, 530 US 290 (2000); *Lee v. Weisman*, 505 US 577 (1992); *Wallace v. Jaffree*, 472 US 38 (1985); *Sch. Dist. v. Schempp*, 374 US 203 (1963); and *Engel v. Vitale*, 370 US 421 (1962).

[175] *Mitchell v. Helms*, 530 US 793 (2000).

[176] See *Estate of Thornton v. Caldor, Inc.*, 472 US 703 (1985) (invalidating state statute mandating that employees be excused from working on their sabbath).

[177] See *Corp. of Presiding Bishop v. Amos*, 483 US 327 (1987), at pp.334–340.

[178] See *Trans World Airlines, Inc. v. Hardison*, 432 US 63 (1977); *Ansonia Board of Education v. Philbrook*, 479 US 60 (1986).

de minimis cost, either in terms of finance, disruption or administrative inconvenience and has allowed courts to find no religious discrimination in cases where affording a degree of accommodation would not have given rise to any economic cost, inconvenience or even co-worker complaints.[179] Similarly, where the defendant can be shown to have acted in good faith and the plaintiff had not suffered any 'irreparable injury'.[180]

Discrimination

Legal issues relating to discriminatory practice are likely to arise when the policies and the above tests which give effect to the First Amendment (specifically the Establishment Clause, the Free Exercise Clause and the Speech Clause) come into conflict with non-discrimination law, in particular with the Title VII exemptions granted to religious organisations under the Civil Rights Act 1964. The Equal Protection Clause of the Fourteenth Amendment, providing protection against religious discrimination, is also relevant. Unfortunately the outcome, in terms of jurisprudence, is far from consistent.[181]

Section 2000a(a) of the Civil Rights Act 1964 declares that 'All persons shall be entitled to the full and equal enjoyment of the goods, services, facilities, privileges, advantages, and accommodations of any place of public accommodation ... without discrimination or segregation on the ground of race, color, religion, or national origin.' It not only prohibits employers from discriminating against employees or prospective employees because of their religion, but it also requires employers to 'reasonably accommodate' the religious practices of employees provided that such reasonable accommodations do not cause the employer 'undue hardship'. Employers may not use the above conditions as a basis for refusing to hire an otherwise qualified applicant, for terminating employment of an individual or to otherwise discriminate against any individual with respect to his/her compensation, terms, conditions or privileges of employment because of race, colour, religion, sex or national origin.[182]

---

[179] *Trans World Airlines* v. *Hardison*, 432 US 63 (1976); *Turpen* v. *Mo.-Kan.-Tex. R.R. Co.*, 736 F.2d 1022, 1027.

[180] *Douglas* v. *City of Jeannette*, 319 US 157 (1943).

[181] As candidly admitted by the highest court in the land: see, *Committee for Public Education and Religious Liberty* v. *Regan*, 444 US 646, 662 (1980).

[182] See, further, at: www.princeton.edu/hr/policies/appendix/a1/_1_1 (accessed 7 January 2014).

HUMAN RIGHTS, DISCRIMINATION & RELIGIOUS CHARITIES 317

The Title VII religious exemptions protect all aspects of religious observance and practice as well as belief. Religion is defined therein in very broad terms to include not only traditional, organised religions such as Christianity, Judaism, Islam, Hinduism and Buddhism, but also religious beliefs that are new, uncommon, not part of a formal church or sect, only subscribed to by a small number of people, or that seem illogical or unreasonable to others. An employee's belief or practice can be 'religious' under Title VII even if the employee is affiliated with a religious group that does not espouse or recognise that individual's belief or practice, or if few – or no – other people adhere to it. Title VII's protections also extend to those who are discriminated against or need accommodation because they profess no religious beliefs. Religious beliefs include theistic beliefs as well as non-theistic 'moral or ethical beliefs as to what is right and wrong which are sincerely held with the strength of traditional religious views'.

When problems arise they often concern the proper test for determining whether an organisation is 'religious', which centres on the tension between Title VII and the First Amendment's religion clauses.

Discrimination and same-sex marriage

In *Baehr* v. *Lewin*,[183] the Supreme Court of Hawaii, interpreting an express prohibition of sex discrimination in the Hawaii Constitution, held that denying same-sex couples the right to marry is *prima facie* sex discrimination and must be justified. Within the next 20 years, nine states in the United States had legalised same-sex marriage, representing 15.7 per cent of the total population.[184]

In all states where same-sex marriage has been legalised the relevant legislation imposes no requirement upon religious organisations and their ministers to provide marriage services (e.g., a celebrant, use of church premises). Most such states include exemption clauses for religious organisations and their ministers (though not Massachusetts) and ensure that eligibility for tax-exempt status will not be adversely affected. The difficulties tend to arise in downstream service provision. While a case may be made for extending such an exemption to premises and services provided by a religious organisation (e.g. education and health care facilities, adoption) it becomes more attenuated and harder to

---

[183] *Baehr* v. *Lewin*, 74 Haw. 530, 852 P.2d 44 (1993).
[184] By the end of 2013, a total of 18 states had enacted legislation permitting gay marriage.

justify when private service providers (owners of hotels, boarding houses, etc.) claim exemption on the grounds of personal religious belief. Presently, there is little consensus and a great deal of controversy throughout the United States on these matters: the US Ninth Circuit Court of Appeals issued a stay on same-sex marriages after it determined California's Proposition 8 was unconstitutional; while the New Jersey State Supreme Court refused to stay a lower court's ruling in favour of marriage equality; in Utah, the state's ban on gay marriages was declared unconstitutional by the 10th US Circuit Court of Appeal on 24 December 2013, when it rejected an application for an emergency stay on a federal ruling allowing such marriages, a decision likely to be appealed to the US Supreme Court. Many have viewed the Defense of Marriage Act, which denied federal benefits to legally married same-sex couples, as effectively legalising discrimination in respect of such couples.[185]

Religious discrimination in practice

In practice it is the exemption for religious organisations that is important. This applies only to those institutions whose 'purpose and character are primarily religious'. The regulatory body charged with enforcing Title VII exemptions for religious organisations is the US Equal Employment Opportunity Commission (EEOC). Factors indicating whether an entity is religious include: whether its articles of incorporation state a religious purpose; whether its day-to-day operations are religious (e.g. are the services the entity performs, the product it produces or the educational curriculum it provides directed towards propagation of the religion?); whether it is nonprofit; and whether it is affiliated with, or supported by, a church or other religious organisation. While this exemption is not limited to religious activities of the organisation, it only allows religious organisations to prefer to employ individuals who share their religion and does not permit discrimination in employment on the basis of race, colour, national origin, sex, age or disability.

The legal complexities involved were well illustrated in the recent case of *Spencer* v. *World Vision, Inc.*,[186] which concerned World Vision, a

---

[185] On 23 June 2013, the US Supreme Court declared the Defense of Marriage Act (Doma) unconstitutional and, in a separate appeal, it also restored the right of same-sex marriage in California, thus dooming Proposition 8.
[186] No. 08-35532, 2011 WL 208356 (9th Cir. 25 January 2011).

nonprofit Christian humanitarian organisation, established to address the causes of poverty and injustice, and heavily funded by government. World Vision is a major Christian global aid and relief organisation with more than 40,000 staff in nearly 100 countries. It carries out a wide range of secular activities involving economic development and disaster relief and is at the centre of an ongoing debate over whether religion-based nonprofits in receipt of government funds should be able to hire only those of their own faith when using those funds. This is a matter of particular significance when, as in the case of World Vision, donor contributions account for only a small proportion of the organisation's annual revenue, with most coming from government grants and gifts-in-kind. The case originated in a 2006 decision by World Vision to terminate the employment of three staff because they had ceased attending daily devotions and weekly chapel services held during the workday and because they had denied the deity of Jesus Christ. In 2007 the staff concerned sued World Vision for unfair dismissal; the latter responded by claiming that it was a religious entity and therefore exempt from Title VII. The protracted court case then got underway.

At the initial hearing before the district court, it was held that World Vision was a 'religious organization' under the terms of the Title VII exemption, and the plaintiffs appealed to the US Court of Appeals for the Ninth Circuit.[187] A three-judge panel, in a divided opinion, affirmed the district court's ruling: the lead opinion stated that the plaintiffs did 'not explain how receipt of government funds undermines World Vision's religiosity or bars its classification as a religious entity'; two of the three judges agreed that World Vision, even though it was not a traditional house of worship, was entitled to the institutional religious liberty accommodation. It found that World Vision was a 'religious corporation' and therefore exempt from a federal law that bars faith-based discrimination. O'Scannlain J stated that:

> I am satisfied that World Vision has met its burden of showing that the 'general picture' of the organization is 'primarily religious ... World Vision is a nonprofit organization whose humanitarian relief efforts flow from a profound sense of religious mission.'

On 7 September 2010 the plaintiffs petitioned the Ninth Circuit for rehearing *en banc*, a petition that was joined by an *amicus brief* submitted by

---

[187] US Court of Appeals for the Ninth Circuit, No. 08-35532, D.C. No. 2:07-cv-01551-RSM (23 August 2010).

320   THE UNITED STATES OF AMERICA

Americans United and three other civil-liberties organisations, out of concern that the language in the above judicial opinions could 'suggest that an organisation's receipt and use of federal funds is never relevant to the application of [the statutory exemption for religious entities] – a suggestion that threatens to effectively decide a complex constitutional issue'. The brief requested the Ninth Circuit to clarify its ruling, specifically asking the court to 'state that it is expressly reserving the question of whether [the statutory exemption for religious entities] may be constitutionally applied to exempt organizations from Title VII's prohibition on religious discrimination in employment with respect to positions that are financed with government funds'. On 25 January 2011 the Ninth Circuit denied the plaintiffs' request for rehearing *en banc* and issued an amended decision that failed to address the impact of a religious organisation's receipt and use of federal funds in determining whether it qualifies for Title VII statutory exemption. While this important decision essentially means that religious organisations can legally factor religion into hiring decisions, it leaves in some uncertainty the ancillary issue of whether or not the law still allows religious groups to discriminate when using federal money to deliver public services.

Unequal but not discriminatory

The law has been somewhat uncertain and inconsistent in this area, but is perhaps merely evolving in keeping with cultural norms.

In an early case, *Braunfeld* v. *Brown*,[188] a Sunday closing law placed a substantial economic burden on some Jewish retailers, but this burden was an indirect consequence of a law which had a legitimate secular purpose. The court found that the law did not forbid or prohibit the religious practice in question, but merely meant that such practices involved a commercial disadvantage. In *Boy Scouts* v. *Dale*,[189] the court ruled that the Boy Scouts have a constitutional right, based on freedom of association, to exclude gays. It is very difficult to reconcile this with prior rulings which held that the government has a compelling interest in ending discrimination and which rejected claims of freedom of association as a basis for violating state laws prohibiting private clubs and groups from discriminating. It has become even more difficult to do so in the light of the recent ruling by the US Supreme Court in *Christian Legal*

---

[188] *Braunfeld* v. *Brown*, 366 US 599 (1961).   [189] *Boy Scouts* v. *Dale*, 120 S Ct 2446 (2000).

Society v. *Martinez*.[190] This case commenced with a suit filed in 2004 after California's Hastings College refused to recognise the student chapter of the Christian Legal Society (CLS): the college had a policy which required all student organisations to operate on an open membership basis, allowing participation regardless of a student's status or beliefs; the CLS required all its officers and voting members to agree with its basic Christian beliefs; certain LGBT students objected when they were denied the opportunity to become voting members. The Court upheld the college policy and denied CLS the protection of the First Amendment. Stevens J noted that CLS refused membership to those who engage in 'unrepentant homosexual conduct', and the same argument could be made by groups that 'may exclude or mistreat Jews, blacks, and women – or those who do not share their contempt for Jews, blacks, and women'.

Unequal but not discriminatory: contractual obligations

In *Corp. of Presiding Bishop of Church of Jesus Christ of Latter-day Saints* v. *Amos*,[191] the US Supreme Court upheld the constitutionality of a law permitting religious organisations to exercise a religious preference when making employment decisions. Such action was found not to violate the Establishment Clause, at least when the discrimination occurs in connection with a religious organisation's nonprofit activities.

Unequal and discriminatory: restricting employment opportunities

Employers may not make employment decisions based on an employee's religious beliefs or practices. Employment decisions include hiring, firing, promoting, demoting and determining assignments and workloads. An exception to this rule exists if an individual's religion is a bona fide occupational qualification, as when it is an essential part of a job description, such as requiring that a Catholic priest belong to the Catholic Church.

The obligation not to allow religious considerations to restrict employment opportunities can come into play at an early stage, as was

---

[190] *Christian Legal Society* v. *Martinez*, (No. 08-1371) 319 Fed. Appx. 645 (2010).
[191] *Corp. of Presiding Bishop of Church of Jesus Christ of Latter-day Saints* v. *Amos*, 483 US 327, 329, 339 (1987).

322   THE UNITED STATES OF AMERICA

demonstrated in a series of rulings upholding applicants' claims of unlawful discrimination. For example, in *EEOC* v. *Covergys Corp.*,[192] when an applicant during the course of his job interview mentioned that he would be unavailable for work on the Jewish sabbath and, allegedly, was then advised that the interview was terminated. Similarly, in *EEOC* v. *Voss Elec. Co. D/B/A Voss Lighting*[193] when, despite being considered qualified for the position, an applicant was denied employment on the basis of his religious beliefs. Nor, as was evident in *Torcaso* v. *Watkins*,[194] can the government require a person to declare his or her belief in God as a pre-condition for becoming a notary.

Employers have a duty to accommodate the religious beliefs of their employees. In *Cooper* v. *Eugene Sch. Dist. No. 4J*,[195] the court upheld a state prohibition on religious dress by teachers as applied to a Sikh who wore a turban and white clothing, on the ground that the statute in question properly sought to ensure avoidance of the appearance of sectarian influence, favouritism or official approval in state schools. Also, in *United States* v. *Board of Educ. Sch. Dist. Phila., 911*,[196] it rejected a claim that application of a similar statute against a Muslim who wore chador covering all but her face while working as a substitute teacher did not violate the Title VII duty of the employer to make reasonable religious accommodations.

Unequal and discriminatory: restricting access to services

The difficulties that have beset Catholic Charities are indicative of the problems that can arise when the traditional values of faith-based organisations encounter modern anti-discriminatory legislation. Between about 1985 and 1995, Catholic Charities of Boston, which contracted with the state's Department of Social Services and accepted state funds in support of their adoption services programme, placed 13 children with gay couples out of 720 adoptions. In December 2005 the lay-dominated board of Catholic Charities of Boston voted unanimously to continue gay adoptions, but in February 2006 when it sought and failed to make the case for an exemption from the state's non-discrimination statute, Catholic Charities announced that the agency would terminate its

---

[192] *EEOC* v. *Covergys Corp.* (E.D. Mo. 2011).
[193] *EEOC* v. *Voss Elec. Co. D/B/A Voss Lighting*, Civil Case No. 4:12-cv-00330-JED-FHM (2013).
[194] *Torcaso* v. *Watkins*, 367 US 488 (1961).
[195] *Cooper* v. *Eugene Sch. Dist. No. 4J*, 723 P.2d 298 (Oregon 1986).
[196] *United States* v. *Board of Educ. Sch. Dist. Phila., 911*, F.2d 882 (3d Cir. 1990).

adoption work rather than continue to place children under the guardianship of homosexuals. This was echoed by a similar decision in Washington, DC in 2010 when the administration declined to renew a contract with the US Conference of Catholic Bishops (USCCB) to provide services for human trafficking victims because the group refused to provide referrals for contraception and abortion to sexual assault victims.[197] In 2012 the Illinois Department of Children and Family Services revoked its contract with Catholic Charities after the Illinois Religious Freedom Protection and Civil Union Act became law. The state administration had then required Catholic Charities, because it accepted public funds, to provide adoption and foster-care services to same-sex couples in the same manner that they serviced different-sex couples. Rather than comply, Catholic Charities closed most of its Illinois affiliates and by October the state had transferred more than 1,000 children from the charity's custody to secular agencies.

Unequal but 'positive action'

The 'permissive accommodations' test referred to earlier clearly envisages a differentiation in resource allocation that would constitute justifiable discrimination, despite it achieving as intended the preferencing of one group at the expense of others. It is well established, for example, that trusts discriminating in favour of traditionally disadvantaged groups may be justified as attempts to address past discrimination or to correct economic or opportunity imbalances.[198]

The 'positive action' issue arose in the context of the Pilot Project Scholarship Program introduced in the 1996–1997 school year, which allowed parents of students in the Cleveland School District to utilise a voucher scheme whereby public money was made available to pay for tuition at private schools, including religious schools. More than 90 per cent of the voucher recipients used their vouchers to transfer to religious schools, triggering a complaint that public dollars were being funnelled

---

[197] Again this was a religious charity in receipt of considerable government funding. The USCCB had seen its share of federal grants from the Department of Health and Human Services jump from $71.8 million in the last three years of the Bush administration to $81.2 million during the first three years of the Obama administration. In fiscal year 2011 alone, the group received a record $31.4 million from the administration.

[198] See The American Law Institute, *The Restatement of the Law, Third, Trusts*, 2012 at: http://mariahbsy.jimdo.com/2013/04/20/restatement-of-the-law-trusts-the-american-law-institute-ebook-downloads (accessed 7 January 2014).

to religious institutions and led to the scheme being challenged in *Zelman* v. *Simmons-Harris*.[199] The Supreme Court found that the programme did not violate the Establishment Clause of the First Amendment, mainly because the programme survived the first prong of the Lemon test as it was enacted for a secular rather than a religious purpose. The point of allowing parents to use public money to send their children to private schools was so that parents in poor areas with failing public schools could get a better education for their children. The fact that parents chose religious schools for their children had no bearing on the government.

So long as the law did not specify or encourage religious schools, the fact that the money mostly went to such schools was ultimately irrelevant. Thus, government support for religion is constitutional so long as it occurs *de facto* and not *de jure*. Formally, the law remained neutral with respect to religion.

Conclusion

The United States, more so than any other common law jurisdiction, has a strong record of enforcing a distinction between Church and State. The effect of the constitutional prohibition on government using its powers and resources in favour of religion per se, or for any particular religion, can be seen in the rigour with which the courts scrutinise issues where there is evidence of that line being crossed: religious charities can only function as secular service providers for government; government cannot fund selective religious bodies nor allow its funding to be used by any such body for purely religious purposes; and, where there is evidence that the latter may be happening implicitly, the courts will intervene. Indeed, because these are fundamental constitutional issues, they arise more frequently and often before the highest court in the land, under this heading, which is untypical of the jurisdictions presently being studied.

---

[199] *Zelman* v. *Simmons-Harris*, 536 US 639 (2002).

8

Canada

Introduction

Canada is a bijural jurisdiction in which, according to s.8(1) of the Interpretation Act 1985,[1] 'both the common law and the civil law are equally authoritative and recognized sources of the law of property and civil rights in Canada'. It is also a federated jurisdiction where the national government, three territories and ten provinces that comprise the governing framework of Canada all have varying levels of jurisdiction over nonprofit organisations and charities, including religious charities. Although the civil law system remains in Quebec, the common law prevails at the federal level and is central to the nationwide decision-making processes of the Canadian Revenue Authority (CRA), which applies the Income Tax Act 1985.[2]

This chapter opens with an overview of the Church–State relationship in Canada, the development of the nonprofit sector and its relationship with government. It then focuses on religious charities and their functioning as part of the nonprofit sector, the proportion of total charities that have religious purposes (numbers, size, wealth, duration, etc.) and notes jurisdiction-specific characteristics. It considers the evolving government policy towards the sector, in particular its funding of charities, before outlining the relevant legal framework, the definition of 'religion' and the requirements for its 'advancement'. It then examines how the donor's discretionary right to choose beneficiaries relates to religious discrimination and public policy. This leads into the central focus of the chapter, which is on the relationship between the Charter of Rights and Freedoms and the contemporary practice of religious charities. This section provides a detailed analysis of relevant case law, at federal and provincial levels, and reveals how the courts and the CRA are currently

[1] RSC 1985, c. I-21.   [2] RSC 1985, c. 1 (5th Supp).

managing the key issues that now dominate the interface between religion, charity and law in Canada. The chapter closes with a review of the law and practice in relation to religious discrimination, with particular reference to how religious charities are now coping with the constraints.

Church, State and religious charities

The mutually dependent relationship of Church and State, not untypical of the post-colonial common law nations, prevailed also in Canada. This preceded and formed a context for the present building of a rapprochement between government and the nonprofit sector. In particular, much of the present institutional and social infrastructure was erected by the Catholic Church which, at least since confederation in 1867,[3] and probably also over many preceding generations, spread its patchwork of educational and health care facilities across the country. The tension between the traditional authority of religious institutions and the secularism now permeating the civic life of the nation may explain the growing volume of litigious disputes along the boundary between the beliefs and practices of religious bodies and the human rights entitlements of Canadian citizens.

Background: government and the nonprofit sector

In Canada, government and the nonprofit sector have taken longer than in many other common law jurisdictions to reach a position where they can formally recognise and negotiate their respective civil society interests. Arguably the reasons for this lie in government policy priorities and certain singular characteristics of the sector.

Government policy

Pluralism has prevailed as governments' preferred mode of nation-building: acknowledging and addressing the needs of different cultural groups, including the Catholic and separatist Quebecois, though arguably at the price of facilitating the growth of a more cohesive civil society. To that extent it differs from the policy formed to govern the more competitive and adversarial social groupings in the United States.

---

[3] See The British North America Act, 1867.

It differs also from the centralist style of government in the United Kingdom as there has been a conspicuous absence of any equivalent to the government–sector dialogue in the latter jurisdiction or of initiatives to put in place the corresponding agencies, processes and procedures that were found necessary to achieve government–sector partnership. Perhaps because of Canada's singular need to ensure equality in its treatment of bijural, bilingual and Indigenous communities, there has instead been a government tendency to pursue a political policy of accommodation.

However, in keeping with the experience elsewhere, as the government reduced its support for public service provision and instead introduced means testing for many health and welfare benefits, so, in the last decades of the twentieth century, Canada experienced a resurgence in community-based health and social care charities, including a strengthening role for those that are religious. Consequently, and again in keeping with their common law counterparts, the Canadian government has found it necessary to embark on charity law reform as a means of both tightening the regulatory framework for the sector and also of revising the distribution of responsibility for public benefit service provision between government and charity.

The nonprofit sector

Canada has a very diverse population, including Indigenous communities with their own distinct cultures, well used to self-reliant, self-governing ways of life. The lack of population homogeneity, the separateness of communities, coupled with a tradition of these being strongly self-reliant relative to the removed and non-intrusive government gave rise, perhaps, to a more attenuated sense of civic responsibility in which citizens looked inward to their communities when it came to volunteering and donating, etc. Charities and voluntary organisations in general, but more so Church bodies, were also very much locally based. The result was a sector considerably more desiccated than its UK counterpart, constituted very largely of institutional religious bodies and an eclectic array of nonprofits, most of which were set up to address the specific needs and issues of local communities.

The challenge of geography, a local community orientation, the lack of leadership and common purpose, together with uncertain funding and, perhaps, a legacy of dominance by institutional religious bodies, have all played their part in inhibiting the forming of a coherent sense of

328 CANADA

sector identity. This has impeded sector capacity to negotiate with government.

Frameworks for facilitating government–sector relationships

The general absence of a nationwide government bureaucracy and of umbrella nonprofit organisations has made it difficult to build a comprehensive and coherent relationship between government and sector. Further complications arise from bijural constitutional arrangements which seek to marry common law and civil code heritages, a legacy from the colonial rule of England and France, respectively, and the presence of a sizeable Indigenous community.

Even allowing for these difficulties, there has been little evidence of mutual commitment towards building a government–sector partnership. The sector has been unable to put forward the representative bodies authorised to negotiate on issues identified as of strategic importance to it. Government has baulked at putting in place the institutions and processes necessary to bridge the gap between it and the sector. The Ontario Law Reform Commission,[4] in the most promising attempt to overcome these difficulties, served only to confirm their severity when its proposal for a principled basis on which government and the sector could jointly embark on modernising charity law was rejected.

In 1995, however, 12 national umbrella organisations covering most parts of the voluntary sector came together as the Voluntary Sector Roundtable to enhance the relationship between the sector and the government, to strengthen the sector's capacity and to improve the legal and regulatory framework governing the sector. The work of the Voluntary Sector Roundtable led to the creation of the Voluntary Sector Initiative and then to its development of an *Accord Between the Government of Canada and the Voluntary Sector*,[5] which was reached by the Joint Accord Table (composed equally of voluntary-sector members and public servants) and signed in 2001. This marked the beginning of a new stage in government–sector relations.

---

[4] See the Ontario Law Reform Commission Report 1996. See, further, at: https://archive. org/details/reportonlawofcha01onta (accessed 7 January 2014).

[5] The Joint Accord Table developed two Codes of Good Practice: the *Code of Good Practice on Policy Dialogue*, intended to encourage voluntary sector participation in the public policy process; and the *Code of Good Practice on Funding*, intended to guide the funding aspect of the relationship between the voluntary sector and the government of Canada and reinforce reciprocal accountability.

CHURCH, STATE AND RELIGIOUS CHARITIES   329

Building a modern Church–State relationship

This relationship has long been characterised as one of cooperation and is therefore quite distinctly different from the explicit separation of Church and State in the neighbouring jurisdiction. In particular, the legacy of religion as an established institution and the close relationship between government and Church leaders, with direct funding arrangements, have continued into present times. Religious bodies have traditionally been given the freedom to organise as they see fit, largely free from government regulatory requirements, and this has included hiring staff on the basis of religious affiliation.

The pre-confederation investment by religious organisations in laying the foundations for the present social infrastructure is apparent, for example, in: the 19 Catholic universities, the colleges and the swathe of primary and secondary schools that now extend across Canada; and in the many hospitals and health care institutions affiliated with that Church, including St. Michael's hospital in Toronto, founded in 1892 by the Sisters of St. Joseph and the Grey Nuns Hospital in southeast Edmonton. This relationship was judicially acknowledged by the Supreme Court in *Adler* v. *Ontario*,[6] when Iacobucci J, on behalf of the court majority, ruled that government funding of both Roman Catholic and public schools, but not private religious schools, was entitled to special protection[7] under s.93 of the Constitution Act 1867.[8]

Religion(s)

Canada has no official religion, and support for religious pluralism is an important part of Canada's political culture. The 2001 Canadian census reported that 72 per cent of Canadians adhered to either Roman Catholicism or Protestantism as their religion – of which those in the first group were by far the majority. The census showed the second largest group as those who subscribed to no religion, at 16 per cent. Statistics Canada projects that by 2017, Muslims, Jews, Hindus, Sikhs and Buddhists will comprise 10 per cent of Canada's population, up from

---

[6] *Adler* v. *Ontario* [1996] SCR 609.
[7] Section 93 of the Constitution Act 1867 was deemed by Iacobucci J to be 'immune from Charter scrutiny' (at p.404). See, further, J. Philips, 'Religion, Charity, and the Charter of Rights', in J. Phillips, B. Chapman and D. Stevens (eds), *Between State and Market: Essays on Charities Law and Policy in Canada*, McGill-Queen's University Press, Montreal, 2002, at p.327.
[8] 30 & 31 Victoria, c. 3.

330   CANADA

6 per cent on the 2001 census (Muslims now comprise the second largest religious group among immigrants, after Catholics, at 15 per cent of the total). The decline in Canada of the number of religiously active Christians to a distinct minority of the total population has been said to have commenced in the 1970s.[9]

Secularisation

Canada would seem to be making the same journey as has occurred in Europe, towards an increased secularisation of social infrastructure and dilution in the religious adherence of its citizens. Arguably, however, the fact that national surveys reveal a marked rise in the numbers declaring no religious affiliation, from less than 1 per cent in 1971 to nearly 23 per cent two decades later, is more an indicator of the resilience than the decline of religious faith in this jurisdiction relative to trends in northern Europe. Secularisation is at a slower pace and is noticeably patchy.

For example, the growing secularism that may be found among the residents of larger conurbations is not matched by their counterparts in rural areas and is generally not typical of the many recent newcomers to Canada who bring with them their Christian, Muslim, Sikh, Hindu and orthodox Jewish beliefs embedded in the cultures of the various less developed nations they have left behind. Moreover, some provinces are more secular than others. Quebec is singular in its relative cultural homogeneity and strong legacy of Catholic religious affiliation: the legislature and judiciary are often at the forefront in tackling the agenda of issues arising at the interface of human rights and religious belief.

An 'established' religion

There is no 'established' religion in this jurisdiction.

Equality of religions

There is no judicial tolerance for a State preference for a particular religion. This was clearly demonstrated in *R. v. Big M Drug Mart*,[10] where the

---

[9] See M. H. Olgivie, *Religious Institutions and the Law in Canada* (2nd edn), Irwin Law, Toronto, 2005.

[10] *R. v. Big M Drug Mart* [1985] 1 SCR 295. Subsequently, however, the ruling in *R v. Edwards Books and Art Ltd.* [1986] 2 SCR 713 permitted Sunday closing laws on

CHURCH, STATE AND RELIGIOUS CHARITIES

presenting issue before the Supreme Court was a clash of interests between commercial and religious bodies. The Court, however, took the opportunity to examine the balance to be struck between religion and secularism in a modern democratic State.

On Sunday, 30 May 1982, Big M Drug Mart in Calgary was charged with violating the Lord's Day Act by opening for business. Big M was acquitted at trial, the appeal being subsequently dismissed by Alberta Court of Appeal, but nonetheless the case was brought before the Supreme Court to determine whether s.2 of the Charter of Rights and Freedoms had a bearing on the matter. The Court was also asked to consider whether the Lord's Day Act placed 'reasonable limits' on those rights, as set out by s.1 of the Charter. The Court ruled the Lord's Day Act unconstitutional because laws must have a secular purpose. They left open the possibility for Sunday closing laws based on secular purposes (e.g. 'rest days'), but a law based on religious reasons and favouring one denomination over others was deemed unconstitutional. As Dickson CJ then explained:

> In proclaiming the standards of the Christian faith, the Act creates a climate hostile to, and gives the appearance of discrimination against, non-Christian Canadians. ... The theological content of the legislation remains as a subtle and constant reminder to religious minorities within the country of their differences with, and alienation from, the dominant religious culture.[11]

This ruling represents an important milestone in the Canadian experience of building a multicultural nation in which the rights of religious minorities would be assured of equal recognition and protection in law.

In *Syndicat Northcrest* v. *Amselem*,[12] the decision of Iacobucci J can be interpreted as conforming to the orthodox judicial view that it is not for the court to test the veracity of religious beliefs:

> It is, of course, axiomatic that Courts of law deal with secular matters only. They do not normally concern themselves with matters of religious

---

a secular basis. Also see *R* v. *Videoflicks Ltd.* (sub nom. *R.* v. *Edwards Books & Art Ltd.*) [1986] 2 SCR 713, 35 DLR (4th) 1, where a Sunday Observance challenge to the Retail Business Holidays Act was found to be *intra vires* because the purpose of the legislation was ruled to be secular.

[11] *R.* v. *Big M Drug Mart* [1985] 1 SCR 295, at p.354.

[12] *Syndicat Northcrest* v. *Amselem* [2004] 2 SCR 551 [67]. As he then commented: 'It is not within the expertise and purview of secular courts to adjudicate questions of religious doctrine.'

332   CANADA

doctrine or government unless those matters become elements in disputes relating to property or other legal rights.[13]

This view is one that has, from time to time, attracted judicial support: 'the truth or falsity of religions is not the business of officials or the courts';[14] 'it is not the role of this Court to decide what any particular religion believes';[15] and, in general, 'the undesirability of a state-conducted inquiry into an individual's religious beliefs'.[16]

Religious organisations and the nonprofit sector

Religious communities in Canada are sizeable and varied. It has been estimated that the Roman Catholic, United and Baptist denominations have 5706, 3909 and 2435 congregations, respectively, while the Pentecostals have 1441 congregations and Jews have 220.[17] Just over half of all religiously active (52 per cent) are Catholics, while non-Christians – comprising Jews, Buddhists, Hindus, Muslims, Sikhs and a few New Age communities – account for only 7 per cent of the religiously active.

Religious charities

The CRA estimates that 94 per cent of religious organisations have charitable status, with places of worship comprising about 40 per cent of all registered charities and receiving about 60 per cent of all receipted donations. Of the current total of 81,601 registered charities, 72,926 are charitable organisations with purposes focused on religion (31,757), welfare (12,620), benefit to the community (12,404), education (11,801) and health (4340).[18] However, while religious organisations have always constituted the largest proportion of Canadian registered charities, their share of the sector is steadily shrinking: in 1967, when charities were first registered, it was calculated that four out of every five were religious

[13] See *Re Christ Church of China* (1983) 15 ETR 272 (BCSC), at p.278.
[14] See *Church of the New Faith* v. *Commissioner of Pay-roll Tax* (1983) 154 CLR 120, *per* Murphy J, at p.150.
[15] See *B.(R.)* v. *Children's Aid Society of Metropolitan Toronto* [1995] 1 SCR 315, *per* LaForest J, at p.866.
[16] See *Edwards Books and Art Ltd. et. al.* v. *the Queen* (1986) 35 DLR (4th) 1 (SCC), at p.26.
[17] See *1997 Yearbook of American and Canadian Churches*, Nashville, Abingdon Press, pp.248–250.
[18] See, further, at: www.statcan.gc.ca (accessed 7 January 2014).

CHURCH, STATE AND RELIGIOUS CHARITIES

bodies; by 1991 they comprised 45.2 per cent;[19] declined to some 41 per cent in 1991; and currently constitute some 40 per cent of total charities. When the National Survey of Nonprofit and Voluntary Organizations published its 2003 report,[20] the proportion had fallen to 19 per cent of the nation's 161,000 nonprofit and voluntary organisations, or almost 31,000 religious organisations. They were then considered to be the second most common type of nonprofit and voluntary organisation in the country, with total annual revenues of $6.8 billion or 6 per cent of the $112 billion total annual revenues for all organisations; 29 per cent have annual revenues under $30,000, while 6 per cent have revenues of $500,000 or more.[21]

Those who regularly attend Church services are credited with contributing about half of all hours volunteered across the country and some 42 per cent of the donations received by direct giving to non-religious charities.

Religious umbrella bodies

The Canadian Council of Christian Charities (CCCC) has created a self-regulatory regime which requires its members to provide documentation relating to matters such as: the identity, location, purpose and governance arrangements of their organisation; an agreement to comply with standards concerning the independence of board members; completion of annual independent audits; public financial disclosure; and the appointment of an audit review committee. It also requires a commitment to the pursuit of integrity, to a declared stewardship policy and affirmation to the Christian faith.

The Office of Religious Freedom

This was first mooted in April 2011 by the Immigration and Citizenship Minister with the explanation that such an office would assist

---

[19] D. Per Sharpe, *A Portrait of Canada's Charities*, Canadian Centre for Philanthropy, Toronto, 1994, p.5. More recent statistics from the Broadbent 1999 study suggest that the religious charity category has decreased to 36 per cent of the total (at p.13).

[20] See Statistics Canada, *Cornerstones of Community: Highlights of the National Survey of Nonprofit and Voluntary Organizations*, Statistics Canada, Ottawa, 2004.

[21] See National Survey of Nonprofit and Voluntary Organizations, *Religious Organizations in Canada*, Imagine Canada, 2006. See, further, at: www.imaginecanada.ca/files/www/en/nsnvo/i_religious_factsheet.pdf (accessed 7 January 2014).

334 CANADA

government to address the many instances of religious oppression in a number of areas of the world. In October 2011 the Canadian Minister of Foreign Affairs hosted a meeting with representatives of Canada's diverse faith community in order to 'exchange ideas on a key priority' for the government of Canada – 'establishing an Office of Religious Freedom'.

Government funding: the sector and religious charities

The dividing line between the public benefit service provision of government bodies and that of charities is somewhat uncertain. As noted in the Johns Hopkins report, 'current government funding practices appear to be turning many nonprofit and voluntary organisations into cost-efficient extensions of government'.[22] This is evidenced by the fact that more than half (51 per cent) of all nonprofit and voluntary sector revenue in Canada comes from government.[23]

Government funding of religious charities: the policy

The provision of funding for religious charities is a long-established aspect of the Canadian government's policy of support for the non-profit sector. Religious charities, in particular, benefit considerably from direct government funding received from all three levels of government, in addition to the benefits derived from their tax-exempt status. In 2007, for example, the combined government funding to religious charities that offered no non-religious programmes totalled some $63 million: almost $21 million from the federal government; $32 million from the provincial governments; and $10 million from the municipal governments. This reflects the privileged relationship enjoyed by such organisations with government, as nonprofits in general have suffered a decrease in direct government funding since the mid 1990s.[24]

---

[22] See, M. Hall, C. Barr, M. Easwaramoorthy, S. Wojciech Sokolowski and L. Salamon, *The Canadian Nonprofit and Voluntary Sector in Comparative Perspective*, Johns Hopkins University, Toronto, 2005, at p.33.
[23] Ibid., at p.22.
[24] F. Boyle, *Charitable Activity Under the Canadian Income Tax Act: Definition, Process and Problems*, Voluntary Sector Roundtable, January 1997.

Government funding of religious charities with discriminatory practices

The guarantee of religious freedom, contained in the Charter of Rights and Freedoms that forms Part I of the Constitution Act 1982, sits somewhat uncomfortably alongside the established government practice of funding charities. This is because the charities in receipt of such funding include those religious bodies that exercise discriminatory preferencing in matters such as the hiring of staff, the type of services they do or do not provide and in the criteria applied to determine potential user eligibility for such services. The precedence for such preferment dates from at least the establishment of denominational schools in the Constitution Act, 1867[25] and continues as the Charter, unlike the US Constitution, does not have an Establishment Clause.

In this context, the decision in *Adler* v. *Ontario*[26] (as mentioned above) is worthy of note because of the Supreme Court's finding that the provision of State funding for Catholic schools does not violate the human rights principle of freedom of religion, nor the equality rights of other religions. However, in *Waldman* v. *Canada*[27] the Human Rights Committee found a violation of Article 26 of the ICCPR (non-discrimination) in the provision made by the Ontario Constitution for the public funding of Roman Catholic schools. Accordingly, the Committee held that public funding should either be withdrawn or made available to other minority religious communities as well.

The continuation of government funding, for the considerable proportion of educational services delivered by such religious organisations, is clearly crucial but it inevitably gives rise to some contention as to whether such a practice constitutes government tax preferencing of some religious bodies to the detriment of others, and to the detriment of non-religious education providers and, if so, whether this amounts to discriminatory practice in violation of human rights principles. In *Heintz* v. *Christian Horizons*,[28] for example, there was considerable judicial examination of the public funding of an institution that faced an allegation of discriminatory hiring and service provision practices (see, further, below).

---

[25] The Constitution Act, 1867 (UK), 30 & 31 Victoria, c. 3.
[26] *Adler* v. *Ontario* [1996] SCR 609.   [27] *Waldman* v. *Canada*, Comm No 694/1996.
[28] *Heintz* v. *Christian Horizons*, 2008 HRTO 22, 2010 ONSC 2105 (Div Ct).

336   CANADA

Charity law and the regulatory framework

As has been pointed out, 'there is no overarching Canadian statutory regime for charities but rather a mix of common law and taxation law combined with some special or sector specific legislation that governs certain charitable activities, such as health care or education'.[29] The current legal and regulatory framework for religious charities in Canada is thus far from coherent, with considerable differences between provinces.

Legislation

The regulatory framework for charities conforms to the traditional revenue-driven model, dominated by tax legislation. This approach places a clear and firm priority on revenue collection as addressed by a distinct body of tax legislation, administered in a standardised fashion by a central government agency. Each province also has its own body of charity-related legislation.

Federal

As the CRA has explained: 'as the Act [the Income Tax Act 1985, *sic*] does not define what is charitable, we look to the common law for both a definition of charity in its legal sense as well as the principles to guide us in applying that definition'.[30] Although the Income Tax Act and provincial charities legislation share a foundation in the common law, recent judicial decisions suggest the beginnings of a divergence.[31]

The Constitution Act 1982 has a bearing on all nonprofits, as it does on other entities, but it has a particular significance for those charities that happen to be religious organisations.[32] The Charter of Rights and Freedoms, which forms part of that Act, guarantees freedom of religion and thereby ensures, for example, the exemption of all places of worship

---

[29] Ibid.
[30] See Revenue Canada, Information Circular CPS-022, *Political Activities*, 2003, at para. 4. See, further, at: http://www.cra-arc.gc.ca/chrts-gvng/chrts/plcy/cps/cps-022-eng.html (accessed 7 January 2014).
[31] See K. Webb, 'Cinderella's Slippers? The Role of Charitable Tax Status in Financing Canadian Interest Groups', SFU-UBC Centre for the Study of Government and Business, Vancouver, 2000.
[32] Schedule B to the Canada Act 1982 (UK), 1982, c. 11; it forms part of the Constitution of Canada, having replaced the British North America Act 1867 (subsequently changed to the Constitution Act, 1867).

CHARITY LAW AND THE REGULATORY FRAMEWORK 337

from government taxes and that donors to such religious organisations are entitled to claim a related income tax deduction.

Province

Under s.92(7) of the Constitution Act, the provinces were given the authority to make laws regarding the 'establishment, maintenance, and management of charities in and for the Province'. This, together with the Quebec Act 1774, guarantees Quebec the right to apply the civil law of gift to charitable donations, while Parliament has given the same jurisdiction to the territories. Although the majority of provinces, with the primary exception of Ontario, do not single out nor regularly supervise charities, some do have charity-specific statutes. Only Ontario has legislated to regulate certain aspects of charitable organisations,[33] though other provinces have introduced statutes to regulate fundraising, and it was this province that initiated the rolling programme of charity law reform that continues to sweep through the main common law jurisdictions.[34] Some courts now consider that Ontario legislation in particular has broadened or liberalised the common law of charities, allowing more charities to qualify for charitable trust status than is compatible with established common law principles.[35] The singular position of Ontario has been further complicated by the introduction of the Not-for-Profit Corporations Act 2010,[36] which replaced the Corporations Act 1917.

The charity regulator

There is no charity-specific regulator. The CRA assumes regulatory responsibility for charities, as it does for all potentially taxable entities, whether or not they are religious organisations.

Charity law

There is no federal, charity-specific statute. While the common law continues to provide the basic platform for defining charities, their

---

[33] The Charitable Gifts Act 1949 (now repealed), the Charitable Institutions Act and the Charities Accounting Act
[34] See the Ontario Law Reform Commission Report 1996. See, further, at: https://archive.org/details/reportonlawofcha01onta (accessed 7 January 2014).
[35] See, for example, Stone J in *Toronto Volgograd Committee* v. *MNR* [1988] 88 DTC 6192.
[36] SO 2010, c. 15.

338   CANADA

purposes and the relevance of their activities, each province has also been
free to augment this through statute law, which they have done in ways
that supplement, or in some cases distort, common law principles.

The common law

The federal Income Tax Act, s.149(1), defines a charitable organisation
in part as 'an organization whether or not incorporated, all the resources
of which are devoted to charitable activities carried on by the organization itself'.[37] Canada applies the traditional common law approach to
'charity', which is broadly in keeping with that which prevailed in
England and Wales prior to the reforms introduced in the latter jurisdiction by the Charities Act 2006: the key common law concepts, *Pemsel*
purposes, rules and case law precedents having an equal relevance to
charity law in both jurisdictions. This source has been approved many
times by Canadian courts, including the Supreme Court.[38] Judicial
decisions with the effect of broadening the interpretation of charitable
purposes to conform more appropriately to contemporary manifestations of social need have been infrequent, which is steadily increasing the
probability that Canada will need to seek federal solutions to address
current failings in its charity law regime.[39]

   While the advancement of religion naturally remains the most important channel for the activities of religious bodies, the latter may choose to
instead pursue their mission through other charitable purposes such as
the advancement of education and by indirect methods such as sport.
Alternatively, the court or regulator may determine that although an
organisation or a gift to it must be refused charitable status under the
third *Pemsel* head, because it is deemed not to meet the definition of
religion, it may nonetheless qualify for registration as a charity. In *Wood*
v. *Whitebread*,[40] for example, while rejecting the claim that a gift for the
Theosophical Society was a trust for the advancement of religion, the

---

[37] See *Alberta Institute of Mental Retardation* v. *The Queen* [1987] 2 CTC 70, 87 DTC 5306
   (FCA), which established that the activities test, rather than the destination of funds,
   would be a determinant of charitable status in Canada. Note also *Christian Homes for
   Children* v. *M.N.R.*, 66 DTC 736, 42 Tax ABC 248.
[38] See *Vancouver Society of Immigrant and Visible Minority Women* v. *Minister of National
   Revenue* (1999) 169 DLR (4th) 34, SC.
[39] Iacobucci J acknowledged as much in *Vancouver Society of Immigrant & Visible
   Minority Women* v. *Minister of National Revenue* [1999] 1 SCR 10, at para. 150, citing
   R. v. *Salituro* [1991] 3 SCR 654, at p.670.
[40] *Wood* v. *Whitebread* (1969) 68 WWR 132 (Sask. QB).

CHARITY LAW AND THE REGULATORY FRAMEWORK   339

court recognised that 'the study of comparative religion, philosophy and society is prima facie charitable'.[41]

In relation to determining the charitable status of religious organisations and of gifts to them, as in all common law jurisdictions, it is the public benefit test that is of central importance. The mix of religion, charity and the law is perhaps particularly evident in the abortion case law. Indeed, the difficulties, uncertainties and extent of litigation generated in regard to this matter can be seen in the many lengthy court battles which have resulted in anti-abortion groups[42] and an anti-pornography group[43] losing their charitable statuses, largely due to the perceived bias of their materials and activities,[44] while abortion clinics[45] and abortion rights groups have maintained such status.

In 1991 the Minister for National Revenue refused to register an abortion clinic, the Everywoman's Health Centre Society, as a valid charity, largely on the grounds that there was no consensus as to whether an abortion clinic met the public benefit test. The Federal Court of Appeal disagreed, holding that the clinic was a valid charity and beneficial to the community.[46] The Everywoman's Health Centre Society was incorporated to provide 'necessary medical services for women for the benefit of the community as a whole' and to 'carry on educational activities incidental to the above'. Its activities were counselling, testing, examinations and abortions, all within the law. As Decary JA noted, 'the controversy that surrounds abortion should not deter us from seeking the true purpose of the clinic, which is to benefit women receiving a legally recognized health care service in a legally constituted clinic'.[47]

In 1998 the Federal Court of Appeal reviewed Revenue Canada's decision to revoke the charitable status of Human Life International on the grounds that it was not devoting substantially all of its resources to charitable activity.[48] The organisation, a registered charity since 1984, had the specific objectives of promoting social welfare and defending the

---

[41] Ibid., at p.284.

[42] For example, *Human Life International in Canada Inc.* v. *Canada (Minister of National Revenue)* FCJ No. 365, 18 March 1998 and *Alliance for Life* v. *Canada (MNR)* 1999 FCJ No. 658, 5 May 1999.

[43] See *Positive Action Against Pornography* v. *MNR* [1988] 1 CTC 232.

[44] See *Interfaith Development Education Association, Burlington* v. *MNR* [1997] 97 DTC 5424.

[45] *Everywoman's Health Centre Society (1988)* v. *Canada (MNR)* [1991] 136 NR 380.

[46] Ibid.   [47] Ibid., at pp.390–391.

[48] *Human Life International in Canada Inc.* v. *Canada (Minister of National Revenue)* [1998] FCJ No. 365, 18 March 1998.

human rights of persons born and unborn, promotion of natural methods of child creation and assistance in the education of persons in their obligation to respect and protect innocent human life. Revenue Canada had been particularly concerned about: bias in the educational material; the explicit discouraging of support from certain corporations (e.g. Proctor and Gamble, Petro Canada) and charities (Planned Parenthood, the United Way); and its activities (urging picketing of abortion clinics for the purpose of putting them out of business). Revenue Canada concluded that Human Life International appeared to be devoting substantial resources to these activities, which were not ancillary and incidental. The Federal Court of Appeal concluded that the appellant's activities did not qualify as educational in nature, given that they were not directed towards the formal training of the mind or the improvement of human knowledge, nor could they qualify under 'other purposes beneficial to the community' because the educational material included in the information kit was biased and political. The Court upheld Revenue Canada's decision to revoke Human Life International's charitable status.

In 1999 the Federal Court of Appeal was called upon to consider a Revenue Canada decision to deregister Alliance for Life, an organisation that had obtained charitable status in 1973 and which had specifically rearranged its organisational structure in accordance with advice given in a Revenue Canada Information Circular.[49] The amended charitable objects were: 'to educate Canadians on ... abortion, chastity, euthanasia and similar issues affecting human life'; 'to provide counselling and referral services to the public with respect to unforeseen pregnancies and post abortion trauma'; and 'to provide educational services and materials for member groups'. Ultimately, Stone JA concluded that the educational materials provided by the organisation could be characterised as political, but not ancillary and incidental to the appellant's charitable activities, and therefore the court upheld Revenue Canada's decision.

Charity law reform

The gestation period of Canadian charity law reform has so far been at least 17 years with little in the way of substantive change. Despite being

---

[49] *Alliance for Life* v. *Canada (Minister of National Revenue)* [1999] FCJ No. 658, 5 May 1999.

the first jurisdiction to launch this reform process[50] (ambitious in scope and watched with optimism and envy across the common law world), it has failed to live up to expectations.

The reforms

The reforms ultimately introduced by government were based on the recommendations made in the 2003 report *Strengthening Canada's Charitable Sector: Regulatory Reform,*[51] all but six of which were accepted and subsequently incorporated into the Tax Act.[52] These included regulatory adjustments to the appeal process in respect of decisions taken by the regulator, changes to the penalties for abuse of charitable status and to fundraising matters. While the internal revision of CRA policies that ensued as a result of the report were viewed favourably by the sector, there is much truth in the observation that 'Canada's attempts at modernising the law of charities have constituted little more than tinkering at the edges.'[53] Unlike other common law jurisdictions, no legislative steps have been taken in Canada to: transfer lead regulatory responsibility from the CRA to a charity-specific (or sector-specific) federal agency; to place the key common law concepts onto the statute books, and thereby equip government with the future capacity to amend charity law as required by changing social circumstances or political expediency; nor to broaden the traditional *Pemsel* list of charitable purposes; or to alter the public benefit presumption. The absence of any alteration to the substance of the definition, or to the categories, of purposes to be recognised as charitable means that the traditional interpretation of 'charity', 'charitable purpose' and 'public benefit', together with accompanying common law rules, continue to form the basis of charity law in this jurisdiction.

The public benefit test and religious organisations

The long-established common law rule that trusts and gifts for the advancement of religion are prima facie charitable and presumed to be

---

[50] See, the Ontario Law Reform Commission Report 1996. See, further, at: https://archive.org/details/reportonlawofcha01onta (accessed 7 January 2014).

[51] See, further, at: www.vsi-isbc.org/eng/regulations/reports.cfm (accessed 7 January 2014).

[52] For an updated version of the Income Tax Act (Canada), see: http://laws.justice.gc.ca/eng/acts/I-3.3 (accessed 7 January 2014).

[53] See B. Wyatt and L. Hunter, 'Charity Law Reforms: Overview of Progress Since 2001', in *Modernising Charity Law*, Elgar Publications, Cheltenham, 2010.

342 CANADA

for the public benefit,[54] although now statutorily repealed in its jurisdiction of origin, continues in effect in Canada.[55]

The test

Both arms of the public benefit test must be satisfied.

• Public

The judiciary and the CRA apply the public benefit requirement to disallow
charitable status to closed and purely contemplative religious orders.[56]

• Benefit

Actual benefit must result from the activities of a religious organisation if
it is to attain or retain charitable status. The benefit must not be merely
secular in nature, such as the provision of welfare services.

Religion, religious beliefs and the advancement of religion

The established common law approach to interpreting the definition of
'religion' and the means for its advancement have been closely followed
in Canada.

Religion

As Monahan P commented in *Re Christian Brothers of Ireland in
Canada*,[57] there is 'a dearth of Canadian case law relating to the definition of religion'. In general the authorities have tended to lean towards
the more traditional and conservative charity law interpretation, requiring a theistic belief and worship as essential components.

Belief in a Supreme Being

A basic requirement for charitable status under the third *Pemsel*
head is that an organisation holds beliefs in a Supreme Being and

---

[54] See, for example, *National Anti-Vivisection Society* v. *IRC* [1948] AC 31 and *Re Watson*
[1973] 1 WLR 1472.
[55] See, for example, *Re Morton Estate* (1941) 1 WWR 311 (BCSC).
[56] The ruling in *Gilmour* v. *Coats* [1949] 1 All ER 848 in respect of closed religious
organisations being followed in Canada.
[57] *Re Christian Brothers of Ireland in Canada*, 184 DLR (4th) 445.

provides for its worship. Thus the Mouvement Raelian Canadien was refused charitable status apparently on the grounds that it did not have a belief in God.[58] Similarly, the Edmonton Grove of the Church of Reformed Druids was rejected, presumably on the same basis (although their practice of animal sacrifice may have played a part).[59] Nor did the court consider the submission from the Coast Salish Indians in British Columbia that hunting deer out of season, for consumption in a tribal gathering, would constitute a religious ceremony.[60]

Worship, religious tenets, doctrines, etc.

To qualify for charitable status under this *Pemsel* head the applicant body must teach belief in a single specified faith or religion. As stated on the CRA website:

> It is a charitable purpose for an organization to teach the religious tenets, doctrines, practices, or culture associated with a specific faith or religion. The religious beliefs or practices must not be subversive or immoral. . . . Teaching ethics or morals is not enough to qualify as a charity in the advancement-of-religion category. . . . There has to be a spiritual element to the teachings, and the religious activities have to serve the public good.[61]

The presence of a body of doctrinal beliefs, together with a commitment to disseminating such doctrines, is essential to the registration of an organisation as a religious charity, the social value of which has been attested to by L'Heureux-Dube J. in *R. v. Gruenke*:

> Religious organisations based on claims to unchanging truths are a stabilizing influence in an increasingly fast-paced and atomised society where bonds of community are scarce and worth preserving.[62]

---

[58] *13 Mouvement raelien canadien* v. *M.N.R.*, FCA, as cited in Carters, (1999) 2:5 *Church & the Law Update* 5. See, further at: www.carters.ca/pub/update/church/volume02/chchv2n5.pdf (accessed 7 January 2014).

[59] See, further, J. Phillips, B. Chapman and D. Stevens, *Between State and Market: Essay on Charities Law and Policy in Canada*, McGill-Queen's Press, Montreal, 2001, at p.338.

[60] See *Anderson, Jack, and George Louie Charlie* v. *Her Majesty the Queen*, Supreme Court of Canada, 31 October 1985.

[61] 'Charitable Work and Ethnocultural Groups – Information on Registering as a Charity, (iii) The Advancement of Religion', Canada Revenue Agency, at: www.cra-arc.gc.ca.

[62] *R. v. Gruenke* [1991] 3 SCR 263.

344   CANADA

Again, in *Re Doering*,[63] it seemed sufficient to point out that:

> The Association of the New Jerusalem Church ... is a religious body
> which professes doctrines ... based on the teachings of Emanuel
> Swedenborg.[64]

The importance of having such a body of beliefs or teachings was demonstrated in the 1977 cases *Re Russell*[65] and *Re Wood* v. *Whitebread*,[66] in both of which it was held that theosophy was not a religion. Subsequently, however, Dickson CJ in *R. v. Big M Drug Mart*[67] seemed to move away from the traditional institutional interpretation of 'religion' to embrace a wider view that respected an individual's human right to adhere to religious beliefs:

> What unites enunciated freedoms in the American First Amendment,
> s.2(a) of the Charter and the provisions of other human rights documents
> in which they are associated is the notion of the centrality of individual
> conscience and the inappropriateness of governmental intervention to
> compel or constrain its manifestation.

While it may not be susceptible to judicial verification, there must actually be a set of beliefs if the claims of any such applicant person or organisation are to be substantiated. The CRA specifically requires applicant organisations to have 'an element of theistic worship, which means the worship of that deity or deities in the spiritual sense. To foster a belief in morals or ethics alone is not enough for a charity to register under this category.'[68] This accords with the views expressed by the Supreme Court of Canada in *Fletcher* v. *A.G. Alta.*, that:

> Religion, as the subject matter of legislation, wherever the jurisdiction
> may lie, must mean religion in the sense that it is generally understood in
> Canada. It involves matters of faith and worship, and freedom of religion
> involves freedom in connection with the profession and dissemination of
> religious faith and the exercise of worship.[69]

---

[63] *Re Doering* (1949) 1 DLR 267 (Ont. HC).   [64] Ibid., at p.279.

[65] *Re Russell* (1977) 1 ETR 285 (Alta. SCTD).

[66] *Wood and Whitebread* v. *the Queen in right of Alberta, Public Trustee of Alberta, The Theosophical Society et al.* (1977) 6 WWR 273 (Alta. SC).

[67] *R. v. Big M Drug Mart* [1985] 1 SCR 295, at p.346.

[68] See, CRA, 'Registering a Charity for Income Tax Purposes', Form T2050, accompanying explanatory note.

[69] *Fletcher* v. *A.G. Alta.* [1969] 66 WWR 513, at p.521.

THE ADVANCEMENT OF RELIGION 345

Philosophy and other value systems

The CRA has ruled that theosophy does not qualify as a religion,[70] nor does Christian Science which, in *Re Cox*,[71] was described by Fitzpatrick CJ as 'rather a theory of all things in Heaven and earth evolved by the Scientists of the Christian Church, rather than a religion as commonly understood'. However, the CRA has registered a wide range of 'religious' organisations not all of which would necessarily meet the traditional conservative view of what constitutes a theistic belief.[72] Buddhist groups have been recognised as charities, as also have Unitarian fellowships and churches, even though these do not acknowledge a deity. At the turn of the century the following were all registered as having charitable status: the Emissaries of the Divine Light; the Khalsa Diwan Society; the Hindu Society of Manitoba; the Alpha and Omega Order of Melchizedek; the Victoria Buddhist Dharma Society; the Zoroastrian Society of Ontario; the Islamic Society of Niagara Peninsula; New Age International; and the Universal Cosmic Light Society.

More recently, in *Blackmore* v. *The Queen*,[73] the presenting issue was eligibility for privileged tax treatment under s.143 of the Canadian Income Tax Act. To be eligible a community had to satisfy all four tests set out in the definition of 'congregation' in the Act.[74] The appellant was the leader of a group called Bountiful, which had an established community in British Columbia, was an offshoot of the fundamentalist Latter Day Saints and practised polygamous marriage. In the course of its deliberations the court considered whether Bountiful satisfied the legislative definition of a 'religious organisation' as 'an organization, other than a registered charity, of which a congregation is a constituent part, that adheres to beliefs, evidenced by the religious and philosophical tenets of the organization, that include a belief in the existence of a supreme being'. The court found that they were not, for several reasons.[75] It held that the community did not meet any of the criteria

---

[70] See *Wood* v. *Whitebread* (1969) 68 WWR 132 (Sask. QB).
[71] *In re Cox* [1953] 1 SCR 94.   [72] See Carters, (1999) 2:5 *Church & The Law Update*.
[73] *Blackmore* v. *The Queen*, 2013 TCC 264 (CanLII).
[74] The definition of 'congregation' in s.143(4) of the Act has four components, being that the members of a community, society or body of individuals, whether or not incorporated: live and work together; adhere to the practices and beliefs of and operate according to the principles of the religious organisation of which it is a constituent part; do not permit any of the members to own any property in their own right; and require the members to devote their working lives to the activities of the congregation.
[75] *Blackmore* v. *The Queen*, 2013 TCC 264 (CanLII), at pp.227–230.

346 CANADA

because it was not a 'religious organization' as defined in the Act, and its members were too integrated into the community, despite their practice of polygamy. This singular case, resting on its own peculiar set of facts, is unlikely to have implications for religion or charity law more broadly, but it does provide an interesting insight into contemporary religious pluralism in Canada.

The advancement of religion

The CRA policy statement on this charitable purpose is unequivocal:

> To advance religion in the charitable sense means to promote the spiritual teachings of a religious body and to maintain doctrines and spiritual observances on which those teachings are based. There must be an element of theistic worship, which means the worship of a deity or deities in the spiritual sense.[76]

Such a clear and inflexible assertion that the traditional definition of 'religion' will continue to determine eligibility for charitable status under this *Pemsel* head is most unusual among the jurisdictions currently being considered. To 'advance' religion, or ensure its promotion, necessitates action to develop and spread the related religious teachings. An onus rests on a religious organisation to pursue its 'religious purpose' by furthering the doctrines and beliefs of the religion, or developing or disseminating its teachings. In *Fuaran Foundation* v. *Canada (Customs and Revenue Agency)*[77] the Federal Court of Appeal held that a proposed 'retreat facility' did not meet this requirement and dismissed the appellant's case because:

> what the Appellant proposes is to simply make available a place where religious thought may be pursued. There is no targeted attempt to promote religion or to take positive steps to sustain and increase religious belief. There seems to be no structured program relating to advancement of religion.

---

[76] Canada Revenue Agency, Summary Policy CSP-R06 (25 October 2002), see, further, at: www.cra-arc.gc.ca/chrts-gvng/chrts/plcy/csp/csp-r06-eng.html (accessed 7 January 2014). Also see *Re Anderson* (1943) 4 DLR 268 (Ont. HC), at p.271. In determining what it means to advance religion, the CRA has followed the traditional English precedents set in *United Grand Lodge of Ancient Free and Accepted Masons of England* v. *Holborn Borough Council* [1957] 1 WLR 1080 and *Keren Kayemeth Le Jisroel Ltd.* v. *The Commissioners of Inland Revenue* [1931] 2 KB 465 (CA).

[77] *Fuaran Foundation* v. *Canada (Customs and Revenue Agency)* (2004) FCA 181, 2004-05-04.

The means for advancing religion

An organisation, or gifts to it, will be advancing religion and thus can be construed as charitable if the purpose is to instruct or edify the public either directly or indirectly: this will be the case if it can show that it is both seeking to advance a specific religion and proposes to do so by relevant and specified means. The courts have adopted a broad and liberal view of this requirement. In *Re Brooks*, for example, the Saskatchewan Court of Queen's Bench held that a gift 'to the work of the Lord' was charitable and not void for uncertainty,[78] while the Nova Scotia Supreme Court ruled in *Re Armstrong* that a direction to a trustee to make payments to a church for ancillary projects was sufficiently closely related to the activities of the Church to be charitable.[79]

In general the judiciary and CRA, in keeping with their counterparts in other common law jurisdictions, have found the requirements for charitable status under 'the advancement of religion' head to be fulfilled by much the same set of organisational activities and gifts, intended to further belief in and worship of the Supreme Being central to the religion in question, including: provision and maintenance of churches, places of worship and ceremonial services; delivering programmes of spiritual and moral education; carrying out, as a practical expression of religious beliefs, other activities (such as conflict resolution or relieving poverty); and provision of social welfare services to those in need.

Public policy, religious charities and common law constraints

The Canadian origins of the present contention regarding the possibly discriminatory practices of religious charities, as in other common law countries, lie in the legacy of its public policy case law.

Testamentary conditions and the common law

Canada, in keeping with other common law jurisdictions, has a significant case law history relating to freedom of testamentary disposition. Although its case law has been broadly in keeping with the traditional benign approach towards testamentary dispositions made subject to religious

---

[78] *Re Brooks* (1969) 68 WWR 132 (Sask. QB).
[79] *Re Armstrong* (1969) 7 DLR (3d) 36 (NS SC).

348   CANADA

conditions, the judiciary made their own singular contribution to present tensions between religious charities and human rights.

Failure due to breach of common law rules

As the Supreme Court ruled in *Canada in Vancouver Society of Immigrant and Visible Minority Women* v. *Minister of National Revenue*,[80] there are two requirements for the registration of a charity: the purpose of the organisation must be exclusively charitable and must define the scope of the activities engaged in by the organisation; and all of the organisation's resources must be devoted to charitable activities. The exclusivity rule is a not infrequent cause of CRA refusal to award charitable status.[81] However, in general, unless a gift by donor or testator fails for technical reasons, is in breach of the criminal law[82] or public policy,[83] is morally subversive,[84] devoid of all merit,[85] made with an improper motive[86] or is compromised by a relationship nexus with the intended beneficiaries,[87] then despite the presence of a religious constraint it will normally be valid.

Bequests subject to a religious condition

That testators' gifts could be made subject to conditions favouring beneficiaries of a particular religious persuasion, virtually immune from public policy constraints, has been contentious.[88] Nonetheless, as Grattan

---

[80] *Canada in Vancouver Society of Immigrant and Visible Minority Women* v. *Minister of National Revenue* [1999] 1 SCR 10.
[81] See, for example, *Fuaran Foundation* v. *Canada (Customs and Revenue Agency)* (2004) FCA 181, 2004-05-04.
[82] See, for example, *R.* v. *Harding* (2001) 52 OR (3d) 714, aff'd 17 December 2001.
[83] See *Canada Trust Co.* v. *Ontario Human Rights Commission* (1990) 69 DLR (4th) 321, *per* Robins JA, where, at para. 38, he reasoned that a 'settlor's freedom to dispose of property through the creation of a charitable trust ... must give way to current principles of public policy'.
[84] *Thornton* v. *Howe* (1862) 31 Beav. 14.
[85] See *Re Watson* [1973] 1 WLR 1472, where it was stated that 'a religious charity can only be shown not to be for the public benefit if its doctrines are adverse to the foundations of all religion and subversive of all morality'.
[86] See *Tempest* v. *Lord Camoys* (1882) 21 Ch D 571 (CA).
[87] See *Re Compton* [1945] Ch. 123.
[88] See, further, S. Grattan and H. Conway, 'Testamentary Conditions in Restraint of Religion in the Twenty-first Century: An Anglo-Canadian Perspective' (2005) 50 *McGill Law Journal* 511.

and Conway have convincingly demonstrated,[89] there is a considerable body of Canadian case law in which bequests made subject to religious conditions, imposed by testators, have been upheld by the judiciary. These include: *Renaud* v. *Lamothe* (the marriages of the testator's children should be celebrated according to the rites of the Roman Catholic Church and any grandchildren should be educated in accordance with its teachings);[90] *Re Patton* ('is and proves himself to be of the Lutheran religion');[91] *Re Curran* ('is at that time a member of a Roman Catholic Parish');[92] *Re Starr* ('rejoin the Catholic Church and practice the Catholic Faith');[93] *Re Kennedy Estate* (be 'married to a Protestant husband of good repute');[94] and *Re Delahey* (not to 'become members of the Roman Catholic Church').[95] Parachin has also catalogued many such discriminatory bequests (see, further, Chapter 1).[96]

Religious preferences and public policy

From at least *Laurence* v. *McQuarrie*,[97] with its forfeiture condition in the event of the beneficiary 'embracing the doctrines of the church of Rome', until the introduction of the Charter of Rights and Freedoms with its s.2 guarantees of freedom of conscience and religion and s.15 guarantee of equality, testamentary conditions in favour of religion had precedence over public policy considerations and went virtually unchallenged by the judiciary. Although, in the immediate post-Charter period it seemed as though Galligan J was right to proclaim a new era – 'It is now settled that it is against public policy to discriminate on grounds of race or religion'[98] – it has proved difficult to leave behind the legacy of preferential judicial treatment for exercises of benevolent donor discretion in favour of religious beliefs.

---

[89] Ibid. [90] *Renaud* v. *Lamothe* (1902) 32 SCR 357.
[91] *Re Patton* [1938] OWN 52 (CA). [92] *Re Curran* [1939] OWN 191 (HCJ).
[93] *Re Starr* [1946] OR 252; [1946] 2 DLR 489 (CA).
[94] *Re Kennedy Estate* (1949) 60 Man. R 1; [1950] 1 WWR 151 (KB).
[95] *Re Delahey* (1950) [1951] OWN 143; [1951] 1 DLR 710 (HCJ).
[96] See A. Parachin, 'The Definition of Charity and Public Law Equality Norms', paper presented at the conference *Private and Public Law – Intersections in Law and Method*, the T.C. Beirne Law School at the University of Queensland, Brisbane, July 2011.
[97] *Laurence* v. *McQuarrie* (1894) 26 NSR 164, at 166.
[98] See *Fox* v. *Fox Estate* (1996) 28 OR (3d) 496, 88 O.AC 201 (CA), *per* Galligan J, at p.502.

Public policy constraints

The courts and regulators have, with some equivocation, held to the principle that a trust in breach of public policy cannot acquire or hope to retain charitable status. This occurred in *Re Drummond Wren*,[99] when a restrictive covenant prohibiting the sale of land to 'Jews or persons of objectionable nationality' was found to be against public policy. Interestingly, when the Supreme Court of Canada considered a similar covenant a few years later in *Re Noble and Wolf*,[100] it struck the covenant solely on the basis of property law considerations. Generally, where a political aspect is present alongside a racial discrimination dimension in the objects or activities of an organisation, then courts and regulators would be more likely to find that the former provided the grounds for justifying a denial of charitable status.

The Canadian Charter of Rights and Freedoms, signed into law by Queen Elizabeth II on 17 April 1982, did, however, prompt a change in the judicial approach to dealing with matters of religious preference and public policy. The best-known Canadian case on the issue of a religious trust being in breach of public policy was determined by the Ontario Court of Appeal in 1990 when it ruled that limiting scholarships to white, Protestant, British subjects was racial discrimination that 'is patently at variance with the democratic principles governing our pluralistic society in which equality rights are constitutionally guaranteed and in which the multicultural heritage of Canadians is to be preserved and enhanced'.[101] This approach was endorsed by the CRA in relation to organisations established to eliminate racial discrimination or foster positive race relations within Canada.[102]

That not all discriminatory bequests necessarily breached public policy was demonstrated, for example, in *Ramsden Estate*,[103] when the court found that a testamentary gift to a university for scholarships for Protestant students was not on par with the discriminatory scholarships in *Canada Trust*,[104] and concluded that there was 'no ground of public policy which would serve as an impediment to the trust proceeding'.[105]

---

[99] *Re Drummond Wren* [1945] 4 DLR 674.   [100] *Re Noble and Wolf* [1951] SCR 64.
[101] See *Canada Trust Co. v. Ontario Human Rights Commission* (1990) 69 DLR (4th) 321.
[102] See the Canada Customs and Revenue Agency, CPS-021, *Registering Charities that Promote Racial Equality*, 2003.
[103] *Ramsden Estate* (1996) 139 DLR (4th) 746.
[104] *Canada Trust Co. v. Ontario Human Rights Commission* (1990) 69 DLR (4th) 321.
[105] Ibid., at para. 13, *per* MacDonald CJTD.

PUBLIC POLICY AND COMMON LAW CONSTRAINTS   351

Again, in *University of Victoria* v. *British Columbia (A.G.)*,[106] the court upheld a scholarship for practising Roman Catholics and distinguished the case from 'the clearly offensive' terms under which scholarships were made available in *Canada Trust*. The court reasoned that a 'scholarship or bursary that simply restricts the class of recipients to members of a particular religious faith does not offend public policy'.[107] It emphasised that even scholarship funds restricted to persons of a particular faith have social utility in as much as they provide educational opportunities to a segment of society.[108]

On the other hand, in some cases the courts clearly established that public policy had been breached, such as when the Ontario Court of Appeal in *Fox* v. *Fox Estate*[109] so ruled in relation to a trustee's use of a power of encroachment to punish the remainder beneficiary for marrying a person not of the Jewish faith. Moreover, in the same year a Sikh organisation with apparent ties to terrorist activities was deregistered,[110] while Jewish charities sending funds to settlers occupying Israeli-occupied territories were the subject of CRA investigations.[111] The decision in *Everywoman's Health Centre Society* v. *Canada*[112] is for present purpose somewhat beside the point, as although the court found the operation of an abortion clinic to be charitable, as being analogous to a hospital, it was unable to establish any linkage between the controversy associated with an abortion service and public policy.[113]

Advocacy

Again, in *Toronto Volgograd Committee* v. *M.N.R.*,[114] an organisation devoted to promoting peace and understanding between Toronto and Volgograd in the USSR through education, public awareness, exchanges and meetings, was denied charitable status because its activities and objects were viewed by the court as 'no more than propaganda'.

---

[106] *University of Victoria* v. *British Columbia (A.G.)* [2000] BCJ No. 520.
[107] Ibid., *per* Maczko J, at para. 25.   [108] Ibid., at para. 17.
[109] *Fox* v. *Fox Estate* [1996] OJ No. 375 (Ont. CA).
[110] See, further, at: http://articles.timesofindia.indiatimes.com/2007-11-30/rest-of-world/ 27956530_1_babbar-khalsa-air-india-bombing-tax-exempt-status (accessed 7 January 2014).
[111] *Per* M. Logan, 'Revenue Canada Probes Charities Donating to Jewish Settlements', *Ottawa Citizen*, 13 October 1996.
[112] *Everywoman's Health Centre Society* v. *Canada* [1992] 2 FC 52.
[113] Ibid., at paras 15–16.
[114] *Toronto Volgograd Committee* v. *M.N.R.* [1988] 1 CTC 365; 88 DTC 6192 (FCA). Also see *Canadian Magen David Adom for Israel* v. *Canada (MNR)* [2002] 4 CTC.

352   CANADA

Indeed, the CRA followed this line (set by the British courts ruling in *Re Strakosch*[115]) until it renounced that approach in 2003.[116]

In *Native Communications Society* v. *M.N.R.*[117] the court held that an organisation involved in publishing a newsletter and in the development of related radio and television productions was charitable under the fourth *Pemsel* category, even though the publication contained some political views. Noting that the organisation also had objectives that included making the community aware of cultural activities and attempting to foster language and cultures, the judges were quite lenient in their interpretation of what was permissible. *Alliance for Life* v. *M.N.R.*[118] is an important case because it describes how a charity can engage in political activities through a 'sister' organisation and not run the risk of losing registered charity status. The organisation had been a registered charity, but the CRA was proposing to revoke the status because it had engaged in a good deal of grass roots political activity.[119] After discussions between the organisation and CRA, it was agreed that Alliance would set up a nonprofit organisation to carry on its non-charitable (political) activities. This was done, but Alliance nonetheless was eventually removed as a registered charity because it continued to use funds raised by the charity for carrying out its political activities.

Proselytism

At the end of the nineteenth century, proselytism was viewed as threatening and there was considerable papal concern that this practice was encroaching on Catholicism. Consequently, Canadian bishops were required to research this issue and report their findings to Rome. The reports compiled and submitted during 1900–1901, by 25 bishops, were somewhat dismissive of the existence or effect of proselytism and broadly concluded that 'Catholics were [not] threatened institutionally or publicly by Protestants'.[120]

---

[115] *Re Strakosch* [1949] 1 Ch. 529 (CA).

[116] See the Canada Customs and Revenue Agency, CPS-021, *Registering Charities that Promote Racial Equality*, 2003.

[117] *Native Communications Society* v. *M.N.R.* [1986] 3 FC 471 (CA).

[118] *Alliance for Life* v. *M.N.R.* [1999] 3 FC 504, available at: www.canlii.org/en/ca/fca/doc/1999/1999canlii8152/1999canlii8152.html (accessed 7 January 2014).

[119] A small amount would have been acceptable, but not to the extent involved in the situation at hand.

[120] See M. McGowan, *Waning of the Green: Catholics, the Irish, and Identity in Toronto, 1887–1922*, McGill-Queen's Press, Montreal, 1999, as cited in T.J. Fay, *History of Canadian Catholics*, McGill-Queen's Press, Montreal, 2002, at pp.143–145.

More recently, in *Zundel* v. *Canada*,[121] where the Supreme Court was concerned with holocaust denial publications, it considered the limitations imposed on proselytism by s.181 of the Criminal Code. This stated that 'Every one who willfully publishes a statement, tale or news that he knows is false and causes or is likely to cause injury or mischief to a public interest is guilty of an indictable offence and liable to imprisonment.' The court found that s.181 violated s.2(b) of the Canadian Charter of Rights and Freedoms, which protects all expression of a non-violent form, because the restriction on all expressions 'likely to cause injury or mischief to a public interest' was far too broad and the penalty of imprisonment for expression was unreasonable as it would have a severely limiting effect on freedom.

The parameters for the reasonable exercise of proselytism are now set by s.319(2) of the Criminal Code, which declares that:

> Every one who, by communicating statements, other than in private conversation, wilfully promotes hatred against any identifiable group is guilty of (a) an indictable offence and is liable to imprisonment for a term not exceeding two years; or (b) an offence punishable on summary conviction.

Again, in *Ross* v. *Canada*, the subject was a former teacher who in his spare time published books and pamphlets and made public statements reflecting his discriminatory views in relation to Jews.[122] The Human Rights Board of Inquiry concluded that he had contributed to a 'poisoned environment' within the school district and recommended that he be transferred to a non-teaching position, which was endorsed by the Supreme Court of Canada and also by the UN Human Rights Committee which concurred that there had been no violation of the freedom of expression as guaranteed by Article 19 of the ICCPR.

Human rights, discrimination and religious charities: contemporary issues

As the above case law makes clear, donor veto does not necessarily constitute discrimination. The issues regarding the line to be drawn between the two, having occasionally surfaced from time to time in a broad public policy context, have in recent years come before the

---

[121] *Zundel* v. *Canada* [1992] 2 SCR 731.
[122] 18 October 2000, Communication No. 736/1997 (UN Human Rights Committee).

354   CANADA

Canadian judiciary and the CRA with ever-increasing frequency. The catalyst that centre-staged a marginal criterion for determining charitable status, transforming it into one of the most highly contentious and frequently disputed aspects of charity law, has been the surge of human rights-related litigation. Unsurprisingly, religious charities, with their inbuilt selective *modus operandi*, have been at the centre of this litigation.

Human rights

In this federated jurisdiction, while the primary body of authority for human rights is to be found in the Constitution, these rights derive added protection from province-level legislation.[123] This second tier of human rights legislation – which followed Canada becoming a signatory to the Universal Declaration of Human Rights 1948, the introduction of the Canadian Bill of Rights 1960, the Canadian Human Rights Act 1985 and the International Centre for Human Rights and Democratic Development Act 1985 – prohibits, among other things, discrimination because of race, religion or creed, colour, nationality, ancestry and place of origin.[124] For present purposes it may be assumed that little consequence for the principles concerned flow from whether adjudication on a particular human rights issue occurs at a federal or provincial level. Indeed, it is well established, for example, that Ontario's Human Rights Code[125] and the Charter share common objectives and should be interpreted in a congruent manner.[126] Moreover, the Supreme Court has advised that courts should develop the common law, which remains the basis for determining charitable status in Canada, 'in a manner consistent with the fundamental values enshrined in the Constitution.'[127]

---

[123] See, for example: British Columbia (Human Rights Code, RSBC 1996, c. 210); Saskatchewan (Saskatchewan Human Rights Code, SS 1979, c. S-24.1); Quebec (Charter of Human Rights and Freedoms, RSQ c. C-1); Newfoundland and Labrador (Human Rights Act, 2010, Chapter H-13.1); Nova Scotia (Human Rights Act, RSNS 1989, c. 214); Nunavut (Human Rights Act, S Nu 2003, c. 12); Prince Edward Island (Human Rights Act, RSPEI 1988, c. H-12); the Yukon (Human Rights Act, RSY 2002, c. 116); and the Northwest Territories (Human Rights Act, SNWT 2002, c. 18).

[124] The Canadian Multiculturalism Act 1985 and the Canadian Race Relations Foundation Act 1991 have also set benchmarks for legislation at provincial and territorial level.

[125] RSO 1990, c. H.19, as amended.

[126] See, for example, *Ontario (Disability Support Program)* v. *Tranchemontagne*, 2010 ONCA 593 (CanLII); *Ball* v. *Ontario (Community and Social Services)*, 2010 HRTO 360 (CanLII); *Mortillaro* v. *Ontario (Transportation)*, 2011 HRTO 310 (CanLII).

[127] See *Retail, Wholesale and Department Store Union, Local 580* v. *Dolphin Delivery* RSC 1985, c. 1 (5th Supp.), *per* McIntyre J., at para. 39.

The Constitution

Following the Preamble declaration, that 'Canada is founded upon principles that recognize the supremacy of God and the rule of law', the Canadian Charter of Rights and Freedoms, Part I of the Constitution Act, 1982, goes on to proclaim:

2. Everyone has the following fundamental freedoms:
   (a) freedom of conscience and religion;
   (b) freedom of thought, belief, opinion and expression, including freedom of the press and other media of communication.[128]

Shortly after the 1982 Act came into force, Wilson J in the Supreme Court advised that the freedom to hold and exercise beliefs was not restricted to beliefs of a religious nature: 'In a free and democratic society "freedom of conscience and religion" should be broadly construed to extend to conscientiously-held beliefs, whether grounded in religion or in a secular morality.'[129]

Section 1 of the Charter qualifies the rights proclaimed in s.2 with the proviso that they are exercised subject to such 'reasonable limits prescribed by law as can be demonstrably justified in a free and democratic society'.[130] Where the purposes of an organisation do in fact breach the fundamental legal principles of the Charter then, as Parachin has noted, 'it cannot be said to be acting in the public benefit and therefore cannot claim or retain charitable status'.[131]

Equality and diversity legislation

Federal legislation and international protocols, as supplemented by a range of statutes at province level, provide additional legal protection on matters of equity, equality and diversity. The Canadian Human Rights Act,[132] passed by the Parliament of Canada in 1977, with the express goal

---

[128] See, Schedule B to the Canada Act 1982 (UK), 1982, c. 11. Note that the Canadian Charter of Rights and Freedoms was introduced partly as a consequence of the Supreme Court of Canada decision in *Gay Alliance Toward Equality* v. *Vancouver Sun*, 1979 CanLII 225 (SCC) [1979] 2 SCR 435.

[129] See *Morgentaler* v. *R* [1988] 1 SCR 30, *per* Wilson J, at para. 251.

[130] The wording of this caveat is very similar to that employed by the ECtHR in its rulings relating to breaches of Article 8 of the European Convention.

[131] Parachin, 'The Definition of Charity and Public Law Equality Norms', citing *Re Drummond Wren* [1945] OR 778; [1945] 4 DLR 674 (HCJ).

[132] RSC 1985, c. H-6.

356   CANADA

of extending the law to ensure equal opportunity for individuals on a set of prohibited grounds – including sex, disability and religion – remains the main statutory basis for ensuring protection for designated groups (women, visible minorities, Aboriginal persons and persons with disabilities). In addition the Canadian government has passed into law a set of regulations, the Federal Contractors Program 1986 and the Employment Equity Act 1996, to address employment opportunities and benefits. As it is anticipated that by 2016 approximately two-thirds of the Canadian population aged 15–64 will consist of citizens belonging to the four designated groups, such targeted statutory protection would seem prudent.

Religious charities, discrimination and exemptions

As Parachin has pointed out, 'many charitable organisations and their activities represent positive discrimination as they undoubtedly intend to benefit some to the exclusion of others'.[133] This, as the Ontario Law Reform Commission foretold with shrewd prescience, would lead to a situation where 'the difficulty will be to define the difference or point of balance between discrimination that is prohibited on the grounds of public policy and discrimination that is permitted because it advances a legitimate interest of a legitimate community'.[134] For religious charities that tipping point typically arrives when religious beliefs conflict with statutorily authorised service provision obligations, as happens most typically in relation to abortion,[135] same-sex marriages and adoptions,[136] together with certain services of various education and social welfare facilities.[137] In keeping with the law of many other common law countries, Canadian religious organisations also have the right to discriminate when employing staff in accordance with 'bona fide occupational requirements' (known as BFOR in Canadian employment law).[138]

---

[133] See A. Parachin, 'The Definition of Charity and Public Law Equality Norms'.

[134] See *Report on the Law of Charities*, Ontario Law Reform Commission, 1996, Chapter 8, at p.21 (as brought to the author's attention by A. Parachin in a note of 13 December 2011).

[135] See *Everywoman's Health Centre Society* v. *Canada* [1992] 2 FC 52.

[136] See *Halpern* v. *Canada (Attorney General)* [2003] OJ No. 2268.

[137] See, for example, *Heintz* v. *Christian Horizons*, 2008 HRTO 22; 2010 ONSC 2105 (Div Ct), where an Evangelical Christian home for the disabled was held to have violated the anti-discrimination laws because it had a code of conduct that forbade, among many other things, homosexual conduct.

[138] See, for example, *Canada Trust Co.* v. *Ontario Human Rights Commission* (1990) 69 DLR (4th) 321, *per* Tarnopolsky J, at para. 98.

Religious charities as public bodies

The right to freedom of religion has a particular bearing on religious charities engaged in 'public' purposes, which will be the case if they are giving effect to statutory powers.[139] Arguably, any such charity that is largely funded by government – and is providing services in accordance with government policy on terms effectively controlled by government – is in such a role. The closer the government–charity relationship approximates a principal–agent relationship,[140] the stronger the presumption that the charity is functioning in law, for all intents and purposes, as a 'public' body.[141]

Freedom of religion

The right to freedom of religion as proclaimed in the Canadian Constitution was analysed as follows by the Supreme Court of Canada in the relatively early case of *R. v. Big M Drug Mart Ltd*:

> The essence of the concept of freedom of religion is the right to entertain such religious beliefs as a person chooses, the right to declare religious beliefs openly and without fear of hindrance or reprisal, and the right to manifest religious belief by worship and practice or by teaching and dissemination. But the concept means more than that.[142]

Further:

> whatever else freedom of conscience and religion may mean, it must at the very least mean this: government may not coerce individuals to affirm a specific religious belief or to manifest a specific religious belief or to manifest a specific religious practice for a sectarian purpose.[143]

In this jurisdiction the freedom of religion and belief has been locked into the Constitution via the Charter and s.2(a) of the latter

---

[139] See *Slaight Communications Inc.* v. *Davidson* (1989) 59 DLR (4th) 416 (SCC).

[140] Note the Supreme Court of Canada's decision in *Gay Alliance Toward Equality* v. *Vancouver Sun*, 1979 CanLII 225 (SCC); [1979] 2 SCR 435, where the majority held that the definition of 'service' was subject to the right of the newspaper to control the content of advertising.

[141] For a case in point, see *Heintz* v. *Christian Horizons*, 2008 HRTO 22; 2010 ONSC 2105 (Div. Ct).

[142] *R. v. Big M Drug Mart Ltd.* [1985] 1 SCR 295, at paras 94–96. See also the Supreme Court of Canada ruling in *Gay Alliance Toward Equality* v. *Vancouver Sun*, 1979 CanLII 225 (SCC); [1979] 2 SCR 435.

[143] *R. v. Big M Drug Mart Ltd.* [1985] 1 SCR 295, at p.362.

358

CANADA

specifically prevents the legislature from discriminating against religious minorities.[144]

Interference with the manifestation of religious belief

Notably, in the *Big M* case, the Supreme Court included within its interpretation of 'freedom' the right to manifest religious belief by the expression and dissemination of information consistent with such beliefs. Such a dissemination issue arose in *Chamberlain* v. *Surrey School District No. 36*,[145] when that Court considered the refusal of the Surrey School Board to approve three controversial books depicting same-sex parented families, which had been promoted as supplementary learning resources, as teaching aids in the family life education curriculum. The Court acknowledged that because religion is an integral aspect of people's lives, religious concerns do have a place in the deliberations on public questions – religion 'cannot be left at the classroom door'.[146] However, it suggested that on matters of public policy, religious concerns cannot exclude the concerns of other members of the community, there was a principle of public decision-making under which 'each group is given as much recognition as it can consistently demand while giving the same recognition to others'.[147] Having provided guidance on the process, the Court returned the approval decision to the Board. Subsequently, the same Court in *Syndicat Northcrest* v. *Amselem* warned that:

> No right, including freedom of religion, is absolute. . . . This is so because we live in a society of individuals in which we must always take the rights of others into account.[148]

---

[144] See, further, S. I. Smithey, 'Religious Freedom and Equality Concerns under the Canadian Charter of Rights and Freedoms' (2001) 34 *Canadian Journal of Political Science/Revue canadienne de science politique*, 85.

[145] *Chamberlain* v. *Surrey School District No. 36*, 2002 SCC 86. See also, *Zylberberg* v. *Sudbury Board of Education* (1989) 65 OR (2d) (Ont. CA), where prescribed religious exercises in Ontario public schools were held to be unconstitutional, because peer pressure and classroom norms operate to 'compel members of religious minorities to conform with majority religious practices' and that the existence of religious exercises 'compels students and parents to make a religious statement', at p.655.

[146] *Chamberlain* v. *Surrey School District No. 36*, 2002 SCC 86, at para. 19.

[147] Ibid.

[148] *Syndicat Northcrest* v. *Amselem*, 2004 SCC 47; [2004] 2 SCR 551, at para. 61.

HUMAN RIGHTS, DISCRIMINATION & RELIGIOUS CHARITIES 359

The Court then took an expansive view of religious freedom and practices connected to it,[149] ruling that a condominium board had to allow a group of orthodox Jewish unit-owners to construct succahs on their balconies as part of the Jewish festival of Succot, despite the prohibition in their condominium contract prohibiting tenants from altering property. Similarly, in *Multani* v. *Commission scolaire Marguerite-Bourgeoys*,[150] the Court ruled that the freedom of a Sikh boy to carry his kirpan outweighed reasons (e.g. alleged safety concerns) to prohibit him from doing so.

There may well be some truth in von Heyking's comment that:

> In cases subsequent to *Big M*, the Court has either upheld the right of religious organizations to discriminate according to 'bona fide occupational requirements', or it has attempted to minimize the conflict between the two stake-holders in a way that diminishes the profundity with which each side regards its own position; it recognizes one by recognizing none.[151]

In general this Court would seem to be striving to apply the principle of 'proportionality' in its weighting of the likely impact of rights enforcement and in choosing the option calculated to achieve a relatively equitable balance or cause minimal impairment, to the rights of the parties before it.[152] In relation to the latter, the Supreme Court in a leading constitutional decision stated that 'the relevance of context

---

[149] Essentially doing so by applying the so-called 'Oakes test' as formulated by Chief Justice Dickson in *R.* v. *Oakes* [1986] 1 SCR 103, which consists of: first, the body making the remedy must have a substantive objective (one that is both reasonable and justified in a free and democratic society); second, the proposed remedy must be rationally connected to the objective; and third, the proposed remedy would have to interfere minimally with the constitutional rights of the respondent.

[150] *Multani* v. *Commission scolaire Marguerite-Bourgeoys* [2006] 1 SCR 256; 2006 SCC 6; see also, *Nijjar* v. *Canada 3000 Airlines Ltd.* (1999) 36 CHRR D/76. An approach earlier adopted by the British Columbia Human Rights Tribunal in *Dhillen* v. *British Columbia Ministry of Transportation and Highways* (1999) 35 CHRR D293 (BCHRT) when it excused a practising Sikh, who wore a turban at all times as required by his faith, from wearing a safety helmet when sitting his motorbike driving test in accordance with normal statutory requirements.

[151] See J. Heyking, 'Civil Religion and Human Rights in Canada', paper presented at the conference *Freedom of Speech, Freedom of Conscience, Right for Unification: International and Russian Experience of Application: The 60th Anniversary of the Universal Declaration of Human Rights*, in Ekaterinburg, Russia, 1998, at p.9.

[152] In keeping with the views expressed by Lamer CJ in *Dagenaise* v. *Canadian Broadcasting Corp.* [1994] 3 SCR 835, when he said, 'when the protected rights of two individuals come into conflict ... Charter principles require a balance to be achieved that fully respects the importance of both sets of rights', at p.877.

360 CANADA

cannot be understated' and that the minimal impairment requirement does not impose an obligation on the government to employ the least intrusive measures available.[153] 'Rather, it only requires it to demonstrate that the measures employed are the least intrusive, in light of both the legislative objective and the infringed right.' In relation to proportionate effect, Dickson CJ stated in *R* v. *Oakes* that:

> Regard must be had to the nature of the right violated, the extent of the violation and the degree to which the measures impact upon the integral principles of a free and democratic society. The more severe the deleterious effects of a measure, the more important the objective must be if the measure is to be reasonable and demonstrably justified in a free and democratic society.[154]

The difficulties in managing such a balancing exercise were, however, demonstrated in *Bruker* v. *Marcovitz*,[155] where one group of judges saw its decision as a minor re-shaping of a religious practice to conform with contemporary public policy, whereas the other regarded it as an impermissible entanglement of the law in religious affairs.

Interference in an individual's right to manifest their religious beliefs does require just cause. In Ontario, the applicant in *Dalliare* v. *Les Chevaliers de Columb*[156] alleged that a monument erected in the grounds of a Catholic church and bearing the inscription 'Let us pray that all life rests in the hands of God from conception until natural death' was offensive and discriminatory because it denounced, victimised and excluded women. While the tribunal accepted that the inscription constituted an expression of religious belief, it considered that the applicant's case was weakened by the fact that the monument in question was located within church grounds and the inscription was not visible to members of the public from outside those grounds. Thus the right of the applicant to exercise their right of religious freedom did not sufficiently and directly impact on the respondent's corresponding right to give the latter just cause to require the removal of the inscription. Similarly, in *Ross* v. *New Brunswick School Dist. No. 15*,[157] when the point was made that the freedom of religion is 'subject to such limitations as are necessary to protect public safety, order, health or morals, or the fundamental rights and freedoms of others'. Just cause was, however, established in

---

[153] *RJR-McDonald* v. *Canada* [1995] 3 SCR 1999.   [154] *R* v. *Oakes* [1986] 1 SCR 103.
[155] *Bruker* v. *Marcovitz*, 2007 SCC 54.
[156] *Dalliare* v. *Les Chevaliers de Columb*, 2011 HRTO 639.
[157] *Ross* v. *New Brunswick School Dist. No. 15* (1996) 25 CHRR D/175.

Streeter v. *HR Technologies*,[158] when the tribunal found that during the course of the applicant's employment with the respondent he was subjected to a religious atmosphere in which he felt compelled to participate as part of his employment. The tribunal then held that the extent of the religious messaging and pressure was such that it violated the Code; the tribunal explained:

> It is important that people in a workplace, including the employer, be able to express their opinions freely (within the confines of the Code). However, as pointed out in the *Dufour* case, the employer must be very careful to not put any unwelcome pressure on an employee such that religion or religious adherence becomes a term and condition of employment.[159]

The closing warning, that any pressure to comply with a prevailing religious ethos could be construed as imputing a requirement for such compliance into the terms and conditions of a contractual arrangement, indicates that religious charities must ensure that such an arrangement is devoid of any suggestion of improper proselytism.[160]

Inter-Church property disputes

In keeping with trends in the United States, and the beginnings of a similar pattern in the United Kingdom and Australia, Canada is also experiencing the property disputes that inevitably follow religious schism. In recent years this phenomenon has been closely linked to the divisions within the Christian religions on issues of same-sex marriages, the ordination of female clergy, etc. Such a dispute was presented before the courts in *Bentley* v. *Anglican Synod of the Diocese of New Westminster*.[161] This case concerned a group of parishioners in British Columbia who sought independence from the mainstream Anglican Church of Canada (ACoC) over what they saw as its anti-Christian trends. Mr. Justice Stephen Kelleher of the British Columbia Supreme Court issued a mixed decision saying that four parishes in the Vancouver area may not keep their buildings if they remove themselves from the

---

[158] *Streeter* v. *HR Technologies*, 2009 HRTO 841 (CanLII).   [159] Ibid., at para. 4.
[160] See also *Caldwell* v. *St. Thomas Aquinas High School* (1984) 6 CHRR D/2643.
[161] *Bentley* v. *Anglican Synod of the Diocese of New Westminster*, 2009 BCSC 1608 (CanLII). Also see *Bentley* v. *Anglican Synod of the Diocese of New Westminster* [2010] BCCA 506, at: www.courts.gov.bc.ca/jdb-txt/CA/10/05/2010BCCA0506.htm (accessed 7 January 2014).

362   CANADA

jurisdiction of the ACoC. Nevertheless, the court ruled, the bishop of New Westminster also does not have the right under civil or canon law to fire the trustees of the parishes. The two sides, he said, are going to have to work out their difficulties outside the courts. An interesting aspect of this case was the Canadian courts' express rejection of the 'neutral principles of law' approach taken by the US courts as not being 'of assistance to us'. Whereas the US courts would defer to the principle of the free exercise of religion, and refrain from engaging in doctrinal argument, in Canada the courts would appear to feel no such constraint and will engage in adjudicating on Church matters, including property disputes, without preference for doctrine but with a forensic respect for trust law and for the right of the Canadian religious organisations to manage their affairs without recourse to doctrinal guidance from elsewhere.

Discrimination

It was in *Canada Trust Co* v. *Ontario Human Rights Commission*[162] that the judiciary first sketched out the areas in which discrimination would be compatible with both charitable status and human rights. This case required the Ontario Court of Appeal to determine whether an *inter vivos* charitable trust for educational purposes (the Leonard Foundation), established in 1923 for the provision of scholarships, but which limited recipients of such scholarships to, amongst others, 'a British Subject of the White Race and of the Christian Religion in its Protestant form',[163] contravened public policy and, if so, whether the *cy-près* doctrine could be applied to save it.[164] The trust included a statement that the 'progress of the World depends in the future, as in the past, on the maintenance of the Christian religion'. Racial and religious restrictions also limited who could participate in the management and administration of the fund. The court emphasised that, although the Leonard Foundation was privately created, it effectively acted in the public sphere by awarding scholarships to study at publicly supported educational institutions to students whose applications were

---

[162] See *Re Canada Trust Co* v. *Ontario (Human Rights Commission)*; *Re Leonard Foundation*; *Canada Trust Co* v. *Ontario Human Rights Commission* (1990) 69 DLR (4th) 321. Also see *Re Murley Estate* (1995) 130 Nfld. & PEIR 271 (Nfld. SC (TD)).

[163] *Re Canada Trust Co* v. *Ontario (Human Rights Commission)*; *Re Leonard Foundation*; *Canada Trust Co* v. *Ontario Human Rights Commission* (1990) 69 DLR (4th) 321, at p.328.

[164] Ibid., at p.326.

HUMAN RIGHTS, DISCRIMINATION & RELIGIOUS CHARITIES 363

solicited from a broad segment of the public; consequently, the Foundation acquired a public or, at least, quasi-public character.[165] It found that it was 'to expatiate the obvious' that a trust premised on notions of racism and religious superiority contravened contemporary public policy imperatives,[166] and ordered, in terms of the *cy-près* doctrine, a striking-out of all references to and restrictions regarding race, colour, creed or religion, ethnic origin and sex as they relate, *inter alia*, to those entitled to the benefits of the trust.

Significantly, Tarnopolsky J stated that scholarships could be restricted to 'women, aboriginal peoples, the physically or mentally handicapped, or other historically disadvantaged groups' and that 'Given the history and importance of bilingualism and multiculturalism in this country, restrictions on the basis of language would probably not be void as against public policy.'[167] Subsequently this view was endorsed by the CRA.[168] This approach, representing an acknowledgement by court and regulator that groups defined along these lines may have distinct needs that are most effectively and efficiently addressed by expert organisations' permitted engagement exclusively with the target community,[169] has since been adopted in a number of cases.

Proportionality

The principle of proportionality was stressed 20 years ago by Latimer CJC in *Dagenais* v. *Canadian Broadcasting Corporation*:

> When the protected rights of two individuals come into conflict ... Charter principles require a balance to be achieved that fully respects the importance of both sets of rights.[170]

In *Alberta* v. *Hutterian Brethren of Wilson Colony*,[171] the Supreme Court of Canada conspicuously relied upon a proportionality approach when determining a freedom of religion issue. The case concerned the Alberta

---

[165] Ibid., at p.333.   [166] Ibid., at p.334.

[167] *Canada Trust Co.* v. *Ontario Human Rights Commission* (1990) 69 DLR (4th) 321, at para. 98.

[168] Canada Revenue Agency CPS-024, 'Guidelines for Registering a Charity: Meeting the Public Benefit Test' (10 March 2006), s.3.2.2. See also Canada Revenue Agency, CPS-023 'Applicants Assisting Ethnocultural Communities' (30 June 2005), at para. 22.

[169] See, further, A. Parachin, 'The Definition of Charity and Public Law Equality Norms'.

[170] *Dagenais* v. *Canadian Broadcasting Corporation* [1994] 3 SCR 835, at para. 31.

[171] *Alberta* v. *Hutterian Brethren of Wilson Colony*, 2009 SCC 37; [2009] 2 SCR 567.

364   CANADA

government's decision to withdraw an exemption previously available to Hutterites (whose religious beliefs prohibited them from willingly allowing their pictures to be taken, while their doctrine of communal living required some of their members to be able to drive in order to maintain the self-sufficiency of their rural communal living) from the requirement that their driver's licences include photographs. The exemption was withdrawn because of a move to introduce a new licensing system that relied upon facial recognition data. In rejecting the applicants' claim, McLachlin CJ acknowledged the perspective of the religious claimants' rights but went on to state 'this perspective must be considered in the context of a multicultural, multi-religious society where the duty of state authorities to legislate for the general good inevitably produces conflict with individual beliefs'. This ruling would seem to carry a warning that where a religious charity operates in a way that is compatible with its beliefs but incompatible with statutory law or public policy, then it may well find that it has both placed itself on the wrong side of the right to freedom of religion and jeopardised its entitlement to charitable status. This right is one that has since been variously iterated in the human rights legislation of the provinces and it is there that much recent case law has been generated.[172]

Discrimination, same-sex marriage and religious organisations

The Ontario Court of Appeal in *Halpern* v. *Canada (Attorney General)*[173] stated that 'The dignity of persons in same-sex relationships is violated by the exclusion of same-sex couples from the institution of marriage' and consequently the 'common-law definition of marriage as "the voluntary union for life of one man and one women to the exclusion of all others" violates s.15(1) of the Charter.' In so doing it triggered a law reform process that culminated in the Civil Marriage Act 2005.

The preamble to the 2005 Act declares 'the freedom of members of religious groups to hold and declare their religious beliefs and the freedom of officials of religious groups to refuse to perform marriages that are not in accordance with their religious beliefs'. The Income Tax Act is correspondingly amended to provide that charitable status will not be

---

[172] See, for example, *Syndicat Northcrest* v. *Amselem* [2004] 2 SCR 551.

[173] *Halpern* v. *Canada (Attorney General)* [2003] OJ No. 2268, at para. 108. Note, however, the 2012 court ruling that non-Canadian same-sex couples cannot marry in Canada unless such a marriage would be lawful in their jurisdiction of origin.

HUMAN RIGHTS, DISCRIMINATION & RELIGIOUS CHARITIES 365

affected by the latter's decision to exercise that right. Current proposed amendments to the Civil Marriage Act will allow a couple's marriage to be dissolved in Canada if they have been separated for a year and living for at least one year in a state that does not recognise the validity of their marriage. This distinguishes the grounds for divorce for same-sex couples (who must only be separated) from divorce for heterosexual couples (cruelty, adultery[174] and separation for a year); also, both partners in the former case must apply. It would seem that while the 2005 Act has achieved the removal of gender discriminatory provisions in respect of grounds for marriage, it has introduced them in respect of the grounds for divorce.

Religious discrimination in practice

Once private beliefs are manifested in action they become a public matter, and when that gives rise to alleged unequal or discriminatory consequences then the matter becomes subject to examination by courts and/or regulators. This can be a complex exercise.

Unequal but not discriminatory

Religious charities that provide public benefit services, as contracted by government, are on a different legal footing from those that engage in mainstream commercial ventures because they are in receipt of public funding. Their service provision role is governed by government public policy and they are accountable to government for all aspects of staffing and service standards relating to that role.

In that context, *Heintz* v. *Christian Horizons*[175] stands as a landmark case in Canadian charity law. Although technically confined by the parameters of Ontario Human Rights legislation, the case addressed fundamental issues of relevance to such charities across Canada. It concerned Christian Horizons, a faith-based ministry, employing over 2500 people to provide housing, care and support to over 1400 developmentally disabled individuals, which it had done for more than 40 years with almost 100 per cent funding from government. Employees

---

[174] Note the decision in *P* v. *P* where the British Columbia Supreme Court ruled that the definition of adultery should include affairs between two people of the same gender (29 August 2005).
[175] *Heintz* v. *Christian Horizons*, 2008 HRTO 22; 2010 ONSC 2105 (Div. Ct).

366 CANADA

were obliged to sign a Statement of Faith and a Lifestyle and Morality Policy, requiring them to abstain from extra-marital affairs, pre-marital sex, homosexual relationships, pornography, the endorsement of alcohol or tobacco and other activities similarly viewed as immoral. This was the subject of a human rights complaint when Connie Heintz, a staff member, resigned after commencing a same-sex relationship and felt she could no longer honour her employee commitment. The decision of the Ontario Human Rights Tribunal (OHRT) at first instance was that the activities of Christian Horizon could not be interpreted as advancing religion because, in practice, these consisted wholly of social services provision on terms and conditions set and paid for by government. It took the view that faith-based bodies, serving public needs on a non-discriminatory basis, could not require employees to share their religious beliefs. As the Human Rights Commission put it:

> the issue in this case [i]s whether an organization which is effectively 100 per cent publicly funded, which provides social services on behalf of the government to the broader community, and offers those services to individuals without regard to their race, creed or cultural background, may discriminate in its hiring policies on the basis of one of the proscribed grounds in the Code.[176]

The tribunal finding, endorsed by the Divisional Court, was that because Christian Horizons provided a service to a broader community than Evangelical Christians, and because the general care of the disabled residents did not require religious observance, therefore adherence to the group's religious doctrine and prohibitions against sexual orientation were not a necessary part of the job. The particular constraint imposed on Ms Heintz was unwarranted. However, the Ontario Divisional Court in upholding the appeal stated that Christian Horizons and other similar groups could maintain a religious identity even though the people they served were not co-religionists. In an important ruling for all religious organisations in Canada, it stated that there is an entitlement to exemption from the law barring discriminatory hiring 'if they are primarily engaged in serving the interests of their religious community, where the restriction is reasonable and bona fide because of the nature of the employment'.

Arguably, however, the fact that despite being wholly public funded and operating almost exclusively as a service provider for government,

---

[176] Ibid., at para. 12.

Christian Horizons should nonetheless seek to rely on the statutory exemption clause to shield its employment practices from the normal requirements of equality and human rights law does give rise to concern. Some may question the diversion of taxpayers' revenue to subsidise the running costs of a partisan organisation, the beliefs of which many taxpayers may well prefer not to support.

Unequal but not discriminatory: contractual obligations

In *Moore v. British Columbia (Ministry of Social Services)*,[177] the presenting issue concerned an employee whose initial knowing commitment to terms and conditions of employment eventually placed her in a position of conflict between job and religious beliefs. Moore, a devout Catholic employed by the Social Services to provide family care advice and assistance, rejected a request from a client seeking assistance to have an abortion, as facilitating abortion was contrary to the tenets of Catholicism. Moore insisted that she would continue to refuse to authorise coverage for abortion, so the Ministry terminated her employment. In its defence, the Ministry argued that accommodating Moore would mean exempting her from cases involving abortions, sterilisation and contraception, causing disruption that would have been 'detrimental to service delivery'. The court ruled in favour of the respondent: by accepting a client she clearly could not serve, Moore had failed to fulfil her duty as a public servant, which was to provide services to the public without discrimination.

In *Caldwell v. St. Thomas Aquinas High School*,[178] in keeping with *Moore*, the issue again turned on the tension between terms and conditions of employment and religious beliefs. Caldwell, the applicant teacher, alleged that her dismissal from a Catholic school following her marriage to a divorced man constituted discrimination based on marital status, religion or dismissal without probable cause. From the perspective of the Catholic Church, Caldwell had knowingly disobeyed two fundamental marital rules: Catholics must marry in a Catholic church and may not marry divorced people. From the point of view of the

---

[177] *Moore v. British Columbia (Ministry of Social Services)* (1992) 17 CHRR D/426 (BCCHR).

[178] *Caldwell v. St. Thomas Aquinas High School* (1984) 6 CHRR D/2643. See also, *Sahota and Shergill v. Shri Gur Ravidass Sabha Temple*, 2008 BCHRT 269, which concerned the exclusion of members of a caste from a religious organisation representing a different caste.

368   CANADA

Catholic school, Caldwell had disregarded a BFOR, according to which Catholic teachers must model Catholicism to their students by living in strict accordance with Church doctrines. The court ruled in favour of the respondent: Catholic teachers must accept and practise the rulings of the Church both inside and outside the school; this principle was stated explicitly in her contract of employment. This rationale was subsequently echoed in *Schroen* v. *Steinbach Bible College*,[179] when the Manitoba Human Rights Commission upheld the right of a Mennonite College to dismiss a secretary who had converted to become a Mormon. She had known that adherence to the Mennonite religious principles would be an aspect of her employment, had willingly placed herself in that position and thus had no just cause for complaint. These rulings, which serve to reinforce the principle that religious compliance can be construed as a bona fide component of the terms and conditions of employment, are of considerable significance to the religious charities engaged not only in the provision of educational services such as in schools, colleges and universities, but also to those involved in health and social care.

Unequal and discriminatory: restricting employment opportunities

As alleged breaches of this right tend to occur most usually in relation to accessing or using services and facilities, the province-level statutes specifically prohibit discrimination in that context. Thus, typically, in Quebec, s.1 of Ontario's Human Rights Code states that:

> Every person has a right to equal treatment with respect to services, goods and facilities, without discrimination because of race, ancestry, place of origin, colour, ethnic origin, citizenship, creed, sex, orientation, age, marital status, family status or disability.[180]

In Ontario, the leading case of *Heintz* v. *Christian Horizons* (see, further, above) provides a good illustration of the approach adopted by the judiciary when faced with work-based discrimination.[181] The finding that the job Ms Heintz was doing was not impacted by her being involved in a same-sex relationship – even though this was contrary to the

---

[179] *Schroen* v. *Steinbach Bible College* (1999) 35 CHRR D/1 (Man. Bd. Adj.).
[180] RSO 1990, c. H.19, as amended. The Code protects the right to manifest religious belief subject to limitations that are similar to those that arise under Article 9.2 of the European Convention.
[181] *Heintz* v. *Christian Horizons*, 2008 HRTO 22; 2010 ONSC 2105 (Div. Ct).

HUMAN RIGHTS, DISCRIMINATION & RELIGIOUS CHARITIES 369

accepted practices of the faith community with which she was serving, and even though she had signed her acceptance of those practices – was a strong reminder that the principle of proportionality should prevail. This decision may be viewed as being at variance with earlier decisions of the Supreme Court of Canada in *Trinity Western*[182] and *Syndicat Northcrest*,[183] which seem to indicate that the law should respect and protect a practice that serves to exemplify a sincerely held religious belief.

Unequal and discriminatory: restricting access to services

In *Brillinger* v. *Brockie*[184] an Ontario Board of Inquiry found that Brockie, a born-again Christian, had discriminated against Brillinger (and the Canadian Lesbian and Gay Archives) on the prohibited ground of sexual orientation by refusing to provide printing services to homosexuals and homosexual organisations, and ordered Brockie and his company to provide the same printing services to lesbians, gays and to organisations in existence for their benefit as they provided to others. However, on appeal the Ontario Superior Court of Justice held that the Board's order went further than was necessary and added a condition to the Board's order to the effect that the order should not require Brockie to print material of a nature that could reasonably be considered to be in direct conflict with the core elements of his religious beliefs. A judicial comment on this added caveat has noted that 'on the above approach the believer is not required to undertake action that promotes that which the essence of the belief teaches to be wrong'.[185]

In *Smith and Chymyshyn* v. *Knights of Columbus and others*,[186] the tribunal found that the respondent's hall did meet the definition of a 'service' or 'facility' and gave short shrift to the respondent's argument that in the light of their belief system and their own right to freedom of religion they could refuse to rent that hall for the celebration of a gay marriage. As this was a matter governed by specific legislation – *viz* the

---

[182] See *Trinity Western University* v. *British Columbia College of Teachers* [2001] 1 SCR 772.

[183] See *Syndicat Northcrest* v. *Amselem*, 2004 SCC 47; [2004] 2 SCR 551.

[184] *Brillinger* v. *Brockie* (No. 3) (2000) 37 CHRR D/15.

[185] See *Christian Institute and Others* v. *Office of First Minister and Deputy First Minister*, Neutral Citation no. [2007] NIQB 66, *per* Weatherup J, at para. 88.

[186] 2005 BCHRT 544 (CanLII). See also *Whiteley* v. *Osprey Media Publishing*, 2010 HRTO 2152 (CanLII).

370 CANADA

Civil Marriage Act,[187] which extended the meaning of marriage to include same-sex relationships under Canadian federal law – the tribunal had little difficulty in finding in favour of the applicants and held that they had been wrongly denied accommodation on the basis of their sexual orientation. This ruling was very much in keeping with the principle established earlier by the Ontario Court of Appeal in *Halpern* v. *Canada (Attorney General)*.[188] In the more recent but not dissimilar case of *Eadie and Thomas* v. *Riverbend Bed and Breakfast and others*[189] a gay couple had reserved a room in bed-and-breakfast accommodation offered by a Christian couple in their own home, but when the husband learned that the couple were gay, the booking was cancelled. Again, the tribunal ruled in favour of the gay couple who had been denied a service.

The case of *Trinity Western University* v. *British Columbia College of Teachers*[190] illustrates the difficulties that can arise when the provision of an education service conflicts with religious principle. In 1995 the British Columbia College of Teachers (BCCT) first refused to accredit the Teacher Training Program at Trinity Western University (TWU), a private institution associated with the Evangelical Free Church of Canada. The TWU had been training teachers for 13 years and its graduates taught in British Columbia public schools. The refusal was based on a TWU requirement that its students sign a Community Standards Contract signalling their condemnation of homosexual behaviour. The BCCT determined that graduates of this private institution would not be adequately prepared to provide educational services without discrimination in British Columbia's diverse public school classrooms. The TWU complained that the BCCT did not have the jurisdiction to refuse accreditation on this ground, as it was an infringement of their right to freedom of religion and association. The British Columbia Supreme Court determined that the BCCT had acted wrongfully, and issued an order of mandamus obliging the BCCT to accredit the TWU. The British Columbia Court of Appeal upheld this decision. The majority of the Supreme Court of Canada upheld both rulings, explaining that the existence of the Community Standards Contract, signed by the students, was insufficient to support the conclusion of the BCCT that

[187] SC 2005, c. 33.
[188] *Halpern* v. *Canada (Attorney General)* [2003] OJ No. 2268, at para. 108.
[189] *Eadie and Thomas* v. *Riverbend Bed and Breakfast and others* (No. 2), 2012 BCHRT 247.
[190] *Trinity Western University* v. *British Columbia College of Teachers* (2001) 39 CHRR D/ 357, 2001 SCC 31.

TWU graduates would behave in a discriminatory manner towards future homosexual students and there was no evidence that this in fact had ever occurred. Delivering the majority verdict, Iacobucci and Bastarache JJ noted that 'for better or worse, tolerance of divergent beliefs is a hallmark of a democratic society'.[191] The Supreme Court was at pains to draw a distinction between religious practice and religious belief, asserting that 'the freedom to hold beliefs is broader than the freedom to act on them'.[192]

Unequal but 'positive action'

In Canada, as elsewhere, the relevant legislation carries an express exemption for charities and charitable donor gifts – from the strictures of human rights provisions – in circumstances where these are dedicated to the benefit of those groups identified as likely to suffer discrimination. An exemption the importance of which was stressed by Justice Tarnopolsky when he declared, as mentioned above, that scholarships could be restricted to 'women, aboriginal peoples, the physically or mentally handicapped, or other historically disadvantaged groups'.[193]

This privilege was triggered by the concerns of religious groups as to whether churches would be required to conduct same-sex weddings after the federal government legalised civil same-sex marriages. So, when the Civil Marriage Act,[194] which extended the meaning of marriage to include same-sex relationships under Canadian federal law and inserted section 149.1(6.21) into the Income Tax Act,[195] was introduced it provided that charities organised for the advancement of religion would not have their charitable registration revoked solely because they or any of their members exercised freedom of conscience and religion in relation

---

[191] Ibid., at p.44.

[192] *Trinity Western University* v. *British Columbia College of Teachers* [2001] 1 SCR 772, at paras 36–37. As Parachin has noted, this dichotomy between religious belief and religious practice has been referred to in other decisions of the Supreme Court, citing: *Amselem*, supra., para. 187; *B. (R.)* v. *Children's Aid Society of Metropolitan Toronto* [1995] 1 SCR 315, at para. 226; *Ross* v. *New Brunswick School District No. 15* [1996] 1 SCR 825, at para. 72. Also those of the lower courts: *Baldasaro* v. *Canada* [2003] FCJ No. 1272 (FC); *Brockie* v. *Ontario (Human Rights Commission)* [2002] OJ No. 2375, para. 42; and *Hall (Litigation guardian of)* v. *Powers* (2002) 59 OR (3d) 423, para. 27 (see, further, Parachin, 'The Definition of Charity and Public Law Equality Norms').

[193] *Canada Trust Co. v. Ontario Human Rights Commission* (1990) 69 DLR (4th) 321, at para. 98.

[194] SC 2005, c. 33.   [195] RSC 1985, (5th Supp.), c. 1, as amended.

372 CANADA

to the meaning of marriage. The issue, however, was never going to be confined to same-sex marriages. The subsequent overspill into associated areas of tension between religious beliefs and human rights, with religious bodies seeking to correspondingly extend their exemption privilege, has continued to frustrate the efforts of judiciary and regulators to build a consistent and coherent body of related jurisprudence. It may at least be said that the exemptions do not provide a blanket *carte blanche* for charities to simply ignore the human rights dimension. Rather, they are expected to follow the example set by the judiciary in *Hutterian Brethren*[196] and adopt a proportionate approach.

Conclusion

The difficulties involved in reconciling the twin principles confidently asserted in the Preamble to the Charter of Rights and Freedoms, 'Whereupon Canada is founded upon principles that recognize the supremacy of God and the rule of law', have become only too apparent in the burgeoning body of related case law. What, in 1982, may have seemed like a safe nod to the traditional pillars of a democratic state has rebounded 30 years later to challenge judiciary and regulators alike, as they field a constant flow of litigious variations on the tension between sincerely held religious beliefs and statutorily guaranteed human rights. Such beliefs, prompting individuals or organisations to transcend the containment of private commitment and extend principles into practice are most likely to conflict with Charter rights and freedoms when they are linked to issues of sex and gender. Most frequently these tend to involve: same-sex marriages; abortion services; and a range of gay,[197] lesbian and transgender[198] lifestyle choices, or the consequences thereof. For religious charities, bound to exclusively pursue their charitable purposes and satisfy the public benefit test, the risks in becoming embroiled in such issues are mainly twofold: any undue narrowing of access to services, or in type of service made available, or in the terms and conditions under which staff are employed, and they may have to forego charitable status; in addition, any compromises made to religious

---

[196] *Alberta* v. *Hutterian Brethren of Wilson Colony*, 2009 SCC 37; [2009] 2 SCR 567.

[197] See *Egan* v. *Canada* (1995) 2 SCR 513, where a statutory definition of 'spouse' which excluded homosexual partners was deemed to discriminate against a homosexual couple.

[198] See, for example, *Vancouver Rape Relief Society* v. *Nixon*, 2005 BCCA 601.

CONCLUSION 373

principle places at risk their affiliation to that religious body, the loyalty of their constituent beneficiaries and their capacity to continue advancing religion. While the secular difficulties of the first set may be eased by statutory exemption privileges, they cannot address the second.

The approach adopted by the judges of the Canadian Supreme Court would essentially seem to be one of accommodation: the greater interest of consolidating a pluralist society requires compromises to be reached between adherents of religious beliefs and the bearers of infringed human rights. As the Chief Justice has explained:

> in Canadian society there is the value we place upon multiculturalism and diversity, which brings with it a commitment to freedom of religion. But the beliefs and actions manifested when this freedom is granted can collide with conventional legal norms. This clash of forces demands a resolution from the courts.[199]

The courts must then 'carve out a space within the rule of law in which religious commitment and claims to authority – sometimes wholly at odds with legal values and authority – can manifest and flourish'.[200]

---

[199] B. McLachlin, 'Freedom of Religion and the Rule of Law: A Canadian Perspective', in D. Farrow (ed.), *Recognizing Religion in a Secular Society: Essays in Pluralism, Religion, and Public Policy*, McGill-Queen's University Press, Montreal and Kingston, 2004, at pp.12–34.

[200] Ibid., at p.19.

9

Australia

Introduction

Historically, the nonprofit sector led by religious charities has been left with considerable freedom and responsibility for delivering basic social services. Now, as Australia's new nationwide regulatory system for the nonprofit sector beds down, the actual success of the long process that produced this outcome has itself raised the question as to whether it might be feasible to repeat the process to address other matters of nationwide importance.

This chapter begins by examining the formative years in the development of the Australian Church–State relationship, considers jurisdiction profile data, identifies the primary religions, traces the emergence and evolving social role of religious charities and considers the issue of government funding for such charities. It then outlines the law, the administrative agencies, the charity law reform process and contemporary changes in the regulatory framework for charities and religious entities. The importance of the 'public benefit test', together with the functions of the Australian Charities and Not-for-Profits Commission (ACNC) and the Australian Taxation Office, in relation to the work of religious charities, are discussed. The definition of 'religion' and the role of doctrines, the significance of a theistic as opposed to a philosophical approach, the meaning of 'religious beliefs' and their manifestation and the different ways of 'advancing' religion are explored. The chapter then focuses on public policy constraints on the discretionary remit of a religiously inspired charitable purpose. This leads into the crux of the chapter, which deals with case law illustrations of the difficulties currently being experienced by religious charities and the new regulator as they relate to a legal environment now structured by a reformed charity, human rights and prohibitions against discrimination.

Church, State and religious charities

The lack of population homogeneity, coupled with a tradition of local communities being strongly self-reliant relative to the more distant and less intrusive government, perhaps resulted in Australians becoming accustomed to looking to their neighbourhoods and to their Churches, rather than to the State, when it came to public benefit service provision. Paradoxically, however, Australia also has a tradition of federal government providing national welfare schemes: it was one of the first countries to introduce a widow's pension, a universal pension system and a generous national health insurance scheme. Some states, such as Queensland, have long had a free hospital service; and in all states and territories there is an efficient government-funded school system.

Historical background: the Church–State relationship

It would be difficult to overstate the 'importance of religion as the midwife to many prominent third sector endeavours in the community services industry'.[1] Up until the Second World War the availability of such health care, education and poverty relief services as existed was due to the efforts of local community-based charities, almost all of which were religious. Subsequently, much of the delivery of such services has remained with religious charities with funding from state and federal governments.

Colonialism and religion

As a British colony, the early settlements in Australia were naturally dominated by British cultural traditions. The administrators, armed forces and missionaries brought with them their allegiance to the Established Church of England which, initially, became part of the ruling institutional framework. The occupants of the large penal colonies, on the other hand, were very often Irish or criminal and seditious elements of English society, and in both cases more likely to belong to the Roman Catholic Church. The foundations of the Australian nation, therefore, reflected to a considerable degree the social class distinction of its early settlers as accurately represented by their respective religious affiliations.[2]

---

[1] M. Lyons, *Third Sector: The Contribution of Nonprofit and Co-operative Enterprises in Australia*, Allen & Unwin, Crows Nest, NSW, 2001, at p.35.
[2] See, further, R. C. Thompson, *Religion in Australia: A History* (2nd edn), Oxford University Press, Oxford, 2002, pp.3–5.

376   AUSTRALIA

This religious divide became more pronounced in the mid nineteenth century in a flare-up over education, which was to rumble on for many years. The strictly secular basis for childhood education, initially State funded but supplemented with a religious input from visiting Anglican and Catholic clergy, was disrupted in 1848 with the introduction of some denominational schools. As the Anglican religious charities seemed poised to colonise the school system, some administrators chose to cease funding faith-based schools. In 1851 the colony of South Australia voted to abolish State funding for religion, an initiative followed in 1879 by New South Wales, while in 1872 the Victorians introduced 'the most secular school system in Australia', with religious education taking place after-hours by permission of local boards.

Religious charities were also prominent in other areas of public benefit services. Prior to federation, as Lucas and Robinson have pointed out, social services were almost entirely delivered by charities, most of which were religious-based. For example, in New South Wales the Benevolent Society was established in 1813 as the first charity in Australia. The men who founded it had mainly served as missionaries of the London Missionary Society and sought to relieve poverty and distress in the process of spreading the gospel. In fairly quick succession district nursing services started (1820), asylums opened for the poor, blind, aged and infirm (1821), maternity hospitals (1866) and the first Women's Hospital in Australia commenced (1901). The Irish Sisters of Charity arrived in 1838, later opening St Vincent's Hospital in Sydney. The Society of St Vincent de Paul started its services in Sydney in 1881. Catholic religious orders such as the St John of God Sisters, Mercy Sisters and Little Company of Mary founded hospitals and hospices throughout Australia in the later part of the nineteenth century.

In 1901 the constituent colonies joined to form the federation of Australia, underpinned by the Constitution in which the limited references to religion and related rights are to be found in s.116.

Building a modern Church–State relationship

Wartime Australia was an interesting period for the Church–State relationship. Whereas the main Christian religions saw it as their duty, as might be expected, to assist the State by joining the armed forces to defeat its enemies, this was not a view shared by other minority religious groups such as Jehovah's Witnesses. Because, on religious grounds, they refused to bear arms, they suffered considerable State persecution

CHURCH, STATE AND RELIGIOUS CHARITIES 377

involving the prohibition of their organisation, banning of their doctrines and confiscation of their property.[3]

It was not until after the Second World War and into the second half of the twentieth century that State provision of social services really developed. As Lucas and Robinson have explained, public benefit service provision then developed quite differently in comparison to equivalent provision in countries such as the United Kingdom and the United States:

> In Australia, government largely took the view that there were already existing charities delivering these services and that it would be more effective and efficient if the increased government funding of these areas occurred through government subsidy of those existing services rather than by a replication of them through the creation or growth of government departments. This decision has had a profound impact on the character, nature and size of charities and nonprofit organisations in Australia compared to the United Kingdom, or, indeed, the USA. Christian charities dominate in Australia in a way that they do not elsewhere.[4]

Such charities, by virtue of their size and longevity, have managed to remain true to their roots as local service providers while also acquiring a nationwide brief: the Brotherhood of St Laurence, based in Melbourne, is a good example; Hammond's Social Services, which had its roots in the Anglican Church, became one of the largest social service providers in Sydney. Now, 23 of the 25 largest Australian charities based on income are Christian. Excluding those focused on education, almost all are engaged in social service delivery, and the number that are Christian is still very high at 19 out of the top 25. In comparison, only three of the largest 25 charities in the United Kingdom are Christian, and one other – Barnardo's – has a Christian heritage. Christian organisations are almost entirely absent at the top of the UK nonprofit sector. Even in the top 50 organisations by income the Christian presence is still less than 20 per cent. However, although government has largely continued to work through the established network of religious service providers, this approach has been diluted in recent years due to factors such as: the declining resources and staff of religious orders available to maintain levels of such provision; the need to extend services to new rural communities; and the inroads on market share made by entrepreneurial business ventures.

---

[3] See, P. Radan, D. Meyerson and R. F. Croucher, *Law and Religion: God, the State and the Common Law*, Routledge, London, 2005, at pp.80–82.

[4] See B. Lucas and A. Robinson, 'Religion as a Head of Charity', in M. McGregor-Lowndes and K. O'Halloran (eds), *Modernising Charity Law*, Elgar Publishing, Cheltenham, 2010, at pp.188–190.

378   AUSTRALIA

Religion(s)

Whereas a century ago almost all religious adherents subscribed to either Anglicanism or Catholicism, together with one or two other minority religions, the 2006 national census revealed the religious affiliation of the Australian population to consist of: Protestants (27.4 per cent) (Anglican 18.7 per cent; Uniting Church, 5.7 per cent; Presbyterian and Reformed, 3 per cent), Catholics (25.8 per cent), Eastern Orthodox (2.7 per cent), other Christian (7.9 per cent), Buddhist (2.1 per cent), Muslim (1.7 per cent), other (2.4 per cent), unspecified (11.3 per cent), none (18.7 per cent). By 2011 the ABS census revealed that: Hinduism was the fastest-growing religion; Christianity remained the most common at 61.1 per cent; the number reporting 'no religion' increased significantly, from 18.7 per cent in 2006 to 22.3 per cent in 2011.[5] The large numbers of immigrants from Asia, particularly from Cambodia and Vietnam, have made Buddhism the third largest religion in Australia.

Secularisation

In the 2006 census, 18.7 per cent of Australians described themselves as having 'no religion'. This was 3 per cent higher than in the 2001 census, and was the largest recorded growth in the total number of any religious option in the census.[6] Interestingly, the number of people responding to the religious affiliation question with an answer that indicated a possible affiliation with 'theism' or 'New Age' had almost doubled between 1996 and 2006. By 2011 census data showed that the percentage of people declaring no religion had risen to 22.3 per cent. The secularisation trend is supported by other data such as: church attendance rates, which are among the lowest in the world and continue to decline;[7] and the increase in non-church weddings from 41.3 per cent in 1988 to 70.1 per cent of all marriages in 2011.[8] Whether this is due to increased prosperity, disillusionment resulting from child abuse scandals involving clergy,

---

[5] See the Australian Bureau of Statistics (ABS), Census of Population and Housing data for 2011, at: www.abs.gov.au/websitedbs/censushome.nsf/home/CO-61?opendocument&navpos=620 (accessed 9 January 2014).

[6] See I. McAllister, 'Religious Change and Secularization: The Transmission of Religious Values in Australia' (1988) 49:3 *Sociology of Religion* 249.

[7] See, for example, National Church Life Survey, Media release, 28 February 2004. See, further, at: www.ncls.org.au/default.aspx?sitemapid=2106 (accessed 9 January 2014).

[8] The 2011 Census of Population and Housing data released in 2012 by the Australian Bureau of Statistics (ABS). See, further, at: www.abs.gov.au (accessed 9 January 2014).

generational attitudes, the attraction of humanist or 'New Age' type organisations or other factors, is uncertain and speculative, but Australia is undoubtedly becoming a more secular nation.

An 'established' religion

In this modern democratic State, situated at the interface of Christian and Eastern religions, there is no indication of any appetite for an 'established' religion. However, although the Australian Constitution closely follows the US model, there is no equivalent to the required separation of Church and State that exists in the First Amendment of the US Constitution.[9] The protections relating to religion are as stated in s.116:

> The Commonwealth shall not make any law for establishing any religion, or for imposing any religious observance, or for prohibiting the free exercise of any religion, and no religious test shall be required as a qualification for any office or public trust under the Commonwealth.

Allegedly based on the wording of the First Amendment, the Australian protective clauses are cursorily stated and have generated very little related case law, unlike their US counterpart. The limitations of s.116 are such that, as Sir Ninian Stephen J once said, it 'cannot readily be viewed as a repository of some broad statement of principle concerning the separation of Church and State, from which may be distilled the detailed consequences of such separation'.[10]

The use of a 'religious test'[11] arose in *Church of Scientology Inc* v. *Woodward*,[12] which concerned the advice allegedly given to government ministers by the Australian Security Intelligence Organisation (ASIO) claiming that certain persons employed or seeking employment in the Commonwealth posed a security risk due to their membership of the Church of Scientology. The plaintiff argued that in effect this amounted to the application of a 'religious test' by the ASIO. The court dismissed the application on a technicality of defective wording. Subsequently, in *Attorney-General (Vic) ex rel Black* v. *Commonwealth*,[13] Stephen J

---

[9] See P. Parkinson, *Tradition and Change in Australian Law* (2nd edn), LBC Information Services, Sydney, 2001, at pp.132–134.

[10] *Attorney-General (Vic) (Ex rel Black)* v. *Commonwealth* (1981) 146 CLR 559.

[11] See, further, L. Beck, 'The Constitutional Prohibition on Religious Tests' (2011) 35 *Melbourne University Law Review* 323.

[12] *Church of Scientology Inc* v. *Woodward* (1979) 154 CLR 79. See also *Sykes* v. *Cleary* (1992) 176 CLR 77.

[13] *Attorney-General (Vic) ex rel Black* v. *Commonwealth* (1981) 146 CLR 559, at p.605.

380 AUSTRALIA

seemed satisfied that the religious test clause 'prohibits the imposition, whether by law or otherwise, of religious tests for the holding of Commonwealth office'. In coming to a majority decision in that case, that indirect government funding of religious schools did not breach the 'establishment' clause of s.116, there was consensus among six of the seven judges that s.116 differed from the corresponding US First Amendment clause in that it did not presume to represent a liberty right but was limited to suppressing any initative by the Commonwealth government to impose a law giving preference to one religion or church.

In any event, the s.116 protections have not impeded the parliamentary standing orders from requiring a full recitation of the Lord's Prayer by the Speaker of the House of Representatives and the President of the Senate at the commencement of each day's business, a practice that is plainly Christian, overtly Protestant, arguably disrespectful of the rights to all other religious adherents and non-believers, but authorised by the highest authority in the land.[14]

Equality of religions

In *Canterbury Municipal Council* v. *Moslem Alawy Society Ltd*,[15] McHugh JA said: 'the preservation of religious equality has always been a matter of fundamental concern to the people of Australia and finds its place in the Constitution, s.116'. That the courts are not in a position to assess the validity or invalidity of the doctrines or tenets of any religion, or to differentiate between them, was established by the High Court of Australia in *Church of the New Faith* v. *Commissioner of Payroll Tax*.[16] As Murphy J then commented:

> The truth or falsity of religions is not the business of officials or the courts. If each purported religion had to show that its doctrines were true, then all might fail.[17]

However, there is a school of thought which argues that the preferential treatment of one religion over another is permissible providing it falls short of seeking the establishment of that religion. In practice, Australia's

---

[14] See, further, G.V. Puig and S. Tudor, 'To the Advancement of Thy Glory? A Constitutional and Policy Critique of Parliamentary Prayers' (2009) 20 *Public Law Review* 56.
[15] *Canterbury Municipal Council* v. *Moslem Alawy Society Ltd.* (1985) 1 NSWLR 525.
[16] *Church of the New Faith* v. *Commissioner of Payroll Tax* (1983) 154 CLR 120.
[17] Ibid., *per* Murphy J, at p.150.

many Churches and religions are all treated equally, at least for tax purposes, by the government.

Religious organisations and the nonprofit sector

Of the 600,000 nonprofits that constitute the sector, the ACNC website estimates that by August 2013 some 58,891 were registered as charities – a considerable increase since October 2010.[18] Of all nonprofits with charitable status, religious organisations are the most numerous and also tend to be the largest, wealthiest and longest-established entities within the sector. Moreover, many large, well-known nonprofits of a seemingly secular standing are in fact owned by religious organisations. Government has largely continued its practice of ensuring the delivery of certain public services by working through the established network of religious service providers.

Religious charities

In Australia, the singular role played by religion, the Churches and religious organisations in the social infrastructure – often the only provider of community services such as education and health care – is a legacy from the colonial era. Recognition that the secular arm of religion in effect functioned as a public service provider was sufficient grounds for tax exemption. As Chia and O'Connell have noted:

> the exemption from income tax for religious institutions is long standing in Australia as elsewhere. It has not depended on advancement of religion being part of charity but rather has stood on its own. The effect is currently to exempt all income whether from business activities, investment or from disposals of property.[19]

There has been considerable controversy as to whether religious bodies should be entitled to be registered and treated as a charity:[20] if they are in receipt of government grants; or if they are endorsed as deductible gift

---

[18] See, further, Australian Charities and Not-for-profits Commission at: www.acnc.gov.au (accessed 9 January 2014).

[19] J. Chia and A. O'Connell, 'The Advancement (or Retreat?) of Religion as a Head of Charity: A Historical Perspective', in J. Tiley (ed.), *Studies in the History of Tax Law*, Volume 6, Hart Publishing, Oxford, 2013, at p.23.

[20] See, e.g. the findings in G. Bouma, D. Cahill, H. Dellal and A. Zwartz, 'Freedom of religion and belief in 21st century Australia', Research report, Australian Human Rights Commission, 2011, at pp.25, 38–39, 55.

382   AUSTRALIA

recipients in respect of the whole of their activities.[21] As the new regulatory regime takes over, the observations made by Kirby J in his strongly worded dissenting judgment in the High Court decision of *Commissioner of Taxation* v. *Word Investments Limited* may well cast a shadow over the future approach to religious charities:

> Charitable and religious institutions contribute to society in various ways. However, such institutions sometimes perform functions that are offensive to the beliefs, values and consciences of other taxpayers. This is especially so in the case of charitable institutions with religious purposes or religious institutions. These institutions can undertake activities that are offensive to many taxpayers who subscribe to different religious beliefs or who have no religious beliefs. Although the Parliament may provide specific exemptions, as a generally applicable principle it is important to spare general taxpayers from the obligation to pay income tax effectively to support or underwrite the activities of religious ... organisations with which they disagree.[22]

His Honour's comments were directed to a matter of statutory interpretation, but they also strongly imply that tax exemptions in favour of religious groups should be supported by a convincing public benefit rationale.

Religious umbrella bodies

Catholic Social Services Australia is the Church's peak national body for the delivery of social services, with 70 member organisations, it represents Catholic religious entities involved in government contracting. Uniting Care is the peak body for the Uniting Church of Australia, which is one of the largest providers of community services in Australia, delivering services to over two million people each year with an annual turnover in excess of $2 billion and employing 35,000 staff and 24,000 volunteers nationally. The National Council of Churches in Australia (NCCA), an ecumenical organisation that coordinates most Australian

---

[21] A deductible gift recipient (DGR) is an organisation that is entitled to receive income tax-deductible gifts and deductible contributions. Charities can receive tax deductible gifts provided the organisation is a deductible gift recipient. Gift deductibility is restricted to a small subset of approximately 27,028 charitable bodies, half of which are Public Benefit Institutions (see, further, *The Perpetual Trustee Co. Ltd.* v. *Federal Commissioner of Taxation* [1931] 45 CLR 224) that focus on directing assistance to the poor and 'helpless'.

[22] *Commissioner of Taxation* v. *Word Investments Limited* (2008) 236 CLR 204, 248 [110] (Kirby J). See also, 249–250 [112]–[116].

CHURCH, STATE AND RELIGIOUS CHARITIES   383

Christian churches, is linked to the World Council of Churches. It succeeded the Australian Council of Churches (ACC) in 1994.

Government funding: the sector and religious charities

In 2010 the ACOSS Community Sector Survey found that 69.6 per cent
of sector funding was from government. As the Productivity Commission
comments, the picture is one of 'government engagement with the sector
primarily as a vehicle for service delivery'.[23]

Government funding of religious charities: the policy

Unlike government policy in the United Kingdom, in Australia the
government has never sought to supplant the well-established public
benefit service provision of religious charities: the policy has consistently
been one of working in partnership with them, maintaining their role
with financial support. This has been specifically continued into the new
regulatory regime by the inclusion of a provision stating: 'Funding
charity-like government entities does not prevent a contributing fund
from being charitable for the purposes of Commonwealth law'.[24]

The extent of government funding directed towards religious bodies
can be on a large scale. The running costs of Hammond Care, for
example, admittedly not representative of such bodies, are very largely
met by government. The annual report of this $140 million organisation,
which proudly describes itself as a 'Catholic, independent, charity',
shows that it is 72 per cent government funded, 18 per cent fee-for-service
funded and only 3 per cent donation funded.

Government funding of religious charities with discriminatory practices

The issue of government funding being directed towards faith-based
charities generates controversy, particularly but not exclusively when
this occurs in the context of education.

In the 1950s and again in the early 1970s, the government decided to
break with its previous policy of abstaining from funding religious

---

[23] Productivity Commission Discussion Paper, *Contribution of the Not for Profit Sector*, at
p.76. See, further, at: http://acoss.org.au/images/uploads/ACOSS_analysis_and_advo
cacy_priorities.pdf (accessed 9 January 2014).
[24] See Charities Act 2013.

schools, especially Catholic schools, prompting opponents to take the question of government funding for Church schools to the High Court in *Attorney-General (vic) (Ex rel Black)* v. *Commonwealth.*[25] The plaintiffs (Defence of Government Schools organisation) sought a court order declaring that State funding of Church schools was in breach of the Constitution. The court rejected the plaintiff's petition and ruled that s.116 of the Constitution does not prevent the 'giving of aid to or encouragement of religion' and therefore could not prevent the government from providing financial assistance to schools operated by religious organisations on the same basis as that assistance was provided to other private schools. Indeed, the ruling permits the preferential treatment of one religion over another providing it falls short of the establishment of religion. Since then the advancement of any or all religion has been deemed permissible under the Constitution.

More recently, the interplay of education, religion and government funding generated further controversy, culminating in *Williams* v. *the Commonwealth of Australia.*[26] This case concerned the National School Chaplaincy Program, introduced in 2007, which uses federal money to fund school chaplaincy services to nearly 3000 schools across Australia. The chaplains are drawn from the National School Chaplaincy Association, a network of Christian chaplaincy organisations, and while they are not permitted to proselytise or evangelise, there has been considerable debate about the provision of a service that is: religious; almost exclusively Christian; and which is paid for by taxpayers, some of whom are atheists, agnostics or belong to non-Christian religions, and many of whom argue that schools should be strictly secular. Mr Williams' claim that he had a right to secure a secular education for his children was rejected by the High Court, which ruled that the case did not impact on the freedom of religion and unanimously dismissed his charge that school chaplains' religious position breached the Constitution. The 'chaplaincy issue' also refers to the long-running controversy regarding the appointment of chaplains to the armed forces. Such appointments are governed by the Defence (Personnel) Regulations 2002 (Cth), which state as a precondition for appointment that the person 'is a member of a church or faith group approved by the Religious Advisory Committee to the

---

[25] *Attorney-General (vic) (Ex rel Black)* v. *Commonwealth* (1981) 146 CLR 559. Also known as the State Aid or Defence of Government Schools (DOGS) case.

[26] *Williams* v. *the Commonwealth of Australia* [2012] HCA 23. See, further, at: www.hcourt.gov.au/cases/case-s307/2010 (accessed 9 January 2014).

CHARITY LAW AND THE REGULATORY FRAMEWORK 385

services'. This, clearly being a 'religious test', has triggered debate as to whether it can be s.116 compliant. So, for example, as in *Kruger* v. *Commonwealth*,[27] the question arises as to whether non-Christians or atheists, caught between the Regulations and s.116, are thus being unfairly treated.

Controversy has also focused on matters such as government funding of faith-based health facilities that refuse to provide vasectomy services on religious grounds and to the Wesley Mission which, on the same grounds, rejected an application from a same-sex prospective adoptive couple in the *OV and OW* case.[28]

Charity law and the regulatory framework

Essentially, the law governing contemporary charities and their activities is derived from the English Charitable Uses Act 1601,[29] has remained true to its common law origins and, with some notable exceptions, generally adopts and follows UK case law developments.[30] The main point of difference has been that in Australia, until November 2012, the determination of both charitable status and eligibility for tax exemption rested with the Revenue agency, the Australian Taxation Office (ATO).

Legislation

As was pointed out in the recent Scoping Study, 'there are more than 178 pieces of Commonwealth, state or territory legislation that involve 19 separate agencies regularly determining the charitable purpose or

---

[27] *Kruger* v. *Commonwealth* (1997) 190 CLR 1, 161.

[28] *OV* v. *QZ (No 2)* [2008] NSWADT 115; *Member of the Board of the Wesley Mission Council* v. *OV and OW (No 2)* [2009] NSWADTAP 57; *OV & OW* v. *Members of the Board of the Wesley Mission Council* [2010] NSWCA 155.

[29] 43 Eliz. I, c.4. This has been repealed with reservations that it will not affect the general law of charity in the Australian Capital Territory: Imperial Acts Application Act 1986 (ACT) s.4(5), New South Wales: Imperial Acts Application Act 1969 (NSW) s.8, and Queensland: Trusts Act 1973 s.103(1). It is not in force in Victoria, but remains in force in the other jurisdictions.

[30] Not always: the ruling in *Gilmore* v. *Coates* [1949] AC 426 (HL) to the effect that a 'closed' religious order could not be charitable was not followed in Australia, and neither did *McGovern* v. *Attorney General* [1982] 1 Ch. 321 nor *Bowman* v. *Secular Society Ltd.* [1907] SALR 190 ever find specific approval in Australia; while the ruling in *Aid/Watch Incorporated* v. *Commissioner of Taxation* [2010] HCA 42; [2009] FCAFC 128 departed significantly from established principles in UK case law.

status of an entity'.[31] However, in practice the legal framework for the sector has consisted mainly of: the common law, governing charities; the Income Tax Assessment Act 1997[32] (as amended), which continues to apply to charities and all other nonprofits; and sundry specialised legislation such as the Corporations Act 2001, which applies to companies limited by guarantee and is supplemented in each state by an association incorporation statute. This will continue until the new nationwide regime for regulating nonprofits is wholly in place.

The charity regulator

The Australian Charities and Not-for-profits Commission Act 2013 and the Australian Charities and Not-for-profits Commission (Consequential and Transitional) Act 2013 enabled the Australian Charities and Not for Profit Commission (ACNC), the new regulator, to commence on 2 December 2012.[33] This national agency now carries responsibility for regulating all charities wishing to avail of federal tax exemptions, including religious institutions, but is intended in due course to extend its remit to the entire Australian nonprofit sector. The Commissioner, appointed by the government and reporting to parliament through the Assistant Treasurer, has sole responsibility for determining charitable and public benevolent institution (PBI) status,[34] and for the health and promotion of charities. The Australian Taxation Office, which by default had until November 2012 been the nonprofit regulator at the Commonwealth level, is transferring its role of determining charitable status and supervising charities to the ACNC, but will still be responsible for determining eligibility for income tax exemption and associated concessions (often called Tax Concession Charity status) and Deductible Gift Recipient (DGR) status. This reserved responsibility is significant. It includes, for

---

[31] See the Treasury, *Scoping Study for a National Notforprofit Regulator: Consultation Paper*, Commonwealth of Australia, January 2011, at para. 33.

[32] In conjunction with the Tax Laws Amendment (2005 Measures No. 3) Act 2005.

[33] See further at the ACNC website: www.acnc.gov.au (accessed 9 January 2014).

[34] A 'public benevolent institution' as defined in *The Perpetual Trustee Co. Ltd.* v. *Federal Commissioner of Taxation* [1931] 45 CLR 224, *per* Starke J, at p.232, is an 'institution organized for the relief of poverty, sickness, destitution or helplessness' and qualifies for donation deductions. Although all PBIs are charities, only about one-third of charities meet this narrower definition.

CHARITY LAW AND THE REGULATORY FRAMEWORK   387

example, the payroll tax exemption,[35] which is available to all religious institutions, all public benevolent institutions and to nonprofits if they have a sole or dominant charitable, benevolent, philanthropic or patriotic purpose and the employees are engaged exclusively in work of a religious, charitable, benevolent, philanthropic or patriotic nature for the institution or nonprofit organisation.[36]

However, the change of government in 2013 brought with it a change in approach towards the proposed new regulatory regime which has left much of the above in doubt. As the new coalition government has a declared intention to repeal the Charities Act after 1 July 2014, it remains to be seen whether once again the Australian law reform process will unravel at the final stage.[37]

Charity law

The Charities Act 2013, effective from January 1 2014, states in s.5 that 'An entity is a charity if it satisfies the following criteria: it is not-for-profit; it has all charitable purposes (other than ancillary or incidental purposes that further or aid the charitable purpose) that are for the public benefit; it does not have disqualifying purposes; and it is not an individual, a political party or a government entity.' Moreover, 'an entity cannot be charitable simply because it is controlled by another entity that is charitable. It is the purpose of the entity itself that must be charitable.' It is important to remember, however, that 'this Act only has Commonwealth application . . . the state laws and common law continue to apply in a non-Commonwealth context'.[38]

---

[35] See, further, *A Protocol for Payroll Tax Harmonisation between Jurisdictions* (2010) at: www.payrolltax.gov.au/harmonisation/2010-harmonisation-joint-protocol (accessed 9 January 2014).

[36] See, e.g. Payroll Tax Act 2007 (Vic) s.48.

[37] As Kevin Andrews, Minister for Social Services, stated in a speech on 4 December 2013 to the National Disability Services Conference:

> the Government has committed to abolishing the Australian Charities and Not-for-Profits Commission, with repeal legislation to be introduced into Parliament next year. In the interim the government is considering what interim measures are available to it in order to begin winding down the Commission's operations.

See, further, at: http://kevinandrews.com.au/media/address-to-the-national-disability-services-ceo-conference (accessed 9 January 2014).

[38] Author acknowledges with thanks the advice of Professor Myles McGregor-Lowndes on this and on the above matter (personal communication, 15 December 2013).

388   AUSTRALIA

Basically, as before, whether or not a body can be defined as a 'charity' is a matter determined with regard to its primary or dominant object as ascertained by reference to the objects as stated in its memorandum of association or other constituent documents and by consideration of its activities.[39] For example, in *Congregational Union of New South Wales* v. *Thistlethwayte*,[40] a religious association had objects which when examined independently were both charitable and non-charitable. The non-charitable objects were maintaining philanthropic agencies, and preserving civil and religious liberty. However, when viewed in the context of the constitution as a whole, the court found that the offending objects were ancillary to the appellant's main object to advance religion.

The 'religious institution' test

A body is regarded as a 'religious institution' if: its objects and activities reflect its character as a body instituted for the promotion of some religious object; and the beliefs and practices of the members of that body constituted a religion.[41] A 'religious institution' is not confined to the major religions such as Christianity, Islam, Judaism and Buddhism – it extends also to religions less well known in Australia, such as Taoism. Private schools, private universities and residential university colleges established or conducted by religious institutions generally, if constituted as separate entities, are not religious institutions for the purposes of the Income Tax Assessment Act (ITAA) and the Fringe Benefits Tax Assessment Act (FBTAA). That question must be determined having regard to the primary or dominant object of the body as ascertained by reference to the objects as stated in its memorandum of association or other constituent documents and by consideration of its activities.[42] Additionally, community care entities established by Churches to give effect to the 'community' aspects of the Church's ministry may also fail the 'religious institution' test unless their activities, objects and purposes remain predominantly religious in character. If such an entity drifts too far into 'secular' activities, such that the religious character fails to be predominant, it may not satisfy the test. On the other hand, seminaries, theological colleges and Bible colleges may qualify, as it is

---

[39] See *Commissioner for ACT Revenue Collections* v. *Council of the Dominican Sisters of Australia*, 91 ATC 4602; (1991) 22 ATR 213.
[40] *Congregational Union of New South Wales* v. *Thistlethwayte* (1952) 87 CLR 375.
[41] See ATO, Taxation Ruling TR 92/17, at: www.ag.gov.au/cca (accessed 9 January 2014).
[42] See *Commissioner for ACT Revenue Collections* v. *Council of the Dominican Sisters of Australia*, 91 ATC 4602; (1991) 22 ATR 213.

CHARITY LAW AND THE REGULATORY FRAMEWORK   389

likely that the primary or dominant object of such a body is religious in character and it will therefore be treated as a religious institution for the purposes of the ITAA and the FBTAA.

Moreover, the requirement that for a trust to be charitable its purposes must be confined exclusively to charitable purposes is one that is binding upon the body seeking that status. In *Commissioner for ACT Revenue Collections* v. *Council of the Dominican Sisters of Australia*,[43] for example, although the ultimate aim of the Corporate Council was to serve the religious ends of its founders, the Council itself sought exemption from payroll tax as a religious institution. The full Federal Court, overturning the tribunal hearing, ruled that the crucial issue was whether the promotion or advancement of religion was the primary and dominant object of the Council, not its founders. Similarly, in *Glebe Administration Board* v. *Commissioner of Pay-roll Tax (NSW)*,[44] the relationship between the Board and a religious institution was one in which the latter created a non-religious Board controlled by, but distinct from, the institution, to raise money in a commercial way for its religious purposes. It was held that the Board was 'a statutory corporation doing commercial work within limitations fixed by reference to religious principles'. Although the Board was controlled by the religious institution, that was insufficient to invest it with a religious purpose. The decision in *Word*[45] temporarily disrupted the settled law regarding subsidiary entities, but this has now been restored by the Charities Act 2013 (see, further, below).

The common law

The courts in Australia, following the *Pemsel* classification, had generally come to recognise the following categories of charity: the relief of poverty; the relief of the needs of the aged; the relief of sickness or distress; the advancement of religion; and the advancement of education. To be entitled to charitable status under the advancement of religion head the promotion or advancement of religion must be the primary and dominant object.[46] The law continues the public benefit presumption in

---

[43] *Commissioner for ACT Revenue Collections* v. *Council of the Dominican Sisters of Australia* (1991) 22 ATR 213; 101 ALR 417; 91 ATC 4602.

[44] *Glebe Administration Board* v. *Commissioner of Pay-roll Tax (NSW)* (1987) 83 ATC 4269.

[45] *Federal Commissioner of Taxation* v. *Word Investments Ltd.* (2008) 236 CLR 204.

[46] See *Commissioner for ACT Revenue Collections* v. *Council of the Dominican Sisters of Australia* (1991) 22 ATR 213; 91 ATC 4602. Also see *Christian Enterprises Ltd.* v. *Commissioner of Land Tax (NSW)* (1968) 88 WN (Pt. 2) (NSW) 112, *per* Walsh JA, at p.123.

relation to the first three *Pemsel* heads and, at all levels of jurisdiction, it applied the common law definitional concepts as they were applied in England and Wales before charity law reform.[47] The Charities Act 2013 (Cth), now defines and extends the *Pemsel* charitable purposes and encodes in statute the existing common law concepts and rules; this includes some adjustment to the public benefit presumption. It also includes the statement in the Explanatory Memorandum that the 'common law ... will ... remain relevant for the purposes of interpreting those principles, concepts and terms that have been derived from the common law and utilised in the statutory definition'.[48]

Charity law reform

In Australia, as the nonprofit sector has frequently pointed out, there have been five different major reviews of the sector in the last 15 years. As elsewhere among the developed common law nations, the principal drivers of charity law reform conformed to a familiar pattern: weaknesses in the common law approach (primarily a sluggish case flow generating few opportunities for judiciary or regulator to broaden the interpretation of charitable purpose to meet contemporary forms of social need, coupled with constraints arising from the archaic nature of the public benefit test and other conceptual benchmarks for identifying 'charity'); and weaknesses in the regulatory framework (primarily the continuation of the traditional Revenue-driven and therefore restrictive interpretation of charitable status, the absence of a charity-specific registration and regulatory system, the many uncoordinated government bodies involved and the often inappropriate legal structures available for housing charitable activity). In addition, the introduction of the New Tax System legislation[49] providing tax concessions for nonprofits also created a fiscal incentive to identify and classify those organisations entitled to the concession, which gave added impetus to the drive for law reform.

Reform process

Australia's most promising early foray into charity law reform process concluded with the 428-page Australian Industry Commission Report,

---

[47] See *Navy Health Ltd.* v. *DFC of T* (2007) ATC 4568.
[48] Explanatory Memorandum, Charities Act 2013 (Cth) 10, at 1.19.
[49] A New Tax System (Goods and Services Tax) Act 1999 (Cth).

Charitable Organizations in Australia, 1995, which was shelved by the government without legislative outcome nor any of its recommendations for change being implemented. At the end of the 1990s, as a result of the introduction of a goods and services tax (GST) under which some charities were not taxable, the government announced its willingness to respond to sector concerns and reconsider the prospect of charity law reform. The Inquiry into the Definition of Charities and Related Organizations was launched in September 2000 amid political rhetoric regarding the need to strengthen regulatory processes, update common law concepts and improve sector capacity.[50] The submission of a report in 2001 led to the drafting of a Charities Bill, but this was withdrawn in May 2004.[51] The collapse of this charity law reform process left behind only the bare remnants to be salvaged by the 2004 Act.[52]

The transition from a Liberal to a Labor government in 2007 saw a transition also in government–sector relations. Among the steps taken by the incoming government to demonstrate its commitment to building a new working relationship with the sector was that of issuing the Productivity Commission in 2009 with terms of reference requiring it to examine how government could engage the sector efficiently and effectively in providing public benefit services, and to assess the related regulatory framework. This was followed by the Henry tax review,[53] by a private bill and by the Economics Legislation Committee report into the Tax Laws Amendment (Public Benefit Test) Bill 2010.[54]

Reform outcomes

Charity law reform concluded on 27 June 2013, when the Australian Charities and Not-for-profits Commission Bill 2012, the Australian Charities and Not-for-profits Commission (Consequential and Transitional) Bill 2012 and the Tax Laws Amendment (Special Conditions for

---

[50] See, further, at: www.cdi.gov.au/html/report.htm (accessed 9 January 2014).
[51] See I. Sheppard, R. Fitzgerald and D. Gonski, *Inquiry into the Definition of Charities and Related Organizations*, CanPrint Communications Pty Ltd, Canberra, June 2001.
[52] The limited reforms introduced by the Extension of Charitable Purpose Act 2004 did no more than extend the *Pemsel* list to include child care, self-help groups and contemplative religious orders.
[53] K. Henry, *Australia's Future Tax System Review*, released 2 May 2010.
[54] The Economics Legislation Committee, *Tax Laws Amendment (Public Benefit Test) Bill 2010 Report*, Canberra, 2010. See, further, at: www.aph.gov.au/binaries/senate/committee/economics_ctte/public_benefit_test_10/report/report.pdf (accessed 9 January 2014).

Not-for-profit Concessions) Bill 2012 were finally passed by both Houses of Parliament.

The new regime is headed by the Australian Charities and Not-for-profits Commission (ACNC), which is charged with registering not-for-profit entities (initially charities) and maintaining a related register. The legislation provides for the powers of the ACNC Commissioner in relation to the regulation of registered entities and sets out the obligations and responsibilities of registered entities. The registration of charities is dependent upon the new statutory definition of 'charity' now to be found in the Charities Act 2013 and the Charities (Consequential Amendments and Transitional Provisions) Act 2013.

The reforms: charitable purposes

To be a charity, an entity must be not-for-profit and have only charitable purposes (other than incidental or ancillary purposes that further or aid the charitable purpose) that are for the public benefit. The statutory categories of charitable purposes are now as stated in the Charities Act 2013, s.12(1): advancing health; advancing education; advancing social or public welfare; advancing religion; advancing culture; promoting reconciliation, mutual respect and tolerance between groups of individuals that are in Australia; promoting or protecting human rights; advancing the security or safety of Australia or the Australian public; preventing or relieving the suffering of animals; advancing the natural environment; any other purpose beneficial to the general public that may reasonably be regarded as analogous to, or within the spirit of, the above purposes; promoting or opposing a change to any matter established by law, policy or practice in the Commonwealth, a State, a Territory or another country, in furtherance or protection of one or more of the above purposes. The specific and freestanding purpose of 'promoting or protecting human rights' as stated in s.12(1)(g) is noteworthy – particularly for present purposes.

Post-reform: the public benefit test and religious organisations

Australia will continue to apply the traditional common law approach to religious organisations as evolved in England and Wales prior to the changes introduced there by the 2006 Act. The somewhat defensive approach taken by the judiciary of both Australia and New Zealand, in upholding the public benefit presumption, remains as expressed by Reynolds JA in *Joyce* v. *Ashfield Municipal Council*:

> This doctrine that religious activities are subject to proof that they are for the public benefit could give rise to great problems in that it might lead to the scrutiny by the courts of the public benefit of all religious practices.[55]

The test

The Charities Act 2013, s.6(1) states that a purpose will be held to be for the public benefit if: (a) the achievement of the purpose would be of public benefit; and (b) the purpose is directed to a benefit that is available to the members of: (i) the general public; or (ii) a sufficient section of the general public. Therefore, the warning emphasised by the ATO that 'a charitable purpose must be for the benefit of the community' remains in place.[56]

Public

The Charities Act 2013 restates the rule that the benefit of a charitable purpose does not have to be available for the whole of the general public; it can be available only to a section, provided that section is not negligible compared to the size of that part of the general public to whom the purpose would be relevant.

A sufficient section of the general public may be a limited number of individuals where the charitable purpose would be relevant to only a small group of people, such as to groups with particular characteristics, residents of a particular geographic area or the followers of a particular religion to which anyone can adhere. Further, the Act clarifies that 'charging fees to members of the public for goods, services, or other benefits where the purpose is otherwise charitable is not inconsistent with a charitable purpose' subject to the customary constraints on private benefit. The accompanying common law rules regarding matters such as incidental or ancillary activities, member benefit and any relationship nexus between donor and prospective beneficiary are reiterated.

---

[55] *Joyce* v. *Ashfield Municipal Council* [1975] 1 NSWLR 744.

[56] See ATO, *Draft Taxation Ruling* TR 1999/D21, at para. 43: 'Charity is altruistic and intends social value or utility. The benefit need not be for the whole community; it may be for an appreciable section of the public.'

Benefit

Section 7 of the new legislation declares that the following are presumed as being for the public benefit, unless there is evidence to the contrary: preventing and relieving sickness, disease or human suffering; advancing education; relieving the poverty, distress or disadvantage of individuals or families; caring for and supporting the aged or people with disabilities; and the purpose of advancing religion. This presumption of public benefit is rebuttable. In relation to open and non-discriminatory self-help groups, and closed or contemplative religious orders that regularly undertake prayerful intervention at the request of members of the public, the Charities Act 2013, s.10, explicitly states that the public benefit test is to have no application, although it will still be necessary for the entity to satisfy the other requirements to be a charity, including having only charitable purposes.

Detriment

The Charities Act 2013, s.6(2)(b), includes a caveat which warns that in determining public benefit, consideration must be given to any possible detriment which arises from the purpose, or would commonly arise, from carrying out the purpose to the general public or a section of the general public.

The public benefit test and 'closed' religious orders

The ruling in *Gilmore* v. *Coats*[57] to the effect that a 'closed' religious order could not be charitable was treated with some equivocation in Australia. Initially the courts seemed persuaded by the House of Lords, and in *A-G (NSW)* v. *Donnelly*[58] chose to follow that precedent. By 1967, however, in *Assoc. of Franciscan Order of Friars Minor* v. *City of Kew*,[59] they had re-considered and when, in 1975, in *Joyce* v. *Ashfield Municipal Council*,[60] a rates exemption case, the NSW Court of Appeal had to determine whether the religious ceremonies of the Exclusive Brethren were for the public benefit, notwithstanding the limited public access to

---

[57] *Gilmore* v. *Coats* [1949] AC 426 (HL).
[58] *A-G (NSW)* v. *Donnelly* (1958) 99 CLR 538.
[59] *Assoc. of Franciscan Order of Friars Minor* v. *City of Kew* (1967) VR 732.
[60] *Joyce* v. *Ashfield Municipal Council* [1975] 1 NSWLR 744.

CHARITY LAW AND THE REGULATORY FRAMEWORK   395

those ceremonies, they had seemingly rejected the *Coats* precedent. Hutley JA, with whom the other judges agreed, was of the view that:

> Even if the ceremonies of the Exclusive Brethren in the hall can be regarded as a temporary withdrawal from the world, those ceremonies are a preparation for the assumption of their place in the world in which they will battle according to their religious views to raise the standards of the world by precept and example ... from the fact that their religious ceremonies cannot be classed as public worship, it cannot be deduced that they are not for the public benefit.[61]

That is, sufficient public benefit could derive from the subsequent inter-action of the religious group with the general public after private worship, which had been the approach of the Australian judiciary before the *Coats* decision.[62] This was reinforced by the decision of the High Court of Australia in *Council of the Municipality of Canterbury* v. *Moslem Alawy Society Limited*,[63] when it decided that to interpret 'place of public worship' in a council planning ordinance as requiring access by the general public would be inconsistent with 'currently accepted standards of religious equality and tolerance in this country'.[64] Again, in *Crowther* v. *Brophy*,[65] the distancing from *Gilmour* v. *Coats* continued when Gobbo J expressed doubt as to whether the latter ruling was followed in Australia and suggested that in finding public benefit from the prac-tice of intercessory prayer, one should look to 'the enhancement in the life, both religious and otherwise, of those who found comfort and peace of mind in their resort to intercessory prayer'. This principle subse-quently received statutory endorsement in the Extension of Charitable Purpose Act 2004, s.5(1)(b) of which defined a group or religious order that 'regularly undertakes prayerful intervention at the request of mem-bers of the public' as being for the public benefit. So it was a little surprising when a year later the Supreme Court of Queensland decided in *Jensen & Ors* v. *Brisbane City Council*,[66] again a rates exemption case,

---

[61] Ibid., at p.751. Reminiscent of Cross J's approach in *Neville Estates* v. *Madden* (1962) Ch. 832, at p.858.

[62] See *Perpetual Trustee Co. Ltd.* v. *Wittscheibe* (1940) 40 SR NSW 501, and *Re a'Beckett, Allard* v. *Lambert* (1941) VLR 283, in which gifts to contemplative religious orders were considered charitable even though their sole purpose was prayerful contemplation without any engagement in society.

[63] *Council of the Municipality of Canterbury* v. *Moslem Alawy Society Limited* (1987) 162 CLR 145.

[64] Ibid., at 149.   [65] *Crowther* v. *Brophy* [1992] 2 VR 97, 100.

[66] *Jensen & Ors* v. *Brisbane City Council* [2005] QCA 469.

that the religious ceremonies in the Brethren hall were not charitable, advising that:

> Private worship by a congregation is not 'public worship', at least insofar as that term is to be understood in the context of rating exemptions, and it does not become public worship because the congregation may decide to permit particular members of the public to attend that worship. 'Public worship' in the present rating context requires that the worship is in a place open to all properly disposed persons who wish to be present without vetting by a gatekeeper.[67]

Government approval of this approach can perhaps be seen in a response to recommendations made by the Senate Economics Legislation Committee Inquiry into the Tax Laws Amendment (Public Benefit Test) Bill 2010, when the government stated that it 'considers that religious observance should not be regarded as a shield behind which breaches of the law can be hidden'.[68] However, any doubts about government intentions have been since laid to rest by the provision in the Charities Act 2013, s.10(2), declaring that the public benefit test does not apply 'if the entity is a closed or contemplative religious order that regularly undertakes prayerful intervention at the request of members of the general public'.[69]

Religion, religious beliefs and the advancement of religion

The Charities Act 2013 offers no definition of 'religion', no reference to the need or otherwise for a god or gods, and makes no reference to non-religious forms of belief. For some decades, however, theistic belief has not been a required component for the advancement of religion in Australian charity law: such belief has traditionally sufficed but, while it continues to be sufficient, it is not strictly necessary; the required belief is no longer one that must be directed exclusively towards a god or gods.

Religion

In Australia the common law interpretation of what constitutes a religion traditionally conformed to the orthodox Judeo-Christian model.[70]

---

[67] Ibid., at para. 49.

[68] See Senate Economics Legislation Committee Inquiry into Tax Laws Amendment (Public Benefit Test) Bill 2010, Government Response at: www.openaustralia.org/senate/?id=2011-02-28.77.2 (accessed 9 January 2014).

[69] Note that the 2004 Act declared closed religious orders to be charitable.

[70] See, further, Thompson, *Religion in Australia*.

THE ADVANCEMENT OF RELIGION 397

Such an understanding has pointedly excluded making any concessions to the beliefs of Indigenous people. In recent years all aspects of Australian law have had to adjust to take account of the cultures of its many Asian immigrants and accordingly charity law has enlarged its understanding of religion to make room for a range of Eastern beliefs. In so doing there are indications that, for the purposes of charity law, there is now a growing willingness to accommodate Indigenous beliefs.

Belief in a Supreme Being

The High Court of Australia, in *The Church of the New Faith* v. *Commissioner of Pay-roll Tax,*[71] considered whether a particular set of beliefs and practices would constitute a religion. The decision reached defined religion very broadly and remains the Australian authority on this subject. Mason ACJ and Brennan J then suggested that:

> for the purposes of law, the criteria of religion are twofold: first, belief in a supernatural Being, Thing or Principle; and second, the acceptance of canons of conduct in order to give effect to that belief, though canons of conduct which offend against the ordinary laws are outside the area of any immunity, privilege or right conferred on the grounds of religion.[72]

It was a ruling that won approval from the Charities Definition Inquiry[73] and marked a turning point for the development of this *Pemsel* head of charity in Australia. Subsequently, in *New South Wales Stewards' Co. Ltd.* v. *Strathfield Municipal Council,*[74] the court fell back on more orthodox principles when it had to determine whether a company, which had among its objects the promotion of the true welfare of humankind in Christian or benevolent principles and the teaching of the word of God, was a 'religious body' and on that basis entitled to a rating exemption. Noting that 'religious body' and 'religion' were not defined in the rating statute, the court found that these terms were to be given their popular meaning – which imputed a belief in a Supreme Being.

---

[71] *The Church of the New Faith* v. *Commissioner of Pay-roll Tax* [1983] HCA 40; (1983) 154 CLR 120 (27 October 1983), per Mason ACJ and Brennan J, at p.137.

[72] Ibid., at p.74.

[73] See I. Fitzhardinge, R. G. Sheppard and D. Gonski, *Report of the Inquiry into the Definition of Charities and Related Organisations*, Legislative Services, Canberra, 2001, Chapter 20, Recommendation 14.

[74] *New South Wales Stewards' Co. Ltd.* v. *Strathfield Municipal Council* (1944) 15 LGR 139.

Philosophy and other value systems

In *Church of the New Faith* the court considered whether the doctrines and beliefs of Scientology could be construed as meeting the definition of religion and, although the five judges were unable to agree on what might constitute such a definition, there was consensus that it should extend to philosophies which 'seek to explain, in terms of a broader reality, the existence of the universe, the meaning of human life and human destiny'.[75] The indicia of religion as discussed by Wilson and Deane JJ were: that the particular collection of ideas and/or practices involved belief in the supernatural, i.e. a belief that reality extended beyond that which was capable of perception by the senses; that the ideas related to man's nature and place in the universe and his relations to things super-natural; that the ideas were accepted by adherents as requiring or encouraging them to observe particular practices having supernatural significance; and that, however loosely knit and varying in beliefs and practices adherents might be, they constituted an identifiable group or identifiable groups.[76] In unanimously concluding that Scientology is a religion, the High Court in Australia reached the opposite decision to that made by the Charity Commission in England and Wales, on the same set of facts (as also occurred in relation to closed religious orders).[77]

Where, however, the purposes of an organisation are clearly antithetical to religion, the Australian judiciary has adopted the same approach as their British counterparts and found that such purposes cannot, by any definition, be said to be 'advancing' religion. The Freethinkers case,[78] for example, concerned a society the beliefs of which included that 'science provides for life and that materialism can be relied upon in all phases of society'. The court considered that as the purpose of the organisation was to work against already established religions or against the idea of religion, this could not itself be a religious purpose and hence the organisation could not be construed as 'religious'.

Worship, religious tenets, doctrines, etc.

In Australia the interpretation given to 'places of worship' is in keeping with its established approach of finding sufficient public benefit in the

---

[75] Ibid., at para. 13.

[76] *The Church of the New Faith* v. *Commissioner of Pay-roll Tax* (1983) 154 CLR 120, at p.174.

[77] For a critique of the decision, see W. Sadurski, 'On Legal Definitions of Religion' (1989) 63 *Australian Law Journal* 834. See also, *Nelson* v. *Fish* (1990) 21 FCR 430.

[78] *Re Jones* [1907] SALR 1990 (Incorporated Body of Freethinkers of Australia).

example set by private piety, in contrast with the equivalent approach in England and Wales, to justify an award of charitable status.

In this jurisdiction, the weight to be placed upon tenets and doctrines was viewed by Mason ACJ and Brennan J in *Church of the New Faith*, as a matter of no great importance:

> The tenets of a religion may give primacy to one particular belief or to one particular canon of conduct. Variations in emphasis may distinguish one religion from other religions, but they are irrelevant to the determination of an individual's or group's freedom to profess and exercise the religion of his, or their, choices.[79]

Instead, the court was of the view that:

> It is more accurate to say that protection is required for the adherents of religions, not for the religions themselves. Protection is not accorded to safeguard the tenets of each religion; no such protection can be given by the law, and it would be contradictory of the law to protect at once the tenets of different religions which are incompatible with one another. Protection is accorded to preserve the dignity and freedom of each man so that he may adhere to any religion of his choosing or to none.[80]

This approach was taken a stage further in the protracted proceedings that constituted the *OV and OW* case,[81] where the central issue turned upon the general exception for 'religious bodies' provided by s.56(d) of the Anti-Discrimination Act 1977 (NSW), which gives protection for the actions of such a body where they conform to the doctrines of its religion.

At the first hearing the Equal Opportunity Division of the Administrative Decisions Tribunal (NSWADT) considered that the issue gave rise to the question: what is a religion? It determined that the relevant religion was the Christian religion. The Wesley Mission sought to rely upon the 'fundamental Biblical teaching that "monogamous heterosexual partnership within marriage" is both the "norm and ideal"'. However, the tribunal found, given the diversity of views across Christendom on this issue, that: 'it does not follow, and nor is it asserted, that that belief can properly be described as a doctrine of the Christian religion'. At the second hearing, the appeals panel found the tribunal to be in error in the

---

[79] *The Church of the New Faith* v. *Commissioner of Pay-roll Tax* [1983] HCA 40; (1983) 154 CLR 120 (27 October 1983), at para. 18.

[80] Ibid., at para. 8.

[81] *OV* v. *QZ (No 2)* [2008] NSWADT 115; *Member of the Board of the Wesley Mission Council* v. *OV and OW (No 2)* [2009] NSWADTAP 57; *OV & OW* v. *Members of the Board of the Wesley Mission Council* [2010] NSWCA 155.

definition it reached, ordered that the matter be reconsidered, and directed the tribunal to ascertain whether 'monogamous heterosexual partnership within marriage is both the norm and ideal' was a doctrine of 'Wesleyanism'. The Court of Appeal disagreed: it found that both the tribunal and appeals panel were in error. Basten JA and Handley AJA stated that 'there is no basis in section 56 to infer that Parliament intended to exempt from the operation of the Anti-Discrimination Act only those acts or practices which formed part ... of the religion common to all Christian churches, or all branches of a particular Christian church (in the sense of a denomination), to the exclusion of variants adopted by some elements within a particular Church'.[82] The consequent search for 'a doctrine of "the Christian religion," and the need to establish conformity or otherwise with the act or practice of the Mission, was misguided. No such doctrine had been found because the evidence was directed specifically to the beliefs and teachings of Methodism or Wesleyism.'[83] The Court of Appeal concluded that this reasoning led to the incorrect finding that, as the actions of the Wesley Mission were not in accordance with its doctrines, it could not therefore enjoy the sanction of the exempting provision in the Act. Instead of adopting a broad focus on the Wesleyan understanding of Christianity, the enquiry should have been confined to the terms of the specific complaint and it should have ascertained whether or not the grounds for complaint conformed to the doctrines of the religion of the Wesley Mission as those doctrines stood at the time of that complaint and not at the time of the founding of the Mission. In reconsidering the matter in December 2010, the NSWADT took the view that 'doctrine' was broad enough to encompass not just formal doctrinal pronouncements such as the Nicene Creed, but effectively whatever was commonly taught or advocated by a body, including moral as well as religious principles. Taking its lead from the Court of Appeal, the tribunal accepted evidence: from the Superintendent and CEO of the Wesley Mission that in 2003 the Wesley Mission had a doctrine that 'monogamous heterosexual partnership within marriage is both the norm and ideal'; and from a minister that the provision of foster care services by a homosexual couple would be contrary to a fundamental commitment of the organisation to the Biblical values as reflected in its doctrines. Hence the defence under s.56(d) was established. It

[82] *OV & OW* v. *Members of the Board of the Wesley Mission Council* [2010] NSWCA 155 (6 July 2010), at para. 41.
[83] Ibid., at para. 40.

concluded that as the cause for complaint conformed with this doctrine which the Mission was, at the relevant time, established to propagate, its decision was protected by the religious exemption found within s.56(d) of the Act. Following the *OV and OW* rationale, Hampel J in *Cobaw Community Health Services Limited* v. *Christian Youth Camps Limited & Anor*[84] determined that, as regards the respondents, the relevant 'religion' was the Christian Brethren denomination of Christianity. Having heard expert evidence from theologians on the meaning of 'doctrines of religion' and the interpretation that should be given to 'conforms with the doctrines of the religion', the judge found that plenary inspiration (the words of the Bible must be believed and acted upon) is a doctrine of the Christian religion. However, and crucially for this and for all subsequent cases which may deal with such issues, the judicial finding included the observation that not everything in the Scriptures amounts to 'doctrine', the prevailing cultural beliefs at the time must also be taken into account. As the evidence showed no reference to marriage, sexual relationships or homosexuality in the creeds or declarations of faith adhered to by members of the Christian Brethren, she held that their beliefs about these matters could not be construed as 'doctrines of the religion'.

Among the implications of these decisions is an awareness that the Australian courts and regulators will hold a firm focus on the doctrines of any organisation seeking to avail itself of the statutory protection provided to religious bodies from allegations of discriminatory practice. In this context the doctrinal focus is more pronounced than in other jurisdictions and is likely to have a considerable impact upon the many religious charities engaged in various forms of service delivery. Moreover, not all adherents of a particular religion need to subscribe to its doctrines; it is sufficient that some do so. Significant also is the finding that when a legal issue arises, which makes it necessary to ascertain the doctrines of a religion, it will be the formulation of those doctrines at the time the issue arose which is crucial: an approach which, by requiring the doctrine to be contextualised within contemporary cultural values and norms, may allow traditional religious dogma to be side-stepped; at least in circumstances where a particular religious group cannot show that it currently wholly or largely subscribes to traditional religious beliefs.

---

[84] *Cobaw Community Health Services Limited* v. *Christian Youth Camps Limited & Anor* [2010] VCAT 1613 (8 October 2010).

Religious and philosophical beliefs

While upholding the orthodox interpretation of what constitutes a religion (belief in a Supreme Being and worship as reinforced by doctrines), the law in Australia now also accommodates a broader view embracing analogous philosophical beliefs. In its report on Article 18, the Human Rights and Equal Opportunity Commission recommended that the Commonwealth Parliament enact religious freedom legislation which would (1) recognise and give effect to freedom of religion and belief in Australia, and (2) make unlawful direct and indirect discrimination on the ground of religion and belief in areas of public life. The Commission recommended only two exemptions broadly reflecting the position at international law. It also recommended that 'religion and belief' should be broadly defined, to encompass theistic, non-theistic and other beliefs, including the traditional belief systems of Indigenous people.

Religious beliefs

It would seem reasonably clear that in determining what constitutes a religious belief the law has not strayed far from its roots: any broadening of interpretation is by analogy and seeks to bring the new belief within the terms of the existing definition rather than view it *sui generis*. The judiciary, so far, have been content to reflect on the potential for a broader interpretation while nonetheless choosing to remain close to standard orthodoxy. The challenge posed by Latham CJ in *Adelaide Co of Jehovah's Witnesses Inc* v. *Commonwealth*,[85] that 'it is not an exaggeration to say that each person chooses the content of his own religion', has yet to be addressed by charity law in Australia. In the *Scientology* case,[86] for example, the initial judgments had rejected the claim that Scientology was a religion, finding instead that it was a philosophy and that the trappings of religion had only been acquired after its establishment in order to give the organisation the semblance of a religion. While this finding was overturned by the High Court,[87] its rationale for doing so was that Scientology beliefs sufficiently approximated religious beliefs to justify extending recognition to it. However, both Mason ACJ and Brennan J were alert to the dangers of overstretching the interpretation of religion to allow for such inclusion and warned that 'the mantle of

---

[85] *Adelaide Co of Jehovah's Witnesses Inc* v. *Commonwealth* (1943) 67 CLR 116, at 124.
[86] *Church of New Faith* v. *Commissioner of Pay-Roll Tax* (1983) 1 VR 97.
[87] *Church of New Faith* v. *Commissioner of Pay-Roll Tax* (1983) 154 CLR 120.

THE ADVANCEMENT OF RELIGION 403

immunity would soon be in tatters if it were wrapped around beliefs, practices and observances of every kind whenever a group of adherents chose to call them a religion'.[88] Although there is also much to be said for Ridge's comment that 'the benefits to society from persons pursuing purely religious purposes have no necessary correlation to the credibility or otherwise of their religious beliefs'.[89]

Indigenous people and religious beliefs

The case for recognising the dreamtime rites as constituting the religious beliefs of Indigenous people – which vary from tribe to tribe in accordance with tribal boundaries, topography and ancestor narratives – has been well made.[90] Despite the analytical difficulties involved, there can be no doubt that the concepts and beliefs of Indigenous culture offer a sufficiently valid and coherent parallel to Christianity, for example, to warrant equal recognition in law. Indeed, Gaudron J clearly subscribed to such a view when in considering, in *Kruger v. Commonwealth*,[91] whether the removal of Aboriginal children breached s.116, she stated that 'the Aboriginal people of the Northern Territory, or at least some of them, had beliefs or practices which are properly classified as a religion'. Indeed, her colleague on the bench, Toohey J, endorsed this and seemed to recognise also the legitimacy of associated manifestations of such beliefs when he commented that: 'It may well be that an effect of the Ordinance was to impair, even prohibit the spiritual beliefs and practices of the Aboriginal people in the Northern Territory.'[92]

The intrusive methods of outsiders seeking to ascertain the genuineness and the extent of Indigenous religious belief may be unwelcome. This was evident in *ALRM v. State of South Australia*,[93] when the Supreme Court of South Australia held that an inquiry into the genuineness of the belief of Ngarrindjiri women, notwithstanding that those beliefs were, under Aboriginal rule, confidential to women, was lawful. However, the importance of their sacred sites to Indigenous people has been judicially recognised, as has the justification for affording

---

[88] Ibid., at p.132.
[89] P. Ridge, 'Religious Charitable Status and Public Benefit in Australia' (2011) 35 *Melbourne University Law Review*, at p.1083. citing *Gilmour v. Coats* [1949] AC 426.
[90] See, for example, W. Gallois, 'On Dreaming Time', in *Time, Religion and History*, Pearson Education, New York, 2007.
[91] *Kruger v. Commonwealth* (1997) 190 CLR 1.   [92] Ibid., at p.86.
[93] *ALRM v. State of South Australia* (1995) 64 SASR 551.

404   AUSTRALIA

protection to lands of religious significance from acquisition under the s.116 'Free Exercise Clause'.[94] Furthermore, among the retrospective objections to the Aboriginals Ordinance 1918 (authorising the forcible 'removal of Aboriginal and half-caste children from their communities') was the argument that in so doing it breached their right to the free exercise of religion under s.116 of the Constitution.[95]

The manifestation of beliefs

The right to 'manifest one's religion' in 'worship, observance, practice and teaching' is protected by Article 18(1) of the International Covenant on Civil and Political Rights (ICCPR). It is also protected by the Australian Constitution. Latham CJ, in *Adelaide Company of Jehovah's Witnesses Inc* v. *Commonwealth*,[96] was clear that the protection afforded by s.116 extended beyond beliefs to include manifestations of such beliefs. Moreover, both Mason ACJ and Brennan J in *Church of the New Faith* v. *Commissioner of Pay-roll Tax (Vict)*[97] were of the view that such beliefs, and manifestations giving effect to them, need not strictly conform to an orthodox theistic religion.

However, this right, to take action in furtherance of religious belief, is constrained in at least two respects. First, the action must be appropriately linked to the belief: clearly not all action taken by a religious person or organisation is necessarily related to, let alone a manifestation of, their religious beliefs. As Dal Pont has expressed it:

> Importantly there must be a connection between a person's belief in the supernatural and his or her conduct as a result of that belief. Conduct such as worship, teaching, propagation or observance is religious only if the motivation for engaging in it is religious.[98]

The Australian courts have, on a number of occasions, found a disconnect between the beliefs of a religious organisation and the means by which it chooses to manifest those beliefs. So, the following are among the activities found insufficient to warrant charitable status: a 'Catholic daily

---

[94] See *Milirrpum* v. *Nabalco Pty Ltd.* (1971) 17 FLR 141 (the Gove Land Rights case) and *Coe* v. *Commonwealth* [1979] HCA 68.

[95] See *Kruger* v. *Commonwealth* (1997) 190 CLR 1, *per* Gaudron J. Note the provision made in the 2013 Act for an Aboriginal Association.

[96] *Adelaide Company of Jehovah's Witnesses Inc* v. *Commonwealth* (1943) 67 CLR 116, 124.

[97] *Church of the New Faith* v. *Commissioner of Pay-roll Tax (Vict)* (1983) 154 CLR 120, 135.

[98] G. Dal Pont, *Charity Law in Australia and New Zealand*, Oxford University Press, Melbourne, 2000, at p.149.

newspaper';[99] the 'formation and advancement of a Catholic Boys' Club';[100] and camping activities.[101] Second, any such action must be proportionate and respectful of the rights of others. There is an important distinction to be drawn between the right to freedom of religion or belief, and the right to demonstrate or manifest religion or belief in worship, observance, practice and teaching. As Hampel J noted in *Cobaw*,[102] the right to hold a belief is broader than the right to act upon it. In particular, she emphasised that the right to freedom of religious belief does not confer a right on members of a religion to impose their beliefs on a secular society.[103]

The advancement of religion

To be charitable, the organisation or gift must 'advance' religion.[104] Once a religious body was recognised as such by the ATO, then, unless the purpose of a gift was clearly in some way illegal or immoral, it was presumed to be charitable. This generous interpretation has been reinforced by the judiciary in cases such as *Roman Catholic Archbishop of Melbourne* v. *Lawlor*,[105] when Dixon J remarked that 'a gift made for any particular means of propagating a faith or a religious belief is charitable; moreover, a disposition is valid which in general terms devotes property to religious purposes or objects'. He added the caveat that 'whether defined widely or narrowly, the purpose must be directly and immediately religious. It is not enough that they arise out of or have a connection with a faith, church or denomination, or that they are considered to have a tendency beneficial to religion, or to a particular form of religion.'[106]

This approach has been continued by the Charities Act 2013, which states that:

> Advancing religion involves the promotion of spiritual teaching and the observances that serve to promote and manifest it. The purpose must be

[99] *Roman Catholic Archbishop of Melbourne* v. *Lawlor* (1934) 51 CLR 1.
[100] *Attorney-General* v. *Cahill* [1969] 1 NSWR 85.
[101] *Cobaw Community Health Services Limited* v. *Christian Youth Camps Limited & Ano* [2010] VCAT 1613.
[102] Ibid., citing both s.14 of the Charter and Article 18 of the ICCPR.
[103] Citing Laws J in *McFarlane* v. *Relate Avon Limited* [2010] EWCA Civ B1.
[104] See, for example, H. Sorenson and A. Thompson, 'The Advancement of Religion is Still a Valid Charitable Object in 2001', *ACPNS Working Paper*, Australian Centre for Philanthropy and Nonprofit Studies, Brisbane, 2002.
[105] *Roman Catholic Archbishop of Melbourne* v. *Lawlor* (1934) 51 CLR 1, *per* Dixon J, at p.32.
[106] Ibid.

directly and immediately religious and involve various ways of advancing religion, including providing and maintaining facilities for worship; supporting religious clergy; missionary bodies; and religious associations.

The means for advancing religion

As Dal Pont explains, 'to advance religion' includes 'to promote spiritual teaching in a wide sense, to spread its message, or to take positive steps to sustain and increase religious belief, via ways that can be described as pastoral or missionary'.[107] Traditionally the most orthodox way of doing so has been through: acts of devotion, prayer, masses for the commemoration of the dead;[108] preaching the Gospel;[109] gifts for missions and missionary work;[110] and participation in collective worship, ceremonies of celebration, etc.; constructing or repairing churches, halls and other buildings used for religious purposes; and missionary work. Picarda draws attention to the fact that:[111]

> in Australia it has been held that the 'purposes' of a particular church are not synonymous with the activities of that church.[112] Moreover, an Australian court has also held that the expression 'Church purposes', whether used generically or in connection with a particular sacred edifice administered by a minister of the Christian religion, denotes religious and prima facie charitable purposes.[113]

So, whereas the purposes of the Roman Catholic Church can be construed as prima facie charitable (the advancement and propagation of Catholicism, the ministering of that religion and the spiritual edification of its members), Roman Catholic purposes are not so privileged. The public benefit presumption would, therefore, be restricted to Church purposes and would not extend, as in *Roman Catholic Archbishop of Melbourne* v. *Lawlor*,[114] to such outreach activity as 'establishing a Catholic daily newspaper'. Again, where the gift is to a religious organisation but is specified for use in furthering a non-religious purpose,

---

[107] See G. E. Dal Pont, *Law of Charity*, LexisNexis Butterworths, Chatswood, NSW, 2010, at p.232.

[108] See *Re Purcell* [1895] 21 VLR 249.   [109] See *Re Flatman* [1953] VLR 33.

[110] See *Re Kenny* (1907) 57 LT 130.

[111] See H. Picarda, *The Law and Practice Relating to Charities* (4th edn), Bloomsbury Professional, Haywards Heath, 2010, at p.374.

[112] Citing *Re Moroney, Maguire* v. *Reilly* (1939) 39 SRNSW 249. See also Dal Pont, *Law of Charity*, at p.153.

[113] Citing *Re Moroney, Maguire* v. *Reilly* (1939) 39 SRNSW 249.

[114] *Roman Catholic Archbishop of Melbourne* v. *Lawlor* (1934) 51 CLR l.

THE ADVANCEMENT OF RELIGION · 407

such as sport or recreation, then the courts tend to find the gift non-charitable.[115]

Where, however, there is a close fit between religious purpose and the means chosen to advance it, then the problem is avoided. So, in *Re Stewart's Will Trusts*,[116] a bequest of land 'to be used for the celebration of Divine Service therein in accordance with the rites and ceremonies of the John Knox Presbyterian Church' was found to be charitable. Similarly, a bequest to a religious organisation to establish a Foundling Hospital, open to all babies without regard for religion or marital status but subject to certain management conditions, was also held to be viable.[117] The principle being as expressed by Mahoney JA in *Presbyterian Church (New South Wales) Property Trust* v. *Ryde Municipal Council*[118] that

> where a church or analogous body has one of the purposes to which its property may be applied a purpose which is not a mere ulterior secular purpose, but one directed at and able to be seen as assisting in the advancement of its religious purpose, then the purpose of that religion will be held to be religious for present purposes.

In this jurisdiction the courts made an early commitment to accepting private devotional activity as contributing to the public good and sufficient to justify charitable status, the rationale for which was stated by Issacs J in *Nelan* v. *Downes*,[119] a case that concerned a testamentary gift for masses to be said for the souls of the testatrix and her husband. Ruling that such a gift was charitable, Issacs J held that the effect of the gift was:

> to provide for a religious act that involves the utmost piety towards the Supreme Being on behalf of an indefinite number of His creatures, and the object of which is to bring to them spiritual assistance, consolation and comfort, vastly surpassing the mere physical assuagement of pain or suffering that would incontestably be admitted to rank as an ordinary charity.

These sentiments were later echoed by Luxmore J in *Re Caus*,[120] when he justified the charitable status of gifts for the saying of masses on the grounds:

---

[115] See, for example, *Attorney General* v. *Cahill* [1969] 1 NSWR 85 (gift for the formation and advancement of a Catholic Boys' Club) and *Re Wilson's Grant* [1960] VR 514 (gift to a Girls' Friendly Society).

[116] *Re Stewart's Will Trusts* [1962] QWN 24.   [117] *Re Quaid* [1972] QWN 22.

[118] *Presbyterian Church (New South Wales) Property Trust* v. *Ryde Municipal Council* [1978] 2 NSWLR 387 (NSWCA).

[119] *Nelan* v. *Downes* (1917) 23 CLR 546, 571.   [120] *Re Caus* [1934] 1 Ch. 162.

408 AUSTRALIA

> first that it enables a ritual act to be performed which is recognized by a
> large proportion of Christian people to be the central act of their religion;
> and secondly, because it assists in the endowment of priests whose duty it
> is to perform that ritual act.[121]

The courts have had little difficulty in finding that missionary work
serves to advance religion. For example, gifts to 'the Christian Brethren',
and to 'foreign missions', have been found to be charitable and the court
will so regard all bona fide missionary work: whether seeking to advance
Christianity in general or the interests of a particular religion. Similarly,
gifts and organisations dedicated to indirectly advancing religion by
providing necessary support services will usually also qualify for charitable status.

Public policy, charity and common law constraints

The traditional presumption that gifts, bequests and organisations dedicated to religious purposes satisfy the public benefit requirement and
warrant charitable status continues in this jurisdiction.

Testamentary conditions and the common law

The resolutely defended principle of free testamentary disposition as
developed in British courts, subject only to the established common law
constraints of no merit, in breach of the law or is contrary to public
policy, has been followed in Australia. Again, as in that jurisdiction, any
bequest may be made subject to a religious condition. Where the bequest
is charitable, then the principle continues to attract such overriding respect
that there is a greater likelihood of an attached condition being found to be
non-charitable because of an infringement of traditional common law
rules for charitable status than because it breaches public policy.

Failure due to breach of common law rules

The construction of a bequest, the actual words used, can defeat a
testator's intention. It has often been the case that a testator's use of
wording confers an undue or uncertain degree of discretion on a named
agent and in so doing constructs a flaw that proves fatal to what would
otherwise have been a good charitable bequest. So, for example, in *Dunne*

---

[121] Ibid., *per* Luxmore J, at pp.169–170.

PUBLIC POLICY AND COMMON LAW CONSTRAINTS   409

v. *Byrne*[122] as in *Queensland Trustees Ltd.* v. *Halse*,[123] where the intent underpinning both testators bequests was undoubtedly charitable, the means of giving effect to it, by conferring discretion upon the Archbishop of Brisbane to deploy the gift 'wholly or in part ... conducive to the good of religion' and 'as he shall see fit ... for the benefit of the said Diocese', respectively, defeated that intent by allowing the Archbishop freedom to select purposes that may not be charitable. In the same way, the wording may introduce uncertainty as in the above *Lawlor* case. This was evident in *Executor Trustee and Agency Co. of Australia Ltd.* v. *Warby*,[124] which concerned a bequest to establish a Church of England hospital, without any additional information, but made subject to a requirement that the Synod give a written undertaking to use the bequest to establish such a facility. In this instance the deficiency was made good by the court adopting a benign approach and affirming the bequest as it found evidence of a general charitable intention. Alternatively, the wording may indicate that any charitable intent is subordinate to other considerations as in *Re Tyrie (deceased)*,[125] where the bequest to erect a Presbyterian church in a specified locality as a memorial to the testatrix's family was found to be non-charitable because, in the words of Gowans J: 'I can discern no dominant concern with the provision of religious amenities for the benefit of the local Presbyterian community.'

However, the case law in this area is far from consistent.

Bequests subject to a religious condition

Although sparse, the case law nonetheless indicates that courts and regulator have tended to follow the lead given by their counterparts in England regarding the well-established principle of a testator's right to make a bequest subject to a religious condition.[126] However, where the imposed restrictive constraint is uncertain in scope this will result in a denial of charitable status. This was the case, for example, in a bequest 'to the Presbyterians the descendants of those settled in the colony hailing from or born in the North of Ireland' in *Davies* v. *Perpetual*

---

[122] *Dunne* v. *Byrne* [1912] AC 407, PC.
[123] *Queensland Trustees Ltd.* v. *Halse* [1949] St R Qd 270.
[124] *Executor Trustee and Agency Co. of Australia Ltd.* v. *Warby* [1973] 6 SASR 336.
[125] *Re Tyrie (deceased)* [1970] VR 264.
[126] See, for example, *Omari* v. *Omari* [2012] ACTSC 33. See, further, P. Butt, 'Testamentary Conditions in Restraint of Religion' (1977) 8 *Sydney Law Review* 400.

410 AUSTRALIA

Trustee Co.[127] Otherwise, conditional gifts requiring adherence to a specified religious belief are not void against public policy. So the bequest to sons, conditional upon their wives converting to Protestantism, in *Trustees of Church Property of the Diocese of Newcastle* v. *Ebbeck*,[128] was valid in itself. Indeed, Windeyer J, in making his determination, declared the general validity of testator-imposed religious restraints on marriage.[129] Partial restraints on marriage, such as preventing marriage to a person of a particular religious denomination, race, ethnicity or class, have also been upheld.[130]

However, although there is no general prohibition on imposing a religious discriminatory condition on a bequest, where the imposition takes the form of a partial restraint and this is worded in such a way that it forces the beneficiary to divorce or prevents them from marrying, then it will be in breach of public policy. This, in fact, was the ultimate outcome in *Ebbeck*.

Religious preferences and public policy

Australian charity law has followed the British approach in developing a benign judicial view towards testamentary dispositions and affords them protection even where they are made subject to a testator's religious preferences which, in other circumstances, would constitute discrimination and a probable breach of public policy. This has been assisted both by the retention of the presumption that gifts for religious purposes are deemed charitable and by relatively weak legislative protection against discriminatory practices.

Public policy constraints

The rationale for imposing such constraints was articulated by Latham CJ in *Adelaide Company of Jehovah's Witnesses Inc* v. *Commonwealth*,[131] when he stated that 'it is consistent with the maintenance of religious

---

[127] *Davies* v. *Perpetual Trustee Co.* [1959] AC 439.
[128] *Trustees of Church Property of the Diocese of Newcastle* v. *Ebbeck* (1960) 104 CLR 394; [1961] ALR 339.
[129] *Trustees of Church Property of the Diocese of Newcastle* v. *Ebbeck* (1960) 104 CLR 394, at para. 5.
[130] *Seidler* v. *Schallhofer* [1982] 2 NSWLR 80.
[131] *Adelaide Company of Jehovah's Witnesses Inc* v. *Commonwealth* (1943) 67 CLR 116, at p.131.

PUBLIC POLICY AND COMMON LAW CONSTRAINTS 411

liberty for the State to restrain actions and courses of conduct which are inconsistent with the maintenance of civil government or prejudicial to the continued existence of the community'. This is an approach also evident in *Krygger* v. *Williams*[132] and *Judd* v. *McKeown*[133] (see, further, below) and continued by the Charities Act 2013, which confines itself to simply restating the existing law:

> A purpose of engaging in, or promoting, activities which are unlawful or contrary to public policy is disqualifying. Public policy refers to such matters as the rule of law and system of government. It does not refer to government policies.

This general common law rule, that to have or retain charitable status an entity must not breach public policy, was stretched to a degree by Santow J in *Public Trustee* v. *Attorney General of New South Wales*.[134] Noting that some states in Australia had not legislated to remove racial discrimination, he ruled that a trust which had such removal as an object could nevertheless be charitable. Santow J distinguished between trusts that were 'contrary to the established policy of the law' and trusts whose object is to 'introduce new law consistent with the way the law is tending'. This ruling indicates that in similar circumstances, a trust with objects that included the removal of religious discrimination would also be eligible for charitable status. It also, more importantly, pushes back the boundary at which trusts risk being denied such status due to a breach of public policy: where there is a reasonable expectation that the law will change, and in doing so remove the present conflict between it and the trust objects, then the latter may be interpreted as anticipating such compatibility rather than as challenging the status quo.

In the rather anomalous case of *Kay* v. *South Eastern Sydney Area Health Service*,[135] the testatrix gave a gift on trust to the Children's Hospital at Randwick – $10,000 for treatment of white (underlined twice) babies. Young J found the condition to be valid, an integral part of the gift and that in its entirety the gift did not breach public policy on the grounds of racism as both the Racial Discrimination Act 1975 (Cth), s.8 and the Anti-Discrimination Act 1977, s.55, expressly provide that any charitable disposition is not subject to the Act. There is no reason to suppose that Young J's decision would have been any different, or any

---

[132] *Krygger* v. *Williams* (1912) 15 CLR 366.   [133] *Judd* v. *McKeown* (1926) 38 CLR 380.
[134] *Public Trustee* v. *Attorney General of New South Wales* (1997) 42 NSWLR 600.
[135] *Kay* v. *South Eastern Sydney Area Health Service* [2003] NSWSC 292.

412 AUSTRALIA

the less unsatisfactory, if the restrictive condition had been religious rather than racist.

Advocacy

The rule prohibiting charities from advocating change in law or policy as their primary purpose,[136] although of less significance in relation to religious charities, has been as troublesome in Australia as in other common law jurisdictions.[137] As the ATO warn in Taxation Ruling TR 2005/21, at para. 111, 'a purpose of seeking changes to government policy or particular decisions of governmental authorities is also not charitable'. This simply confirms long-standing case law to the same effect: in *Re Cripps* establishing a trust for the purpose of promoting temperance through the introduction of legislation was found to be not charitable as being essentially political;[138] similarly in *Bacon* v. *Pianta*, when a gift to the Communist Party for its sole use was found to be non-charitable on political grounds.[139]

However, if the purpose is charitable, the presence of political or lobbying programmes and activities will not detract from charitable status, provided these are merely incidental to the charitable purpose. This allows charities to engage in many forms of political activity, including advocacy and campaigning to change law or policy. This approach is continued by the Charities Act 2013.[140]

Proselytism

The dividing line between persuasion as to the merits of one religion and deriding the absence of any in another is not always respected; often both constitute part of quite legitimate proselytising activity. Where, however, the latter takes the form of vilification of another religion or religious beliefs, then this breaches the right to religious freedom which is legislatively protected in a number of states. Typically, for example, in

---

[136] See ATO State in Taxation Ruling TR 2005/21, at para. 111, which states that 'a purpose of seeking changes to government policy or particular decisions of governmental authorities is also not charitable'.

[137] See, in particular, *AID/WATCH Incorporated* v. *Commissioner of Taxation* [2009] FCAFC 128.

[138] *Re Cripps* [1941] Tas SR 19.   [139] *Bacon* v. *Pianta* [1966] ALR 1044.

[140] Commencing on 1 January 2014. Also see, *AID/WATCH Incorporated* v. *Commissioner of Taxation* [2009] FCAFC 128.

Victoria s.8(1) of the Racial and Religious Tolerance Act 2001 states that 'a person must not, on the ground of the religious belief or activity of another person or class of persons, engage in conduct that incites hatred against, serious contempt for, or revulsion or severe ridicule of, that other person or class of persons'. While Australia has generated a number of cases on alleged vilification,[141] there would appear to be none on improper proselytism.

An absence of case law on proselytism seems propitious, as indicating no serious disputes, but it does seem a little suspect. The long history of competitive proselytism by Christian religions, Mormons,[142] etc., directed towards the conversion of members of the Indigenous community, might have been expected to trigger some litigious issues. Again, given the current level of dissension within the Catholic and Protestant Churches, with New Age and Evangelical movements developing a growing presence, the resulting competition for adherents (if not Church property) might also be expected to do so. Perhaps, in this jurisdiction, a high free speech threshold accommodates low-level improper proselytism and matters only reach the courts when the line is crossed by the abusive or coercive conduct of religious advocates.

Human rights, discrimination and religious charities: contemporary issues

The 2011 census showed that 24.6 per cent of Australians were born overseas, with the four largest overseas birthplace groups being the United Kingdom, New Zealand, China and India, which have remained as the principal sources of migrants over the past ten years, while some 2.5 per cent of the population identified as Aboriginal or Torres Strait Islanders. In keeping with this rapid growth in ethnic and cultural diversity, the religious affiliation of Australian citizens has also undergone considerable change. The burgeoning diversity requires a uniform nationwide legal framework of human rights and equality legislation to promote and safeguard a pluralistic society. This is not yet in place. Consequently, perhaps, there is relatively little case law to reveal how

---

[141] See, for example, *Deen v. Lamb* [2001] QADT 20 and *Catch the Fire Ministries Inc v. Islamic Council of Victoria Inc* [2006] VSCA 284 3751.

[142] See, further, 'LDS Outreach among the Indigenous Australians (Aborigines) of Australia' at: www.cumorah.com/index.php?target=view_other_articles&story_id=538&cat_id=30www. cumorah.com/index.php?target=view_other_articles&story_id=538&cat_id=30 (accessed 9 January 2014).

414   AUSTRALIA

Australia is coping with the tensions between religious beliefs and
human rights.

Human rights

Australian law provides only limited recognition for human rights: there
is neither a formal Bill of Rights or as extensive a human rights legislative
base as can be found in most European countries; nor does the Constitution
ensure rights to equality and non-discrimination.[143] However, it does have
a Human Rights and Equal Opportunity Commission (HREOC) established under the Human Rights and Equal Opportunity Commission Act
1986 (Cth), and each state has a form of human rights commission.
Further, the Human Rights (Parliamentary Scrutiny) Act 2011 (Cth),
which took effect on 4 January 2012, requires all new legislation introduced to the Federal Parliament to be assessed for compatibility with
human rights and it also established a new parliamentary joint committee on human rights.

A degree of protection can be found in s.116 of the 1901 Constitution
and in the provisions of certain international human rights law to which
Australia is a signatory.[144] Of the latter, the ICCPR, as ratified by
Australia in 1980,[145] is of particular importance, especially: Article
18(1), which protects the right to 'manifest one's religion' in 'worship,
observance, practice and teaching'; and Articles 2(1) and 26, which
protect the right not to be discriminated against in relation to discrimination on the basis of religion. Also relevant is the Declaration on the
Elimination of All Forms of Intolerance and of Discrimination Based on
Religion or Belief,[146] which elaborates upon the right to 'manifest' one's
religion in Article 18 of the ICCPR.

---

[143] See, further, G. Williams, *Human Rights under the Australian Constitution*, Oxford
University Press, Melbourne, 1999.

[144] Currently, Australia is a party to seven core international human rights treaties: the
International Covenant on Civil and Political Rights; the International Covenant on
Economic, Social and Cultural Rights; the International Convention on the
Elimination of All Forms of Racial Discrimination; the Convention on the
Elimination of All Forms of Discrimination against Women; the Convention against
Torture and Other Cruel, Inhuman or Degrading Treatment or Punishment; the
Convention on the Rights of the Child; and the Convention on the Rights of Persons
with Disabilities.

[145] Opened for signature 16 December 1966, 999 UNTS 171 (entered into force 23 March
1976).

[146] GA Res 36/55, UN GAOR, 36th sess, UN Doc A/36/684 (25 November 1981).

The Constitution

The Constitution came into effect on 1 January 1901. In general terms, the legislative capacity of the Commonwealth Parliament is limited by the Constitution: neither religion nor human rights are included among the 'heads of power' available to Parliament for legislative purposes. While this does not prevent Parliament legislating on some aspects of these matters, it can only do so tangentially.

The limitations of the constitutional references to the right of religious freedom in s.116 have been noted by the High Court of Australia, which has advised that the only laws invalidated under the establishment clause are those which: entrench 'a religion as a feature of and identified with the body politic'; 'constitute a particular religion or religious body as a State religion or State church'; or require 'statutory recognition of a religion as a national institution'. As s.116 refers only to the Commonwealth, its constitutional protection does not apply to the states or to local government; the states are basically free to make such laws relating to establishing a religion or regarding the exercise of a religion as they see fit. Over the intervening century since its inception, this section has been the subject of judicial deliberation on only four occasions, during which time the social and religious context has wholly changed.

Equality and diversity legislation

At the Commonwealth level, the Fair Work Act 2009 (Cth)[147] extends the specific legal protection previously given to religious non-discrimination in the workplace. At the state level, both the Racial Discrimination Act 1975 (Cth) and the Anti- Discrimination Act 1977 (NSW) contain substantive equality provisions; though both s.8(2) of the former and s.55 of the latter specifically exempt charitable gifts in wills. The Equal Opportunity Act 2010 (Vic), which took effect in August 2011, replaces the Equal Opportunity Act 1995 and strengthens discrimination laws in Victoria. It aims to encourage the identification and elimination of discrimination, sexual harassment and victimisation and their causes, and to promote and facilitate the progressive realisation of equality.

Conflicts between the right to religious freedom and the right to freedom of speech have been brought before the Australian courts on a

---

[147] Replacing the Workplace Relations Act 1996 (Cth).

416 AUSTRALIA

number of occasions.[148] Most recently, this was the focus of concern in *Catch the Fire Ministries Inc* v. *Islamic Council of Victoria Inc*,[149] when the Victorian Court of Appeal considered a ruling by the Victorian Civil & Administrative Tribunal that Catch the Fire Ministries (an incorporated association which carries out Christian activities within Australia) had engaged in conduct that contravened s.8 of the Racial and Religious Tolerance Act 2001 (Vic). This prohibits a person, on the ground of religious belief, from engaging in conduct that incites hatred against, serious contempt for, or revulsion or severe ridicule of, another person or group. Section 11 of that Act provides a defence to s.8 if the conduct was reasonable and in good faith in the course of any statement, publication, discussion or debate made or held, or any other conduct engaged in, for any genuine academic, artistic, religious or scientific purpose. The conduct complained of included statements made at a seminar presented by Catch the Fire Ministries in 2002, publication of a newsletter by Catch the Fire Ministries in 2001 and publication of an article on the Catch the Fire Ministries website in 2001. Some of the impugned statements included that: the Koran promotes violence and killing; the Koran teaches that women are of little value; Allah is not merciful; that Muslims practising Jihad are following the Koran and a number of other statements. Nettle J in the Court of Appeal suggested that the legitimacy of the defence hinged on whether the conduct was engaged in 'reasonably' for a genuine religious purpose such as would naturally reflect the views of reasonable members of a tolerant, multicultural society. Ultimately, the appeal was allowed, the court ruled that the orders of the tribunal be set aside as there had been no incitement to hatred of Muslims because of their Islamic faith.[150]

Equality legislation and exemption for charities

Australian legislation does not comprehensively address human rights and equality issues. It fails, for example, to provide specific protection

---

[148] See, for example: *Fletcher* v. *Salvation Army Australia (Anti Discrimination)* [2005] VCAT 1523 (1 August 2005); *Bropho* v. *Human Rights and Equal Opportunity Commission* [2004] FCAFC 16; *Judeh* v. *Jewish National Fund of Australia Inc* [2003] VCAT 1254; and *John Fairfax Publications Pty Ltd.* v. *Kazak* [2002] NSWADTAP 35.

[149] *Catch the Fire Ministries Inc* v. *Islamic Council of Victoria Inc* [2006] VSCA 284 3751.

[150] See, further, P. Parkinson, 'Enforcing Tolerance: Vilification Laws and Religious Freedom in Australia', 2005, at: http://sydneyanglicans.net/blogs/indepth/enforcing_tolerance_patrick_parkinson (accessed 9 January 2014).

against discrimination on the grounds of sexual orientation, gender identity, religion or social status. Moreover, certain bodies are privileged by being granted exemption from statutory constraints, for example under the Sex Discrimination Act 1984 (Cth), sporting clubs, religious bodies and charities are permanently exempt from the operation of the Act.

Religious charities, discrimination and exemptions

Although there is little in the way of state legislation providing direct human rights protection that has any bearing on the charitable status of Australian religious groups,[151] such as there is usually exempts religious organisations from most of its provisions. For example: s.54 of the Anti-Discrimination Act 1977 (NSW) provides: 'nothing in this Act affects . . . any other act or practice of a body established to propagate religion that conforms to the doctrines of that religion or is necessary to avoid injury to the religious susceptibilities of the adherents of that religion'; s.35 of the Age Discrimination Act 2004 exempts an act or practice of a body established for religious purposes that conforms to the doctrines, tenets or beliefs of that religion or is necessary to avoid injury to the religious sensitivities of adherents of that religion; and so, in identical terms, does s.37 of the Sex Discrimination Act 1984 (it also exempts a number of other activities such as the ordination or appointment of priests or other members of any religious order or the training or education of such persons and educational institutions established for religious purposes). However, the Sex Discrimination Amendment (Sexual Orientation, Gender Identity and Intersex Status) Bill 2013 has now amended the Sex Discrimination Act 1984 by inserting new protections from discrimination on the basis of sexual orientation, gender identity and intersex status. It is interesting that religious charities neither sought nor were permitted an extension of their religious exemption privileges to include those with a trans-sexual identity.

Religious charities as public bodies

Where it can be shown that the extent of control exercised by government over the activities of a charity – by means such as funding, policy

---

[151] See the Charter of Human Rights and Responsibilities Act 2006 (Vic) ss.14 and 19, and the Human Rights Act 2004 (ACT) ss.8, 11, 14 and 27.

418   AUSTRALIA

and activities – has reached a point where the latter has surrendered its independence, then a principal–agency relationship can be said to exist between the two parties (see also, Chapter 3). This matter arose for consideration in the *Central Bayside* case when, on appeal,[152] Gleeson CJ, Heydon and Crennan JJ strongly denied that such a relationship had arisen:

> The mere fact that the appellant and the government both have a purpose of improving patient care and health does not establish that the appellant has the purpose of giving effect to government purposes, abdicating any independent fulfilment of its own. The appellant's purpose is charitable. It remains charitable even though the government is the source of the funds it uses to carry out that purpose. Its consent to the attachment by the government of conditions to the employment of those funds does not establish that the appellant is not independently carrying out its purpose.[153]

Ordinarily, a religious charity that has in fact assumed such a relationship with government is liable to be treated as a proxy government entity and be required to forego any statutory exemption privileges to which it might otherwise be entitled. However, in Australia, following the decision in *Commissioner of Taxation* v. *Word Investments Limited*,[154] the legal situation became quite different from elsewhere in the common law world.

Traditionally, where a principal–agent relationship existed between two entities, both had to independently satisfy the charitable purpose and activities test if they were to qualify as charities: the approach of the courts in *Dominican Sisters*,[155] *Glebe Administration Board*[156] and *Theosophical Foundation*[157] demonstrated that control by another entity did not determine character or purpose. As Mason ACJ and Brennan J

---

[152] *Central Bayside Division of General Practice Ltd.* v. *Commissioner of State Revenue* (2003) 53 ATR 473; *Central Bayside Division of General Practice Ltd.* v. *Commissioner of State Revenue* (2005) 60 ATR 151.

[153] *Central Bayside* (2006) 228 CLR 168, 185 [40]. See also at 214 [144] (Kirby J), 230 [185] (Callinan J).

[154] *Commissioner of Taxation* v. *Word Investments Limited* (2008) 236 CLR 204.

[155] *Commissioner for ACT Revenue Collections* v. *Council of the Dominican Sisters of Australia*, 91 ATC 4602; (1991) 22 ATR 213.

[156] *Glebe Administration Board* v. *Commissioner of Pay-roll Tax (NSW)* (1987) 10 NSWLR 352; 87 ATC 4825; 19 ATR 297.

[157] *Theosophical Foundation Pty Ltd.* v. *Commissioner of Land Tax (NSW)* (1966) 67 SR (NSW) 70.

pointed out in *The Church of the New Faith* v. *Commissioner of Pay-roll Tax (Vic)*:

> It does not follow that the common religion of a group stamps a religious character on an institution founded, maintained or staffed by members of that group or that the purpose or activity of such an institution is religious.[158]

That approach was challenged by the decision in *Word*,[159] which concerned a nonprofit company of that name, founded by members closely associated with Wycliffe, a religious charity. In the period 1996–2002, Word operated a business of conducting funerals, the profits from which were used to support Christian activities in the form of Bible translation and missionary work largely carried out by Wycliffe. So, basically, Word was solely engaged in for-profit commercial activity. In rejecting an application from Word for charitable tax exemption, the ATO explained that 'commercial enterprise entities are not considered to be charities. This is the case irrespective of whether charitable consequences flow from the entity's activities.' Ultimately, however, the High Court, upholding the decision of the federal court in favouring charitable status, ruled that Wycliffe was at liberty to select any method it chose for the purpose of effectuating translations of the Christian Scriptures. This finding, that activities undertaken by an entity need not be intrinsically charitable for the entity to be a charity so long as they are directed to aiding or furthering the charitable purpose, was specifically negated by the Charities Act 2013. The new statutory provision, which repeats earlier ATO guidance and returns the law to pre-*Word*, states that:

> An entity must have only charitable purposes and must not have an independent, non-charitable purpose. An entity may have incidental or ancillary purposes that may be non-charitable when viewed in isolation, but which must aid or further the charitable purpose.

Freedom of religion

While the right to freedom of religion is not absolute, and nor does every breach of it necessarily constitute a breach of s.116, its importance should not be underestimated. As Mason ACJ and Brennan J asserted in *Church of the New Faith*: 'freedom of religion, the paradigm freedom

---

[158] *The Church of the New Faith* v. *Commissioner of Pay-roll Tax (Vic)* (1983) 154 CLR 120, at pp.128–129.
[159] *Commissioner of Taxation* v. *Word Investments Limited* (2008) 236 CLR 204.

420   AUSTRALIA

of conscience, is of the essence of a free society'. They also stressed that the protection of s.116 extends to those without religious belief and can accommodate all nascent minority religions that may yet emerge:

> Protection is accorded to preserve the dignity and freedom of each man so that he may adhere to any religion of his choosing or to none. . . . [T]he variety of religious beliefs which are within the area of legal immunity is not restricted.[160]

Interference with the manifestation of religious belief

In *Grace Bible Church* v. *Reedman*,[161] the court gave short shrift to the appellant's claim that 'there was an inalienable right to religious freedom'. Parliament, as White J commented, had 'an absolute right to interfere with religious worship and the expression of religious beliefs at any time that it liked'.[162]

That the judiciary could also so interfere was demonstrated a century ago in *Krygger* v. *Williams*,[163] when the court declined to hold that the compulsory military service provisions of the Defence Act 1903 prohibited a Jehovah's Witness, with religious objections to military service, from freely exercising his religion. The then Chief Justice, Sir Samuel Griffith, described such a proposition as 'absurd' and added that s.116 only protected 'the doing of acts which are done in the practice of religion. To require a man to do a thing which has nothing to do with religion is not prohibiting him from a free exercise of religion.' Subsequently, Higgins J in *Judd* v. *McKeown*,[164] where the appellant had been convicted of failing to vote 'without a valid and sufficient reason' contrary to the compulsory voting provisions of the Commonwealth Electoral Act 1918 (Cth), suggested that a religious duty not to vote would, in the light of s.116, be 'a valid and sufficient reason' for refusal to do so, emphasising (in a minority view) that the subjective perception of the person with religious belief would be the critical determinant. In *Adelaide Company of Jehovah's Witnesses Inc* v. *Commonwealth*,[165] at the height of the Second World War, Latham J commented that 's.116 is required to protect the religion (or absence of religion) of minorities and, in particular, of unpopular minorities'. He also rejected any suggestion that s.116 restricted the

---

[160] *Church of New Faith* v. *Commissioner of Pay-roll Tax* (1983) 154 CLR 120.
[161] *Grace Bible Church* v. *Reedman* (1984) 36 SASR 376.   [162] Ibid., at p.385.
[163] *Krygger* v. *Williams* (1912) 15 CLR 366.   [164] *Judd* v. *McKeown* (1926) 38 CLR 380.
[165] *Adelaide Company of Jehovah's Witnesses Inc* v. *Commonwealth* (1943) 67 CLR 116.

freedom of religion to freedom of thought or opinion. Instead, the use of the word 'exercise' suggested that 'the section goes far beyond protecting liberty of opinion. It protects also, acts done in pursuance of religious belief as part of religion'.[166]

Discrimination

At the Commonwealth level, anti-discrimination provisions are to be found in the Age Discrimination Act 2004, the Disability Discrimination Act 1992, the Racial Discrimination Act 1975, the Sex Discrimination Act 1984 and the Australian Human Rights Commission Act 1986. Some legislation, such as the Fair Work Act 2009 (Cth), offers limited protection against discrimination on the basis of religious belief. In November 2012, the government released a draft of its Human Rights and Anti-Discrimination Bill 2012, which is intended to consolidate Commonwealth anti-discrimination law and replace the above five existing Acts. Then, in March 2013, the Sex Discrimination Amendment (Sexual Orientation, Gender Identity and Intersex Status) Bill 2013 was introduced in Parliament. This amends the Sex Discrimination Act 1984 by inserting new protections from discrimination, and extending the ground of marital status to marital or relationship status to provide protection from discrimination for same-sex de facto couples.

In general, discrimination on the basis of religion is usually prohibited with respect to: employment, the provision of goods and services, accommodation, education, membership of clubs and participation in sporting activity and provision of government services.

Discrimination and same-sex marriage

In Australia, same-sex relationships became decriminalised following *Toonen* v. *Australia*,[167] and same-sex civil unions then became possible in Queensland, Tasmania, Victoria, New South Wales and ACT – but same-sex marriage remains impossible throughout the country. The latter is partially due to the passing of the Marriage Amendment Act 2004, which amended the Marriage Act 1961 by the insertion of the words 'marriage means the union of a man and a woman to the exclusion of all

---

[166] See P. Radan, D. Meyerson, R. F. Croucher, *Law and Religion: God, the State and the Common Law*, Routledge, London, 2005, at p.82.

[167] Communication No. 488/1992, UN Doc CCPR/C/50/D/488/1992.

others, voluntarily entered into for life', despite the well-documented history of polygamy in the country.[168] Any legislative process initiated to add Australia to the list of 14 countries that have so far legalised same-sex marriage will now necessarily be more complex. Currently, in South Australia a same-sex marriage bill has been introduced in the State parliament while the briefly returned Prime Minister Rudd had given advance notice of his intention to see this also happens at the Commonwealth level. It would seem probable that any such legislation will exempt religious organisations from a statutory obligation to either conduct same-sex wedding ceremonies or allow their churches to be used for that purpose.

Religious discrimination in practice

Religious bodies may avail of statutory protection from alleged discriminatory acts or practice when they can show that such conduct is required by or conforms to their religious doctrine. One consequence of the ruling in the *OV and OW*[169] case is that an act or practice will be exempt where required by a religious doctrine, even where the doctrine is held by only some elements in a particular denomination. Further, the exemption applies to the contemporary doctrines of the religious body. The doctrines are not required to be those that applied at the time of a religious body's establishment.

Unequal but not discriminatory

As in other federated jurisdictions, there is a lack of consistency across Australia as regards many aspects of discrimination: equality can be geographically determined. Same-sex couples, for example, are able to adopt only in Western Australia, New South Wales and the ACT.

In the protracted proceedings that constituted the *OV and OW* case much consideration was given to the exemption from the prohibitions on discriminatory conduct granted to religious bodies contained within s.54 of the Anti-Discrimination Act 1977 (NSW), which provides: 'nothing in this Act affects ... any other act or practice of a body established to propagate religion that conforms to the doctrines of that

---

[168] See, further, C. Evans and B. Gaze, 'Between Religious Freedom and Equality: Complexity and Context' (2008) 49 *Harvard International Law Journal* 40.

[169] *OV v. QZ (No 2)* [2008] NSWADT 115; *Member of the Board of the Wesley Mission Council* v. *OV and OW (No 2)* [2009] NSWADTAP 57; *OV & OW* v. *Members of the Board of the Wesley Mission Council* [2010] NSWCA 155.

religion or is necessary to avoid injury to the religious susceptibilities of the adherents of that religion'. In 2002, OV and OW, partners in a same-sex relationship, had sought to be authorised as foster carers by an agency of the Wesley Mission. They were informed that an application from them would not be accepted because of their relationship as a 'homosexual couple'. The claimants challenged that refusal claiming that it contravened the prohibition against discrimination on the grounds of homosexuality and marital status under the Anti-Discrimination Act 1977 (NSW). The Wesley Mission argued that they were exempted from the prohibition on discrimination because of the general exception provided for 'religious bodies' under s.54. The question for the court was whether Wesley Mission's refusal to consider the couple's application conformed to the relevant doctrines of the religion that the Wesley Mission was established to propagate.

In finally concluding the matter in December 2010, the NSWADT determined that the decision of the Wesley Mission to reject the applicants fell within one of the arms of the religious exemption found in s.54(d), and therefore did not breach the Act. As the form of words expressing the terms of exemption under this Act can be found in similar exemption provisions in much Australian legislation, this decision has potentially widespread ramifications.

Unequal but not discriminatory: contractual obligations

In concluding the *OV and OW* case, the tribunal also considered the relationship between the terms of the government funding contracts Wesley Mission had entered into, which prohibited discrimination on the grounds of sexual preference, and the exemption within the Act. In a helpful clarification for religious bodies operating under government funding contracts, the tribunal held that 'the terms of the agreements cannot override the provisions of the statute'.[170]

Unequal and discriminatory: restricting employment opportunities

Part 4 of the Equal Opportunities Act 2010 (Vic) prevents religious groups from discriminating in hiring staff on religious grounds, unless

---

[170] *OV & OW* v. *Members of the Board of the Wesley Mission Council* [2010] NSWCA 155, at para. 24.

424   AUSTRALIA

the organisation can identify how a person's sexual orientation or gender identity affects their ability to meet the inherent requirements of the job.

Unequal and discriminatory: restricting access to services

The *OV and OW* case was essentially concerned with the right of the Wesley Mission to withhold services, by not accepting an application to place a child in the foster care of a same-sex couple who were living in a homosexual relationship, on the grounds that its religious beliefs would be breached if it treated them the same as it did those whose status complied with the core Wesleyan doctrine of 'monogamous heterosexual partnership within marriage'. Ultimately, the court rejected the allegation of discrimination on finding that the Wesley Mission was able to avail of the s.54(d) protection as, at the relevant time, their doctrines were binding upon the Mission and could be construed as religious (see, further, above). By way of comparison, and to illustrate that doctrinal issues are not necessarily as restricting for other Christian charities, the practice of Uniting Care Burnside, part of the Uniting Church, has long held progressive attitudes towards homosexuality and it has a non-discriminatory policy when looking for safe environments in which to place foster children.

Again, in *Cobaw Community Health Services Limited v. Christian Youth Camps Limited & Anor*,[171] the issue was whether a religious body could claim statutory exemption from what would otherwise be discriminatory practice. This case concerned the WayOut project ('WayOut'), a youth suicide prevention initiative operated by Cobaw Community Health Service ('Cobaw') that targets homosexual young people in rural Victoria. Its attempt to make a booking at a resort operated by Christian Youth Camps Limited (CYC), a religious commercial entity established for purposes connected with the Christian Brethren religion, was rejected. Consequently, Cobaw alleged discrimination in contravention of the Equal Opportunity Act 1995 (Vic). CYC responded by claiming an entitlement to refuse service provision to people because of their sexual orientation, on the grounds of its religious beliefs. Hampel J found that CYC had refused to accept WayOut's booking for accommodation on the basis of sexual orientation and rejected the distinction

---

[171] *Cobaw Community Health Services Limited* v. *Christian Youth Camps Limited & Anor* [2010] VCAT 1613. See, further, at: www.austlii.edu.au/au/cases/vic/VCAT/2010/1613.html (accessed 9 January 2014).

HUMAN RIGHTS, DISCRIMINATION & RELIGIOUS CHARITIES 425

drawn between sexual orientation and promoting homosexuality. However, she was not satisfied that the purposes of CYC in the conduct of the adventure resort were religious and instead found that, although CYC's constitution declared its establishment was inspired by a religious motive, its purposes were not directly and immediately religious and neither were the camping activities it provided for both secular and religious groups.[172] She took the view that there was no evidence to suggest that conformity with their beliefs about marriage and sexuality required CYC to avoid contact with people who were not of their faith and who did not subscribe to their beliefs about God's will in respect of sex and marriage. Justice Hampel ultimately concluded that it was not necessary for the respondents to refuse the booking in order to comply with their genuine religious beliefs and in taking that step they had committed an act of discrimination in breach of the Act.

The exemption privileges traditionally exercised by religious charities must now be revised in the light of the Sex Discrimination Amendment (Sexual Orientation, Gender Identity and Intersex Status) Bill 2013. In particular, and very importantly, the provision of care services for the elderly by religious charities (which constitute approximately one-third of total aged care provision in Australia) will no longer be subject to opt-out caveats that previously permitted a refusal of services to those whose sexual orientation or gender identity offended the beliefs of service providers.[173] However, the exemption privileges will continue to allow religious charities to discriminate on such grounds in relation to health care, education and employment.

Unequal but 'positive action'

In *Kay* v. *South Eastern Sydney Area Health Service*,[174] a fund for the treatment of white babies was upheld as charitable. This might well be seen as a somewhat perverse interpretation of 'positive action', in that it clearly indicates an intention to discriminate against non-white babies which (certainly as regards those born to Indigenous parents) are more

---

[172] See also *Attorney-General* v. *Cahill* [1969] 1 NSWR 85, and *Roman Catholic Archbishop of Melbourne* v. *Lawlor* (1934) 51 CLR 1, where again the main secular activities of religious organisations were judged not to be a necessary means for advancing their religious purposes and were therefore not charitable.

[173] The faith-based aged care providers Mission Australia and Uniting Care strongly supported the removal of the religious exemption in this context.

[174] *Kay* v. *South Eastern Sydney Area Health Service* [2003] NSWSC 292.

likely to be socially disadvantaged, in need of the testator's bequest and representative of the targeting that underpinned the legislative intent. In reaching its decision, the court relied on the fact that charities are expressly exempt from anti-discrimination legislation and also upon the ground that 'the receipt of a fund to benefit white babies would just mean that more of the general funds of the hospital would be available to treat non-white babies so that, in due course, despite the testatrix's intention things will even up'.

Conclusion

In Australia, community and geographic links are attenuated, social cohesion is complicated by disparate patterns of immigration and by the presence of Indigenous people with their own distinct culture, while organisational capacity is fragmented by state-based administrative systems. After many false starts, the charity law reform process has now concluded with a legislative basis for a comprehensive regulatory system that will govern all nonprofits, including religious charities. This success is likely to be shortly followed by a not dissimilar initiative to consolidate, at federal level, the various state laws relating to human rights, discrimination and equality. In the course of preparing such new, streamlined and inclusive legal frameworks it would seem probable that room will be made to legalise same-sex marriage and address the related exemption privileges of religious bodies on the same nationwide basis. The end result will be a different, more joined-up and human rights-oriented environment, within which religious charities may have greater difficulty in claiming exemption than they formerly experienced. However, it will be some years before this new world takes shape. In the meantime, the judicial guidance available – e.g. in *Church of the New Faith*, *Word*, *OV and OW* and *Cobaw* – indicates that this jurisdiction will carve out its own path in regulating Church–State relations, relatively unconstrained by precedents set elsewhere in the common law world or by the establishment clause in the Constitution.

10

New Zealand

Introduction

In New Zealand, the original and continuing presence of Māori, with their distinctive culture and spiritual beliefs, together with the proximity of Pacific Island cultures and the influx from many other non-Christian cultures, have always challenged and stimulated government efforts to build a coherent pluralistic society. This prolonged exposure to the problems inherent in managing the mix of religions, charity and different cultural heritages makes the New Zealand experience of developing an appropriate legal framework particularly interesting.

This chapter begins by considering the Church–State relationship and the profile of the nonprofit sector, noting: the proportion of total charities with religious purposes (numbers, size, wealth, duration, etc.); the role played by religious charities within the sector; and the importance of government funding. It then outlines the charity law framework, describing and analysing the process of charity law reform and assessing the importance of reform outcomes. Attention then focuses on religion, religious type beliefs and the activities of charities dedicated to the purpose of the advancement of religion. This is followed by an examination of how public policy and certain common law rules have acted to constrain religion and charity in New Zealand. All of which leads up to the bulk of the chapter dealing with human rights, discrimination and religious charities. Essentially this is the case law section which explores the relatively few judicial and regulatory reported cases that illustrate the changes made in recent years to the law governing religion and religious discrimination.

Church, State and religious charities

From an early stage this jurisdiction has been reliant upon charities, most often religious organisations and church-centred community groups, to fill the gaps in public services by providing the health and social care facilities that the government could not afford. Not unlike Ireland, the working relationship between religious organisations and government prepared the ground for the contemporary government–sector partnership.

Background: government and the nonprofit sector

New Zealand has a proud tradition of self-reliance – of looking to family and community-based organisations rather than to government for support in times of need.[1] This has allowed or required charities, in common with other nonprofit bodies, to find their own space and develop as independent entities relatively free from regulatory restraint.

Government policy

In New Zealand, government policy must be set against the principles[2] embodied in that country's founding document, the Treaty of Waitangi,[3] as interpreted and applied in a contemporary context. As has been said: 'The Treaty has to be seen as an embryo rather than a fully developed and integrated set of ideas.'[4] Although its initial terms of reference were confined to the interests of the parties concerned, the Treaty has provided a 'constitutional' basis for recognising legal rights and for testing government policy in respect of all citizens: Treaty compatibility is now a political if not a legal imperative for all government policy initiatives. The broad umbrella of the Treaty has come to accommodate the common law and international conventions.

The installation of a new Labour government in 1999 triggered a series of measures, replicating those taken in the United Kingdom and foreshadowing those to come in Australia, to put in place mediatory

---

[1] See M. Tennant, *Paupers and Providers: Charitable Aid in New Zealand*, Allen & Unwin, Wellington, 1989, cited in G. Dal Pont, *Charity Law in Australia and New Zealand*, Oxford University Press, Melbourne, 2000, at p.78 *et seq.*

[2] See, for example, New Zealand Maori Council (*New Zealand Maori Council* v. *Attorney-General*) [1987] 1 NZLR 641.

[3] Signed on 6 February 1840 by representatives of the British Crown, and Maori chiefs from North Island at Waitangi on the Bay of Islands in New Zealand, and eventually consolidated by the Treaty of Waitangi Act 1975.

[4] See (*New Zealand Maori Council* v. *Attorney-General*) [1987] 1 NZLR 641, *per* P. Cooke.

CHURCH, STATE AND RELIGIOUS CHARITIES 429

structures that would give institutional recognition to the new government policy of rapprochement with the nonprofit sector. The appointment of a minister with specific responsibility for the sector in 1999, the Statement of Government Intentions for an Improved Community–Government Relationship (SOGI) in 2001 and the creation of the Office for the Community and Voluntary Sector in 2003, together with the establishment of the Charities Commission in 2005, all illustrate a movement towards closer relationships. A range of other initiatives followed, such as increased tax relief for contributions to nonprofit organisations.[5] Drawing on SOGI principles, which provided the framework for the State's approach to its relationship with the sector, a number of government agencies established national mechanisms for building and developing relationships with nonprofit organisations in their respective sectors (e.g. in health, housing, sport and recreation, international aid and development and services for children and families).

The nonprofit sector

In the 1980s–1990s, the switch in government funding tactics from grants aiding the sector to service contracts with targeted nonprofit providers marked a significant change in government policy and a period of deterioration in government–sector relations. Smith noted 'the new relationship which gives Government considerably greater control of that voluntary sector activity which it funds',[6] whereas Wilson argued that government funding redefined the nature of the relationship between the State and nonprofit organisations as 'Government has moved from investment in voluntary organizations to purchase of core government services, with voluntary organizations becoming alternative rather than complementary service providers.'[7] This was a period of

---

[5] See, further, M. Gousmett, 'The History of Charitable Purpose Tax Concessions in New Zealand' (2013) 19 *New Zealand Journal of Taxation Law and Policy* 139.

[6] V. Smith, 'Contracting for Social and Welfare Services: The Changing Relationship between Government and the Voluntary Sector in New Zealand', research paper presented at the Australian and New Zealand Third Sector Research Conference, Wellington, 2–5 July 1996.

[7] C. Wilson, *The Changing Face of Social Service Volunteering: A Literature Review*, Ministry of Social Development, Wellington, 2001, at p. 132. See also Baxter, K., 'Community–Government Relationships: Issues in Establishing Formal Linkages Between Central Government and the Community Sector', paper for presentation at the

430 NEW ZEALAND

well-recorded dissatisfaction with the contract culture[8] and consequent soul searching for the sector.[9]

Building a modern Church–State relationship

In the Constitution Act 1986 there is neither provision for the separation of Church and State nor for establishing a specific religion. Indeed, there is no New Zealand constitution as such.[10]

Religion(s)

New Zealand has a population of about 4.2 million, of which approximately 78 per cent identify with European ethnic groups, mostly British or Irish. According to the 2006 Census,[11] just over two million people, or 55.6 per cent of those answering the religious affiliation question, affiliated with a Christian religion (including Māori Christian), compared with the 60.6 per cent of people who did so at the 2001 Census. Despite an overall decrease in Christian religions, some Christian denominations increased; the five largest in 2001 – Anglican, Catholic, Presbyterian (Congregation and Reformed), Christian not further defined and Methodist – remained the largest in 2006.

The Indigenous Māori people are the largest non-European ethnic group, accounting for 14.6 per cent of the population of New Zealand. For Māori, in common with Indigenous people generally, religion and culture are closely interwoven: their religious or spiritual beliefs form the shared reference points for daily life.

Strengthening Communities Through Local Partnerships symposium, University of Auckland, 12 April 2002.

[8] See, e.g. G. Nowland-Foreman, 'Can Voluntary Organizations Survive the Bear Hug of Government Funding under a Contracting Regime? A View from Aotearoa/New Zealand' (1997) 3 *Third Sector Review* 5; J. Cribb, 'Accounting for Something: Voluntary Organizations, Accountability and the Implications for Government Funders' (2005) 26 *Social Policy Journal of New Zealand* 43.

[9] See M. O'Brien, J. Sanders and M. Tennant, *The New Zealand Non-Profit Sector and Government Policy*, Office for the Community and Voluntary Sector, Wellington, 2009, at p.13.

[10] See, further, at: www.beehive.govt.nz/release/govt-begins-cross-party-constitutional-review (accessed 10 January 2014); and at: www.radionz.co.nz/national/programmes/constitutional-review (accessed 10 January 2014).

[11] The planned 2011 Census was postponed to 2013 following earthquake disruption. See, further, at: www.census.govt.nz (accessed 10 January 2014).

Secularisation

As the Human Rights Commission point out: 'New Zealand is a secular State with no State religion, in which religious and democratic structures are separated',[12] albeit within a distinct Christian colonial heritage. This would appear to be borne out by the 2006 Census statistics, which indicate that the proportion of the population without any religious belief continues to increase: in 2006, 34.7 per cent stated that they had no religion, compared with 29.6 per cent in the 2001 Census. Arguably, however, Māori culture – conflated with its distinctive heritage of spiritual beliefs and reinforced by the Treaty of Waitangi – has grown to exercise a considerable 'establishment' presence.

Secular education is provided for in the Education Act 1964, which specifies that teaching in primary schools 'shall be entirely of a secular character' and only permits religious instruction and 'observances' within defined conditions.[13]

An 'established' religion

There is no suggestion of an 'established' religion, nor of any appetite for one, in this jurisdiction.

Equality of religions

As in other common law jurisdictions, the judiciary have been at pains to emphasise their independence and impartiality when considering religious issues, as was evident in *Liberty Trust* v. *Charities Commission*[14] when Mallon J pointed out that: 'it is not for the Court to impose its own view as to the religious beliefs that are advanced through the scheme'.[15] Moreover, as Gresson J pronounced in *Watch Tower Bible and Tract Society* v. *Mount Roskill Borough*, 'every person is free to choose the context of his own religion and it is not for a Court, in a field in which it can profess no competence, to disqualify upon some *a priori* basis

---

[12] See, further, at: www.hrc.co.nz/report/chapters/chapter09/religion02.html (accessed 10 January 2014).

[13] See A.-M. Mooney Cotter, *Heaven Forbid: An International Legal Analysis of Religious Discrimination*, Ashgate, Surrey, 2009, at p.79.

[14] *Liberty Trust* v. *Charities Commission*, HC WN CIV 2010-485-000831 [2 June 2011].

[15] Ibid., at para. 125.

certain beliefs as incapable of being religious in character'.[16] It is important to bear in mind, however, that this was not always the case: the Tohunga Suppression Act 1907 specifically discriminated against Māori spiritual beliefs;[17] it has been observed that 'this Act forms part of a particularly shameful part of the history of Māori/Pakeha relations, and no doubt forms part of the various Treaty breaches for which the government has been apologising and paying compensation in more recent times'.[18]

Religious organisations and the nonprofit sector

Because of the historical lack of any system for registering their existence, it has been difficult to estimate trends in the number and type of charities in New Zealand, let alone gauge their impact.[19] While there can be little doubt that religious organisations constitute the oldest and wealthiest part of the nonprofit sector, acquiring accurate information as to their number, geographical spread and denominational affiliation is problematic.

Religious charities

In New Zealand, as in other common law jurisdictions, religious organisations have traditionally made a significant contribution to sector capacity, particularly as regards service provision in the areas of education, health and social care. From an early stage the prevailing policy has been to encourage charities, usually Church-based community groups, to fill the gaps in public services by providing the health and social care facilities for the poor, ill or those otherwise disadvantaged. The last two

---

[16] *Watch Tower Bible and Tract Society* v. *Mount Roskill Borough* [1959] NZLR 1236, at p.1241.

[17] 7 Edw. VII No. 13. This being 'An Act to suppress Tohungas.' It was an Act of two pages containing only four sections. The Act was not repealed until 1962 – see Māori Community Development Act 1962 No. 133 (14 December 1962) at Schedule 44 Enactments repealed (author is indebted to Michael Gousmett for this information).

[18] Susan Barker, personal communication, 24 July 2013.

[19] See G. Hawke and D. Robinson (eds), *Performance Without Profit: The Voluntary Sector in New Zealand*, Institute of Policy Studies, Wellington, 1993. Also see, reports commissioned by Philanthropy New Zealand in 1996, 1998 and 2002 to measure philanthropic funding; and the most recent and comprehensive source of information, Robinson and Hanley's report Funding New Zealand (2002). See, further, at: www.philanthropy.org. nz/sites/all/files/funding-NZ-2002.pdf (accessed 10 January 2014).

decades of the nineteenth century, for example, saw the Women's Christian Temperance Union well established in the colonial settlements of New Zealand.

Currently, religious organisations constitute the third largest sector group (10.2 per cent) in terms of numbers of nonprofits (9890), with the second largest number of institutions (1910) employing staff, but only the fifth largest number of employees (9390). A total of 80.7 per cent of these organisations rely entirely on volunteers to maintain their operations. Their main source of income is from donations, memberships and grants (71 per cent). Religious charities are also strongly represented in other sector groups such as education and research, and in social services.[20] Of the 26,259 charities registered with the Charities Commission in June 2013, the second largest single group (1205 organisations) comprised those involved in religious activities.[21]

Religious umbrella bodies

The New Zealand Council of Christian Social Services is an umbrella organisation that now provides representation for the Anglican Care Network, Baptist Churches of Aotearoa New Zealand, Catholic Social Services, Presbyterian Support NZ, the Methodist Church and the Salvation Army.

Government funding of religious charities: the policy

Traditionally, the nonprofit sector as a whole has been very dependent upon government funding, either directly or through funding streams overseen by government, such as the state-controlled lotteries system, state-regulated gaming machine proceeds and statutory community trusts. By the turn of the century the New Zealand Council of Christian Social Services had identified a government preference for contract-based funding of nonprofit activity.[22] This strategy became more evident

---

[20] See Office for the Community & Voluntary Sector at: www.dia.govt.nz/Decommissioned-websites---Office-of-the-Community-and-Voluntary-Sector-website (accessed 10 January 2014).

[21] Charities Commission, *A Snapshot of New Zealand's Charitable Sector*, Charities Commission, Wellington, 2011. See, further, at: www.charities.govt.nz (accessed 10 January 2014).

[22] New Zealand Council of Christian Social Services, *Towards a Real Partnership: A NZCCS Review of the Relationship Between Voluntary Social Services and NZ Community Funding Agency*, New Zealand Council of Christian Social Services, Wellington, 1998.

in 2003 with the Labour-led government policy programme 'Funding for Outcomes', and in particular by the 'Pathway to Partnership' programme in 2008, which signalled a desire to move towards more grant-like funding arrangements for what were described as essential social services.[23] Despite the extent of government funding, it has been reported that the sector generates most of its own income.[24]

Government funding of religious charities with discriminatory practices

As elsewhere in the common law world, current government funding policy of social infrastructure facilities initially created by religious organisations is a telling indicator of Church–State relationships, particularly in relation to the provision of a national education system. In New Zealand, the Private Schools Conditional Integration Act 1975 brought private, faith-based and other schools, many with charitable status, into the public-funded state education system. In 2005 government funding to the 239 Catholic schools and 75 other denomination-specific schools was provided on condition that such schools also enrolled children of other faiths; the proportion of annual school intake reserved for that purpose is unknown.[25] The role of religious organisations in the school system, and the channelling of government funds to them, has proved to be as contentious in this as in other common law jurisdictions.

Charity law and the regulatory framework

Until the partial introduction of the Charities Act in July 2005 there was no system of registration,[26] no regulatory framework and no central regulatory body for charities in New Zealand. This may have been due

---

[23] www.msd.govt.nz/about-msd-and-our-work/work-programmes/initiatives/pathway-to-partnership/key-information (accessed 10 January 2014).

[24] See G. Nowland-Foreman, 'No Longer Overlooked and Undervalued', at the launch of the New Zealand Non-Profit Sector in Comparative Perspective, Wellington, 12 August 2008. See, further, at: www.communityresearch.org.nz/research/no-longer-overlooked-and-undervalued-launch-of-the-new-zealand-non-profit-sector-in-comparative-persp ective (accessed 10 January 2014).

[25] However, note the Private Schools Conditional Integration Amendment Act 1977, ss.3 and 4, which provide powers to 'preserve and safeguard the special character of the education provided by the school'.

[26] There was no systematic system of registration until the 2005 Act. As at 23 July 2013 there were 26,459 charities on the charities register.

CHARITY LAW AND THE REGULATORY FRAMEWORK   435

to an implicit understanding between government and the charitable sector that a self-regulatory approach from within the sector rather than an imposed State system was more appropriate. The charity law reform process, which concluded with the Charities Act 2005, introduced some change to the established and typical common law regulatory framework, if rather less than anticipated. The Charities Commission was positioned, if briefly, as the centrepiece of a new regulatory framework. More recently, the government has embarked upon further reform by developing a new rebate regime for charities as evidenced by the changes introduced in the 2007 budget and, crucially, by disestablishing the Commission as an independent entity.

Legislation

The Charities Act 2005, together with the Income Tax Act 2007, now provides the legislative framework for charities (in conjunction with the Incorporated Societies Act 1908, the Trustee Act 1956, the Charitable Trusts Act 1957 and the Companies Act 1993). The 2005 Act neither repeals nor significantly amends any previous legislation,[27] nor have any legislative steps been taken to broaden the traditional *Pemsel* list of charitable purposes or to alter the public benefit presumption. However, New Zealand's Charities Commission has stated that:

> all charities must have public benefit. When we look at that, we look at, firstly, whether there is a benefit, which means that we will also look at whether there are harms that are caused; and, secondly, we look at the extent to which the charity is accessible to the public.[28]

A review of the Charities Act, including the legal definition of 'charitable purpose', scheduled for completion in 2015, has now been cancelled.[29]

---

[27] However, it inserts slight amendments to the Estate and Gift Duties Act 1968, the Incorporated Societies Act 1908, the Tax Administration Act 1994, the Income Tax Act 2004, the Crown Entities Act 2004 (2004 No. 15) and the Ombudsmen Act 1975 (1975 No. 9).

[28] Mr Trevor Garrett, Chief Executive, Charities Commission New Zealand, Committee Hansard, 28 June 2010, at p.25. As cited in the Economics Legislation Committee, *Tax Laws Amendment (Public Benefit Test) Bill 2010 Report*, Economics Legislation Committee, Canberra, 2010, at p.18.

[29] Information provided by Susan Barker (personal communication, 24 July 2013). See, further, at: http://my.lawsociety.org.nz/news/charities-act-review-cancelled (accessed 10 January 2014).

436 NEW ZEALAND

The Charitable Trusts Act 1957

This statute, which remains unaltered by the 2005 Act, provided further consolidation of previous legislative provisions and the rudiments of a supervisory system.

Section 2 explains that 'charitable purpose' means every purpose which in accordance with the law of New Zealand is charitable; and, for the purposes of Parts I and II, includes every purpose that is religious or educational, whether or not it is charitable according to the law of New Zealand. Section 61A specifically retains the principle that a trust or institution must be for the public benefit to be charitable.

The charity regulator

Part I of the Charities Act 2005 established a new Autonomous Crown Entity (ACE),[30] the Charities Commission, to implement and maintain a registration, reporting and monitoring system for charities and for investigating complaints.[31] While retaining its responsibilities in relation to donee status, the Inland Revenue Department transferred to the Charities Commission the power to grant an organisation 'charitable status' for income tax purposes, but only if that organisation satisfied four requirements:

(1) it must be carried on exclusively for charitable purposes;
(2) it must not be carried on for the private pecuniary profit of any individual;
(3) it must have a provision in its rules requiring the assets of the organisation to be transferred to another entity with charitable purposes if the organisation ceases to exist; and
(4) it must not have the power to amend its rules in such a way as to alter the exclusively charitable nature of the organisation.

Once registered, charities are generally eligible for exemptions from income tax on some, or all, of their income and need not apply to Inland Revenue for those exemptions.

In May 2012 the Commission was disestablished as an ACE and merged with the Department of Internal Affairs (DIA); its registration

---

[30] An ACE is an organisation that is independent of government but must 'have regard' for government policy when directed by the responsible minister.

[31] As recommended by the Working Party and earlier by the 1989 Spencer Russell report, the report of the Accountability of Charities and Sporting Bodies Working Party and in the more recent Statement of Government Intentions.

CHARITY LAW AND THE REGULATORY FRAMEWORK   437

and deregistration duties were transferred to the Charities Registration Board. This body is now responsible for the administration of the Charities Act 2005, while amendments to the Income Tax Act 2004 and the Estate and Gift Duties Act 1968[32] have ensured that since July 2008 only those registered as 'charitable entities' are exempted from income tax, and gift duty is now entirely abolished.[33]

Charity law

An understanding of what constitutes a charity has been developed by applying common law principles and remains based on the Preamble to the Statute of Charitable Uses,[34] even though the statute never had any direct application to New Zealand. This heritage, as extended by following case law precedents established in England and by broadening its contemporary relevance under the 'spirit or intendment' rule[35] within the *Pemsel*[36] classification of charitable purposes, formed a foundation for the development of charity law in this jurisdiction: a foundation which it has now outgrown. The Religious, Charitable and Educational Trusts Act 1908, as subsequently amended in 1928, consolidated the law relating to charitable trusts and, as Dal Pont notes, under s.3 defined 'charitable purpose' as every other purpose which in accordance with the law of England is a charitable purpose.[37]

The common law

By the time this jurisdiction acquired a measure of independence in 1840, the development of its legal framework for charities was rooted in common law principles.[38] The characteristic hallmarks of charity law as

---

[32] The Charities Act Commencement Order 2006 came into force on 1 July 2008, inserting amendments to the Income Tax Act 2004 (ss.64–68) and an amendment to the Estate and Gift Duties Act 1968 (s.72).

[33] See, further, M. Gousmett, 'Examinations and Inquiries into Charities' (2013) April *New Zealand Law Journal* 97.

[34] Statute of 43 Eliz. 1 cap. 4.

[35] See *Commissioner of Inland Revenue* v. *Medical Council of New Zealand* [1997] 2 NZLR 297, when Thomas J expressed the view that the 'spirit and intendment' rule should be used with more attention to contemporary circumstances than to case precedents.

[36] See *Income Tax Special Commissioners* v. *Pemsel* [1891] AC 531.

[37] See Dal Pont, *Charity Law in Australia and New Zealand*, at p.81.

[38] For further information on the legislative history, see Dal Pont, *Charity Law in Australia and New Zealand*, at p.78 *et seq.*

established in England and Wales (see, further, Chapter 2) have played their customary role and, subject to some specific adjustments, continue to do so under the 2005 Act.

Charity law reform

Following on from its largely tax-centred attempts at reform in 1979,[39] 1989,[40] and 1998,[41] government in New Zealand completed its charity law reform process with the launch of the Charities Act 2005, which is seen as a cornerstone of its partnership policy. As a minister declared: 'This legislation is a symbol of this government's commitment to growing the relationship between government and the charitable sector.'[42]

Reform outcomes

Decoupling the responsibilities for determining charitable status and eligibility for tax exemption has been the principal reform outcome, with the former being subsequently, if briefly, vested in the Charities Commission. The Charitable Trust Act 1957 continues in effect.

However, on 31 May 2012, as part of sweeping cost-cutting measures, Parliament passed the Charities Amendment Act (No. 2) 2012, which wound up the Charities Commission as of 1 July, and moved its core functions to the DIA. The disestablishment of the Commission was followed by the creation of a statutory three-person Charities Registration Board, which now has responsibility for registration and deregistration decisions and for related functions, while the DIA is vested with monitoring, investigating and prosecuting functions. Although viewed by many in the nonprofit sector as a retrograde step, this development has at least served to consolidate the functions of the Charities Commission and the Office for the Community and Voluntary Sector under the roof of the Department of Internal Affairs.

---

[39] Property Law and Equity Reform Committee, *Report on the Charitable Trusts Act*, Property Law and Equity Reform Committee, Wellington, 1979.

[40] Working Party on Charities and Sporting Bodies, *Report to the Minister of Finance and the Minister of Social Welfare by the Working Party on Charities and Sporting Bodies*, Treasury, Wellington, 1989.

[41] Committee of Experts on Tax Compliance, *Tax Compliance: Report to the Treasurer and Minister of Revenue*, Inland Revenue Department, Wellington, 1998.

[42] From media statement made by the Honourable Judith Tizard, Associate Minister of Commerce, announcing the new legislation on 14 April 2005.

CHARITY LAW AND THE REGULATORY FRAMEWORK   439

Charitable purposes

The Charities Act 2005 incorporated the established common law governing charities into legislation. The four *Pemsel* heads of charity, together with the accompanying common law rules and concepts (which require, for example, that an organisation be established and maintained exclusively for charitable purposes,[43] be for the public benefit and that no private profits accrue to any individual), were placed onto the statute book, thereby, in keeping with the UK and Irish jurisdictions, giving the legislature the future capacity to amend and extend the *Pemsel* list and adjust the public benefit rules. Otherwise, no alteration was made to the long-established substance of the law; in particular, and unlike those jurisdictions, there was no inclusion of a *Pemsel*-plus list of purposes.[44] The public benefit presumption prevails in regard to the first three *Pemsel* heads but 'the question whether a gift is or may be operative for the public benefit is a question to be answered by the Court by forming an opinion on the evidence before it',[45] whereas it must be expressly proven in respect of the fourth.[46]

The public benefit test and religious organisations

The new legislation is said to provide the most stringent test of purpose while strengthening the enforcement of the existing exemptions and providing a basis for policy review of their scope.[47] For present purposes,

---

[43] See *MK Hunt Foundation Ltd.* v. *Commissioner of Inland Revenue* [1961] NZLR 405, where the presence of non-charitable objects was fatal to a claim for charitable status. See also *Auckland Medical Aid Trust* v. *Commissioner of Inland Revenue* [1979] 1 NZLR 382 and *New Zealand Society of Accountants* v. *Commissioner of Inland Revenue* [1986] 1 NZLR 147, *per* Somers J, at p. 157. But note that the Privy Council stated in *Latimer* v. *Commissioner of Inland Revenue* [2004] 3 NZLR 157 (PC) that trusts are not required to be established and maintained for exclusively charitable purposes. This was reflected in the income tax legislation, which in turn is reflected in the two tests in ss.13(1)(a) and (b) of the Charities Act 2005 (information provided by Susan Barker, personal communication, 24 July 2013).

[44] Note, however, that clause 7 of the Statutes Amendment Bill (No. 2), introduced on 22 February 2011, proposes to amend the definition of 'charitable purpose' in the Charities Act to include an entity that promotes sport, if the purpose is 'expressed to be, and is in fact, the means by which a charitable purpose (such as the promotion of health or education) will be achieved'.

[45] *Molloy* v. *Commissioner of Inland Revenue* [1981] 1 NZLR 688, at p.695.

[46] *Canterbury Development Corporation* v. *Charities Commission* [2010] 2 NZLR 707.

[47] www.community.net.nz/hottopics/charities/publicationsresources/guidance.htm (accessed 10 January 2014).

440 NEW ZEALAND

the main point is that the 2005 Act did not alter the presumption that charities for the purpose of advancing religion are for the public benefit. As Mallon J noted in *Liberty Trust* when dealing with a trust which has as its purpose the advancement of religion, 'the starting assumption is that it has a public benefit'.[48]

The test

A trust or institution must be for the public benefit to be charitable.[49] As Gallen J put it in *Educational Fees Protection Society Inc* v. *Commissioner of Inland Revenue*,[50] when evaluating the presence of the requisite public benefit the question to be addressed was whether the Society was 'substantially altruistic in character'. Both arms of this test must be satisfied.

- Public

In *Travis Trust* v. *Charities Commission*,[51] the first of many unsuccessful challenges to Commission decisions, the High Court upheld the Commission's decision to refuse to register the trust as a charitable entity, stating that, as its membership was not open to the public generally, the club was not 'the community' – or a sufficient section of it – to amount to 'the public' as was required to satisfy the public benefit test. Again, in 2009, the Freemasons lost the charitable status it had held since 1933 when Simon France J, rejecting a subsequent appeal, ruled that the activities of the Grand Lodge, and freemasonry in general, 'do not benefit the public other than indirectly and intangibly by seeking to produce members who are better citizens'.[52] The importance of the 'public' dimension was also noted by Mallon J in *Liberty Trust* when, in affirming the charitable nature of the Trust's mortgage lending scheme, she commented that 'the benefits of the scheme are not focused too narrowly on

---

[48] *Liberty Trust* v. *Charities Commission* [2011] NZHC 577, *per* Mallon J, at para. 125.
[49] See C. Rickett, 'A Statutory Charitable Trust' (2000) March *New Zealand Law Journal* 59.
[50] *Educational Fees Protection Society Inc* v. *Commissioner of Inland Revenue* [1992] 2 NZLR 115.
[51] *Travis Trust* v. *Charities Commission*, CIV-2008-485-1689, HC, Wellington (3 December 2008).
[52] *Re The Grand Lodge of Ancient Free and Accepted Masons in New Zealand* (High Court of New Zealand, Simon France J, 9 August 2010). See, further, at: www.nzlii.org (accessed 10 January 2014).

CHARITY LAW AND THE REGULATORY FRAMEWORK 441

its adherents. It is open to anyone and the money donated is "recycled" for the benefit of others'.[53]

- Benefit

This arm of the test will be breached if anything other than incidental benefit accrues to members of a charitable organisation.[54] Curiously, this proposition was applied in a sequence of cases concerning Church financial schemes.

In *Presbyterian Church of New Zealand Beneficiary Fund* v. *Commissioner of Inland Revenue*,[55] a superannuation scheme for retired ministers of the Presbyterian Church was accepted as a charity. While recognising the financial benefits to be provided to particular persons – the ministers – the court viewed them as incidental to the advancement of religion. The importance of the ministry to the Church and the life-long commitment were particular features influencing the decision. In *Hester* v. *Commissioner of Inland Revenue*,[56] however, the Church of Jesus Christ of Latter-day Saints Deseret Benefit Plan was not accepted as a charity. It covered employees of two of the Church's entities, employed in administration and education. The court distinguished the circumstances from those in the Presbyterian Church of New Zealand Beneficiary Fund case. It covered employees generally, whose roles were more transferable to other employment, and whose employment activities were not 'essential' to the operation of the Church. The court declared the Presbyterian Church of New Zealand Beneficiary Fund to be an exceptional case, and that it did not authorise the proposition that any Church-controlled superannuation scheme for its employees would be a charity. Then, in *Liberty Trust* v. *Charities Commission*,[57] the High Court reinstated a Christian mortgage lending scheme as a charity after it was struck off the Register of Charities by the Charities Commission. The latter had taken the view that the scheme, run in accordance with

---

[53] *Liberty Trust* v. *Charities Commission* [2011] NZHC 577, *per* Mallon J, at para. 125.

[54] See *Latimer* v. *Commissioner of Inland Revenue* [2004] 3 NZLR 157 (PC), at 35. See also *New Zealand Society of Accountants* v. *Commissioner of Inland Revenue* [1986] 1 NZLR 147 (CA), at 152.

[55] *Presbyterian Church of New Zealand Beneficiary Fund* v. *Commissioner of Inland Revenue* [1994] 3 NZLR 363.

[56] *Hester* v. *Commissioner of Inland Revenue* (2004) 21 NZTC 18, 421.

[57] *Liberty Trust* v. *Charities Commission*, HC WN CIV 2010-485-000831 [2 June 2011]. See, further, at: https://wiki.qut.edu.au/display/CPNS/Liberty+Trust+v+Charities+Commission (accessed 10 January 2014).

'biblical principles' and funded largely by donations,[58] was not for the advancement of religion as there was no public benefit. The benefits arising under the scheme were purely private (see, further, below).

Religion, religious beliefs and the advancement of religion

In New Zealand it would seem at first sight that the traditional approach to the definition of 'religion' continues to hold sway: the twin common law requirements of belief in a Supreme Being and worship of that Being are evident; accompanied by the customary necessity for tenets, canons or doctrines. Indeed, the activities of organisations registered as for the purpose of the advancement of religion also appear to be largely of the traditional orthodox variety, mainly concerned with promoting the work of the church and in education and health care service provision. In fact, however, the reality is a little different.

Religion

The referencing of traditional hallmarks is clearly present in the leading Australian case, *Church of the New Faith* v. *Commissioner of Pay-roll Tax.*[59] This has been followed by the New Zealand judiciary, particularly the judgment delivered by Mason ACJ and Brennan J that these requirements are to be interpreted broadly and flexibly:

> first, belief in a supernatural Being, Thing or Principle and second, the acceptance of canons of conduct in order to give effect to that belief, though canons of conduct which offend against ordinary laws are outside the area of any immunity, privilege or right conferred on the grounds of religion. Those criteria may vary in their comparative importance and there may be a different intensity of belief or of acceptance of canons of conduct among religions or among the adherents to a religion. The tenets of a religion may give primacy to one particular belief or to one particular canon of conduct. Variations in emphasis may distinguish one religion from other religions, but they are irrelevant to the determination of an

---

[58] As explained on their website:

> Since 1989 Liberty Trust has been teaching & enabling New Zealanders to follow God's financial principles of giving, lending and borrowing without interest, in order to assist those in financial difficulty, relieve financial burdens and advance the Kingdom of God.

See, further, at www.libertytrust.org.nz (accessed 10 January 2014).

[59] *Church of the New Faith* v. *Commissioner of Pay-roll Tax* (1983) 154 CLR 120.

THE ADVANCEMENT OF RELIGION   443

individual's or a group's freedom to profess and exercise the religion of
his, or their, choice.[60]

As Dal Pont has noted, the other members of the Bench – Wilson and
Deane JJ – added three further indicia of a religion: 'that its ideas relate to
man's nature and place in the universe and his or her relation to things
supernatural; that its adherents constitute an identifiable group or groups;
and that its adherents themselves see the collection of ideas and/or
practices as constituting a religion'.[61] Dal Pont makes the point that,
given the Pacific Rim cultural context of Australia and New Zealand, the
judiciary in this and other cases can be seen interpreting 'religion' so as
to give recognition to the fact 'that some, mostly Eastern religions are not
theistic which [sic] thereby releases the law from Judeo-Christian
notions'. This prompted the New Zealand and Australian judiciary to
digress from the traditional formulaic definition of 'religion' at an earlier
stage than their contemporary English counterparts (see also, Chapter 9).[62]

Belief in a Supreme Being

The principles stated above by Mason ACJ and Brennan J in *Church of
the New Faith* were accepted and applied by Tomkins J in the New
Zealand case *Centrepoint Community Growth Trust* v. *Commissioner of
Inland Revenue*,[63] which concerned an incorporated community of like-
minded persons who shared the common purpose of advancing the
spiritual education and humanitarian teachings of Herbert Thomas
Potter and 'of all the messengers of god'. These were 'the founders' of

---

[60] Ibid., at p.136.
[61] See Dal Pont, *Charity Law in Australia and New Zealand*, at p.148.
[62] Ibid., at p.149. Citing, for example, *Re South Place Ethical Society* [1980] 1 WLR 1565,
per Dillon J, at 1571 (religion is concerned with man's relation to God); and *Barralet* v.
Attorney General [1980] 3 ALL ER 918, *per* Dillon LJ, at 924 (two of the essential
attributes of a religion are faith and worship: faith in a God and worship of that God).
[63] *Centrepoint Community Growth Trust* v. *Commissioner of Inland Revenue* [1985] 1
NZLR 673. It is notable that Tomkins J declared that he was not aware of any New
Zealand authorities on the meaning of 'religion' nor on what might constitute its
'advancement' and therefore he proposed to rely on English and US case law (see,
further, D. Poirier, *Charity Law in New Zealand*, at: www.charities.govt.nz/news/
charity-law-in-new-zealand, p.233 (accessed 10 January 2014)). For a case comment
on Centrepoint Community Growth Trust, see A. W. Lockhart, 'Case Comment:
Charitable Trusts – *Centrepoint Community Growth Trust* v. *Commissioner of Inland
Revenue*' (1984–1987) 5 *Auckland University Law Review* 244.

444 NEW ZEALAND

the world's revealed (or Abrahamic) religions, a term which included the community's own named 'spiritual leader'. In addition to its intimate, mutually assisting lifestyle, the community was engaged with the public in counselling and psycho-therapy, plus some commercial activities, the latter of which supplied funding to the corporate community. The court, at first instance, found that while some members of the community believed in a supernatural being, others held:

> a belief in the supernatural in the sense of reality beyond that which can be perceived by the senses. An exemplification [in the witnesses' evidence] of that type of belief is in the expression that frequently recurs of creative energy.

Included in these beliefs were concepts that related not only to man's relationship to man but also to his relationship to the supernatural in the sense of a Being or a reality beyond sensory perception. The court held that in terms of their formal association, and in their beliefs and practices, the members were engaged in the advancement of religion.[64]

Worship, religious tenets, doctrines, etc.

As Mason ACJ and Brennan J acknowledged in *Church of the New Faith*, tenets in themselves are not a determining constituent of religion:

> we would not deny the character of a religion to a set of beliefs and practices which would otherwise qualify merely because its tenets aver or admit that knowledge of the supernatural is partial or otherwise imperfect or because the tenets offer no solution to some of the abiding and fundamental problems of man's existence.[65]

However, as they went on to explain, in order to verify that adherents' beliefs and actions together are sufficiently coherent to constitute a religion, the court needs to establish a binding link. Doctrines can provide that link, but in their absence, or guided only by vague doctrines, the court or regulator will be faced with correspondingly greater verification difficulties.

---

[64] *Centrepoint Community Growth Trust* v. *Commissioner of Inland Revenue* [1985] 1 NZLR 673, citing as a guiding precedent the earlier ruling in *Church of the New Faith* in the High Court of Australia.

[65] *Church of the New Faith* v. *Commissioner of Pay-roll Tax* (1983) 154 CLR 120, at p.139.

Philosophy and other value systems

The broad view of what constitutes 'religion' in New Zealand, as expounded by Mason ACJ and Brennan J, is reflected in the record (limited though it may be) of instances in which recognition of charitable status has been extended to organisations at a time when this was likely to have been denied in the United Kingdom and elsewhere.

In *Centrepoint Community Growth Trust* v. *Commissioner of Inland Revenue*,[66] Tompkins J found that the Trust was charitable as it was established for the advancement of religion. In December 2002 the New Zealand Inland Revenue notified the Church of Scientology that 'the advancement of Scientology meets the requirements of the definition of Charitable Purpose in . . . the Income Tax Act of 1994' and 'the Church of Scientology of New Zealand is a "society or institution established exclusively for charitable purposes"'. The New Zealand Humanist Society has also been awarded charitable status.

However, the *Exodus Ministries Trust Board* and other cases involving religious charities coming before the Commission (or Board, as it now is), have led the latter to comment that religious status alone may not constitute tangible public benefit under the terms of the Charities Act sufficient to warrant registration as a charity. This warning is one that acknowledges the continuing presumption of public benefit in relation to religious charities but is also a reminder that, presumption or not, all charities must nonetheless show how they benefit the public: religion is not necessarily for the public benefit; which would seem an appropriate corollary to an expansive interpretation of 'religion'.

The advancement of religion

The Charities Act 2005 has essentially left unaltered the presumption that gifts and organisations for the advancement of religion satisfy the public benefit test; though this may be affected by the legislative caveat that registration requires evidence that activities comply with objects.[67]

---

[66] *Centrepoint Community Growth Trust* v. *Commissioner of Inland Revenue* [1985] 1 NZLR 673.

[67] This reference to an 'activities test' is not borne out by evidence that it is applied with any rigour. For example, with respect to 'Sanitarium' and the Seventh-day Adventist Church, there is no evidence as to what the latter organisation does in the community apart from hold church services. There is no evidence of the other activities as stated in the Churches Deed of Trust, such as homes for the destitute, schools or hospitals and no explanation of what the Church did in 2012 with the distribution of $10.2 million to its

446 NEW ZEALAND

The means for advancing religion

As Dal Pont has clearly demonstrated,[68] there is little jurisdictional difference between New Zealand and Australia in the interpretation given by their courts and regulators to the means for advancing religion:[69] both jurisdictions uphold the time-honoured range of gifts and activities so recognised throughout the common law world (see, further, Chapter 2).

The continuing presumption of public benefit will similarly continue the eligibility of such gifts and activities for charitable status. So, also, will gifts for masses to be said for the soul of the deceased testatrix,[70] for church organs[71] and retired clergy.[72] In *Shears* v. *Miller*,[73] Chisholm J followed the earlier English Court of Appeal decision and similarly found that Freemasonry did not advance religion.

However, in *Liberty Trust* v. *Charities Commission*,[74] Mallon J considered the approach adopted by the Commission in deregistering the Trust to be too narrow and conservative, likely to confine the advancement of religion 'to praying, preaching and building churches or looking after priest, minister, nuns and the like'.[75] Contrary to the Commission, she was of the view that the Trust was not engaged in a purely secular activity in promoting budgeting and financial advice, since it presented its information about these matters as part of 'the Word of God': its teachings were biblical teachings; its loan scheme was a practical outworking of the Christian faith; and, therefore, it was 'advancing religion'. Mallon J found the reasons given by the Commission for rejecting the Trust's charitable status unconvincing: first, the Trust, as an organisation, was clearly operating in a religious context; second, advancement of religion does not have to take place within a church building; and third, educating people about biblical financial principles was clearly

---

77 churches and 12,000 members in New Zealand. (Information provided by Michael Gousmett, personal communication, 23 July 2013).

[68] See G. Dal Pont, 'Advancement of Religion', in *Charity Law in Australia and New Zealand*, Oxford University Press, Melbourne, 2000, at pp.147–171.

[69] Aside from the decision in *Commissioner of Taxation of the Commonwealth of Australia* v. *Word Investments Ltd.* [2008] HCA 55 (High Court of Australia, 3 December 2008), an initiative resisted by the judiciary and regulators in New Zealand.

[70] Such a gift was found to be charitable in *Carrigan* v. *Redwood* (1910) 30 NZLR 244.

[71] See *Methodist Theological College Council* v. *Guardian Trust and Executors Co. of New Zealand Ltd.* [1927] GLR 297.

[72] See *Re Burke (deceased)*, 16.03.94 HC Christchurch M 92/93, *per* Neazor J.

[73] *Shears* v. *Miller*, 30.05.2000, HC Timaru CP 10/99.

[74] *Liberty Trust* v. *Charities Commission*, HC WN CIV 2010-485-000831 [2 June 2011].

[75] Ibid., at p.89.

THE ADVANCEMENT OF RELIGION 447

propagating a Christian doctrine. She concluded that: 'given the assumption of public benefit, and the Court does not intrude into matters of faith except where they are contrary to public policy, it is not for the Court to say that teaching biblical financial principles is not a public benefit'.[76]

This decision is important because of the broad judicial interpretation of the advancement of religion as a charitable purpose coupled with the re-affirmation of the public benefit presumption favouring such purposes in this jurisdiction.

It is, perhaps, a decision that strengthens the position of other religious organisations engaged in secular activities and which may similarly claim that in so doing they are also pursuing an outworking of their Christian faith. However, the further removed the activities are from religion the greater the difficulty in sustaining a claim that these represent a manifestation of religious belief.[77] This becomes more compounded where the activity is on a scale and generating such profit margins as to enable a religious organisation to dominate a sector of the commercial market. Arguably there is a line to be drawn between the outworkings of religious faith that, being ancillary and incidental in nature, can be seen to manifest an organisation's religious beliefs, and those that are disproportionate and unrelated to such an organisation and its beliefs.[78] While that line was decisively crossed by the Australian judiciary, with the ruling in *Word Investments*,[79] it was subsequently reinstated by the government. In New Zealand there has never been any corresponding judicial ruling, but in practice the activities of organisations such as Sanitarium indicates a similar disproportionate relationship between business and religious belief and this practice would seem to be condoned by the regulating authorities.

---

[76] Ibid., at p.102.
[77] An alternative view is put forward by Sue Barker: 'I see *Sanitarium* as a practical application of cases like *Re Resch's Will Trusts* etc: that charities can run businesses, any business, even a wholly unrelated business, provided the proceeds must be plied back in furtherance of their charitable purposes. The real problem arises when funds are accumulated, and potentially used anti-competitively' (personal communication, 11 September 2013).
[78] Sanitarium, for example, a wholly owned subsidiary of the Seventh-day Adventist Church, with a multi-million dollar annual turnover, produces Weet-bix, New Zealand's most popular breakfast cereal.
[79] *Commissioner of Taxation of the Commonwealth of Australia* v. *Word Investments Ltd.* [2008] HCA 55.

448   NEW ZEALAND

Public policy, charity and common law constraints

The governing dictum expressed by Upjohn LJ some 50 years ago that 'to establish that a condition is void on the grounds of public policy, it must be shown that it will have a tendency to produce injury to the public interest or good or to the common weal' has prevailed in New Zealand.[80]

Testamentary conditions and the common law

The standard rules as embodied in case law precedents (see, further, Chapter 2) are applied in New Zealand.

Failure due to breach of common law rules

Of the common law rules governing charitable testamentary dispositions the one generally most likely to breach eligibility for charitable status is the requirement that the objects and activities of a charity be dedicated exclusively to furthering the charity's purpose; subject to the 'incidental and ancillary' caveat.[81] The problem often arises due to uncertainty in the wording of a bequest such as to 'any good work' in *Re Aston (deceased)*,[82] but in this jurisdiction it has no particular application to religious charities.

Bequests subject to a religious condition

Such bequests benefit from a long-standing assumption that they are not contrary to public policy. In the early twentieth century, bequests subject to a condition that the prospective beneficiary 'be of the Lutheran religion'[83] or be 'in the Protestant faith'[84] were acceptable charitable bequests in this jurisdiction as they would have been elsewhere in the common law world. However, by the mid twentieth century, Smith J in *Re Lockie*,[85] when considering a gift accompanied by a condition that discriminated on grounds of religion, took quite the opposite approach and refused to recognise such a gift as charitable on the grounds that the testator's blatant religious discrimination had irredeemably corrupted

---

[80] *Re Neeld, Carpenter v. Inigo-Jones* [1962] Ch. 643, at p.680.
[81] See, for example, *Commissioner of Inland Revenue v. New Zealand Council of Law Reporting* [1981] 1 NZLR 682.
[82] *Re Aston (deceased)* [1955] NZLR 192.   [83] *Re Carleton* [1909] 28 NZLR 1066.
[84] *In Re Gunn* [1912] 32 NZLR 153.   [85] *Re Lockie* [1945] NZLR 230, at p.240.

PUBLIC POLICY AND COMMON LAW CONSTRAINTS   449

any charitable intent. As he explained: 'it is better that what appears to be the testator's manifest object should be defeated, unless he has complied with the rule in all its strictness, rather than that the control of one person's religion by another, by the method of material reward, should be encouraged'. This approach was then followed in relation to attached conditions intended to prevent 'contracting marriage outside the Jewish faith'.[86] The absence of rulings upholding the right of testators to make testamentary dispositions subject to discriminatory religious conditions is a noticeable feature of New Zealand case law, which differentiates it from that of countries such as England, Canada and Ireland.

Religious preferences and public policy

Charitable status is required to be public policy compliant. The public benefit presumption will not save the otherwise charitable status of an organisation, or gift dedicated to the advancement of religion, where this is found to be illegal,[87] immoral or in breach of the prevailing public policy.

Public policy constraints

Under ss.10(j) and (k) of the Charities Act 2005, there is provision that in some instances, registration can be withheld or withdrawn on evidence that an organisation's activities are not primarily directed at charitable objectives, and that political purposes are in fact its main objective. In *Molloy* v. *Commissioner of Inland Revenue*,[88] for example, the Society for the Protection of the Unborn Child was denied charitable status, as its main object was to preserve the current law on the subject, which fatally compromised its charitable purpose. Similarly, in *Knowles* v. *Commissioner of Stamp Duties*,[89] an organisation ostensibly established to promote temperance in alcoholic consumption was determined to be non-charitable on the grounds that its main purpose was in fact to effect changes in the law.

---

[86] *Re Biggs, Public Trustee* v. *Schneider* [1945] NZLR 303, 307; and *Re Myers, Perpetual Trust Estate and Agency Co of New Zealand* v. *Myers* [1947] NZLR 828, 834.
[87] See, for example, abortion and *Auckland Medical Aid Trust* v. *Commissioner of Inland Revenue* [1979] 1 NZLR 382, *per* Chilwell J, at p.395.
[88] *Molloy* v. *Commissioner of Inland Revenue* [1981] 1 NZLR 688.
[89] *Knowles* v. *Commissioner of Stamp Duties* [1945] NZLR 522.

Advocacy

There have been some recent cases in this jurisdiction which, while not specific to religious charities, serve to clarify the law relating to the lobbying activities of all charities.

For example, in 2012, Greenpeace New Zealand won its case to have its charitable status reconsidered after the Court of Appeal set aside an earlier ruling by the Charities Commission rejecting such recognition. The Charities Commission had ruled Greenpeace's promotion of disarmament was a political purpose that was not 'charitable' under the Charities Act 2005. That decision was upheld by the High Court in 2011,[90] which followed the ruling in *Molloy*,[91] but was then overturned by the Court of Appeal.[92] The latter stated that it would not depart from *Molloy*, which had effectively been endorsed by the Charities Act 2005 and which determined that a society established for contentious political purposes is not founded principally for charitable purposes. It noted that while the prohibition on political purposes no longer applied in Australia, following the *Aid/Watch* decision,[93] it remained part of the current law of New Zealand. However, given the amendments made to Greenpeace objects in the interim between court hearings, it was satisfied that the 'advocacy' purpose was intended to be ancillary to and not independent from Greenpeace's primary charitable purposes. The amended object would then meet the requirements of ss.5(3) and 5(4) of the Charities Act and would support Greenpeace's contention that it is now established 'exclusively for charitable purposes'.

More recently, the independent Charities Registration Board (formerly known as the Charities Commission) announced, early in 2013, its decision to deregister Family First NZ, a charity known for its open espousal of partisan political allegiances and for lobbying in support of causes such as the parental right to administer corporal punishment and against gay marriage. It was explained that:

> The Board's position is that Family First's main purpose is to promote particular points of view about family life. Under the Act promotion of a controversial point of view is a political purpose.

The charity declared its intention to appeal the decision.

---

[90] See *Re Greenpeace New Zealand Inc* [2011] 2 NZLR 815.
[91] See *Molloy* v. *Commissioner of Inland Revenue* [1981] 1 NZLR 688 (CA).
[92] *Re Greenpeace New Zealand Inc* [2012] NZCA 535.
[93] See *Aid/Watch* v. *Commissioner of Taxation* [2010] HCA 42.

Proselytism

As Dal Pont has noted 'inherent in advancing religion is the object of converting persons from one faith to another'. He then goes on to comment that 'it must be queried whether such an object, though it may advance religion, can safely be assumed to be for the public benefit'.[94] While he is surely right, it is nonetheless difficult to see in what circumstances, given that the public benefit test remains unaltered in this jurisdiction, the courts or regulator could now find proselytism to be non-charitable.

Human rights, discrimination and religious charities: contemporary issues

The presence of Māori, traditionally renowned for their robust and assertive culture, has more recently acted as a catalyst for developing a human rights and non-discriminatory environment in New Zealand; often, in practice, a challenge that has not always worked to their advantage. The current statistics illustrate the continuing relative disadvantages suffered by this group: the median age for Māori is around 22 years and 55 per cent of the population is under 25 years, compared with only 34.6 per cent of non-Māori; in general, they have lower incomes and larger households than non- Māori and are more likely to be living in one-parent households; they are disadvantaged by age, geographical distribution, low standards of education and skills and levels of unemployment; and are over-represented in prisons and drug/alcohol rehabilitation units.[95]

The Māori factor also brought into play a conflation of ethnic culture and religion which perhaps gave this jurisdiction an early opportunity to rehearse the problems of pluralism that now face all Western societies as they struggle to accommodate Muslim, Sikh and other cultures.

Human rights

New Zealand has ratified a number of international conventions relating to non-discrimination and to fundamental rights for all citizens,

---

[94] See Dal Pont, *Charity Law in Australia and New Zealand*, at p.165.
[95] See Statistics of New Zealand, *Census of Population and Dwellings*, Wellington, 2013, at www.stats.govt.nz (accessed 10 January 2014).

452 NEW ZEALAND

including minority groups.[96] It is a signatory to the Universal Declaration of Human Rights, and as such is bound by Article 18(1), which states that everyone has the right to freedom of thought, conscience and religion; this right includes freedom to change his religion or belief, and freedom, either alone or in community with others and in public or private, to manifest his religion or belief in teaching, practice, worship and observance. However, it was one of only four countries to refuse to sign the recent UN Declaration of Rights of Indigenous Peoples.[97]

The Constitution

New Zealand does not have a Constitution as such,[98] though the principles embodied in the Treaty of Waitangi have an overarching constitutional effect.[99] Domestic legislative provisions governing human rights, with particular reference to rights relating to religious freedom, are to be found in the Constitution Act 1986, the New Zealand Bill of Rights Act 1990 and the Human Rights Act 1993.

Articles 2 and 3 of the Treaty of Waitangi both provide protection for Māori to observe and practice their religions and beliefs. Article 2 does so by reference, in the Māori version, to taonga, that is, 'everything that is held precious'. Article 3 provides for Māori to have 'the same rights as those of the people of England'.

The Constitution Act 1986, New Zealand's primary constitutional legal instrument, consolidated the institutional and statutory powers necessary to clarify its relationship with the UK government and monarchy, provide for more coherent domestic governance and affirm its (relatively) independent status. The New Zealand Bill of Rights Act 1990:

---

[96] International Convention on the Elimination of All Forms of Racial Discrimination; International Covenant on Civil and Political Rights; International Covenant on Economic Social and Cultural Rights. See, further, at: www.hrc.co.nz/report/chapters/chapter09/religion02.html (accessed 10 January 2014).

[97] On 13 September 2007, the General Assembly adopted a landmark declaration outlining the rights of the world's estimated 370 million Indigenous people and outlawing discrimination against them: 143 Member States voted in favour; 11 abstained; and four – Australia, Canada, New Zealand and the United States – voted against the text.

[98] It does, however, have a collection of Acts that make up an 'unwritten' constitution and this is currently being scrutinised by an Advisory Panel. See, further, at: www.justice.govt.nz/policy/constitutional-law-and-human-rights/consideration-of-constitutional-issues-1/members-of-the-constitutional-advisory-panel (accessed 10 January 2014).

[99] See, further, R. Ekins and D. Tomkins, *Constitutional Theory for the Constitutional Review*, Maxim Institute, Auckland, 2013.

declares the right to freedom of thought, conscience, religion and belief (including the right to hold and embrace views without interference); protects the right to express religion and belief in worship, observance, teaching and practice; and affirms the right of minorities to be free from discrimination.

The Human Rights Act 1993 (amalgamating the Race Relations Act 1971 and the Human Rights Commission Act 1977) prohibits discrimination based on religious and ethical belief (defined as lack of a religious belief, whether in respect of a particular religion or religions or all religions) in employment, in partnerships, in access to places, vehicles and facilities, in the provision of goods and services and in the provision of land, housing and accommodation.[100] The Human Rights Amendment Act 2001 restructured the Human Rights Commission and introduced additional safeguards against discrimination on grounds such as age, disability or sexual orientation in the policies and practices of government agencies.

Equality and diversity legislation, public bodies and exemption for charities

New Zealand has in place a not untypical platform of equality legislation including the above Human Rights Act 1993, the Equal Pay Act 1972 and the Employment Relations Act 2000 (which repealled the Employment Contracts Act 1991) and has introduced other legislative and policy frameworks to promote equality.[101] The task of interpreting and applying the 2000 Act falls to the Employment Relations Authority, the Employment Court and the New Zealand Court of Appeal.

The New Zealand courts, while maintaining a conservative approach that seldom strays far from mainstream common law jurisprudence, have cautiously sought to make links between national statutory human rights provisions and the developing international law on discrimination and

---

[100] There are 13 grounds on which it is unlawful to discriminate against people: sex (including pregnancy and childbirth), marital status, religious belief, ethical belief, colour, race, ethnic or national origin (including nationality or citizenship), disability, age, political opinion, employment status, family status and sexual orientation. See, further, at: www.hrc.co.nz/report/chapters/chapter03/equality01.html#2 (accessed 10 January 2014).

[101] Citizenship Act 1977; Immigration Act 1987; State Sector Act 1988; Ethnic Perspectives in Policy 2003.

equality. In *Quilter* v. *Attorney-General*,[102] for example, the Court of Appeal noted that equality is one of the core principles underlying New Zealand's law on discrimination, even though that law contains no express reference to equality.

Religious charities, discrimination and exemptions

Under s.28 of the Human Rights Act 1993, specific 'Exceptions for purposes of religion' are provided as follows:

(1) Nothing in s.22 shall prevent different treatment based on sex where the position is for the purposes of an organised religion and is limited to one sex so as to comply with the doctrines or rules or established customs of the religion.
(2) Nothing in s.22 shall prevent different treatment based on religious or ethical belief where:
   (a) that treatment is accorded under s.65 of the Private Schools Conditional Integration Act 1975; or
   (b) the sole or principal duties of the position (not being a position to which s.65 or the Private Schools Conditional Integration Act 1975 applies):
      (i) are, or are substantially the same as, those of a clergyman, priest, pastor, official or teacher among adherents of that belief or otherwise involve the propagation of that belief; or
      (ii) are those of a teacher in a private school; or
      (iii) consist of acting as a social worker on behalf of an organisation whose members comprise solely or principally adherents of that belief.
(3) Where a religious or ethical belief requires its adherents to follow a particular practice, an employer must accommodate the practice so long as any adjustment of the employer's activities required to accommodate the practice does not unreasonably disrupt the employer's activities.

While religious purposes exemption from the prohibition against discrimination in relation to employment is specified in s.28(2), provision for educational establishments to be maintained wholly or principally for students of one religious belief is to be found in s.58(1).

---

[102] *Quilter* v. *Attorney-General* [1998] 1 NZLR 523.

Religious charities as public bodies

It is clear that government activities are required to be compliant with anti-discrimination standards, including discrimination on grounds of sexual orientation, as set out in s.19 of the New Zealand Bill of Rights Act 1990 and s.21 of the Human Rights Act 1993.[103] The extent to which religious organisations when delivering public services on behalf of government are thereby acting as public bodies and are similarly bound by the same provisions, is an open question.

Freedom of religion

As Mason ACJ and Brennan J stressed in *Church of the New Faith*, the law governing religious freedom, as expressed in the New Zealand Bill of Rights Act 1990, is intended to preserve the dignity and freedom of persons to adhere to the religion of their choice.[104]

Interference with manifestations of religious belief

The Bill of Rights Act 1990, s.15, deals specifically with the manifestation of religion and belief; it provides for the right of any person to manifest their religion or beliefs through worship, observance, practice or teaching, either individually or in community, in public or in private. This right is one that under s.5 'may be subject only to such reasonable limits prescribed by law as can be demonstrably justified in a free and democratic society'.

One such manifestation of religious belief, which has caused difficulty for the Jewish community in this and other jurisdictions, is the requirement that the slaughter of animals for human consumption be conducted without stunning. The New Zealand animal welfare code states that all animals set for commercial consumption must be stunned prior to slaughter so that they are treated 'humanely and in accordance with good practice and scientific knowledge'. While this requirement accords with the expectations of the rest of society, it offends the Jewish community as their kosher laws necessitate slaughter by shechita or without stunning. In November 2010, the New Zealand Jewish community reached agreement with the Minister of Agriculture, enabling the shechita of poultry to continue in New Zealand and orders putting that agreement into effect were issued by the High Court in Wellington.

---

[103] See the Human Rights Amendment Act 2001.
[104] See *Church of the New Faith* v. *Commissioner of Pay-roll Tax* (1983) 154 CLR 120, at p.132.

456   NEW ZEALAND

Discrimination

The Human Rights Act 1993 (HRA) prohibits discrimination on various
grounds, as noted above. Under s.21(1) of the Act (as amended) discrimination is expressly prohibited in relation to: (c) religious belief and;
(d) ethical belief, which means the lack of a religious belief, whether
in respect of a particular religion or religions or all religions.[105] The
Employment Relations Act 2000 (ERA), in conjunction with the
Employment Contracts Act 1991, provides employees with the right to
take allegations of discrimination to the Employment Court. The customary definition of 'discrimination' as either direct or indirect applies
in this jurisdiction, as does the caveat favouring 'affirmative action' to
counteract inequality.

Reasonable accommodation

The HRA, s.28(3), requires employers to accommodate the religious
or ethical belief practices of an employee as long as any adjustment
required 'does not unreasonably disrupt the employer's activities'.
The term 'reasonable accommodation', like 'reasonable measures',
signifies that the law is to be applied with some flexibility: there is
an expectation that employers will be prepared to make some adjustments to terms and conditions of employment to accommodate the
religious beliefs of staff, and that those with such beliefs will accept
that working arrangements may impose a degree of inconvenience.[106]
This has to be balanced against health and safety considerations
in the work environment: if making allowances for religious beliefs
gives rise to a risk of harm and measures can be taken to reduce that
risk without unreasonable disruption but with consequences for the
exercise of beliefs, then the provider or employer should take those
measures.

Discrimination, same-sex marriage and religious organisations

Following a succession of cases in which the judiciary wrestled with new
definitions of 'family' and with the problems entailed in transposing

---

[105] See Mooney Cotter, *Heaven Forbid*.
[106] 'Reasonable accommodation' resonates strongly with the 'permissive accommodations
test' in the United States, which asks what religious accommodations are allowed – but
not required (see, for example, *Corp. of Presiding Bishop* v. *Amos*, 483 US 327 (1987)).

HUMAN RIGHTS, DISCRIMINATION & RELIGIOUS CHARITIES 457

familiar concepts into a reconfigured and more challenging social and legal landscape,[107] the Court of Appeal in *Quilter*[108] considered same-sex marriage. It held that the Marriage Act 1955 applies to marriage between a man and a woman only and that excluding same-sex couples does not constitute discrimination.[109] It also, however, noted that equality is one of the core principles underlying New Zealand's law on discrimination: the Human Rights Amendment Act 2001 requires that government activities be subject to the anti-discrimination standards set out in s.19 of the New Zealand Bill of Rights Act 1990 and s.21 of the Human Rights Act 1993. Prohibited grounds of discrimination include sexual orientation.

The government was, therefore, obliged to rectify the inequitable if not discriminatory provisions in marriage law. Acknowledging that making separate and different provision for same-sex couples (by way of civil partnership) would not address issues of either discrimination or equality, it was felt necessary to amend the Marriage Act to make marriage as available to same-sex couples as it is for heterosexual couples. Consequently, on 17 April 2013 the New Zealand Parliament passed the Marriage (Definition of Marriage) Amendment Act 2013, enabling gay, bisexual, lesbian, trans-sexual and inter-sex marriages to be legal. New Zealand's legalisation of same-sex marriages makes it the first country in Asia-Pacific to make the change and the thirteenth country in the world to do so.

Religious exemption privileges

Under s.29(2) of the 2013 Act:

> no celebrant who is a minister of religion recognised by a religious body enumerated in Schedule 1,[110] and no celebrant who is a person

---

[107] See, for example: *VP* v. *PM* (1998) 16 FRNZ 61 (lesbian mother retains custody of two children); *Re An Application by T* [1998] NZFLR 769 (second parent adoption by lesbian mother of partner's child by donor insemination refused); *A* v. *R* [1999] NZFLR 249 (non-biological mother in *Re An Application by T*, ibid., held liable for child support payments as a step-parent); and *Re application of AMM and KJO to adopt a child* [2010] NZFLR 629 ('spouse' includes de facto heterosexual couples).

[108] *Quilter* v. *Attorney-General* [1998] 1 NZLR 523.

[109] Although Tipping J did bluntly state: 'I see the inability of homosexual and lesbian couples to marry as involving (indirect) discrimination against them on the grounds of sexual orientation', at pp.575–576 (admittedly obiter).

[110] Schedule 1 lists Baptists, Anglicans, Congregational Independents, the Greek Orthodox Church, 'All Hebrew Congregations', Lutherans, Methodists, Presbyterians, Catholics and the Salvation Army as the relevant enumerated religious bodies.

458   NEW ZEALAND

> nominated to solemnize marriages by an approved organisation, is
> obliged to solemnize a marriage if solemnizing that marriage would
> contravene the religious beliefs of the religious body or the religious
> beliefs or philosophical or humanitarian convictions of the approved
> organisation.

This discretionary opt-out clause is problematic. The right to exercise discretion would seem to rest with an organisation rather than an individual: a celebrant prepared to conduct a same-sex marriage can be prevented from doing so if their religious body determines that this would be in breach of its beliefs; and yet the term 'is obliged' suggests some indeterminate scope of decision-making by a willing celebrant. Given the increasing weight of case law affirming the decisive importance of an individual's interpretation of religious belief, it is noticeable that this clause does not functionally address any possible issues arising from the tension between institutional religion and individual religious beliefs. The Human Rights Commission has drawn attention to persistent contention over the employment of clergy and religious officers, noting, for example, that where an appointment to the post of religious officer is refused because of the applicant's gender or sexual orientation this is discrimination and constitutes a breach of the applicant's human rights. In 2003 the Commission sought the opinion of four experts on the question of the employment of gay and lesbian clergy, a key question being whether clergy are in fact 'employed' as such. Three of the experts were of the view that they are not, and that the prohibition on employment does not therefore generally apply. This view finds support in a 1998 decision of the New Zealand Court of Appeal that (for the purposes of the Employment Contracts Act and in relation to the situation prevailing in the Methodist Church) the relationship between clergy and the Church is not an employment relationship. Accordingly, the question of whether the discrimination exception provision for churches in the HRA is applicable does not arise, because the parties are not in an employment relationship. The alternative view was that, under the HRA as opposed to the Employment Contracts Act, clergy are in an employment relationship with their Church authorities, which is why the s.28 exemption (allowing discrimination to be lawful) exists. All the opinions thus lead, by differing reasoning, to the same conclusion: that the HRA allows Churches to discriminate on grounds of sex (including sexual orientation) with respect to the engagement of clergy.

HUMAN RIGHTS, DISCRIMINATION & RELIGIOUS CHARITIES 459

Religious discrimination: equality in practice

Discrimination, as Tipping J said in *Quilter* v. *Attorney-General*,[111] can be discerned in 'the difference of treatment in comparable circumstances. For discrimination to occur one person or group of persons must be treated differently from another person or group of persons.' Each case must, of course, turn on its own set of facts.[112] The lack of religious discrimination case law in this jurisdiction perhaps testifies to the effectiveness of the mediation service introduced by the Human Rights Commission in 2002, or to the relative lack of disputes in this area;[113] certainly, by 2006, when the Commission published *Ten Cases that Made a Difference*, it referenced only one such case. In its 2010–2011 annual Activities Report, the Commission stated that it had received 71 discrimination complaints in 2010 on the grounds of religious or ethical belief.[114] This was slightly up from 67 in 2009, 57 in 2008 and 69 in 2007. Forty-four of the complaints were about discrimination against someone of a specific religion, spirituality or belief system.

Unequal but not discriminatory

Māori and their culture pre-date the settler social infrastructure and contemporary institutions. One aspect of that culture that has always differentiated it from Western practice is adoption. The difference has its origins in the Māori belief system.

For many centuries Māori have had a practice known as whangai or atawhai,[115] or customary adoption whereby a collective decision is taken, usually as a result of ongoing consultation between all members of the extended families or communities involved, that a particular child would be given to relatives for them to raise. Whangai has few of the legal characteristics of adoption in Western societies and is not recognised

---

[111] *Quilter* v. *Attorney-General* [1998] 1 NZLR 523.

[112] See *Orlov* v. *Ministry of Justice and Attorney-General* [2009] (NZHRRT 28, 14 October 2009).

[113] The Human Rights Commission annual report for 2010–2011 records that the Office of Human Rights Proceedings provided representation in only one case of ethical belief discrimination in services provision. See, further, at: www.nzlii.org/nz/cases/NZHRRT (accessed 10 January 2014).

[114] See, further, at: www.hrc.co.nz (accessed 10 January 2014).

[115] See, for example, D. Durie-Hall and D. J. Metge, 'Kua Tutu Te Puehu, Kia Mau Maori Aspirations and Family Law', in M. Henaghan and W. Atkin (eds), *Family Law Policy in New Zealand*, Oxford University Press, Oxford, 1992, pp.54–82.

within the statutory adoption framework of New Zealand, but is none-theless still in use by Māori. Generally, a whangai placement was practised within a hapu or iwi as a means of strengthening relations and tradi-tionally had the advantage of ensuring that land rights were consolidated within the tribe – though placements were sometimes made with rela-tives by marriage. Because the severing of blood-ties was regarded as a betrayal of origins, breaking the spiritual links with ancestors and com-promising the future spiritual path, a child from outside the whanau, hapu and iwi would seldom be adopted. Adoption by 'strangers', the foundation stone of the practice in Western societies, has been deliber-ately avoided in Māori culture. Māori and Western-style adoptions, with their different legal attributes, continue to co-exist alongside each other.

Unequal but not discriminatory: contractual obligations

Complaints alleging religious discrimination are relatively rare, consti-tuting approximately 10 per cent of annual complaints received by the Human Rights Commission. The most common area of complaint noted by the Commission in its 2010–2011 annual report (19 complaints) concerned employment. No particular denomination predominated, but various Christian beliefs were the most common. Fourteen com-plaints related to discrimination based on religious or ethical belief, and five were about being subjected to the beliefs of others in the workplace.

The HRA, s.28(3), requires employers to accommodate the religious or ethical belief practices of an employee as long as any adjustment required 'does not unreasonably disrupt the employer's activities'. An example of a breach of this provision occurred in 2003 when the Office of Human Rights Proceedings determined a case concerning a Seventh Day Adventist who had been required, by his employer, to work on his Saturday sabbath contrary to his religious beliefs.

Unequal and discriminatory: restricting employment opportunities

During the period 2007–2010, the Human Rights Commission received 249 complaints on the grounds of religious and/or ethical belief. Of these, 33 related to employment, including enquiries from employers about accommodating the religious requirements of their staff or poten-tial employees, and complaints from people who were asked about aspects of their religious belief during job interviews. In a number of

HUMAN RIGHTS, DISCRIMINATION & RELIGIOUS CHARITIES 461

these cases, the issues involved the person not being of a certain religion (for example, non-Catholics working in Catholic schools), rather than discrimination because of their specific religious beliefs.

An ongoing case before the Human Rights Tribunal, *Gay and Lesbian Clergy Anti-Discrimination Society Inc* v. *Bishop of Auckland*,[116] is interesting as it concerns a gay man who alleges he has been barred from training to become an Anglican priest because he is in an 'active' homosexual relationship. The Anglican Church presently only permits gay persons in a celibant relationship to become priests. Should this person now avail of the changed marriage laws to marry his partner – or should the Tribunal, in the light of that change, adopt the recent judicial interpretation of 'spouses'[117] – then, if the Anglican Church continued to deny training on that ground, it would be placed in a position where it would have to either be seen to discriminate or have to claim statutory exemption under s.28 of the 1993 Act.

Unequal and discriminatory: restricting access to services

Many religious discrimination complaints noted by the Human Rights Commission in its annual reports concern matters of dress and appearance that are religion- or culture-specific. In 2004, for example, a district court in Auckland was called upon to resolve an issue raised by lawyers for the defence, who objected to two Muslim women wearing the burqa (covering their faces except for their eyes) while giving evidence as Crown witnesses. The judge called for submissions on the matter and ultimately decided in January 2005 to allow screens to be used to ensure that only the judge, counsel and female court staff were able to observe the witnesses' faces.[118] There was also controversy about a Christchurch secondary school which provided a purpose-built prayer room for Muslim students. More recently, in 2010, a Sikh businessman who was refused service at a golf-club bar because he was wearing a turban received a written apology. Also that year, the Cosmopolitan Club voted to maintain its policy forbidding the wearing of headwear on its premises. At the club's annual meeting a majority of members voted to maintain the ban, which includes turbans.

---

[116] See, further, at: www.justice.govt.nz/tribunals/human-rights-review-tribunal (accessed 10 January 2014).
[117] See, *Re application of AMM and KJO to adopt a child* [2010] NZFLR 629.
[118] See, further, at: www.hrc.co.nz (accessed 10 January 2014).

462   NEW ZEALAND

The Marriage (Definition of Marriage) Amendment Act 2013, though legalising gay marriages, is nevertheless problematic in terms of guaranteeing access to a marriage service. While it is clear that a religious organisation is now enabled to conduct such a marriage ceremony, it remains somewhat uncertain as to what happens if celebrant clergy refuse to officiate and/or the couple are denied the use of their chosen church.

An ancillary matter is the availability of adoption services. In New Zealand, as in many other common law countries, this is fraught with religious discrimination issues. For example, s.3 of the Adoption Act 1955 provides for adoption by one person or by '2 spouses jointly' and to that extent is discriminatory in relation to applicants in a same-sex partnership. Discriminatory restrictions are also apparent in the role of public benefit service agencies belonging to religious organisations, such as Catholic Social Services in Christchurch and the Latter Day Saints Social Services, which are restricted by their religious beliefs in the range of services they can offer. Specifically, although both engage in ancillary adoption work, their discriminatory beliefs exclude the possibility of contracting with same-sex prospective adopters and they are therefore excluded from registration and regulation by government as adoption agencies.

Unequal but 'positive action'

The Bill of Rights Act 1990, s.19(2), states that:

> Measures taken in good faith for the purpose of assisting or advancing persons or groups of persons disadvantaged because of discrimination that is unlawful by virtue of Part II of the Human Rights Act 1993 do not constitute discrimination.

This and similar provisions in the HRA require, as a pre-condition, that any such measures are actually needed: the intended recipients must be disadvantaged relative to others; and they must need, or be reasonably supposed to need, assistance in order to achieve equality. This was clearly established in *Amaltal Fishing Co. Ltd.* v. *Nelson Polytechnic (No.2)*,[119] where the court focused on the prerequisite that the target group did not occupy an equal place with others in a particular community and that the intended measure was necessary for them to achieve that equality. This

---

[119] *Amaltal Fishing Co. Ltd.* v. *Nelson Polytechnic (No.2)* (1996) 2 HRNZ 225.

CONCLUSION   463

principle, of compensatory intervention justified by the relative disadvantages of the recipients' circumstances, also underpinned the decision in *Avis Rent A Car Ltd.* v. *Proceedings Commissioner.*[120]

In a religious charity context, the Partnership Schools/Kura Hourua project provides an example of positive action. In June 2013, following the passing of the Education Amendment Bill 2012, the legal framework was created for a third type of state-funded school, Partnership Schools/Kura Hourua (in addition to state schools and state-integrated schools), which is to be accountable to government for raising achievement through a contract to deliver specific outcomes. In return they will have more flexibility to make decisions about how they operate and use funding (e.g. the number of teachers employed, rate of teachers' pay, the length of the school day and the purchase of school resources). In addition to guaranteed government funding of $9.5 million over five years, the religious charity Sanitarium and Fonterra will expand their free breakfast programme to such schools. This government initiative is a response to the recommendations of an expert advisory group on child poverty.

Conclusion

This small nation is unique among the jurisdictions presently being considered due to its experience in marrying the cultural heritage of its assertive Indigenous Māori population with that of successive waves of settlers. The associational structures of Māori society formed a relatively intact, homogenous culture in which religious beliefs and practices were wholly subsumed into family and social life: there was no separation of the sacred and the secular; nor was there any room for non-believers. While this has undoubtedly loosened up during the course of the latter part of the twentieth century, the preceding centuries of prolonged exposure to the complexities involved in bridging the cultural gap between the social institutions of the immigrant population and the tangata whenua have given the government many opportunities to develop the strategies necessary to build and sustain a pluralist society.[121]

---

[120] *Avis Rent A Car Ltd.* v. *Proceedings Commissioner* (1998) 5 HRNZ 501. The tribunal then held that the practice of rental car companies of passing on to the client the higher insurance cost they incurred by hiring vehicles to drivers under the age of 25 was justified, provided that the difference could be established by reference to statistical or actuarial data.

[121] Tangata whenua is a Māori term that loosely translates as 'people of the land'.

The Charities Act 2005 settled for little more that the statutory encoding of already established common law rules and principles, together with the introduction of a now defunct Charities Commission, a register for charities, and was accompanied by some tactical amendments to the Income Tax Act 2007. The same prudent tendency would seem characteristic of the judicial approach to human rights issues as evidenced in the *Quilter* ruling.[122] Although the 2013 Act has now legalised gay marriages, it remains to be seen how the ancillary issues such as the availability of church marriage services and adoption services for such couples will work out.

---

[122] *Quilter v. Attorney-General* [1998] 1 NZLR 523.

PART III

Future directions

11

A conflict of laws

Canon law, charity law and human rights law

Introduction

This concluding chapter considers some of the more significant jurisdictional differences in the law governing the relationship between religion and charity, as illustrated in the cases, that have emerged in recent years. It identifies – from the perspectives of canon law, charity law and then human rights law – the main respective characteristics of each that are now leading to conflict between those bodies of law and it considers the differences in jurisdictional response. This leads into an examination of the 'moral imperatives', or the red line issues for those with and those without religious belief. These deeply divisive, morally driven issues, would seem to have in common a concern for 'life' – the means of engendering and terminating it – or for the meaning of 'marriage' and 'family', often with an added suggestion of 'sinfulness', particularly where sexuality is involved. At a different level, the issues also indicate tensions in the relationship between the State and religion. They are matters that seem to be stuck at the intersection of the three branches of law. Their irresolvability has come to symbolise the nature of some deep divisions in society and may well constitute one of the more profound dilemmas to face the developed nations at the outset of the twenty-first century.

Canon law: the need for god(s)

For almost all of the two millennia that have so far measured the progress of Christianity, and indeed from much earlier as Lucretius,[1] among others, has observed, there have been religious disputes. These have tended to be rooted in perceptions of a 'true' or 'false' God and the righteousness or otherwise of his adherents. The modern permutation of

---

[1] The Roman poet, Lucretius (96 BC–55 BC). See, further, 1911 Encyclopedia Brittanica at: www.studylight.org/enc/bri/view.cgi?n=20770&search=span (accessed 10 January 2014).

467

such disputes has now broadened to include participants of no belief (neither in God nor religion) and those who do believe (but in a philosophy or way of life) without any need for a God. This is a relatively recent development (treatment meted out in the past to those deemed to be 'heretics', 'heathens', 'pagans' or 'witches' being a considerable deterrent to non-believers). The UK jurisdictions have now taken the unprecedented step of placing on the statute books a clear declaration that the definition of 'religion' includes 'a religion which does not involve a belief in a god'.[2] This unavoidable concession to human rights principles established by the ECtHR would have been unimaginable to previous generations in the jurisdictions currently being studied.[3] They would have regarded such a parliamentary initiative as undermining not only Christianity, but also the foundations of theological study that have accompanied civilisation since the Greek empire. This excising of any future need for what has been religion's core component is a development which opens wide the opportunities for a limitless range of alternative belief systems to acquire parity with religion as traditionally understood, while also sharpening the edges of the Church–State interface and dissolving any rationale for an 'Established' Church.

Religion, theism, Christianity and canon law

A *sine qua non* of religion is a requirement for belief in matters not amenable to objective proof. This transcendental aspect has traditionally been met by a belief in God – a Christian God in the common law countries.

Theism

Christianity, or more specifically Protestantism, was the midwife to charity law. From its earliest beginnings, the advancement of religion as a charitable purpose bonded exclusively with Christian principles. The necessity of a theistic component for the advancement of religion was

---

[2] For England and Wales, see the Charities Act 2011, s.3(2).

[3] See, for example, the ECtHR rulings extending protection to include: Scientology, in *X and the Church of Scientology* v. *Sweden* (1976) 16 D&R 68; Druidism, in *Chappel* v. *UK* (1988) 10 EHRR 510 (Eur. Comm. HR), *Pendragon* v. *UK* (1998) EHRR CD 179; Divine Light Zentrum, in *Swami Omkaramamda and the Divine light Zentrum* v. *Switzerland* (1981) 25 D&R 105 (Eur. Comm. HR); and Krishna Consciousness, in *ISKCON* v. *UK* (1994) 76A D&R 90.

CANON LAW: THE NEED FOR GOD(S)

thus regarded as a given, almost exclusively interpreted as monotheism; this has remained the case in all common law jurisdictions until comparatively recently.

Theistic religions, including Christianity, would seem to generally require a body of doctrines or tenets, priests or other clergy, places and modes of worship, sacraments, blessings, ceremonies, rites and devotional objects such as rosaries and scapulars.

Canon law

Perhaps in order to substantiate the transcendental, the Catholic and Protestant strands of Christianity accumulated a considerable body of canon law, revered and passed on through successive generations, which has served both as an evidential basis for that religion while simultaneously grounding the beliefs of adherents. Canon law, which is rooted in the Scriptures: identifies God, his lineage and spiritual context; details the essential doctrines, tenets, spectrum of beliefs and rules for their adherence; specifies modes and places of worship, prescribes ceremonial occasions and provides for the veneration of sacraments; directs the roles of clergy and laity; and generally outlines the morality and conduct required of adherents. For present purposes it is important to note that the canon law injunctions governing morality and conduct are wholly integrated into Christianity and essentially prescribe a way of life that adherents must commit to in order to demonstrate the veracity of their professed Christian religious convictions (see also, Chapter 1).

Canon law and morality

During the formative years in the development of the British colonies, Christianity and its canon law precepts provided a unifying thread, linking their development, giving them a shared cultural identity and preparing the ground for the subsequent similar evolution of associated bodies of law. This was particularly evident in family law: matters relating to immoral conduct were rigorously policed by the Ecclesiastical Courts. Canon law morality, drawing heavily from the Scriptures, dwelt at length on sexual activity which was to be confined within a marital relationship and be for the purposes of procreation. Such was the enduring authority of canon law that it was only in the mid nineteenth century that the Ecclesiastical Courts surrendered their jurisdiction in relation to marriage and divorce. The basic principles, having gained common law currency, continued to produce an almost identical jurisprudence schematic on family law and related moral matters well into the twentieth century. Although such law still remains recognisably similar in the common law jurisdictions, the evolving cultural differences, including the drift towards secularism, have now resulted in the civil law of some countries remaining closer to their canon law heritage (e.g. Ireland), further away in others (e.g. the United States), while in all a patchwork of competing morality-based subcultures is emerging. The challenge for civil law in the jurisdictions studied, as regards how to accommodate and manage these competing cultures within a morality-coherent legislative framework, is becoming steadily more real.

Christianity and canon law

Given that Christianity is defined by canon law, the beliefs of a professed Christian must be governed by its provisions. For this to be established there has to be corroborating evidence demonstrating an informed understanding of and commitment to a coherent blend of canon law principles, together with a consistent record of conduct commensurate with such understanding and commitment. Routine attendance at places of worship – let alone a commitment limited to being christened, married and buried in accordance with Christian ceremonial requirements – will not in itself suffice. The collective Christian religion may claim the individual as an adherent (on the basis of being christened and church attendance) but, strictly speaking, the latter cannot meet that definition unless he or she satisfies the canon law requirements; any more so than someone born a Muslim, but living their life in ignorance of the Quran, could be defined as an Islamist.

Religion and religious beliefs

However, recent developments in human rights and charity law have ruptured the hitherto solid ties between the *locus standi* of religion and the religious belief of an individual. The right of those who wish to perpetuate traditional beliefs, modes of worship and means of socially manifesting religious beliefs is unquestionable. But as far as the law of the land is now concerned, canon law in itself is no longer necessary and, more importantly, for religious adherents it is insufficient, to substantiate the professed religious beliefs of an individual.

Canon law, modern belief systems and the human rights/charity law frame of reference

Canon law is now compromised: it sits uneasily alongside a human rights/charity law definition of religion. This frame of reference, being no longer reliant on the need for God, is freed from any necessity to have his existence substantiated by and for adherents in the traditional way. Without the cohering force of monotheism, the need for a framework to demonstrate collective religious belief falls away, taking with it the ancillary need to conform to the supporting and regulating effect of rules governing modes of worship.

Alternative belief systems and the subjective religious experience

The commitment to and experience of religious belief (or, for that matter, philosophical, moral, ethical or other forms of belief) is clearly private and personal; verifiable, if at all, only within the matrix employed by the individual concerned. Consequently, there is now a considerable body of case law illustrating the painstaking efforts of the judiciary to establish: first, whether the beliefs held by an individual can be construed as having a religious quality;[4] and second, if so, whether his or her conduct conforms to such beliefs,[5] and whether that conduct in fact constitutes a reasonable manifestation of that belief[6] (and, then, whether the conduct impacts disproportionately upon the rights of others[7]).

The first step in this approach is one which upholds the subjective and personal in favour of the collective interpretation of religion.[8] It allows for the legal recognition of beliefs that have nothing to do with God[9] nor with the transcendental, and may have formerly been derided as specious,[10] and looks to the coherence of beliefs and related actions to test and authenticate the religious nature of an individual's purported convictions.[11] The concern is primarily with establishing the authenticity (not the validity)

---

[4] *Campbell and Cosans* v. *United Kingdom* [1982] 4 EHRR 293 (corporal punishment) and *H* v. *UK.* (1993) 16 EHRR CD 44 (veganism).

[5] *Arrowsmith* v. *the United Kingdom*, App. No. 7050/75, Comm. Report para. 71 DR 19.

[6] *Otto-Preminger-Institut* v. *Austria* (1994) 19 EHRR 34.

[7] *D.H.* v. *Czech Republic*, App. No. 42393/98, 2001-V Eur Ct HR 449.

[8] *Ghai, R (on the application of)* v. *Newcastle City Council & Ors* [2010] EWCA Civ 59.

[9] *Grainger* v. *Nicholson* [2009] UKEAT 0219 09 0311 (EAT).   [10] Ibid.

[11] *R (On the application of Begum (by her litigation friend, Rahman))* v. *Headteacher and Governors of Denbigh High School* [2006] UKHL 15 (HL).

of an individual's religious beliefs. The courts have been at pains to stress that in secular terms it is of little or no consequence that the beliefs of an individual do not correlate with those of a particular religion to which he or she 'belongs':[12] they cannot judge whether a particular interpretation of any religion is more correct than any other;[13] an individual is free to follow their own subjective interpretation and to change it as they see fit,[14] so long as their beliefs at the relevant point in time are cogent, authentic and appropriately supported by their conduct, they may then be confirmed as 'religious beliefs'.[15] All that is required is evidence to substantiate the subjective, informed (even if clearly wrong or misguided – though there may well be an issue here of weighting) commitment to specific beliefs.

The second step requires the individual to show that the manner of giving effect to their beliefs is necessary and appropriate, not merely incidental. The court or regulator will need to be assured that, given the authenticity of beliefs held, the related conduct is a reasonable manifestation of them. This injects an objective test; it must be demonstrably clear that the conduct in question represents an important aspect of those beliefs, is proportionate and not to do such an act would constitute a serious breach in personal belief commitment.

Christianity, canon law and the subjective religious experience

The inevitable corrolary to the above approach is that it must also be applied to test and authenticate the actual beliefs of those who claim their actions appropriately manifest their commitment to Christianity:[16] the subjective religious experience must be disentangled from the collective; it is insufficient for an individual to claim that membership of a Christian Church means, *ipso facto*, that he or she therefore subscribes to and their conduct conforms with canon law. The '*Playfoot*' factor,[17] a health and safety alert for religious banality, has to be a benchmark standard for assessing the veracity of an individual's 'religious' belief and the authenticity

---

[12] Ibid.   [13] Ibid.   [14] Ibid.

[15] See *Grainger v. Nicholson* [2009] UKEAT 0219 09 0311 (EAT).

[16] See, for example, *Jehovah's Witnesses Inc.* (1943) 67 CLR, *per* McTiernan J, who noted that conduct which consists of worship, teaching, propagation, practices or observances may be held to be religious, only if the motivation for engaging in the conduct is religious, i.e. if the person who engages in the conduct does so in giving effect to his particular faith in the supernatural (at p.135).

[17] See *Playfoot (a minor), R (on the application of) v. Millais School* [2007] EWHC 1698 Admin. (purity ring).

of its related social manifestation – regardless of whether he or she belongs to a traditional institutional religion or subscribes to an esoteric philosophy. This constitutes a very significant step away from the 'corporate Christianity' view that 'no prophecy of the scripture is of any private interpretation'.[18] The civil law focus has shifted from religion as an institution to the authenticity of an individual's subjective interpretation and experience of it.[19] 'Christians' can, of course, still meet the definition of such within canon law and within the human rights/charity law frame of reference by fulfilling the traditional criteria, but it would seem that to meet the definition of religious belief a 'Christian' would need only to produce evidence of an authentic personal interpretation of that religion, supported by appropriate conduct, which need not be referenced wholly or in part to canon law.

The cultural context of canon law

Naturally there is a difficulty in transferring and applying principles forged in the circumstances of one cultural context to fit those of another. Much of canon law draws from the Scriptures, and the moral imperatives of early Christianity do not always fit well with contemporary circumstances. In common with all law, it could be argued that the principles given effect by canons must be contextualised to take account of other laws currently governing the relevant circumstances. Recent case law in Australia would seem to indicate that some members of the common law judiciary are prepared to construe traditional religious doctrines in the light of contemporary social circumstances and related jurisprudence.[20]

The social role of religion

The morality that infuses canon law, often reinforced by secular legislation (including charity law), was transferred and policed by the clergy and governors of the British administration throughout its Empire. It was transmitted through the contribution to education and health care

---

[18] See the Second Epistle of Peter.

[19] See P. W. Edge, 'Determining Religion in English Courts' (2012) *Oxford Journal of Law and Religion*, doi: 10.1093/ojlr/rwr005.

[20] See *OV & OW* v. *Members of the Board of the Wesley Mission Council* [2010] NSWCA 155 (6 July 2010).

474   A CONFLICT OF LAWS

infrastructure made by Christian religious organisations in all common law nations and further afield through their missionary activities. The social status of the Church was also transferred to establish the clergy as figures signifying respectability, moral approbation and a degree of social authority in the parishes, communities and political circles of those nations.

The life cycle and 'sacraments'

Christianity has interposed a sacramental gateway at crucial stages in the human life cycle – a ceremonial blessing that marks the passage from one stage to another[21] – which tends to be interpreted by secularists as a religious hijacking of normal life events. For present purposes the role of sacraments is relevant as there is considerable controversy surrounding the marriage ceremony. Matrimony has been traditionally claimed as a significant sacrament for at least the Catholic and Protestant strands of Christianity. Who may be married, where and whether with or without clergy officiating and/or giving a blessing, are currently pressing issues in all jurisdictions studied. An ancillary issue has been the validity of female clergy undertaking the role of priest or bishop in officiating on sacramental occasions.

Conflating culture and religion

Some countries have been stamped with a particular religious ethos for so long and so pervasively – permeating their customs, art, architecture and often language, dress and family names – that their cultural identity has become immersed in and emblematic of that religion. Italy, Ireland, Spain and the former Spanish colonies of South America are thus associated with Catholicism and, similarly, England, Scotland and the Scandinavian countries with Protestantism.[22] In such countries, a single dominant religion has long been such a defining influence on culture that national identity and social cohesion would be severely impaired by the secular stripping out (if that were possible) of the religious component.

---

[21] The Catholic Church, for example, recognises seven such sacraments: baptism, confirmation, the eucharist, penance, anointing of the sick, holy orders and matrimony. Other religions also have ceremonial ways of marking 'rites of passage'.

[22] Equally, of course, mapping countries against religion/culture would, for example, show Iran and Pakistan as distinctively Islamist.

By extension, the same argument holds good for those geographic regions within a country where the religious cultural identity of a particular group has long been dominant – such as the Amish in the counties of Lancaster and Chester in Pennsylvania or the Hutterites in western Canada.

The promotion of pluralism needs to take account of such a context. There is clearly a case to be made for protecting cultural/religious identity (as with any endangered species) where that has proved to be an authentic and self-supporting entity, giving security and nurture to successive generations and offering respect to its neighbours: ethnic groups such as Rastafarians, religions such as the Jews and territorally based religious organisations such as the Amish come to mind. Equally, of course, the reverse case could be made where such an entity uses its social cohesion to act as an aggressor to those it perceives as religious/cultural inferiors: Kosovo, Northern Ireland and the Middle East, not to mention the treatment of Indigenous populations by colonial settlers, offer many examples of situations in which the behaviour of groups could have been usefully moderated by positively implementing a social policy of pluralism.

Contemporary moral issues and social policy

Transmitting canon law – mainly through the Protestantism that characterised the British colonial administration – to inform the civic morality of its settlements, inevitably laid the foundations for the current divisive disputes that are now such a feature of society, mainly in the United States, but also to a varying degree in all the common law jurisdictions (see, further, below). As new discoveries push back the boundaries of science and medicine, while legal rights/human rights further shrink the space left to religion, and secularists and other belief systems continue undermining the once pervasive Christian morality, the range of such social policy issues and the accompanying acrimonious contention can only increase.

Some current and significant jurisdictional differences

While largely retaining loyalty to their Christian heritage, all the jurisdictions studied have since broadened it to also include the Eastern religions, which may be non-theistic or multi-theistic,[23] but they vary in the extent to which their respective interpretations of 'religion' have

---

[23] See, for example, Theravadan Buddhism, the Samkhya school of Hinduism and Taoism.

accommodated beliefs that are more moral, ethical or philosophical in nature, with the judiciary in the United States and the United Kingdom taking a particularly generous view, although their counterparts in Canada and Ireland have remained close to the traditional, conservative reliance upon a theistic component. This expansion in the range of religions and religious beliefs has, paradoxically, been accompanied by an increase in the proportion of the population that eschews religion, faith and matters of belief for a more secular approach. As a consequence, the traditional Christian religions, with their canon law and Scriptural underpinnings, are steadily becoming less representative of contemporary culture in the developed common law nations. While an increasing proportion of the population in each jurisdiction is thus unencumbered by canon law morality and able to respond positively to evolving human rights principles, traditional Christians are less able to do so. Instead, the latter are finding themselves morally embattled in their own countries and are now communing more, and building solidarity, with their counterparts in the developing nations of the southern hemisphere, where the reach of human rights legislation is not yet quite so tenacious.

Religion and religious belief

A belief in God or a Supreme Being is no longer regarded as essential to the legal definition of religion in many of the countries studied,[24] and some have now followed the UK example and specifically legislated to that effect – Ireland, New Zealand, Canada and Australia being exceptions. Where the definition has been extended to include non-theistic beliefs, this has sometimes fallen short of accommodating those of a philosophical, moral or ethical nature – as is the case in Canada, while in Ireland the lobby to include in the Charities Act 2009 a specific reference to humanism or to secular philosophical beliefs was rejected.

The proliferation and infinite variety of new forms of belief systems, movements and cults that seemed to spring up in the aftermath of the 1960s hippy culture challenged judicial efforts to find a test that could be uniformly applicable in identifying those that constituted a 'religion'. At first the approach adopted was to judge the new in accordance with the accepted specification of the old: the traditional need for doctrines, tenets,

---

[24] See, in the United States, *United States* v. *Kauten* (1943) 133 F(2d) 703, *United States* v. *Ballard* [1944] USSC 72 (88 Law Ed 1148) and *Welsh* v. *United States* [1970] USSC 147 (26 Law Ed (2d) 308.

worship, celebrants, etc. that typified collective religious belief was used as a template for assessing whether new forms conformed to that model. This was defeated by the diversity and mutation of belief systems and also by the perceived unfair advantage in terms of public credence that might be gained by those that were modelled on traditional religions.[25] Now there is widespread consensus that an individual's religious beliefs cannot be determined by virtue of their adherence to a collective religion but must be ascertained by examining personal convictions and related conduct.[26] Again, however, it is unlikely that this approach will find early acceptance in Ireland.

Need for doctrines, tenets, etc.

The common law jurisdictions have moved at a variable pace – some if at all – in leaving behind the customary reliance upon supportive evidence of worship and the accompanying need for doctrines, tenets, etc. So, again in Ireland, the 2009 charity law provisions pointedly repeated the wording in the 1961 legislation to require that 'a charitable gift for the purpose of the advancement of religion shall have effect, and the terms upon which it is given shall be construed, in accordance with the laws, canons, ordinances and tenets of the religion concerned'.[27] In Canada there tends to be a similar reliance upon a body of doctrines. In Australia and New Zealand, however, as in the United Kingdom, the judiciary would seem firmly convinced that there is no longer a necessity for an entity to have such a body of liturgical and ecclesiastical teachings in order to substantiate its status as a 'religion'.[28]

Charity law: the need for public benefit

Whether religion should have a social utility function has long been a matter of contention. The UK legislators responded in the affirmative when they reversed the public benefit presumption in favour of the advancement of religion, which it had enjoyed for centuries, thereby presenting a very real challenge for the future of this charitable purpose.

---

[25] *Gillette* v. *United States* [1971] USSC 45; (1971) 401 US 437 (28 Law Ed (2d) 168.
[26] See, in the United States, *United States* v. *Seeger* [1965] USSC 49 (13 Law Ed (2d) 733.
[27] Charities Act 2009, s.3(6), repeating verbatim the Charities Act 1961, s.45.
[28] See *The Church of the New Faith* v. *Commissioner of Pay-roll Tax* [1983] HCA 40; (1983) 154 CLR 120 (27 October 1983).

This initiative constitutes a fundamental readjustment of the core component of charity law, comparable in its effect to the redefinition of 'religion' that removes any need for a god or gods. Together these changes have significantly altered the traditional relationship between law, religion and charity in the United Kingdom.[29] Because of the well-established practice of looking to, and most often following, the lead given by the progenitor charity law jurisdiction, it is highly probable that in due course other jurisdictions will adopt the same approach but, even if they choose not to, the effects of this initiative will impact upon them due to the resulting variation in charitable status for the many international religious entities based or operating in the United Kingdom. However, as religion and religious organisations with few exceptions have always striven to make a positive contribution to improving the environment within which they operate there is some uncertainty as to the actual difference that the UK change will make.

Religion and the public benefit

Ultimately, the benefit of religion most probably lies in the eye of the beholder. For those of religious belief, the benefits are axiomatic and largely spiritual: they cannot believe otherwise. Those without such belief may well see what largely amounts to member benefit activity, with any wider social benefit being due to the palliative effect of religion on its adherents, resulting in a greater amount of mutual support and a more peaceful and ordered society.

One way forward may be to recognise the intrinsic characteristics of religion – those that fall at either extreme – acknowledging that the balance to be stuck between them will vary according to the social context.

Religion as intrinsically beneficial

The benefits of religion and other forms of belief can be most clearly seen in their direct effect on adherents: in the peace and equanimity instilled

---

[29] The controversy generated by the present statutory requirement that religion be subject to a public benefit test has some way to run and may yet cause Parliament to review this provision. See, for example: P. Luxton, *Making Law? Parliament* v. *The Charity Commission*, Politeia, 2009; P. Luxton and N. Evans, 'Cogent and Cohesive? Two Recent Charity Commission Decisions on the Advancement of Religion' (2011) 75:2 *Conveyancer and Property Lawyer* 144; and H. Picarda, *The Law and Practice Relating to Charities* (4th edn), Bloomsbury Professional, Haywards Heath, 2010 at pp. 36–39, 80–87, 135–138.

by the prospect of eternal salvation or other forms of redemption; and on communities of the like-minded, by being part of a collective bound by the same values and modes of worship. For the general public the benefits are more indirect: in the main these result from the exposure to the modelling of responsible civic conduct, and the dissemination of related virtuous teachings; by leading a good life and doing good works, the spiritual welfare of the believer – and the more secular welfare of the beneficiary and the wider community – may be furthered.

There are other benefits that may be seen as intrinsic to religion and which enhance the community and public life more generally. These would include: its physical presence in the form of churches and other places of worship which represent pastoral care and signify a source of solace, a refuge or somewhere to turn for those in need; the moral leadership practised by the clergy; the body of acquired theological and legal knowledge; and the churches, cathedrals, ceremonies, music, literature, sculpture and other artefacts which are culturally enriching. Religious principles of good and evil, justice and mercy continue to inform and set boundaries for acceptable social relationships and the heritage of values centred on generosity, altruism, philanthropy and care for the poor and needy – generated by religious doctrines, teachings and practice – has done much to counterbalance other social pressures. As a 'pillar of society', religion (together with other forms of faith and belief) continues to uphold and represent virtuous and decent behaviour and serves as a reminder to citizens that 'good works' are needed if society is to be a better place.

Religion as intrinsically detrimental

Religion's innate capacity for generating and maintaining social cohesion has a dark side. Whether or not it is essentially member benefit in its orientation, it does tend to be perceived by others as excluding and marginalising them, which can lead to polarisation and mutual antipathy within and between communities. Arguably, religion is fundamentally discriminatory. Throughout the centuries, it has demonstrated an ability to cause social divisions and provoke violent confrontations. Most recently this was illustrated by the experience in Northern Ireland. Where religion or other forms of belief veer off towards the closed-group thinking typical of cults, then the sense of separateness is exacerbated, which can be destructive for both the group and the wider community.

Religion may also incline its adherents towards attitudes of acceptance of the status quo and deference to higher authority and thereby act as a

480 A CONFLICT OF LAWS

conservative force in politics: possibly explaining why it has traditionally earned its reputation as 'a pillar of society'.

The public benefit test

All common law jurisdictions will require in the future, as in the past, that a religion, religious organisations (as variably extended to belief systems), and gifts to such must be for the public benefit if they are to warrant charitable status. Of the minority of those jurisdictions that embarked on charity law reform processes, only in the United Kingdom was the outcome a legislative commitment to changing the presumption that such entities are public-benefit compliant: the Irish jurisdiction statutorily substituted a rebuttable for the previous irrebuttable presumption that they are;[30] while Australia has more recently legislated for the same rebuttable approach.

The UK initiative to require both positive proof of public benefit and an absence of any outweighing detrimental effect is seen by some as a fundamental devaluation of religion. The imposition of a flat rate public benefit test across all charitable purposes, reinforced by an 'activities test', is viewed as secularising the value of religion, which in turn then raises the question: what remains of this charitable purpose to warrant its continued legal classification as a separate and distinct branch of charity? Is there an added-value religious premium which should be factored in as a way of computing its distinctive contribution, or is the future of this purpose to be reduced to its secular function, weighed and measured in terms of its proven usefulness (with due regard for possible detriment), as any other charitable purpose? Would there then be anything left that was intrinsically religious in 'the advancement of religion'?

The choices would seem to be limited. The current default approach, as applied in all jurisdictions other than the United Kingdom, which essentially presumes that religion and associated faiths or beliefs are inherently for the public benefit unless evidence to the contrary is available, is not wholly satisfactory. Religious organisations are not by nature transparent and are unaccustomed to external processes of accountability, so evidence of non-compliance with public benefit is not readily forthcoming. Also, this approach: allows for the benefit to

---

[30] Note that as most of the Charities Act 2009 has yet to be implemented, the presumption currently remains irrebuttable.

be spiritual or otherwise intangible; the advancement of religion can be purely self-advancement and, arguably, socially divisive with no benefit dividend to the general public as when it takes the form of proselytism or its secular activities are overtly partisan in religiously unstable societies; and it does not specifically require a secular benefit, quantifiable and significant, to be delivered to non-members.

Alternatively it might be possible to separate religion, belief systems and related organisations from their secular functions and regulate them differently, with charitable status being restricted to the latter, if they satisfy the public benefit test, and designated in accordance with their secular contribution (i.e. under education or health care, etc.). After all, in an increasingly secular society, it is not a given that the additional 'religious' premium that comes with the delivery of an educational or health service by a religious organisation produces a greater quotient of public benefit than the same service delivered by a secular organisation. Such a formal organisational separation would set aside and give special recognition to religion and associated beliefs which, unlike other charitable purposes, will always have only an incidental relationship with charity as their identity and orientation lies with the spiritual. Again, as would seem to be the intention in the United Kingdom, a religion/belief system and its secular functions, if any, could be treated as one and charitable status awarded in accordance with the flat rate test (subject to the 'member benefit' and 'private profit' rules being applied to ensure that benefit also accrues to those who are not adherents of the religion concerned). However, can there ever be a 'flat rate' public benefit test that applies to religion and to religious matters in the same way as it does to other charitable purposes?

The test in a human rights context

The considerable contention as to whether the traditional treatment of religion within charity law is human rights compatible would seem to have been readjusted to focus on whether the UK changes to the public benefit test have increased or diminished that compatibility. In theory, subjecting the advancement of religion and beliefs to the test, thereby achieving parity in terms of onus of proof with all other charitable purposes, must remove any discriminatory preferencing in favour of religion/beliefs, their organisations and related gifts and activities. Much, however, depends on the nature of the test and the permitted exemptions.

The test and the advancement of religion

As has been pointed out: 'The difficult question is how to identify the necessary public benefit, especially in relation to purely religious purposes (for example, prayer, worship, ritual and ceremonial practices, preaching or evangelism) that cannot be subsumed under other charitable heads such as the advancement of education or the relief of poverty.'[31] This is true and the difficulties are likely to increase when the test is applied to the many and varied forms of belief with their equivalent types of worship, rituals and ceremonial accoutrements that will invite parity of treatment. However, arguably a bigger problem lies with proselytism. This has been a well recognised means of advancing religion in all the jurisdictions studied – but it has never before been subject to a positively applied public benefit test (and, of course, for the foreseeable future will continue not to be in all jurisdictions other than the United Kingdom). It is difficult to see how such activity can now be said to be in the public interest: where is the benefit to the general public in an agency persuading persons to leave one religion and join another or acquire rather than reject religious beliefs?[32] Even leaving aside the added onus to show public benefit that now distinguishes the UK approach, the questionable practice of sustained proselytising by sophisticated evangelical representatives among the Indigenous people of Australia, for example, is probably open to challenge on the grounds of using undue influence or manipulation in respect of a dependent group – if not of violating cultural integrity.[33]

Applying the test: the 'public' arm

There is an argument that submitting religion/beliefs to a positive public benefit test breaches the right to manifest religion as provided for in Article 9 of the Convention and in equivalent national legislative provisions.[34]

---

[31] See P. Ridge, 'Religious Charitable Status and Public Benefit in Australia' (2011) 35 *Melbourne University Law Review* 1071, at p.1073.

[32] Having the British taxpayer subsidise the smuggling of Bibles into Eastern Europe, for example (as per the disclosures of Archbishop Welby), with the attendant risks of adding further to the social instability in that region, would seem to be of doubtful benefit to the British public.

[33] The example set in the United States by the decision in *Americans United For Separation of Church and State* v. *Prison Fellowship Ministries*, 432 F. Supp. 2d 862 (SD Iowa 2006) being a case in point.

[34] See, for example, M. Harding, 'Trusts for Religious Purposes and the Question of Public Benefit' (2008) 71 *Modern Law Review* 159, at pp.179–180.

This would clearly come into play most forcibly in relation to private piety. When practised by a closed contemplative religious order, this way of manifesting religious belief has long been a point of jurisdictional difference in terms of meeting the public benefit test, and one which has remained unaltered by the various charity law reform processes. While the United Kingdom and the United States resolutely deny charitable status to closed religious orders, Ireland, Australia, New Zealand and Canada continue to endorse it. The eligibility of private piety for charitable status has also long been contentious when it takes the form of intercessory prayer, private masses, masses dedicated to a restricted group such as family members, etc. From a human rights perspective, a problem now arising as a consequence of extending recognition to philosophical, ethical, moral and other such belief systems is whether commensurate recognition should not be similarly extended to those whose beliefs also require contemplative practices? The permissive parameters of private piety as a legitimate manifestation of 'religious belief' – warranting charitable status and tax exemption on the grounds of its net contribution to public benefit – is likely to be increasingly contentious.

Arguably, also, the public benefit test is likely to favour the traditional institutional religions at the expense of those that are newer, smaller and less well known or are concerned more with ethical, moral or philosophical beliefs.

Applying the test: the 'benefit' arm

To submit to the regulator's public benefit test carries a price tag. For the newer and smaller non-religious belief entities this is likely to be disproportionately onerous in terms of the inescapable routine submission of paperwork, but also as regards compiling the evidence necessary to demonstrate public benefit compliance. There is an argument, therefore, that complying with the public benefit test makes it more costly to manifest religion and this may violate the right to freedom of religion.[35]

Public benefit and government funding

The public benefit principle provides the basis for a natural synergy between government and charity and the rationale for the former to

---

[35] See Ridge, 'Religious Charitable Status and Public Benefit in Australia', at p.1091.

484 A CONFLICT OF LAWS

fund or help fund education, health, social care and other such services provided by the latter: case law has long ago endorsed as charitable those organisations which do that which government would otherwise be obliged to do.[36] In the United Kingdom and most other common law jurisdictions, though not in the United States,[37] this understanding probably worked well enough and charities became accustomed to having their public benefit role subsidised by government grant aid. However, by the closing decades of the twentieth century diminishing tax revenues coupled with the rapidly climbing costs of services (health care for the elderly, drugs, etc.) meant that government had to rely on charity to assume proportionately more responsibility for public benefit service provision but, for the same reason, it could no longer afford to offset the costs of this by way of grant aid.

Government preference for partnership with charities – because of the latter's resources, experience and established bonds with service users and, not least, because the cost of the services they provide is subsidised by public donations – survived the change in funding policy from grants to contracts. Of those charities, religious organisations were particularly well positioned to prosper in the new open market environment. Many of the initial hospitals, social care services, schools and colleges were founded by religious charities. The experience of being embedded in – through ownership, management and a long cultivated customer base – much social infrastructure (now in prime downtown locations) over many generations, subsidised by public and private donations, by tax privileges and by direct government grants, placed religious organisations in a dominant competitive position to further develop their public benefit service provision. Which is largely what has happened in the jurisdictions concerned. Faith-based provision – most obviously in education but also in health and elderly care – has become the preferred government option, leading to a noticeable scaling up in the level of schools and residential care facilities provided on a religion-specific basis in the United Kingdom and the United States.

The stepped-up faith-based contribution to public service provision brought with it a more vociferous challenge from secularists. Whereas

---

[36] See, for example, the US case *Jackson* v. *Phillips*, 14 Allen 539 (1867), 'lessening the burdens of government', *per* Gray J at p.536.

[37] The open market economy of the United States has always accommodated a mix of competing charitable, non-profit and for-profit entities in public benefit service provision, where the boundaries are blurred by the role of insurance companies.

CHARITY LAW: THE NEED FOR PUBLIC BENEFIT   485

the public policy debate had previously been concerned with unfair competition resulting from the effect of tax concessions to charities on the principle of competitive neutrality, it now developed a new twist and focused on the use of public benefit service provision as a platform for showcasing religion, for religious evangelising and for discriminatory practice. There were and are several different aspects to this challenge, including: that government should not be in the business of strengthening the social role of religion,[38] let alone any particular religion; that public benefit service providers should deliver on a religion-free basis; that recipients should have a choice not to be dependent upon making concessions to a particular religion, nor to any, in order to access such services; that when acting as government service delivery agents, religious organisations should be required to act in a non-discriminatory fashion, not just as regards service access, but also in relation to the nature of the services delivered and in the hiring of staff to be employed in the delivery of such services. These matters have been particularly contentious in the United States, where they trigger constitutional issues regarding the separation of Church and State (see, further, below).

In short, the public benefit principle that drives charity and government binds both to ensure that public benefit service delivery is wholly human rights compliant – meaning that when engaged in such delivery as a government agent, a religious organisation must respect public service neutrality: public benefit goods are paid for by taxpayers without a religious premium, and should be made available and delivered to all on the same basis.

Some current and significant jurisdictional differences

To acquire or retain charitable status, religion, religious organisations and gifts to them have always been required to be for the public benefit. However, following the many recent disclosures of abuse by Christian clergy, there is now a greater willingness than formerly to question the public benefit compliance of religious organisations and religious persons. This, perhaps more than anything else, has triggered a general disquiet among regulators about continuing the traditional approach to such entities and led to the UK initiative. Placing the burden of proof on all religions, faiths, beliefs and religious entities to show how they are

---

[38] A policy most contentious in the United States; see, for example, *Dodge* v. *Salvation Army* 1989, WL 53857 (SD Miss).

486   A CONFLICT OF LAWS

bringing benefit to the public – not just to their own adherents – is a development that has significantly changed the *locus standi* of religion in charity law, even if for the present this change is confined to the United Kingdom.

Public benefit and equality

Primarily, it has been the need to synchronise the public benefit test with the equality demands of human rights legislation that caused the UK jurisdictions to take the initiative and reverse the compliance presumption. As this step was taken with an eye to ensuring that in future all entities and purposes would bear the same burden of proof, thereby achieving equality of treatment from a human rights perspective, there could be no question of exempting religion, religious organisations and gifts to them – although this approach is currently confined to the United Kingdom. Until all jurisdictions find, or re-find, parity in their regard for the need for such entities to demonstrate a social utility function (accompanied by no evidence of any detrimental social effects), there will be some confusion – not least among religious organisations as to their role and how they are perceived by society.

In theory there is an argument that equality is all very well but when religion conflates with culture to give a nation or region a coherent identity, and all that goes with it in terms of a secure sense of belonging for successive generations (generating its distinctive art, artefacts and other cultural characteristics) for the citizens and communities concerned then, in such a case, it is not feasible to regard religion as separable from culture. The meaning of 'freedom of religion' and 'manifestations of religion' can be susceptible to cultural translation which makes jurisdictional comparisons difficult. In terms of achieving equality, it may also mean that it would be unreasonable to expect any such religiously/culturally coherent jurisdiction to jettison such customs and practice: it would in fact be treating any such nation or region unequally, relative to other more pluralist societies, by requiring a devaluation of the role traditionally played by religion in order that parity be achieved. This would not be to the benefit of the public in the nation or region concerned (any 'regime change' strategy initiated from outside that regime must always be suspect).

However, it is a bit late for any such argument to have much traction. Pluralism has taken hold on all developed Western societies: there is little credence in special pleading on behalf, for example, of 'Catholic Ireland'

CHARITY LAW: THE NEED FOR PUBLIC BENEFIT 487

any more so than for 'Protestant England'; the management of diversity has become the more pressing contemporary social policy issue and aligning the public benefit principle of charity law with the equality principle of human rights legislation would seem crucial to the success of that policy.

Calibrating the test

It can be argued that persons and other entities engaged in furthering this charitable purpose do not lend themselves to measurement by any standardised public benefit calibration. Religion per se does not require a social utility function: the effects of intercessory prayer are not measurable. Religion is surely, above all else, directed towards the salvation of the soul or souls in the next life and thus is not readily amenable to a quality audit in this one. Where there is social utility it may well be wholly extraneous and unrelated to the core nature of this charitable purpose, if that purpose is essentially concerned with the spiritual welfare of the individual. There may be, after all, some validity in the observation of the Nathan Committee, in relation to almsgiving (but perhaps infinitely applicable in the context of religion) that this was 'more a means to the salvation of the soul of the benefactor than an endeavour to diagnose and alleviate the needs of the beneficiary'.[39]

Moreover, the test itself is not a value-free, neutral tool capable of measuring 'benefit' according to fixed, standardised criteria and with forensic detachment: arguably it is formulated and applied subject to an overarching national religious ethos. In Ireland, for example, where Christianity and specifically Catholicism is constitutionally preferenced, the 'benefit' is determined in accordance with the intentions of the donor: if these are not in breach of the law or public policy, and the traditional common law rules are satisfied, then the subjective wishes of the donor rather than the objective assessment of the court or regulator will decide whether the public benefit requirement is satisfied. This ensures that in Ireland public benefit will continue to be found in donor gifts for private prayerful activity and in masses for the dead, but not so in the United Kingdom, where the more objective (and traditionally Protestant) assessment of such gifts will, in such instances, prevail over donor intentions.

---

[39] See the Nathan Committee, *Report of the Committee on the Law and Practice Relating to Charitable Trusts*, London, HMSO (Cmd 8710), at para. 36; cf. *In re Delany: Conoley* v. *Quick* [1902] 2 Ch. 642, *per* Farwell J, at p.648.

488 A CONFLICT OF LAWS

Countering the national religious ethos to provide a means of calibrating public benefit equitably for all religions and other forms of belief, in keeping with human rights requirements will be a challenge – particularly in countries with a long 'established' national religion.

There is also now the issue of whether there can be any calibration of public benefit that could be equally applicable to the traditional and more institutional religions as to the very varied range of newer faiths and beliefs – some quite transient or in a fairly constant process of mutation. It is hard to see what these can contribute in terms of benefit to society that would bear comparison with the greatly valued cultural heritage that accompanies the Christian and other traditional religions. How to measure and weigh the respective social utility of both types in such a way that satisfies the principles of public benefit and equality is another significant challenge – presently, at least, for the UK jurisdictions.

Government preferencing of particular religions as service providers

There is little wiggle room available when considering the role played by government in some countries in the selection of faith-based service providers. In particular, the 'established' nature of the Church of England, with its very substantial contribution to educating the nation's children, has assured it of continuing government support; currently very evident as the Church commits to adopting the government's policy for 'academies' and takes full advantage of the funding available to do so. In Ireland the proportion of the nation's children being taught in schools owned and very largely controlled by Catholic organisations, but funded by government, is even greater than that of the Church of England in the neighbouring jurisdiction. In both cases this is to a considerable degree an inherited legacy from a time when both populations were more homogenous and their societies cohered naturally around their respective religions – a legacy which will prove difficult to adjust if these jurisdictions are to fully respond to the pressures of pluralism. Other common law jurisdictions further removed from the heart of what was the British Empire have managed things differently. Of note has been the vigour with which the courts in the United States have ensured that government avoids 'excessive entanglement' with religion per se, let alone any preferencing of a particular religion.[40] This has not impeded

---

[40] See *Agostini* v. *Felton*, 521 US 203 (1997).

successive governments from pursuing a policy of expanding faith-based public benefit service provision.

Human rights law: the need for religious pluralism

Cultural dissonance has become a serious threat to social stability. Whether within families and communities, between Indigenous people and others, between settled communities and immigrant groups and between such groups, and indeed between nations, a lack of mutual understanding and willingness to respect and value cultural difference is causing destructive tensions. Similar tensions are also evident on a more domestic social level in terms of inequities rooted in such differentiating factors as gender, disability, mental health, age, etc. Where the fact or perception of inequity caused by such differences is not acknowledged or is unaccompanied by actions demonstrating good faith in dealing with them, then the disadvantaged can quickly become alienated. Human rights legislation has grown to play a crucial role in setting the parameters for legitimate manifestations of social difference; identifying the acceptable means for asserting identity issues and the processes for resolving any related conflict.

Religion is layered into culture and can often provide the trigger that turns cultural dissonance into dissension with long-lasting destructive consequences, as evidenced by the pattern of deterioration in places such as Northern Ireland. For that reason, of all possible breaches of human rights, religious discrimination has the potential to be particularly harmful. While charities in general, as dispensers of goodwill and public benefit services, can play an important role in mediating along the interfaces between mutually estranged social groups, religious charities have the potential to compound the tensions. Recent judicial exploration of human rights provisions relating to religious discrimination and the exemption privileges attached to religious belief have demonstrated the need for legal checks and balances that could promote a new religious pluralism.

Religious belief, charity and taxation

In the developed Western world, religion and its adherents are ostensibly diminishing relative to secularists. There is an absence of hard evidence of this (in terms of those who, despite non-Church attendance or even despite forthright renunciation of 'religion', nonetheless subscribe to some personal version of the transcendental and quietly abide by related rules of private piety). There is no doubt, however, as to the growing confidence with which the secular challenge is now being levelled in relation to the privileges traditionally enjoyed by religious entities.

Religious belief and tax exemption

It is not always clear what type of religious conduct qualifies for tax privileges. Establishing the ground rules for eligibility is not straightforward and has generated a good deal of not always consistent judicial guidance.

The spectrum of beliefs of a person or organisation now recognised as meeting the definition of 'religion', and therefore presumed charitable in most common law jurisdictions, is very broad and shows every indication of becoming more so. This suggests that it may well be questionable whether all should be equally entitled to have their beliefs subsidised by taxpayers: but what criteria would exclude groups such as vegetarians from entitlement to parity of treatment with, for example, the Church of England; when is a 'belief' simply incidental or just derivative?

Taxation

Tax can give rise to issues of equity and diversity when applied in a context where religion, charity and human rights interface. The right of religious parents, for example, to expect that their contribution as taxpayers will result in their child accessing education within a school that promotes their particular religious beliefs may well conflict with the equal right of non-religious taxpaying parents to expect a secular education for their child. Similarly, perhaps: taxpayers who fund public services have a right to expect that children in care will be placed by agencies for adoption in accordance with the needs of the child regardless of adopters' gender; that mosques and Christian churches will not preach that homosexuality is wrong when it is a right permitted by civil law; and likewise that teachers in faith schools will not teach that abortion is wrong (these may be challenged as unethical or immoral, perhaps, but 'wrong' is to refute prevailing civil law). Taxpayers might, not unreasonably, expect that the price for any such practice would be at least the denial of tax exemption charitable status. The same taxpayers might wish to question the government subvention of religion through national lotteries and the discrete political massaging of value-added tax, goods and services tax and donor incentive schemes – such as Gift Aid, public benevolent institution status, etc. – that tend to favour religious organisations. Then there is the more vexed issue of direct government channelling of tax revenues through religious organisations to pay for religious-flavoured public benefit services, including those provided in the United States to fund faith-based penitentiary rehabilitation schemes, not to mention the Charitable Choice programme.

For many secularists and the public in general, these issues give rise to a basic question as to what exactly it is about religion and related entities that warrants such a double take on the tax revenue base – privileged by exemptions and preferential donor incentive schemes, etc., and also recipients of targeted government funding?

Freedom of religion

There are few fundamental freedoms that can be found as frequently and widely stated in international conventions, national constitutions and jurisdiction-specific legislation as the right to freedom of religion.

The right

This right is easily stated and was once as readily understood. In recent years, however, the definition of 'religion' has been enlarged to accommodate not only an ever growing range of new religions and assorted faiths and beliefs, while allowing for changes in religious commitment, but it has also been stretched to include the right to atheism and agnosticism. As Nicholls LJ observed, in *R (Williamson)* v. *Secretary of State for Education and Employment*,[41] 'the atheist, the agnostic, and the sceptic are as much entitled to freedom to hold and manifest their beliefs as the theist'. In addition, all legislative declarations of this right are accompanied by caveats acknowledging that its exercise is subject to restrictions, mainly regarding the rights and freedoms of others, and the judiciary are increasingly demonstrating a willingness to impose further limits. Consequently, the boundaries of the right to freedom of religion are now very uncertain.

Of particular importance has been the judicial weighting given relatively recently to the subjective understanding of the individual as the

---

[41] *R (Williamson)* v. *Secretary of State for Education and Employment* [2005] 2 AC 246.

key determinant of religious belief.[42] This would seem to have brought to an end the traditional assumption that religious belief was simply a derivative of religion: once the identity of the 'religion' was established the prescriptive nature of the associated 'beliefs' could be safely assumed. Religious adherents now have the legal (if not the theological) right to interpret their religion as they see fit: the new faiths and forms of belief provide limitless opportunities for individuals to find their own religion (which, subject to the public benefit test, will be recognised as a charitable entity), construe the associated beliefs and change these as their understanding develops – provided that any such interpretation relates to a significant and substantive belief, is cogent, is authentically held and is not inappropriate in a democratic society. This is accompanied by the subsidiary right to advance that religion through activities such as proselytism.

The traditional religions continue to register much the same institutional presence, with accompanying social role and functions. They provide a model for the associated rights now also held by the new forms of faith and belief, including: collective worship; body of doctrines, tenets, etc.; the freedom to choose their religious leaders, priests and teachers; the freedom to establish seminaries or religious schools; and the freedom to prepare and distribute religious texts or publications, etc. It is, however, a model that may be intimidating for emerging religions and beliefs, as well as for immigrant ethnic groups, all of whom may consider that they cannot possibly 'measure up'. Taylor warns of the risk of 'needlessly limiting the religious freedom of immigrant minorities, on the strength of our historical institutional arrangements, while sending a message to those same minorities that they by no means enjoy equal status with the long-established mainstream'.[43]

As religion and religious belief become more individualised, at least for legal purposes, so the importance attached to private piety is acquiring greater salience. The individual who worships through solitary prayerful activity is making a legitimate choice regarding the manner in which they give effect to their religious beliefs and this is an aspect of the right to freedom of religion which is finding international recognition. There is, however, considerably less jurisdictional consensus as to whether private piety also constitutes the advancement of religion.

---

[42] See, for example, *Ex parte Williamson* [2005] UKHL 15; [2005] 2 AC 246 (HL).

[43] See C. Taylor, 'Why We Need a Radical Redefinition of Secularism', in E. Mendieta and J. Vanantwerpen (eds), *The Power of Religion in the Public Sphere*, Columbia University Press, New York, 2011, at p.48.

The right to manifest religious belief

International and national legislation recognise that the right to manifest religious beliefs, whether individually or communally, can be legitimately restricted when it interferes with the rights and freedoms of others. Essentially, this is interpreted as being justified only when 'prescribed by law', proportionate and 'necessary to protect public safety, order, health, or morals or the fundamental rights and freedoms of others'.[44] However, there is considerable jurisdictional inconsistency as to the circumstances justifying imposing such restrictions on religious freedom.

The right to publicly worship or celebrate religious belief attracts the highest degree of legal protection when this is undertaken collectively by adherents in furtherance of an important aspect of their religion. Similarly, the attendant right to erect churches and other places for collective worship and to build facilities for the outworkings of religious belief such as seminaries, cloistered religious premises, community centres, etc. will normally be assured of State protection. The standards set by the ICCPR find general acceptance, and communal religious practices are unlikely to attract State intervention unless they present a clear threat to democratic society.[45]

Most often it is when the manifestation of religion or belief by way of 'worship, observance, practice and teaching'[46] is undertaken publicly by an individual that the State may be prompted to impose restrictions. Difficulties may then arise due to the individual misconstruing the manifestation as religious when in fact it is merely idiosyncratic. For example, a person may hold Christian beliefs but their decision to wear a purity ring would not be construed as a necessary manifestation of that belief.[47] The problem here is that, given the judicial weighting now placed upon the subjective interpretation of religious belief, it is difficult to draw a line between conduct (short of breaching law or public policy) that the adherent believes to be both appropriate and a duty (as opposed to a discretionary obligation) and that which is open to an objective challenge as unreasonable. On the other hand, by placing themselves in a position where they could reasonably anticipate that their religious beliefs would be compromised, an individual may have negated any

---

[44] As stated in the ICCPR, Article 18(3).

[45] See, for example, *Reynolds* v. *United States* (1879) 98 US 145, at p.167; 25 Law Ed 244.

[46] As stated in the ICCPR, Article 18(1).

[47] See *Playfoot (a minor), R (on the application of)* v. *Millais School* [2007] EWHC 1698 Admin.

494   A CONFLICT OF LAWS

justification for subsequent conduct undertaken to manifest those beliefs.[48]

Discrimination and the religious exemption

Of all aspects of the law relating to the freedom of religion, none is so well established nor so frequently and clearly stated in national and international legislation as the prohibition against religious discrimination.

Discrimination

With its holocaust resonances, religious discrimination is an invidious and universally recognised taboo. It also continues to be worryingly prevalent.

Traditionally, the significance of religion would seem to be culturally embedded, accompanied by a sense that some importance should be attached to religious difference. In the developed common law countries presently being considered, religion itself has largely lost its former power to label and alienate persons and divide communities in mutual enmity: although, as always, it is newcomers who tend to attract discrimination and there is good reason to believe that it is the minority religions and the newly emerging faith or belief groups that are now particularly vulnerable.[49] Its latent destructiveness tends to emerge tangentially as when, for example, a person brings a symbol of their private religious belief – of their not belonging to the prevailing culture – into a public place.

The case law indicates that religious discrimination conforms to much the same pattern in the jurisdictions studied and the related prohibitive provisions – whether in international conventions and protocols or in national constitutions, human rights statutes or equality legislation – are also similar in their listings of settings and practices which may provide 'occasions' for such discrimination. Notably different, however, is the judicial experience in the United States where religious discrimination is treated not only as a matter of private civil law, but also very much as public law and as often giving rise to constitutional issues.

---

[48] See *McClintock* v. *Department of Constitutional Affairs* [2008] IRLR 29 and *McFarlane* v. *Relate Avon Ltd.* [2010] EWCA Civ B1 (29 April 2010).

[49] See, further, Ridge, 'Religious Charitable Status and Public Benefit in Australia'.

The exemptions

The traditionally privileged position of religion in society has been respected, throughout the common law jurisdictions studied, by exemption clauses built into human rights legislation that allow religious persons and/or organisations to be excused from requirements that are binding on all others.[50] Typically, they are excused from liability for conduct which would otherwise be discriminatory whether occurring in the workplace, when providing goods, facilities and services, when exercising public functions, in the disposal and management of premises or in education. Religious belief provides, for example, a free pass exempting religious organisations from many equality provisions, including employment laws, thereby enabling the selection of clergy for its churches or of staff for its public benefit facilities such as hospitals and schools on the basis of religious affiliation, gender and sexual orientation. Although staff selection criteria for employment in a facility such as a faith-based school could more reasonably include a criterion of belonging to that faith for the post of teacher (a 'bona fide occupational requirement' in Canada) than for a janitor, it is hard to be sure where along the spectrum of school education posts that line is to be drawn and what allowances can reasonably be made for conditional beliefs (e.g. the pro-choice Christian teacher).

There is, of course, a secularist argument that there can be little justification in exempting those of religious belief from the penalties associated with discriminatory behaviour – thereby benefitting those ostensibly more morally cognisant than others – while the resulting tax burden for that privilege is met by those others. The point of domestic civil rights legislation is surely to draw a line underneath what is acceptable conduct in a civil society; those of religious belief might be expected to be more respectful and supportive of that legislative purpose than other sections of society.

The underlying issue is perhaps around whether religious entities – persons, organisations or churches – should be required to choose between

---

[50] There is a view that 'exemption clauses' in human rights legislation is a misguided use of language. Fr Brian Lucas makes the case that:

> There are two competing values and the law must accommodate them. One is not an exemption from the other. To pretend that it is, is to give priority to one world view (usually a secular one) over the other (usually the religious).   (Personal communication, 12 September 2013)

an entitlement to charitable status (with tax privileges) or an entitlement to discriminate on the basis of their beliefs. As Morris comments:

> It could be argued that public benefit cannot be achieved through discrimination. Conferral of charitable status should bring with it the responsibility to ensure observance of equal opportunities for beneficiaries, volunteers and trustees, the denial of which is contrary to the public benefit principle.[51]

Therefore, the choice to discriminate should entail foregoing charitable status and the accompanying tax privileges. After all, human rights legislation ensures that all religious entities are entitled to fully manifest their beliefs (subject to the rights of others), so there is no threat to religion or to those of religious belief. Why, then, should religious entities be singled out for indemnity against what would otherwise be discrimination and be subsidised by taxpayers to do so? If the clash between canon law and human rights law must result in the non-compliance of religious entities there is an argument for at least making such non-compliance less profitable.

Some current and significant jurisdictional differences

While all the jurisdictions studied had developed quite pluralist societies in recent years, not all had adjusted their primary sources of law accordingly. Consequently, in some there is now a significant disconnect between modern equality legislation (which all have in place) and their overarching constitutional provisions and arrangements which pre-date pluralism and reflect the concerns of a more homogenous and distinctly Christian society.

Freedom of religion and the Church–State relationship

The paradox of England being the first of the jurisdictions presently considered to impose a flat rate public benefit test upon all charitable purposes, including religions/faiths/beliefs and related organisations, while also being the only one to retain an 'Established' Church, is striking. In a human rights context it simply isn't credible for the State in such circumstances to maintain that all religions etc. are being treated equally: the binary authority and weighting of the Church–State relationship

---

[51] See D. Morris, 'Charities and the Modern Equality Framework: Heading for a Collision?' (2012) 65 *Current Legal Problems* 295, at p.300.

clearly confers greater advantages upon the Church of England, its adherents and its public benefit facilities, relative to all others. At the other extreme, the vigour with which the courts in the United States police any possible infringement of the Free Exercise Clause in the First Amendment, cultivating a succession of rules to assist in that task, is also striking. In the United States such is the intensity of the focus on ensuring that 'the wall' separating Church and State remains intact that comparatively little case law (at least not at US Supreme Court level) is generated by religious discrimination disputes. Ireland lies some way between England and the United States in its balancing of Church–State relationships: on the one hand, its Constitution is weighted in favour of Christianity, preferencing the position of the Catholic Church; but on the other it certainly does not have an established religion and it does tend to look to the US Free Exercise Clause on the few occasions it has had to interpret the Free Practice Clause in Article 44.2.1 of the Irish Constitution.[52] New Zealand is currently closer to Ireland than to either England or the United States on such matters, but this may change following the results of the current constitution reform inquiry. In neither of the federated jurisdictions of Canada and Australia is there the same constitutional and therefore judicial concern for policing the Church–State relationship as in the United States; although, that said, the Supreme Court of Canada has adjudicated a number of important cases concerning the freedom of religion.[53]

Traditional institutional religions and the subjective interpretation of religious belief

In those jurisdictions where the traditional Christian religions have long maintained an institutional presence, there are correspondingly fewer opportunities for the subjective interpretation of beliefs and for their idiosyncratic public manifestation. This is most evident in England and Ireland, where the vast majority of religious adherents subscribe to a set of beliefs – embedded in the Scriptures and canon law, filtered through the ministry of the clergy and celebrated in collective worship – that have remained recognisably the same for centuries. In the United States and

---

[52] The Irish Constitution states that 'the free practice and profession of religion . . . subject to public order and morality' is 'guaranteed to every citizen'.

[53] See, for example: *R.* v. *Big M Drug Mart Ltd.* [1985] 1 SCR 295; *Fletcher* v. *A.G. Alta.* [1969] 66 WWR 513; *Adler* v. *Ontario* [1996] SCR 609; and *Heintz* v. *Christian Horizons Horizons*, 2008 HRTO 22; 2010 ONSC 2105 (Div. Ct).

to a lesser extent in Canada, this is not so much the case, and for constitutional and demographic reasons there have been opportunities for the courts to explore the boundaries of religious freedom and its public manifestations as subjectively understood. So far, New Zealand and Australia would seem to be comparatively conservative in their approach to these matters.

As the ECtHR and the courts more generally protect the rights of individuals to find and publicly or privately manifest their own interpretation of 'religion' or 'belief', subject to the rights of others, it is clear that all the common law jurisdictions currently being considered will encounter much the same type of legal issue. The range of those with religious or other forms of belief is set to multiply, the traditional Christian religions will have to endure repeated schisms, the essentially monolithic religion of Islam (mainly Sunni and Shia) will continue to expand, while the secularists grow in number and in assertiveness. The tensions between these groups will be a challenge for civil society everywhere.

The contemporary agenda of 'moral imperatives' and the conflict of laws

For all the jurisdictions studied, the initial common law definition of 'religion' was Christian and therefore exclusively monotheistic, rooted firmly in canon law and the Scriptures, and accompanied by prescribed forms and places of worship. Over the subsequent centuries, this shared Christian context nurtured not only an evolving charity law, and the particular interpretation given to the advancement of religion, but it also generated a shared sense of civic morality that informed the cultural development of those jurisdictions.

The synthesis of canon law-inspired Christianity and related civic morality was always particularly evident in family law. The observation of Finlay LC in *Bowman* v. *Secular Society Ltd.*,[54] when reflecting on previous centuries of case law, applied throughout what was then the British Empire:

> It has been repeatedly laid down by the Courts that Christianity is part of the law of the land, and it is the fact that our civil polity is to a large extent based upon the Christian religion. This is notably so with regard to the law of marriage and the law affecting the family.[55]

---

[54] *Bowman* v. *Secular Society Ltd.* [1917] AC 406 (HL). Also see *R* v. *Dibdin* [1910] P 57, CA.

[55] Ibid., citing: *Briggs* v. *Hartley* (1850) 19 LJ (Ch.) 416; *Cowan* v. *Milbourn* (1867) LR 2 Ex. 230; *De Costa* v. *De Paz* (1754) 2 Swanst, 487; and *In re Bedford Charity* (1819) 2 Swanst 470, 527.

He was quite clear that up until then the courts would have considered themselves bound by Christian principles (understood in terms of canon law as referenced to the Scriptures) when called upon to interpret 'religion'.[56] The jurisdiction-specific chapters in this book clearly demonstrate that such principles were applied with equal vigour in those countries.

By the closing decades of the twentieth century, however, families and communities had become more diffuse, science had pushed back the boundaries of the unknown, societies were stretched to accommodate new cultural groups and secularism was growing in strength. The hitherto joint stand of Church and State on moral matters, particularly those affecting the family, began to unravel – a trend accelerated by developments in human rights law and the accompanying equalities legislation, leading to an emphasis on the fundamental rights of the individual as opposed to the prescribed duties of the collectively religious. Most recently, charity law reform has introduced changes to the definition of 'religion', its 'advancement' and (in some jurisdictions) its relationship to public benefit. These changes have had the net effect of aligning the charity law and human rights approaches to religion while distancing both from canon law. The lack of synch between these areas of law is now such as to be benchmarked by a growing number of polarising social issues which have acquired the status of 'moral imperatives'.

'Moral imperatives'

This term, meaning the necessity to 'do the right thing', most probably has its origins in Kant's 'categorical imperative',[57] but may also owe something to Sartre's later theorising on existentialism,[58] and can be traced back to the concern of Socrates and Plato that we should act virtuously for the sake of others. In contemporary Western culture it has come to be associated with those socially divisive, morally driven issues,

---

[56] A long catalogue of cases beginning with *De Costa* v. *De Paz* (1754) 2 Swanst 487, Chancery, including *Lawrence* v. *Smith, Murray* v. *Benbow* (1822) *The Times* 2 February 1822, *Briggs* v. *Hartley* (1850) 19 LJ (Ch.) 416, and ending with *Pare* v. *Clegg* (1861) 29 Beav. 589, 54 ER 756, established that 'the Courts will not help in the promotion of objects contrary to the Christian religion'.

[57] See Kant, *Groundwork for the Metaphysics of Morals*, 1785 (republished by Hackett, 3rd edn, 1993).

[58] See J. P. Sartre, *Existentialism and Human Emotions*, Carol Publishing Group, Secaucus, NJ, 1995.

in regard to which each set of protagonists feels equally strongly that they are right and wholly justified in their actions, that 'God is on their side' and their opponents are wholly wrong and must be seen to be publicly defeated. The term identifies issues which touch upon matters of public rather than private morality; they crystallise a moral dilemma considered to have profound implications for the wellbeing of society. In practice there is no reason why they should be seen as limited to Christian matters, nor is there any suggestion that the issues generating most heat are also necessarily more 'moral' or 'imperative' than others. For present purposes, however, and given the decidedly Christian cultural heritage shared by the jurisdictions being considered, the relevant moral imperatives can be viewed in that context and – it is argued throughout this book – can be seen as representing principles drawn from canon law that are now in conflict with those of charity law and/or human rights.

Culturally determined

Within the Christian nations, practices that may be acceptable for one generation can be rejected by those that follow: over a period of centuries there was nothing incompatible with Christianity and, for example, slavery, colonialism, restricted suffrage, patriarchy, the criminal responsibility of children, the absence of 'civil rights' and the death penalty; all were Scriptually compliant, if not mandated, activities. In due course, each in turn became the moral imperative of its generation. The religious/cultural practices of one social group can also become the moral imperative of another: so female genital mutilation, a traditional African practice (in countries such as Ethiopia, Sudan and Mali) is now not unknown in the developed West where, in many of those host countries, it has attained moral imperative status. Curiously, the AIDS crisis in America in the latter half of the 1980s was first viewed by many as a moral imperative, in a way that its current manifestation in Africa is not. So, also, the Arab Spring phenomenon was seen in that light, as was the related Western intervention (as also in Kosovo); which was viewed as morally justified by one culture in order to bring the benefits of democracy to another. Wars in general are usually justified on the same basis.

In broad terms a more modern agenda of such imperatives includes matters that transcend national and cultural boundaries and do not necessarily have a religious dimension. Some, such as combating poverty, preventing disease and increasing literacy, are the unfinished business of previous generations and are largely focused on certain cultures in the

'MORAL IMPERATIVES' AND THE CONFLICT OF LAWS   501

southern hemisphere. Others, such as managing climate change, are more global and therefore political in nature; though probably driven by Western culture.

Family oriented

For Christianity, the more immediate moral imperatives tend to be associated with the family, particularly with matters relating to sexuality (see, further, Chapter 1).

In that context, the ideal family unit has been one that conformed to the 'Nazarene' model, consisting, like the original family of Christ in Nazareth, of married parents and the children of their marriage. Drawing from that model, the Christian principles governing marriage, as alluded to in *Bowman* above, traditionally included: monogamous, heterosexual marriage for life; the sanctity of marriage to the exclusion of non-marital sex, any children thereof and unmarried partnerships; the criminalisation of homosexuality; and the repudiation of all other forms of non-marital sex. This was in keeping with many centuries of Christian religious doctrine, underpinned by statute and common law, which prohibited any infringement of Christian approved marital family relationships (e.g. bigamy, incest, abortion, sodomy, etc.). The marital family unit provided the only Scripturally permissible context for sexual activity. Anything else offended both Church and State and was treated, respectively, as a sin and a crime. In particular, both viewed homosexuality as a deviant form of sexual activity, not only sinful and illegal, but singled out for particular opprobrium which continued long after its decriminalisation (in England in 1967). It is condemned in the Scriptures as sinful regardless of the context and there are several references in both the Old and the New Testaments to a homosexual lifestyle being expressly forbidden.[59] As an ancillary point, it was also traditionally rejected by Christianity on the grounds that it defines sexuality in purely hedonistic terms as it cannot fulfil the procreative purpose assigned to sexuality within a marital relationship.

---

[59] See, for example, Leviticus (18:22 and 20:13), Romans (1:26–32) and in 1 Corinthians 6:9–10 it is declared: 'Do you not know that the wicked will not inherit the kingdom of God? Do not be deceived:

> Neither the sexually immoral nor idolaters nor adulterers not male prostitutes nor homosexual offenders nor thieves nor the greedy nor drunkards nor slanderers nor swindlers will inherit the kingdom of God.'

502 A CONFLICT OF LAWS

By the mid twentieth century, however, Church and State in the still largely Christian common law nations had begun to disentangle their hitherto joint stand on such family matters as 'illegitimacy', the indissolubility of marriage and birth control. These and associated criminal offences, such as 'unlawful carnal knowledge', including homosexuality, became the moral imperatives for Christians until each in turn was legislatively resolved – though retaining their aura of venality.

The contemporary agenda of 'moral imperatives'

The irreconcilability of some traditional religious beliefs with the values and lifestyle choices of modern civil society would seem to be driving a wave of didactic moralism,[60] polarising views and politicising the role of religion within the developed common law nations presently being considered. Beginning, possibly, with the 'pro-life' campaigns against abortion, a number of such issues are now hotly contested by those with and by those without religious belief as secularists contest the moral ground previously held by the Church. Of these, gay marriage is currently the most socially divisive issue, or at least it is the one currently commanding most media interest, but in the long run is unlikely to prove the most important.

Family-oriented moral imperatives

The agenda of such imperatives currently includes: the use of contraception, artificial insemination and abortion; same-sex marriage, adoption and access to services; genetic screening, programming, cloning and modification; the use of human tissue, DNA patenting, research involving human embryos and stem cells; the general use of medical intervention to aid human reproduction and death; and the rejection of a Darwinian approach to the meaning of 'life'. In that context, the recent US Supreme Court ruling that, in the words of Clarence Thomas J, 'a

---

[60] See J. Grote, *A Treatise on the Moral Ideals*, 1876 (republished by Kessinger Publishing, 2004), at p.476, who explains:

> Didactic moralism proceeds always more or less on something of a previously formed ideal of what a man ought to be, and might be, and refers the particular actions to this rather than dissects them by themselves. This is an approach that has fuelled a degree of moral judgmentalism among some religious groups, certainly in America and to a lesser extent in England, in recent decades.

naturally occurring DNA segment is a product of nature and not patent eligible merely because it has been isolated',[61] is an interesting example of the current deeply divisive social debates on morally driven issues centring on the parameters of the medical right to intervene (allied to commercial opportunism in this case) in matters fundamental to 'life'. These and many other such matters are associated with the morality that flowed from canon law and 'natural law' to set the social norms in the jurisdictions studied. They comprise an agenda that promises to be further extended in keeping with the ebb and flow of advances in science, the collapse of confidence in social institutions and retreat into conservative if not fundamentalist values (see, further, Chapter 3).

Although, by the latter half of the twentieth century, Christianity had given ground or compromised on many matters traditionally regarded as imperatives (e.g. abortion and contraception), certain core issues were seemingly securely ring-fenced by the Scriptures. Of these, the nature of marriage was a red-line issue. The traditional characteristics of marriage, as outlined in the Scriptures and adhered to by Church and State (at least until the introduction of divorce), have always been understood to be monogamy, heterosexuality and lifelong duration.[62] That it could be redefined to accommodate same-sex couples was theologically inconceivable. The challenge of gay marriage for canon law-based Christianity is certainly significant: it negates the 'Nazarene' family model; reverses centuries of canonical rejection of relationships seen as virtually heretical; impairs the social contract between family and State; and threatens to rupture Christian solidarity, ending the years of incremental progress towards a rapprochement between its different denominations. Indeed, Pope John Paul II denounced it as 'a serious threat to the future of the family and society'.[63] Whether the worst fears, of it eventually causing

---

[61] See *Association for Molecular Pathology* v. *Myriad Genetics*, 569 US Supreme Court, No. 12-398 (2013); but, note an earlier decision to the opposite effect in *Cancer Voices Australia* v. *Myriad Genetics Inc* [2013] FCA 65, when the Federal Court in Australia ruled in favour of Myriad Genetics, enabling them to continue to hold the patent in respect of the gene BRCA1. It should be noted that the US ruling leaves open the possibility that synthetic molecules known as complementary DNA can be patented 'because it is not naturally occurring'. Given the genetic engineering expertise now available, the artificial replication of patentable DNA material can be anticipated.

[62] Jesus is held to have taught that marriage is for life. See, for example: Mk 10:9; Jn 8:11; Mt 5:28; and Mk 7:21–23.

[63] On 22 February 1994, Pope John Paul II in his weekly address on St. Peter's Square denounced an earlier resolution by the European Parliament, calling on Member States to end discriminatory practices against their lesbian and gay citizens as 'inappropriately

schisms in Protestantism and fundamental rifts in Christianity, will be realised remains to be seen.

For the immediate future, gay marriage remains a high-profile moral imperative. It joins the list of other contemporary contentious moral issues – on abortion, between pro-choice and pro-life groups; and on traditional family units, between LGBT libertarians and Christian conservatives – that are derived from the core moral values instilled by Christianity and headlined in the Scriptures.

Religious pluralism

Emerging from the United States in the latter decades of the twentieth century, and now making inroads in the United Kingdom, an explosion of some innovative and many derivative religious groupings has cumulatively broadened the spectrum of what could be construed as a 'religious belief' well beyond the imaginings of early traditionalists. It's not just the profusion of revisionist versions of Christianity (e.g. Progressive Christians and Pentecostal Christians), although evangelicalism in its many forms is itself a phenomenon, but Christian-related entities such as Christian Science and wholly original ones such as Scientology are also very evident. There are also a host of African/ American churches and a stream of 'New Age' religions and semi-philosophical or mystical belief systems, some touching upon Gaia or other 'mother earth' ideologies and most concerned with relating to immediate environmental and lifestyle issues. This is accompanied by the steady growth of Islam. While other traditional non-Christian religions are also becoming more conspicuous in the common law jurisdictions – Sikhs and Hindus, for example – none are expanding so rapidly or registering such a strong presence as Muslims, with their very coherent culture that includes some family values at variance with those of Christianity. The challenge that these multiple variants of belief systems present for traditional, orthodox and institutional Christian religions such as Catholicism and Protestantism is very real.

In particular it is hard to see how canon law, as traditionally interpreted, can wholly retain its authority when so many evangelical

---

conferring an institutional value on deviant behavior'. He called on European countries to ignore the resolution. That same day, the Pope also issued a letter denouncing same-sex unions as 'a serious threat to the future of the family and society', adding that only 'heterosexual unions can be recognized as a marriage in society'.

Christian churches – together with other religions, new belief systems, etc. – now welcome those of LGBT orientation as both adherents and clergy. As the proportion of human rights-compliant religious entities increases, the moral imperative resting on the remainder to make the adjustments necessary to achieve a greater degree of compliance, or at least forfeit a continuing entitlement to charitable status, will surely similarly increase.

Social inclusion and diversity

Leaving aside the specific challenges of religious pluralism, a looming imperative for Christianity in the jurisdictions studied is to demonstrate its relevance to the new patterns of social need that are forming as a consequence of prolonged economic recession, the cumulative effects of immigration that have brought in so many disparate and displaced ethnic groups and the failure of multiculturalist policies to secure their integration. The institutional infrastructure of the traditional religions, together with their accumulated cultural baggage, must be perceived as intimidating by those who need assistance and assurance of their social worth. Their sense of marginalisation is likely to be exacerbated by government-funded faith-based service provision, especially in relation to schools, and by the widespread practice of fee-based access to religious facilities.

Being more accessible to the needs of the disadvantaged will also require religious entities to review their present stance in relation to statutory exemption privileges – indeed, there is considerable irony in specifically allowing religious organisations to practice religious and other forms of discrimination. Why exactly is it that human rights are trumped only by religious beliefs? Arguably, there is a moral imperative resting on religious entities, particularly on those belonging to the more traditional religions, to move away from their institutionalised ways of relating to the community, rise above the accumulating child abuse stigma and find new ways of reaching out to the socially marginalised. It is not possible to both demonstrate moral leadership and simultaneously claim exemption from discriminatory practices that are statutorily declared immoral. Whether or not evidence of actual public benefit is to be required, evidence of non-dependency upon State protectionist policies, to avoid liability for practices prohibited to all other citizens, may well be perceived as reassuring by those citizens.

Equality

The challenge presented by the equality principle is the broader and more fundamental moral imperative for religion. In the current context this has a particular relevance for Christianity which underpins the culture of the jurisdictions presently being considered (needless to say, it has implications for other religions such as Islam). It is a challenge also for charity, both being inherently discriminatory. The fusion of religion and charity in the charitable purpose 'advancement of religion', as pursued throughout the common law jurisdictions, provides a sharp focus for the imperative and one which may have been eased in the UK jurisdictions by being made statutorily subject to the public benefit principle.

Equality of access to marriage may be the most prominent and pressing area of incompatibility with canon law, but it is not the only one. Other areas of difficulty arise in relation to discriminatory policies regarding gender and sexuality as preconditions for clergy appointments. The former is clearly demonstrated in the prohibition against female ordination in the Catholic Church,[64] and the equivocation within Protestantism regarding the appointment of female bishops. This refusal to extend to women the same opportunities afforded to men is indefensible, contrary to convention principles and is particularly contrary to the Convention on the Elimination of all Forms of Discrimination Against Women (CEDAW), in which discrimination is defined as:

> any distinction, exclusion or restriction made on the basis of sex which has the effect or purpose of impairing or nullifying the recognition, enjoyment or exercise by women, irrespective of their marital status, on a basis of equality of men and women, of human rights and fundamental freedoms in the political, economic, social, cultural, civil or any other field.[65]

The latter is linked to the canon law renunciation of non-marital sexuality, and is evident in the current Church of England policy of not appointing actively homosexual clergy. Both may be viewed as morally untenable and legally inequitable. Also associated with canon law is the

---

[64] Usually justified by reference to 1 Tim. 2:11–14, 1 Cor. 11:3, 1 Cor. 14:34–38 and Gen. 3:16.

[65] Adopted in 1979 by the UN General Assembly, it is often described as an international bill of rights for women.

'MORAL IMPERATIVES' AND THE CONFLICT OF LAWS 507

policy of some Christian charitable organisations refusing to provide, or continue to provide or work with, legally mandated services such as adoption and youth or community forms of provision that have an LGBT orientation.

Equality and 'islands of exclusivity'

Rivers, in his masterly *The Law of Organised Religions*, has championed the Esau thesis of 'islands of exclusivity',[66] stating that:

> While the State may legitimately adopt a particular, more or less controversial, conception of equality, it should not impose such a conception uniformly on the whole of civil society. Protection from uniform State ideologies is one of the main points of collective religious liberty.[67]

There will be few who will disagree with their joint views about the dangers of giving permission for the State to impose an ideology – any ideology. However, it must be open to question whether pursuing a social policy of equality really amounts to any such thing. The problem with this approach – requiring a policy of equality to be subject to privileged exemptions – is much the same as the problem with 'multiculturalism': the more reinforcement is given to separate identities, and the more communal civic space is fragmented to accommodate expressions of difference, the less integrated and coherent is society as a whole. Balance is everything and if there is to be a veto, by religious entities on matters of equality that are binding on the rest of society, its exercise must somehow be conditional upon this being demonstrably compliant with the best interests of that society; particularly if tax exemption and/ or government funding is involved.

The prolonged intensity of the multicultural impact upon the jurisdictions considered has resulted in societies that, over a relatively short period, have developed an unforeseen complexity. They are now layered with a mix of overlapping cultures – the many ethnic identities imported intact from their countries of origin, together with minority group identities acquired as a consequence of welfare rights labelling (as disabled,

---

[66] A. J. Esau, 'Islands of Exclusivity: Religious Organisations and Employment Discrimination' (2000) 33 *UBC Law Review* 719. Also see A. J. Esau,'Islands of Exclusivity Revisited: Religious Organizations, Employment Discrimination and *Heintz* v. *Christian Horizons*' (2009–2010) 15 *Canadian Labour & Employment Law Journal* 389.

[67] See J. Rivers, *The Law of Organised Religions*, Oxford University Press, Oxford, 2010, at p.136.

elderly, youths, etc.) – their differences and separateness reinforced by government funding policies. The hierarchically structured Christian religions, emulating their host societies (note, for example, the 26 Anglican bishops in the House of Lords), currently seem more inclined to add to the social fragmentation through schisms than to model equality in their organisations or practice it in relation to those who do not share their beliefs. All this, together with the proliferation of new religions, faiths and forms of belief – they and their adherents all being entitled to equality of treatment with the traditional religions – does need a nuanced rather than an ideological response from the State but, if the Northern Ireland experience is anything to go by, the 'islands of exclusivity' approach is unlikely to prove conducive to promoting a balanced and healthy society.

Conclusion

It was inevitable that the twenty-first century would see a clash between the Scripture-led canon law of Christianity and the equality-led provisions of the European Convention on Human Rights (or its national, constitutional or legislative equivalent). In some common law jurisdictions it has been further complicated by the introduction of new domestic legislation following processes of charity law and equality law reform. The importance of this conflict of laws would be difficult to overstate. How it is resolved will have consequences for social cohesion in the countries concerned (of which those presently studied are a small minority), for Christian theology and for any prospect of a continuing theological solidarity among the Christian common law nations.

~

Conclusion

This book started with a question: what is it about the same agenda of 'moral imperatives' that is causing much the same difficulties for law and social policy at much the same time in a number of leading common law jurisdictions?

The answer would seem to lie in the shared background of those jurisdictions: specifically in the developmental history of the religion–charity–law relationship. The agenda – relating to matters concerning 'life', 'family' and 'marriage' – reflects a cultural background which owes a great deal to norms of civic morality as originally instilled by canon law precepts. On one level these agenda issues – of which abortion was perhaps the earliest and gay marriage the latest – simply indicate a conflict of values. On another they may be seen as the product of what has grown to become a classic conflict of laws: representing an asymmetry of principles; Christian (derived from the Scriptures) and human rights (derived from the European Convention or national, constitution and legislative equivalents). Thus far no single issue has proven to be of great magnitude in itself, in terms of significance to either society or jurisprudence, but when charity law statutorily encoded a reframed legal definition of 'religion' and 'religious belief', the stage was then reset for the conflict to become more broadly confrontational. For those intent on consolidating civil society in the common law jurisdictions, the ongoing friction – triggered by the ever-expanding and levelling effects of a human rights and equality paradigm as it runs up against traditional religious beliefs – is creating a series of sizeable bumps along that road.

There is no doubting the polarising effect of these social issues with a religious resonance: not only for those of religious belief; and between them and those of no belief; but the latter are often also divided. The difficulty in finding common ground on which opposing sets of irreconcilably entrenched advocates can begin to negotiate a way forward has been only too apparent in relation to abortion and gay marriage. Sadly, arguments based on Scripture or religious principles often find no

510   CONCLUSION

credence with those who take an ideological stand on equality as an overriding norm or with secularists who insist on translating a religious premise into its measurable social effects. There would seem to be little traction and limited scope for negotiation between those divided on the basis of 'belief'. For the traditional or 'organised religions' and their adherents the challenges are particularly acute.

Given the impasse and the importance of finding a way forward, this would seem an appropriate time to pause and reflect – to take stock of the positive gains that have brought us to this point and strive for a sense of perspective – before taking any precipitous steps. The cautionary advice of Mendelsohn in *Waiting for the Barbarians*[1] seems apt. He suggests that Cavafy's poem of that title:[2]

> may well be a parable about artistic growth – the unexpectedly complex and even, potentially, fruitful interaction between old cultures and new, between (we might say) high and low; about the way that what's classic is always being refreshed by new energies that, at the time they make themselves felt, probably seems barbaric to some. ... As Cavafy knew well ... there rarely are any real 'barbarians'. What others might see as declines and falls look, when seen from the bird's-eye view vantage point of history, more like shifts, adaptations, reorganizations.[3]

The need to accommodate canon law doctrine within a modern human rights environment has now become one of the greatest challenges to face the traditional Christian religions. It will also be a serious stress test for modern pluralist societies. The potential for religion to trigger social disruption has been sufficiently well demonstrated over past millennia for the present difficulties to warrant close attention.

It would be overreaching the scope of this short legal study to venture into the realm of politics and social policy with suggestions as to how the above complex sets of relationships might be readjusted. Certainly there is no magic formula: any such strategic re-alignment could only be undertaken in relation to the particular unfolding cultural context of each jurisdiction. It might, however, be permissible to make some tentative observations.

First, it does seem to this observer that something like a deconstruction of 'religion' is occurring – at least in relation to Christianity – which

---

[1] See D. Mendelsohn, *Waiting for the Barbarians*, New York Review of Books, New York, 2012.

[2] See D. Mendelsohn (trans.), *Cavafy, C.P., Collected Poems*, Alfred A. Knopf, New York, 2009.

[3] Ibid., 'Foreword', at pp.x–xi.

CONCLUSION 511

raises a serious question as to what its future role in society might look like. If true, it's a development that may well present a challenge not just for those who remain devout adherents to the traditional religions, but also for everyone else. This is not just about the steady growth of a more confident secularism undermining the role of religion in the public arena and becoming louder in its insistence that the arena be neutralised. Nor is it about the unmistakeable drift towards fundamentalism for a small but sizeable proportion of adherents in all the traditional religions, which is very evident in relation to the 'moral imperatives'. Even the phenomenon of evangelism, the schisms within Christianity and the real prospect of deep divisions opening up within Protestantism are not in themselves a huge threat to the accustomed role of religion in the common law jurisdictions. It is more to do with the number, variety and the relatively insubstantial nature of the new religions, faiths and forms of belief that are constantly emerging[4] – seemingly to seize the zeitgeist and with an intent to address the secular as much as the sacred. The internet has, naturally, played a role in this as in all other forms of communication. The safe anonymity of social networking sites has permitted a transference from physical participation in public worship (with all the self-sustaining, mutual reinforcement and accountability that accompanies person-to-person and collective engagement in religious activity) to a virtual communing with religious and non-religious groups which can be transient and shallow. It is as though consumerism has finally reached the realm of the sacred and transcendental. The multiple variants of current belief systems would seem to fit into a social context of fluid marital and parenting arrangements where mobile nuclear family units are accustomed to needs-led, user-driven choices in which most attachments are negotiable. Religious affiliation is among the choices on offer to the discerning consumer: selection being determined on the basis of personal lifestyle, convenience, degree of user involvement, the perceived relevance of social and environmental issues addressed by religious leaders and by add-on loyalty benefits such as access to creche facilities, faith based schooling, networking opportunities, etc. It's not unusual for personal commitment, or 'brand loyalty', to now pass through a number of sequential or even coterminus phases

---

[4] See, for example, the Sunday Assembly which describes itself as 'a godless congregation that meets to hear great talks, sing songs and generally celebrate the wonder of life. It's a service for anyone who wants to live better, help often and wonder more.' See, further, at: http://sundayassembly.com (accessed 10 January 2014).

(perhaps beginning with adherence to a birth religion, then Zen Buddhism or other such meditative or philosophical discipline, then a form of evangelism, before returning to birth religion or concluding in atheism) and extend only as far as the next best offer: religion, faith and other forms of belief may now be selected, customised or traded-in to suit individual evolving lifestyles.[5] This makes it increasingly difficult to know what weighting to give to the next new association (or transient mutation) of believers, and how to gauge their theological and social significance, relative to that of the traditional religions. While the latter, having survived many challenges over the past millennia will surely endure, they may not do so in the same form. As attendance rates for public worship in the Catholic and Protestant churches of these jurisdictions continue to fall, questions arise as to whether this trend will result in orthodox Christianity becoming ever more a matter of private piety, just as Islam would seem to be resolutely heading in the opposite direction, while both continue to generate a fringe capacity for fundamentalism. Such trends may gradually push more serious questions regarding the politics of religion before government in the jurisdictions presently being considered.

Second, given that the doors to legal recognition of what might legally constitute a religion have been flung wide open, it seems only prudent to review the public role and social value of religious entities and to have clear basic ground rules for managing the State–Church relationship. The rights to freedom of religion and to form associations are unquestioned, but that does not preclude questioning such entities in relation to: their public benefit premium and consequent entitlement to privileges such as charitable status and tax exemption; their role in the provision of public goods such as education; and the propriety of their being recipients of government funding. It must require stringent policing of the circumstances whereby religious bodies acquire the responsibilities of a proxy government service provider and of the implied terms and conditions of that role (i.e. being wholly bound by statute laws and regulations without any exemption privileges). It also raises questions regarding their entitlement to statutory exemption from the rules and obligations of citizenship, such as: discrimination in the employment of staff; the pursuit of trading or other practices (e.g. in relation to animal slaughter) that are at variance with normal legal requirements. Any such revisionist approach will have implications for the charitable purpose of advancing religion. The number and variety of new

---

[5] See, for example, the findings reported in the Pew Forum on Religion & Public Life, *U.S. Religious Landscape Survey*, 2007 at: http://religions.pewforum.org.

CONCLUSION 513

'religious' entities (including many derived by schism from old religions) must call into question whether the benefit of the general public is really equally well served by each engaging in: competitive proselytism; sending missionaries abroad; building new places of worship, maintaining related fixtures and conducting ceremonies of worship (whether in public or private); and providing support services for clergy. There is no doubting the lawfulness of such activities, only whether there is sufficient non-member benefit for all new forms of religion and systems of belief to justify extending the taxpayer subsidy. It may be that the definition of 'religion' has become so broad and diluted as to question the continued justification of its advancement as a charitable purpose: if all are equally entitled to be so defined then perhaps none should be entitled to such a subsidy; and each should look to their adherents, to discretionary public donations or to commerce for financial subvention.

Thirdly, leaving aside the role of religion as an institution and the functioning of religious organisations, there is the question of accommodating private manifestations of religious belief in the public sphere. There are many ways in which this can become an issue, but perhaps the most common are: wearing religious clothing in public, which is particularly contentious when worn by persons in the course of their public-service role (e.g. as a teacher); the refusal of service on grounds of religious objection to a customer, again more contentious in a public-service context (e.g. registrar and same-sex married couples); and when employers refuse to make allowances for the religious observance requirements of staff (e.g. not working on days of particular religious significance). Given the long-standing traditional religious/cultural practices regarding crucifixes in class-rooms, prayers at the opening of meetings in public institutions, etc., it might be appropriate to err on the side of inclusiveness and presume such personal displays of religious affiliation are socially acceptable, unless there is a weight of evidence to the contrary.

Finally, if something like the deconstruction of religion as it has been traditionally known in the common law jurisdictions is underway, then it may be best to accept this and allow the process the space to play out as visibly and transparently as public order permits. Pluralism – religious and cultural – are perhaps only aspects of a more basic reworking of social identities – the culture wars – that indicate a profound 'work in progress' in these jurisdictions. As globalisation further erodes national identities, the long-term effects on citizenship currently remain a matter of conjecture – but some key reference points that guided previous generations now seem prone to slippage. Of these, the sense of belonging – of attachment and loyalty to family, community and nation, to culture and religion – and of trust in institutions and authority are not the norms they once were. Arguably, this is reflected in the current relationship between religion, charity and the law – and will determine how that relationship is rebalanced in the future.

INDEX

abortion, 2, 5, 38–40, 75–77, 235–236, 339–340, 367, 501–504, 509
  clinics, 36, 339–340, 351
  services, 351, 372
abuse of charitable status, 145, 240, 341
acceptance, 11, 31–32, 37, 87, 94–96, 128, 442, 477, 479
accountability, 19, 28, 56, 65, 91, 101, 240, 292, 295
ACEs, *see* Autonomous Crown Entities
ACNC, *see* Australian Charities and Not-for-profits Commission
ACoC (Anglican Church of Canada), 361
activities test, 64, 418, 480
ad pias causas, 44–45
adoption, 106, 220–221, 317, 322–323, 459–460, 462, 490, 502, 507
  services, 219–220, 462, 464
adoptive parents, 220–221
advancement
  contemporary types of, 68–69
  definition, 64
  traditional types of, 65–68
advancement of education, 52, 68, 211, 239, 242, 338, 389, 392, 394
advancement of human rights, 150, 199, 255
advancement of religion, 50–54, 64–69, 103–106, 192–193, 241–243, 346–347, 371–374, 405–408, 440–442, 444–449
  Australia, 405–406
  Canada, 346
  England and Wales, 192–193
  Ireland, 247–249
  New Zealand, 445

and public benefit test, 482
  United States, 300
advocacy, 21, 88, 104–106, 122, 137, 254, 412
  in the advancement of religion, 106
  Australia, 412
  Canada, 351
  England and Wales, 198
  Ireland, 254
  New Zealand, 450
  United States, 305
affiliation, religious, 157, 163, 218, 265, 329, 330, 378, 413, 512–513
affirmative action, 135, 456
Africa, 40, 116, 167, 500
agnostics, 29, 119, 182, 190, 231–233, 384, 491
  and atheism, 29–30
aid, 50, 103, 116, 284, 286, 291, 384, 387, 392
aims, legitimate, 126, 134, 141, 202–207, 210, 220–221
altruism, 9, 16–17, 50, 97, 293, 440, 479
  definition, 16
Anglican Church, 13, 220, 377, 461
Anglican Church of Canada (ACoC), 361
Anglicanism, 158, 161–163, 223, 378
anti-discrimination standards, 455–457
anti-semitism, 41
anti-terrorism measures, 98, 110, 116–117
appreciation, margin of, 119, 131–134, 141, 200, 201, 256
armed forces, 31, 34, 167, 375–376, 384
association, freedom of, 81, 86, 118, 320

515

associations, 79, 84–86, 127, 182, 185, 202–204, 274, 277, 308–309
atheism, 23, 28–29, 119, 161, 190, 231–233, 384–385, 491, 512
  and agnostics, 29–30
ATO, *see* Australian Taxation Office
Australia, 3, 6, 58, 62, 113, 115, 142, 143, 148, 149, 150, 374–426, 476, 477
  advancement of religion, 405–406
  advocacy, 412
  belief in Supreme Being, 397
  bequests subject to a religious condition, 409
  charity law, 387
    reform, 390
    and regulatory framework, 385–396
  charity regulator, 386–387
  Church
    State and religious charities, 375–385
  colonialism and religion, 375–376
  common law, 389
  Constitution, 415
  courts, 395–398, 401, 404–406, 415, 447
  discrimination, 421
    and same-sex marriage, 421
  equality and diversity legislation, 415
  equality legislation and exemption for charities, 416
  equality of religions, 380–381
  established religion, 379
  failure of testamentary dispositions due to breach of common law rules, 408–409
  freedom of religion, 419
  government funding, 383–385
  historical background, 375
  human rights
    discrimination and religious charities, 413–426
  interference with the manifestation of religious belief, 420
  legislation, 385
  manifestation of beliefs, 404–405
  means for advancing religion, 406–408

modern Church–State relationship, 376–377
philosophy and other value systems, 398
positive action, 425
proselytism, 412
public benefit test
  and 'closed' religious orders, 394–396
  and religious organisations, 392–394
public policy
  charity and common law constraints, 408–413
  constraints, 410–412
reform
  charitable purposes, 392
  outcomes, 391
  process, 390
religion
  religious beliefs and advancement of religion, 396–408
religion(s), 378
religious beliefs, 402–403
  and Indigenous people, 403–404
religious charities, 381–382
  discrimination and exemptions, 417
  as public bodies, 417–419
religious discrimination in practice, 422
religious institution test, 388
religious organisations and nonprofit sector, 381
religious preferences and public policy, 410
religious umbrella bodies, 382
secularisation, 378
testamentary conditions and common law, 408
unequal and discriminatory treatment
  restriction of access to services, 424–425
  restriction of employment opportunities, 423
unequal but not discriminatory treatment, 422
  contractual obligations, 423

INDEX

worship
  religious tenets
    doctrines, etc., 398–401
Australian Charities and
        Not-for-profits Commission
        (ACNC), 374, 386, 391–392
Australian Taxation Office (ATO), 374,
        385, 393, 405, 412, 419
Austria, 126–128, 140–141, 149
authenticity, 4, 180–183, 232, 471–473
Autonomous Crown Entities
        (ACEs), 436

belief in Supreme Being, 57
  Australia, 397
  Canada, 342
  England and Wales, 181–182
  Ireland, 246
  New Zealand, 443–444
  United States, 298
belief systems, 77, 80, 180, 203, 468,
        471, 475–477, 480–481, 483
beliefs, 10–14, 119–126, 183–188,
        189–191, 297–300, 399–405,
        442–444, 452–460, 468–472
  Christian, 44, 129, 214, 257, 460, 493
  ethical, 317, 453–456, 459–460
  non-religious, 189, 205
  non-theistic, 183, 476
  philosophical, 120, 123–125,
        130–132, 180, 183–185,
        189–190, 192, 245–247, 402
  Scientology, 398, 402
  spectrum of, 469, 490
  theistic, 128, 317, 342, 345, 396
believers, 12–13, 114, 119, 126, 181,
        191–192, 272, 369, 479
benefactors, 45, 89, 487
benevolent institutions, public, 387
bequests, 30–32, 63, 66–67, 194–197,
        241–242, 250–253, 303,
        407–410, 448
  charitable, 29–30, 32, 63, 302, 305, 448
  ordinary, 63
  subject to a religious condition
    Australia, 409
    Canada, 348
    England and Wales, 195–196

Ireland, 252
New Zealand, 448
United States, 303
birth control, *see* contraception
bishops, 44, 103, 176, 217, 352, 362, 474
Blackstone, 160
blasphemy, 13, 22, 23, 160–161
blood donation, 16
bonding, 9, 18, 35, 80
boundaries, 9, 24, 43, 69, 75, 109, 115,
        491, 498–499
  between individual/family/society,
        75–80
Brady, J.C., 234
bridging, 9, 18, 35–36, 80, 463
Buddhists, 10–12, 24, 278, 329,
        332, 378
burqa, 164, 461

campaigning, 56, 106, 412
Canada, 3, 6, 10, 128, 142, 143, 148,
        149, 151, 325–373, 476, 477,
        495, 497, 498
  advancement of religion, 346
  advocacy, 351
  belief in Supreme Being, 342
  bequests subject to a religious
        condition, 348
  charity law, 336–342, 365
    reform, 340
    and regulatory framework, 336–342
  charity regulator, 337
  Church
    State and religious charities,
        326–335
  common law, 338–340
  Constitution, 355
  discrimination, 362–363
    same-sex marriage and religious
        organisations, 364
  equality and diversity legislation, 355
  equality of religions, 330–332
  established religion, 330
  failure of testamentary dispositions
        due to common law rules, 348
  frameworks for facilitating
        government–sector
        relationships, 328

518 INDEX

Canada (cont.)
freedom of religion, 357–358
government and nonprofit sector, 326
government funding, 334–335
government policy, 326
human rights
discrimination and religious
charities, 353–372
inter-Church property disputes, 361
interference with the manifestation
of religious belief, 358–361
legislation, 336–337
means for advancing religion, 347
modern Church–State
relationship, 329
nonprofit sector, 327
Office of Religious Freedom,
333–334
philosophy and other value
systems, 345
positive action, 371
proportionality, 363
proselytism, 352–353
public benefit test and religious
organisations, 341
public policy
constraints, 350–351
religious charities and common
law constraints, 347–353
reforms, 341
religion
religious beliefs and the
advancement of religion,
342–347
religion(s), 329
religious charities, 332
discrimination and exemptions, 356
as public bodies, 357
religious discrimination in
practice, 365
religious organisations and
nonprofit sector, 332
religious preferences and public
policy, 349
religious umbrella bodies, 333
secularisation, 330
testamentary conditions and
common law, 347

unequal and discriminatory
treatment
restriction of access to services,
369–371
restriction of employment
opportunities, 368–369
unequal but not discriminatory
treatment, 365–367
contractual obligations, 367
worship
religious tenets
doctrines, etc., 343–344
Canadian Revenue Authority (CRA),
325, 336–337, 341–342,
345–347, 350–354, 363
canon law, 5–9, 11–13, 40–41, 247, 467,
469–477, 496–504, 506–510
alternative belief systems and
subjective religious
experience, 471–472
and Christianity, 470
Christianity and subjective religious
experience, 472
conflation of culture and religion, 474
cultural context, 473
definition, 11, 13–14
doctrines, tenets, etc., 477
jurisdictional differences, 475
life cycle and sacraments, 474
modern belief systems and human
rights/charity law frame of
reference, 471
morality, 469, 476
religion and religious belief, 470,
476–477
and religious doctrine, 11
social policy and contemporary
moral issues, 475
and social role of religion, 473
canons, 13, 152, 208, 223, 245–246,
442, 473, 477
capital, social, 9, 18–19, 68, 80, 147
capitalism, 19, 112–113
care services, 14, 400, 425, 484
Catholic Care, 219–221
Catholic Church, 46, 49, 217–220,
225, 260–261, 321, 326,
349, 367

INDEX

Catholic schools, 217, 335, 367, 384, 434, 461
Catholicism, 22, 24, 158–159, 226–229, 232, 250, 255, 258, 264
Catholics, 248, 252, 260, 278, 285, 326, 330–332, 376–378, 382–383
celebration of masses, 66, 227–228, 248
censuses, 163, 231, 329–330, 378, 413, 430–431
ceremonies, 18, 68, 248, 300, 395, 406–407, 469, 479, 513
Chancery, 29, 43–51
chantries, 45, 49, 67, 227
chapels, 18, 160, 167, 175, 227
charitable activities, 51, 62, 68, 102, 147–148, 274, 336–338, 339–340, 348
charitable bequests, 29–30, 32, 63, 302, 305, 448
Charitable Choice, 274, 284, 288–289, 491
charitable gifts, 43, 49, 61, 81, 137, 227, 232, 245–246, 252
  valid, 228
charitable intention, 84, 196–197, 249, 409
charitable objects, 48, 72, 175, 252
charitable organisations, 53, 81, 84, 137, 145, 284, 292–294, 332, 337–338
charitable purpose constraints, 82
charitable purposes, 50–56, 103–111, 145–150, 171–174, 195–199, 385–394, 445–450
  Australia, 392
  England and Wales, 173–174
  Ireland, 241–242
  New Zealand, 439
  and religion, 54–64
  religious, 151–153
charitable sector, 144, 294, 341, 435, 438
charitable status, 60–61, 174–178, 239–246, 254–255, 339–343, 345–350, 407–408, 445–450, 483–485
  abuse of, 145, 240, 341
  denial of, 56–58, 66, 72, 105, 175, 338, 343, 350, 351

charitable tax exemption, 1, 35, 419
charitable trusts, 32, 46–51, 69–70, 72, 84–86, 90, 107, 158–159, 239
  emergence from ecclesiastic origins, 47–48
  religious, 247, 300
  valid, 253
charities, 16–21, 41–56, 87–93, 97–117, 142–151, 202–207, 209–227, 237–241, 332–344
  basic legal structures for charitable and nonprofit activity, 84
  core conceptual requirements, 55–57
  faith-based, 28, 220, 383
  independence, 56
  as legal entities, 83–88
  and political activity, 103–105
  public, 292, 294
  as public bodies, 89
  and public policy constraint, 107–109
  register of, 148, 241, 441
  registered, 92, 177, 332, 339, 345, 352
  religious, 102–112, 152–158, 166–168, 225–226, 281–285, 324–327, 334–336, 372–376, 425–427
Charities Regulatory Authority, 237, 241
charity
  definition, 16
  and faith-based provision, 38
  and nonprofit sector, 114–115
  and political frame of reference, 100–101
  and politics, 19
  and religion, 19–20, 93–100
  and theocratic rule, 23
Charity Commission, 150, 157, 162, 170–172, 174–181, 183, 198–199, 207, 209
charity law, 5–6, 30–32, 49–51, 150–158, 223–228, 237–238, 294–296, 498–500
  Australia, 385–396, 410
  basic structures uniting holy and secular, 44–45
  Chancery, 48

520   INDEX

charity law (cont.)
   Commissioners for Special Purposes
      of Income Tax v. *Pemsel*, 52
   constraints, 104–105
   contemporary constraints, 100–107
   and definition of religion, 57–59
   early judicial developments, 51
   Elizabethan legislative
      developments, 48–49
   Elizabethan Poor Laws, 49
   emergence of charitable trusts from
      ecclesiastic origins, 47–48
   England and Wales, *see* England and
      Wales, charity law
   equity, 53
   government preferencing of
      particular religions as service
      providers, 488
   Ireland, *see* Ireland, charity law
   jurisdictional differences, 485
   medieval origins, 43–44
   Morice v. *Bishop of Durham*, 51–52
   mortmain, 46, 227
   need for public benefit, 477–489
   New Zealand, 434–442
   public benefit
      and equality, 486–487
      and government funding, 483–485
      test, *see* public benefit, test
   reform, 2, 142–153, 390–391,
      426–427, 435, 438, 480, 483
      Australia, 390
      Canada, 340
      England and Wales, 172–180
      Ireland, 239–240
      New Zealand, 438
      United States, 294–295
   Reformation, 47
   religion
      as intrinsically beneficial, 478
      as intrinsically detrimental,
      479–480
      and public benefit, 60–64, 478
      and state, 46
   and religions, 59
   Statute of Charitable Uses 1601, 42–43,
      49–51, 73, 226, 238, 437
   and tax law, 53–54

   and taxes, 53
   United States, 291–297
   Williams Trustees v. *IRC*, 52
charity regulators, 172
   Australia, 386–387
   Canada, 337
   Ireland, 237–238
   New Zealand, 436–437
   United States, 292
child abuse, 4, 78, 115, 378
children, 75–76, 130–132, 218–220,
      258–263, 266–270, 272,
      286–289, 322–324, 500–501
Christian beliefs, 44, 129, 214, 257,
      460, 493
Christian marital family unit, 76
Christian religions, 12, 22, 103, 233,
      361–362, 399–401, 406, 413,
      430
Christianity, 3–5, 20–22, 102, 131,
      159–160, 401–403, 467–470,
      472–474, 500–508
   and canon law, 470
   and subjective religious
      experience, 472
Church
   and State, 16, 21–29, 38, 41, 76–79,
      158, 497–499, 501–503
      relationships, 3, 6, 21, 223, 228,
      375–376, 427–430, 434,
      496–497
         symbiotic, 79, 225
      separation of, 28, 279–281, 329,
      379, 430, 485
Church of England, 3, 161, 169–170,
      196, 208, 216–217, 223,
      488–490, 497
   doctrines, 73, 196
   special position, 161–162
Church of Ireland, 229, 231, 264
Church of Scientology, *see* Scientology
Church property, 103, 410, 413
Churches, 26–28, 66–68, 103–106,
      160–162, 167, 279–284,
      345–349, 380–381, 405–407
   and fixtures, 66
citizenship, 109, 245, 255, 279, 368,
      512–513

INDEX

521

civic morality, 13, 475, 498, 509
civic responsibility, 17–19, 42, 147,
    192, 277, 327
civil law, 1, 14, 39, 325, 337, 470, 490
civil partnership, 202, 213, 457
civil rights, 294, 325, 500
civil society, 19, 112, 114, 146–147, 150,
    495–498, 502, 507, 509
clergy, 1, 458, 469, 473–474, 479, 495,
    497, 505, 513
  gifts for support of, 66
climate change, 101, 184
closed religious orders, 68, 83, 175, 243,
    252, 398, 483
  Australia, 394–396
cogency, 4, 123, 181, 184, 189–190
cohesion, 30, 123, 181, 184,
    189–190, 222
Cold War, 112–113
collective worship, 406, 492–493, 497
collectivism, 86–87
  and organisational structures, 86–87
colleges, 197, 226, 321, 329, 368, 484
colonialism, 20–21, 226, 375, 500
*Commissioners for Special Purposes of
    Income Tax* v. *Pemsel*, 52
common law
  Australia, 389
  Canada, 338–340
  conceptual constraints, 82
  constraints, 43, 74, 81–83, 194, 250,
    301, 347, 408
  context, 6, 21, 24, 42–73, 295
  England and Wales, 172
  Ireland, 239
  jurisdictions, 1–5, 41–43, 53–59,
    83–86, 150–158, 291–297,
    337–341, 431–434, 506–509
  New Zealand, 437
  and religious conditions, 72–73
  rules, 251, 254, 302, 341, 348, 408,
    411, 439, 448
  and testamentary conditions, 194,
    250, 301, 408
  United States, 292–294
communism, 102, 112–115
communities, religious, 26, 39, 59, 68,
    103, 166, 335, 366

community benefit societies, 88
compelling interests, 312–313, 320
competition, 4, 37, 89, 413
  from old and new legal forms of
    nonprofit activity, 91–92
compromise, 15, 56, 61, 208, 215, 223,
    372–373
conditions of employment, 214,
    367–368, 456
conduct, 94–96, 125, 188, 411, 413, 416,
    458, 469–473, 493–495
  canons of, 397–399, 442
conflict of laws, 467–508
  and moral imperatives, 498–508
conflict resolution, 68, 150, 199, 242,
    255, 347
congregations, 59, 80, 281, 332, 345,
    396, 430
conscience, 119–120, 132, 138,
    212–214, 256, 259, 355, 357,
    452–453
constitutionality, 261, 269–270, 287, 321
constitutions, 228–229, 233–236,
    256–257, 258–270, 275–277,
    308–311, 354, 384, 414–415
  Australia, 415
  Canada, 355
  Ireland, 257–258
  New Zealand, 452–453
  United States, 308–309
constraints, 17, 37, 74, 89, 99–103, 199,
    225, 293, 304
  public policy, *see* public policy,
    constraints
  religious, 82, 195, 348
  statutory, 46, 417
contemplative religious orders, 230,
    296, 342, 394, 396
contemporary religious states, 23–24
contraception, 101, 127, 225, 232, 323,
    367, 502–503
  improved, 75–77
contracts, 76, 81, 85–89, 150, 205, 212,
    284, 288, 323
contractual obligations, 211, 270–271,
    321, 367, 423, 460
control, 85, 90, 96, 168, 172, 204, 270,
    417, 418

controversy, 1, 17, 28, 339, 351, 381, 383–385, 461, 474

Convention rights, 128, 171, 201, 206, 212

convents, 231, 248–249

cooperatives, 74, 88, 92

core doctrines, 11, 153

corporal punishment, 125, 160, 183, 450

corporations, 49, 53–54, 85–86, 292, 340
   religious, 86, 281, 290, 300, 309, 319

costs, 17–19, 26, 91, 145, 151, 169, 277, 484

counselling, 58, 214, 285, 339–340, 444

covenants, 100, 135, 350

CRA, *see* Canadian Revenue Authority

credit unions, 88, 92

criminalisation of homosexuality, 232, 501

cults, 10, 54, 246, 298, 476–479

cultural diversity, 199, 413

cultural values, 35, 401

culture wars, 5, 39, 75, 95, 96, 278, 513
   and moral imperatives, 39–40

cultures, 82, 87, 459–461, 486, 489, 500, 506, 510, 514

cy-près doctrine, 148, 302, 305, 362–363

Dal Pont, G., 404–406, 437, 443, 446, 451

de Tocqueville, Alexis, 9, 276, 281

deductible gift recipient (DGR), 381, 386

democracy, 17, 25, 33, 38, 86, 96, 112–115, 218, 500
   and secularism, 38

democratic society, 96, 100, 119–120, 126, 138, 189–190, 355, 360, 492–493

denial of charitable status, 56–58, 66, 72, 105, 175, 338, 343, 350, 351

denominational schools, 261–262, 270, 335, 376

denominations, 159–162, 229, 234, 261–264, 270, 278, 331, 400, 405

detriment, 131, 175, 179–180, 208, 335, 394, 480

developed nations, 38, 40–41, 74, 91, 93, 102, 111, 113, 225

DGR, *see* deductible gift recipient (DGR)

didactic moralism, 9, 38, 502

direct discrimination, 135, 196, 216–219

direct funding, 235, 329, 334

direct government funding, 288, 334

disability, 98–99, 123, 202, 234, 259, 263, 267, 356, 368

disadvantaged groups, 32, 36, 150, 222, 323, 363

discretion, 1, 56, 69, 89, 129, 161, 179, 194–195, 251
   donor, 21, 43, 69, 81, 85, 98
   judicial, 48–53

discrimination, 121–123, 133–136, 201–203, 207–214, 217–225, 255–259, 267–268, 421–427, 453–460
   see also non-discrimination
   affirmative action, *see* affirmative action
   against a class, 136
   Australia, 421
   Canada, 362–363
   conflated, 136
   direct, 135, 196, 216–219
   England and Wales, 207–209
   and human rights law/legislation, 494
   indirect, 135, 202, 212–214, 218, 268, 402
   Ireland, 267–268
   laws, 259, 289, 309, 415
   New Zealand, 456
   and organisational issues, 139–140
   positive, 136, 266, 271, 272, 356
   racial, 219, 302–303, 350, 411
   religious, 2–5, 69–70, 136, 209, 270–271, 272, 459–461, 494
   and religious organisations, 137
   sex, 202, 317, 417, 421
   sexual orientation, 140, 201, 216, 220
   United States, 316–317
   unlawful, 222, 322

INDEX

discriminatory practices, 137, 141,
169, 170, 236, 335, 401,
410, 424
discriminatory religious conditions, 69
dismissal, 140, 212–213, 271, 367
diversity, 33, 54, 301, 309, 399, 413,
477, 487, 490
  cultural, 199, 413
  ethnic, 9, 32
  legislation, 258, 309, 355, 415, 453
  religious, 31, 114, 297
  and social inclusion, 505
divorce, 14, 232, 279, 365, 410,
470, 503
doctrines, 11–12, 59, 126, 343–346,
362–364, 398–402, 422–424,
444, 476–477
  body of, 4, 469, 477, 492
  core, 11, 153
domestic constraints, 74–109
donor constraints, 81–82
donor discretion, 21, 43, 69, 81, 85, 98
donors, 16–17, 32, 45–46, 72–74,
81–85, 107–109, 243,
250–251, 487
  intention, 48, 55, 69, 108, 487
  and public policy, 107–108
duties, 208, 211–214, 260, 266, 271–272,
315, 322, 364, 367

Eastern Europe, 102, 112, 113, 114
education, 50–52, 88–91, 120, 130–132,
169, 234–239, 242–244,
260–263, 266–270
  advancement of, 52, 68, 211, 239,
242, 338, 389, 392, 394
  moral, 68, 121, 130, 347
  primary, 236, 260
  religious, 269, 376
  secular, 384, 431, 490
educational institutions, 302, 309,
362, 417
educational pluralism, 132
educational services, 261, 335, 340,
368, 370
Elizabethan legislative developments in
charity law, 48–49
Elizabethan Poor Laws, 49

employees, 139, 212–214, 270–271,
309–310, 316–317, 321–322,
365–367, 456, 460
employers, 89, 211–214, 222–223, 316,
321–322, 361, 454, 456, 460
employment, 122–123, 207, 211–214,
267–271, 316–320, 361,
366–368, 453, 454–460
  decisions, 309, 321
  fair, 98–99
  tribunals, 184, 189, 213, 216
enforcement, 13, 45, 96–97, 259,
318, 439
England and Wales, 3, 6, 42, 142, 144,
147, 148, 150, 157–223, 390,
392, 398, 399
  advancement of religion, 192–193
  advocacy, 198
  belief in a Supreme Being, 181–182
  beliefs
    the believer and manifestations of
belief, 191
  bequests subject to a religious
condition, 195–196
  charitable purposes, 173–174
  charity law
    reform, 172–180
    and regulatory framework,
170–193
  Church
    State and religious charities,
158–170
  common law, 172
  detriment, 179–180
  differences in approach to
religious and philosophical
beliefs, 189
  discrimination, 207
    and same-sex marriage, 208
  Equality Act 2010
    public bodies and exemption for
charities, 202–203
  equality of religions, 166
  established religion, 164–165
  European Convention, 201–202
  failure of testamentary dispositions
due to breach of common law
rules, 194–195

INDEX

England and Wales (cont.)
freedom of religion, 205
government funding, 167–170
historical background, 158
human rights
discrimination and religious
charities, 199–222
interference with the manifestation
of religious belief, 205–207
legislation, 171–172
legitimate aim, 207
manifestation of beliefs, 192
means for advancing religion, 193
modern Church–state
relationship, 162
non-philosophical beliefs, 189
non-religious beliefs, 189
personal nature of beliefs, 191–192
philosophy and other value systems,
183–185
positive action, 222
proportionality, 208
proselytism, 199
public benefit, 173
test and religious organisations,
174–180
public policy
constraints, 198
and *Pemsel*-plus charitable
purposes, 199
religious charities and common
law constraints, 194–199
religion
religious beliefs and the
advancement of religion,
180–193
religion(s), 163
religious beliefs, 185–188
religious charities, 166, 204–205
discrimination and exemptions,
203–204
as public bodies, 204–205
religious discrimination in
practice, 209
religious organisations and
nonprofit sector, 166
religious umbrella bodies, 167
secularisation, 163–164

special position of Church of
England, 161–162
State
Protestantism
charity and religious
discrimination, 158–159
state enforcement of Christianity,
159–161
testamentary conditions and
common law, 194
unequal and discriminatory
treatment
restriction of access to services,
218–221
restriction of employment
opportunities, 215–218
unequal but not discriminatory
treatment
contractual obligations, 211–215
worship
religious tenets
doctrines, etc., 182–183
entrenched interests, 34, 263
equality, 1–2, 98–99, 103, 241–242,
414–415, 453–454, 457–459,
486–488, 506–510
see also discrimination;
non-discrimination
definition, 29
gender, 20, 103
and islands of exclusivity, 507–508
legislation, 1, 3–5, 31, 102, 223,
453, 494
principle, 79, 208, 487, 506
and public benefit, 486–487
of religions, 28
Australia, 380–381
Canada, 330–332
England and Wales, 166
Ireland, 233–234
New Zealand, 431
United States, 280
equitable owners, 49
equity, 1, 53, 85, 93, 97, 105, 128,
355, 490
universal standards of, 98–99
Established Church, 3, 9, 31–32, 34, 38,
47, 158–165, 279, 468

INDEX

established religion
  Australia, 379
  Canada, 330
  England and Wales, 164–165
  Ireland, 232–233
  New Zealand, 431
  United States, 279–280
Establishment Clause, 280–288, 308,
    310–316, 321, 324, 380,
    415, 426
ethical belief, 317, 453–456, 459–460
ethnic diversity, 9, 32
ethnic groups, 32, 35, 112, 137, 430,
    475, 492, 505
ethnic identity, 35, 507
ethnic minorities, 222
ethos, religious, 98, 139, 215, 258–263,
    269–271, 361, 474, 487–488
EU, *see* European Union
European Union (EU), 113, 118, 256
evangelism, 78, 137–139, 482, 511–512
Everywoman's Health Centre Society,
    339, 351
exclusion, 29, 101, 133, 137, 182, 206,
    247, 356, 364
exclusiveness, 14, 18–19, 55, 149, 239
exclusivity, islands of, 218, 507–508
exemption doctrine, 312
exemption privileges, 1, 4–5, 216, 222,
    263–264, 372–373, 425–426,
    505, 512
exemptions, religious, 262, 312,
    315–317, 401, 417, 423,
    457, 494

fair employment, 98–99
faith communities, 168, 170, 334, 369
faith schools, 164, 170, 219, 490
faith-based charities, 28, 220, 383
faith-based initiatives, 153, 277, 283,
    287–288
faith-based organizations (FBOs), 28,
    168, 217, 288–289
faith-based schools, 1, 36, 115, 139,
    169–170, 495, 511
family, 22, 30, 74–76, 258, 283, 285,
    428–429, 463–467, 498–503
  changes in, 75–76

Christian marital family unit, 76
marital, 76, 258
modern family and traditional
    religious belief, 127–128
Nazarene family model, 38,
    127, 503
non-marital, 258
family law, 39, 469–470, 498
family life, 118, 128, 450
family-oriented moral imperatives,
    502–504
family support, and professional
    services, 76–77
fathers, 126, 303
FBOs, *see* faith-based organizations
federal grants, 284
First Amendment, 280, 285–287, 298,
    300, 305–309, 316–317, 321,
    324, 379–380
Fishman, J.J., 291, 294
forfeiture, 71, 195–197, 349
for-profit sector, 26–27, 34, 37,
    115, 419
France, 127, 134, 141, 328
franchising, 28
fraternity, 53–54
Free Exercise Clause, 264, 298,
    303–306, 308, 311–312,
    315–316, 404, 497
Free Practice Clause, 264–266, 497
freedom, 119–129, 134–138,
    212–215, 262–266, 308–311,
    353–359, 360–364, 369–374,
    491–494
  of association, 81, 86, 118, 320
  of religion, 119–123, 212, 310–311,
    335–336, 357, 360–364,
    369–373, 419–420, 491–494
    Australia, 419
    Canada, 357–358
    and Church–State relationship,
      496–497
    England and Wales, 205
    and human rights
      law/legislation, 491–492
    Ireland, 263–264
    New Zealand, 455
    United States, 310–311

526 INDEX

freedom (cont.)
religious, 122, 138–139, 308–310,
333–335, 359, 360, 412–415,
452, 492–493
of speech, 203, 415
of testamentary disposition, 197, 347
friendship, 20–21
fundamental freedoms, 99, 355, 491, 506
fundamental human rights, 110, 117
fundamentalism, 40, 78, 115, 162, 512
and moral imperatives, 41
funding, 34, 219–222, 235, 285,
288–290, 324, 334–335,
375–376, 383
direct, 235, 329, 334
government, *see* government
funding

gay marriage, 2, 98, 106, 115, 450, 462,
464, 502–504, 509
see also same-sex marriage
gays, 36, 220, 320, 369, 372,
457–458, 461
gender, 1, 5, 32, 137, 140, 216–217,
258–259, 489, 490
gender, identity, 417, 424–425
gender equality, 20, 103
gift relationship, 16–18, 84
gifts, 42–50, 55–57, 59–66, 68–70,
194–197, 227–232, 242–246,
247–253, 405–411
charitable, *see* charitable gifts
for support of clergy, 66
testamentary, 197, 350, 407
for upkeep of graves, 66
God(s), 3–4, 44, 58, 126, 223, 230,
298–299, 468–471, 476
goods, 49, 81, 92, 129, 316, 368,
391, 393
provision of, 207, 259, 267, 421, 453
public, 18, 485, 512
government bodies, 85, 91, 147, 166,
204, 238, 275, 334, 390
government funding, 1, 3, 260–261,
272–274, 288–290, 334–335,
383–385, 427–429, 433–434
Australia, 383–385
Canada, 334–335

direct, 288, 334
England and Wales, 167–170
indirect, 380
Ireland, 235–237
New Zealand, 433–434
and public benefit, 483–485
of religious charities, 27–28
United States, 283–288, 289
government grants, 37, 85, 168–169,
285, 319, 381
government policy, 33, 105, 112,
116–117, 222–223, 232,
411–412, 428
government service provision, 53, 90,
289, 421
government–sector relations, 151, 276,
327–328, 391, 429
grants, 27–28, 35, 46–47, 168, 197, 284,
433, 436
see also government funding
federal, 284
graves, upkeep of, 66, 249
Greece, 86, 118, 129, 139

Habermas, J., 13, 25–26, 39
hapu, 460
hardship
religious, 313
undue, 315
Hart, H. L. A., 75, 95–96
Hart–Devlin debate, 95–96
health, 113, 116, 119–122,
146, 150, 360, 368,
432, 484
care, 3, 37, 68, 225, 235, 375, 381,
481, 484
heresy, 12, 22, 23, 96
hijab, 213, 271
Hindus, 10, 24, 188, 278, 329–332, 504
historical background, 42–73, 158,
225, 375
religious organisations
charity and the common law,
43–54
homosexual marriage, *see* gay
marriage
homosexual relationships, 123, 127,
366, 424

INDEX

homosexuality, 40, 95, 131, 157, 214–216, 401, 423–425, 490, 502
  criminalisation, 232, 501
hospitals, 61, 69, 226, 231, 235–236, 275, 283, 290, 294–297
  religious, 285, 290
House of Lords, 159–162, 176, 185–187, 194, 198–200, 210–211, 218, 227, 394
housing, 47, 77, 90, 92, 217, 304, 365, 390, 429
human rights, 2–6, 117–118, 133–137, 153–157, 307, 353–354, 413–414, 451–452, 505–509
  advancement of, 150, 199, 255
  Australia, 414
  Canada, 354
  commissions, 362, 366, 414, 431, 453, 459–461
  England and Wales, 200–201
  fundamental, 110, 117
  Ireland, 256
  law/legislation, 5–6, 22, 354, 364, 367, 467, 495–496, 499
    and discrimination, 494
    and freedom of religion, 491–492
      and Church–State relationship, 496–497
    jurisdictional differences, 496
    need for religious pluralism, 489–498
    religious belief
      charity and taxation, 489
      and tax exemption, 490
    religious exemptions, 495–496
    right to manifest religious belief, 493–494
    and taxation, 490
    traditional institutional religions and subjective interpretation of religious belief, 497
  principles, 4, 103, 180, 335, 468, 476
  and religion, 118–119
  United States, 307

identity
  ethnic, 35, 507

gender, 417, 424–425
  religious, 267, 276, 366
ideological change, 112
ideology, 39, 87, 101, 112–114, 507
improper proselytism, 137–138, 361, 413
income, 14, 20, 54, 167, 240, 377, 381, 433–434, 436
  tax, 52, 381–382, 436–437
    exemption, 67, 386
independence, 18, 57, 85, 90, 226, 228, 277, 431, 437
Indigenous peoples, 10, 301, 327, 397, 403, 413, 426, 482
  and religious beliefs, 403–404
indirect discrimination, 135, 202, 212–214, 218, 268, 402
indirect government funding, 380
indoctrination, 130–133, 139, 288, 291
  religious, 286, 291
informal public sphere, 26
infrastructures, social, 3, 42, 74, 93, 112–114, 237, 326, 330, 381
institution of marriage, 258, 364
institutional infrastructures, 129, 150, 505
institutions, 14–15, 26, 30–31, 129–130, 195, 250–251, 270–271, 382, 419
  public, 31, 79, 513
  public benevolent, 387
  religious, 63, 195, 244, 250, 324, 326, 381–382, 386–387, 388–389
  social, 20–21, 39, 41, 127, 463, 503
  state, 79, 98, 255
intangible rewards/benefits, 18, 179
intentions
  charitable, 84, 196–197, 249, 409
  donors, 48, 55, 108, 487
  testators, 194–197
intercessory prayers, 62, 395, 483, 487
interference
  State/government, 25, 141, 264, 277, 308
  with the manifestation of religious belief
    Australia, 420
    Canada, 358–361

interference (cont.)
England and Wales, 205–207
Ireland, 264–267
New Zealand, 455
United States, 311–316
international aid/trade, 116
international context, 6, 110–153
international dimension and religion, 99–100
international human rights law, 414
intolerance, 31, 41, 111, 122, 414
Ireland, 6, 34, 35, 39, 147, 149, 150, 151, 152, 224–273, 470, 476, 477, 483, 487, 488, 497
advancement of religion, 247–249
advocacy, 254
belief in Supreme Being, 246
bequests subject to a religious condition, 252
charitable purposes, 241–242
charity law
reform, 239–240
and regulatory framework, 237–245
charity regulator, 237–238
Church
State and religious charities, 226
common law, 239
Constitution, 257–258
discrimination, 267–268
equality and diversity legislation
public bodies and exemption for charities, 258–259
equality of religions, 233–234
established religion, 232–233
European Convention, 256
failure of testamentary dispositions due to breach of common law rules, 251–252
freedom of religion, 263–264
government and nonprofit sector, 226–237
government funding, 235, 237
human rights, 256
discrimination and religious charities, 255–272
interference with manifestations of religious belief, 264–267
legislation, 237
means for advancing religion, 249–250
modern Church–State relationship, 228
Northern, 5, 30, 147, 187, 475, 479, 489
philosophy and other value systems, 247
pious uses, 238
positive action, 272
private piety, 230–231, 243
proselytism, 254–255
public benefit test and religious organisations, 242–245
public policy
charity and common law constraints, 250
constraints, 253–254
and *Pemsel*-plus charitable purposes, 255
reform outcomes, 241
reform process, 240–241
religion
religious beliefs and the advancement of religion, 245–250
religion(s), 229
religious charities, 234, 260–263
discrimination and exemptions, 259–260
as public bodies, 260–263
religious discrimination in practice, 268–269
religious organisations and nonprofit sector, 234
religious preferences and public policy, 252
religious umbrella bodies, 234
secularisation, 231–232
State
Catholicism and charity, 227–228
testamentary conditions and common law, 250
unequal and discriminatory treatment
restriction of access to services, 272

INDEX 529

restriction of employment
opportunities, 271
unequal but not discriminatory
treatment, 269–270
worship
religious tenets
doctrines, etc., 246–247
irrebuttable presumptions, 480
IRS (Internal Revenue Service), 274,
281–282, 291–296, 298–301,
303–304
Islam, 20, 25, 38, 40, 115, 498, 504,
506, 512
islands of exclusivity, 218, 507–508
isolationism, 36
Israel, 39, 40, 303
Italy, 24, 79, 131, 133, 138, 474

Jehovah's Witnesses, 139–141, 180,
306, 308, 376, 404, 410, 420
Jewish faith, 159, 196, 303, 351, 449
Jews, 12, 127–128, 265, 278, 321, 329,
332, 350, 353
jilbab, 187, 211
judiciary, 48–54, 83–86, 174–175, 199,
296–299, 347–349, 372,
402–405, 476–477
justice, 12, 75, 118, 129, 137, 160,
219, 241
and morality, 93–100
social, 75, 98–99, 306

Koran, 416

land ownership, 44, 227
language, 35, 72, 99, 133, 186, 320, 352,
363, 474
law and principles, 93–95
law reform, 110, 149, 294, 390
process, 147, 225, 296, 364
legacies, 16, 194, 224, 255, 272,
327–329, 347–349,
381, 488
legal frameworks, 113, 143, 146, 267,
295, 386, 413, 427, 437
legal owners, 49
legal positivism, 93–94
legal presumptions, 60, 152, 300–301

legal rights, 75, 76, 93, 97–98, 110, 225,
332, 428
charity and religion, 97
legal structures, 84–86, 148, 238, 390
legitimate aims, 126, 134, 141,
202–207, 210, 220–221
legitimate secular purposes, 320
liberty, 121, 160, 253, 309, 311, 380, 419
religious, 312, 388, 410, 507
life cycle, 474
litigation, 97, 143, 240, 275, 339, 354
lobbying, 20, 34, 56, 167, 302, 305,
412, 450

management, 14, 139, 260–261, 296,
337, 362, 484, 487
manifestation of beliefs
Australia, 404–405
England and Wales, 192
manifestation of religious belief, 130,
205–206, 264, 311–313, 358,
420, 447, 455
Māori, 3, 427, 430–432, 451–452,
459–460
margin of appreciation, 119, 131–134,
141, 200, 201, 256
marital family, 76, 258
relationships, 38, 501
unit, 38, 258, 501
marital status, 216, 258, 268, 367–368,
407, 421, 423, 506
markets, 80, 89, 91–93
marriage, 70–72, 75–76, 123, 364–365,
370–372, 399–401, 424–425,
457–458, 501–503
gay, 2, 40, 106, 115, 450, 462, 464,
502–504, 509
heterosexual, 23, 501
homosexual, *see* gay marriage
institution of, 258, 364
law of, 22, 457, 498
sanctity of, 23, 501
marriage services, 36, 317, 462
marriages
same-sex, 103, 209, 356, 361, 372
married parents, 76, 501
masses, 44, 49, 62, 227–228, 243, 248,
406–407, 483, 487

530 INDEX

masses (cont.)
  celebration of, 66, 227–228, 248
  private, 62, 68, 230, 483
maternity, 75–77, 97, 202
means for advancing religion
  Australia, 406–408
  Canada, 347
  England and Wales, 193
  Ireland, 249–250
  New Zealand, 446–447
  United States, 300
medicine, 75–77, 475
member benefit, 9, 18, 35, 393,
    478–479, 481
  vs. public benefit, 18–19
membership, 14, 34, 196, 210, 253, 259,
    421, 433, 440
military service, 141, 299, 420
ministers, 19, 26, 317, 400, 406, 438,
    441, 446, 457
minorities, 11, 24, 34, 40, 124–126,
    149–151, 163, 187, 420
  ethnic, 222
  religious, 24, 159, 272, 331, 358
minority groups, 18, 32, 34–35,
    129–131, 192, 200, 267,
    304, 452
missionaries, 67, 193, 375–376, 406
missionary purposes, 239, 249–250
missionary work, 67, 103, 250,
    406–408, 419
modern Church–State relationship
  Australia, 376–377
  Canada, 329
  England and Wales, 162
  Ireland, 228
  New Zealand, 430
  United States, 277
modes of worship, 469–470, 479
monarchs, 161
monasteries, 45–47
monotheism, 228, 469–471
monuments, 294, 360
moral education, 68, 121, 130, 347
moral imperatives, 2, 6–9, 22, 38–39, 467,
    473, 499–502, 505–509, 511
  agenda of, 4, 39
  and conflict of laws, 498–508

  and culture wars, 39–40
  family oriented, 502–504
  and fundamentalism, 41
  and theocratic rule, 22–23
moral principles, 94–95
moralism, didactic, 9, 38, 502
morality, 75, 76, 93–96, 100, 109,
    243–245, 259, 263–264,
    469–470
  civic, 13, 475, 498, 509
  and justice, 93–100
  private, 96, 500
  public, 2, 81, 253, 257
  shared, 17
morals, 105, 119–122, 137, 205, 232,
    245, 343–344, 493, 500
Mormons, 10, 176, 206, 278, 304, 311,
    368, 413
mortmain, 46, 227
mothers, 219
multiculturalism, 9, 30–33, 41, 150,
    255, 363, 373, 507
  promotion of, 31, 150, 255
  and subsidies, 34–35
Muslims, see also Islam, 12, 24, 103,
    128, 167, 187, 231–233, 322,
    329–332
mutual benefit and other
    organisational structures,
    88–89

Nation of Islam, 313
national origin, 309, 316–318
Nazarene family model, 38, 127, 503
negotiated rights, 89
neutrality, 129, 132, 165, 280, 314
  test, 314–315
New South Wales, 68, 376, 407, 422
New Zealand, 3, 6, 24, 142, 143, 148,
    151, 218, 300, 427–464,
    476, 477
  advancement of religion, 445
  advocacy, 450
  belief in Supreme Being, 443–444
  bequests subject to a religious
    condition, 448
  charitable purposes, 439
  charity law

INDEX

reform, 438
and regulatory framework, 434–442
charity regulator, 436–437
Church
State and religious charities, 427–434
common law, 437
Constitution, 452–453
discrimination, 456
same-sex marriage and religious organisations, 456
equality and diversity legislation
public bodies and exemption for charities, 453–454
equality of religions, 431
failure of testamentary dispositions due to breach of common law rules, 448
freedom of religion, 455
government and nonprofit sector, 428
government funding, 433–434
human rights
discrimination and religious charities, 451–463
interference with the manifestation of religious belief, 455
legislation, 435
means for advancing religion, 446–447
modern Church–State relationship, 430
philosophy and other value systems, 445
positive action, 462–463
proselytism, 451
public benefit test and religious organisations, 439–442
public policy
charity and common law constraints, 448–451
constraints, 449
reasonable accommodation, 456
reform outcomes, 438
religion
religious beliefs and the advancement of religion, 442–447
religion(s), 430

religious charities, 432–433
discrimination and exemptions, 454
as public bodies, 455
religious discrimination in practice, 459
religious exemption privileges, 457–458
religious organisations and nonprofit sector, 432
religious preferences and public policy, 449
secularisation, 431
testamentary conditions and common law, 448
unequal and discriminatory treatment
restriction of access to services, 461–462
restriction of employment opportunities, 460
unequal but not discriminatory treatment, 459
contractual obligations, 460
worship
religious tenets
doctrines, etc., 444
niqab, 163
non-charitable objects, 239, 252, 388
non-charitable purposes, 55–56, 65, 194–195, 251–252, 419
non-discrimination, *see also* discrimination, 93, 97–99, 103, 129, 133, 139–140, 263, 335, 414
non-philosophical beliefs
England and Wales, 189
non-political purposes requirement for charities, 56, 104
nonprofit activity, 84, 91, 433
non-profit distributing characteristic of charities, 55–56, 82, 172
nonprofit sector, 83–86, 88–93, 113–115, 144–146, 275, 293–296, 325–327, 332–334, 426–429
and charity, 114–115
and citizens, 80

non-religious beliefs, 205
  England and Wales, 189
non-theistic beliefs, 183, 476
Northern Ireland, 5, 30, 147, 187, 475,
    479, 489, 508
nurses, 69, 271, 272

objects, 56–58, 64, 72, 180–182,
    251–253, 351–352, 388, 411,
    445–451
  charitable, 48, 72, 175, 252
  non-charitable, 239, 252, 388
  political, 105
obligations, 85, 90, 121, 125, 137, 208,
    214, 382, 392
  contractual, 211, 270–271, 321, 367,
    423, 460
  perceived, 188, 222
observance, 119–121, 127, 131, 205,
    403–405, 452–453, 455,
    493, 496
  religious, 317, 366, 379,
    396, 513
occupational requirements, 211, 216,
    356, 359, 368, 495
Office of Faith-Based and Community
    Initiatives, 283, 287
Office of Religious Freedom,
    333–334
ordination, 217–218, 417
organisational issues, and
    discrimination, 139–140
organisational structures, 102
  and collectivism, 86–87
organisations, voluntary, 168, 327,
    333–334, 429
outworkings, 1, 107, 199, 446–447, 493
owners, 81, 92, 194, 318
  equitable, 49
  legal, 49
ownership, 81, 227, 260–261, 484
  land, 44, 227

pacifism, 184
papal supremacy, doctrine of, 198
Parachin, A., 71, 195, 252, 349,
    355–356
parenting, 75–77

parents, 77, 120–121, 130–133, 139,
    237, 258, 266, 269–270,
    323–324
  see also fathers; mothers
  adoptive, 220–221
  married, 76, 501
  religious, 490
parish churches, 45, 80
parishes, 45, 194, 361–362, 474
parity, 34, 36, 256, 468, 481–482,
    486, 490
partnerships
  civil, 202, 213, 457
    see also same-sex marriage
  government–sector, 151, 327–328
paternity, 75–77
patriarchy, residual traces of, 75–77
Pemsel classification, 82–83, 145, 149,
    173, 239, 241, 338, 342–343,
    389–390
permissive accommodations test,
    315, 323
perpetuity, 46, 55, 85, 227, 248
pervasively sectarian test, 284, 288,
    313–314
philanthropy, 26, 80, 88, 114, 479
philosophical beliefs/convictions, 120,
    123–125, 130–132, 180,
    183–185, 189–190, 192,
    245–247, 402
philosophy, 26, 80, 131, 183, 191, 339,
    345, 398, 402
Picarda, H., 160, 406
pious uses, 238
pluralism, 9, 30, 41, 78, 269, 272, 475,
    486–488
  challenge of, 33–41
  educational, 132
  and religion, 35
  religious, 3, 245, 329, 346, 489,
    504–505
  and religious charities, 37
pluralist societies, 34, 38, 223, 267, 350,
    373, 413, 486, 496
political activity, 43, 56, 103–106, 254,
    293, 300, 352, 412
  and charities, 103–104
political objects, 105

INDEX

political purposes, 104, 199, 254,
 449–450
politics, 14–15, 19, 75, 100–102, 109,
 299, 307, 480, 510
 and charity, 19
 constraints on, 101–102
 and religion, 15–16
 and religion, 102
positive action, 66, 204
 Australia, 425
 Canada, 371
 England and Wales, 222
 Ireland, 272
 New Zealand, 462–463
 United States, 323–324
positive discrimination, 136, 266, 271,
 272, 356
positive public benefit test, 482
positivism, legal, 93–94
poverty, 19, 27, 35, 47, 113–114, 116,
 167, 175, 207
 relief of, 37, 52, 68, 239, 242,
 375–376, 389, 482
powers, 46, 48, 124, 130, 240–241, 247,
 274–275, 436
 discretionary, 48, 262
 prerogative, 51
 state, 46, 275
 statutory, 144, 357, 452
practice of religion, 233, 260, 265, 420
prayers, 44, 58, 62, 65, 165, 217, 227,
 246, 249
 intercessory, 62, 395, 483, 487
 private, 36, 68, 248
precepts, 5, 9, 166, 249, 395
preferential treatment, 170, 233, 262,
 380, 384
pregnancy, 75–77, 202, 340
prerogative powers, 51
Presbyterians, 264, 378, 409, 430, 441
presumptions, 19, 54, 63–65, 83, 145,
 243, 272, 440, 445
 irrebuttable, 480
 legal, 60, 152, 300–301
 public benefit, 149, 152, 171–174,
 239, 244, 389–390, 393–394,
 435, 445–449
 rebuttable, 137, 243

priests, 408, 417, 446, 454, 461, 469,
 474, 492
primary education, 236, 260
primary schools, 260, 431
primary teachers, 271, 272
principal–agency relationship, 90–91,
 260, 291, 418
principles and law, 93–95
prisoners, 50, 139, 287–289
prisons, 161–162, 287–288, 313, 451
private benefits, 61, 175, 293, 301, 393
private interests, 14–15, 31, 41, 98
private masses, 62, 68, 230, 483
private morality, 96, 500
private piety, 4, 15, 20, 36, 61, 247, 483,
 490, 492
 Ireland, 230–231, 243
private schools, 290, 310, 323–324, 384,
 388, 454
privileges, 26, 42, 141, 162, 234, 244,
 316, 490, 495
professional services, and family
 support, 76–77
profit margins, 297, 447
profits, 56, 61, 64, 88, 275, 419
proof, 20, 62, 137, 145, 174, 190–192,
 393, 481, 485–486
 objective, 11, 468
propaganda, 105, 199, 302, 305–306
property, 14, 17–18, 45–47, 70–71, 72,
 133, 297, 405, 407
 law, 71–72, 325
proportionality, 118, 134, 141, 201–202,
 208, 215, 218, 359, 369
 Canada, 363
 England and Wales, 208
 reasonable, 134, 207
proselytism, 103, 107, 137, 199, 203,
 254–255, 352–353, 481, 482
 Australia, 412
 Canada, 352–353
 competitive, 413, 513
 England and Wales, 199
 improper, 137–138, 361, 413
 Ireland, 254–255
 New Zealand, 451
 and religious beliefs, 137–139
 United States, 306

534 INDEX

protected characteristics, 204, 207, 209–210, 217, 222
Protestantism, 16, 22, 24, 158, 161, 468, 474–475, 504, 506
public arena, 25, 31, 34, 79, 511
public benefit, 1–3, 60–65, 172–174, 177–180, 240–244, 392–395, 439–442, 445–447
  activity, 35, 42, 255, 294
  constraints, 83
  England and Wales, 173
  and equality, 486–487
  and government funding, 483–485
  need for, 477–489
  presumption, 149, 152, 171–174, 239, 244, 389–390, 393–394, 435, 445–449
  principle, 94, 483–485, 487, 496, 506
  and religion, 478
  requirement, 62, 171, 296, 342, 408, 487
  service provision, 92, 113–115, 145–146, 277, 327, 334, 375–377, 484–485, 489
  test, 247–249, 295–296, 339, 341–342, 390–391, 392–394, 396, 439–440, 480–481, 483
    and advancement of religion, 482
    application, 482–483
    Australia, 392–396
    benefit arm, 483
    calibration, 487–488
    Canada, 341
    England and Wales, 174–180
    in human rights context, 481
    Ireland, 242–245
    New Zealand, 439–442
    positive, 482
    public arm, 482–483
    United States, 296–297
  vs. member benefit, 18–19
public benevolent institutions, 387
public bodies, 89–91, 202–204, 210, 256, 258–261, 289–291, 357, 453, 455
public charities, 292, 294
public funding, *see also* government funding, 236, 261, 335, 365

public good, 16–19, 28, 35–36, 294, 343, 407
public goods, 18, 485, 512
public institutions, 31, 79, 513
public interests, 14
public law, 53, 90, 98, 494
public money, 308, 323–324
public morality, 2, 81, 253, 257
public order, 100, 119, 205, 257–259, 263–264, 513
public policy
  constraints, 75, 304, 348, 374
    Australia, 410–412
    Canada, 350–351
    and charities, 107–109
    England and Wales, 198
    Ireland, 253–254
    New Zealand, 449
    United States, 304
  and donors, 107–108
  and *Pemsel*-plus charitable purposes, 199
  and religious preferences, 196–198, 252, 304, 321, 349–350, 410, 449
public policy and *Pemsel*-plus charitable purposes, 255
public schools, 324, 329, 370
public service provision, 49, 93, 234, 327, 484
public services, 61, 213, 221, 320, 381, 428, 432, 455, 490
public sphere, 15, 130, 165, 362, 513
  informal, 26
public trust, 84, 115, 379
public utilities, 52, 92
public worship, 177, 279, 395–396, 512
  homage of, 233, 263
  place of, 395
publicly funded schools, 266, 270
punishment, corporal, 125, 160, 183, 450

racial discrimination, 219, 302–303, 350, 411
reasonable accommodation, 316
  New Zealand, 456
reasonable justification, 124, 134, 207, 256

rebuttable presumptions, 137, 243
Reformation, 13, 21, 41, 47, 54, 66, 79,
    194, 227
registered charities, 92, 177, 332, 339,
    345, 352
regulatory framework, 144, 147,
    291–292, 327–328, 336, 374,
    385, 390–391, 434–435
  Australia, 385–396, 410
  Canada, 336–342, 365
  England and Wales, 170–193
  Ireland, 237–245
  New Zealand, 434–442
  United States, 291–297
regulatory responsibility, 100, 337, 341
relief
  of poverty, 37, 52, 68, 239, 242,
    375–376, 389, 482
  of sickness, 69, 389
religion, 11
  advancement of, 50–54, 64–69,
    103–106, 192–193, 241–243,
    246–249, 346–347, 405–408,
    440–442, 444–451
  changes in, 77
  and charitable purposes, 54–64
  and charity, 19–20, 93–100
  definition, 10
  established, 27, 78, 164, 223, 232,
    272–274, 279, 379, 431
  freedom of practice of, 265
  and international dimension, 99–100
  as intrinsically beneficial, 478
  as intrinsically detrimental, 479–480
  legal definition, 58, 64, 151, 246, 476
  per se, 16, 25–26, 54, 324, 487–488
  and pluralism, 35
  and politics, 15–16
  and public benefit, 478
  and secularism, 78
  social role, 1, 3, 6, 78, 102, 115, 473, 485
religion(s)
  Australia, 378
  Canada, 329
  England and Wales, 163
  Ireland, 229
  New Zealand, 430
  United States, 278

religions
  and charity law, 59
  equality of, 28, 166, 233, 280, 330,
    380, 431
religious activities, 28, 36, 133, 249,
    312–314, 318, 343, 393, 433
religious adherents, 11, 30, 65, 115,
    163, 378–380, 470, 492
religious affiliation, 157, 163, 218, 265,
    329, 330, 378, 413, 512–513
religious beliefs, 2–5, 120–129,
    183–193, 206–215, 360–374,
    402–405, 454–467, 470–473,
    492–496
  Australia, 402–403
  England and Wales, 185–188
  groups with and without, 79–80
  and indigenous people, 403–404
  manifestation of, 125–127, 130,
    205–206, 264, 311–313, 358,
    447, 455
  and proselytism, 137–139
  and state, 129
  subjective interpretation, 493, 497
  traditional, 22, 38, 131, 153, 401,
    502, 509
religious bodies, 63–67, 244–245,
    261–263, 326–329, 344–346,
    372–373, 399–401, 422–423,
    457–458
religious charitable purposes, 151–153
religious charities, 102–112, 128–129,
    152–158, 166–168, 225–226,
    283–285, 324–327, 334–336,
    372–376, 425–427
  Australia, 381–382
  and definitional common law
    conceptual components of
    'charity', 55
  England and Wales, 166, 204–205
  Ireland, 234, 260–263
  New Zealand, 432–433
  and pluralism, 37
  as public bodies
    Australia, 417–419
    Canada, 357
    England and Wales, 204–205
    Ireland, 260–263

536 INDEX

religious charities (cont.)
New Zealand, 455
United States, 289–291
and secularism, 26–27
United States, 281–282
religious communities, 26, 39, 59, 68,
103, 166, 335, 366
religious conditions, 30–31, 71–73,
195, 250–252, 303, 347–349,
408, 409, 448–449
and common law, 72–73
discriminatory, 69
and public policy, 70–72
testators, 30–31
and unlawfulness, 69–70
religious convictions, *see also* religious
beliefs, 12, 78, 130, 184, 216,
220, 257, 313, 469
religious corporations, 86, 281, 290,
300, 309, 319
religious denominations, *see*
denominations
religious differences, 14, 40, 494
religious discrimination, 2–5, 136, 209,
270–271, 272–275, 325–326,
459–461, 494
charities and law in pre-human
rights era, 69–73
religious diversity, 31, 114, 297
religious doctrine, 9, 12–13, 22, 24, 59,
232, 235, 245, 422
and canon law, 11
religious duty to assist others, 20–21
religious education, 269, 376
religious entities, 162, 166, 310,
315, 319–320, 495–496,
505–507, 512
religious ethos, 98, 139, 215, 258–263,
269–271, 361, 474, 487–488
religious exemptions, 262, 312,
315–317, 401, 417, 423, 457
human rights
law/legislation, 495–496
religious faith, 4, 41, 192, 330,
344, 447
religious freedom, 122, 138–139,
308–310, 333–335, 359, 360,
412–415, 452, 492–493

religious groups, 140–141, 149,
177–178, 180, 281, 315–317,
320, 364, 423–425
religious hardship, 313
religious identity, 267, 276, 366
religious indoctrination, 286, 291
religious institution test, 388
religious institutions, 63, 195, 244, 250,
324, 326, 381–382, 386–387,
388–389
religious instruction, 57, 71, 261,
272, 431
religious liberty, 312, 388, 410, 507
religious minorities, 24, 159, 272,
331, 358
religious observance, 317, 366, 379,
396, 513
religious orders, 46, 65, 234, 239, 297,
310, 376–377, 395, 417
closed, 68, 83, 175, 243, 252, 394,
398, 483
closed contemplative, 61, 248, 483
contemplative, 230, 296, 342,
394, 396
religious organisations, 3–5, 174–182,
242–245, 281–282, 286–288,
315–320, 341–346, 432–434,
484–486
and discrimination, 137
religious parents, 490
religious pluralism, 3, 245, 329, 346,
504–505
need for, 489–498
religious practices, 62–63, 289, 300,
310, 312–314, 316, 320,
357–360, 371
religious preferences and public policy,
196–198, 252, 304, 349–350,
410, 449
religious premium, 480–481, 485
religious principles, 106, 127, 368, 370,
389, 400, 479, 509
religious purposes, 63, 194–195,
247–250, 274–275, 324, 389,
403–408, 410, 416–417
religious schism, 102, 361
religious schools, 285–286, 323–324,
329, 380, 383, 492

INDEX

religious service providers, 3, 28, 283, 377, 381
religious states, contemporary, 23–24
religious tenets, *see* tenets
religious tests, 379–380, 385
religious tolerance, 28, 32
religious umbrella bodies
    Australia, 382
    Canada, 333
    England and Wales, 167
    Ireland, 234
    United States, 282
religious worship, *see* worship
resources, 25, 37, 85, 100–102, 113–117, 175, 324, 338, 339–340
respect, 171–173, 189–190, 232–233, 235, 258–263, 316–318, 340–341, 365, 368–369
responsibility, 28, 49–50, 142–146, 261–263, 291–292, 295, 310–311, 386, 436–438
    civic, 17–19, 42, 147, 192, 277, 327
    regulatory, 100, 337, 341
righteousness, 20, 467
rights, 97–100, 117–120, 133–135, 205–206, 212–214, 307–310, 331, 353–359, 452
    civil, 294, 325, 500
    to manifest religious belief, 493–494
    and religion, 123
rituals, 11, 18, 68, 121, 265, 310, 482
Roman Catholic Church, *see* Catholic Church
Roman Catholicism, *see* Catholicism

sacraments, 76, 469, 474
salvation, 14, 20, 43–45, 227, 230, 487
same-sex couples, 77, 127–128, 208, 220–221, 317, 323, 364–365, 422–424, 457
same-sex marriage, 103, 157, 208–209, 267–268, 317, 356, 361, 364, 372
    see also gay marriage
    Australia, 421
    Canada, 364
    England and Wales, 208

    foreign, 268
    legalised, 317, 371, 422
    New Zealand, 456
    United States, 317
sanctity of marriage, 23, 501
school chaplains, 269, 384
schools, 93–95, 204–205, 211, 218–219, 236, 260–262, 266–271, 314–315, 384
    Catholic, 217, 335, 367, 384, 434, 461
    denominational, 261–262, 270, 335, 376
    faith-based, 1, 36, 115, 139, 169–170, 495, 511
    free, 50, 169
    primary, 260, 431
    private, 290, 310, 323–324, 384, 388, 454
    public, 324, 329, 370
    publicly funded, 266, 270
    religious, 285–286, 323–324, 329, 380, 383, 492
    secondary, 131, 260, 461
    state, 125, 132, 170, 183, 322, 463
scientific rationality, 77–78
Scientology, 58, 124, 181, 182, 299, 301, 379, 398, 402, 445, 504
    beliefs, 398, 402
Scotland, 142, 147, 148, 161, 167, 235, 242, 474
Scottish state schools, 125, 183
Scriptures, 12, 223, 469, 473, 497–499, 501–504, 508–510
secondary schools, 131, 260, 461
secular activities, 102, 234, 314, 319, 388, 446–447, 481
secular education, 384, 431, 490
secular purposes, 65, 286, 308, 331
    legitimate, 320
secular 'sense of mission', 80
secular service providers, 324
secular society, 52, 181, 224, 247, 405, 481
secularisation, 40, 75, 93, 133, 307, 330
    Australia, 378
    Canada, 330
    England and Wales, 163–164

538 INDEX

secularisation (cont.)
 Ireland, 231–232
 New Zealand, 431
 United States, 278–279
secularism, 4–5, 25–26, 39–41, 78, 79,
  130–132, 474–475, 489–491,
  498–499
 definition, 25–26
 and democracy, 38
 and religion, 78
 and religious charities, 26–27
 and State, 129–133
security, 75, 83, 392
separation of Church and State,
  24, 28, 281, 287, 314, 379,
  430, 485
 definition, 24
service delivery, 90–91, 142, 168, 235,
  383, 401, 485
service providers, 1, 27, 222, 235, 284,
  288, 366, 425, 488
 faith-based, 3, 283
 government preferencing of
  particular religions as, 488
 religious, 3, 28, 283, 377, 381
 secular, 324
service provision, 19, 27, 37, 89,
  150–153, 424, 432
 government, 53, 90, 289, 421
 public benefit, 92, 113–115,
  145–146, 277, 327, 334,
  375–377, 484–485, 489
services, 36–37, 202–210, 218–222,
  288, 316–318, 366–368,
  372–377, 382–384, 484–485
 abortion, 351, 372
 educational, 261, 335, 340, 368, 370
 public, 61, 213, 221, 320, 381, 428,
  432, 455, 490
 social, *see* social services
sex, 133, 316–318, 356, 363, 368, 372,
  454, 458, 462
sex discrimination, 202, 317, 417, 421
sexual orientation, 187, 201–202, 210,
  215–216, 220, 369–370, 417,
  424–425, 455–458
 discrimination, 140, 201, 216, 220
 of staff, 141

sexuality, 216, 223, 255, 425, 467,
  501, 506
shared faith, 58, 246
shared morality, 17
Sikhs, 10, 128, 218, 322, 329–332,
  451, 504
sin, 14, 22, 227, 501
Singapore, 142, 143, 147, 148, 150
social capital, 9, 18–19, 68, 80, 147
social care, 68, 85, 90–91, 113, 146, 166,
  234, 368, 432
social care facilities/services, 1, 14, 428,
  432, 484
social cohesion, 1, 21, 68, 97, 147,
  224–226, 426, 474–475, 479
social enterprises, 74, 92
social inclusion, 505
social infrastructure, 3, 42, 74, 93,
  112–114, 237, 326, 330, 381
social institutions, 20–21, 39, 41, 127,
  463, 503
social justice, 75, 98–99, 306
 charity and religion, 98
social policy, 41, 101, 150,
  507–509, 510
 and contemporary moral issues, 475
social roles, 9–10, 21, 41, 73, 75, 93,
  374, 492
 of religion, 1, 3, 6, 78, 102, 115, 485
 and canon law, 473
social services, 235, 281, 288, 322,
  366–367, 376–377, 433–434
 delivery of, 288, 377, 382
souls, 12–14, 18–20, 43–49, 62, 66,
  227–228, 407, 446, 487
speech, freedom of, 203, 415
spiritual teaching, 57, 346, 405–406
spiritualism, 183
spouses, 76, 461–462
State
 and religion, 79
 and religious belief, 129
 and secularism, 129–133
State, and Church, *see* Church, and
  State
State, secularism and religious
  charities, 26–27
State institutions, 79, 98, 255

INDEX

State interference, 25, 141, 264, 277, 308
State powers, 46, 275
State religions, 23, 415, 431
State schools, 125, 132, 170, 183, 322, 463
Status
  charitable, *see* charitable status
  marital, 216, 258, 268, 367–368, 407, 421, 423, 506
  tax exempt, 241, 300, 317, 334
Statute of Charitable Uses 1601, 42–43, 49–51, 73, 226, 238, 437
statutory powers, 144, 357, 452
subjective interpretation, 4, 183, 191, 472–473, 497
  of religious belief, 493, 497
subjective religious experience, 471–472
  and Christianity, 472
subliminal permeation, 14
subsidies, 24, 34–35, 513
  and multiculturalism, 34–35
Sunday, 212, 320, 331
support services, 67, 408, 513
Supreme Being, 42, 64, 152, 160, 181, 245–246, 272, 298–300, 442–443
  belief in, *see* belief in Supreme Being
  worship of, 58
surrogacy, 75–77
symbols, 129–132, 138, 186, 438, 494

tax administration, 239–241, 295–296
tax exempt status, 241, 300, 317, 334
tax exemption, 42, 302, 304, 381–382, 385, 483, 490, 507, 512
  charitable, 1, 35, 419
tax law, and charities, 53–54
taxes, 17, 50, 113, 125, 141, 274, 281, 296, 308
  and charity law, 53
taxpayers, 5, 28, 287, 367, 382, 384, 485, 490, 496
teachers, 205, 217, 270, 310, 322, 454, 490, 492, 495
  primary, 271, 272
temperance, 105–106, 412, 449
temples, 18, 176–177, 206, 284

tenets, 11, 182–183, 245–246, 298–299, 343, 398–399, 442–444, 469, 476–477
tensions, 52, 56, 194, 197–199, 367, 372, 458, 467, 489
testamentary bequests, religion and public policy, 108–109
testamentary conditions, 194, 347–349, 408, 448
  and common law, 194, 250, 301, 408
testamentary disposition, freedom of, 197, 347
testators, 30–31, 70, 108–109, 194, 249–251, 301–303, 348–349, 409–410
  intent, 194–197
  religious conditions, 30–31
theism, 232, 378
theistic beliefs, 128, 317, 342, 345, 396
theocracy, 21, 112, 166
theocratic rule, 9, 21–22, 23, 38
  and charity, 23
  and moral imperatives, 22–23
theosophy, 193, 344–345
Titmuss, R. A., 16–18
tolerance, 119, 126, 371, 392, 395
  religious, 28, 32
trade unions, 89, 113
traditional family units, 14, 279, 504
traditions, 35, 70, 131, 165, 192, 231, 246, 303–305, 375
  Judeo-Christian, 38, 128
trustees, 45, 56, 84, 90, 148, 179, 194–195, 347, 362
trusts, 52–54, 60–62, 72–73, 84–85, 158–160, 177–179, 195–198, 302–303, 411–412, 445–446
  charitable, *see* charitable trusts
  religious, 50
turbans, 125, 163, 213, 218, 461
Turkey, 126, 129

umbrella bodies, religious, *see* religious umbrella bodies
unemployment, 113, 451
unincorporated associations, 84–86
United Kingdom, *see* England and Wales; Scotland

United States, 16, 275, 276
  advancement of religion, 300
  advocacy, 305
  belief in Supreme Being, 298
  bequests subject to a religious
      condition, 303
  Charitable Choice, 274, 284,
      288–289, 491
  charity law
    reform, 294–295
    and regulatory framework,
      291–297
  charity regulators, 292
  Church
    State and religious charities,
      275–291
  common law, 292–294
  compelling interests, 312–313, 320
  Constitution, 308–309
  discrimination, 316–317
    and same-sex marriage, 317
  equality and diversity
      legislation, 309
  equality of religions, 280
  established religion, 279–280
  exemption doctrine, 312
  failure of testamentary dispositions
      due to breach of common law
      rules, 302–303
  First Amendment, 280, 285–287,
      298, 300, 305–309, 316–317,
      321, 324, 379–380
  frameworks for facilitating
      government–sector
      relationships, 276
  freedom of religion, 310–311
  government and nonprofit
      sector, 275
  government funding, 283–288
  government policy, 275
  human rights, 307
    discrimination and religious
      charities, 307–324
  interference with the manifestation
      of religious belief, 311–316
  IRS (Internal Revenue Service), 274,
      281–282, 291–296, 298–301,
      303–304

legislation, 291
means for advancing religion, 300
modern Church–State
    relationship, 277
neutrality test, 314–315
Office of Faith-Based and
    Community Initiatives,
    283, 287
permissive accommodations test,
    315, 323
pervasively sectarian test, 284, 288,
    313–314
philosophy and other value systems,
    299–300
positive action, 323–324
proselytism, 306
public benefit test and religious
    organisations, 296
public policy
  charity and common law
      constraints, 301–307
  constraints, 304
reforms, 295–296
religion(s), 278
  religious beliefs and the
      advancement of religion,
      297–301
religious charities, 281–282
  discrimination and
      exemptions, 309
  as public bodies, 289–291
religious discrimination in practice,
    310–320
religious organisations and
    nonprofit sector, 281
religious preferences and public
    policy, 304
religious umbrella bodies, 282
secularisation, 278–279
unequal and discriminatory
    treatment
  restriction of access to
      services, 322
  restriction of employment
      opportunities, 321
unequal but not discriminatory
    treatment, 320
  contractual obligations, 321

worship
  religious tenets
    doctrines, 298
unity, 59
universal standards of equity, 98–99
unlawfulness and religious conditions,
  69–70
upkeep of graves, 66, 249

valid charitable gifts, 228
validity, 29, 70, 94, 186, 196–197,
  227–232, 471, 474, 487
values, cultural, 35, 401
veneration, 58, 181–182, 246,
  298, 469
vocational training, 123, 259, 267–269
voluntary organisations, 168, 327,
  333–334, 429
voluntary sector, 328, 429, 438
vulnerable groups, 201, 287

wealth, 21, 32, 46, 239, 325, 427
Western society, 31, 33, 37, 41, 77–78,
  98, 451, 459–460, 486
White House Office of Faith-Based
  and Community Initiatives,
  283, 287
Williams Trustees v. *IRC*, 52
women, 122, 128, 230–232, 236, 268,
  321, 356, 363–364, 506
workplaces, 97, 129, 139, 202, 214, 222,
  232, 361, 415
worship, 58, 119–121, 175–177,
  181–182, 245–246, 342–347,
  402–406, 469–471, 476–479
  collective, 406, 492–493, 497
  modes of, 469–470, 479
  public, *see* public worship
  of Supreme Being, 58
worship services, 68
  generic, 313

For EU product safety concerns, contact us at Calle de José Abascal, 56–1°,
28003 Madrid, Spain or eugpsr@cambridge.org.

www.ingramcontent.com/pod-product-compliance
Ingram Content Group UK Ltd.
Pitfield, Milton Keynes, MK11 3LW, UK
UKHW020451090825
461507UK00007B/179